THE ROAD TO DALLAS

THE ROAD TO DALLAS

The Assassination of John F. Kennedy

David Kaiser

THE BELKNAP PRESS OF HARVARD UNIVERSITY PRESS

CAMBRIDGE, MASSACHUSETTS, AND LONDON, ENGLAND 2008

Library of Congress Cataloging-in-Publication Data

Kaiser, David E., 1947–
The road to Dallas : the assassination of John F. Kennedy / David Kaiser.
   p.   cm.
Includes index.
ISBN-13: 978-0-674-02766-4 (alk. paper)
ISBN-10: 0-674-02766-3 (alk. paper)
1. Kennedy, John F. (John Fitzgerald), 1917–1963—Assassination.   I. Title
E842.9.K25 2008
973.922092—dc22   2007027305

In memory of Charles A. Beard, Fawn Brodie,
Archibald Cox, W. E. B. Du Bois, Sam Ervin,
Edward R. Murrow, Drew Pearson, Randy Shilts,
and all the other great Americans who knew
that the truth does not kill

CONTENTS

The White Rabbit put on his spectacles. "Where shall I begin, please your Majesty?" he asked.

"Begin at the beginning," the King said gravely, "and go on till you come to the end: then stop."

—Lewis Carroll, *Alice in Wonderland*

"Murder will out, 'tis sure, and never fails."

—Chaucer, *Canterbury Tales*

Introduction

Sometime in the last week of September or the first few days of October 1963, three men knocked at the door of Silvia Odio, a young divorced Cuban woman living in the Magellan Circle apartments in Dallas, Texas. Odio, who had four small children, was packing up for a move with the help of her younger sister Annie. Their parents were in prison in Cuba, where they had been arrested after participating in an unsuccessful assassination conspiracy against Fidel Castro in the summer and fall of 1961. Silvia Odio belonged to JURE, the Revolutionary Junta in Exile, an anti-Castro organization composed mainly of disaffected Castroites who had left the Cuban government—and the island—when Fidel Castro started turning toward Communism. By the fall of 1963 JURE had established a training base in Venezuela and was preparing, with covert American assistance, for a descent upon Cuba.

Two of the three men identified themselves as "Leopoldo" and "Angelo" and spoke Spanish. They claimed to be Cubans, but Silvia Odio suspected they were actually Mexicans. They also claimed to know her father, and identified him and her mother by their underground "war names." The third man, a young, slim American introduced as "Leon," said almost nothing. The men asked her assistance in identifying possible Dallas-area donors to the Cuban cause and writing letters to them soliciting funds. She was polite but noncommittal, and they left saying they were going on a trip.

A day or two later, she received a phone call from "Leopoldo." The call, she surmised, reflected some romantic interest on his part, but he also asked what she thought of "the American." When she had nothing to say, he explained that "the American" was a former Marine and an ex-

cellent shot, a slightly crazy fellow who might do anything. He speculated that "Leon" might be able to shoot Castro if he could be gotten
into Cuba illegally, and also reported that Leon himself commented
that Cubans should have shot President Kennedy after the Bay of Pigs.
As Silvia Odio explained to the Warren Commission investigating the
assassination of John F. Kennedy many months later, she felt they were
feeling her out to see if she had contacts in the Cuban underground that
they could use. But she had no such contacts and did not reciprocate
Leopoldo's romantic interest. The conversation ended uneventfully. A
little less than two months later, after the assassination of President Kennedy, she saw Lee Harvey Oswald's picture and recognized him as Leon,
and became distraught. Within two weeks she gave the essence of her
story to the FBI, but the agency did nothing to pursue it for more than
six months.

The Odio incident, as it is called among experts on the Kennedy assassination, was immediately recognized by Warren Commission investigators and by readers of the commission's 1964 report as one of the most
provocative pieces of evidence in the case. Investigators for both the
Warren Commission and the House Select Committee on Assassinations, which convened in 1977–78, found Silvia Odio highly credible.
But it has taken more than forty years, and the release of millions of pages
of original documentation on the case in the late 1990s, to finally identify who Odio's visitors were and how their visit confirms that President
Kennedy was assassinated by a conspiracy for which Lee Harvey Oswald
was simply the trigger man. As it turns out, the visit links Oswald and his
crime to an enormous network of mobsters, anti-Castro Cubans, and
right-wing political activists. Together with other new evidence, it allows
us to name several of the key players in the conspiracy.

The men who visited Silvia Odio that night were almost certainly
Loran Hall, Lawrence Howard, and Oswald.[1] Hall was an American veteran and part-time mercenary who went to Cuba in 1959, joined Fidel
Castro's army as a trainer, and then spent several months in a Cuban transit prison after falling afoul of Cuban authorities. In the same prison at
the same time was one of the United States' most notorious criminals,
Santo Trafficante, Jr., owner of several Havana casinos and mob boss of
northern Florida. During that summer Trafficante was also visited in his
cell by a Dallas club owner named Jack Ruby. Hall re-established contact

with Trafficante in Florida during the first half of 1963. Now he and Lawrence Howard, his fellow mercenary, were transporting a truckload of arms to Florida from southern California, where Hall had been speaking to right-wing extremist groups and raising money. They intended to use the arms in a raid on Cuba.

Loran Hall had been involved in many discussions of assassination plots against Castro—including one failed attempt known as the Bayo-Pawley raid in the previous June—and had also heard a good deal of talk about assassinating President Kennedy. As he implied to Silvia Odio, he realized that in Oswald he had come across a man willing to do either job. Hall, moreover, was not the only Trafficante associate in Dallas early that fall. His visit coincided with a talk by John Martino, another mobster who was involved in gambling in both the United States and Havana and who had been jailed from 1959 through 1962 by Castro for trying to smuggle money out of Cuba after the revolution. Once released and repatriated to the States, Martino became a link between Trafficante and anti-Castro Cubans in the Miami area, and he actually helped mastermind the Bayo-Pawley raid in June.

Martino made another unexplained trip to Dallas on October 27, 1963. Sometime in the next few weeks Martino was watching the television news with his family when the newscaster referred to President Kennedy's trip to Texas. "If he goes to Dallas," Martino remarked, "they are going to kill him."[2] After the assassination, Martino led an effort to exploit Kennedy's death by linking Oswald to Fidel Castro in an attempt to provoke an invasion of Cuba.

The Central Intelligence Agency had nothing to do with Kennedy's assassination, but it was involved with organized crime figures while pursuing anti-Castro activities, including assassination plots against Fidel. In late 1960, agency operatives used a "cut-out"—the private investigator Robert Maheu—to recruit mobsters, particularly those who had lost their Havana casinos, to kill Castro. The most important mob figures in that conspiracy were Johnny Roselli of Los Angeles and Las Vegas; Sam Giancana, boss of Chicago; and Trafficante. New evidence suggests that Carlos Marcello of New Orleans was also involved. Their efforts continued well into 1963. Both the Eisenhower and Kennedy administrations allowed the CIA to create a large zone of illegality within which it carried out various acts of sabotage, propaganda, and conspiracy against Castro. Trafficante, Martino, Roselli, Giancana, Hall, Marcello, and other shadowy figures, including Jimmy Hoffa, all operated effectively within that zone.

In all probability, Oswald's attempt to reach Cuba via Mexico City—a trip he undertook either immediately after or immediately before "Leopoldo" introduced him to Silvia Odio—was designed to give him a chance to assassinate Castro. The Cuban consulate in Mexico City immediately smelled a rat and refused to grant him a visa. Oswald then returned to Dallas, and within five weeks he accepted the assignment of assassinating President Kennedy in exchange for a significant sum of money if he succeeded.

Oswald himself, just twenty-four years old in 1963, grew up with a single parent in New Orleans and joined the Marines at the age of seventeen. Immediately after his discharge in 1959 he traveled to the Soviet Union and publicly defected. Three years later, he managed to return to the United States with a Russian wife, Marina, and a new baby. Within a few months he began corresponding with American Communist and Socialist groups, and in the spring of 1963, after moving from Dallas to New Orleans, he formed a one-man chapter of a Communist front organization, the Fair Play for Cuba Committee. For four and a half decades, these activities have convinced most Americans that Oswald was a sincere leftist in 1962–63.

But the evidence suggests otherwise. His activities only embarrassed the FPCC and the Castro cause in the New Orleans area, and his behavior throughout resembled that of an *agent provocateur* rather than a genuine left-wing activist. His activities fit into a well-documented, broader effort by the FBI and independent right-wing groups to discredit left-wing organizations in the 1950s and 1960s, especially in the South.

The organized crime bosses whom the CIA recruited to help assassinate Castro masterminded the killing of President Kennedy. They did this because of Attorney General Robert Kennedy's unprecedented, all-out effort to put the American mob out of business. That effort included intensive surveillance and harassment of Sam Giancana in Chicago, similar treatment for Trafficante in Tampa and Miami, and a three-year effort to deport Carlos Marcello, who had two direct links to Lee Harvey Oswald. Robert Kennedy's other key target was Jimmy Hoffa of the Teamsters Union, who had close business ties with Giancana, Marcello, and Trafficante and shared a lawyer, Frank Ragano, with Trafficante.

In May 1963 Ragano delivered a message from Hoffa to the two mob bosses: that it was time to execute the contract on President Kennedy. Both Marcello and Trafficante had already discussed or foretold the killing of the President in private conversations, and Giancana frequently expressed his resentment of the Kennedys in conversations recorded by the FBI. Jack Ruby, who killed Oswald just two days after the Kennedy assassination, had links to all three of these men. In addition to visiting Trafficante in his Cuban prison cell in 1959, Ruby was very friendly with former Trafficante employee and mobster Lewis McWillie. He grew up among Chicago mobsters and was in touch with a number of Chicago mob figures through long-distance telephone calls in the months leading up to the assassination. He operated a strip club in Dallas, which was within Marcello's territory. The killing of President Kennedy, followed by the resignation less than a year later of Robert Kennedy as attorney general, seriously curtailed the government's effort to clean up organized crime—just as it was intended to do.

The Kennedy assassination, then, must be understood in the context of two much larger stories. The first is the government's campaign against organized crime, which actually began in the late 1950s after an infamous Mafia conclave was discovered in Appalachin, New York, proving that a national crime syndicate existed. The campaign accelerated dramatically under Robert Kennedy. The second story recounts the efforts of two administrations, and various private groups as well, to bring down Fidel Castro. A great deal has been written on these two subjects in the last thirty years, much of it exaggerated and far off the mark. The truth provides ample interest.

The Eisenhower administration recruited top mobsters to assassinate Castro, and their plots continued during the Kennedy years, though the Kennedy administration thought they had stopped. On the other hand, JFK's administration clearly viewed the assassination of Castro as a possible solution to the problem of Communism in Cuba, and it encouraged the CIA to bring about that result without involving the mob. Even after the Cuban missile crisis of October 1962, when President Kennedy promised the Soviets not to invade the island, the U.S. government hoped that either the assassination of Castro or a significant internal uprising would provide the opportunity for groups of exiles or American forces to land on the island and remove the rest of the Castro regime. Ironically, however, the administration's failure to support the Bay of Pigs invasion in 1961, combined with its refusal to take military action during the missile crisis, convinced most Cuban exiles that John and Robert Kennedy had no intention of toppling Castro. The Kennedys' favoritism toward relatively leftist exiles angered conservative Cubans and their American allies still further.

The assassination of the President was not a random event. At bottom it grew out of moralistic obsessions in American life: the insistence on outlawing the satisfaction of certain human appetites for gambling, sex, and drugs, which created and sustained organized crime; and the refusal (and not only during the Cold War) to respect the rights of foreign regimes that seem to threaten American values and interests. Those two broader problems made the assassination possible; the actions of particular men made it happen. Lee Harvey Oswald was an extraordinarily useful assassin, and his sudden death at the hands of Jack Ruby—despite its highly suspicious nature—made it much harder for the truth to emerge. In the 1970s, when key events in the background to the crime became known to law enforcement agencies, the additional murders of Sam Giancana and Johnny Roselli kept the details secret for two more decades and shielded living conspirators from legal action. The only prosecution of the crime, by Jim Garrison in New Orleans, was a farce, and those conspirators who can now be identified are long since dead. But the truth of the assassination, its historical impact, and the ways in which it is still with us can now be told.

This book has been written as a result of the release during the 1990s of enormous documentation on all aspects of the Kennedy assassination by the Kennedy Assassination Records Collection Act of 1992 and the very thorough and intrepid work of the Review Board, led by historian Anna K. Nelson, which was appointed to implement it. Those records include not only all the original FBI files on the investigation of the assassination itself but also FBI files on numerous key organized crime figures, including Giancana, Marcello, and Trafficante. More astonishingly, the CIA was persuaded to release not only all the materials it had provided to the House Select Committee on Assassinations (HSCA) in 1977–78 but also individual 201 files on a large number of Cuban exiles and exile groups.

While many of the files released by the CIA provide important information, they also make clear how tenaciously the agency can protect itself when it feels a need to do so. Unfortunately, a few important files were overlooked, and it has now become harder than ever to secure their release in usable form. Still, the new CIA and FBI materials have allowed me to tell far more of the assassination story than has ever been told before, and also to evaluate, based on the original FBI reports, many of the key incidents in Lee Harvey Oswald's life. Also released was all the original testimony before the Church Committee of 1975–76, which was convened to study governmental operations with respect to intelligence activities. This testimony included a great many important facts that did not make it into the committee's final report. The files of HSCA, which looked into many other neglected areas, have also been made available. This committee concluded that President Kennedy had "probably" been assassinated by a conspiracy involving organized crime figures.

Hundreds of books on the Kennedy assassination have appeared, but this is the first one written by a professional historian who has researched the available archives. Partly because of the evidentiary excesses or deficiencies of so many other authors, I have written this book not only to show what happened but to make clear how we know it. I have not, however, attempted to tell the story of either the Warren Commission or the HSCA investigations. Instead, I have used the raw data they had available—and a great deal more that they did not have—to tell the story from the beginning. And while I have not hesitated to draw on the work of many authors who have already published books on the case, I have not attempted to mention every instance in which my conclusions differ from theirs, or to explain why. Such a task would have required another book.

Jack Ruby's murder of Lee Harvey Oswald and the apparent improbability of some of the critical evidence in the case—including the single-bullet theory, which the HSCA very convincingly determined to be true—got research into the Kennedy assassination off to an unfortunate start. Much of this early work became an exercise in trying to show that Oswald, who was indeed guilty, did not commit the crime. On the other hand, most of those who believed that Oswald *was* the assassin (with the very important exception of the HSCA) have argued vehemently, in the face of a great deal of contrary evidence, that he acted without any help or encouragement from anyone.

The truth lies squarely between these two extremes—the image of

Oswald as a lone, nutty gunman, and the image of Oswald as an innocent patsy caught up in an enormous web of conspiracy that included the federal government itself. A true understanding of President Kennedy's assassination requires the reconstruction of a complex network of relationships among mobsters, hit men, intelligence agents, Cuban exiles, and America's Cold War foreign policy. *The Road to Dallas* puts each of these bricks in its place, so that careful readers can see exactly who did what with whom—when and where.

The story of President Kennedy's death touches on an extraordinary range of locales and includes a remarkable cast of characters. It involves presidential intimates, down-and-out mercenaries dreaming of glory, mobsters and their show-business paramours, hot-headed Cuban exiles, duplicitous CIA agents, FBI bugs in Chicago restaurants, a mysterious white Russian whose vast circle of friends included Jacqueline Kennedy, Lee Harvey Oswald, and George H. W. Bush, American surveillance of embassies in a foreign capital, extreme right-wing businessmen and activists, the moribund and persecuted Communist Party of the United States, and a dogged FBI agent who never quite caught up to Lee Harvey Oswald in the weeks before the assassination. It also involves the paradoxical policies of John F. Kennedy himself, who sought the relaxation of the Cold War but apparently could not resign himself to the continuance of the Castro regime. And there are heroes as well, such as the hundreds of FBI agents who carefully and zealously put information to paper, the investigators for the House Select Committee on Assassinations, and a few CIA operatives who in the 1970s believed that the American people deserved to know the truth. And now, at long last, we can see how all these various paths converged, and how a conspiracy of mobsters and misfits got away with assassinating a President.

PART I

Criminals, Cubans, Kennedys, and the CIA

Organized Crime in the 1950s

Ever since the Pilgrims landed in Plymouth in 1620 to create a new and more holy community, American society has struggled with those who provide it with forbidden fruits. These have included illegal drugs (and, from 1920 to 1933, beer, wines, and liquors), gambling, and commercial sex. The gangs that have controlled such ventures at least since the nineteenth century have invariably broadened their field of activity to include simple theft, fraud, and extortion from legitimate enterprises. By trying to outlaw activities that cater to essential human desires, society has created a zone of illegality in which other kinds of crime—including intimidation, beatings, and murders—become commonplace.

Organized crime has had contradictory effects on American political life. On the one hand, mobsters frequently corrupt both law enforcement professionals and politicians. But they also provide opportunities for honest, crusading leaders to win favor and renown by sending notorious lawbreakers to prison, whether or not they reduce the extent of the criminal enterprise in the long run. While local, state, and sometimes even national politicians frequently yield to temptation behind the scenes, a knight in shining armor periodically emerges to slay a wicked dragon or two, usually in search of higher office as well as justice.

During the 1920s Prohibition gave organized crime a huge new source of income while thrusting racketeers like Al Capone into the national spotlight. In the 1930s Thomas Dewey, a crusading young New York prosecutor, parlayed the conviction of New York mobster Charles "Lucky" Luciano into three terms as state governor and two unsuccessful runs for the presidency. In 1950, in response to some widely read newspaper reporting and an attorney general's conference on organized crime, a young, ambitious Democratic senator from Tennessee, Estes Kefauver, helped create a Senate Special Committee to Investigate Crime in Interstate Commerce. Kefauver held televised hearings in various cities from May 1950 through May 1951, and they raised citizens' awareness of the problem to a new level while turning him into a national figure and presidential candidate.

The Kefauver Committee's report concluded that a crime syndicate definitely existed, although it did not identify any single boss.[1] It named Frank Costello, Joe Adonis, and Meyer Lansky as the leading figures on the East Coast and reported that the "Capone Syndicate" continued to run Chicago. Lucky Luciano, who in 1946 had been released from a New York prison and deported to a life of semi-retirement in Italy—reportedly in return for favors and intelligence he helped provide American troops in Italy during the war—remained the head of the Mafia's international narcotics trade.[2]

Narcotics, the committee found, flowed from Sicily to Marseilles to Tampa, Florida, and thence to Kansas City. New Orleans was a second entry port for illegal drug traffic. Another major organized crime activity investigated by the committee involved the national wire services, controlled by Cleveland and Chicago interests, whose competition for the right to send gambling information around the country resulted in a series of spectacular murders. The wire services in turn led the Kefauver Committee to gambling, which took up much of its report. In South Florida, gambling kingpins Meyer and Jake Lansky, Joe Adonis, and Vincent "Jimmy Blue Eyes" Alo (caricatured in the film *Godfather II* as Johnny Ola) apparently had the sheriffs of both Broward County and Miami on their payroll. Gambling money also played a critical role in the local politics of Kansas City. Tampa was another gambling center, where Santo Trafficante, Sr., ran the bolita, a Cuban numbers game.

In New Orleans, Kefauver identified mob leader Carlos Marcello as "one of the most sinister criminals encountered by the committee anywhere." Marcello, born in Tunisia in 1909, remained an alien, and Kefauver complained that numerous attempts to secure his deportation had failed. Gambling was "wide open" in New Orleans until 1946, and Frank Costello told the committee that he had been discussing the legalization of slot machines with Louisiana's Huey Long just before Long was assassinated in 1935. Bourbon Street, in New Orleans, was also a hub of the sex trade—an enterprise that drew relatively little attention from the committee even though the mob was heavily involved.[3]

The committee discovered considerable mob influence in labor–management disputes. Detroit mobsters had corrupted the waste handlers unions and provided strike-breaking thugs to Harry Bennett of Henry Ford's Ford Service Bureau. Hoodlums were also prominent in the trucking business. In Hollywood, several mobsters from the Chicago area, including Willie Bioff and Johnny Roselli, were convicted in the early 1940s of using their control of certain motion picture unions (notably the International Alliance of Theatrical Stage Employees) to extort huge payments from studios.

The Kefauver Committee recommended the formation of a national crime commission and laws against interstate transmission of information related to gambling. It gingerly suggested that the FBI—whose formidable director, J. Edgar Hoover, had not shown much interest in the national crime syndicate—be more generous with information in its files. Dramatic televised hearings (the first in a long line that would include the Army-McCarthy probes of 1954, the Watergate hearings of 1973, and the Iran-Contra hearings of 1987) made Kefauver a national figure, and he challenged President Truman for the Democratic nomination in 1952.

Yet the hearings had negative political repercussions as well. They exposed the extensive corruption of law enforcement officials and political leaders in Chicago, New Orleans, and Kansas City, President Truman's own home base, where his late political mentor, Tom Prendergast, was specifically implicated. Truman, who prized loyalty above all else, never forgave Kefauver, and after withdrawing from the presidential race himself, he helped make sure the nomination went to Adlai Stevenson, governor of Illinois, whose own proposal for a state crime commission had died in the Illinois legislature.

Kefauver himself learned the wisdom of the Biblical parable of the first stone. Sidney Korshak, a Chicago attorney who in the 1940s became the Chicago mob's representative in Hollywood, managed to avoid appearing at the committee's Chicago hearing by directing a young woman to seduce Kefauver—who, like so many politicians of his generation, was a notorious womanizer. The senator's assignation was photographed at his hotel, and Korshak did not testify.[4]

The Kefauver Committee mentioned Dallas only briefly, but the mob's presence there was already in the news. Jack Ruby, who moved from Chicago's West Side to Dallas in 1947, was managing a strip club there at the time of Kefauver's report. Born Jacob Rubinstein in 1911 to a large and troubled family of Russian Jewish immigrants, Ruby grew up in a tough neighborhood among several friends who became prominent within the Chicago mob, including boxer Barney Ross, labor racketeer Alan Dorfman, and hit man Dave Yaras.[5] After trouble with truancy and a stint in foster homes, Jack quit school at age sixteen. It is not altogether clear how he spent his time from 1927 to 1933, when he moved to San Francisco for four years, but apparently he never held a steady job and tried to make a living scalping tickets. While in San Francisco, he sold newspaper subscriptions and racing tip sheets.[6]

From 1937 to 1940 Ruby became involved in another mob activity, the infiltration of unions. He worked in an undefined capacity for Local 20467 of the Scrap Iron and Junk Handlers' Union—one of many dominated and exploited by the Chicago mob. Ruby left the union after Leon Cooke killed the local president, John Martin, in December 1939 during an argument over funds. Cooke successfully pleaded self-defense at his trial. Paul "Red" Dorfman, Ruby's childhood acquaintance and later an important associate of Jimmy Hoffa, took over the union, and Ruby apparently would not or could not remain under the new regime. He worked for the next three years selling various cheap novelties and served without major incident in the Army Air Corps from 1943 to 1946. Shortly after his discharge, he moved to Dallas.[7]

The woman behind Ruby's move to Dallas was his slightly older sister, Eva Grant, who had some mob connections of her own. Mobster Paul Roland Jones explained to the FBI in December 1963 that Eva Grant brought Ruby along to a meeting in the fall of 1946 in Chicago with two men from the slot machine business—another mob specialty—which she arranged. The two men, Paul Labriola and James Weinberg, were eventually found garroted in 1954.[8] In 1946 Jones was leading an attempt by Chicago mobsters to take over the Dallas rackets—an attempt that he discussed in secretly recorded conversations with Dallas sheriff Steve Guthrie. The recordings led to Jones's arrest in late 1946 and his eventual conviction on bribery charges the next year.

Meanwhile, Eva Grant moved to Dallas and become the reputed

owner of a "dance hall" called the Singapore Club. Jones approached Ruby on Eva's behalf and persuaded him to come to Dallas and take over the operation of the club, which he did around the middle of 1947.[9] Eva herself told a Dallas friend during the 1940s that she belonged to the Capone gang.[10] When Jones was arrested in late 1947 for smuggling narcotics from Mexico into Texas, a review of his phone calls disclosed that he was in touch with both Ruby and his brother, Hyman Rubinstein.[11]

Ruby eventually renamed the Singapore Club the Silver Spur, and in 1953 he began running another club, called the Vegas, with a Chicago native named Joe Bonds. Bonds in 1954 went to prison on sodomy and prostitution charges. Meanwhile, Ruby became friendly with mob figure Lewis McWillie. Born in Kansas City in 1908, McWillie ran dice and card games in Dallas all through the 1940s and early 1950s. An FBI report of 1953 stated that McWillie had been working in Dallas for Benny Binion, a major gambling figure who later ran a casino in Las Vegas. In 1946 McWillie shot and killed a certain George Arthur McBride. He escaped with a plea of self-defense, but Dallas sources believed this was a gangland murder on Binion's behalf.[12]

McWillie later explained that he met Ruby in 1951 and straightened out a curfew problem at Ruby's club with the help of one of his gambling patrons, a liquor distributor. McWillie remained in Dallas until leaving to work in Havana casinos in 1958, and he continued to see Ruby frequently. McWillie ran card games at private clubs, and his clients included oil men Sid Richardson and H. L. Hunt. When the House Select Committee on Assassinations (HSCA) asked him whose permission—on either side of the law—he needed to run card games, he claimed to have no idea.[13]

The answer, almost certainly, was Joseph Civello, the Dallas co-proprietor of Civello Imports and Liquors, who was born in 1902 in Port Allen, Louisiana, and who admitted in 1958 that he was a long-time friend of Carlos Marcello of New Orleans. Although Civello maintained one of the lower profiles among Mafia bosses in major cities, he suddenly engaged the attention of federal authorities when he turned up at the famous Appalachin, New York, conclave of mob bosses in November 1957. Civello told the FBI that he was in New York on business and traveled to Appalachin to play in a crap game, but rumors suggested that he was there representing Marcello, who did not attend. An official of the federal narcotics bureau described Civello as a leader of the drug trade.[14] The FBI in 1959 concluded that Civello's rise began in 1928 after he shot one Joe De Carlo in a drugstore. Convicted of narcotics trafficking in 1937, he served seven years of a fifteen-year sentence before being paroled. He became the Dallas boss in 1956. In November 1963 a former Civello employee remembered Ruby visiting a gambling house behind a liquor store in which Civello was involved.[15]

Two other prominent Dallas mobsters were Joe and Sam Campisi, owners of the Egyptian Lounge, a successful restaurant that doubled as an after-hours gambling house. Dallas police authorities were not very concerned about Civello and the Campisis, apparently. Beginning in the late 1950s, Sheriff Bill Decker and Dallas police lieutenant Jack Revill told FBI agents that neither Civello nor the Campisi brothers were engaged in illegal activities anymore because of their own crackdowns. Years later, in 1966, Joe Campisi reportedly remarked that he hoped Sheriff Decker, who was stepping down, would be replaced by his assistant rather than by another candidate from the Dallas police who, he believed, would give bookmakers a much harder time.[16]

New Orleans got much more attention in the Kefauver Committee report, which described Carlos Marcello's gambling and vice empire. Ironically, that empire would help shape the childhood and adolescent environment of Lee Harvey Oswald, who was born in New Orleans in 1939, a few months after the death of his father from a heart attack. His widowed mother, Marguerite Claverly Oswald, had difficulty supporting and raising her three sons (John Pic, the child of an earlier marriage, and Robert Oswald were the others), and Lee spent his first four years in the home of a maternal aunt and uncle, Charles "Dutz" and Lillian Claverly Murret. After living in Texas and New York City in the late 1940s and early 1950s, Marguerite and her son, Lee, returned to New Orleans in 1954. For the next two years, while Lee finished junior high school, they lived in an apartment above a poolroom and gambling hangout on Exchange Alley, in the heart of the vice district of the French Quarter.

By this time, Lee's Uncle Dutz Murret, who had been a boxer, boxing manager, and dockworker, was a successful bookmaker working with Sam Saia, long known as a major New Orleans gambling figure and associate of Carlos Marcello. The Oswalds visited the Murret household frequently during the mid-1950s, and Murret apparently remained a bookmaker until his death from cancer in October 1964, just a few months after he testified briefly before the Warren Commission. The commissioners did not ask any questions about how he earned a living.

Lee's mother, Marguerite, had her own mob connections. In the mid-1950s she was friendly with Clem Sehrt, a New Orleans lawyer who in turn was closely associated with Louis Roussell, a banker involved in several attempts to corrupt public officials. Marguerite worked for Raoul Sere, an attorney employed by the New Orleans District Attorney's Office during a period in which it was notoriously corrupt. Aaron Kohn of the New Orleans Crime Commission believed Sere was involved in attempts to influence justice. Marguerite Oswald also enjoyed a long friendship with Sam Termine, who once served simultaneously as Carlos Marcello's chauffeur and as a member of the Louisiana State Police.[17]

The Kefauver Committee focused on activities within the continental United States and therefore had relatively little to say about a critical offshore territory—the island of Cuba, where American mobsters played an increasingly important role since at least the 1930s. In September 1933, Fulgencio Batista led a group of Cuban Army officers that seized political power, and he immediately struck deals with four major Mafia leaders, including Meyer Lansky and Santo Trafficante, Sr., of Tampa, along with an Italian and a Corsican. Lansky received the gambling concession at the Hotel Nacional in Havana.

In 1944, in the middle of World War II, the United States insisted that Batista give way to an elected ruler, and Grau San Martin returned to power. Mob influence continued, however, and in late 1946 Lucky Luciano journeyed from Italy to Havana for a major mob conclave that included Lansky, Trafficante, and Vito Genovese of New York. Pressure from Washington forced Luciano to depart for Italy early the next year. In 1948 a new Cuban president, Carlos Prio Socarras, was elected on a reform platform, but Prio proved as corrupt as any of his predecessors. On March 10, 1952, Batista returned from eight years of exile in Florida and overthrew Prio, who managed to reach Florida with tens of millions of dollars—money that he subsequently used to finance revolutionary activities against both Batista and his successor, Fidel Castro.[18]

By 1957 a handful of Americans, including Lansky and his brother Jake, Dino Cellini, Norman Rothmann, Mike McLaney of New Orleans, and Santo Trafficante, Jr. (who inherited his deceased father's bolita empire in Tampa in 1954), controlled perhaps half a dozen hotels and casinos in Havana. In addition to these gambling activities, two other key mobsters, Marcello of New Orleans and Sam Mannarino of Pittsburgh, began purchasing heroin in Central America and shipping it to Rothmann at the Sans Souci.[19] The Cuban Treasury theoretically received twenty percent of gambling profits, but much of that money actually went to the officials who collected it and to Cuban police.[20]

Attempts by New York mobsters to take over a share of the Cuban gold mine threatened to provoke an all-out war. Its most famous episodes included the shooting of Albert Anastasia, formerly of Murder, Inc., in a Park Sheraton Hotel barber chair on October 25, 1957, and the nonfatal shooting of Frank Costello some time earlier. Although neither crime was ever solved, many suspected Santo Trafficante, Jr., as Anastasia's killer. He stayed at the Waldorf, where Anastasia hung out, just two days earlier. To avoid questioning, Trafficante shifted his base of operations to Cuba sometime later. Equally significantly, the shooting led to the national Mafia conclave at Appalachin, New York, on November 13–14, 1957. An alert state trooper, noticing out-of-state luxury cars near the home of Joseph Barbara, Sr., set up a check point and eventually identified fifty-nine well-known criminals there, including mob leaders from Detroit, Buffalo, New York City, and California, along with Trafficante of Florida.

The Appalachin meeting got the attention of the FBI and led to a new federal effort against organized crime. In 1958 a detailed FBI study confirmed the conclusions of the Kefauver Committee regarding mob activity in narcotics, loan sharking, gambling (with particular reference to Trafficante's activities both in the southeastern United States and in Cuba), garbage hauling, and labor racketeering. It also noted the mob's involvement in liquor retailing, the garment industry, race tracks, banking, and financing. A map of the United States showing the provenance of sixty-one visitors to Appalachin the previous year included California, Colorado, Texas, Missouri, Illinois, Ohio, Pennsylvania, New Jersey, Massachusetts, Florida, and Cuba. A summary also referred to a number of successful attempts to corrupt local officials.[21] Even before the study was completed, J. Edgar Hoover and the FBI started a "Top Hoodlum" program in late 1957, designed to identify and intensively investigate about two dozen leading mobsters all over the country. Meanwhile, by a fateful coincidence, the issue of organized crime also engaged the attention of a young, ambitious Massachusetts senator, John F. Kennedy, and his younger brother Robert.

The Kennedy family, led by its patriarch Joseph P. Kennedy, had been working for decades toward the election of one of its members as President of the United States. Joe himself was forced to abandon his political ambitions after his pro-appeasement stance as ambassador to Britain put him at odds with Franklin Roosevelt in 1940. He had already begun grooming his oldest son for the role when Joseph, Jr., died during a dangerous combat mission in Britain in 1944. In 1946 second son John took over and was elected to Congress at age twenty-nine with the help of his brother, Robert, who was only twenty-one at the time of the 1946 campaign. In 1952, after completing Law School at the University of Virginia, Robert managed his brother's narrow victory over Senator Henry Cabot Lodge in Massachusetts, despite the Eisenhower landslide.

When the new Congress met, old Joe—a strong supporter of Senator Joseph McCarthy, a fellow anti-Communist Irish Catholic—got Robert a job as assistant counsel of McCarthy's Permanent Subcommittee on Investigations of the Senate Government Operations Committee. Robert lasted only six months before falling out with McCarthy, but he returned in early 1954 as the committee's minority (Democratic) counsel, just in time for the Army-McCarthy hearings that led to Senator McCarthy's downfall.

The Democrats took over the Senate in the 1954 elections and Robert Kennedy, now twenty-eight, became the majority counsel of the committee. In 1956 John Kennedy, still only thirty-nine years old, decided to seek the vice-presidential nomination after Adlai Stevenson won a lengthy primary fight against Senator Estes Kefauver. At the Chicago Convention, Stevenson threw the selection of his running mate open to the delegates, and Kefauver defeated Kennedy on the second ballot. It was the last selection of a presidential or vice-presidential candidate by a major party convention that required more than one ballot—in short, the last prolonged nominating contest on a convention floor.

The Permanent Subcommittee on Investigations—now headed by John McClellan of Arkansas, and joined in 1957 by Senator Kennedy—mutated into the Select Committee on Labor Racketeering, and Chief Counsel Robert Kennedy decided in early 1957 to investigate the influence of organized crime on labor unions, and in particular the activities of the Teamsters Union. Robert's decision angered his father, who feared that antagonizing organized labor would hurt Jack's chances for the White House. Robert, however, knew a number of young journalists who were investigating the mob and the Teamsters, including Clark Mollenhof, Ed Guthman, John Siegenthaler, and Pierre Salinger—the last three destined for roles in the Kennedy administration. The investigation he began early in 1957 rapidly turned into a crusade.[22]

Like so many members of large, close-knit families in public life, young Robert faced a dual problem: how to contribute to the broader goals of the family, centered in his case on his brother's presidential ambitions, while carving out an identity of his own. He had already distinguished himself as being by far the most religious of the Kennedy men; he was the first of Joe's children to become a husband and father (and, in the latter role, the most prolific). He had demonstrated good judgment and organizational skills during his brother's campaigns, particularly in 1952. But he suffered from a generational frustration as well. Like most men born in 1925, he did not complete his military training in time to go overseas before the Second World War ended. While brother Joe died in action and brother Jack returned home from the Pacific a war hero, Robert missed being part of the great crusade to rid the world of evil—a circumstance that left him and others of his generation with a measurable sense of inferiority to those who had taken part.[23]

Robert Kennedy's discovery of the influence of organized crime on unions—especially the Teamsters Union—gave him a chance to do battle with an evil enemy. The 1957 investigation turned into a three-year campaign that the chief counsel (with the help of committee staffer John Siegenthaler) described in a book entitled *The Enemy Within*. Published in 1960, it became an instant best-seller in both hardcover and mass market paperback. This helped catch him up to his brother Jack, the author (also with considerable help) of *Profiles in Courage*. But what is most noteworthy about Robert's book, in retrospect, is the language in which it describes the investigation and its targets.

Kennedy and his staff discovered enormous abuses in the Teamsters Union, the nation's largest. Dave Beck, its president, was caught financing the construction of his own house with union funds and paying consultancies to Chicago mob figures. Beck immediately became a target of

Kennedy's moral righteousness, and a scalp he intended to take in the cause of justice. "By end of our hearing in March [1957]," he wrote, "Dave Beck had been shown to be cruel, stingy, avaricious and arrogant."[24] But by then Beck was already losing his status as number one target to the man who was about to succeed him after he was indicted, tried, and sentenced—James R. Hoffa of Detroit.

Hoffa was, indeed, at the center of the alliance between mobsters and corrupt unions whose surface Kennedy was just beginning to scratch. Born in 1913, Hoffa rose to prominence in the Detroit area during the 1940s when he enlisted organized crime figures to defeat a rival CIO union in a violent jurisdictional conflict. He survived indictments for extortion and antitrust charges in the early 1940s and helped organize the mob-dominated coin machine business after the war. Another violent organizing drive corralled truckers in the southeastern United States in the early 1950s. Hoffa dominated the Teamsters' Central States Council and its huge pension and welfare funds, which were already being used to finance mob enterprises in various parts of the country. He was also involved in several successful attempts to corrupt the criminal justice system on behalf of himself and various associates and had acquired the confidence—which eventually ruined him—that a mixture of money and intimidation could fix absolutely anything.[25]

No sooner did RFK's investigation begin to threaten Beck than Hoffa hired a New York attorney, John Cye Cheasty, to get a job with the new committee and report on its doings. Cheasty, evidently the wrong man for the job, immediately contacted Kennedy, who introduced him to J. Edgar Hoover, who turned him into a double agent. After agents photographed Cheasty handing Hoffa committee documents and receiving an envelope with $2,000 in cash, Hoffa was arrested and put on trial. Young Kennedy declared that he would jump off the Capitol if Hoffa were not convicted, but things turned out not to be so simple.

Hoffa retained Washington's leading defense attorney, Edward Bennett Williams, who decided to appeal to a Washington jury composed of eight African Americans and four whites. Hoffa's friend, Chicago mobster Paul Dorfman, arranged for retired heavyweight champion Joe Louis to appear in the courtroom and demonstrate his good will toward the accused, and Hoffa, testifying, argued that he simply retained Cheasty as an attorney, nothing more. The jury voted to acquit. Hoffa survived a trial on two wiretapping charges in New York City the next year as well, and despite a raft of continuing investigations—several destined to lead to more indictments—Jimmy Hoffa was elected Teamster president to succeed Beck.

Although the Rackets Committee hearings were never nationally televised, Robert Kennedy wrung all the drama he could out of them. He called many witnesses, such as Hoffa associate and strongarm Rolland McMaster, Paul Dorfman of Chicago, and Dorfman's stepson Allen, and questioned them at length even though it was clear they would take the Fifth Amendment in every case. Hoffa proudly promised to answer all questions and endured a marathon session before the committee in the summer of 1957. It was focused largely on his business relationship with convicted New York murderer Johnny Dio. The hearings led to state and local investigations of numerous Teamster officials.[26]

During its three years of existence, the committee used tactics reminiscent of the House Un-American Activities Committee and McCarthy's subcommittee on investigations. Sessions of the committee focused on particular instances of labor racketeering and usually began with testimony from victims of intimidation, local law enforcement authorities, or even investigators for the committee such as Walter Sheridan or future White House press secretary Pierre Salinger about abuses they had uncovered. Then after these crimes had been fully aired, the committee would call the accused, who usually took the Fifth. Like Senator McCarthy, Robert Kennedy felt no compunction about filling pages and pages of the committee record with leading and abusive questions answered by endless repetitions of the witness's constitutional privilege. Such proceedings were obviously designed, like McCarthy's, to humiliate and disgrace individuals whom law enforcement, for a variety of reasons, was unable to convict, and to generate publicity in the witnesses' home cities.

The scope of the investigation gradually broadened until by 1959 it was delving into almost anything having to do with organized crime. On March 23–24 of that year the committee focused on the operation of juke boxes, slot machines, and pinball machines in Louisiana. On the first day, Aaron Kohn, the director of the independent New Orleans Crime Commission since 1954, testified at length about Carlos Marcello's political power, criminal activities, and corruption of the justice system. The Supreme Court had ordered his deportation nearly four years before, but various appeals managed to delay it. Robert Kennedy elicited this testimony even though Marcello's power had very little to do with labor unions or racketeering, since, as Kohn explained, unions had made very few successful inroads into Louisiana.

Kohn was followed by several bar owners who detailed the pressure they were under to use machines from Marcello-controlled companies. The next day Marcello took the stand, and, when asked by Chief Counsel Kennedy for his occupation, replied cleverly, "I decline to answer that on the ground it may intend to incriminate me." "On the ground it may 'intend' to incriminate you?" asked Senator McClellan. "Yes, sir," said Mr. Marcello, who proceeded to repeat the same answer over many pages of printed testimony. Three Senators became intrigued with the failure of the government to carry out its deportation order and suggested that the committee send an inquiry to the Justice Department to ask for an explanation. Robert Kennedy evidently remembered Marcello's ability to avoid his deportation very well.[27]

The Select Committee on Labor Racketeering and its chief counsel refined its dramatic techniques somewhat by June 1959, when it spent seven full days hearing testimony about gambling, juke box, and prostitution activities in Lake County, Indiana, just across the border from Chicago. On June 9 the committee called Sam Giancana, the reputed deputy mob boss of Chicago, who was subpoenaed in Las Vegas after eluding committee investigators for over a year. Giancana immediately took the Fifth, much to the disgust of Chairman McClellan, and Kennedy called committee investigator Pierre Salinger as a witness. As Salinger detailed Giancana's criminal record, including seventeen arrests and two major convictions, both McClellan and Kennedy interspersed Salinger's testimony with questions for Giancana, every one of which, of course, was met with a refusal to answer "because I honestly believe my answer might tend to incriminate me."

Salinger quoted from a recent interview in the *Chicago Tribune* in which Giancana bragged about how he evaded the committee investigators by taking the Fifth even though he would prefer "to tell them to go to hell," and about how he avoided the draft by telling his draft board that he was a thief. "Are you happy in being a thief; is that what you are laughing about?" McClellan asked him after that passage was read. Salinger's testimony—essentially hearsay, albeit probably accurate—

linked Giancana to extortion in the restaurant business, to fraud in the record industry, to a double gangland slaying, and to a Chicago Teamsters local. Kennedy then asked Giancana five questions about specific accusations, receiving the standard answer every time. "Would you tell us anything about any of your operations or will you just giggle every time I ask you a question?" Kennedy asked in exasperation. "I decline to answer because I honestly believe my answer might tend to incriminate me," Giancana replied. "I thought only little girls giggled, Mr. Giancana," Kennedy retorted.[28]

The Kennedy brothers attempted to integrate the hearings into a broader political strategy. Arguing that their quarrel was merely with corrupt unions rather than the mass of organized labor—a pillar, of course, of the Democratic Party whose nomination they sought—John Kennedy joined with New York Senator Irving Ives to introduce the Kennedy-Ives Bill, which sought to make it easier to deal with corrupt officials while preserving labor's organizing rights. But Kennedy, the AFL-CIO, and the Democrats were outmaneuvered in 1959, when a conservative coalition managed to substitute the Landrum-Griffin Bill, which imposed restrictions on picketing designed to block organizing drives in the South, for the renamed Kennedy-Ervin bill. Labor emerged weaker, not stronger, despite the massive Democratic congressional landslide in 1958.

Still, as Robert Kennedy commented rather ruefully in oral history interviews in 1964, his labor investigations won him considerable credit among southern Democrats. "All the Southerners were very much in favor of my being Attorney General," he said late that year, "because I had been investigating labor unions. They didn't like labor unions much."[29] Still, most unions supported John F. Kennedy against Richard Nixon in 1960.

The exception, of course, was the Teamsters. In May 1960 Jimmy Hoffa sued Robert Kennedy and late-night talkshow host Jack Paar for $2.5 million, claiming that Kennedy had libeled and slandered him on four different appearances on Paar's show.[30] Jimmy Hoffa attended the Democratic Convention in Los Angeles in 1960 and pulled every string he could to secure the nomination of Lyndon Johnson. Hoffa claimed later to have contributed a good deal of money to LBJ as well.[31] Never a man to put all his eggs in one basket, however, Hoffa also made contact with Vice President Richard Nixon, the likely Republican candidate, in late 1959. The intermediaries were I. Irving Davidson, a Washington public relations man, arms dealer, and fixer who was already arranging loans from the Teamsters' Central States Pension Fund, and a California Republican former congressman named Allan Oakley Hunter, who met Hoffa in Miami Beach on December 13, 1959. During the meeting, Hoffa complained of discriminatory treatment from the Justice Department and speculated that an open endorsement of Nixon by himself might do more harm than good, but offered the cooperation of locals around the country.

Hoffa "gave the impression," Hunter wrote Nixon, "that as between those candidates for President on the horizon at the present time he definitely favored you." At the Republican Convention in Chicago, after Kennedy won the Democratic nomination, Davidson and Hunter met Hoffa again and secured his support. In September, federal prosecutor James Dowd was about to ask an Orlando, Florida, grand jury for an indictment of Hoffa when he was called to Washington and ordered to delay action—which he did. After the election, on January 4, 1961, columnist Drew Pearson published two letters from Congressman Hunter indicating that Nixon had spoken to Attorney General William Rogers and had persuaded him to delay indicting Hoffa in connection with the construction of his Sun Valley resort in Florida. Hoffa, Pearson wrote, provided Nixon some important help in the key state of Ohio, but now that the election was over and Nixon had lost, Nixon was unable to stop the indictment from going forward.[32]

Hoffa's ability not only to withstand a whole series of federal investigations but also to continue making friends and influencing people at the highest levels of American politics testified to the power he commanded by virtue of the allegiance and resources of the Teamsters Union—regardless of how he acquired that power and how tightly the Teamsters were tied to the mob in various parts of the country. But Robert Kennedy's feelings about his investigations and what they had uncovered transcended politics. During the Senate hearings, he wrote, Hoffa often gave the Kennedys "the look of a man obsessed by his enmity . . . There were times when his face seemed completely transfixed with this stare of absolute evilness." The Teamsters, he repeatedly reminded his readers, controlled a major portion of the transportation system of the United States. He concluded, literally, with a call to arms.

> Neither the labor movement nor our economic system can stand this paralyzing corruption. Premier Khrushchev has said that we are a dying house, a decadent society. That he says it does not make it true. But that corruption, dishonesty and softness, physical and moral, have become widespread in this country there can be no doubt.
>
> The great events of our nation's past were forged by men of toughness, men who risked their security and their futures for freedom and for an ideal . . . And because of what they and countless others like them achieved, we are now a powerful and prosperous country.
>
> But have the comforts we have bought, the successes we have won, the speeches that we make on national holidays extolling American bravery and generosity so undermined our strength of character that we are now unprepared to deal with the problems that face us? The records of the McClellan Committee are studded with disturbing signs that we are not prepared. Dangerous changes are taking place in the moral fiber of American society . . .
>
> It seems to me imperative that we re-instill in ourselves the toughness and idealism that guided the nation in the past . . .
>
> To meet the challenge of our times, so that we can later look back on this era not as one of which we need to be ashamed but as a turning point on the way to a better America, we must first defeat the enemy within.[33]

Although Robert Kennedy did not yet know that his brother would be elected president in the next year and that he would become attorney general, he had already stepped into Estes Kefauver's shoes as the leading foe of organized crime in national politics. And when in 1961 he rose to the pinnacle of the Justice Department, organized crime in general—and Jimmy Hoffa, Carlos Marcello, and Sam Giancana in particular—became his top priorities.

Meanwhile, both the government of the United States and the leadership of the mob became deeply preoccupied by events ninety miles off the coast of Florida, on the island of Cuba.

Castro Takes Power

The network of relationships that eventually brought about John F. Kennedy's assassination began to take shape in 1959, as a result of Fidel Castro's ascent to power. An astonishing number of key figures in the drama found themselves in Cuba during that year, their lives irrevocably altered by the emergence of the first Communist regime in the Western Hemisphere.

Castro's rise shook American foreign policy and the intelligence establishment to its foundations. It also created a new domestic and exiled revolutionary movement against Castro's regime and dealt a major blow to American mob interests. Perhaps most important, it brought to Cuba a remarkable collection of miscellaneous Americans whose names remained prominent in anti-Castro circles for years and whom we shall encounter again and again on the road to Dallas. Within a year of Castro's assumption of power, officials at the highest levels of the U.S. government, along with conservative American businessmen, mobsters, and independent Cuban exile groups, were all scheming to overthrow the dictator, and the complex relationships among these various contingents form the background of the Kennedy assassination in November 1963.

The island of Cuba—finally liberated from Spain in 1898 with American help—was one of the first and most disastrous of the United States' attempts to spread its values and system of government by force of arms. As so often happens, Washington soon found itself torn between two priorities: its genuine support for Cuban independence and its wish to control Cuban politics. These conflicting interests were embodied in the 1903 Platt Amendment to the Army Appropriations Act, which gave the United States the right to intervene in Cuba "for the preservation of

Cuban independence, the maintenance of a government adequate for the protection of life, property, and individual liberty," or simply to enforce the payment of Cuba's debts. When in 1933 President Ramon Grau San Martin unilaterally declared the humiliating amendment null and void, U.S. Ambassador Sumner Welles convinced Washington to support the overthrow of his government by a group of Army officers led by Fulgencio Batista. Although Batista yielded power in 1944, he returned in 1952 to overthrow the elected government of Carlos Prio Socarras.

In the mid-1950s Batista's rule was challenged by at least three powerful factions. Fidel Castro's 26th of July Movement commemorated the attack the twenty-six-year-old lawyer staged against the Moncada Barracks on that date in 1953—a bloody failure that landed Castro in jail for two years. After his release in 1955, he traveled to the United States and then to Mexico to raise money for revolutionary activities, and in December 1956 he managed to land a small group of men in Cuba. A few months later, on March 13, 1957, an internal revolutionary group, the Directorio Revolucionario (DR) or Revolutionary Directory, made an unsuccessful attempt on Batista's life by attacking the Presidential Palace. By 1956 both Castro and the DR were receiving help from Carlos Prio, who had taken tens of millions of dollars with him when he fled from Cuba to Miami in 1952. Prio eventually claimed to have given Castro $125,000—as it turned out, a very poor investment from Prio's perspective.[1]

Three North American entities developed an intense interest in Cuba's fate: the U.S. government in Washington, legitimate American businessmen, and mob figures who controlled Havana's rich casinos. All three tried in different ways to keep Batista in power, and all three rapidly became embroiled in attempts to overthrow or assassinate Fidel Castro after Batista fell. Both the State Department and the CIA criticized the brutal tactics of the "Tigers," a private pro-government militia run by Cuban Senator Rolando Masferrer, and eventually declared an arms embargo on Batista. Beginning to doubt that Batista could survive, the CIA may have even funneled some money to Fidel Castro, who at that time had no official Communist connections despite a good deal of socialist and anti-American rhetoric.

The American mob also faced a characteristic dilemma. For twenty-five years they had enlarged their interests in Cuban broadcasting and the press, as well as in casinos and the drug trade. And now, in 1958, they were planning the construction of a new resort hotel, the Havana Monte Carlo, twenty miles outside the capital. Its board of directors included several Hollywood figures and prominent hotel owners. Frank Sinatra was arranging to spend a good deal of time at the resort; leading Cuban banks were providing financing; and the developers planned a promotional campaign to rehabilitate Batista's image.[2] Meanwhile, however, the revolution—and especially the arms deals to which it gave birth—offered new opportunities for American mobsters, all the more so since Prio, who made plenty of mob connections of his own while Cuba's president, was financing some of them. And arms for Castro, of course, might provide insurance in case the bearded rebel managed to take power.

The Neutrality Act of 1937 barred Americans from independent military activities designed to affect the outcome of foreign wars, and several mob figures were caught attempting to sell arms—sometimes stolen arms—to Cuban rebels in 1957–58. Norman Rothmann, the owner of the Sans Souci casino in Havana, was arrested in late 1958 for transporting arms stolen from a National Guard Armory in Canton, Ohio, to Pittsburgh, the home base of his collaborator, Sam Mannarino. In 1960 Carl Noll, a New Orleans mobster who became a government informant, told the FBI that Carlos Marcello was deeply involved in this deal as well.[3] The *Chicago Sun-Times* reported that the arms were destined for Fidel Castro.[4] Like other casino owners, Rothmann had to flee Cuba after Castro's takeover in January 1959. He settled in Miami and immediately began promoting an anti-Castro coup.

A second, larger arms operation involved Pedro Diaz Lanz, later chief of Castro's air force, and Frank Fiorini (or, to use the name he had adopted some years earlier, Frank Sturgis), a thirty-five-year-old American veteran, former policeman, and bartender. Sturgis left the bar he ran in Norfolk, Virginia, in 1957 after kiting some checks and somehow made contact with the Cuban revolutionary movement in Miami.[5] Sturgis told a New York *Daily News* reporter in 1975 that he met Prio through a family connection and went to work for him in 1958, buying cars in Miami, filling them with arms, and shipping them to Cuba. He was arrested for arms trafficking and deported from Cuba in July of that year, after which U.S. Customs officials apparently decided to investigate him. A raid on his Miami house netted over 250 guns and 50,000 rounds of ammunition, and he was arrested for Neutrality Act violations.

In September 1958 Sturgis—a chronic exaggerator and self-promoter—told the Miami FBI that he once traveled to Cuba to offer Castro $100,000 for the release of some kidnapped Americans on behalf of no less a figure than Vice President Richard Nixon, for whom Sturgis became a "plumber" in the Watergate break-in thirteen years later. Meanwhile, he told an informant that he was looking for racketeers who might provide arms for Castro.[6] Undeterred by the FBI's interest, Sturgis went on a long trip in November that took him, Pedro Diaz Lanz, and others to California, Arizona (where they picked up a C-46 cargo plane), and Venezuela. They were arrested in Mexico, along with a huge cache of arms. Sturgis and Diaz Lanz managed to make contact with the CIA—which up until then had not, apparently, shown any interest in Sturgis—and the men were released after about ten days. In early 1959, after Castro took over, Sturgis claimed to have been his chief arms buyer in Miami.[7]

Yet another arms channel involved the exiled Cuban president, Prio. The FBI watched him closely from the moment he came to the United States in 1952 and continually uncovered new arms deals and expeditions to Cuba in which he was involved.[8] On February 13, 1958, the Justice Department indicted Prio for violating the Neutrality Act.[9] Also arrested were several Houston men, led by a reputed smuggler named Robert Ray McKeown, whose daughter was said to be Prio's girlfriend. McKeown had used Prio's money to purchase a safe house near Houston for storing five loads of arms prior to their shipment to Cuba, and he had been organizing an actual landing in Cuba, led by Jorge Sotus of the 26th of July Movement. McKeown pled guilty at his trial in October 1958 and received an eighteen-month suspended sentence. He eventually told the *Houston Post* that Prio promised him a half interest in the Sevia Biltmore hotel in Havana, in return for his cooperation. His arrest and trial received substantial press coverage throughout Texas and came to the attention of Dallas club owner Jack Ruby.[10]

Batista, meanwhile, attracted the help of Irving Davidson, a Washington public relations consultant, agent of foreign governments, and arms dealer who by 1958 was already working closely with Jimmy Hoffa.

Born in Pittsburgh in 1924, Davidson became a player in Washington by the mid-1950s, representing among others the Somoza government in Nicaragua, to which he managed to sell a shipment of Israeli weapons. "My specialty," he told an FBI source in 1955, "is to furnish anyone, anywhere, whatever armaments and other equipment they need as long as no questions are asked." Reports during the 1950s connected him to the Murchisons in Dallas—a family of oil barons who started the Dallas Cowboys—and identified him as a middleman for several loans from the Teamsters' Central States Pension Fund. He kept in intermittent touch with both CIA and FBI officials, apparently to stay in their good graces.[11] In November 1958 the FBI heard that Davidson had received a $260,000 letter of credit from the Cuban government to purchase more arms from Israel.[12]

In 1957 a Hoffa-connected arms dealer, Dominick Bartone of Ohio, formed a company, Akros Dynamics, to finance the purchase of eleven C-74 Globemaster aircraft from the U.S. government for $1.5 million to sell to Batista. Over the next two years, Bartone and various partners tried to arrange a loan from the Teamsters to finance the deal, but they had not been successful at the time of Batista's fall.[13] The mob, however, was apparently playing both sides of the street, trying to insure itself against a Castro takeover on the one hand while simultaneously seeking to eliminate the troublesome revolutionary altogether. As early as March 1958, the well-informed columnist Drew Pearson heard that the Mafia had put a $5 million price on Castro's head because his guerrilla campaign was damaging the tourist business.[14]

Meanwhile, the federal government's attempt to moderate Batista's rule failed. The dictator suspended constitutional guarantees in March 1958 and eventually staged a farcical election for president in November, in which a tiny turnout cast their ballots for his hand-picked candidate. Castro was clearly getting stronger, and in a show of strength in June he kidnapped fifty Americans and held them for a month—the Americans whom Sturgis claimed to have tried to ransom on behalf of Nixon. By the second half of 1958 the American ambassador to Cuba, Earl Smith, had concluded that Castro was a Communist, but the U.S. government, while continuing to make arrests of arms traffickers to the rebels, had not managed to come up with any new options for dealing with him. In fall 1958 a key CIA operative visited Havana to survey the situation and concluded that Batista was doomed.[15] But in the waning days of that year an American businessman, William Pawley, contacted Washington in an attempt to save Batista's government, if not the dictator himself.[16]

Pawley was both a former diplomat and a semi-professional intelligence agent. Born in South Carolina in 1896, he spent some of his youth in Cuba, and during the 1920s and 1930s he established himself as a player in the fledgling aircraft industry there, as well as in China and India. In 1940–41 Pawley became deeply involved in the formation of the American Volunteer Group, also known as the Flying Tigers—an American-piloted air force that the Roosevelt administration recruited for Chiang Kai-Shek. Active in various business enterprises catering to the Flying Tigers, Pawley eventually managed to collect a commission of $250,000 on one hundred P-40 planes that the new air force purchased from the Curtiss-Wright Corporation. The force's commander, General Claire Chennault, told federal investigators in 1944–45 that Pawley was guilty of attempted bribery.[17] But President Truman nevertheless appointed him as ambassador to Peru in 1945–46 and to Brazil in 1946–1948.

Pawley was also friendly with Henry Luce, the publisher of *Time* and *Life* magazines, and by 1949 he shared Luce's view that a foolish or treacherous clique of Foreign Service officers had handed China to the Communists. He began a parallel campaign against several diplomats, led by one Spruille Braden, a determined opponent of right-wing Latin American dictatorships which—he implied to the FBI—were giving similar aid and comfort to Communists in Latin America.[18] During the 1950s Pawley worked on two occasions with the CIA, which briefly cleared him as a source in 1952 despite several reports of his dishonesty and appointed him to the advisory Doolittle Committee in 1954.[19] He claimed in 1967 that he had somehow participated in the CIA-sponsored overthrow of the Arbenz government in Guatemala in 1954. According to his account, he had been a friend of Batista for about thirty years.[20]

By the 1950s Pawley owned the Havana street railway system and was developing business interests in the Dominican Republic. He had also become friendly with President Eisenhower and CIA Director Allen Dulles, and in November of 1958 he talked them into sending him on a private diplomatic mission to persuade Batista to step down in favor of a junta of more moderate army officers. On December 9, 1958, Pawley made the approach, together with the chief of the Havana CIA station and with J. C. King, chief of the CIA's Western Hemisphere branch. Batista declined to step down.[21]

Batista finally left Cuba on the last day of 1958. Prio's trusted associate Antonio Varona returned to Cuba and tried frantically to organize a "Third Force" at the last minute, but he failed. Fabian Escalante, a retired Cuban intelligence-officer-turned-historian, later wrote that a CIA contract agent in Havana, David Atlee Phillips, had been pushing a similar scheme.[22]

Although the American business community in Cuba shared Pawley's horror at Castro's triumph, a few American adventurers suddenly found themselves in new positions of power and influence, and others—including several recent veterans of the military—flocked to Cuba for reasons that are not entirely clear. Arms buyer Frank Sturgis, who by 1959 had reverted to his original name of Frank Fiorini, contacted the CIA station in Santiago de Cuba and offered to supply information on the new government in exchange for help in dealing with possible charges against him in the United States and the threatened loss of his U.S. citizenship. CIA headquarters advised the station to proceed without making any commitments, and Sturgis reported in March that he was now both chief security officer for the Cuban air force and an inspector for gambling.[23] During April, he visited the United States, presented himself at FBI headquarters, and warned several agents of growing Communist influence in Cuba. He claimed that the brothers Pedro and Mario Diaz Lanz of Castro's air force shared his concerns.[24]

Another ex-serviceman who apparently gave more than a passing thought to going to Castro's Cuba was Lee Harvey Oswald. He joined the Marines in 1957 and returned to the United States from a tour in the Far East in late 1958. Stationed at El Toro in southern California, Oswald and fellow Marine Luis Delgado talked about heading to Cuba when they were discharged later in 1959 and training soldiers to fight elsewhere in Latin America. Delgado told the Warren Commission that Oswald visited the Cuban consulate in Los Angeles during 1959, that he received mail from them, and that a visitor from the consulate came all the way out to the El Toro Marine base to talk to Oswald.[25] But when Oswald was discharged from the Marines in September, he changed his mind, took a boat to Europe, and traveled from Helsinki to Moscow in order to defect to the Soviet Union instead.

Three critical figures in the Kennedy assassination also turned up in Cuba during 1959. Loran Eugene Hall—who, with Lee Harvey Oswald in tow, stood at Silvia Odio's door in the fall of 1963—arrived on the island almost immediately after Castro's takeover. After Army service in Germany from 1947 to 1952, Hall spent seven difficult years in Wichita, enduring a broken marriage, an arrest for bad checks, and a new role as a police informer on local gambling activities. In 1957 he suffered a mental breakdown and spent six months in a VA hospital, and in March 1959, without warning, he left his parents' house and went directly to Cuba. Introduced shortly thereafter to Frank Sturgis, he landed a job as a trainer of troops for a planned invasion of Nicaragua. This coup was designed to overthrow the Somoza brothers, Anastasio and Luis—just the kind of work Oswald had contemplated. Hall rapidly fell afoul of his Cuban commanders, however, and was arrested on suspicion of being an American agent. He was released in July after three months' incarceration and returned to the United States, but not before he met Tampa mobster Santo Trafficante at a detention camp.[26]

Trafficante controlled five casinos or hotels to varying degrees, including the Sans Souci, the Hotel Comodoro, the Hotel St. John, the Hotel Deauville, and the Hotel Capri. He had settled in Cuba to evade the service of a subpoena in New York concerning the 1957 murder of Albert Anastasia. He also wanted to avoid answering questions about the Appalachin meeting, which had led to the indictment on May 21, 1959, of twenty-seven mobsters from around the country for obstruction of justice and the conviction of twenty of them in January 1960.[27]

Having given Castro some help and having already survived two major Cuban regime changes in 1944 and 1952, Trafficante, Meyer Lansky, and the rest of the casino owners probably expected simply to have to renegotiate and redirect their payoffs, but they were wrong. To many of Castro's rebels, the mob-owned Havana casinos looked like outposts of the Batista regime. Victorious soldiers trashed several of them on January 1, 1959, and the new government immediately banned gambling. Although Castro initially reopened the casinos in February to promote employment, he made it clear that Trafficante would not be able to continue operating the Sans Souci because of his former relationship to Batista's brother-in-law, Roberto Fernandez Miranda.[28]

During the next two months Trafficante arranged a false sale of the Sans Souci to Eufemio Fernandez Ortega, once the Secret Police chief under Prio. Castro responded by closing the Sans Souci on April 13, but Trafficante still hoped to remain in Cuba. When Jake Lansky and Dino Cellini, two fellow casino owners, were arrested for narcotics trafficking on May 6, Trafficante went into hiding. A month later one of his associates was arrested for offering the director general of public order $4,000 to call off the search for him.[29]

One of Trafficante's men had even worse luck. John Martino, who eventually admitted his role in the JFK assassination to three different people, first came to the attention of the FBI in the 1930s as a gambler, bootlegger, extortionist, and possible kidnapper in Atlantic City. In 1935 he moved to Miami and became deeply involved in gambling there. He was closely associated with Trafficante, and by the mid-1950s he was supplying gambling and security equipment to the casinos in Havana. Martino knew how to make roulette wheels that could stop on command, and he had also designed communications equipment to get the results of horse races to gamblers before they reached bookies through official channels.[30] Martino flew to Havana in January 1959 after Castro took power and made approximately half a dozen return trips to Miami during the next six months. Years later he admitted that he had been smuggling out money.[31]

On July 23 Martino was arrested in Havana for flying into the country illegally with his twelve-year-old son Edward and was subsequently charged with trying to sneak Cuban counter-revolutionaries out of the country. A Cuban doctor who treated him told the FBI that Martino was close not only to Trafficante but to a number of high officials of the Batista government, including former senator Rolando Masferrer, and had offered the doctor the job of house physician in a brothel he hoped to start.[32] Martino did not go to trial until December 1959.

Trafficante was also reported to have made contact with certain Americans in the Cuban Revolutionary Army, who could easily have included Frank Sturgis and the American soldier of fortune William Morgan. On June 9 he was finally arrested, but in recognition of his promi-

nence and financial resources he was held at Trescornia, a holding area
for immigrants, rather than in a prison, and was allowed to have his own
food and wine brought in while he tried to arrange his release. One of
his cellmates was Hall, and this marked the beginning of an intermittent
association that lasted for at least twenty years.[33]

During his confinement, Trafficante received another visitor—Jack
Ruby. In the mid-1950s Ruby was still running the Vegas Club, which
he had started with his partner Joe Bonds, now in prison on sodomy and
white slave charges. Dallas police had arrested Ruby several times over
fights with customers and liquor hour violations, but he had no significant convictions.[34] Indeed, he was already buttering up the Dallas police by encouraging them to frequent his clubs and hiring them as
bouncers.[35] In the late 1950s, living hand to mouth, Ruby took out several loans of one to three thousand dollars, secured by his cars, which he
repaid in installments.[36] Like so many minor underworld figures, he was
continually looking for the big score—ranging from a new invention to
the career of a dancer/singer he discovered at one of his clubs—and in
early 1959 he tried to get into the Cuban arms business.

Around that time, Robert Ray McKeown was awaiting sentencing in
Houston for making arms deals and planning invasions of Cuba in 1958.
To keep himself busy, he ran a drive-in in nearby Seabrook, financed by
his friend and collaborator Prio. Not long after Castro took power, a local deputy sheriff visited McKeown to tell him that someone was trying
frantically to locate him through the sheriff's office on "a life or death
matter." About an hour after giving the sheriff his number, McKeown
got a call. A Dallas man identified himself as "Rubinstein" and explained
that he wanted to help free three men who were being held by Fidel
Castro. He offered a ransom of $5,000 for each man, the money to be
supplied by unidentified Las Vegas interests. McKeown asked for the
money up front, and Rubinstein promised to get back to him.

Rubinstein never called back, but several weeks later a man whom
McKeown believed to be Ruby showed up at the drive-in with a somewhat different proposition—an offer to sell a large number of jeeps in
Shreveport, Louisiana, to Castro. McKeown offered him a letter of introduction to Castro for $5,000, and the man promised to bring the money,
but he never returned. McKeown, Ruby, and the deputy sheriff all confirmed this story in 1964.[37] In his deposition for the HSCA in 1978,

McKeown opened up another possible connection between Ruby and Cuba. Asked if he knew the prominent restaurateurs and mobsters Joe and Sam Campisi of Dallas—with whom Ruby was well acquainted—McKeown replied that while he had not met them, Prio had identified them as friends of his cause.[38]

Nothing, apparently, came of Ruby's jeep scheme, but he had definitely discovered that certain prominent Americans in Cuba needed help getting out. During 1959 Ruby was pushing forward on several fronts. In March he contacted an FBI agent, Charles Flynn, and offered to serve as an informant. He met with an agent eight times between March and October but never provided any useful information.[39] Criminals frequently open up a channel to law enforcement when they are embarking on a new and potentially hazardous enterprise.[40] Flynn simply used their meetings to ask Ruby for information about recent crimes, mainly robberies, and Ruby did not have any to give.[41] Significantly, he never told Flynn anything about Cuba—which remained very much on his mind.

It may also have been during the summer of 1959 that Ruby made contact with the Fox brothers Pedro and Martin, the Cuban owners of the Tropicana Hotel and Casino in Havana, where mobster Lewis McWillie, Ruby's old friend, worked.[42] As Ruby explained to the Warren Commission, he had had dinner with one of the Fox brothers and two Dallas attorneys with shady connections of their own, David McCord and Alfred E. McLane. The Fox brothers had come to Dallas to collect a gambling debt from the owner of a cotton gin company. If the dinner took place in early 1959, Ruby might well have heard about the continuing arms market in Cuba or about Castro's detention of mob figures connected with the casinos. Certainly he became interested in these issues around that time.[43]

In May 1959 a woman named Elaine Mynier, who had met Ruby while working for National Car Rental in Dallas, took a trip to Havana. Ruby gave her a coded message for McWillie, indicating that Ruby himself was coming to Havana soon. "He's crazy," McWillie remarked, when Mynier delivered the message.[44] About six weeks later, on July 1, Ruby rented a safe deposit box in a Dallas bank, which he visited frequently during the next few months.[45]

Ruby never told the whole truth about his Havana visit. A Cuban government tourist card showed that he entered Cuba on August 8.

During the next ten days he evidently visited Trafficante, still being held in Trescornia, more than once. That information was given to the CIA in London on November 26, 1963—the day after Ruby became world famous for killing Lee Harvey Oswald—by a British journalist named John Wilson-Hudson, who had been arrested in Cuba in July 1959 for his involvement in a plot to invade Nicaragua (the same round-up, apparently, that snared Loran Hall, who also spent time in Trescornia). Wilson-Hudson was held for about sixty days. He remembered an American gangster, "Louis Santos"—an alias Trafficante frequently used in Cuba—who enjoyed unusually comfortable accommodations and who was "frequently" visited by "another American gangster type named Ruby." Trafficante was released on August 18, ten days after Ruby's arrival.[46]

This, however, was only the first chapter in Ruby's Cuban odyssey. Around the time of Trafficante's release, he apparently managed to get out of Cuba without the knowledge of Cuban authorities. He was back in Dallas using his safe deposit box on August 21, met with FBI agent Flynn on August 31 (although without mentioning his travels to Cuba), and visited the safe deposit box again on September 4, the Friday before Labor Day. He evidently flew back to Havana immediately thereafter, since three Chicagoans vividly remembered a conversation with Ruby at the Tropicana during that weekend.[47] Ruby flew to Miami on September 11, where he met an old gambling friend of his and McWillie's from Dallas, Meyer Panitz, and then returned to Havana on September 12. He left for New Orleans the next day.[48] It seems reasonable to suppose that Ruby, like Martino, was flying money out of Cuba. But unlike Martino, who on December 28, 1959, was sentenced to thirteen years in prison for attempting to smuggle the family of a war criminal off the island, Ruby got away with it.[49]

While the Havana casino owners struggled to get themselves and their money out of Cuba, other American mob interests tried to play it both ways. Akros Dynamics—the Ohio-based organization that had sought Teamsters money to finance the sale of surplus planes to Batista—attempted early in 1959 to sell several planes to the new Cuban government. Dominick Bartone and some of his associates also made trips to Cuba to try to work out a deal. Jimmy Hoffa's role in the financing of Akros Dynamics had already come to the attention of the Senate Rackets Committee and Robert Kennedy, and publicity forced the Teamsters to drop out of the deal—at least overtly. Many years later, Edward Partin, a Louisiana Teamster who became the government's key informant against Hoffa in 1962, commented, "The whole thing was purely and simply Hoffa's way of helping some of his mob buddies who were afraid of losing their businesses in Cuba . . . They were trying to score points with Castro right after he moved in."[50]

By May, however, Bartone had worked out another deal to sell a consignment of arms to a group of Batista supporters that had formed inside the Dominican dictatorship of General Rafael Trujillo. On May 22 Bartone and several confederates were arrested in Miami as they tried to fly a planeload of arms and ammunition to the Dominican Republic, and they were charged with bribing a customs official and conspiring to export arms illegally.[51]

In July 1959 an American journalist, William Attwood, made one of his many visits to Cuba. A distinguished foreign correspondent and editor of *Look* magazine, Attwood had interviewed Castro at length before and after the revolution. He later became ambassador to Guinea under President Kennedy. During a party at a well-appointed Havana house, Attwood heard several Americans openly discussing the imminent assassination of Castro. "As a matter of fact," he said, "I was introduced to two alleged assassins, people who had been selected to do the job, which actually dumfounded me." Attwood also heard from the multimillionaire banker and sugar magnate Julio Lobo that "there was a contract out" on Castro, that he "would not live out the year." Other party-goers said the talkative Americans were CIA.[52]

Attwood had probably stumbled upon a budding conspiracy involving mobsters, Batistianos in the Dominican Republic, and the American William Morgan, who had fought for Castro and was now operating as a double or triple agent. Bartone contacted Morgan by May 1959 and heard of the Trujillo-backed plan to overthrow Castro. On July 30 an informant told the FBI in Havana that he had seen the Dominican consul general give Morgan $200,000 in Bartone's presence. Morgan was rumored to be planning Castro's assassination in conjunction with a planned invasion from the Dominican Republic.[53] In 1978 the former arms trader and convicted securities swindler Edward Browder not only told almost exactly the same story to HSCA investigators but added that the assassination was supposed to take place at Cojimar, a favorite resort of Castro's, and that CIA agents had personally furnished Morgan with the weapons to do it. Browder said that Morgan double-crossed his confederates and gave the weapons and the money to Castro.[54]

In Washington, FBI headquarters heard about the proposed invasion in early May from several sources, including General Manuel Benitez, former Cuban legislator and head of the National Police, and lobbyist Irving Davidson. Some weeks later, on June 30, Davidson met with FBI assistant director August Belmont on behalf of Julio Lobo in an attempt to secure official U.S. backing for another group of conservative exiles, the Crusade of Revolutionaries against Communism (CRAC). Davidson threatened that Lobo and CRAC would have to associate themselves with the imminent invasion from the Dominican Republic if they did not get U.S. backing.[55] But on August 13 the invasion of Cuba from the Dominican Republic failed disastrously after Morgan and Castro associate Eloy Gutierrez Menoyo turned double agents and betrayed the plot, leading to the arrest of several thousand Cubans who had planned to assist the invasion force.[56] The first major effort to topple Fidel Castro had failed. Morgan, who had a history of mental illness as well as crime, apparently continued playing one side against the other until November 1959, when Cuban police arrested him for trying to organize guerrilla resistance against Castro. He was executed in 1960.

The highest levels of the United States government reacted more slowly to Castro's takeover. After the revolutionaries executed several hundred Batistianos, CIA director Dulles warned the National Security Council on February 12 that Castro intended to lead a revolution throughout Latin America. In April, however, when Castro visited the United States, Vice President Nixon talked to him at some length and concluded that the U.S. government had no choice but to try to influence Castro, a natural leader of men, in the right direction. Huge May Day celebrations and the announcement of a new Agrarian Law on May 17—which had dire implications for American sugar properties—aroused more concern. But in June the State Department sent an urgent telegram to Latin American missions, warning of a possible invasion of Cuba by pro-Batista forces in the Dominican Republic.[57]

Some evidence suggests, however, that American intelligence agents in Cuba were taking a more alarmed view of the Castro regime, and were even beginning to act on it. The Agrarian Reform Law and the increasing influence of Raoul Castro and Che Guevara led to the formation of an organized opposition within Cuba during the summer of 1959, including both veterans of the guerrilla war in the Sierra Maestra like Huber Matos, Humberto Sori Marin, and Manuel Artime, and Autenticos like Prio and Varona. The CIA maintained contact with them through Bernard Barker, a former Batista intelligence operative and future Watergate burglar. In September, Artime suggested that the opposition might rebel to provide a pretext for American intervention, but within another month Matos was arrested and Artime had fled the country.[58]

In 1975 in testimony before the Rockefeller Commission and in an interview with the New York *Daily News,* Frank Sturgis told how he was recruited by Park F. Woolam, a CIA agent in Santiago de Cuba, just before Castro took power, and how he then began working with the military attaché in Havana, a Colonel Nichols, who, he believed, worked with CIA. Sturgis's CIA 201 file, which was opened in 1958 when his arms dealings became known to government authorities, confirms that he did offer his services to a CIA agent in Santiago de Cuba on January 6, 1959, expressing some fear that he might lose his U.S. citizenship as a result of continuing to work for Castro. "Base should deal with subject under strict [deleted] cover and not make any commitments which might later be construed as [U.S. Government] approval [of] his activities," the Western Hemisphere branch replied on January 13.[59]

Sturgis claimed that he immediately began recruiting agents and was involved as early as February 1959 in the first of several plots to assassinate Castro and the rest of Cuba's top leadership. He said he informed Colonel Nichols of the plots but was told not to go ahead. He said that he helped arrange the dramatic escape of himself and Pedro Diaz Lanz, the commander of Castro's air force, who flew to the United States on July 1, 1959, testified before a Senate committee, and began dropping leaflets over Cuba. Sturgis himself eventually fled the island in 1960.[60] The CIA has not released documents that would confirm or refute Sturgis's story. But in the 201 file the CIA released to the Assassination Records Review Board, there is not a single document from the period between January 13, 1959, when headquarters authorized Sturgis's use as a source, and January 10, 1961, when the CIA's Miami station reported on his activities in terms that suggest the station had no idea he had worked for the agency in Cuba. Sturgis frequently embellished his exploits when talking with the press, but given that he clearly *was* recruited in 1959, it seems that either the CIA opened a new file for him under a different name when he became a source or agent, or that some of his file was never released.[61]

Not until the fall of 1959 did the highest levels of the U.S. government decide that Castro had to go. In October, after another blood-curdling anti-American speech, the State Department concluded that regime change would be necessary to achieve U.S. objectives in Latin America, and that the United States should begin working toward this goal without "giving the impression of direct pressure or intervention." Secretary of State Christian Herter, who replaced the mortally ill John Foster Dulles, passed this recommendation on to President Eisenhower, but meanwhile the State Department was trying to stop unauthorized raids against Castro by Cuban exiles.[62] In December the joint chiefs of staff—prodded by the militant chief of naval operations, Admiral Arleigh Burke—were asking for a plan to invade Cuba.

The Eisenhower administration's policy of seeking the overthrow of leftist Latin American regimes, adopted in 1954, marked a break from Franklin Roosevelt's Good Neighbor Policy of 1934, in which FDR renounced decades of American military intervention around the Caribbean. In the Rio Treaty of 1947 and the charter of the Organization of American States in 1948, the United States and the rest of the Latin American republics reaffirmed the principle of nonintervention in one another's internal affairs. But within just a few years, the Truman administration was struggling with the issue of how to reconcile that principle with the possible need to move against Communism in Latin America. It never reached a definite conclusion.[63] The Truman administration also tried to coexist peacefully with the Arbenz regime in Guatemala after Jacobo Arbenz Guzman was elected president in 1950, despite its nationalization of large properties owned by the United Fruit Company.

Within a year of taking office, Eisenhower decided that Arbenz was under the control of international Communism, and after failing to secure the endorsement of the OAS for the regime's overthrow, the administration decided to proceed covertly. The CIA under Allen Dulles was rapidly emerging as the preferred action arm against hostile Third World regimes. It had successfully overthrown the nationalist and leftist government in Iran in 1953. A year later, it orchestrated a small two-hundred-man invasion of Guatemala from Honduras, which, along with air strikes, persuaded the Guatemalan military to move against Arbenz. During the 1950s the CIA also tried and failed to eliminate the neutralist Prince Sihanouk of Cambodia, maneuvered a weak pro-Western government into power in Laos, and started a failed rebellion in Tibet and an unsuccessful secessionist war in Sumatra.[64] The agency was certain to play an important role in dealing with Castro as well.

On December 12, J. C. King, chief of the CIA's Western Hemisphere branch, wrote a memo for Dulles, his boss, predicting terrible consequences if Castro remained in power for as much as two years. Thorough consideration, he argued, should be given "to the elimination of Fidel Castro." In a foretaste of the rhetorical prudery that characterized many such discussions over the next four years, someone bracketed "elimination" and wrote "removal from Cuba" above it in ink.[65] A month later King cabled the Havana station chief about the possibility of using chemicals to make Castro's beard fall out.[66]

King was already supervising attempts to unify the Cuban exile community, partly with the help of William Pawley, who had tried and failed to get Batista to step down in late 1958. According to a report from King's Miami representative in early October, Pawley was "a staunch believer in the value of a certain kind of dictatorship for certain Latin American countries," including the Dominican Republic, where he and his brother had business interests and were close to Trujillo. Because he was in frequent touch with Cubans within Batista's inner circle—including some of those associated with Lobo's CRAC and with the Dominican invasion fiasco—Pawley suggested that the CIA install a recording device in his own Miami office, which technicians did in mid-October 1959.[67]

Pawley communicated frequently with Dulles, a personal friend, as well as with King, and on December 22 he was given covert security approval and assigned the cryptonym QDDALE. With CIA help, he began building anti-Castro organizations both inside and outside Cuba. He was, in effect, an informal case officer.[68] On January 9, 1960, Pawley had some intense discussions about the Cuban problem during a lunch with Vice President Nixon, who regarded him as a close adviser and to whom

Pawley presented a handsome dress watch. At Nixon's suggestion, Pawley invited President Eisenhower for a weekend of hunting at his Virginia farm.[69]

The National Security Council reviewed policy on January 14, 1960, and Livingston Merchant of the State Department explained that his agency was "cooperating with CIA in action [deletion] designed to build up an opposition to Castro. The NSC members discussed different legal bases for intervention, and Nixon, whose campaign for President was warming up, suggested "that Latin America was better prepared for what might happen in Cuba than it had been for events in Guatemala."[70] Eisenhower, however, gave the opposite impression in a press conference and in an official statement on January 22. While the President declared that he was "perplexed" and "concerned" by Castro's anti-American rhetoric, the statement reaffirmed the OAS treaty's commitment to "the policy of non-intervention in the domestic affairs of other countries, including Cuba." It also claimed that the United States was continuing to prevent aggressive acts against Castro mounted from within U.S. territory, and it recognized Cuba's right to undertake domestic reforms.[71]

Pawley may actually have sold President Eisenhower on the assassination of Castro. He met with the President, who had confidence in his judgment on Latin American matters, for about an hour on February 15. Two days later Eisenhower discussed pending proposals for covert action in Cuba with two NSC staffers, Gordon Gray and General Andrew Goodpaster. Eisenhower questioned why plans were proceeding "on such a narrow basis [and] said that he wondered why we weren't trying to identify assets for this and other things as well across the board, including even possibly things that might be drastic. He thought it would be a good idea for the Group to talk with a man he had talked with as Government officials interested in the problem."[72] Five days later, Pawley called one of his CIA contacts to report that Matthew Slepin, chairman of the Dade County Republican Party, had promised twelve Cuban exiles either $20 million or $200 million on behalf of Vice President Nixon to finance the overthrow of Castro. The story was never confirmed.[73]

President Eisenhower left on a tour of South America just a few days later. There, he witnessed abject poverty and received a warm personal reception, but faced resolute opposition to any intervention in Cuba's internal affairs. In Brazil, Argentina, Chile, and Uruguay, his public statements reaffirmed his commitment to nonintervention while extolling the growth of freedom and resistance to tyranny of all kinds.[74] By early March, however, Castro had proceeded from the nationalization of American enterprises to the exploration of weapons purchases from the Soviet Union—the exact steps that had provoked the administration to overthrow the Arbenz regime in Guatemala just six years earlier.[75]

The Eisenhower administration's approval of covert action to overthrow Castro came during the spring of 1960, some months after the CIA actually began work on the project. High-level meetings and papers consistently used language that concealed certain aspects of their strategy. Although the Eisenhower NSC customarily registered any change in policy in a formal document, a State official explained that they did not want to do so this time, since the desired change in government must be brought about by "highly intricate and delicate operations in daily coordination with each other" by State, CIA, and USIA.[76]

The administration established a "Special Group" with responsibility for covert action. It included one representative each of the White House, State Department, Defense Department, and CIA. On March 16 the Special Group (also known as the 5412 Committee) submitted a program of action to bring down the Castro regime.[77] "The purpose of the program outlined herein," it read, "is to bring about the replacement of the Castro regime with one more devoted to the true interests of the Cuban people and more acceptable to the U.S. in such a manner as to avoid any appearance of U.S. intervention." To accomplish this, the CIA intended to organize political leadership within the Cuban exile community and to continue work on forming a "covert intelligence and action organization" inside Cuba that could provide intelligence, infiltrate and exfiltrate agents, distribute propaganda, and attempt to secure the defection of key individuals.

Meanwhile, the CIA planned to take six to eight months (roughly the period of time before the November election) to train a paramilitary force somewhere outside the United States. The paper budgeted $4.4 million for the program during fiscal 1960—a figure that eventually fell short by an order of magnitude. Contacts with the force, the paper claimed, would be handled by "a carefully screened group of U.S. businessmen with a stated interest in Cuban affairs and desire to support the opposition." That statement, as it turned out, was false. The so-called businessmen were actually CIA case officers *posing* as American business-men—a ruse that certainly did not fool the Cuban exiles they were sup-porting.[78] Eisenhower endorsed the plan firmly in a March 17 meeting with various CIA agents but emphasized that everyone involved "must be prepared to swear that he has not heard of it."[79]

Although March 1960 was a pivotal moment in U.S. policy toward Castro, at least one mystery remains unsolved. We do not know if the CIA had anything to do with the explosion of the French ship *La Coubre* in Havana harbor on March 4, 1960. The ship was loaded with arms, and two separate explosions killed a total of eighty-one crew members and Cubans. Castro immediately blamed the U.S. government, which, whether or not it was responsible for this particular outrage, was on the verge of undertaking to overthrow his regime.[80]

Thus began the CIA's first attempt to remove Castro from power. Af-ter the disaster at the Bay of Pigs, this operation was summarized in some detail by Lyman Kirkpatrick, a rising star in covert operations in the early 1950s who became the agency inspector general after a crippling polio attack. Kirkpatrick's report—of which Richard Helms, then the deputy director for plans and chief of covert operations, ordered all copies de-stroyed but one—did not see the light of day until the late 1990s, despite the efforts of no less a figure than President Richard Nixon to get his hands on it. Nixon undoubtedly hoped that it would definitively assign blame for the failure of the Bay of Pigs to John Kennedy, but it did not. The inspector general's report was a remarkably frank and informative document that laid the vast majority of the blame on the agency itself.[81]

According to the report, in January 1960 the CIA formed a new branch, the Western Hemisphere branch 4 (WH4), to deal with Castro. Headed by J. D. Esterline, it included eighteen headquarters personnel, twenty agents in Havana, and two in Santiago de Cuba. In April they re-ceived the right to recruit personnel from any covert operations branch, and by April 1961 they had grown to a strength of 588. Many of the re-cruits, Kirkpatrick found, were low-quality people whom their home of-fices were delighted to get rid of, and relatively few of them spoke Span-ish.[82] The effort did not go well.

Poor organization—frequently a problem in the compartmentalized CIA during this period—plagued the project. Richard Bissell, the deputy director for plans, insisted on remaining in charge but gave some respon-sibility to his deputy for covert action, Tracy Barnes. J. C. King, chief of the Western Hemisphere branch, intermittently inserted himself between Bissell and the actual project coordinator, Esterline. Meanwhile, both headquarters and the Miami station frequently competed for the same agents—a problem that persisted throughout the early 1960s. When the Cuban stations closed down in January 1961 after breaking off diplomatic relations, the Miami station (now named JMWAVE) expected to take over agents still remaining in Cuba, but headquarters took them over instead.[83]

Plagued by divided lines of authority and conflicts between headquarters and the new Miami station (JMWAVE), the project moved forward on at least three fronts: counterintelligence, politics, and military training. In July 1960 the Miami station—increasingly a contender for power—began training a couple of hundred Cubans in counterintelligence, hoping to develop the nucleus of a post-Castro security organization in Havana. According to a Cuban authority, this group included Bernard Barker and Eugenio Martinez (both of Watergate fame) and Felix Rodriguez, who emerged in 1986 as a key figure in the Iran-Contra affair.[84] These men became important CIA and FBI sources on exile activity all through the 1960s.

On the political front, the agency made a firm decision not to help anyone associated with Batista, but it failed to stop its informal case officer, William Pawley, from doing just that.[85] In May 1960 the CIA arranged the formation of the Frente Revolucionario Democratico (FRD), with Antonio Varona as coordinator. The front also included his fellow Autentico party leader Aureliano Sanchez Arrango and three defectors from Castro's revolution: Manuel Artime of the Movimiento Revolucionario de Recuparacion (MRR), Juan Antonio Rasco of the Movimiento Democratico Cristiano (MDC), and Manuel Ray of the Movimiento Revolucionario Popular (MRP).[86] All these men would remain leaders of Cuban exile groups for the next four years. Ray, who openly pressed for "Fidelismo sin Fidel" (Castroism without Castro), immediately became a very controversial figure, and by March 1961 Pawley was complaining to the State Department that Ray was already making promises to the Russians and arguing that four more conservative leaders should join the FRD.[87] The struggle between former Castro associates who had turned against Communism on the one hand and former Batistianos on the other was destined to continue all the way through the Kennedy administration.

The FRD's first CIA case officer, Gerald Droller—a leftish German using the name Frank Bender—was now replaced by the much more conservative E. Howard Hunt. The FRD fell apart in November 1960, but by the following March it was reborn as the Cuban Revolutionary Council, led by a new defector, another diplomat, Jose Miro Cardona.[88] The controversy was a portent of things to come. Both the Eisenhower and Kennedy administrations recognized that they could not sponsor anything that looked like a restoration of the Batista regime, but their patronage of left-leaning activists infuriated established Cuban exiles and, as time went on, some of their right-wing American supporters as well.

On the military front, the project eventually established bases at four locations in Florida, at one location near New Orleans, and at others in Puerto Rico, Panama, Nicaragua, and above all Guatemala. Though the CIA decided as early as December 1959 to train some kind of paramilitary force outside Cuba, the main base in Guatemala did not open until late October 1960, and American Special Forces instructors did not arrive until January 1961. By the end of that month the base had 644 trainees, and the number more than doubled during the next three months. Manuel Artime became the commander of the force, which was christened Brigade 2506. Although the Eisenhower administration was never convinced that this force alone would overthrow Castro, the Guatemala base, Kirkpatrick found, became the focus of the agency's hopes for success. Its American trainers frequently treated the Cubans with contempt, however, and kept political leaders of the FRD/CRC from visiting the base until the eve of the actual Bay of Pigs invasion. Dissension resulted, and the Cubans came to view the paramilitary force as an entirely American project.[89]

Thousands of Cubans, including many young men of military age, were now emigrating to the United States, and several significant underground movements were still carrying on resistance within Cuba during 1960. However, the CIA's directorate of plans—its covert arm—was simply not suited to mobilizing the masses. Its case officers were accustomed to the clandestine exploitation of individual sources or small networks for the purpose of collecting intelligence—a process very different from instigation and management of a political movement, much less the training and deployment of an army. While agency officers spent months trying to bring various groups together in the FRD and CRC, they refused to give Cuban political leaders any authority over the 1,500 men they were training to invade. Cuban leaders believed that the CIA was ignoring them, and when the Bay of Pigs failed, many exiles became convinced that the agency could never deliver on its promises.[90]

Inevitably, given the broad spectrum of opposition to Castro, the complexity of Cuban politics, and the rampant individualism of young male Cubans, as shown by the multiple splits within Castro's own coalition during 1959–60, some Cuban groups began operating independently. In September 1960 the CIA learned of the formation of the Insurrectional Movement for Revolutionary Recovery (MIRR), led by two veterans of Castro's revolution: Orlando Bosch Avila, a former provincial chief of Castro's 26th of July Movement, and Victor Paneque Batista, known as Commandante Diego, who had been a high police official under Castro in 1959. Paneque expressed distrust for the FRD, arguing that "the CIA was in such a hurry to get married that it picked the wrong girl." He claimed to have formed a loose alliance with Artime's MRR and other groups and discussed plans to infiltrate ninety guerrillas into the Escambray, where he had fought Batista. The agency was leery of Paneque, fearing he might be a Castro agent, but he somehow acquired enough money to purchase arms for one hundred men inside the United States.[91]

By the end of the year Bosch and Paneque were receiving recruiting assistance from two Americans: Frank Sturgis, who had returned from Cuba, and Alex Rorke, a television journalist and friend of President Eisenhower who had contacts with the New York office of the CIA.[92] In December the FBI informed the CIA that it was investigating Sturgis for Neutrality Act violations, and the agency replied equivocally that while it did not yet have an interest in the MIRR, it might acquire one. Bosch traveled back and forth to Cuba in early 1961, but a huge offensive by Castro's militia rolled up most of the Escambray guerrillas in March. Bosch complained bitterly that no equipment had ever been airdropped by Varona and the FRD.[93]

Another new factor in the exile community was the revived DRE, or Student Revolutionary Directorate, which the CIA helped put together in Miami in October 1960. The original Directorio Revolucionario had been a key part of Castro's revolutionary coalition, and in early 1960

Castro appointed one of its leaders, Rolando Cubela, to head the Federation of University Students. Cubela immediately began purging and driving into hiding any students who opposed the turn toward Communism.[94]

Two student leaders, Alberto Muller and Manuel Salvat Roque, managed to reach the United States in June 1960, and the CIA helped them set up the DRE in September with Muller as leader and Salvat as propaganda chief. During the next six months the DRE did what it could to arrange attacks on radio stations, other sabotage actions, and a general student strike in April 1961. But the CIA treated the DRE as a propaganda operation and does not seem to have given any assistance beyond infiltrating Muller and Salvat back into Cuba. Salvat eventually returned to the United States through Guantanamo, but Muller remained inside.[95] In the summer of 1963, the DRE would have a well-publicized confrontation with Lee Harvey Oswald in New Orleans.

Official Cuban-American relations deteriorated significantly during the second half of 1960. In May Castro demanded that American and British oil refineries on Cuban soil must begin processing Soviet crude, and when they refused, he nationalized them in late June. A week later President Eisenhower announced that the United States would cancel Cuba's huge sugar quota, and Khrushchev immediately promised to take up the slack. The Soviet premier also made a vague but threatening promise of military support for Cuba, including "rockets." In August Castro began nationalizing the remaining American properties, and in September he traveled to New York to attend a session of the United Nations and meet with Khrushchev.[96] Eisenhower's last major public statement on Castro during 1960 came on August 24, when he told a press conference that he did not regard the situation as "irretrievable." After reviewing the history of Cuban-American relations, he went on to say that the United States had "tried to keep our hands out of their internal political affairs."[97]

Presidential candidates John F. Kennedy and Richard Nixon took a different view. From the beginning of his campaign, Kennedy declared that Cuba had definitely gone Communist on the Eisenhower administration's watch. In his fourth televised debate with Nixon, he specifically advocated helping and arming exiles in an effort to overthrow the Castro regime, pointing out, correctly, that many of the arms Castro had used to topple Batista had come from the United States. There is no evidence that Kennedy was briefed about the forthcoming invasion, which had not yet leaked to the American press, though Nixon later claimed that he was. Nixon replied that Kennedy's proposals would alienate the OAS and the United Nations and invite Khrushchev to come into Latin America. He suggested instead that Castro might be toppled by "isolating" him, the way that the United States had isolated the Arbenz government in Guatemala in 1954—an ironic suggestion, since Arbenz had actually been felled by a CIA covert operation.[98]

On November 29, 1960, after Nixon had lost the election, the senior leadership of the Eisenhower administration discussed the Cuban situation for the last time. News of the Guatemala training camp had now leaked, but President Eisenhower insisted that it continue as long as it was not obvious that the United States was behind it—a rather optimistic underestimate of the perceptive capabilities of the Latin American public. Eisenhower had just come from another forty-five minutes with Pawley, who entreated him to purge Manuel Artime from the FRD on the grounds that he was a Communist, to increase the size of the brigade, and to put one man—Pawley himself—in charge of the whole effort. Pawley had been lobbying for such an appointment for about six months, and Ike, while acknowledging that Pawley was "a zealot," seemed to like the idea. Allen Dulles and his senior cabinet secretaries disagreed.[99]

On December 8, CIA representatives presented a new plan to the Special Group in charge of covert activities. It called for preliminary air strikes launched from Nicaragua against Cuban military targets, followed by a landing of exiles that was expected to rally dissidents and trigger an anti-Castro uprising. The group authorized the agency to proceed. A last CIA study, prepared just four days before Kennedy took office, expressed doubt that the Cuban force would be able to effect a "lodgment" on its own and implied that American military intervention would be necessary. On his last day in office on January 19, Eisenhower told Kennedy that the project was going well and that he had a "responsibility" to do "whatever is necessary" to make it work.[100]

By the time of that meeting, co-existence with Castro was no longer an option. In early December 1960 the American Embassy in Havana—which obviously had not been apprised of decisions in Washington—recommended that the United States take a series of measures to bring about Castro's fall, even if OAS and NATO help were not forthcoming. These included the rupture of diplomatic relations, which the embassy suggested in a further dispatch of December 16, despite the intelligence disadvantages that would accrue from the departure of CIA agents working within the embassy and various consulates. Eisenhower decided on December 29 to break off relations, two days after yet another meeting with Pawley, who was just back from Argentina and who thought that some Latin American governments would support that step.[101]

The embassy warned that the United States would do well to take the initiative in this matter, but Washington did not move quickly enough. On January 2, 1961, the Cuban government gave the Havana embassy a note informing it that both the Cuban Embassy in Washington and the American Embassy in Havana must be reduced to eleven persons within forty-eight hours. The next day, a meeting of senior officials at the White House decided to break relations even though the President noted that this would make it much harder to know what was happening in Cuba. The officials also decided to increase the size of the guerrilla force in training to about 1,500 men. The break was consummated that very day.[102]

The paramilitary effort to topple the Castro regime, while covert, figured in numerous high-level administration discussions and gradually leaked to the press. But the assassination of Castro himself, and possibly of other Cuban leaders as well, was handled with a much greater emphasis on secrecy. The Eisenhower administration was committed to this mission by mid-1960, and to carry it out the CIA recruited three prominent organized crime figures: John Roselli of Los Angeles, Sam Giancana of Chicago, and Santo Trafficante of Tampa and Miami.

3

The CIA Enlists the Mob

In May 1960, Nikita Khrushchev shocked the United States and the world by announcing that the Soviet Union had shot down an American spy plane over its territory and captured the pilot, Francis Gary Powers. Responding at a news conference on May 11, President Eisenhower commented on "the nature of intelligence-gathering activities" of a "special and secret character. They are, so to speak, 'below the surface' activities . . . They are divorced from the regular visible agencies of government which stay clear of operational involvement in specific detailed activities . . . a distasteful but vital necessity."[1]

Eisenhower was referring specifically to the collection of intelligence, but his administration had also overseen a vast expansion of CIA covert political activity. Eisenhower and his leading subordinates had undertaken highly sensitive covert operations which, in some cases, might be known to only two individuals outside the CIA, the President and the secretary of state. CIA agents, meanwhile, treated the secrecy of their sources, methods, and operations as a fundamental requirement that must never be compromised. Against this background, in the summer of 1960 the Eisenhower administration authorized and mounted several assassination plots against troublesome foreign leaders, including Fidel Castro.

The CIA-Mafia plot against Castro—which lasted from 1960 until at least the late spring of 1963—raises profound questions for the historian. Planned at the highest level, it took place in such complete secrecy that the American people might never have heard of it at all. Although the affair left a few paper traces in some parts of the government, everything we know suggests that it would never have come to light had not the legislative and executive branches of the government caused trouble for some of the key participants. In March 1967 Edward Morgan, an attorney for one of the principals, leaked the essence of the story to the muckraking columnist Drew Pearson, who published it in his column *The Washington Merry-Go-Round*. Publicly, the story went nowhere; privately, Pearson also gave the story to President Johnson, who in turn asked CIA director Richard Helms to look into it, triggering an investigation by a new CIA inspector general, J. S. Earman. The office of the IG completed the report two months later, on May 23, 1967. As the authors of the report explained, they found no documentation in the files directly relating to the assassination plan and had to rely on the sometimes erratic recollection of the participants.

The IG report came to the attention of President Gerald Ford in early 1975 after a famous leak of widespread CIA wrongdoing to Seymour Hersh of the *New York Times* in the previous December. The 1967 document then became the basis for the Senate Select Committee on Intelligence Activities' report, *Alleged Assassination Attempts against Foreign Leaders,* published later that year. But neither the Church Committee report (named after the committee chairman, Senator Frank Church) nor the IG report itself, which was finally released in 1993, told anywhere near the whole story about the U.S. government's attempts to assassinate Fidel Castro.[2]

Written by lawyers, the Church Committee report focused on very specific questions concerning high-level authorization of, and responsibility for, the assassination plots. The secret testimony on which it was based is now fully available in the JFK collection at the National Archives, and it contains much key information not included in the report. It also documents the ethos of the CIA at the height of the Cold War and gives a unique glimpse into the agency's inner workings. While witnesses like Richard Bissell, the deputy director for plans, and his deputy and successor, Richard Helms, worked very hard not to provide any information that the Church Committee did not already have, a few others, like William Harvey, Sam Halpern, and E. Howard Hunt, were much more forthcoming. Most importantly for history, Halpern in particular did the committee (and now historians) the service of making it quite clear that the agency had the means and the will to conceal sensitive information forever, if it so chose.

As we have seen, the idea of assassinating Fidel Castro was spreading through Cuba as early as the middle of 1959. In July, William Attwood heard both private American and Cuban interests (including the banker Julio Lobo) and reputed intelligence agents promising the imminent assassination of Cuba's leader. In this era the CIA sometimes began operations before they had been approved at the highest levels, and in this case the possibility of Castro's killing did not become the focus of recorded discussions until early 1960. J. C. King wrote Allen Dulles on December 12, recommending that the "elimination" of Castro receive thorough consideration. The CIA heard in January that the American cattleman Robert Kleberg, the owner of the King Ranch and properties in Cuba, was working with a representative of the United Front and some Cuban exiles, including Emilio Nunez Portuondo, who was close to William Pawley, to arrange the assassination of Fidel, his younger brother Raoul, and Che Guevara.[3] Two months later, on March 10, Admiral Arleigh Burke also suggested to the National Security Council that Fidel's death might not help the United States unless Raoul and Che Guevara could be eliminated as well. Four days later, the NSC Special Group discussed "the effect on the Cuban scene" if those three leaders should "disappear simultaneously."[4]

On April 3 the irrepressible Pawley told Dulles himself "that if CIA is interested in quickly removing Fidel Castro such could be arranged through [deleted]. He said that [deleted] has two men of his confidence who are with Fidel frequently, and they would be prepared to eliminate CASTRO for a price." Dulles "jokingly remarked that he would turn this over to his 'assassination department,'" but Pawley "closed by saying that he believed this matter should be given consideration as it would save time, lives, and money."[5] Assassination was almost certainly one of the "drastic" options that Pawley had pressed upon President Eisenhower on February 15.[6]

E. Howard Hunt also helped get the assassination plot going. A CIA operative for two decades, he returned from overseas in March 1960 to work on the new Cuba project, and he became its director of political action, with responsibility for organizing exile groups. In his memoir *Give Us This Day*, which refers to other participants with a mixture of true and false names, Hunt made clear that he resented the insistence of J. C. King and Gerald Droller ("Frank Bender") that Batistianos be excluded from the CIA's plans, and he confirmed that both William Pawley and Vice President Nixon were trying to promote more conservative elements. Hunt made a trip to Cuba in spring 1960, and when he returned he told Bissell that "Cuban patriots" should be given the job of assassinating Castro. Later he asked Bissell about the fate of that recommendation and testified that Bissell said it was "in the hands of a special group." Hunt was not sure whether Bissell was referring specifically to *the* Special Group (the 5412 Committee) charged with approving covert actions.[7]

In 1978 the convicted arms dealer and securities swindler Edward Browder told investigators from the House Select Committee on Assassinations that he participated in two major CIA-sponsored assassination plots against Castro during the second half of 1960. In the first plot, he claimed he received about $50,000 and a promise of $250,000 more to arrange for Castro's exposure to a lethal dose of radiation during an interview with the Canadian Broadcasting Company. In the second, the CIA gave him a van of plastic explosives to ship to Havana through Mexico, where it would be detonated outside one of Castro's favorite cafés—a scheme that CIA files also mention.[8]

In late July an unidentified Cuban approached a CIA man in Havana and offered to kill Raoul Castro. The duty officer at headquarters immediately cabled Tracy Barnes, the deputy director for plans, and King of the Western Hemisphere branch. "Possible removal top three leaders is receiving serious consideration at HQs," they replied, and asked whether $10,000 would do the job with respect to Raoul. The unidentified case officer made a deal on that basis, but twenty-four hours later headquarters changed its mind. In any case, the Cuban reported that he had been unable to arrange an "accident" involving Raoul.[9]

Cuba was not the only target for assassinations. The Third World was becoming a major battleground in the Cold War, and during the summer of 1960 Washington faced alarming developments on several continents. The American position in Laos was beginning to crack, and the independence of the former Belgian Congo had unveiled another challenge—the leftist and nationalist prime minister Patrice Lumumba. Meanwhile, Soviet-American relations, which in 1959 had appeared to thaw during Nikita Khrushchev's visit to the United States, were taking a drastic turn for the worse. The loss of the U-2 spy plane over the Soviet Union and the capture of its pilot in early May led to the collapse of a summit conference in Paris and the cancellation of Eisenhower's return visit to the Soviet Union. In this atmosphere, every Third World crisis took on heightened significance.

Africa was emerging as a new front in the Cold War, and the Congo was one of its largest and potentially richest nations. The Belgian government attempted to give the Congo a sham independence on June 30, 1960, under an arrangement that would have left Belgians in control of the army and of state bureaucracies. Lumumba delivered a blunt, nationalistic attack on Belgian rule at the independence ceremony, and the Congolese troops promptly revolted against their old masters. The Belgians sent in more troops, and Khrushchev, then in his most aggressive mood, began airlifting soldiers from two other anti-Western African states, Ghana and Guinea, into the Congo.

In late July, Lumumba made a brief, disastrous visit to the United States. President Eisenhower remained out of town the whole time, just as he had for Castro fifteen months earlier, but Lumumba struck Undersecretary of State Douglas Dillon as out of touch with reality. He also offended the sensibilities of white Americans by requesting a blond female companion at a moment when reports of the rape of white women by Congolese soldiers were reaching the United States. Official Washington decided that he had to be removed.[10]

Although the Eisenhower administration avoided putting anything on paper, it seems clear that the President ordered the assassinations of both Lumumba and Castro in August 1960. The Church Committee found that officials in NSC meetings tended to speak more bluntly about Lumumba—perhaps because of his racially offensive behavior—and one witness, a relatively junior staffer named Robert Johnson, distinctly remembered Eisenhower ordering that Lumumba be killed, probably on August 18. Just one week later, according to minutes of an August 25 meeting of the Special Group overseeing covert action, Allen Dulles recognized the "extremely strong feelings on the necessity of very straightforward action in this situation" and promised that CIA planning would not rule anything out. These decisions received further confirmation at meetings of the NSC on September 7 and of the Special Group on September 8, and the agency was actively working toward Lumumba's assassination by the end of the month. In October or November 1960 a CIA case officer recruited a European criminal, code-named QJWIN, to travel to Leopoldville and carry out the assassination.[11] But the following

January, before the CIA's man could get close to Lumumba, the prime minister was killed by his Congolese enemies.[12]

The U.S. government was also turning to assassination to solve another problem in Latin America—the dictatorship of Rafael Trujillo in the Dominican Republic. Trujillo, who had held power for thirty years, not only ran one of the most brutal dictatorships in Latin America but also caused a considerable scandal in 1956 by kidnapping and murdering a Dominican critic with American citizenship in the United States itself. Washington sent Florida Senator George Smathers and the ubiquitous William Pawley to ask Trujillo to step down in early 1960, but he refused. Taking on Trujillo simultaneously with Castro might rally more Latin American support for intervention in Cuba, and Trujillo did not help his own cause by trying to arrange the assassination of Venezuelan President Romulo Betancourt in June 1960. Later that month, on June 28, a State Department official agreed with J. C. King of the CIA to provide Dominican dissidents with rifles, telescopic sites, and ammunition to deal with the problem. This project stalled when the dissidents suggested international action instead.

In August 1960, Secretary of State Herter tried to persuade the OAS to depose Trujillo and hold free elections in the Dominican Republic, but the Latin American governments refused to pass judgment on the internal regime of a neighbor. After yet another attempt by Pawley to get Trujillo to step down failed, the CIA in October 1960 began planning to dispatch arms to overthrow the dictator, and on January 12, 1961, the Special Group approved the transfer of arms to dissident elements. After a few months of haggling and disputes over procedures, several pistols reached the rebels. Trujillo was finally gunned down on May 30, 1961, but no one has ever determined whether American weapons were used.[13]

Perhaps because the U.S. government would come under great suspicion in the event of Castro's death, the elaborate and multiple plans for his assassination seem to have left much less of a paper trail than the Congolese and Dominican plots. Still, all the evidence indicates that Dulles and Bissell received parallel authorizations to proceed against the Cuban leader in August 1960. At least one mob figure had already offered help against Castro. Three months earlier, in May, former casino owner Norman Rothmann let the U.S. government know through his lawyer that he could arrange for either Castro's death or improved U.S.–Cuba relations, whichever the United States preferred, in exchange for help with his own legal problems. In a second interview some time later, Rothmann attached this carrot to an implied blackmail threat against Vice President Nixon, who, he claimed, had welshed on a substantial gambling debt at his Miami Sans Souci casino in the early 1950s.[14]

In September, Bissell apparently asked Sheffield Edwards, director of the Office of Security, to recruit members of the Mafia (referred to in the 1967 inspector general's report as the "syndicate") who had lost their interests in Cuba to do the job. Although the Office of Security did not fall under the Directorate of Plans—the agency's convert branch— it apparently performed operational tasks from time to time because of special expertise in particular fields.[15] The legendary CIA counter-intelligence chief James Jesus Angleton may also have been involved in the plot. The name of Angleton, whose constant searches for moles in-side the agency wreaked considerable havoc for more than two decades, does not appear in either the IG or Church Committee reports. But in HSCA testimony a fellow CIA operative, John Whiten, linked Angleton to plots to kill Castro, and a British intelligence operative, Peter Wright, had a provocative conversation with Angleton about Castro's assassina-tion.[16]

The CIA apparently failed to seek any authorization for this project from the Special Group, but a loophole allowing it to dispense with this procedure was written into NSC 5412/2 on December 28, 1955. Para-graph 7 of that document provided for consultation with representatives of State, Defense, and the President "except as the President otherwise directs"; and a further annex of March 26, 1957, stated that the "standard procedure . . . shall not apply to the case of a particularly sensitive project which relates exclusively to U.S. foreign policy and which does not in-volve military implications." Mere approval by Secretary of State John Foster Dulles—who was the brother of the director of Central Intelli-gence—would suffice in such a case, although the Department of Cen-tral Intelligence was also supposed to "report any such exception (with-out identification)" to the Special Group.[17]

Edwards now turned to a private investigator and former FBI agent, Robert Maheu. In 1954 when Maheu struck out on his own as a Wash-ington private investigator, Edwards put him on a modest retainer and assigned another former FBI man, James P. O'Connell, as his case officer.

Maheu, O'Connell explained, was used for certain jobs which the agency preferred to avoid being associated with directly, including sur- veillance operations inside the United States and the procurement of women for foreign dignitaries. (The details of the latter assignment re- main classified.) Although Maheu's office was still in Washington in 1960, he was doing more and more work in Hollywood and Las Vegas. Maheu agreed to approach the underworld. Like the CIA case officers overseeing the Bay of Pigs invasion, he was instructed to claim that he represented wealthy businessmen with Cuban interests who would pay $150,000 for the death of Fidel Castro. O'Connell remained Maheu's case officer for this new operation.[18]

Sometime in the late 1950s Maheu made the acquaintance of John Roselli, who represented the Chicago mob in Los Angeles and Las Vegas, and O'Connell met Roselli at Maheu's home. Roselli, who claimed to have been born in 1904 in Chicago, muscled in on the Los Angeles wire service and a gambling parlor in the 1930s, and in 1944 he was convicted of extorting Hollywood studios, along with Willie Bioff of the mob- dominated International Alliance of Theatrical Stage Employees. Sen- tenced to ten years, he and several other defendants were paroled after only three. Roselli immediately began working again in Hollywood as an assistant producer and technical adviser on crime pictures. The paroles caused a scandal, and the Federal Parole Board tried to revoke them in 1948, but Roselli won his freedom.[19]

Bioff and another co-defendant who turned state's evidence were murdered in 1954 and 1955. By this point Roselli was dividing his time between Las Vegas and Los Angeles, where he was prominent in the Hollywood party scene. A short man with a distinguished appearance, he was described by a 1953 California Governor's Crime Commission re- port as a socially well-connected hoodlum. Roselli was identified as a West Coast representative of the East Coast mob and became the subject of a renewed investigation by the Los Angeles FBI office in early 1958. In 1960 an informant suggested that Roselli had taken "a rap" for the "big eastern boys." During testimony before the Kefauver Committee, Roselli had admitted knowing Frank Costello, Mickey Cohen of Los Angeles, the late Bugsy Siegel, Meyer Lansky, Lucky Luciano, and many other organized crime figures. Other reports speculated that Roselli's as- sociate Louis Lederer was fronting for him in the West Side Holding

Company of Chicago, and possibly in a projected Havana casino in 1958.[20]

Given the FBI's intensified interest in Roselli, Maheu's approach must have come as a welcome surprise. (The CIA did not approach the bureau for information about him or any of the other underworld figures who became involved in anti-Castro plots.) During lunch at the Brown Derby in Los Angeles, Maheu immediately dropped his cover and told Roselli he was recruiting him on behalf of a government agency. The project, he said, was designed either to assassinate Castro or to develop intelligence sources inside Cuba. When Roselli insisted on meeting a government official, arrangements were made for him to travel to New York in September to meet O'Connell. O'Connell repeated the original cover story that Maheu was acting on behalf of business interests, but Maheu told Roselli that O'Connell was with the CIA. O'Connell then accompanied Maheu and Roselli to Miami to meet with other key participants in the anti-Castro plot.

Meanwhile, in Washington, Edwards gave a progress report to his superiors, Bissell, Allen Dulles, and Deputy Director General Charles Cabell.[21] But despite this briefing, on November 3 when Livingston Merchant of the State Department raised the possibility of assassinating Fidel, Raoul, and Che, General Cabell told Merchant that these assassinations were "beyond our capabilities." And Bissell acknowledged that the Special Group overseeing covert activities—which was well informed about both the Lumumba and Trujillo plots—never heard about this one.[22] The CIA, in its talks with other agencies, repeatedly professed opposition to certain courses of action even when the agency was already pursuing those courses covertly.

The CIA inspector general's report of 1967—the initial source of all information on the assassination plots—focused on O'Connell, Maheu, Edwards, Roselli, and Giancana because (as we shall see) they were caught undertaking an illegal surveillance operation in Las Vegas which generated a paper trail. The Church Committee's report concentrated on the Castro assassination alone. As a result, both of these official reports underestimated not just the scope of the operation but also its objectives. They mention only three mobsters and two Cubans who became involved in the Castro assassination plot, but Maheu testified that he, O'Connell, Roselli, and Giancana spent about seven months, from October 1960 through April 1961, in Miami making contacts related to the project. And the testimony of Roselli, of his attorney Edward P. Morgan, and of William Harvey, who later took over from O'Connell as Roselli's case officer, makes clear that the CIA was not only attempting to find an assassin but also to use the mob's extensive pre-Castro connections to set up the broadest possible intelligence network, including sources close to Fidel himself.[23] The use of Roselli (who consistently represented himself to Cubans as "Mr. Rawlins") as a mob cut-out could also have been a way to maintain contacts with ex-Batista associates whom the CIA's Western Hemisphere branch had decided to shun.

It was Roselli who now introduced Maheu to the second major player in the assassination scheme, Sam Giancana—who in these meetings used the name Sam Gold. Born in Chicago in 1908, Giancana was the subject of perhaps the most intensive FBI investigation of any mobster in the country, thanks to the diligence of Chicago Special Agent Ralph Hill. Giancana took over the Chicago mob in 1957 after "Tough Tony" Accardo went into retirement.[24] His interests included a gambling casino in Wheeling, West Virginia; several bars, restaurants, and motels (at least one of which doubled as a brothel); bail bondsmen in a number of major cities; and several unions. Bugs and phone taps revealed his associations with hit men Lenny Patrick and Dave Yaras of Chicago (both childhood friends of Jack Ruby) and included references to payoffs of numerous local and state law enforcement officials.

The Chicago mob, certainly one of the most powerful in the country, had interests in all the major "open cities" around North America, including Las Vegas, Miami, and Havana. Giancana's financial wizard Murray Humphreys had worked with Meyer Lansky and Bugsy Siegel to build the Flamingo in Las Vegas in the 1940s, and phone taps confirmed that Roselli represented Giancana in Las Vegas and was causing him some concern by getting into trouble there. Charles "Babe" Baron looked after Giancana's interests in the Riviera in Havana. A notorious womanizer, Giancana began an affair in mid-1960 with Phyllis McGuire of the singing McGuire Sisters. The FBI bugged motel rooms where the couple spent weekends.[25] Giancana also associated with Frank Sinatra, who in 1960 was campaigning vigorously for John F. Kennedy's election.

Whatever Giancana's exact connection to gambling in Havana—and Roselli's approach to him suggests that it was significant—he had clearly given the problem of Castro's assassination some thought. "The Agency," the CIA inspector general wrote in his 1967 report, "had first thought in terms of a typical, gangland-style killing in which Castro would be gunned down. Giancana was flatly opposed to the use of firearms. He said that no one could be recruited to do the job, because the chance of survival and escape would be negligible. Giancana stated a preference for a lethal pill that could be put into Castro's food or drink." He referred to another associate, "Joe the courier," who could contact a disaffected Cuban official close to Castro to do the job.[26]

"Joe the Courier" turned out to be Santo Trafficante, Jr., who was spending most of his time in Miami after his release from Trescornia in the summer of 1959. Trafficante won an acquittal on tax charges in Tampa early in the year and managed to make a few more trips to and from Cuba in the first half of 1960—suggesting that he managed to pay off authorities in the new government both to secure his release and to make it possible to continue to look after some of his interests in the few casinos that remained open.[27] The extent of Trafficante's role in the conspiracy has consistently been downplayed, suggesting that he effectively warned his co-conspirators, including Roselli, never to mention his name. Maheu managed to avoid doing so throughout his four appearances before the Church Committee in 1975–76. But despite this silence, Trafficante's long residence in Cuba and his intimate connections with both the Batista and Prio governments suggest that he was almost certainly the key to the CIA's Castro assassination plot.

Trafficante himself did not have to talk to the Church Committee until the fall of 1976, about a year after their assassinations report appeared. He explained that he had known Roselli since the mid-1950s, although he denied any business relationship, and that he and Roselli decided on Rafael "Macho" Gener, a former official of the Prio government, as their main Cuban contact. This in turn led them to another close Prio associate, Tony Varona, who was currently serving as the head of the CIA-sponsored Cuban Revolutionary Council. Varona arranged a large meeting of Cuban exiles with Trafficante, Roselli, and Maheu, who introduced himself as the representative of a group of Cuban businessmen. Prio himself was playing no role because in 1959 he had returned to live on his Cuban estate. The meeting, Trafficante claimed, generally discussed resistance to Castro.[28] Trafficante may have successfully concealed his identity at least from O'Connell, and possibly from Maheu as well. O'Connell and a friend of his, a Washington policeman named Joe Shimon, said that they did not identify Trafficante until January 1962, when his picture appeared in a *Parade Magazine* story identifying ten of the most wanted mobsters in the country.[29]

Looking for a contact within Cuba to carry out the assassination, the conspirators hit upon Juan Orta, a member of Prio's faction who had been living in Florida during Batista's last years. He was arrested in 1958 for arms trafficking, but he was now working closely with Castro in Havana. Orta, like Prio, had apparently received mob kickbacks in the late 1940s and early 1950s and would have welcomed the return of the American gamblers and their largesse. Trafficante had known Orta in Havana, and he told Giancana and Roselli that Orta would be able to place a poison pill in Castro's food or drink.[30]

The CIA had independently decided on the use of poison. As the inspector general's report noted in 1967, the CIA's Technical Services Division was already at work on effective poisons, as well as cigars so thoroughly treated with lethal agents that they might kill Castro even before he had time to light one up.[31] Two unrelated CIA cables confirm that a poisoning plot was already afoot in late 1960. One, from the Havana station, gave a detailed account of what Castro had eaten in one of his favorite restaurants on September 13 and mentioned that only one bodyguard had accompanied him, and the second referred to the possibility of a contact's giving an "H capsule" to Rolando Cubela, the former DR leader who was now a disaffected associate of Castro, in December.[32] This may well have been the same plot, since Trafficante had also known Cubela at least since 1959.[33] Six months later, on March 28, 1961, the CIA station in Miami cabled headquarters that Cubela and Orta wanted to be "exfiltrated" from Cuba, and headquarters replied expressing interest—suggesting that the two men may have been working together.[34]

More significantly, the assassination plot—as Maheu testified in 1975—was being coordinated with the Bay of Pigs invasion. Although Bissell purposely made himself the only link between Edwards's plan and J. D. Esterline's Guatemala-trained invasion force, and although Varona never told E. Howard Hunt, his case officer, about the plot, it seemed designed either to trigger an invasion or to ensure the invasion's success. That was why Maheu, O'Connell, and Roselli spent the better part of seven months in Miami, from October 1960 through April 1961, and why Maheu, after the operation was compromised, lied to the FBI for four months, until after the invasion had failed.

Trafficante apparently promised to get the poison to Orta; but before any new steps could be taken, the CIA discovered the perils of using mobsters as agents. In October John Teeter, the husband of Phyllis McGuire's sister and co-performer Christine, contacted the FBI with a remarkable story. The Chicago FBI office apparently passed it directly to headquarters.

> Giancana, Phyllis McGuire and Christine McGuire had dinner at the LaScala Restaurant, in New York City, recently and during the dinner Fidel Castro and Cuba was discussed. Giancana stated that Castro was to be done away with very shortly and when the girls registered doubt about this happening, Giancana assured them that it was to occur in November, and that he had met with the "assassin" on three occasions. Teeter said that the "assassin" was the term used by Giancana, who said that he last met with the "assassin" on a boat docked at the Fontainbleau Hotel, Miami Beech, Florida, and that everything had been perfected for the killing of CASTRO. Giancana said that the "assassin" had arranged with a girl, not further described, to drop a pill in a drink or some food of Castro's. Giancana also told the sisters that Castro was at that time in the advanced stages of syphilis and was not completely rational.[35]

The assassin in question was probably Richard Cain, born Richard Scaletti, a handsome, charming, extremely intelligent former Chicago policeman and investigator. As phone taps eventually showed, Cain was actually a full-fledged member of the Mafia who was detailed to infiltrate law enforcement. He had already become involved with Cuban exiles in both Chicago and Miami. Born either in 1924 or 1931, Cain spent four years as a Chicago vice cop but quit the force in 1960 before he and his partner could be fired for killing a convict in what was reported to be an extortion scheme.[36] Cain also liked to cultivate the Chicago CIA office and the FBI, and in October and November 1960 he told the chief of the Chicago CIA Domestic Contacts office that he was trying to go to Cuba on behalf of Carlos Prio to place some phone taps. Cain also claimed to have a contract with *Life* magazine to take photographs on the island, and he gave the FBI information on Soviet and Czech arms arriving in Cuba. By December Cain's trip had fallen through, but he continued hanging around the office of Varona's FRD. The trip was probably part of the assassination plot.[37]

Giancana's indiscretion with the McGuire sisters set off alarm bells at the FBI, where someone must have had an idea of what the CIA was doing. On October 18, J. Edgar Hoover conveyed the substance of the report almost verbatim to Dulles and Bissell. Bissell evidently spoke to Edwards at once, no doubt telling him to get Giancana to shut up. Meanwhile, however, O'Connell and Maheu had to deal with another related problem in the mobster's life.

The extensive stays of Edwards's conspirators in Miami were creating problems in their private lives. Maheu was just beginning his long association with the eccentric industrialist Howard Hughes, and Hughes was now ordering him to come out to California to respond to accusations that he had given a $200,000 sweetheart loan to the brother of presidential candidate Richard Nixon. In an effort to buy himself more time in Miami, Maheu left his hotel—which he believed was under FBI surveillance—went to a pay phone, called Hughes, and told him exactly what he was doing in Miami and for whom. Giancana was demanding to return to Las Vegas to check on his girlfriend, Phyllis McGuire, who was rumored to be having an affair with comedian Dan Rowan of the comedy team Rowan and Martin. Desperate to keep Giancana in Miami, Maheu offered to arrange for surveillance of Rowan instead. Giancana agreed, and Maheu cleared the operation with Edwards through O'Connell.[38] The Church Committee later wondered why Maheu went to such lengths to keep Giancana around. Roselli, in his testimony, insisted that Giancana knew very little about Roselli's dealings with Gener and Varona, and if that is true, it tends to confirm that Giancana was supervising a separate assassination plot of his own.[39]

On October 31, just two weeks after Hoover's memo to the CIA, Las Vegas police arrested a Miami private investigator named Arthur J. Balletti. The manager of the Riviera had gone to see Balletti after his hotel bill reached $100, and he found notes and a large cache of wiretapping and bugging equipment in Balletti's room. The notes led the manager to Rowan's room, where he found a wiretap and promptly called the police. Both Rowan and McGuire, whose conversations had been recorded, wisely denied any knowledge of who might have planted the bug, and twenty-four hours later Rowan declined to press charges on the advice of two of the hotel's owners. Balletti blamed the operation on his missing hotel roommate, who had registered as J. W. Harrison but whom Balletti now described as Mr. Harris.[40]

It took another month, until December 8, for someone at FBI headquarters to conclude that Giancana, whose affair with McGuire was well documented, might be behind the tap. Only then did the Miami office interview Edward Dubois, Balletti's Miami employer, who explained that he had been contacted by Walter Fitzpatrick, representing Robert Maheu of Washington, D.C. Dubois claimed that Maheu asked him to purchase plane tickets for two of Dubois' employees, only to announce that one of the tickets would be used by the mysterious J. W. Harrison instead.[41]

It took several more weeks, until January 4, for the Washington Field Office to find Maheu in his DC office, by which time Maheu had decided, presumably with O'Connell's encouragement, to brazen it out. The former bureau agent explained that a mysterious Los Angeles attorney whom he could not name had simply asked him to recommend someone to do investigative work in Los Angeles for a client of his, and that he recommended Balletti. Not until January 30 did Maheu get back to the Washington agents to repeat that the Los Angeles attorney refused to let Maheu reveal his name.[42] Maheu was desperately trying to stall the FBI until the assassination of Castro and the invasion of Cuba had taken place. O'Connell, Edwards, and Bissell must have concluded—accurately, as it turned out—that J. Edgar Hoover would not react favorably to hearing the truth about the CIA's Cuba activities.

Pressing on with its investigation without any help from the principals, the FBI discovered that Maheu had been staying at the Kenilworth Hotel in Miami Beach for about twenty days with a certain J. A. Rollins. Maheu stuck to his story in another interview on February 8 and did not reveal that Rollins was in fact Johnny Roselli. Shortly thereafter he called the Washington office to say that he had "just received a phone call and if this matter could be held up a few days it would be straightened out."[43] Maheu was anticipating the success of the Cuban operation. O'Connell had given Roselli three pills destined for Orta sometime after February 10, and Roselli eventually told O'Connell that Trafficante had managed to get the pills to Orta, but that Orta had gotten cold feet. In fact, Orta had fallen out with Castro and lost his position in the prime minister's office on January 26.[44]

When it became clear in early 1961 that the Orta channel had dried up, Trafficante suggested to Roselli that he go back to the former Autentico leader Tony Varona, who enjoyed the confidence of both the mob and some former Batistianos, including Orlando Piedra, whom the CIA identified as having been "in charge of all matters pertaining to gambling, rackets and contraband" under Batista.[45] Piedra was now working with former Batista senator Rolando Masferrer, and the Castro government regarded him as one of the leading war criminals in the United States.[46] Two years later, after Piedra moved to New Orleans, his address found its way into Lee Harvey Oswald's address book.

Trafficante had already introduced Varona to Roselli, who identified himself as Mr. Rawlston. Some money changed hands, although subsequent accounts differed on the nature of the arrangement. Varona welcomed the funds to buy arms and equipment and said he knew a Cuban chef who might be able to poison Castro. Trafficante gave Varona the poison pills. Roselli's approach must have intrigued Varona, since he had been complaining to the State Department and to his case officer, E. Howard Hunt, that he and the FRD were being kept away from the invasion force in Guatemala and that they were being refused any input regarding Cuba's political future as well. He had previously told State Department officials that the FRD was having trouble raising money from American businessmen, who feared being accused of violating the Neutrality Act, and so Roselli's generosity must have been a welcome change. The FBI office in Tampa heard that Trafficante was in touch with Cuban exiles but had no idea of the plot. Nothing, however, came of all this before the Bay of Pigs fiasco.[47]

The FBI's Las Vegas investigation continued. In new interviews during March, Balletti assigned more and more of the blame to the mysterious J. W. Harrison, whom no one could find. By April 12 FBI agents finally figured out that "Rollins" might in fact be Johnny Roselli.[48]

On April 18, as anti-Castro forces were fighting on the beaches at the Bay of Pigs, Maheu contacted the Washington Field Office of the FBI to say that the invasion now allowed him to furnish "further information" regarding the wiretapping case. In an obviously well-prepared story, Maheu "insinuated" that he had been working for the CIA for some time, and referred FBI agents to "Shef Edwards" for details. He heard in October, he said, that an unidentified individual from Chicago (he specifically denied knowing Giancana's last name) had leaked information to Phyllis McGuire. Learning that McGuire would be "visiting" Dan Rowan in Las Vegas, he authorized "coverage of the meetings"— but not, he insisted, telephone taps.

Still denying any knowledge of J. W. Harrison, Maheu said he had no desire to furnish any additional information. A high-level interoffice FBI memorandum passed this information on, adding, "Maheu advised that he was quite disturbed by our investigation because it could possibly have jeopardized the work he has been doing." "It is immaterial how disturbed he gets," wrote J. Edgar Hoover. "He is no good."[49] Maheu's and Giancana's role in the assassination plots was over, but Roselli's continued for at least two more years.

This elaborate scheme was not, however, the only CIA assassination plot against Castro before the Bay of Pigs or the only attempt by the mob to bring Castro down. Indications of at least half a dozen others have surfaced. In testimony given to the Church Committee in 1975, CIA General Counsel Laurence Houston vividly remembered that in late 1960 the agency sent a sniper rifle to Havana via diplomatic pouch. The incident stuck in his mind because he feared that Swiss diplomats would discover it when they took over the American Embassy after the break in relations.[50] While training the Bay of Pigs force, the CIA was also attempting both to supply existing underground forces in Cuba and to infiltrate agents into Cuba for "paramilitary activities." Agents went into Cuba either legally, by sea, or, on March 29, through the U.S. naval base at Guantanamo Bay.[51] Some of them, evidently, had the mission of assassinating Fidel Castro.

In 1975 Senator George McGovern traveled to Cuba and received a bound "Black Book" of data on assassination plots against Castro from the Cuban leader himself. McGovern provided the Black Book to the Church Committee, which queried the CIA for comment. The agency conducted an internal study and reported to the committee that its files failed to verify that it had actually directed any of the twenty-four plots that Castro tied to the CIA, although it acknowledged connections with some of the individuals involved in nine of them. That was merely a way of saying that they had not put the assassination missions down on paper.[52]

Specifically, the Black Book reported that in March 1961 "various counterrevolutionary groups" trained and armed by the agency were infiltrated by the CIA to assassinate the premier and support the coming invasion. Among them were Castro's former collaborator Humberto Sori Marin and thirteen others. The internal CIA study confirmed that Sori Marin had been in contact with the agency and that four other men arrested in the plot had been trained for paramilitary operations and infiltrated into Cuba, some of them with weapons and explosives. No evidence in the files indicated that they had been asked to assassinate Castro, however. Most of the fourteen were captured in March and executed in April 1961. Given that the agency *was* trying to secure Castro's assassination by other means, it seems unlikely that the CIA-trained-and-equipped infiltrators developed the idea on their own.

Of several additional plots identified in Castro's Black Book as having occurred during the late spring and early summer of 1961, the most interesting was one said to be directed by the FRD-CRC leadership, including Varona, Aureliano Sanchez Arrango, and Manuel Ray. The agents arrested claimed to have received support through Guantanamo. The Church Committee confirmed that naval intelligence officers at Guantanamo had been supporting assassination attempts from May through July of 1961.[53] What is not clear is whether any or all of these infiltrations were completely separate plots or whether Roselli was involved in arranging them. Since they were not fully documented, we may never know.

The CIA was aware of at least one other plot at the time. In 1960 Antonio Veciana was a young Cuban accountant for banker Julio Lobo, who had joined Manuel Ray's MRP. Veciana told the Church Committee in 1976 that in the spring of 1960 he was recruited by an American businessman with a Belgian passport named Maurice Bishop, who approached him after hearing about his disillusionment with Castro, possibly from his boss, Lobo. Bishop, whom Veciana believed to be a Texan, turned him over to a man named Melton for classes in organization and sabotage in a building that also housed a Berlitz language school. Melton gave him the names of three contacts at the U.S. Embassy: Colonel Sam Kail, who appears to have been an Army intelligence agent, Ewing Smith, and Vice-Consul Joe Acosta. In late 1960 Veciana began planning the assassination of Fidel Castro.[54]

In 1976 he helped draw a sketch of Bishop that bore a remarkable resemblance to David Atlee Phillips, a long-time CIA operative who was indeed in Havana as a contract agent from 1958 through most of 1960 and who then became one of the directors of the Bay of Pigs project and associated propaganda activities. Veciana dropped his biggest bombshell when he told the Church Committee that he saw Lee Harvey Oswald meeting with Bishop in Dallas in the late summer of 1963. Cuban intelligence services concluded independently that Bishop was Phillips and Gaeton Fonzi, the Church Committee and HSCA investigator who worked with Veciana, has since stated that Veciana identified Phillips as Bishop off the record, although he declined to do so under questioning by the committee. During the HSCA investigation, a JMWAVE case officer named Ross Crozier, when asked for the identity of any CIA officer who used the name "Bishop," replied spontaneously after a couple of days of thought that David Atlee Phillips used the name Maurice Bishop.[55] All evidence, in short, suggests that Maurice Bishop and David Phillips were the same man.

Phillips was working in Havana under contract while running a public relations firm, and this may have given him more freedom than usual to operate independently of the CIA. Agency records contain no indication that Phillips or any other CIA officer recruited Veciana in 1959–60.[56] Richard Helms, however, acknowledged in his memoirs that the agency recruited many Cubans for the Bay of Pigs without going through customary checks.[57] In 1975, another extremely informative CIA officer, Sam Halpern, told the Church Committee that operational branches would not necessarily reveal a covert relationship to an agent in response to a security check in any case but would merely send over biographical information in their files.[58]

In Phillips's second appearance before the House Select Committee on Assassinations in 1978, he was questioned closely about the possibility that he might have once been Maurice Bishop. While he denied having known Veciana or using the name Maurice Bishop, he acknowledged knowing Veciana's boss, Lobo, and another close friend of Veciana's. He also agreed that Lobo probably suggested people for him to recruit and provided funds to others at the suggestion of the CIA. Asked whether he knew a man named Melton, he indicated that he thought he once did, and he even connected him spontaneously with the Berlitz language school, which Veciana had placed in the building where Melton held classes in sabotage. Phillips denied that "Bishop" was among the hundred or so aliases he used with agents but admitted that the sketch Veciana supervised resembled himself.[59] In short, Phillips's denials of any relationship with Veciana are not credible, both because he confirmed so many background details and because Phillips definitely tried to deceive the committee on other points as well.[60]

One CIA cable definitely confirms much of Veciana's story. On December 12, 1960, he called on the Havana Embassy, along with another man who also claimed to be working with the MRP. "No station traces," cabled the Havana CIA, confirming that there was no record of Veciana's recruitment. Veciana spoke to "Olien," which may be a cryptonym for the military attaché Colonel Kail. He claimed to have developed a plan to kill Castro and his top associates—a scheme known only to two men outside Cuba and a handful inside. One of those on the outside was presumably Bishop, with whom he later claimed to have discussed it. He wanted U.S. visas for the families of the four men involved, and four M-1 rifles with grenade adapters. Veciana said that he spoke previously with an unidentified embassy political officer, which that officer subsequently confirmed, and gave Lobo as a reference. In reply, headquarters confirmed that Lobo thought highly of Veciana but added, "In any case [this from director] agree Havana should not in any way encourage radical schemes this kind particularly when presented this cold approach manner. Accordingly prefer no action on visas."[61]

Headquarters apparently, by this time, had developed a policy of refusing unsolicited offers to assassinate Castro to avoid being entrapped, while mounting its own attempts. Veciana was forced to abort one planned assassination in May, and most of his network was arrested before another one could be attempted in November. Among those arrested that month was Amador Odio, a wealthy landowner on whose estate some conspirators had taken refuge and whose daughter, Silvia—already a refugee—found Lee Harvey Oswald standing at her front door in the fall of 1963. Veciana himself managed to escape to the United States and told the Miami press that the assassination plan failed when a bazooka misfired.[62]

The alliance between mobsters and anti-Castro Cubans, which at the highest level included Trafficante's CIA-sponsored approach to Varona, extended into other parts of the country as well. Jimmy Hoffa and the

Teamsters attempted to finance a sale of airplanes to Castro through Dominick Bartone of Cleveland and Akros Dynamics, as we have seen, and Norman Rothmann was now in Miami managing a hotel and working with Santo Trafficante. And although the CIA officers involved managed to limit the agency's specific disclosures about mob figures to Roselli, Giancana, and Trafficante, evidence indicates that Roselli drew in additional mobsters too.

In 1975 *Time* magazine quoted CIA sources to the effect that Russell Bufalino, a Pennsylvania mob boss with close ties to Hoffa, was also asked by the CIA to set up an intelligence network in Cuba during the months before the Bay of Pigs.[63] And in 1978 the imprisoned mobster and arms dealer Edward Browder told HSCA investigators that he participated in assassination plots against Castro in 1959 and 1960 that involved Bartone, Meyer Lansky's lieutenant Jimmy Alo, and, he claimed, CIA support.[64]

More significantly, Carlos Marcello of New Orleans also seems to have been involved. He had reportedly been shipping narcotics and arms to Cuba since the 1950s, including heroin delivered to Rothmann's hotel.[65] In late January 1961, while Maheu, Roselli, and Trafficante were in Miami trying to organize Castro's assassination, New Orleans officials of National Airlines told the FBI that Marcello flew to Miami for two days as well. At about the same time, he indirectly contacted the Cuban FRD representative in New Orleans, Sergio Arcacha Smith, a former Cuban diplomat who defected. In January 1961 a New Orleans arms dealer named William Dalzell offered Arcacha Smith $200,000 on Marcello's behalf to overthrow Castro in exchange for gambling concessions and citizenship in a post-Castro Cuba. The figure is suspiciously similar to the $250,000 that Roselli was promising anyone who could do the job. Arcacha Smith explained to the FBI that he turned down the offer because he had no way of overthrowing Fidel.[66]

Confronted in 1959–60 with the disastrous threat of a Communist Cuba but unwilling to revive the policy of the Platt Amendment and simply send in the armed forces, the Eisenhower administration turned to desperate measures that expanded and solidified networks of Cuban exiles, mobsters, and right-wing Americans. Prodded by businessmen like William Pawley and Robert Kleberg, the administration and the CIA launched a multi-front war on Castro, including the training of an exile invasion force, attempts to enlarge the Cuban underground, a propaganda war, and several assassination attempts. The leaders of CIA-sponsored Cuban exile organizations came mainly from Carlos Prio's Autentico party and from revolutionaries who had turned against Castro, including Manuel Artime, Manuel Ray, and Pedro Diaz Lanz. Although the U.S. government's firm resolve not to aid Batistianos was weakening somewhat, exiles like Rolando Masferrer, Jose Rubio Padilla, and Orlando Piedra were operating either independently or with the help of Americans like Pawley, Washington mob-connected lobbyist Irving Davidson, and many more.

Meanwhile, the CIA was organizing a combined intelligence/assassination effort against Castro that involved a host of American Mafia leaders, including Roselli, Giancana, Trafficante, Bufalino, Rothmann, and Marcello. That network continued to operate under two different CIA case officers well into 1963. It mounted at least half a dozen serious assassination plots against Fidel, and it generated some important intelligence. But most important, by 1963 the network had evidently developed the capability of acting on its own, in its own interests, and for its own reasons.

On November 8, 1960, the American people turned the Republican Party out of the White House and elected John F. Kennedy president by a razor-thin margin. In January, Kennedy inherited crises in the Congo, Laos, Berlin, Vietnam, and Cuba. While eager in many ways to change the Eisenhower administration's foreign policy, the new President—who as a candidate had demanded *more* support of Cuban exiles in a televised debate—was equally eager to do something about Castro. His younger brother Robert shared that view, but he was also determined, in his new position as attorney general, to mount an offensive against organized crime in general, and Jimmy Hoffa of the Teamsters Union in particular. The country, now led by its first president from what is now known as the "greatest generation," moved optimistically into a new era. Behind the scenes, however, the election had ignited a highly combustible mixture.

4

The Kennedys Take Over

Almost half a century after his death, John F. Kennedy remains a source of enormous fascination, not least because of the contradictory elements of his character. A recent and justly acclaimed biography contrasts Kennedy's vigorous image with his chronically poor health; his attractive and beloved family with his numerous extramarital affairs; and his straightforward powers of expression—so characteristic of the best of his generation—with his remarkable capacity for duplicity.[1] At ease with everyone, he revealed himself fully to no one. Any balanced judgment of him must rest on both his words and his actions.

Contradictions also marked JFK's policies toward Latin America in general and Cuba in particular. His concern for what was to become known as the Third World extended to the United States' neighbors to the south, where he believed that poverty and political oppression might cause a shift toward Communism. On March 13, 1961, in a highly publicized address to Latin American diplomats, the President announced the Alliance for Progress, designed to combine political reform with economic aid—something Truman and Eisenhower both had declined to do.[2] But with respect to Castro's regime in Cuba—toward which he had already endorsed a hostile, activist policy during the campaign—he did not reverse his predecessor's course, either before or after the debacle of the Bay of Pigs. Despite some reservations, he authorized the covert action to go forward in a long series of meetings, and he intermittently pursued the overthrow of Castro until the day of his death.

Accusations by Richard Nixon to the contrary, Kennedy did not receive an actual CIA briefing on the Bay of Pigs until after his election, although he and Robert Kennedy had heard about the training camp in

Guatemala well before that.[3] An initial series of meetings during the first month of the administration, however, revealed serious problems in the current plan. Richard Bissell, J. C. King, and the rest of the CIA leadership declined to promise that the invasion force could do more than seize a beachhead and ask for American military intervention, which the State Department continued to oppose as being politically disastrous. One Pentagon planner offered a way out of this conundrum: if the invasion failed, the exiles might move into the interior to fight a guerrilla war or be evacuated by sea.

On February 17 Bissell claimed that the landing would lead to either a general uprising against Castro or a guerrilla war, and warned the President that disbanding the force in Guatemala would have a catastrophic effect on pro-American regimes. The next day Kennedy approved continued preparations for the invasion but made clear that he would prefer a less visible, large-scale infiltration of guerrillas. On March 11 a similar exchange took place, with Bissell asking for a full-scale landing and Kennedy asking for a plan that would make the U.S. role "less obvious."[4] Years later Bissell still resented the series of "large meetings" at the White House that discussed what was supposed to have been a highly secure CIA operation. Once an operation had been authorized, Bissell and his CIA colleagues obviously expected the details to remain within the agency.[5]

While Kennedy's participation in planning the Bay of Pigs is clear, his involvement in CIA assassination plots is harder to establish precisely. But at some point he became aware that the idea of eliminating Castro was being pursued by the CIA, and he apparently did not try to stop it. When the Church Committee took testimony from officials of the Eisenhower and Kennedy administrations in the summer of 1975, nearly every witness showed extraordinary loyalty to the President he had worked for. With respect to Kennedy, Bissell denied ever having briefed the President or anyone outside the agency about the assassination plots—although he assumed, he said, that Allen Dulles (who died in 1969) had informed both Eisenhower and Kennedy. All the senior officials of the Kennedy administration who were available for questioning, including McGeorge Bundy, Robert McNamara, Dean Rusk, and Richard Goodwin of the White House staff, denied any knowledge as well. Numerous authors have treated this testimony with skepticism, but in fact what evidence we have suggests that Bissell discussed the assassination of Castro with only one of his new superiors, National Security Adviser McGeorge Bundy, and only in the most general terms.

With plots against Lumumba, Trujillo, and Castro under way and QJWIN already recruited to assassinate Lumumba, Bissell was apparently trying to improve both the organization and execution of an ongoing assassination project carried forward from the Eisenhower administration. Sometime in January 1961, he asked William Harvey, then chief of a CIA station overseas, to establish an " 'executive action capability,' which would include research into a capability to assassinate foreign leaders." Harvey, a gun-toting alcoholic who left the FBI in 1947 and joined the CIA, had recently supervised the construction of a tunnel into East Berlin that enabled the agency to listen to enemy communications. Not surprisingly, his reputation among his colleagues was controversial. Harvey's notes on his conversation with Bissell were dated January 26, 1961. He was also briefed by Sheffield Edwards regarding Roselli and the plots against Castro.[6]

Within the CIA, the new assassination program, code-named ZRRIFLE, was officially listed as an FID operation, which ostensibly meant entering safes and kidnapping couriers.[7] This designation shows the care with which the agency, even internally, avoided the use of sensitive language. Bissell and Bundy eventually agreed that they had discussed ZRRIFLE, but Bundy told the Church Committee that while he knew about the program in general, he had no knowledge of any specific operations that it had undertaken. Bissell, however, slipped in response to a telling question from the committee, confirming that he might well have mentioned Castro, Lumumba, and Trujillo while discussing the Executive Action program with Bundy, "because these were the sorts of individuals at that moment in history against whom such a capability might possibly have been employed." Bundy, Bissell said, seemed to approve the program. We do not know whether that conversation took place during the first five days of the new administration, that is, before Bissell's conversation with Harvey.[8]

Evidence suggests that President Kennedy himself was informed at least generally about the ongoing assassination plots against Castro (and thus, quite possibly, about the Trujillo plot as well) before the Bay of Pigs invasion. In early 1961 the President asked Florida Senator George

Smathers, who was close to the Cuban community in Florida, for his opinion of the reaction in Latin America if Castro were assassinated. When Smathers, by his own account, strongly disapproved of the idea, Kennedy said he agreed with him.[9]

Meanwhile, plans for the Bay of Pigs invasion were advancing, with the knowledge and approval of the President. To broaden the political base of the Cuban invasion somewhat, the administration reorganized the Frente Revolucionario Democratico (FRD) in March 1961, just weeks before the operation was scheduled to unfold. The new Cuban Revolutionary Council (CRC) replaced the FRD, and Dr. Jose Miro Cardona took over from Tony Varona as its chief. Varona, now deeply involved in at least one CIA plot to kill Castro, continued to complain to his case officer, E. Howard Hunt, that Cubans, not Americans, should control the invasion. The reorganization allowed Manuel Ray and the leftist MRP to affiliate with it, much to the disgust of William Pawley and Hunt, who neither trusted Ray nor valued his help. Angry over this decision, Hunt resigned as the main contact with the Cuban political leadership and began working with David Atlee Phillips on propaganda instead.[10]

A long series of meetings in late March culminated in final approval of the invasion. The State Department decided that the force would have to seize a substantial amount of territory before the United States could recognize a new government. Kennedy insisted not only on a pre-dawn landing in an attempt to make the operation surreptitious but demanded that leaders of the brigade be specifically informed that U.S. forces were not going to intervene. Asked whether they still wanted to go ahead with the operation, the leaders responded affirmatively.[11]

Unfortunately, by this time the Guatemala project had become isolated and self-sustaining. Its only intelligence unit came under the command of its paramilitary chief, Marine Colonel "Rip" Robertson, and could not provide independent advice. Although Castro in the first few months of 1961 had been busily rolling up opposition elements within Cuba and arresting an important group of infiltrators sent to assassinate him, the invasion project was still counting on a widespread popular uprising. The CRC leadership, though finally allowed to pay brief visits to the Guatemalan camp, was given no authority over what was happening. Many of the camp's trainers treated their Cuban recruits with contempt.

For all these reasons, the operation would go down in history as an American-controlled fiasco.[12]

On March 29, with the invasion only weeks away, a CIA agent in Cuba reported that a plan was in place to assassinate Castro on April 9 while he was giving a speech at the Presidential Palace. The agent desperately requested CIA approval, but no reply has been released. Further cables on April 5 repeated the intention to assassinate the Cuban leader but warned that American military intervention would be essential to overthrowing the government after Castro's death.[13] This certainly sounds like the plot that Maheu and Roselli were hatching.

On April 12 President Kennedy stated publicly that "there will not be, under any conditions, any intervention in Cuba by United States armed forces," and promised to make sure that no Americans would be "involved in any actions inside" either.[14] This enraged CRC chief Cardona, who told White House aide Arthur Schlesinger, Jr., that the United States simply had to join any prolonged conflict and demanded to know what the American plan really was.[15] At about the same time, perhaps in order to make clear that the United States was not trying to restore Batista's dictatorship, authorities in Washington arrested Rolando Masferrer, a former senator and Batista militia leader who had sponsored his own small, futile landing in Cuba during October 1960.[16] On April 12 Bundy informed Rusk, McNamara, and Dulles that "the specific plan for paramilitary support, Nestor, has been rejected, and the President does not wish further planning of any such operations for an invasion of Cuba. There will be quiet disengagement from associations developed in connection with Nestor."[17] No surviving documents or witnesses seem to give any clue as to what Nestor was.

During the first half of April, "Frank," an army colonel at the training camp in Guatemala, warned two Cuban commanders of the invasion force that figures within the administration opposed the Bay of Pigs landing and wanted to stop it. If orders to stand down arrived, he said, the Cubans should put their American leaders under house arrest and proceed with the original plan. The two Cubans were shocked but agreed to the procedure.[18]

Kennedy's public statements pledging no military action apparently served their purpose as disinformation. Soviet sources show that Castro was genuinely surprised by the series of air strikes that began the attack on April 15. A good many American planes were lost, and those that returned claimed to be Cuban pilots defecting from Castro's air force. Castro immediately blasted the United States, and the next day UN Ambassador Adlai Stevenson expressed his extreme displeasure at having to defend the official line. That evening—a Saturday—Rusk informed CIA Deputy Director General Charles Cabell that the second round of air strikes would be canceled. Cabell did not take up Rusk's offer to call the President, who was weekending at Glen Ora, Virginia, to protest that decision. A diversionary landing planned for a different site in Cuba was also canceled.[19] Cabell and Bissell chose to ignore the opinion of Esterline, the project chief, that the second round of air strikes was essential to success.[20]

The landing itself on April 17 surprised the Cubans as much as the air strike had, although Castro's security services were already rounding up thousands of suspected opponents of the regime. A combination of Castro's massive counter-invasion force and Cuba's air superiority—which led to the sinking of two invasion ships, including one full of ammunition—doomed the force within three days. In a strange decision that has never been fully explained, the CIA had persuaded the leaders of the CRC to sequester themselves in a Miami safe house during the battle. In the midst of the debacle, Kennedy put his chief of naval operations, Admiral Arleigh Burke, in charge and briefly provided some air cover over the beach from supposedly unmarked airplanes. But the tiny force of 1,500 men, surrounded by thousands of Castro's troops, could not possibly melt into the interior and become guerrilla fighters, as Bissell had imagined.[21]

On April 19, as the fighting on the beaches was coming to a close, Attorney General Robert Kennedy made a determined effort to find a way to restore the administration's prestige. He wrote his brother a rare memorandum warning of the danger of a Soviet-armed Cuba. While noting that the President had rejected an American invasion of the island "for good and sufficient reasons (although this might have to be reconsidered)," he asked whether a showdown might better occur now than in a year or two. Cuba, he argued, was more critical to American survival than Laos, the Congo, or anywhere else.[22] His always calmer older brother did not reply. That evening, the battle was over, and by every measure the young Kennedy administration had suffered a humiliating defeat.[23] In Cuba, Castro's supremacy was reaffirmed as never before, while at the UN, international reaction, led by Mexico, was very hostile to the United States. But the failure seems to have enflamed Robert Kennedy's passion all the more.

In two meetings during the remainder of April, the attorney general demanded an immediate, greater effort against Castro, and he dealt brutally with any suggestion that the United States was on the wrong path and should let the situation quiet down. The military began producing new invasion plans, which the President welcomed but did not commit himself to executing. As cooler heads prevailed, in practice if not in theory, the National Security Council on April 22 decided to reduce, for the time being, its financial support of resistance elements in Cuba, except in cases of a "moral obligation" or to help them survive or evacuate, and to begin building an international political case against the Castro regime.[24] The President appointed a board led by retired General Maxwell Taylor to hold secret hearings and issue a report on the Bay of Pigs, with recommendations for future action. Robert Kennedy, Admiral Burke, and Allen Dulles were members of this panel.

As it turned out, other events quickly forced Cuba out of the headlines. During the first week of June, Kennedy met with Nikita Khrushchev in Vienna, and the Soviet leader's threats of nuclear war inaugurated the most serious stage of the crisis over the fate of West Berlin. Kennedy replied by mobilizing large numbers of reserves and calling for fall-out shelters, whereupon Khrushchev resumed atmospheric nuclear testing. But behind the scenes, the government continued to ponder the situation in Cuba and its stance toward Cuban exiles. By the end of JFK's first year in office, the dilemmas that would plague the administration until his own assassination had begun to emerge.

To begin with, despite some enthusiastic calls for intervention from Admiral Burke and Air Force Chief of Staff Curtis LeMay (who characteristically offered to topple Castro with air power alone), the administration rejected immediate military intervention in Cuba, while asking the commander-in-chief for the Atlantic region to prepare larger-scale invasion plans. Both the State and Defense departments regarded an invasion as excessively costly to America's reputation; yet they agreed that invasion of Haiti or the Dominican Republic would be required should either of those states suddenly be threatened by Communist revolution.

Kennedy approved this mix of policies on May 5. Intervention remained an option, but now was not the time.[25] This policy did not change even after the Taylor Board issued its secret report on June 13 calling, guardedly, for American action to overthrow Castro.[26]

The same series of meetings deferred a decision on new covert operations. The CIA and State Department eventually settled on a program designed to strengthen internal resistance elements in Cuba and to undertake a limited program of sabotage and, possibly, paramilitary actions intended mainly to improve agent recruitment and opposition morale. The government, in short, wanted to keep opposition to Castro alive, unify it politically to the extent possible, and wait upon events. While this policy suited the administration's broader international goals, it was bound to anger the Cuban exiles, who wanted an all-out effort as soon as possible. Having argued during 1960–61 that they could overthrow Castro themselves if Washington would simply provide the money, the exile leaders now had to deal with the disastrous aftermath of an American-led failure.

Despite continuous U.S. support, the director of the CRC, in a talk with presidential assistant Richard Goodwin, threatened to quit without a firm American commitment to overthrow Castro. A letter from President Kennedy asking Cardona to remain until Cuba "[has been] liberated from the tyranny which has been imposed upon it" managed to avert a public relations debacle but did little to resolve the underlying problem—that the Cubans wanted more of a commitment than the President (who was now telling Latin American leaders that he did *not* intend to invade Cuba) was willing to give.[27]

Although the CRC continued to exist and distribute money among selected exile groups, the botched invasion put an end to any chance the U.S. government ever had of controlling all the exiles and their American patrons in the criminal and business worlds. Those exiles who participated in the invasion were now in Cuban prisons, and those who did not participate had lost all faith in the organizational ability of the CIA. Some Cubans traveled to Washington to meet with high-ranking American officials, some built up relations with the CIA, and some struck out on their own, forming networks that remained active for at least the next three years, and in some cases for much longer.

The MIRR, led by Orlando Bosch, Victor Paneque Batista, and

Evelio Duque Milar, who had run anti-Castro guerrillas in the Escambray Mountains in the months before the Bay of Pigs, immediately made its displeasure known. In a May 15 article in the Sunday supplement *Parade,* Jack Anderson wrote glowingly of the repeated trips in and out of Cuba made by "Frank Fiorini" (Sturgis), who with Orlando Bosch and Victor Paneque was building an underground movement that, Anderson reported, would finish the job the CIA had failed to accomplish weeks earlier at the Bay of Pigs.[28] On May 20 Bosch published a large ad in the Miami Cuban newspaper *Diario Las Americas* which blamed CIA incompetence for the bungled invasion and specifically attacked the agency for failing to come to the assistance of Duque's guerrillas in the Escambray. The CIA eventually established formal relationships with both Duque and Bosch, despite Bosch's repeatedly critical public statements.[29]

In mid-1961 the MIRR established a relationship with Gerry Patrick Hemming, a young Marine Corps veteran who had gone to Cuba for the first six months of 1959. Hemming, who apparently wanted to work for the CIA, provided the agency with a series of reports on his time in Cuba after returning to Los Angeles in fall 1960, and he popped up in Miami the following spring. By July 5 he was promoting himself as the leader (along with Sturgis) of Interpen, the Intercontinental Penetration Force, which he acknowledged had been founded by the Batistiano Rolando Masferrer. Exaggerating his activities, as was his wont, he claimed two hundred members for Interpen and mentioned a well-publicized parachute drop he and Sturgis had staged on July 2. In an attempt to avoid Neutrality Act charges, Hemming told the FBI that he was running training exercises, nothing more.[30]

No one seemed to know where these various groups were getting their funds, but the most likely suspects seemed to be exiled Cuban sugar barons like Julio Lobo, dispossessed mobsters, supporters of Prio and Batista, and wealthy Americans like Pawley. Sturgis's International Anti-Communist Brigade, one mercenary speculated, might be "financed by dispossessed hotel and gambling room owners who operated under Batista."[31]

Another new player on the Cuban-exile scene was Prio himself, who had spent most of the 1950s organizing arms purchases and expeditions to overthrow Batista and regain his position as Cuba's president. He had also given Castro critical financial help and spent the first two years of the revolution living quietly on his estate in Cuba before returning to the United States in January 1961. Even though Prio's old comrade Tony Varona was by then the head of the FRD, the former president had apparently arrived too late to join it. He immediately managed to establish a relationship with Army intelligence, but was less successful securing appointments with leading Washington figures or getting the CIA to take any interest in him.

On April 2, 1961, Prio told his U.S. Army contact that he had joined a coalition of non-CRC groups called Unidad Revolucionaria (Revolutionary Unity), and gave an account of the organization's plans, which sounded like an expanded version of the forthcoming landings at the Bay of Pigs, about which he seemed to know a great deal.[32] After the landing failed, Prio sponsored the formation of a Cuban government in exile led by Dr. Julio Garceran, who had been a Supreme Court justice at the time of Batista's coup and could be regarded as the legitimate ruler of Cuba under the 1940 Constitution. Some evidence suggests he began recruiting his own mercenaries.[33] He also made a trip to Central America looking for help. The Kennedy administration regarded him as a rival patron of the exiles, but with the Bay of Pigs force in Castro's prisons, it had little choice but to tolerate independent exile activity.[34] And within a few more months, the administration had launched another initiative designed to topple the regime.

With respect to Cuba, then, the Kennedy administration inherited an existing project of invasion and assassination, tried unsuccessfully to modify this plan along less dangerous lines, and suffered a disastrous failure. With respect to organized crime, the new attorney general, Robert Kennedy, vastly expanded the federal government's efforts in an already growing field.

Beginning in 1961, the Kennedys, sensitive to accusations of nepotism, created a rather clever myth: that their father, Joe, had insisted, almost out of his own personal vanity, that Robert Kennedy become attorney general. As Robert Dallek showed in his 2003 biography of JFK, this was a fairly typical maneuver. John Kennedy excelled at concealing not necessarily what he had done but why he had done it. In talks with his informal adviser Clark Clifford, John implied that he was not really responsible for the very controversial choice of his younger brother for a key cabinet post—just as he sometimes implied that the critical selection of Lyndon Johnson as his vice president had come about almost by accident. But in fact, the two brothers decided on the appointment within five weeks of the election. John wanted his brother close at hand, and Robert wanted the opportunity to continue his crusade against organized crime in general, and Jimmy Hoffa in particular.[35]

Although both J. Edgar Hoover and the Eisenhower Justice Department had stepped up efforts against organized crime after the mob's conclave in Appalachin, New York, Robert Kennedy's moves in this arena were unprecedented, most notably in their focus on specific targets. Kennedy chose Jack Miller to head the Criminal Division of the Department of Justice. Miller had been a lawyer for a court-appointed Board of Monitors supervising Teamster activities during the late 1950s, in response to investigations by the Rackets Committee (where Robert was chief counsel). As head of the Criminal Division, Miller quadrupled the size of the Organized Crime and Racketeering Section to sixty lawyers, and to fill these new positions he recruited recent graduates from the country's best law schools. Many of these men, such as William Hundley, Charles Schaeffer, G. Robert Blakey, and James Neal, became leaders in the criminal law field during the next few decades as both prosecutors and defenders, most notably during the Watergate era. Within the Organized Crime section, Miller created a Labor Racketeering Subdivision—known internally as the Get Hoffa Squad—under Walter Sheridan, an investigator for the Rackets Committee who was a former FBI agent but not a lawyer. Sheridan reported directly to the attorney general.[36]

Convinced that organized crime represented a threat to the security of the United States, RFK focused on finding new ways to put criminals behind bars. To that end, he insisted on sharing information among various agencies. Building on the Al Capone precedent that had sent the legendary mobster to Alcatraz for tax evasion, he convinced his former law professor, the new IRS commissioner Mortimer Caplan, to move tax cases against organized criminals to the top of the pile. Lawyers in the Organized Crime section mined the statute books for rare offenses with which mobsters might be charged. They scanned mobsters' loan and licensing applications for trivial false statements and brought indictments for perjury. One Chicago mobster was indicted and convicted for having too many mourning doves in his freezer, but the conviction was overturned on appeal.

In his first months in office Robert Kennedy pushed several new anti-crime bills through Congress, making the interstate transportation and communication of information and equipment related to illegal gambling a crime. Senate Judiciary Committee Chairman James Eastland, an ultra-conservative segregationist, helped rush the bills through, and the Justice Department reciprocated by approving the appointment of Eastland's law partner (as well as a number of other white southern conservatives) to fill some of the newly created positions on the federal bench. Kennedy and his subordinates intended to weaken and eventually destroy organized crime through prosecution, publicity, and harassment—and they enlisted the FBI in their campaign.

The Top Hoodlum program, which had led to intense surveillance of the Chicago mob under Eisenhower, expanded in May 1961 to include Sam Giancana, Murray Humphreys, and Gus Alex of Chicago, several New Yorkers, and Santo Trafficante, who was now dividing his time between Tampa and Miami—for a total of twenty. Crucially, Hoover demanded daily airtels, or telegrams, reporting the activities of each of these men.[37] The daily missives became a bureaucratic nightmare that undoubtedly wasted many agent man-hours. In Chicago, several well-placed bugs made the airtels relatively easy to fill with specific information; but for Trafficante, Joe Civello of Dallas, and some others, the reports simply related comings and goings without developing any information of significance. The surveillance, however, undoubtedly raised the tension between Hoover's men and the mob. Four individual targets were of particular interest to the Justice Department: Trafficante, Carlos Marcello, Sam Giancana, and Jimmy Hoffa. At least two of them—Trafficante and Giancana—were involved with the CIA's assassination plots against Castro.

The war-within-a-war against Jimmy Hoffa got off to an unpromising start. Hoffa's own huge and resourceful legal staff had something of a jump on the new unit in the Justice Department, and in late February it successfully overturned a court order that had established the neutral Board of Monitors to oversee Teamster affairs. Within months a new convention re-elected Hoffa, increased his salary, committed the union to paying his legal bills, more than doubled members' and locals' contributions to the national office, and removed some procedural obstacles from his path. Shortly thereafter, his attorneys secured the dismissal of a Florida indictment against him on procedural grounds. Hoffa scored a personal victory over RFK in late 1961 or early 1962 when private threats managed to prevent any Hollywood studio from shooting a movie script based on Kennedy's book *The Enemy Within*.[38]

All was not going well for Hoffa, however. Several important locals were moving to disaffiliate themselves from the Teamsters despite heavy pressure from Hoffa's large band of henchmen. Meanwhile, Justice Department attorneys and investigators were looking into possible jury tampering in Hoffa's New York state trial for wiretapping, where he had been acquitted, and loans from the Central States Pension Fund for projects in New Orleans, Atlanta, Miami, and Los Angeles. Late in 1961, Hoffa angrily claimed that he personally was the target of twenty-nine grand juries, half the lawyers in the Justice Department, and half the agents of the FBI. The true figures were thirteen grand juries, sixteen attorneys, and about thirty FBI agents. Six grand juries returned indictments against Hoffa or his associates before the end of 1961.[39]

Hoffa had close connections to many of the country's leading mob bosses. In Chicago, Paul and Allen Dorfman controlled enormous flows of money out of the Central States Pension Fund, some of which bankrolled various Las Vegas casinos. Hoffa apparently had never met Trafficante, but in 1957 one of his leading lieutenants, Rolland McMaster, secured Trafficante's cooperation in starting a Miami local that fronted for gambling activities.[40] In mid-1961 Hoffa recruited one of Trafficante's attorneys, Frank Ragano, to act as local counsel in his indictment for misuse of funds to build his Sun Valley, Florida, resort. Trafficante, Ragano wrote thirty years later in his autobiography, recommended Ragano through Paul Ricca, one of the retired bosses of the Chicago mob. Trafficante declined to meet Hoffa but told Ragano to say Hoffa should regard him as a friend with whom he could exchange favors. Within two years this association led to new attempts by Trafficante and Ragano to secure loans from the Pension Fund for local developments—loans from which they would take a cut.[41]

The paradox of the Kennedys' crusade against organized crime, particularly in Chicago, was the family's own indirect connections to the mob. Such connections have in recent years been exaggerated in a number of sensational books and television programs, and by now the fiction in such accounts has come to outweigh the fact. Stories about the mob's purported relations with Joe Kennedy and about Sam Giancana's pivotal role in the 1960 election have never been substantiated. But an indirect link most certainly existed, and it complicated the campaign against Giancana and the Chicago mob from 1961 until JFK's death.

The most durable legend regarding the Kennedys and Chicago mobsters is also the one that has been most decisively disproved: that vote fraud by a coalition of Mayor Richard Daley's Democratic machine and its mob allies gave Illinois' electoral votes to JFK in the 1960 election and thus awarded him the presidency. In fact, Robert Kennedy made an enemy of Giancana in 1959 by humiliating him before the Rackets Committee, and Robert's prime target, Jimmy Hoffa, had numerous ties to Chicago mobsters as well. As a result, Hoffa was firmly in the Nixon camp. But it would not have been impossible or unprecedented for a mobster like Giancana to try to buy some insurance by helping the Kennedys—and evidence shows that Giancana made such a donation through Frank Sinatra.[42] Nevertheless, a careful analysis of the 1960 campaign in Illinois, published in 1988 by the political scientist Edmund Kallina, has shown clearly that the Illinois presidential vote was *not* stolen for Kennedy by the mob or anybody else.[43]

Kallina discovered that the Chicago Democratic organization led by Daley paid relatively little attention to the presidential campaign. Instead, they focused on defeating Cook County State Attorney Benjamin Adamowski, a renegade Democrat turned Republican who had recently embarrassed several party officials with investigations into links between law enforcement and organized crime. Observers during the fall of 1960 noted that his campaign for re-election against the Democrat Daniel Ward was much harder fought than the Nixon-Kennedy battle.[44] Kallina also found that press accounts in the days after the election, in which Kennedy carried Illinois by just 8,858 votes out of almost five million cast, did not contain any allegations of irregularities or late reporting of precinct totals. Only some days later, when it became apparent that absentee ballots would give California to Richard Nixon and that a similar shift in two other close states such as Illinois, New Jersey, or Texas might have changed the outcome of the presidential race, did the conduct of the Chicago election become controversial.[45]

On December 20 Adamowski, who had been defeated by about 26,000 votes, challenged the outcome and was granted a recount in paper-ballot precincts. This gave both Nixon and Adamowski small and far from decisive gains. In an attempt to lay the issue to rest, Kallina made the generous assumption (generous, that is, to the Republicans) that vote fraud took place on the same scale in voting-machine precincts as in paper-ballot precincts. Two different methods of estimating the result yielded quite extraordinary but consistent conclusions. According to these extrapolations, Nixon gained either 7,968 net votes or 4,674 net votes—not enough to reverse the outcome. Adamowski gained either 31,284 net votes or 32,391 net votes, and thus was very possibly the real winner of the election, even though his legal challenge failed.

If the Chicago Democratic machine stole an election in November 1960, it was not the contest between Kennedy and Nixon. And since the mob itself had even less influence over voters than the Democratic machine as a whole, it could not have been responsible for more than a fraction of any fraud that occurred. Despite later claims to the contrary, Giancana and company did *not* hand Illinois to Jack Kennedy, and even if they had, Nixon would have needed another medium-size state to change the final outcome of the presidential election.[46]

The Kennedys' relationship with Giancana did not come from any political alliance but rather from their mutual ties to Hollywood and the entertainment world. The family's connections in Hollywood went back to the 1920s and 1930s, when Joseph P. Kennedy ran a studio, fell in love with actress Gloria Swanson, and cut a wide swathe through the town. The Kennedys acquired an additional tie to Hollywood in 1954 when sister Patricia married the British actor Peter Lawford. Family members were no strangers to Palm Springs or Las Vegas, and by the late 1950s Jack, through his brother-in-law, became friends with Frank Sinatra, who certainly had connections to the mob. He had known Sam Giancana since at least the 1950s and had performed several times at one of Giancana's clubs in Chicago. One FBI informant even claimed that Giancana received a share of Sinatra's earnings.[47]

Sinatra worked in Adlai Stevenson's presidential campaigns of 1952 and 1956, and he recorded campaign songs for Kennedy before the 1960 primaries. But Sinatra and Kennedy had more in common than the entertainment world and politics. Like Sam Giancana, they were compulsive womanizers. In March 1960 Los Angeles private investigator Fred Otash informed the FBI that he was asked by *Confidential* magazine, a notorious scandal sheet, to investigate "indiscreet parties" involving Kennedy, Lawford, and a name the bureau blanked out—almost certainly Sinatra. Otash declined.[48]

In his rich and varied life, John Kennedy demonstrated an extraordinary ability to feel comfortable in the most incongruous milieus—among British aristocrats, Boston Irish politicians, Hollywood actors and actresses, diplomats from around the world, sports figures, hookers, and intellectuals of the highest order. The records of his administration, including tapes of meetings and conversations with foreign leaders, show an unusual capacity to focus on the task—and the person—at hand, a skill that also enabled him to compartmentalize his life. Despite Sinatra's mob connections, any conflict between his friendship with the presidential candidate and Robert Kennedy's crusade against organized crime does not seem to have occurred to Jack or Bobby Kennedy as yet. But by February 1960, this friendship had already compromised the President, when he allowed Sinatra to introduce him to Judith Campbell, a beautiful young woman whose life might in an earlier age have found its way into a novel by Emile Zola.

Although Judith Campbell's associations with both President Kennedy and Sam Giancana figured in numerous FBI documents in 1961–62, the entire story did not come to light until the Church Committee's investigations in 1975. The book that Campbell—by then Judith Campbell Exner—later co-authored with Ovid Demaris documented her movements and meetings with remarkable accuracy, thanks, she said, to scrapbooks and clippings she saved over the years.[49] A young divorcée living in the Los Angeles area, Campbell claimed to have met Sinatra, along with Peter and Pat Kennedy Lawford, late in 1959 and had subsequently been Sinatra's guest in Hawaii and Las Vegas. She met then-Senator Kennedy in Las Vegas during a February campaign trip, and their affair began in New York City on March 7.

At Sinatra's invitation, Campbell went from New York to Miami Beach to stay at the Fontainebleau Hotel. During that visit she met "Sam Flood" of Chicago, who turned out to be Giancana. She continued to see both Kennedy and Giancana during 1960, although in her book she claimed she had not yet had sexual relations with Giancana. In 1961 Campbell also began spending time with John Roselli, whom she met years earlier in Hollywood.[50] Although the FBI identified Campbell as a friend of both Roselli and Giancana, by the spring of 1961 the bureau apparently had not yet secured her phone records and discovered a series of calls to presidential secretary Evelyn Lincoln.

During the whole first half of 1961, Giancana endured perhaps the most intense FBI surveillance of any mobster in the country. Bureau agents bugged hotel rooms where he stayed with Phyllis McGuire, even though these bugs never seemed to generate anything but the gory details of their relationship. Giancana remained a highest-priority target of the FBI, the Justice Department, and Attorney General Robert Kennedy himself.

On April 1, J. Edgar Hoover told RFK that a Giancana lieutenant, Joe Pignatello, was trying to get liquor and gambling licenses for a Las Vegas restaurant that he planned to buy, and that Frank Sinatra had recommended Pignatello to Las Vegas authorities. Kennedy asked Hoover to have the Las Vegas FBI office call those authorities on his behalf to dissuade them from granting it. A special conference at FBI headquarters on April 7–10, 1961, designated Giancana and his Chicago associates Gus Alex and Murray Humphreys as three of the top nine hoodlums in the country. In response, the Chicago office generated a report of several hundred pages on Giancana's business interests, political and law enforcement connections, potential tax problems, and the general results of intense surveillance. Sinatra, interviewed on April 25, admitted knowing Giancana but denied intervening on behalf of Pignatello in Vegas. Hoover forwarded the report to RFK and assured him that a grand jury should shortly be called.[51] The attorney general obviously felt no obligation to Sinatra or Giancana because of any help they might have provided during the previous fall election.

It was exactly at this moment, of course, that Giancana's CIA connection began to emerge. On April 18, in the midst of the Bay of Pigs landing, Robert Maheu finally explained the genesis of the tap on Dan Rowan's telephone to Washington FBI agents. After "insinuating" that he was working for the CIA and referring the agents to Sheffield Edwards for confirmation, Maheu said that in the course of his recent travels he learned of a possible leak of crucial information through an individual from Chicago. Asked by an alert agent whether it was Sam Giancana, he denied knowing his last name, but indicated that the man was in love with Phyllis McGuire and that the tap had been placed to see whether Giancana was the source of the leak. (Since the FBI itself had reported

Giancana's leak six months earlier, this story was not likely to hold up.) Maheu claimed that he sent investigators to plant a bug, not a telephone tap, and that he had no intention of violating the law. A senior FBI official recommended that the CIA be contacted immediately both to verify Maheu's story and to find out whether the agency had authorized him to undertake surveillance.[52]

The FBI interviewed Edwards on May 12, and Hoover passed the results along to the attorney general on May 22. Edwards explained that he had selected Maheu in the fall of 1960 as a cut-out to contact Giancana because he believed that the underworld still had "sources and contacts in Cuba which perhaps could be utilized successfully in connection with CIA's clandestine efforts against the Castro government." Giancana had cooperated, he continued, and while "none of Giancana's efforts have materialized to date," several were in progress and "might eventually 'pay off.'" But Edwards denied that he had any specific knowledge of the methods the two men were using or that he had authorized or discussed any technical surveillance. Since neither Maheu nor Edwards mentioned the name of Jim O'Connell—the link between them—Edwards could deny his own knowledge.

Moving on to more sensitive matters, Edwards said that only Bissell and two other CIA officials knew "of the Giancana-Maheu activity," and added that Bissell, during recent conversations with General Taylor and the attorney general in connection with the Taylor Board's inquiry into the Bay of Pigs, "told the Attorney General that some of CIA's associated planning included the use of Giancana and the underworld against Castro." Bissell certainly never referred to this operation in his voluminous testimony before the Taylor Board, and he essentially refused to confirm this in testimony before the Church Committee. In an obvious (and successful) attempt to keep the operation going, Edwards carefully avoided mentioning the names of John Roselli—Maheu's true original contact— or Santo Trafficante.[53]

"Courtney," wrote Robert Kennedy on his copy of this memo to Courtney Evans, his personal FBI liaison with Hoover, on June 3, "I hope this will be followed up vigorously." In response, Evans wrote to his superior, August Belmont, that the CIA, while acknowledging their relationship with Maheu, denied authorizing any surveillance, and that "the field has been instructed to press this investigation vigorously." During the next few days alert FBI agents in Los Angeles concluded that Roselli was the "J. A. Rollins" who had registered at the Kenilworth Hotel along with Maheu, and Maheu eventually admitted that he had contacted Giancana through Roselli. It proved impossible, however, to tie Roselli directly to the wiretapping, since Balletti had never met him and he had not been in Las Vegas at the time. When the FBI approached Roselli on July 7 in Beverly Hills, he refused to discuss the matter at all. Maheu, meanwhile, repeated that he ordered the bug to check on Giancana's leak and that Giancana knew nothing about it—a tactic that made any prosecution of Giancana much more difficult.[54]

On June 22 Hoover ordered new attempts to locate and interview Giancana himself.[55] Surveillance continued more intensely than ever as Giancana spent much of June and early July in Las Vegas with McGuire. On July 11 the couple tried to evade surveillance by driving a Cadillac he had recently given her to Phoenix at speeds of over 100 mph in the middle of the night, and taking a plane from Phoenix to Chicago. Agents stayed with them every step of the way and met both of them at the airport the next morning, where they attempted to interview Sam and Phyllis separately.

Bitter and humiliated, Giancana complained of the bureau's "persecution of Italians" but refused to leave before McGuire's interview—which was more polite but also unproductive—was over. "Now you can tell your super chief you talked to me and he can tell the super super chief all about it," the FBI report quoted him as saying the next day, "and all of them can go fuck themselves." Asked to identify the super bosses, he replied, "The Kennedys, who else." In his memoir, Agent William Roemer, who was present, rendered the exchange as follows: "Fuck you. Fuck your boss. Fuck your boss's boss . . . You'll rue this day. I'll get you."[56] He refused to comment on the bugging of Rowan's hotel room and denied knowing Maheu. Giancana, the agents reported, was behaving erratically and "might explode." Two days later Hoover forwarded a summary of the confrontation to the attorney general.[57] Giancana's intense surveillance continued through the rest of the year, but in September the U.S. attorney in Las Vegas informed Washington that he did not think he could get an indictment in the wiretap case.[58]

The target of RFK's first and most dramatic anti-racketeering initiative after becoming attorney general was Carlos Marcello of New Orleans. In early 1960 the government got a break in its campaign against Marcello when Carl Noll, an inmate in Lewisburg Federal Penitentiary who was facing another indictment, decided to talk to the Immigration and Naturalization Service. In a long and fascinating interview, Noll, a former football player at Ohio State, described his own involvement in heroin imports from Guatemala and Honduras. Some of them were destined for the Sans Souci casino in Havana owned by Norman Rothmann and Santo Trafficante. After getting in some trouble in New Orleans, Noll—with Marcello's help—had gone to work for Sam Mannarino, the Pittsburgh area mobster who was involved with Marcello in slot machine shipments to Cuba and who planned the robbery of the Canton, Ohio, armory for arms to ship to Castro.

Most interesting of all, Noll told the investigators how he had traveled to Guatemala in April 1956 to get Marcello a false birth certificate in a remote Guatemalan village with the help of the country's attorney general. Noll estimated that Marcello owned perhaps fifty gambling establishments around the South and might be worth $20 million. During 1960, however, the FBI held off opening any new cases against Marcello, pending further action in his deportation proceedings. In an effort to avoid being deported to Italy, the New Orleans boss had indeed given Italian authorities a copy of his forged Guatemalan birth certificate, which would have relieved the Italian government of any responsibility for him.[59]

In late December 1960 the New Orleans *Times-Picayune* called publicly for the attorney general–designate to push forward with Marcello's deportation. Robert Kennedy needed no encouragement. While the FBI laid plans to install bugs in one or two of Marcello's favorite hangouts, Kennedy during his first week in office told the INS, which fell under his jurisdiction, to get to work on the case. Meanwhile, Marcello was visiting Washington and trying to contact some important political figures, including Louisiana Democrat Hale Boggs. In the last few days of January he visited Miami, where Maheu, Giancana, and Trafficante were working to arrange the Castro assassination. On March 3, INS Commissioner Joseph Swing told the FBI that the attorney general was demanding to deport Marcello as soon as possible and that he was trying to find a country which would accept him. The country must be easily accessible, however, because if Marcello had to wait even a few hours before boarding a plane to get there, his attorney could file a new motion to block his deportation. The INS and the CIA, he explained, were working to get the Guatemalan government to accept him, but he worried that Marcello's own Guatemalan connections might tip him off.[60]

That problem was solved after Robert Kennedy met with Undersecretary of State George Ball to get things moving. The Italian government obligingly provided Washington with a copy of Marcello's phony birth certificate, Washington showed it to the Guatemalan government, and it agreed to receive him.[61] On April 4 Marcello made a routine appearance at the New Orleans INS office and was accosted by two border patrolmen who bundled him into a car, drove him to Moisant Airport, and put him on a plane to Guatemala. These summary proceedings immediately raised some eyebrows in the legal community and in the press, and on April 6 Robert Kennedy disingenuously told journalists that he had not been aware of what was about to happen and that he would have used "different steps" had he been in New Orleans. The border patrol reported to the FBI the next day that RFK had been completely informed in advance.[62]

Marcello was already working closely with Washington lobbyist and Hoffa ally Irving Davidson, and Davidson apparently managed to arrange a telephone interview on April 9 between Marcello and columnist Drew Pearson, whose office was in the same building as Davidson's. Marcello claimed he was a Guatemalan citizen and carefully avoided blaming the attorney general.[63] New legal action began in the United States, and RFK had Jack Miller of the Criminal Division ask the FBI about securing the telephone records of Marcello's attorney, Jack Wasserman.[64] The Guatemalan president, Manuel Ydigoras, now blamed Marcello's purported Guatemalan citizenship on his predecessor. He ordered Marcello flown back to the United States on May 3, but three airlines refused to accept him. Instead, Guatemalan police drove him to the El Salvadorean border and expelled him.[65]

The El Salvadorean police reportedly turned Marcello and his lawyer loose in the wilderness, forcing them to walk for miles. During the journey Marcello fell and broke two ribs.[66] After some unexplained travels through the Caribbean, apparently including a stop in the Dominican Republic where his friend Irving Davidson had connections, Marcello arrived back in the United States in early June. With his fortune intact, the legal battle began again. Within a few days he was indicted for illegal re-entry into the country, and in late October he was accused of falsely submitting the Guatemalan birth certificate and swearing to its validity.[67] Carl Noll, on whose testimony the latter case would largely depend, was now out of jail and living in Baltimore, and in September two men approached him to tell him that he was "owed a lot of money" and that he knew who owed it to him. Noll assumed they were referring to $100,000 that Marcello had promised him years before.[68]

Backed by the resources of the Justice Department, RFK was now deeply involved in life or death struggles with Hoffa, Giancana, and Marcello—and all of them would became more, not less, intense during the next two years. Inevitably, these underworld figures began thinking about ways to stop him, or even to retaliate.

5

Operation Mongoose

The Berlin Crisis, the Congo imbroglio, and the Soviets' resumption of nuclear testing preoccupied the Kennedy administration in the summer and early fall of 1961, but Cuba remained a key issue as well. The CIA now settled on a modest program of continuing intelligence and paramilitary operations, and the agency argued with the State Department over whether to continue supporting Cuban political groups through the Cuban Revolutionary Council. In August, White House assistant Richard Goodwin attended an OAS meeting in Uruguay and had a lengthy conversation with Che Guevara. Upon his return he suggested that an eventual understanding with the Castro regime might be possible, but proposed a campaign of economic pressure, isolation, and sabotage in the meantime. The President concurred.

Latin America as a whole, meanwhile, was moving to the forefront of the administration's agenda. The August Uruguay meeting also launched the Alliance for Progress, the Kennedy administration's plan to promote economic development throughout the continent. During the same month, a political crisis shook South America's largest nation, Brazil. Leftist, neutralist President Janio Quadros suddenly resigned, citing opposition from the forces of reaction, and Vice President Joao Goulart—another leftist and trade union leader—took office only after the Brazilian constitution was modified to weaken the office of president and create a strong prime minister. The administration was apparently evolving a three-track strategy: first, to promote economic justice and democracy; second, to watch carefully and try to head off any new leftist gains; and third, to see what could be done, once again, to bring about the fall of Fidel Castro.

In early October, President Kennedy himself initiated a new burst of activity relating not only to Cuba but potentially to the assassination of its leader. On October 5 Thomas Parrott, a CIA official working in the White House for General Maxwell Taylor, who was brought into the inner circle as the President's special military representative after the Bay of Pigs, informed two State Department officials—Assistant Secretary Robert Woodward and Wymberly Coerr—of a new "requirement" regarding Cuba.

> I said that what was wanted was a plan against the contingency that Castro would in some way or other be removed from the Cuban scene. I said that my understanding was the terms of reference governing this plan should be quite broad; we agreed, for example, that the presence and positions of Raoul and Che Guevara must be taken into account. We agreed that this was an exercise that should be under the direction of State with participation by Defense and CIA. I also pointed out to Mr. Coerr that Mr. Goodwin had been aware of this requirement.

Critically, Parrott also noted that this new requirement came to him through Taylor from the President himself, but that Taylor told him to keep that a secret. When Parrott asked Tracy Barnes, Bissell's deputy at CIA, to furnish an immediate "up-to-date report on what was going on and what was being planned," he discovered that Barnes had already heard about the requirement and the President's interest from Goodwin.[1] The President's request—combined with a conversation he had with *New York Times* reporter Tad Szulc a few weeks later—confirms that he was aware, as he had been in the spring before the Bay of Pigs, that the assassination of the Cuban leadership was still regarded as a live option within the government and that he had some interest in it himself.

The surprising responses Taylor received from the CIA illustrate how hard it is to uncover the agency's behavior based on written documentation, especially documentation circulated outside the agency itself. The Western Hemisphere branch responded just twenty-four hours later with a pessimistic report. Castro's death, "whether by natural causes or assassination," would have little chance of changing the regime, and the four most likely successors—led by Raoul Castro and Che Guevara—would probably pursue the same course.[2] The author said nothing about any past or present plots, either because he did not know about them or because he thought any mention of them outside the agency was inappropriate. A subsequent CIA analysis by the Office of National Estimates also argued that Castro's death would not prove fatal to the regime.[3]

Meanwhile, the State Department was directing an interdepartmental effort to answer the White House's question. On November 1 Goodwin, who had been taking some public heat for his meeting with Guevara, wrote the President a memorandum on the Cuban problem.

> I believe that the concept of a "command operation" for Cuba, as discussed with you by the Attorney General, is the only effective way to handle an all-out attack on the Cuban problem. Since I understand you are favorably disposed toward the idea I will not discuss why the present disorganized and uncoordinated operation cannot do the job effectively.
>
> The beauty of such an operation over the next few months is that we cannot lose. If the best happens we will unseat Castro. If not, then at least we will emerge with a stronger underground, better propaganda and a far clearer idea of the dimensions of the problems which affect us.
>
> The question then is who should head this operation. I know of no one currently in Cuban affairs at the State Department who can do it. Nor is it a very good idea to get the State Department involved in depth in such covert activities. I do not think it should be centered in the CIA. Even if the CIA can find someone of sufficient force and stature, one of the major problems will be to revamp CIA operations and thinking—and this will be very hard to do from the inside.
>
> I believe that the Attorney General would be the most effective commander of such an operation. Either I or someone else should be assigned to him as Deputy for this activity, since he obviously will not be able to devote full time to it.[4]

Two days later, the President met with Bissell, Robert Kennedy, General Taylor, Goodwin, and various Cuban specialists from CIA and State. Differing accounts of the meeting illustrate the gulf that divided the insular CIA from the rest of the government. A contemporary note by the attorney general echoed Goodwin's memo.

> McNamara, Dick Bissell, Alexis Johnson, Paul Nitze, Lansdale (the Ugly American). McN said he would make latter available for me—I assigned him to make survey of situation in Cuba—the problem and our assets. My idea is to stir things up on island with espionage, sabotage, general

disorder, run & operated by Cubans themselves with every group but Batistaites & Communists. Do not know if we will be successful in overthrowing Castro but we have nothing to lose in my estimate.[5]

When Bissell returned to CIA headquarters, he told his deputy, Sam Halpern, that he had been "chewed out" by the President and the attorney general "for, as he put it, sitting on his ass and not doing anything about getting rid of Castro and the Castro regime." Halpern and the chief of Western Hemisphere branch 4, whom he did not identify, were given that task. "There was no limitation of any kind. Nothing was forbidden, and nothing was withheld," Halpern said. Since President Kennedy almost never chewed out anyone, especially in a large meeting, one can reasonably assume that his brother did most of the chewing. Halpern, who was probably the most forthcoming CIA witness before the Church Committee (and who did a long and very informative oral history of his CIA years for an agency historian in the early 1980s), clearly regarded this as a directive to the CIA, quite independent of the new structure that the meeting was setting up. On November 4, RFK and Bissell agreed that large-scale sabotage actions would be carried out by both CIA-controlled assets and independent Cuban groups as quickly as possible.[6]

In succeeding weeks Robert Kennedy made it clear that he did not want J. C. King to remain in charge of CIA affairs in Cuba because of his role in the Bay of Pigs. In December the new director of Central Intelligence, John McCone—who replaced Allen Dulles because of the invasion fiasco—announced that Richard Helms would take charge of Cuban affairs. Helms succeeded Bissell as deputy director for plans a couple of weeks later. Helms split Cuban affairs off from the rest of the Western Hemisphere branch, and in February William Harvey returned from Europe and took over Task Force W, the new CIA office charged with Cuba.[7]

At the same time, Robert Kennedy's new interdepartmental initiative was christened Operation Mongoose, and General Edward Lansdale was chosen to head it late in November. Lansdale was famous outside the government and highly controversial within it. He had already played major roles helping President Magsaysay of the Philippines defeat a Communist insurgency and installing President Ngo Dinh Diem's government in South Vietnam. Moreover, he was the model for the hero of two best-selling novels, *The Quiet American* by Graham Greene and *The Ugly American* by Eugene Burdick and William J. Lederer (to which Robert Kennedy's note referred). He had alienated most of the U.S. government, however, including the State Department and the CIA, which had blocked his return to Saigon on two occasions during 1961.

Although other officials regarded Lansdale as impossible, he was indeed a legend, and his reputation as an independent operator apparently appealed to the attorney general. Originally, he hoped to give Lansdale a task force of his own composed of officers detailed from CIA, State, and Defense for his exclusive use, but the agencies firmly resisted that solution. Lansdale had to be content with a team of agency representatives who reported to him. He in turn began reporting to a new Special Group (Augmented), a revised 5412 Committee that now included Robert Kennedy, General Taylor, National Security Adviser McGeorge Bundy, U. Alexis Johnson from State, and Roswell Gilpatric from Defense.

Despite its initial designation as a "command operation," Mongoose was only one element of the administration's campaign against Cuba. Latin American attitudes remained the key obstacle to armed intervention, and in February 1962 the administration secured new OAS resolutions isolating Cuba, though not the blanket authorization it wanted to deal with the problem. Meanwhile, the Pentagon worked hard to update its contingency plans for invasion.[8]

The dilemmas Operation Mongoose faced, which persisted right up until the end of the Kennedy administration, emerged during the first four months of the project. Both the President and his brother established a maximum objective, albeit with some qualifications regarding the role of the United States. "We will use our available assets to go ahead with the discussed project in order to help Cuba overthrow the Communist regime," read a presidential memorandum of November 30. Robert Kennedy told the Mongoose team on January 18 that "the solution to the Cuban problem" is "top priority," and no assets were to be spared: "It's got to be done and will be done."[9] But McCone at CIA repeatedly warned the attorney general that the organization of effective resistance to a well-armed authoritarian regime was going to be a very difficult and long-term job. He explained on December 27 that the CIA had only twenty-eight agents in Cuba. Seven more who had infiltrated on December 19 were captured and had confessed on Cuban TV four days later.[10]

Lansdale's impossible task reflected the Kennedy administration's refusal simply to invade Cuba without the permission of the OAS, which the United States had been unable to secure. Harvey complained bitterly in 1975 that Robert Kennedy wanted his agency to overthrow Castro entirely with covert means and without the slightest taint of American involvement.[11] But another way of handling this problem had already surfaced in response to the President's covert October request for analysis of the impact of Fidel Castro's sudden death. In early November Robert Hurwitch of State—an action officer on Cuba—drafted a long memorandum "to determine the courses of action which the U.S. would follow with reference to Cuba in the event of Fidel Castro's death in order to insure the replacement of the Castro regime with a friendly government." It assumed that Castro might die suddenly and violently, that the United States would be blamed for his death, that Raoul Castro would become prime minister, and any outbreak of resistance would be crushed. The United States would immediately mobilize its forces and invade, provided that the regime was carrying out widespread atrocities, a rebellion was in progress, the rebels called for American help, and the U.S. government concluded that the Soviets would not go to war.

The paper proposed giving the task of "creat[ing] the above-described minimum desirable conditions in Cuba" to CIA, Defense, State, and the U.S. Information Agency. Ironically, it illustrates the greater willingness of State officials to discuss the assassination of Castro in writing than their more active CIA counterparts, and it laid out a scenario that found its way into Mongoose and resurfaced in a slightly different form in the middle of 1963.[12] It seemed to match American capabilities fairly well. Assassinating Castro could be accomplished far more easily than the gigantic task of creating an effective revolutionary movement, and the American military presumably could, if turned loose with a suitable pretext, finish the job of dealing with his decapitated regime. The joint chiefs approved a revised operational plan to invade Cuba on five days' notice late in that same month.[13]

The President's interest in such a plan seemed to be confirmed by his November 9 conversation with reporter Tad Szulc, who had recently spent time in Cuba. Szulc lunched with RFK at the Justice Department and then, at the attorney general's request, met with the President, along with Goodwin. JFK, who always delighted in first-hand reports on situations in foreign countries, drew Szulc out regarding Castro's personality and the strength of his regime. He asked whether new U.S.-sponsored guerrilla operations would make sense, and "talked about the need of controlling CIA in some way so that CIA wouldn't construct another operation like [the] Bay of Pigs."

> Then, suddenly, Pres leaned forward and asked me, "What would you think if I ordered Castro to be assassinated?" I said this would be terrible idea because a) it probably wouldn't do away with regime; on contrary it would strengthen it, and b) I felt personally US had no business in assassinations. JFK then said he was testing me, that he felt the same way—he added "I'm glad you feel the same way"—because indeed US morally must not be party to assassinations. JFK said he raised question because he was under terrific pressure from advisers (think he said intelligence people, but not positive) to okay a Castro murder. Said he was resisting pressures.[14]

Like Kennedy's conversation early in the year with Florida Senator George Smathers, this one confirms that the topic of assassination had been discussed at the highest level. Although Szulc suggested to the Church Committee that Kennedy would hardly have tipped his hand to a journalist if he knew an assassination was in the works, his behavior does seem to indicate some genuine interest.[15] Nor was this the first time that Kennedy had attributed an unpopular idea to someone else. On November 16—exactly one week later—the President actually raised the issue in a speech at the University of Washington.

> As the most powerful defender of freedom on earth, we find ourselves unable to escape the responsibilities of freedom, and yet unable to exercise it without restraints imposed by the very freedoms we seek to protect. We cannot, as a free nation, compete with our adversaries in tactics of terror, assassination, false promises, counterfeit mobs and crises. We cannot, under the scrutiny of a free press and public, tell different stories to different audiences, foreign and domestic, friendly and hostile.[16]

Despite these words, Kennedy, who consistently refused to make final decisions until it was absolutely necessary, apparently had not ruled out assassination, especially as part of a broader uprising. More than a year later, in a conversation with Guatemalan President Ydigoras, he expressed the opinion that Castro's sudden disappearance might well mean the end of his regime.

Assassination was certainly an option in the plan that Lansdale was developing to overthrow the Castro regime. Completed by February 20, this scenario envisioned the infiltration of several small teams of "pathfinder" agents over the next few months, followed in June by three larger "resistance teams" that would establish bases for guerrilla activity. During the next three months guerrillas would escalate resistance and sabotage, attempt to get key Cuban leaders to defect, and in September mount an "attack on the cadre of the regime, including key leaders." October would see a full-scale revolt, the proclamation of a new government, and possibly armed U.S. intervention, which Lansdale asked the Pentagon to prepare.[17]

The CIA, however, immediately argued that at least six months must be added to the October deadline, and Secretary of Defense McNamara agreed with the agency, even though the joint chiefs had already declared the completion of new invasion plans to be their "first priority." Lansdale in early March began discussing other possible pretexts for intervention, such as purported Cuban plots in Latin America or a simulated Cuban landing in Guatemala. In the end, a new set of "Guidelines for Operation Mongoose" established intelligence as the first objective, called for political, economic, and covert tactics that would *not* be sufficient to start a revolt, and asked the joint chiefs to plan for military intervention. The President approved these guidelines on March 14, while expressing skepticism that the conditions for American intervention would arise any time soon.[18]

The CIA's operations during the first half of 1962 illustrate how impossible it was to influence such a fully compartmented and isolated organization from outside. Mongoose was RFK's attempt to do just that— to integrate the CIA's operations into a broader strategy. The agency detailed first Helms and then Harvey as its Mongoose representative, to try to satisfy the Special Group (Augmented) that it was doing its part. Yet no one in the CIA regarded Mongoose as much more than a bureaucratic response to the administration's political embarrassment over the Bay of Pigs. Thus, McCone, as the new director of Central Intelligence, was arguing by early March that armed U.S. intervention to remove Castro was both necessary and advisable.[19] Yet meanwhile, CIA agents James O'Connell and William Harvey were keeping the mob assassination plot alive, outside the knowledge not only of Lansdale and the Special Group but also of the agency's own director.

The FBI's Las Vegas wiretap investigation had forced Sheffield Edwards and Robert Maheu to confess their part in the operation to kill Castro, but no one outside the CIA had learned about O'Connell's involvement. He was perfectly free to pursue the assassination plot through Johnny Roselli, whose central role had also been concealed. O'Connell continued meeting with Roselli during 1961 and into 1962. On November 15, 1961, Bissell told Harvey that he would be taking over the Castro assassination project from Edwards and O'Connell. By April 1962 Roselli had apparently informed O'Connell that Tony Varona was willing to make another assassination attempt in return for some arms and equipment, and during that month O'Connell accompanied Harvey to Miami to meet Roselli for the first time. There, Harvey gave Varona new poison capsules and supervised the transfer of a truckload of arms provided by Ted Shackley, chief of Miami's CIA Station JMWAVE. Varona said, apparently, that he had a team ready to enter Cuba.[20]

Meanwhile, the Las Vegas wiretapping case itself was nearing resolution. On January 31 Jack Miller of the Criminal Division of the Justice Department asked Edwards about a possible prosecution of Maheu. Edwards replied a week later that the CIA "would object to any prosecution which would necessitate the use of CIA personnel or CIA information. He pointed out that an introduction of any evidence concerning the CIA operation would be most embarrassing to the US Government."[21] On April 2 Edwards told Sam Papich, the FBI liaison agent, that "he had no desire to impose any restriction which might hinder efforts to prosecute any individual but that he is firmly convinced that prosecution of Maheu undoubtedly would result in most damaging embarrassment to the U.S. Government." In view of this, "his Agency objects to prosecution of Maheu."

"This is an outrage," J. Edgar Hoover wrote when he saw the account of this conversation.[22] When apparently the attorney general himself demanded a briefing, Edwards and CIA general counsel Laurence Houston—who had no first-hand knowledge of the events—met with him on May 7. On May 9, in a face-to-face meeting with Hoover, Robert

Kennedy discussed what he had learned. According to Hoover's memo, Kennedy told him that the CIA authorized Maheu to offer Giancana $150,000 to hire gunmen to kill Castro. "I expressed astonishment at this," Hoover wrote, "in view of the bad reputation of Maheu and the horrible judgment in using a man of Giancana's background for such a project. The Attorney General shared the same views." Kennedy also told Hoover that the CIA admitted it had not cleared this decision with the Justice Department and promised never to take such steps without checking with Justice again.

Edwards's memorandum for record was much more circumspect, referring only to "a sensitive operation against Fidel Castro." It did acknowledge the central role of Roselli as Maheu's primary contact, but it did not name Trafficante as the "courier" through whom the operation was arranged. None of the Cubans involved, Edwards claimed, had discovered that the federal government was behind the project. "After the failure of the invasion of Cuba," Edwards wrote, "word was sent through Maheu to Roselli to call off the operation and Roselli was told to tell his principal that the proposal to pay one hundred fifty thousand dollars for completion of the operation had been definitely withdrawn."[23]

The Hoover memorandum of his conversation with Robert Kennedy is noteworthy because neither man seems to have expressed any reservations about the CIA's assassination plot in principle, but both objected vehemently to the personnel the agency chose to carry it out. And knowing, apparently, that the administration would welcome Castro's disappearance, CIA personnel now decided to continue the operation anyway, under a new case officer. Edwards and O'Connell had already turned Roselli over to Harvey, who had just given Varona new poison pills for Castro in Miami. Seemingly troubled by this chain of events and anxious to purge any evidence of it from the record, Edwards on May 14—the same day that he wrote his memo to the attorney general—dictated an internal memorandum for the record claiming that Harvey called him and announced that he was "dropping any plans for the use" of Roselli in the future. That, Harvey told the Church Committee, was a lie, as both he and Edwards knew. Harvey then discussed the situation with Helms, and they agreed not to brief McCone.[24]

The new CIA director had quickly emerged as a man of keen intelligence and strong opinions, who carefully recorded all his dealings with his superiors. Both he and his deputy, Walter Elder, told the Church Committee that McCone did not learn of the mob plot until September 1963, and McCone stated that he would never have approved assassination.[25] The 1967 inspector general's report recorded the reasoning behind Edwards's and Harvey's decision to keep McCone in the dark. Edwards, the report said, had not informed McCone, his deputy, General Carter, or Helms of his meeting with the attorney general. "He felt that, since they [McCone and Carter] had not been privy to the operation when it was under way, they should be protected from involvement in it after the fact." The report also inadvertently explained how CIA subordinates interpreted the significance of a change of directors. Edwards informed the inspector general "that at the time of the bugging incident and the flap that ensued those (Dulles and Bissell) who had given the initial approval of the plan to assassinate Castro through the gambling syndicate were gone. As no one else in authority (including Mr. Helms) had been cut in on the operation, Edwards dealt with [the FBI] without reference to anyone else in the Agency." The reference to Helms was at best a half-truth, but the underlying philosophy—once authorized, always authorized until further notice—was clear enough.[26]

And although Harvey gave the Special Group (Augmented) an immediate report on his trip to Miami and his attempts to infiltrate sabotage teams, he told neither them nor Lansdale about the assassination plot.[27] Halpern remarked to a CIA historian many years later that Harvey was a man who could keep a secret, and Harvey's own Church Committee testimony actually explains his behavior very well. Questioned in detail about how he could have kept the plot away from Lansdale and the Special Group, he replied that because the operation had begun before the SGA had been created, it did not fall under its authority. Asked at one point whether one could assume that a new director (McCone) would have been briefed on any really sensitive operation by his predecessor (Helms), he replied that directors apparently did not always brief their successors.[28]

These remarks indicate both how the CIA worked and how it saw its relationship to the rest of the United States government. Once an operation was authorized, it took on a life of its own, until and unless it was compromised and led to a public embarrassment. In the case of the assassination plot against Castro, the agency dealt with the public embarrassment of the phone taps by eliminating from the assassination operation those who were definitely implicated in lawbreaking—Giancana, Maheu, O'Connell, and Edwards—and by turning Roselli, who was mentioned only peripherally, over to Harvey, who, as far as anyone else knew, had nothing to do with the plot at all.

Harvey obviously viewed his work with Lansdale and the Special Group as a separate effort designed to satisfy the attorney general and the administration, and he did not really believe that he fell under the Special Group's command. By December 1961 Lansdale had heard something about the CIA's mob contacts, and in an early memo on Mongoose he had proposed that the agency use "American links to the Cuban underworld," with FBI cooperation.[29] To Harvey, apparently, that proposal did not imply that the agency had to let Lansdale know about its existing efforts—as both of them told the Church Committee in 1975. Nor did the director have to learn anything either, until (as actually happened over a year later) another public embarrassment developed.

As for Helms's role in keeping the matter away from McCone, he merely claimed one of his many failures of memory during his first appearance under oath before the Church Committee. But in his second appearance he made two very revealing comments about the nature of the CIA and the way it saw itself in relation to the rest of the government. The committee, he suggested, could find no explicit authorizations of assassination plots because assassination would not have become part of a discussion among "a large group of people sitting around a table in the United States Government." "In other words, when you establish a clandestine service as was established in the Central Intelligence Agency, you established something that was totally different from anything else in the United States government. Whether it's right that you should have it, or wrong that you should have it, it works under different rules and ground rules than any other part of the government."

His second revealing statement came in the context of explaining Edwards's submission of a false memorandum about Harvey and Roselli. Helms remarked:

If I had, or any other Director of the Agency, had thought at any time during these years since 1947 that our records would be the basis for an interrogation on matters of action that were taken and actions that were not taken, I can assure you it would have been a very different record and we would have done things a very different way, and I don't think that any sane Director would have taken any oral word of any kind at any point, if this was going to be the way it was going to turn out, that we would ask for everything in writing.[30]

In short, documents within the CIA did not have the same purpose as documents in other parts of the federal government, that is, to convey a record of the truth to anyone who wanted to know it. The information they contained was designed to protect ongoing operations and contacts.

Exactly whom Varona sent into Cuba in April has never been made clear. Roselli was now dealing directly with not only Varona but another unidentified Cuban, possibly related to Varona, who owned a speedboat.[31] Around that time, Castro's government discovered several new assassination plots. On May 8 the national coordinator of the CIA-assisted MRR, Juan Falcon Tamar, was arrested in Cuba. Two months later, in a July 7 interview on Cuban television, he confessed to participating in a CIA-sponsored assassination plot and displayed a pistol with a silencer. Falcon described an elaborate plan to kill Fidel, Raoul, and other leaders of the Castro regime on its national holiday, July 26th. It is not clear whether Harvey, Roselli, and Varona had anything to do with this particular plot.[32] In late August the Cuban government broke up another plot, this one hatched by the Armed Forces of Liberation (FAL) and designed to assassinate several regime leaders on August 30. One captured man linked the plot to the DRE.[33]

In mid-July Lansdale initiated a review of Operation Mongoose activities and asked for interagency comment on four new options: (A) to abandon the overthrow of the Castro government; (B) to do whatever the United States could to incite a revolt but without pledging U.S. military intervention; (C) to make a commitment to Cuban exiles to help overthrow the Castro regime with American armed forces, if necessary; or (D) to stage a provocation as a pretext for an invasion. The State Department, he mentioned, still opposed option C as too unpopular within the hemisphere, and certain to leak as soon as the exiles got the word.[34] Replies from Defense and CIA evinced little enthusiasm for continuing along current lines. The Pentagon did not make a firm recommendation but expressed a preference for course D over C, because it would allow the United States to time the invasion.

Writing the CIA's response, Harvey outlined the scale of the effort the agency was making against the Castro regime. Four hundred and seventy-seven CIA personnel were now working on Cuba full time—most of them at the Miami JMWAVE station—and a number of agents, including third-country recruits, were operating inside Cuba. But only eleven out of twenty-three planned teams had actually infiltrated the island, and some Cubans had quit out of dissatisfaction with America's timid military policy. Lansdale's option C, he said, might still be possible by the end of the year, but without American military support any revolt would certainly be crushed. Should higher authorities reject the two most drastic options, he recommended cutting back the current effort. Should the President choose option D, he said, CIA would be glad to help stage the provocation.[35]

On July 25 when Lansdale summarized these recommendations in a memorandum for the Special Group (Augmented) and other senior administration figures, General Taylor showed the memo to Bundy, the President's national security adviser, who checked option B: "Exert all possible diplomatic, economic, psychological, and other pressures to overthrow the Castro-Communist regime without overt employment of U.S. military."[36] Undeterred, Lansdale submitted a memorandum on July 31 describing his option C—a revolt leading to U.S. military intervention. After Lansdale met with Taylor and Robert Kennedy on August 1, the Special Group met on August 8 to discuss a "stepped up Course B." It included major acts of sabotage, overflights, the use of submarines, the infiltration of up to two hundred more men into Cuba during the coming months, and accelerated military preparations. In response to a recent development on the intelligence front, Lansdale also spoke optimistically of splitting the Cuban leadership. Robert Kennedy endorsed this new option "Mongoose B+" and wrote Taylor that he was in favor of pushing ahead, not taking any step backward.[37]

An expanded meeting of the Special Group (Augmented) on August 10, which included McCone, McNamara, Rusk, and USIA Director Edward R. Murrow, along with the regulars, had a wide-ranging discussion of objectives in Cuba. McCone clearly favored American intervention, but Rusk argued that no pretext for it could be found short of a Soviet move against Berlin, and McNamara wanted to reduce the attributability of certain actions to the United States. The group did not approve the B+ course of action and instead asked McCone to develop a new program designed to split the leadership of Castro's regime.[38]

Over the course of this rambling discussion, according to several witnesses, McNamara at some point argued that more consideration should be given to the assassination of Castro and other Cuban leaders. Several of those in attendance, led by Murrow, immediately responded that assassination was out of the question, and the matter was dropped. Nonetheless, after the meeting Lansdale wrote an August 13 memo asking Harvey to prepare new political options for Cuba, "including liquidation of leaders." Harvey wrote Helms the next day that McNamara had raised "the question of assassination, particularly Fidel Castro . . . on 10 August," and a clear consensus emerged "that this is not a subject which has been made a matter of official record." Harvey explained that he called Lansdale's office to protest "the inadmissibility and stupidity of putting this type of comment in writing." The CIA, Harvey wrote revealingly, "would write no document pertaining to this and would participate in no open meeting discussing it." Four key words, "including liquidation of leaders," were removed. Once again, Harvey—the only person at the session who knew for a fact that assassination plots were in progress— was carefully distinguishing between secure CIA operations and projects that might be discussed in writing or with other agencies.[39]

Having failed to convince his superiors to commit to armed intervention, Lansdale on August 14 produced a new revised course B: continuing present efforts on the diplomatic, propaganda, economic, and intelligence fronts; mounting sabotage operations against economic targets; looking for opportunities to split the Cuban leadership; and being "prepared to capitalize on any significant uprising." The Special Group gave it provisional approval on August 17 and asked Lansdale to submit a list of proposed sabotage operations. Taylor in the meantime had written President Kennedy that despite eight months of work, the group saw no prospect of overthrowing Castro without American military force. He suggested that the United States might have to react to an uprising, and indicated that the "'noise level' of Mongoose operations will probably rise in the course of the new phase and there will always be the chance that the participation of some U.S. citizens may become known."[40] After more haggling, the Special Group finally approved the revised course B on September 14.[41]

Although on August 10 McCone evidently opposed assassination, a partially declassified document suggests that he might have been having second thoughts, or that he was in favor of fomenting some kind of uprising to trigger an American invasion. On August 21 he set down a new plan of action for meeting the Cuban threat in view of the massive Soviet build-up there. One can only do justice to the released version of the key paragraphs by quoting them in full:

> (1) An immediate continuing aggressive political action designed to awaken and alarm all of Latin America and all of the free world as to the extreme dangers inherent in the present Cuban situation. Appropriate actions should be taken through domestic and foreign press media to inform and alarm the people, through the United Nations, through the Organization of American States and its subcommittees, by contact with each free world country at the level of head of state, foreign minister and ambassador, and through semi-public or private organizations such as labor, church, farm cooperatives, youth groups, et cetera.
>
> (2) [5 lines of source text not declassified]
>
> (3) The instantaneous commitment of sufficient armed forces to occupy the country, destroy the regime, free the people, and establish in Cuba a peaceful country which will be a member of the community of American states.
>
> It is possible, though in my opinion improbable, that actions taken under (1) above would in themselves be sufficient to cause destruction of the Castro regime from dissension and disaffections within the regime itself which would obviate steps (2) or (3).[42]

All this time, the Harvey-Roselli-Varona assassination plot against Castro was proceeding apace. In September, Roselli told Harvey that Varona had verified that the pills delivered in April were still in place, and that Varona was sending another three-man team into Cuba to try to infiltrate Castro's militia and find a way to administer them. Years later, Cuban General Fabian Escalante claimed that in early September Varona, working with the Office of Naval Intelligence at Guantanamo, infiltrated "the men from the commando unit from Miami with the collaboration of the omnipresent Mafia." Their plans included an attempt on Castro's life and an attack against Guantanamo by a unit supposedly trained near New Orleans. The Guantanamo attack would serve as a provocation for American military intervention. This certainly sounded like Varona's three-man team, and it cast doubt on Harvey's claim to the inspector general that the team never left the States.

Escalante also described a plot organized by a CIA agent, Norberto Martinez, who had infiltrated into Cuba in early 1962 and recruited several members of Rescate. Working with the niece of former Cuban President Ramon Grau San Martin and with an old friend of Santo Trafficante, he spent 1962 and early 1963 trying to organize the poisoning of Fidel Castro with capsules mailed to the Spanish Embassy. Castro failed to show up at the Hotel Havana Libre at the key moment.[43]

In July 1962 the CIA made an important breakthrough in its assassination plans when it re-established contact with Rolando Cubela, the former DRE assassin from the Batista era was now a high Cuban government official and evidently had been involved in the late 1960 poisoning plots against Castro. Since March 1961, when Cubela met a CIA man in Mexico City, the agency had received several indirect reports of his intention to defect because of unhappiness with Fidel's turn to Communism. Some of these reports came through a long-time friend of his, a jeweler named Carlos Tepedino who had moved to the United States and now lived in New York. Tepedino had run a jewelry store in the Trafficante-owned Havana Hilton in the pre-Castro days. In April 1962 Tepedino said that Cubela was going to attend the Communist-sponsored World Youth Festival in Helsinki, Finland, later that month and wanted to defect dramatically to embarrass the Cuban government. The CIA prepared to meet him and gave Tepedino and Cubela the code names AMWHIP and AMLASH, respectively.[44]

Things took on a different cast after CIA operatives finally had several long discussions with Cubela in Helsinki between August 16 and September 2, 1962. He immediately made it clear that he had no interest in defecting but wanted to overthrow Castro by assassinating the Soviet ambassador, one or two other officials, and Castro himself. He did not believe, he said, that either Raoul Castro or Che Guevara would be able to rally the country once Fidel was dead, and he claimed to have about seven confederates willing to help him with the plot. Were he to defect, he said, he would become just another Miami exile. He insisted that no one in Miami must learn anything about his plans, since the exiles were hopelessly selfish and deeply penetrated by Castro's agents. While he would have preferred to do without the CIA altogether, he recognized that he would need help.

The agents who spoke with Cubela gave him some training and set up a mail drop in Madrid for his use. They were not certain about his reliability and noticed that he resented the use of the verb "assassinate" to describe his plans ("eliminate" was acceptable), perhaps because he had been known as an "assassin" in the Batista days.[45] This was exactly the kind of penetration Operation Mongoose had hoped for, but things moved very slowly, and the agency received only one letter from AMLASH for the rest of the year.[46]

Robert Kennedy's intense personal interest in the Cuban question continued to cause problems for the CIA. Because his support for Cuban rebels was well known, exile groups made many attempts to contact him. On September 24 the attorney general visited with Ernesto Betancourt, leader of a small Cuban Liberation Army (Ejercito de Liberacion Cubana, or ELC), which had apparently opened a modest training camp in Florida with the tolerance, if not the active supervision, of the CIA.[47] Kennedy told the CIA deputy director that, according to this group, an armed uprising was about to take place in Cuba, and they needed help. The attorney general went on to say "that Betancourt's group and its plans might fall within the framework of decisions reached by the Special Group about a month ago, and that, therefore, someone appearing to be other than a CIA officer should get in touch with Betancourt" and find out what was happening.

In an attempt to confirm this story, an unidentified CIA agent spoke to Eduardo Perez Gonzales, also known as Captain Bayo. He had worked in 1961 as a crew member on the CIA-sponsored boat *Tejana*, which had been active in the waters around Cuba before the Bay of Pigs. Bayo confirmed what Betancourt said. He predicted an uprising of 15,000 men on September 30 and asked an American representative to meet with its leaders at Guantanamo on September 28. The agent, known as Charles Ford, advised the Cubans to stop the uprising, which was also supposed to involve the assassination of Fidel and Raoul Castro and Che Guevara. JMWAVE reported that Bayo claimed to have swum from Guantanamo into Cuba and met with rebel leaders in mid-month. But when the agency asked the Office of Naval Intelligence at Guantanamo, they replied that Bayo had not made it into Cuba at all. By October 4 a presumably exasperated William Harvey informed the attorney general that Bayo's story did not hold up and that nothing was to be gained by any further contact with him.[48] Despite Bayo's lies, no one seriously investigated the possibility that the whole story—and especially the request for a meeting in Guantanamo—might have been a Castro-inspired provocation.

By October the Kennedy administration was becoming more and more concerned about the obvious Soviet military build-up in Cuba, even though only McCone thought the Soviets were introducing medium- and intermediate-range ballistic missiles (MRBMs and IRBMs). The President on September 4 issued a statement protesting the establishment of surface-to-air (SAM) batteries in Cuba and warning against the installation of MRBMs or IRBMs.[49] At another meeting of the Special Group on October 4, Robert Kennedy once again complained strenuously about the lack of sabotage, and Lansdale confirmed that Mongoose had not as yet undertaken any operations. The next day, McCone blamed the lack of progress on the State Department's overreaction to a couple of raids by exile groups, and Bundy suggested that unless the Soviets put missiles into Cuba—which he did not believe they would do—the United States might have to decide to live with Castro.[50]

On October 14 a U-2 flight discovered the construction of Soviet missile bases in Cuba. Within a few days the administration's leading figures were discussing the massive Soviet military build-up in Cuba that had begun during July, the possibility that it might include nuclear warheads, the possible interrelationships among Soviet missiles in Cuba, American nuclear missiles in Turkey and Italy, and the ever-present threat of a Soviet move against West Berlin.

Torn by conflicting objectives, the administration was essentially pursuing a compromise policy against Cuba that was not, in fact, likely to achieve very much. While planning a possible military intervention, trying without success to remove the diplomatic obstacles to such a course, and covertly organizing resistance in Cuba, the administration was also overseeing talks between attorney James Donovan and the Castro regime, with the purpose of agreeing on a ransom for more than one thousand prisoners from the Bay of Pigs. This mix of policies did nothing to assuage the concerns of Cuban exiles, who enjoyed various kinds of relationships with U.S. government agencies and were increasingly inclined to act on their own.

By 1962 at least half a dozen distinct exile and American groups were operating against Castro, with or without American support, and many more existed on the fringes. U.S.-supported organizations included the groups affiliated with the much-weakened Cuban Revolutionary Council, still led by Miro Cardona, including the Catholic MDC; Manuel Ray's new Revolutionary Junta in Exile (JURE); the very active and determined DRE; and, apparently, Alpha-66, led by Antonio Veciana. Independent operators included the MIRR run by Orlando Bosch and Victor Paneque Batista; the MIRR-linked American mercenaries, including Gerry Hemming, Frank Sturgis, Alex Rorke, and their Cuban associate Pedro Diaz Lanz; former Batistianos, including Rolando Masferrer; and former Cuban president Carlos Prio Socarras. None of these groups and individuals, except perhaps Alpha-66, seem to have understood exactly what the Kennedy administration's policy toward Cuba was, and all of them were becoming increasingly restive in the course of 1962.

Having been given maximum visibility with minimum power, the CRC showed the lowest morale and the most frustration. Cardona and Varona met State Department officials in late February 1962, in order to find out whether military action was imminent, but State officials warned about Soviet retaliation in Berlin or elsewhere and cautioned patience.[51] By June the CIA case officer at JMWAVE reported that the CRC leadership was convinced that the U.S. government would do nothing—a rather ironic situation, given the debates over Operation Mongoose going on at that time. The CIA replied by asking them to beef up intelligence collection. Cardona traveled to Washington to talk to Robert Kennedy, whom the Cubans now recognized as a key administration figure on Cuba. He returned concerned that the administration was once again putting its trust in the leftist Manuel Ray.[52]

Originally the head of the MRP, Ray was the leading proponent of a pro-U.S. but largely socialist Cuba that would incorporate many of Castro's revolutionary changes—a plan his opponents liked to refer to as "Fidelism without Fidel." As a genuinely popular figure, he enjoyed favor with the Kennedy administration, and during the summer of 1962 Ray was busy forming his new organization, JURE. He announced this initiative in July and began discussions with CIA representatives. Agency headquarters, which had already adopted a policy of helping some groups independently of the CRC, urged JMWAVE officers to continue these contacts because of Ray's potential usefulness.[53]

The militant MIRR was drifting away from CIA control. On March 13, 1962, one of its leaders, Victor Paneque Batista, joined Laureano Batista Falla of the MDC (Christian Democratic Movement) at a Miami rally celebrating a hunger strike Paneque was conducting to protest the administration's inaction on Cuba. Speakers at the rally said the strike would show the U.S. government that Cubans were willing to die in exile if denied the opportunity to liberate their country. They attacked the CRC as traitors to their cause and asked President Kennedy for guns.[54]

Orlando Bosch remained a favorite of the JMWAVE station despite his public criticisms of the U.S. government in general and the CIA in particular. During the spring, case officers began negotiating with him and Evelio Duque over possible operations in Cuba. Typically, Duque wanted arms for hundreds of men to start a resistance movement, while the agency wanted him to agree to infiltrate a few of Harvey's five-man teams to collect intelligence. On April 26—the eve of a planned infiltration—Duque met a case officer and withdrew from the operation because he refused to follow "WAVE operational concepts." He realized this was the end of CIA support and actually seemed relieved. In September Bosch published another aggressively anti–United States and anti-CIA pamphlet, and the station at last allowed his operational approval to expire.[55]

Around this time, Gerry Patrick Hemming emerged as a young man forty years ahead of his time. By late March 1962 he was writing Costa Rican President Jose Figueres, explaining that his organization, Interpen, wanted to train anti-Communist guerrilla fighters to serve all over the world as a more militant counterpart to the Peace Corps. Later, he wrote a similar letter to the White House. Having tried and failed to secure employment with the CIA in late 1961, he apparently wanted to establish himself as a military contractor, training paramilitaries for any private group or government that would take an interest in him. His letter to Figueres claimed "favorable relations" with a long string of Cuban leaders. "Here in the U.S.," he claimed, "we have made contact with many prominent and wealthy persons that just recently have been organizing and concentrating their efforts on anti-Communist propaganda . . . Among those very patriotic Americans can be found many Senators, Congressmen, Doctors, lawyers, and military officers on retirement from active duty." He compared his efforts to those of William Pawley, Claire Chennault, and the Flying Tigers, "which stopped the Japanese advance in China." Since Pawley was pushing that analogy himself, it sounds as though Hemming had made contact with him as well.[56]

By April 1962 Hemming had thrown in his lot with a mixed Cuban-American band that included Larry Laborde and a former Castro revolutionary, Antonio "Tony" Cuesta, both of whom had crewed on the CIA's *Tejana*.[57] Laborde, whom the agency had recently dropped, had contacts in New Orleans, where he was trying to secure a new boat. Hemming and another friend, Howard Davis, visited New Orleans in late June and met with Frank Bartes and Luis Rabel, the leaders of the New Orleans branch of the CRC. Bartes immediately informed the New Orleans CIA office that the three men hated the CIA and complained that it was preventing anyone from doing anything about Castro. This was true—Hemming was actually circulating a story from the *Denver Post* that accused the agency of stopping operations, shutting down training camps, spying on exiles, and providing faulty equipment. The CIA report on this contact does not, however, explain what the Cubans' meeting with Laborde and Hemming was about.[58]

An answer emerged in two press stories that Hemming evidently managed to get into the *New Orleans States-Item* on July 21 and the *Miami Herald* on July 22. In the first, columnist Bill Stuckey wrote that New Orleans Cubans had been supplying "Jerry Patrick"—an alias Hemming used as his war name—with military equipment since an earlier visit in February. In the spring, Stuckey claimed, an anonymous American donor offered Patrick a large tract of land, including an air strip, on the north shore of Lake Pontchartrain for a training camp. The Miami leadership of the CRC, he claimed, vetoed the plan. Stuckey also mentioned Patrick's links to Frank Sturgis and speculated that Carlos Prio Socarras was bankrolling him. James Buchanan's story in the *Miami Herald* the next day told essentially the same tale, adding that Luis Rabel of the New Orleans CRC confirmed it.[59] Later events suggested that the anonymous American donor could have been Mike McLaney, a former Havana casino operator with property in the area who was taking a keen interest in anti-Castro activities.[60]

Returning to Miami, Hemming struck up alliances with Sam Benton, a shady figure who claimed, falsely, to be an attorney, and former Senator Rolando Masferrer, now living in New Jersey, who provided arms and men for a training camp. By the fall he was running a camp for about ten Americans and ten Cubans. Officially, of course, this was a violation of the Neutrality Act, and Hemming evidently had no CIA sponsorship.[61]

The mob was remaining active in exile activities in other ways as well. In early 1962 the FBI delegated information that Prio, who had been involved with mob figures in numerous arms deals before 1959, had asked for financial assistance from Jimmy Hoffa. Hoffa's Puerto Rico Teamster lieutenant Frank Chavez told FBI agents on March 1 that Prio asked him for help obtaining arms, equipment, and about 150 men to seize a small island just off Cuba and begin shelling the mainland. Prio asked to meet with Hoffa during the Teamster convention, but Hoffa refused to see him. The FBI also heard that Sturgis claimed he was going to be Prio's military coordinator.[62]

Chavez, like Hoffa, was under investigation in early 1962, and he and Hoffa may have reasoned that they could not afford to risk a further indictment for Neutrality Act violations. Hoffa, Chavez, and Trafficante were sharing the same attorney, Frank Ragano, who explained in his autobiography that Trafficante was trying to arrange various loans from the Teamsters' legendary pension funds. Since Trafficante knew Prio and Varona from the 1940s and 1950s, he may easily have played some role in Prio's approach to Chavez.[63]

Antonio Veciana—the accountant who was recruited by "Maurice Bishop" in Havana in 1960 and fled Cuba in November 1961 after his assassination plot against Castro collapsed—became a player in his own right in 1962. In March 1978, during the HSCA investigation, the CIA told the committee, "There has been no Agency relationship with Veciana," but that was not entirely true.[64] In December 1961 a CIA case officer named Calvin Hicks asked for and received a provisional operational approval, or clearance, to use Veciana in sabotage operations, and the Cuban was given the cryptonym AMSHALE-1.[65] By the middle of 1962, however, Veciana had emerged as the leader and chief fundraiser of Alpha-66, an organization of Cuban professionals dedicated to the violent overthrow of the Castro regime.

In fundraising meetings, Veciana told wealthy Cubans that they needed the organization because the United States government was too frightened of Soviet retaliation to do anything against Castro, and Alpha-66 would carry out a program of sabotage, outside the control of the CIA. In July Veciana told a CIA informant that Manuel Ray was supporting him and that he planned five major acts of sabotage in the near future: the demolition of a power plant, an oil refinery, and a Soviet ship, and the assassination of a leading foreigner in Cuba (perhaps the Soviet ambassador) and the highest possible official of the Castro regime. In late July he asked a representative of the CIA Domestic Contacts division in New York for rifles with telescopic sights, C-4 explosives, and American and Cuban currency. In asking for the CIA's help, he insisted to the agent that his organization would have no explicit CIA connection and that the agency's refusal to provide these items would delay, but not stop, the actions he intended to take. Veciana's file does not indicate that this conversation was followed up.[66]

In late August and early September rumors buzzed around Miami and San Juan, Puerto Rico, where Alpha-66 was active, of an impending sabotage operation, and on September 11 JMWAVE reported that a boat with a .57 recoilless rifle had carried out such a raid on a Cuban barge and a British ship on September 9. Interagency traffic certainly suggested that Veciana was acting on his own. In a widely reported San Juan press conference on September 12, he took credit for the attacks and promised more sabotage, but the October missile crisis put an end to such plans.[67] In November, sources reported a violent split within Alpha-66 because of Veciana's new alliance with former July 26th leader Eloy Gutierrez Menoyo, who had now formed a similar organization, the Second National Front of the Escambray (SNFE).

Another organization that eclipsed Alpha-66 with its determined mix of sabotage and wide-ranging propaganda was the Revolutionary Student Directorate, or DRE. It was an indirect descendant of the Batista-era DR, one of Castro's most important allies in his 1959 revolution. In 1960, after Rolando Cubela of the old DR became head of Castro's new Student Federation (FE), several independent student leaders fled to the United States and created the DRE. Two of them, Alberto Muller and Manuel Salvat Roque, infiltrated into Cuba late in 1960, and a third, Isidro Borja, got back inside by swimming to Mexico, his birthplace, and traveling to Cuba as a tourist.

In his 2004 book on the assassination, *El Complot,* retired Cuban intelligence chief Fabian Escalante claimed that David Atlee Phillips recruited Salvat for the CIA in 1959–60. Phillips confirmed that he worked with "student groups" around that time, including DRE leaders in Florida during the run-up to the Bay of Pigs, and referred to the group as a very important student organization both in Cuba and in the United States.[68] After some narrow escapes following the Bay of Pigs fiasco, Salvat managed to return to Florida, but Muller was eventually captured in Cuba.[69] The DRE's CIA case officer, Ross Crozier, described Salvat as "organizer and action type. Driver, perserverant, headstrong but fearless. Cool operator in spite of temper . . . In support matters, is demanding and insistent."[70] By mid-1962 he seemed to personify the organization itself.

The DRE left the CRC in spring 1962, complaining bitterly about the failed attempt to ransom the Bay of Pigs prisoners—and enhancing its reputation for independence. Crozier estimated that by this time the DRE had five thousand members in the United States and all over Latin America, where it maintained offices in many capitals. Its main function—and, if the CIA had its way, its exclusive one—was spreading anti-Castro propaganda throughout the region. It now received $44,000 a month from the agency to support its leadership, its branch offices in the United States (which eventually included both New Orleans and Dallas), and its propaganda operation. It also purchased arms and started an independent training camp in the Florida Everglades. Because the organization appeared to have lost its leadership in Cuba, Luis Fernandez Rocha successfully infiltrated back onto the island in May, without CIA help, and remained there for several months.[71]

By late summer 1962 Crozier was involved in a bitter argument with DRE leaders over their skimming from the monthly support payments to build a war chest, and their refusal to stick to propaganda alone. On August 24 two DRE vessels sailed to within sight of Havana and shelled the Sierra Maestra Hotel, home to numerous Soviets and Czechs, and the Blanquita Theater, where Castro was thought to be speaking. A communiqué announced that the attack was responding to the Soviet build-up (about which the DRE was the best-informed organization in America) and called into question President Kennedy's promise not to abandon Cuba. They missed assassinating Fidel but put themselves on the map in the United States.[72]

Fernandez Rocha, who by this time had returned from his secret mission to Cuba, proudly appeared on Miami television to take independent responsibility for the attack. Isidro Borja also discussed it on the popular NBC news program *Meet the Press.* Helms immediately asked Harvey whether the DRE could be reined in, and Harvey replied that it was hopeless.[73] By late August, JMWAVE, concerned that a planned DRE attack on a Soviet ship might trigger a full-scale war, had raised the issue of terminating support for the organization, but no decision had been reached.[74]

The August 24 attack apparently got the attention of William Pawley, however. Pawley had known the playwright and politician Clare Boothe Luce and her husband Henry for more than twenty years. As she explained in 1975, Pawley told her (and presumably other wealthy friends as well) that the DRE was playing the role of the Flying Tigers against the Japanese in China, and convinced her to sponsor a DRE boat in the same way that she and her husband had sponsored Flying Tiger aircraft. Manuel Salvat confirmed DRE contacts with Pawley in an interview with HSCA investigators. Luce immediately agreed, and, she said in 1975, passed on DRE reports of Soviet missiles landing in Cuba to New York Senator Ken Keating, who did indeed declare on October 10 that he had "confirmed" the construction of Soviet missile bases.[75]

Ironically, despite all the efforts of leading administration figures to start a rebellion in Cuba, the more militant exiles in the States were now convinced that the administration had no intention of doing anything at all, and they were showing less and less respect for the CIA. The missile crisis that broke into the open during the third week of October seemed initially to offer fresh hope that Castro might be eliminated, but its denouement left the exiles more bitter than ever and seemed to bring Operation Mongoose and its planned activities to an end.

Meanwhile, however, Robert Kennedy's other war—against American organized crime—was proceeding apace in Chicago, Detroit, New Orleans, and Tampa, and on many other fronts all over the United States.

6

Crusaders and Gangsters

In addition to his role overseeing Operation Mongoose, Attorney General Robert Kennedy was emerging during 1962 as a national and international figure in his own right. Early that year he took a much-publicized trip around the world, and in April he played a key role in the administration's successful effort to overturn a steel price increase. In the fall he became involved in his first critical civil rights battle—the admission of the first black student, James Meredith, to the University of Mississippi—and he was a major player during the Cuban missile crisis in October. Yet within the Justice Department his top priority remained organized crime, and Sam Giancana, Jimmy Hoffa, Carlos Marcello, and Santo Trafficante were among his critical targets.

Sam Giancana was still getting the most attention from the FBI. During 1961 agents kept track of his frequent travels to Las Vegas, New York City, the Philadelphia area, and elsewhere, usually to visit Phyllis McGuire while she was performing. During a three-day weekend in August when their motel room was bugged, one FBI report stated, McGuire "referred to subject [Giancana] as 'Sam,' 'Momo,' and Mr. Flood,' in addition to numerous obscenities."[1] In October the Chicago office reported that the IRS agent assigned to Giancana's tax case was not pursuing the matter very vigorously, and Courtney Evans passed this information on to Robert Kennedy.[2]

In the same month microphones picked up news of Jimmy Hoffa informing Giancana of an important upcoming meeting, and of Giancana advising an Italian-American politician not to attend a Columbus Day observance in Chicago at which Robert Kennedy would be present.[3] In November and December Giancana and McGuire made a long trip to

London, Rome, and Puerto Rico, where he was scouting for new casino locations. In January federal microphones overheard him discussing the possibility of buying a hotel in Jamaica and complaining about Frank Annunzio, his hand-picked alderman in Chicago's First Ward, whom he called a "double-crosser" for inviting Robert Kennedy to the Columbus Day festivities.[4]

On December 8, 1961, a bug overheard a conversation between Giancana and Johnny Roselli that has been misreported and misunderstood by a number of authors but which clarifies the relationship between Giancana, the Kennedys, and Frank Sinatra. Roselli reported on a recent meeting with Sinatra during which he asked if the entertainer had interceded with "the Kennedys" on Giancana's behalf. Roselli repeatedly suggested that Sinatra approach old Joe Kennedy, who, he claimed, telephoned Sinatra several times during his visit, but Sinatra replied that he did not think the Kennedy sons were "faithful" to their father. Roselli continued:

> He's got big ideas, Frank does, about being an Ambassador or something. You fuck them, you pay them, and then they're through. You've got the right idea, Moe, so . . . fuck everybody . . . They only know one way. Now let them see the other side of you . . .
>
> I said, Frankie, can I ask one question? He says, Johnny, I took Sam's name, and wrote it down, and told Bobby Kennedy, this is my buddy. This is my buddy, this is what I want you to know, Bob. And he says, Johnny, he . . .

Giancana laughed and interrupted: "You could have answered it yourself."

"Concerning the next Presidential campaign," the FBI report read, "Giancana indicated that he would not donate one penny toward any such campaign and furthermore stated 'that [obscene] better not think of taking this [obscene] state.'" The report continued:

> Giancana claimed that he made a donation to the recent presidential campaign of Kennedy and was not getting his money's worth because if he got a speeding ticket "none of those [obscenes] would know me." The informant [that is, bug] further related that John, in an attempt to persuade Giancana that Sinatra had attempted to intercede for Giancana,

stated "Frank says to me, Johnny, he (Giancana) ain't being bothered." Giancana then screamed "I got more [obscene] on my [obscene] than any other [obscene] in the country." He then continued railing and stated that every place he goes there are "twenty guys next door, upstairs, downstairs" and that he is surrounded. John asked him where this took place and he said "right here in Russia, Chicago, New York and Phoenix."[5]

This report—which Hoover immediately passed on to Robert Kennedy—was evidently the source of the legend that Giancana felt the Kennedys had betrayed him after he stole the election for them in 1960. It actually confirms what we have already seen—that there is no evidence for that scenario at all. It *does* confirm that Sinatra collected a campaign contribution from Giancana in 1960, but suggests that Sinatra never even told Robert Kennedy that Giancana had given the money. Sinatra had incurred a debt to a powerful patron upon which he could not make good. Two years later, as we shall see, his son may have been kidnapped as a result. One would certainly like to know exactly why Roselli thought Joseph P. Kennedy (who would soon be disabled by a stroke) might be a promising channel, but evidently Sinatra refused to try him out. What remains unmistakably clear is that RFK felt no debt to Giancana, nor did he have the slightest interest in easing the pressure on him by one iota.

A month later, Giancana was talking to ward committeeman John D'Arco (whose office was bugged by the FBI) about an Illinois politician named Spencer. "Spencer is like Kennedy," Giancana said. "He'll get what he wants out of you, but you won't get anything out of him." "That fucker Kennedy!" D'Arco replied. "Is Sinatra gonna work on . . . ?" "No," said Giancana. "He can't get change of a quarter." "Sinatra can't?" asked D'Arco, who had heard that the President was spending time with Sinatra in California. "That's right," said Giancana. "Well, they've got the whip and they're in office and that's it . . . So they're going to knock us guys out of the box and make us defenseless."[6] "Moe," wailed D'Arco in early January, "it's a shame. They want us out of politics. We got to think this thing over. This . . . is coming on, it's all over the country, that fucker Kennedy is laughing about it, boasting about it. We're supposed to be politicians, we aren't supposed to be hoodlums, know what I mean? So we go along . . . what do we do?"[7]

On February 2, in another conversation at the Armory Lounge, D'Arco and Giancana worried about the FBI's recent interview of Alderman Annunzio, part of a new bureau strategy of grilling politicians about their ties to Giancana. According to D'Arco, Annunzio told the agents that President Kennedy could thank Italian ward politicians for having won the presidential election. D'Arco moaned that because of the government's campaign against organized crime, "We are through, there is no place to go," and Giancana added, "This is it, don't worry about it, we'll make a living somehow, history repeats itself . . . I told everyone they're on their own, go ahead and make a living, but you're on your own."[8] "I remember you telling me before Kennedy came in that there was gonna be fireworks," another associate told Sam in early February, "but I never expected nothing like this." "They are only investigating certain individuals, in certain cities in certain areas," Giancana replied—including himself.[9]

On February 15, 1962, J. Edgar Hoover informed his Chicago office that given Giancana's importance in Chicago and elsewhere, "it is deemed imperative that an all-out effort be launched to develop details of the violations he is engaged in so that he may be successfully prosecuted and convicted for these offenses." Chicago replied on February 28 by listing several possible areas of interest, including organized crime murders.[10] Meanwhile, columnists in New York and Chicago published the story of the Giancana-McGuire romance.

Coincidentally, the attorney general learned that same week about another series of romances, one that connected Roselli, Giancana, and the President of the United States. On February 23 the Los Angeles FBI office reported on its investigation of Roselli. Checking the telephone records of Roselli's new girlfriend, Judith Campbell, they found that not only was she in touch with Sam Giancana but that she had also placed calls to President Kennedy's secretary, Evelyn Lincoln, on November 7 and November 18. On February 27 Hoover passed this information along to the attorney general and to Kenneth O'Donnell, who was White House appointments secretary and formerly RFK's college roommate.[11] No reactions to this interesting news made their way onto any typed sheets of paper, and O'Donnell insisted to the Church Committee in 1975 that this was routine information that he would never have bothered to follow up, even with Mrs. Lincoln.[12]

On March 15, however, Courtney Evans, RFK's liaison to Hoover, wrote FBI Assistant Director August Belmont a further memo detailing Campbell's relationships with Giancana and Roselli and her calls to Mrs. Lincoln. He added that a Los Angeles private investigator and FBI informant, Fred Otash, had discussed Campbell's simultaneous affairs with Roselli and the President, and that some months earlier, in August 1961, Otash had a conversation with a noted freelance wiretapper, Bernard Spindel. Spindel told Otash that his client, Jimmy Hoffa, wanted information about West Coast prostitutes who might have slept with either John or Robert Kennedy—information that Hoffa felt would allow him to "bury" the Kennedys.[13]

News of the President's indiscretions, indeed, had traveled through mob circles around the country. "Since when is fucking a federal offense?" an FBI bug heard an unidentified mobster complain around this time. "And if it is, I want the President indicted, because I know he was whacking all those broads Sinatra brought him out . . . I would gladly go to the penitentiary for the rest of my life, believe me," the man continued, if he could manage to kill "Kennedy." Having accepted favors, he seemed to be saying, the Kennedys had no right to move so hard against the mob.[14]

Just a week after Evans's memorandum, on March 22, Hoover lunched privately with the President. According to the Church Committee report, the White House phone logs showed that "the last telephone contact between the White House and the President's friend [Campbell] occurred a few hours after the luncheon."[15]

The Church Committee report also pointedly mentioned that on the next day, March 23, Hoover formally requested the CIA's written opinion as to whether Robert Maheu could be prosecuted for tapping the phone in the Las Vegas hotel room to check on Phyllis McGuire and comedian Dan Rowan. Since the tap was put in place to pacify Giancana, who was in Miami rounding up potential assassins in the CIA's anti-Castro plot, the committee implied that Hoover might have been trying to close the case to protect the President from possible embarrassment. However, FBI documents that the committee did not see decisively disprove this theory. Almost two weeks later, on April 4, Hoover reiterated the need to "vigorously pursue investigation of every aspect of [Giancana's] activities in order that a prosecutable violation can be developed with all possible speed." Hoover and his men were still going full speed after Giancana right up until May 10.[16]

"I told the Attorney General we also were bearing down on Giancana," Hoover wrote that day in a memorandum for his six top assistants.[17] That was when Kennedy told him the whole story of the CIA's hiring of Maheu and Giancana to assassinate Castro. Hoover told Kennedy this was a "most unfortunate development," all the more so since "gutter gossip" held that Giancana had escaped prosecution through the good offices of his own friend, Frank Sinatra, "who, in turn, claimed to be quite close to the Kennedy family." Robert replied that he knew that, and it made him all the more concerned about what he had learned from the CIA about Maheu and Giancana's involvement with them. But Kennedy "stated that he felt notwithstanding the obstacle now in the path of prosecution of Giancana, we should still keep after him. He stated of course it would be very difficult to initiate any prosecution against him because Giancana could immediately bring out the fact that the United States Government had approached him to arrange for the assassination of Castro."[18]

Though unable to prosecute Giancana, the FBI maintained its surveillance of him at about the same level into 1963, gathering endless information about his political influence, especially in Chicago's First Ward, and his connections with Sinatra, Dean Martin, Sammy Davis, Jr., Eddie Fisher, and other entertainers. In November 1962 Giancana opened a new Chicago nightclub, the Villa Venice, and the FBI heard from an informant that Giancana, using the name Sam Mooney, had just met with Fisher and Sinatra in Reno. Shortly thereafter, Sinatra called Fisher to tell him that his forthcoming appearance at the Desert Inn, Las Vegas, for $100,000 per week had been canceled and that he was going to help open the Villa Venice in early November in Chicago for $15,000 a week instead. Interviewed on November 20, 1962, Fisher said he made the appearance as a favor to Sinatra. Though he admitted recognizing "Sam Mooney" as Phyllis McGuire's boyfriend, he denied knowing that he was Sam Giancana.[19]

The FBI sent further shockwaves through Chicago on November 29, when two agents walked into the Czech Lounge, where they had been unable to place a bug, and confronted Giancana in the company of John D'Arco and the known hoodlum Paul Ricca. The agents had already overheard Giancana discussing D'Arco's projected resignation as alderman for feigned health reasons and his possible replacement by Giancana's nephew, Anthony De Tolve.[20]

Cuba and the Kennedy administration figured in two overheard conversations involving Giancana. On October 29, the day after Khrushchev's promise to remove missiles from Cuba, "Giancana took off against Democratic Administration, criticized President's handling of Cuba, stated if Administration spent less time attempting to put people in jail and more on international situation this country would not be in its present shape."[21] And on January 14, after the Kennedys ransomed the Bay of Pigs prisoners, a leading Giancana mob associate, Chuckie English, was overheard complaining that the "Federal Government is closing in on the organization and there apparently is nothing that can be done about it. English made various and sundry inflammatory remarks re Kennedy Administration, pointed out that the Attorney General's raising of ransom moneys for Cuban invaders was muscle which would make Chicago syndicate look like amateurs."[22]

But in late February, when Giancana's candidate, Mike Fio Rito, won the election for First Ward alderman, replacing the "double-crosser" Frank Annunzio, Sam remarked, "That little [obscenity] the Attorney General, he opens his mouth, but he found out who runs things around here."[23] Within two months, however, Fio Rito's own voter registration was being investigated, and he too had become a liability. In early April a tap overheard Giancana's chauffeur, John Matassa, describe Jimmy Hoffa's "recent tirade against Attorney General Kennedy," whom Hoffa accused of "conducting a personal vendetta against hoodlums at government expense."[24]

Giancana's FBI file, with its many wiretap records, does not confirm certain other well-publicized stories about him, however. Despite numerous discussions among his associates of Phyllis McGuire, singer Keely Smith, and other women in his life, after spring 1961 not a single word was overheard about Judith Campbell or her connection to the President, much less about the President's other romantic interest, Marilyn Monroe, who died from a prescription drug overdose in August 1962.[25] Giancana said almost nothing about his relations with other bosses around the country, although the FBI picked up news of several big meetings in Florida, and he never mentioned his involvement in Castro assassination plots after his indiscretion at the dinner party with the McGuire sisters late in 1960. But the tapes leave no doubt that Giancana was suffering a multi-front attack from the Justice Department and the FBI, and the struggle would only escalate during the second half of 1963.

In contrast with Giancana and his CIA connections, Robert Kennedy had no inconvenient obstacles to overcome in going after Jimmy Hoffa. The government's cases against Hoffa were rather technical matters involving his use of union funds—particularly pension funds—to enrich himself and others. Most of the evidence against him was developed by the McClellan Committee in the late 1950s, and several of its investigators, led by Walter Sheridan, had moved to the Justice Department to form the Get Hoffa Squad. Sheridan, who was a former FBI agent but not a lawyer, apparently attracted more than his share of J. Edgar Hoover's animus against former agents.[26]

The Sun Valley case in Florida, for which Hoffa temporarily escaped indictment in 1961, involved inflation in the price tag on a tract of Florida land which—through a complicated series of transactions—was supposed to become a Teamster retirement community. The case that ultimately brought Hoffa down involved the Test Fleet Corporation, a trucking company that Hoffa and an associate incorporated under their wives' names. Test Fleet immediately managed to borrow $50,000 to purchase its equipment from the Commercial Carriers' Corporation, a trucking outfit that was fighting a wildcat strike. After making the loan to Hoffa, the company's labor troubles mysteriously disappeared.[27]

The third and by far the most serious case, involving kickbacks from Teamster pension fund loans, did not come to trial until 1964. Both Hoffa and the government were now working with multimillion-dollar budgets, and their legal fights were becoming more and more complicated. In March 1962, during hearings on the Sun Valley case, in which the Justice Department was seeking a new indictment, Hoffa tried to subpoena a raft of senatorial and federal officials to prove that the case against him drew on illegal wiretaps. The judge denied most of the subpoenas. The defendant ran into more problems in May, when another Teamster official, Frank Baron, accused Hoffa of beating him up after an argument at Teamster headquarters in Chicago.[28]

During the next few weeks, Hoffa's Florida indictment in the Sun Valley case was reinstated, he pled not guilty to a new Test Fleet Corporation indictment in Nashville, and the U.S. attorney in Washington, D.C., investigated Baron's complaint. Hoffa suffered a big blow on July 19 when the U.S. Court of Appeals in Washington ruled that he could not draw on union funds to pay for his defense. In an effort to stave off disaster, Hoffa's attorneys now began arguing that the Sun Valley trial, which they had spent several years delaying, had to take place before the Test Fleet proceedings.

Hoffa may have been waging a counteroffensive on another front as well. FBI agents were still surveilling Judith Campbell in early August 1962. One night they observed two men drive up in a car with Texas license plates and climb onto her balcony. One of them entered the apartment. The car turned out to be registered to a former FBI agent named Hale, and the two men, the bureau discovered, matched the description of his sons, one of whom had been married to the daughter of Texas Governor John Connolly. The bureau seems never to have found out exactly who they were working for or what they wanted, but Hoffa almost surely knew about Campbell and the President through Otash and through his own wiretapper, Spindel, and may have sent them to look for proof.[29]

As the head of a union with tens of thousands of members and tens of millions of dollars in its treasury, Hoffa inevitably enjoyed enormous political influence. Beginning in August 1962, more than a dozen congressmen and senators, ranging from the Indiana conservative Republican Homer Capehart to Oregon liberal Democrat Wayne Morse, complained on the floor of the House and Senate that Justice Department tactics were depriving Hoffa of various constitutional rights. (Both Capehart and Morse were involved in re-election fights.) Many of their statements used almost identical language. Meanwhile, behind the scenes, the man who eventually sent Hoffa to jail came forward with an amazing story.[30]

Edward Grady Partin was the secretary-treasurer of the Teamsters local in Baton Rouge, Louisiana, in the heart of Carlos Marcello country. His checkered past included a bad conduct discharge from the Marine Corps, a conviction for breaking and entering, and a manslaughter indictment (apparently related to a traffic accident). In September 1962 he was in jail on a $50,000 bond, charged with forging a union member's signature and embezzling the funds of his local. He had also been accused of kidnapping, a charge that apparently grew out of assistance he provided a friend in a child custody dispute.[31] After a few days in jail, he told the district attorney that he had information vital to national security and asked to see federal authorities. The DA called the U.S. attorney, who called Frank Grimsley of the Get Hoffa Squad, who called his boss, Walter Sheridan, who told Grimsley to go to Baton Rouge. On the night of October 1, Grimsley talked with Partin from 3:00 a.m. to 6:00 a.m. and heard his story.

Partin said he visited Washington, D.C., in June and talked with Hoffa alone. During their conversation, Hoffa asked him if he knew anything about plastic bombs. "I've got to do something about that son of a bitch Bobby Kennedy," he claimed Hoffa said. "He's got to go." Saying that he was checking on the attorney general, Hoffa reported that RFK drove around by himself in a convertible and swam alone, without guards, in his McLean, Virginia, home, offering two possible targets for explosives. Hoffa also said he knew where he could get a silencer, Partin claimed. When Sheridan heard Grimsley's account of the conversation, he immediately talked to Jack Miller, head of the Criminal Division, and they decided to give Partin a lie detector test.

Writing in 1972, Sheridan, who had devoted more than a few years of his life to putting Jimmy Hoffa behind bars, claimed that Partin passed the test. That statement, it turns out, was not entirely accurate. The original FBI report on Partin's first polygraph examination reads, in part: "Although significant reactions indicating possible deception to some of the relevant questions were noted during this examination, Partin's responses to other questions were so erratic that it was not possible for the polygraph operator to reach a definite conclusion as to whether Partin was telling the truth or lying about his alleged conversation with Hoffa regarding plastic bombs, Hoffa's intention to inflict physical harm on you or Hoffa's access to a silencer."

During the initial interview with Grimsley, Partin also admitted that he was a habitual liar, especially when trying to negotiate union contracts. He also claimed that he had not slept for three nights when he took the polygraph test and he wanted to retake it. Five days later, after his bond was reduced from $50,000 to $5,000, Partin emerged from jail, took a second polygraph test, and passed. The FBI still did not trust

Partin, but Sheridan wanted to try him out as an informant. Partin promised to immediately contact Hoffa, apparently offered to record any further conversations with the union leader, and promised more information on assassination plots and other matters.[32] On October 18 Partin reached Hoffa, who asked to meet him in Nashville the following week, where the Test Fleet trial was about to begin. Partin immediately joined Hoffa's enormous entourage of Teamster officials, mob-connected figures like Allen Dorfman, Irving Davidson (a Washington contact for both Hoffa and Marcello), and Puerto Rico Teamster Frank Chavez.

Years later, long after the two Kennedy brothers and Jimmy Hoffa were all dead, a prominent labor attorney remarked that Hoffa's downfall stemmed from his belief that he could "fix" anything. Hoffa faced only a misdemeanor charge in the Nashville Test Fleet case, with a maximum penalty of a year in jail. Yet as Partin reported to Sheridan in the first week of the trial, Hoffa, Dorfman, and another man were planning to fix the jury. No sooner had proceedings opened than a juror reported a $10,000 bribe attempt to the judge and was excused. The trial lasted for two months, during which Partin made frequent trips back and forth from Baton Rouge to Nashville and continually kept Sheridan and the prosecution staff informed of the Hoffa camp's attempts to bribe two more jurors, both of whom were eventually removed from the panel. Hoffa took the stand and claimed that he had no personal connection to Test Fleet and had not profited from it, even though it was incorporated in his wife's name. The jury eventually deadlocked seven to five for acquittal, but the government immediately announced that it was opening a new jury tampering case. That one took over a year to come to trial.

Although Hoffa was undoubtedly guilty of jury tampering (here and probably in some earlier acquittals as well), of misusing union funds, violent intimidation, and a host of corrupt relationships with mobsters who benefited from his loans, the scope and obsessiveness of Robert Kennedy's campaign against him raised many eyebrows. The attorney general took an almost daily interest in the progress of the campaign, even during the Cuban missile crisis, which happened to coincide with the first week of the unsuccessful Nashville trial.[33] And after Partin's testimony finally sent him to jail for jury tampering, no less a figure than Chief Justice Earl Warren dissented from his brethren's opinion affirming Hoffa's jury tampering conviction in 1967, citing Partin's character, the circumstances under which he came to the government, and the favors (including effectively the dismissal of all charges against him) that he had received.

Although Partin eventually became the instrument of Hoffa's downfall, and all the information he provided during the Nashville trial was easily verified, it is certainly far from clear that his story about Hoffa's plan to assassinate RFK was true. In fact, as we will see, Carlos Marcello may have put him up to making it. Curiously enough, Robert eventually passed information about the plot along to his brother Jack, but in an exaggerated form, stating that Hoffa hired a "hoodlum," gave him a pistol with a silencer, and ordered him to go to Washington to kill the attorney general.[34] Hoffa was right about one thing—Robert Kennedy would never rest until he had put the Teamster leader behind bars.

The campaign against Hoffa was only the biggest of the Justice Department's offensives against major organized crime figures, many of whom, like Marcello and Trafficante, stood to lose a great deal should Hoffa's imprisonment cost them their access to Teamster pension funds. And by late 1962, fearing enormous pressure from the government's investigations, they were discussing assassination as a possible way out—not only killing the attorney general but the President himself.

The government was still having great difficulty securing the prosecution of many major mob bosses. Because nothing like today's RICO (Racketeer Influenced and Corrupt Organizations) Act was on the statute books in the 1960s, and because securing the safety of witnesses against organized crime figures was very difficult, the FBI's effort focused on intelligence, surveillance, and harassment—much as it had done when going after the American Communist Party in the 1950s—rather than investigations designed to lead to federal prosecution. But the FBI's shift of its targets from leftist activists to mobsters necessitated some amusing procedural adjustments. For example, according to one young attorney in the Organized Crime section, agents bugging the homes of crime figures began by planting their bugs in the bedroom, where Communists had carried on a good deal of their political talk. Such tactics had to be abandoned when they discovered that gangland figures were much less likely to mix business with pleasure than were leftists.[35] The FBI's pursuit extended not only to leading criminals themselves but to many of their close associates, including their girlfriends. This escalation outside the bounds of "business" naturally aroused a great deal of resentment. But the bureau did, from time to time, turn up some interesting information about the activities of leading mobsters.

Trafficante proved one of the most elusive targets. From late 1961 through 1962 he shuttled between Tampa, Miami, San Juan, Puerto Rico, and points unknown, and the FBI agents assigned to keep tabs on him had to report again and again that they had not seen him for weeks. By September 1961 the Tampa office was trying to install bugs in his house, in one of his businesses, and in the home of one of his associates, and were under orders to cover his mail. An informant reported that Trafficante wanted to eliminate Sam Kay, a Miami financier who refused to return a $50,000 deposit on a Havana hotel. In September he met in a Miami hotel with two other former Havana casino owners— Dino Cellini, whom the FBI linked to Tony Varona, and Martin Fox, who once had dinner in Dallas with Jack Ruby.[36] Another informant reported that Trafficante was living in the Florida Keys under the name Louis Santos—the exact name the British expatriate remembered him using at the Trescornia detention center in 1959, when he was visited by Jack Ruby.[37]

Robert Kennedy enlisted the IRS in his fight, and on January 11, 1962, the U.S. attorney in Tampa filed a complaint against Trafficante and three of his brothers, alleging specifically that Santo owed more than $46,000 in back taxes. A few weeks later, his attorney, Frank Ragano— whom Trafficante was about to lend to Jimmy Hoffa to help him with the Sun Valley case—said Santo wanted to sue the government for libel because of recent stories in the local press, but Ragano advised against it.[38]

Word of new business opportunities soon reached the FBI. In March, the Miami office heard that Trafficante and Angelo Bruno, another top hoodlum based in Philadelphia, were starting a pest control business. And in September, Miami law enforcement officials told the bureau that Larry de Joseph, a former Tropicana Hotel casino employee from Havana, was working with Trafficante to open a new casino in Guatemala. Two other partners were identified as Aureliano Sanchez Arrango, a leader of Varona's Autentico party and former member of the CRC, and Donald "Red" Sanders, a close associate of Frank Sturgis.[39] Trafficante was clearly remaining active in the Cuban exile community, even as he, like Giancana, looked for foreign opportunities that might eventually compensate for the loss of the Havana casinos.

Another associate from Trafficante's past re-emerged in October 1962. John Martino had supplied gambling and monitoring equipment to the casinos in Cuba and had apparently been caught smuggling money out of the country. He was arrested in Cuba in 1959 and sentenced to twelve years in prison. He spent most of the next two and a half years at the La Cabana fortress in Havana, suffering from a kidney ailment that required a narcotic drug he was not given. His fellow prisoners included three CIA agents who had been caught trying to bug the new Chinese Embassy in Havana.[40] In October 1962, after many appeals by his wife, Martino was released. Why exactly remains somewhat mysterious, and raises the question of whether Trafficante, Martino's former employer, still had some connections inside Castro's government. Castro was negotiating the ransom of the Bay of Pigs prisoners at that very moment, and William Pawley had recently ransomed three Cubans from Castro's jails as well.

When the FBI debriefed Martino on October 18, he claimed that he had been imprisoned because he identified Castro as a Communist on a Miami radio program in early 1959. He also blamed Dr. Estevez, the Cuban doctor who at the time of his arrest told the FBI in Havana that Martino was connected to both Trafficante and Rolando Masferrer. Cuban authorities linked him to Masferrer at his trial. In a CIA debriefing, he bitterly complained that the American Embassy refused him asylum. He gave the CIA man the names of six Cuban fellow prisoners who had been released and deported to the United States, including one, he said, who was now living in New Orleans.[41] Gerry Hemming, who was running a Florida training camp with the help of Masferrer in fall 1962, said later that Martino immediately showed an interest in organizing raids on Cuba.[42]

The FBI agent noted that Martino was obviously looking for publicity. Somehow he acquired a ghostwriter named Nathan Weyl, a former Communist who had become a violent anti-Communist. Weyl was connected to both Victor Lasky, author of an anti-JFK campaign book in 1960, and to William Buckley, and had published *Red Star over Cuba* in 1960. The new book he and Martino turned out over the next few months, entitled *I Was Castro's Prisoner*, accused Castro of drug trafficking and Adlai Stevenson of sabotaging the Bay of Pigs landing. Echoing Pawley, Weyl also argued that Franklin Roosevelt and Sumner Welles staffed the Latin American bureau of the State Department with Communists and homosexuals.[43]

In January of that year, a bug in a North Miami Beach restaurant recorded a long conversation among Trafficante and two Florida associates, James Palmaisano and Anthony "Pussy" Russo. "Let me tell you this," Trafficante complained, using mob slang terms "S" and "G" for state and federal authorities,

> This is what happens to me. Now, I don't give a [obscenity] about the S & G, I know when I'm beat, you understand. I got a numbers office in Orlando. They grab everybody, forty or fifty people. Forty or fifty thousand in bond, no evidence, but they get through with you it costs . . . thousands. I got another office in St. Cloud, Florida. You can't even find St. Cloud on the map of here, but the [obscenity] G found it—Kennedy's right hand man—he goes through [obscenity] nigger town. Must have been two thousand niggers and makes a [obscenity] big raid over there . . . I used to have over a hundred thousand dollars worth of numbers business, every week, Florida, Georgia and Alabama, three states. I talked to a cop one time for five minutes. It cost me about five thousand and half a million dollars lawyer's fee—six years lawyer's fee, and six years later, I beat it.[44]

Alone among the major mob bosses, Carlos Marcello was the object of active federal civil and criminal proceedings after his return from deportation to Central America. And like Hoffa, he seemed able to muster financial and legal resources comparable to those ranged against him. The government indicted him for illegally re-entering the country on June 8, 1961—just days after he came back to the States. On July 9 the INS issued another deportation order, and Marcello appealed again. The INS now hoped to deport him to Italy on the grounds that his parents were Italian, but any permission to travel issued by Rome would have a time limit, and Marcello could almost certainly delay his deportation until it passed.[45]

Opening another front, the government began an investigation of perjury and conspiracy regarding Marcello's submission of the false Guatemalan birth certificate in August 1961. An indictment came down two months later.[46] But Marcello and his lawyers fought back on at least two fronts. The basis for his deportation was a 1938 marijuana conviction, which became grounds for deportation under a 1952 law that specifically applied to prior as well as future convictions. His attorneys filed a writ of coram nobis in December 1961 in an attempt to set the conviction aside based on a lack of proper representation.[47] Not until late October 1962 was his writ formally denied by a federal district judge, and his lawyers promptly began another appeal. Meanwhile, he evidently began a rather careful campaign to influence Carl Irving Noll, his ex-employee, who had given the INS the story of the fake Guatemalan birth certificate back in 1960.[48]

On March 22, 1962, an anonymous informant told a long story to an FBI agent in Milwaukee. About a year earlier, he claimed, he arranged a meeting in Washington, D.C., between Marcello and a Washington lobbyist named James Donohue who was trying to negotiate a deal that would allow Marcello to settle in the Dominican Republic in exchange for a $200,000 payment to General Rafael Trujillo. The story made sense: Marcello had been in Washington in January 1961, and he had an indirect connection to Trujillo through I. Irving Davidson, a Washington lobbyist and arms middleman whom he had known since the late 1950s.[49]

According to one report, the Dominican Republic was Marcello's last stop before he returned to the United States from Guatemala a few months later, but that visit coincided almost exactly with Trujillo's assassination.[50] Now, the informant continued, Marcello's deportation was once again a high priority, but not so high as putting Jimmy Hoffa into jail. He had the impression that Marcello hoped to get his deportation proceedings dropped in return for providing witnesses against Hoffa. The deal, he claimed, had been worked out through La Verne Duffy, a McClellan Committee investigator described as RFK's "right-hand man." The informant claimed to have talked very recently to Sam Marcello, Carlos's brother, to ask him whether a promised $1 million to stave off deportation was still available. "Don't spend a buck on it," Sam told him, "it's all taken care of."[51]

La Verne Duffy was indeed a McClellan Committee investigator who worked on Hoffa investigations before 1961, but the FBI does not seem to have contacted him to ask him about this allegation, perhaps because of the bad relations between present and past McClellan Committee staffers and the FBI. But since in September 1962 the jailed Teamster Ed Partin told his story of Hoffa's plans to assassinate the attorney general and became an informant against Hoffa, one cannot help wondering if Marcello told Partin to make this accusation.

Marcello seems to have been staying in touch with Trafficante. He visited Miami in August 1961, when he reportedly inquired about moving to Fort Lauderdale, and again in November 1962.[52] Late that month, the Los Angeles FBI got new information about Marcello from an informant named Edward Becker, who claimed that he was involved with Carlos Marcello's nephew, Carl Roppolo, in a scheme to promote an oil additive called Mustang. When Becker returned to Los Angeles, he told the FBI that he had met with Marcello about the project. (Although Becker told the bureau that Roppolo was Marcello's nephew, the HSCA later found that their families merely had a long relationship.)

Five years later, Becker's story reached journalist Ed Reid, who was working on a book about the Mafia entitled *The Grim Reapers*. On May 9, 1967, Reid showed a draft of his book to a Los Angeles FBI agent. It claimed that at a meeting with Marcello at his Churchill Farms, Louisiana, estate, Marcello spoke bitterly of RFK's campaign against him and uttered a Sicilian curse, "Take this stone from my shoe." But, he said, if they killed Bobby, the President would send the Marines after them. So in order to get Bobby, they would have to kill the President, and someone had to be "peppered up" to do the job.

Becker claimed that he repeated the story to two FBI agents a few days later and gave their names. Reid's interlocutor immediately confirmed that such an interview took place, but the agents denied hearing anything more than what was in the original report. Becker's story apparently set off some alarm bells within the mob, because Sidney Korshak, a notorious mob lawyer, got word to the FBI a few days later that Becker was claiming to be Reid's collaborator and shaking people down in return for keeping them out of the book. After hearing that rumor from FBI agents, Reid promised to delete the story, but in the end he did not. The bureau made no attempt to contact Roppolo.[53]

The alliance among Trafficante, Hoffa, and Marcello around the idea of assassinating the President tightened during the first seven months of 1963, according to Ragano, who was now representing Hoffa as well as

Trafficante. In March 1963, Hoffa told Ragano to go to New Orleans to investigate rumors of new investigations of Teamster pension fund loans there, loans in which Marcello was involved. When Ragano told Trafficante about it, Trafficante decided to accompany him to a meeting with Marcello at his headquarters, the Town and Country Motel in New Orleans. At a second meeting they commiserated about Robert Kennedy's investigations of themselves and of Hoffa, and Marcello, according to Ragano, commented angrily that "some one ought to kill all those goddamn Kennedys." Later in the evening, Trafficante told Ragano that Carlos controlled the rackets in Dallas through Joe Civello, who Ragano remembered had represented Marcello at the 1957 Appalachin meeting. He also claimed that Joseph P. Kennedy, Sr., had been a bootlegging partner of Frank Costello. Before leaving, Ragano found there had been no improprieties involving the Teamster loan for a new Fontainebleau Hotel in New Orleans.[54]

In late March, Ragano attended a card game with Hoffa and two Chicago associates, Gus Zappas and Joey Glimco, a Chicago Teamsters leader who was also close to Giancana. Hoffa casually asked Ragano and another of his attorneys, William Bufalino, about the possible consequences of the demise of the attorney general or the President or both. They agreed that while the President would replace Robert Kennedy with someone even worse, Lyndon Johnson would surely appoint a new attorney general.

In May and June Hoffa was indicted for jury tampering in the Test Fleet case and for a complex series of frauds involving the pension fund. Ragano claimed that Hoffa and Robert Kennedy had a violent confrontation in the Justice Department in July when he and Hoffa went there to examine documents in these cases. On July 23, Ragano wrote, he met Hoffa in Washington before leaving for New Orleans to discuss pension fund loans again with both Marcello and Trafficante. Hoffa took a moment alone to ask him about them, and when he learned about the trip, he gave him a new mission. "Something has to be done," he said. "The time has come for your friend [Trafficante] and Carlos to get rid of him, kill that son-of-a-bitch John Kennedy. This has got to be done. Be sure to tell them what I said. No more fucking around. We're running out of time—something has to be done."

Although Ragano did not take the request seriously, he felt he had to pass it on. He arrived in New Orleans that very night, he said, and met with Marcello and Trafficante in the Royal Orleans Hotel the next morning. He decided to take a light-hearted approach and treat the matter as a joke. "Marteduzzo [Hoffa, the 'little hammer'] wants you to do a little favor for him," he said, and paused for effect. "You won't believe this, but he wants you to kill John Kennedy . . . He wants you to get rid of the President right away." The two men looked at one another in icy silence and did not respond. The conversation then moved on to other matters.[55]

Just two months later, in September 1963, the FBI got new reports about Trafficante from a very wealthy Cuban exile, Jose Aleman, whose father had been a minister under Carlos Prio and who had testified against mobster Norman Rothmann in Rothmann's trial for arms dealing. Aleman explained that he had met Trafficante during the first half of that year through a mutual friend, Rafael "Macho" Gener, who had cooperated with Trafficante, Roselli, Varona, and Maheu in setting up the failed Castro assassination plot back in 1960–61. Aleman said, however, that he did not learn Trafficante's name until July. After that, he explained, they began working on a deal for a low-cost housing development in the Dominican Republic, where Aleman had connections. A month later, Aleman reported that Philadelphia mobster Angelo Bruno was also a partner in the deal.[56]

Thirteen years later, in 1976, Aleman told the Washington journalist George Crile a somewhat different story. He explained that he had another connection to Trafficante—his cousin, Rafael Garcia Bongo, who represented Trafficante in Cuba and had gotten him out of jail in 1959. He told Crile that his discussions with Trafficante in 1963 also involved a loan from the Teamsters Union to re-establish his failing personal finances. He acknowledged that he had become an FBI informant, which agents confirmed to Crile. Aleman's FBI file, however, indicates that he did not officially become an informant until early fall 1963, much later than he told Crile. It would have been natural to buy some insurance with the FBI by providing some information about another, more innocent project, while negotiating for the loan.

Aleman, however, added in 1976 that one evening, while discussing the loan, Trafficante turned to national politics. Kennedy, he claimed, was dishonest. "Have you seen how his brother is hitting Hoffa, who is a worker, a man who is not a millionaire, who is a friend of the blue col-lars?" he said. "He doesn't understand that this kind of encounter is very delicate. Mark my words, this man Kennedy is in trouble, and he will get what is coming to him." Aleman protested that Kennedy would be re-elected in 1964. "You don't understand, Jose," Trafficante replied. "He is going to be hit."[57]

The FBI reports of talks with Aleman in 1963 do not include this story, and when it broke in 1976 the agents who had interviewed him then denied ever having heard it. Testifying in 1978, after the death of John Roselli, Aleman confirmed Trafficante's words but denied that they referred to assassination.[58]

Ragano wrote his book in the early 1990s with the help of a re-spected organized crime reporter named Selwyn Raab. Like Judith Campbell, he apparently drew on records he had kept to tell a very detailed story, complete with dates, about his involvement with several of the most notorious criminals in America. His credibility increased because of the corroboration provided independently by Becker and Aleman, who heard Marcello and Trafficante talking in the same vein. By the time Ragano delivered Hoffa's message to Marcello and Trafficante, Lee Harvey Oswald, whose Uncle Dutz Murret was a bookmaker in the Marcello organization, was already living in New Orleans.

The Mob Enlists the CIA

On October 14, 1962, a U-2 overflight—the first in weeks—photographed Soviet medium-range and intermediate-range ballistic missile bases in Cuba. It took another day to analyze the photographs, and on October 16 the Executive Committee of the National Security Council (EXCOM) met for the first time to decide what to do. By Monday, October 22, the President had rejected proposals for an immediate air strike and invasion in favor of a quarantine of Soviet missiles. That night he announced his decision to the American people.

Well before delivering his speech, JFK had anticipated that the crisis might be settled diplomatically, in a deal involving the withdrawal of American missiles from Turkey. For the next six days, until October 28, the world teetered on the brink of local or total war. On that Sunday, after receiving private assurances from Robert Kennedy the day before that the United States would shortly withdraw its missiles from Turkish soil, Khrushchev announced that Soviet missiles would be removed from Cuba. In return, President Kennedy pledged not to invade the island.[1]

The missile crisis showed John F. Kennedy at his best as a leader, diplomat, and strategic thinker. It also inaugurated a new era in Soviet-American relations, leading initially to the Test Ban Treaty in July 1963, an end to the standoff in Berlin, and, after a hiatus occasioned by the Vietnam War, the era of détente in the 1970s. But despite these broader shifts in its foreign policy, the administration's approach to Cuba did not undergo a dramatic change. Although Operation Mongoose shut down, the Kennedys did not abandon their objective of overthrowing Castro. Despite JFK's no-invasion pledge and a general easing of international tensions, by the middle of 1963 the administration returned to the same strategies it had adopted in 1961–62. These included scenarios that depended on either a split within the Cuban leadership or the sudden death of Castro by assassination. By September 1963 a young Lee Harvey Oswald found himself in the middle of one of these Castro assassination plots.

In early October 1962, before the missile crisis exploded, the Special Group (Augmented) had not been able to agree on a sabotage program. The CIA's William Harvey, director of Task Force W and the agency's representative for Operation Mongoose, was feeling increasing frustration over pressure from General Lansdale and the attorney general to magically bring about the overthrow of Castro. The discovery of missiles only increased the strain.

On October 16, the day the crisis began, Robert Kennedy took time between the first two EXCOM sessions to meet with the various Mongoose representatives from the CIA, including Richard Helms, who came instead of Harvey. RFK expressed "the general dissatisfaction of the President" with the progress of Mongoose and complained specifically that no sabotage had taken place. In an effort to increase the pressure, Kennedy scheduled a daily 9:30 a.m. meeting with Mongoose representatives (including Lansdale). His appointment calendar shows that such meetings took place on the next two mornings, but after that, unsurprisingly, they lapsed.[2]

As the missile crisis heated up, Harvey—according to his own later testimony—"put into Cuba, or put in train to put into Cuba, for the purpose of supporting any military effort that might have to be engaged into, every single team and asset that we could scrape together." By the time RFK found out about this, in a Special Group meeting at the height of the crisis, he was more concerned with avoiding the outbreak of war, and ordered Harvey to pull back in no uncertain terms. Harvey later explained that RFK held a low opinion of him, originating from the time when Harvey told him that the CIA simply could not clandestinely arrange the overthrow of the Castro regime without any possible attribution to the United States. After this episode, Harvey told Helms that he was willing to quit. That turned out to be unnecessary.[3]

President Kennedy, in an October 27 letter to Khrushchev that attempted to resolve the crisis, promised both to lift the quarantine of Cuba and "to give assurances against an invasion of Cuba."[4] But in fact, the crisis dragged on in muted form for another month, over the removal of Soviet IL-28 bombers and Castro's refusal to admit on-site inspections. It was eventually concluded to the satisfaction of Kennedy and Khrushchev on November 20. Unbeknown to the Americans, the Soviets also insisted, over Castro's objections, on removing the tactical nuclear weapons they had sent along with their ground troops.[5] Two weeks earlier, on November 5, a CIA official had already begun putting Operation Mongoose to bed and re-establishing the firewall between the agency and the rest of the government.

That official, George McManus, argued that Mongoose essentially died when Kennedy and Khrushchev exchanged letters on October 27–28. While military intervention still remained a possibility until the IL-28 crisis was solved, once that was settled Cuba would become a "denied area" which the agency would treat like other similar areas. "Looking back to the origins of Mongoose," he wrote, "one finds the Attorney General and Mr. McNamara seeking primarily to remove the political stain left on the President by the Bay of Pigs failure. Both the A.G. and the Secretary of Defense felt it necessary for political reasons that some action be taken with respect to Cuba to insure the President's future. In a nutshell, they were out to dump Castro or to make him cooperate."

While Mongoose had focused upon creating internal resistance that could trigger U.S. intervention, McManus's review of the year before the missile crisis showed policymakers generally shying away from both military intervention and sabotage. Robert Kennedy, Robert McNamara, McGeorge Bundy, and other officials, he wrote, "viewed the project in a strictly political light. Hindsight must now reveal to others, as well as it has to us, that a Chief of Operations (i.e. Lansdale) was never actually needed." McManus was now determined to remove Harvey's Task Force W from General Lansdale's orbit by reorganizing it and putting it back under the control of the Western Hemisphere branch. While he opposed any CIA effort to unseat Lansdale, partly because McNamara, Gilpatric, and the attorney general still had some belief in him, "everyone at the operating level agrees that Lansdale has lost his value . . . With a political solution to the Cuban problem in hand reflecting great credit on the part of the President, the A.G. will drop Lansdale like a hot brick."[6]

McManus's paper makes interesting reading almost half a century later, since he apparently but mistakenly hoped that the missile crisis would put an end to the "no war, no peace" policies of the last three years—policies that had left the CIA with an impossible task. But the administration—led by the President himself—was not prepared to go that far. In a November 20 EXCOM meeting, JFK rejected a formal no-invasion pledge to the United Nations, although (against the opinion of the attorney general) he advocated reiterating a private, informal pledge to Khrushchev. The next day, in another meeting, he hinted at his hopes for the future.

> The President agreed that we could abandon insistence on ground inspection, but he felt that the proposed no-invasion assurances were too hard. He said our objective is to preserve our right to invade Cuba in the event of civil war, if there were guerrilla activities in other Latin American countries or if offensive weapons were reintroduced into Cuba. We do not want to build up Castro by means of a no-invasion guarantee. The pertinent sentence in the declaration which we would make to the UN Security Council was revised.[7]

Just a few days later, a perceptive William Harvey viewed the situation more realistically than McManus in a memorandum for CIA director John McCone. In light of the no-invasion pledge, he wrote, agency-controlled paramilitary and guerrilla operations would now be "unacceptable as a matter of policy." And this promised to make an impossible mission even more difficult. "Higher authority" would probably continue to pressure the CIA for a maximum effort, even though the regime probably could not be overthrown without the use of U.S. forces and even though the government was not prepared to admit this to Cuban exile groups. "In view of these factors," he continued, "the so-called 'Track Two' course of action, i.e., unlimited support of Cuban exiles and exile groups with no real control or objective purpose in the hope that these groups will be able to shake the Castro regime will, although unrealistic, become increasingly attractive at various levels in the US government"—a prediction that rapidly proved correct. Training facilities for the Cubans outside the United States would be "both necessary and desirable."

Harvey resurrected another element of American strategy, however: "Take maximum action to induce a split in the Cuban regime and maintain the capability of capitalizing immediately through clandestine means to the extent possible on any significant uprising, revolt, resistance, split in the regime, or strains and stresses among Cuban leadership or in Cuban/Bloc relationships." Given Harvey's aversion to blunt language and the agency's ongoing contacts with Rolando Cubela—the disaffected Cuban official involved in plots to poison Castro in 1960—it seems fair to assume that Harvey had in mind a coup triggered by Castro's assassination.

"The effectiveness of assets aimed at actually splitting the regime, i.e., a palace revolt, will of course depend, to an extent, on the willingness of the United States Government to support them and it is entirely possible that any such effort might fail" without American military support. He recommended turning political relations with the exile groups over to the State Department, reducing Task Force W, moving it back into the Western Hemisphere branch "under different direction" (an indication that he was eager to give up Cuba and move back to Europe himself), abolishing "the operational Mongoose mechanism," and reducing supervision by the Special Group (Augmented).[8]

Within a month, Task Force W under Harvey mutated into the Special Affairs Staff (SAS), and Harvey turned its direction over to another senior agency operative, Desmond Fitzgerald, a veteran of the failed attempt in 1957 to bring about Sumatra's rebellion against Indonesia, who as late as 1962 was still working in the Far East.[9] But the SAS was not brought back under the authority of the Western Hemisphere branch. It continued to operate independently and to pursue the assassination of Castro by various means.

JFK, vacationing in Palm Beach, Florida, approved this reorganization during the first week of January.[10] A Cuba Coordinating Committee headed by Sterling Cottrell, who became director of the State Department's Office of Cuban Affairs, replaced Mongoose and Lansdale as the interdepartmental coordinator of Cuban policy. EXCOM, under the President himself, retained responsibility for deciding policy, and the 5412 Committee—as distinct from its now-deceased child, the Special Group (Augmented)—retained authority over covert action. Even Robert Kennedy delegated the task of working out the new arrangements to his deputy, Nicholas Katzenbach.[11]

Cottrell promptly tried to define U.S. policy but discovered a difference of opinion between the State Department, which simply wanted to continue isolating Castro to the maximum extent possible, and Defense, represented by Assistant Secretary Cyrus Vance, which wanted the United States once again to commit itself to overthrowing Castro. On January 25 the President approved a program that called for the support of anti-Castro Cubans inside and outside Cuba, and for "being prepared to meet, with the employment of appropriate U.S. combat elements and/or logistical support, the wide variety of military contingencies that may arise from pursuit of the foregoing objectives."[12]

The President continued to place U.S. policy toward Cuba in a broader international context. As he made clear to the National Security Council on January 22, he wanted up-to-date contingency plans for an invasion of Cuba in case the Soviets made a sudden move in Berlin. Cuba, he argued, was now the Americans' hostage, just as West Berlin was the Soviets' hostage. After two years of Berlin crises, Kennedy had evolved a solution to the strategic nightmare of a Soviet invasion and occupation of West Berlin—which the West could not possibly prevent—that would not necessarily unleash a general war in Europe.[13] About a month later, on February 25, after some reports of a failed uprising inside Cuba, Kennedy told the joint chiefs of staff that he wanted to introduce troops immediately if a revolt showed any chance of success.[14] For three months since the Soviets announced the withdrawal of their missiles, administration officials, while backing away from Operation Mongoose, had been groping for a new policy. In March, the exiles finally forced their hand.

Relations with Cuban exiles entered a new phase after the missile crisis. When President Kennedy announced the quarantine of Cuba on October 22, the exiles believed that the hour of liberation was at hand. The announcement of the Kennedy-Khrushchev agreement six days later and the lifting of the quarantine on November 21 were terrible shocks. Jose Miro Cardona, still head of the Cuban Revolutionary Council, took weeks to make a statement before declaring, on November 21, that the President's speech did *not* mean the end of the struggle. Rogelio Cisneros, who along with Manuel Ray was leading the left-wing exile organization JURE, also supported the President and claimed that JURE believed that only Cubans could liberate Cuba. The Second National Front of the Escambray (SNFE), one of the independent, action-oriented organizations, welcomed the end of the blockade since it allowed for the resumption of raids against Cuba.[15] But the DRE—whose relations with its CIA sponsor were already desperate when the missile crisis broke out—refused to toe the line.

The DRE had run afoul of its case officer, Ross Crozier (who worked under the name of Harold Noemayr) during 1962, because of the group's refusal to spend all its money as ordered or to confine its activities to propaganda rather than sabotage. Things got worse during the missile crisis, when a DRE leader complained in a press interview that the CIA had refused to help them and had confiscated their arms after the August 22 raid on Havana. "Now we have to work in an underground way," one student said. "The prices of things are high, and we have to deal with anybody we can, the Mafia and all. They don't say they are the Mafia, but you ought to see their faces. One man right over there in a Miami Beach hotel looked like a gangster in a movie. We argued about the prices."[16] With financial backing from rich cold warriors like William Pawley and Clare Boothe Luce and arms contacts with mobsters, the DRE was on its way to setting up an independent military capability.

Ted Shackley, chief of the CIA's Miami station JMWAVE, met with DRE leader Luis Fernandez Rocha, believing it essential, "in order to assure that we were not nurturing an uncontrollable organism capable of inflicting even greater public damage to CIA's reputation," to get "some evidence of a readiness to cooperate with basic operational caveats under which CIA must operate . . . In this hope we were disappointed." The DRE leadership, Crozier reported, "fanatically" believed they could dictate the terms of collaboration and displayed "a flagrant disregard for the recent months of patient efforts in which we have sought to foster [DRE] programs along lines of mutual interest—during which time CIA has been the sole and generous supporter of a consistently intractable" DRE. The station, he reported, was considering dropping the whole project: DRE "simply does not wish to be bound to policies of prudence whensoever it may opt for unilateral adventures of its own devising."[17]

When Crozier met with Fernandez and his military chief, Manuel Salvat Roque, on November 16, they spoke bravely about raising $15,000 recently in Chicago and Puerto Rico and negotiating with Texas industrialists for help.[18] By that time, DRE leaders had already successfully outflanked Crozier by traveling to Washington to meet with Helms on November 15. After a morning session in which the DRE claimed that

Soviet missiles were being hidden in Cuban caves, rather than with-drawn, in the afternoon they turned to their stormy relationship with the agency.

Fernandez began by apologizing for his October press interview, and Helms, after warning that the DRE might not like pending American policy decisions on Cuba, said he was replacing Crozier as the organiza-tion's main point of contact. Fernandez replied that the relationship would have to end if the United States opted for co-existence with Cas-tro. Helms made clear that he hoped the DRE would continue intelli-gence collection, with or without operations, and asked to be warned about press conferences. He and Fernandez, Helms said, were both "re-sponsible" men. Helms invited him to submit new military plans to their contact. In a later meeting with another Langley official, Fernandez re-fused, once again, to submit to lie detector tests. The whole episode must have confirmed the DRE's view that they could bully the agency.[19]

On December 10 JMWAVE was informed that Crozier had been re-placed by George Joannides, who worked under the name of Walter Newby. Joannides had joined the CIA in 1951 and spent the last ten years working in his native Greece.[20] Three days later, Fernandez released a letter to President Kennedy expressing fears that talks with the Soviets would eventually lead to co-existence with Castro's Cuba. "Should the end of the crisis tend to prolong the agony of our people," he continued, "Cubans will never renounce the right to fight, by every means possible, those who have seized our national sovereignty; and in identical fashion, we have never renounced the right to carry the struggle to the enemy at every single opportunity."[21] Meanwhile, on December 10 JMWAVE of-ficers confirmed press reports that the federal government intended to crack down on unauthorized military operations.[22]

The crackdown had already begun on December 3, when U.S. Cus-toms arrested thirteen men training under Gerry Patrick Hemming, the American ex-Marine and mercenary, on Sombrero Key, near Marathon Key. Deputy Attorney General Nicholas Katzenbach immediately asked J. Edgar Hoover about their status, and Hoover assured him they had no official sanction. The government confiscated quite a few weapons and charged the men with violating the Neutrality Act, and Hoover spe-cifically commended the Miami office of the FBI for helping to head off a potentially embarrassing action. Hemming, however, apparently knew enough CIA personnel to make a trial embarrassing, and the charges were dropped just six weeks later.[23] Hemming continued to pursue aggressively his career as a free-lance guerrilla trainer and intelligence source for the rest of the year. The FBI evidently wanted to continue its crackdown, however, and in late December the bureau asked the CIA about its relationship to various Cuban groups.[24]

Meanwhile, the Kennedy administration, led by the attorney general, took another public and dramatic step to help erase whatever political stain the Bay of Pigs had left. In summer 1961, not long after the landing, President Kennedy had encouraged Milton Eisenhower (younger brother of Ike), Eleanor Roosevelt, and labor leader Walter Reuther to form the Tractors for Freedom committee, designed to ransom the prisoners with agricultural equipment. The committee became politically controversial, undergoing attacks from, among others, former Vice President Nixon, and its efforts fell apart within a year. A renewed effort began in April 1962, when the prisoners were sentenced to thirty years of hard labor or a $50 million fine. A committee of families hired attorney James Donovan to negotiate with Castro, and he traveled to Cuba in September and October to discuss agricultural and pharmaceutical items that Castro might receive as ransom.

On November 30, 1962, after the final settlement of the missile crisis, RFK put Don Oberdorfer, head of the Tax Division of the Justice Department, in charge of working out the ransom. Critically, the Justice Department not only exempted pharmaceutical firms from the Trading with the Enemy Act but agreed that the firms could deduct from their taxable income the full retail value of donated drugs. Since corporate profits were taxed at the rate of about 50 percent at that time and drug companies often sold drugs for ten times their unit cost, the companies made a substantial profit on the drug giveaway. After intense negotiations that lasted less than a month, the Bay of Pigs prisoners came back to the United States on Christmas Eve 1962.[25]

The President personally met with several brigade leaders at his vacation home in Palm Beach a few days later, and in his December 29 address at the Orange Bowl, he said this: "I want to express my great appreciation to the brigade for making the United States the custodian of this flag. I can assure you that this flag will be returned to this brigade in a free Havana." Cubans, he declared, now lived in slavery, but the brigade and the United States government shared a commitment to freedom throughout the Americas. "I can assure you," he concluded, "that it is the strongest wish of the people of this country, as well as the people of this hemisphere, that Cuba shall one day be free again, and when it is, this brigade will deserve to march at the head of the free column."[26]

The brigade's return made new leadership available to the Cuban exile community, and the administration, led once again by RFK, rapidly settled on one of its commanders, Manuel Artime, as their most important organizer. The freed commander had contempt for the CRC and Cardona, and RFK informed Artime in early January that he would be getting support funds from a "separate channel" in Miami rather than through the CRC, as indeed he did. Soon Artime was in almost daily contact with a CIA case officer whom he called in Washington on a secure line, and by March RFK had promised him, through Enrique Ruiz Williams, another brigade veteran, that he would help him find a new base outside the United States. In that same month, Artime visited Nicaragua to discuss a possible base with longtime president Luis Somoza.[27] President Kennedy met the leaders of all the Central American nations in Costa Rica in late March, and some indications suggest that he encouraged them to host Cuban exile bases.[28]

The other major beneficiary of the administration's new policy was Manuel Ray Rivera, Castro's old July 26 associate who in the fall of 1962 founded JURE (Junta Revolucionaria in Exilo). The CIA in January 1963 claimed only a casual relationship with Ray, but by early February the agency acknowledged that he was receiving important support from leftist Caribbean governments and from the United States. In January 1963 he was promised one bolivar, peso, or dollar per member of the Venezuelan Workers Union, the Confederation of Workers in Costa Rica, the Workers Union in Costa Rica, and the Workers Union in Puerto Rico, and he was now getting $6,000 U.S. monthly "through an unidentified mechanism of the Venezuelan government" for operational expenses for JURE.[29] Ray had told another CIA informant in early January that he wanted to infiltrate the Cuban militia to arrange the "assassination [of the] Cuban government hierarchy," which he saw as the only means of doing anything about Castro in the short run.[30]

Working through the CIA, the administration was planning to establish new exile bases in Central America that could allow the Cubans to strike directly at Castro again without bringing undue embarrassment upon the United States. But at the same time, the agency's own plot to assassinate Castro with the help of Roselli was continuing apace. Contrary to the conclusions of two official investigations, that plot did not terminate after the missile crisis. Fitzgerald, Harvey's replacement at Task Force W, was equally committed to the assassination of Castro, as his deputy Sam Halpern testified, and Harvey continued to run Roselli's operation.

In 1967 the CIA inspector general, relying, presumably, on William Harvey, described events at the turn of 1962–63 as follows.

> Harvey was in Miami between 22 December and 6 January. He saw both Roselli and Maceo several times during that period. He made a payment of $2,700 to Roselli for passing to Varona for the expenses of the three militia men. Harvey and Roselli had telephone discussions of the operation between 11 and 16 January. Harvey says that Roselli wasn't kidding himself. He agreed with Harvey that nothing was happening and that there was not much chance that anything would happen in the future. As far as Harvey knows, the three militia men never did leave for Cuba. He knows nothing of what may have happened to the three reported to have been sent to Cuba.

> February 1963
> Harvey was in Miami 11–14 February. He had no contacts with any of the principals, but he left word for Maceo that there was nothing new and that it now looked as if it were all over. (Just how Harvey left this word for Maceo is not clear.) Harvey left Miami on 15 February to meet with Roselli in Los Angeles. They agreed at the Los Angeles meeting that the operation would be closed off, but that it would be unwise to attempt a precipitate break between Roselli and Varona. Roselli agreed that he would continue to see Varona, gradually reducing the frequency of contact until there was none.

> April–May 1963
> Harvey says that he received two telephone calls from Roselli during this period. Harvey decided that it would be best to have one last meeting with Roselli before he left for his assignment in [deletion]. He states that he reported this decision to Mr. Helms who gave his approval.[31]

Evidently this was not the truth. The team had in fact infiltrated into Cuba in March 1963 and were captured by Cuban security forces on March 9. They had planned to kill Castro from a rooftop near the University of Havana on March 13. The team entered through Guantanamo (where earlier assassination conspiracies had originated) with the help of an associate of Roselli's on the base.[32] The Black Book that Fidel Castro gave George McGovern in 1975 lists five men who were involved in this plot but does not make clear how many took part in the actual attempt. By the time the Black Book was published, Roselli had already identified the team as his own.

The capture of the team figured in the stories that Edward Morgan, Roselli's and Maheu's attorney, gave to Drew Pearson and to the FBI in January and March 1967, respectively, although Morgan provided only an approximate date.[33] In both cases, Morgan added that the team had been tortured and captured and had confessed that they were on an official mission for the U.S. government; and that this led to Castro's decision to arrange the assassination of Kennedy. Pearson passed the story on to President Johnson, who called Helms at the CIA and persuaded him to initiate the inspector general's investigation that resulted in the 1967 IG report.

The story of the March 1963 attempt also appeared in several columns by Jack Anderson, Pearson's collaborator, after Pearson's death in 1969. Anderson originally revived the story in two columns on January 18 and 19, 1971, referring specifically to a team that was apprehended on a rooftop "around the last of February or the first of March, 1963." Although the first story actually named Roselli, Maheu, Jim O'Connell, and Harvey, Pearson and Anderson had always been maverick journalists, and the major media outlets ignored the story for almost four more years. In March 1975, as the assassination plot was finally becoming known, Anderson retold the story, referring to five different assassination attempts between the Bay of Pigs and the final one in late February or early March.[34]

Roselli himself, in his three appearances before the Church Committee, acknowledged that he never told his Cuban contacts that the deal was off. But despite all this, the committee's report, which was rushed to press in the fall of 1975, simply followed the line of the inspector general's report that nothing had happened after the missile crisis.[35] The

House Select Committee on Assassinations, in turn, followed the Church Committee's lead four years later.[36]

Harvey and Roselli got away with concealing their failed attempt to assassinate Castro. To have revealed the truth in 1975–76 would have compromised a hitherto secure operation, and this Harvey evidently refused to do. He did have to admit that he remained in contact with Roselli, because FBI surveillance detected a June 1963 meeting between them in Washington, well after Fitzgerald had taken over the Cuban operation and Harvey had moved on to Rome. Apparently, Harvey remained, in effect, Roselli's case officer even then. Another witness claimed that Roselli was still hard at work on conspiracies in Florida in the second half of 1963.[37] Neither the IG in preparing his report nor the Church Committee seems ever to have asked Harvey whether he briefed his successor on the ongoing Mafia plot. Fitzgerald himself died suddenly in July 1967, just months after the IG report was prepared.

But Fitzgerald probably would not have objected to what Harvey was doing, because he had made the assassination of Castro a high priority of the Special Affairs Staff. In early 1963 he ordered the staff to come up with a workable scheme, and he told his deputy, Halpern, that he had received orders from "on high," though he did not explain whether that meant inside or outside the agency. At some point during 1963, Fitzgerald himself initiated a plan to kill Castro while he was skin diving. The scheme involved either exploding sea shells or a poisoned diving suit that he might receive from Donovan, who had just accomplished the prisoner exchange. The agency still regarded the assassination of Castro as simply an ongoing project requiring no further consultation or authorization.[38]

While the assassination plot ultimately failed, the issue of sabotage came onto the radar screen again as 1962 turned into 1963. The relationship between the CIA and autonomous action groups led by Alpha-66 and its splinter organization, Commandos L, remained murky around that time. The agency's own clearance of Antonio Veciana lapsed in November 1962, but Veciana apparently had a new connection to Army intelligence.[39] When the FBI queried the CIA about its relationship with various exile groups, JMWAVE commented that it did not trust Alpha-66 or Commandos L because it suspected Eloy Gutierrez Menoyo, the 1961 defector who led Commandos L, of being an undercover agent for

Castro. It added, however, that JMWAVE retained a marginal interest in these two groups because they could take credit for CIA covert actions.[40]

On March 18 Alpha-66 forced the administration's hand, announcing that it had carried on two more raids on a Russian ship and a Russian training area in Las Villas province. The State Department immediately issued a highly critical statement, and on April 11 President Kennedy assured Khrushchev that the United States opposed raids that violated U.S. laws.[41] Three EXCOM meetings on March 26, 28, and 29 showed utter confusion at the highest levels of the administration. McCone, who never reconciled himself to Castro's rule, wanted the raids to continue, but the attorney general, surprisingly, now wanted to crack down on all unauthorized activity. Vice President Johnson vociferously agreed with him. The President, however, recognized that raids were less dangerous and more spectacular that infiltrations. While not arguing against them, he wanted the CIA to provide the raiders with direction and, following Secretary of State Rusk's recommendation, wanted the raiders to shift to Cuban rather than Soviet targets. In the end, the President asked the CIA to give the Cuban exiles guidance while the FBI cracked crack down on unauthorized groups and arms dealers.[42]

The missile crisis was over, but substantial numbers of Soviet troops remained in Cuba, and the thaw in Soviet-American relations was just beginning. McCone still believed that Castro had to go; McNamara agreed; and the Kennedy brothers remained sufficiently interested to ask the CIA on April 3 to estimate the maximum action against Castro they could undertake.[43] In the first week of April the new Cottrell Committee decided to recommend that the Army train Cuban exile infiltrators on military reservations, that balloons drop leaflets, and that the CIA mount a sabotage campaign against Cuban ships in foreign ports. On April 15 McCone met with Kennedy in Palm Beach and argued that the United States had only two choices: either to establish relations with Castro and persuade him to expel the Soviet troops and reorient his foreign policy, or to arrange for the removal of Soviet troops and to overthrow him. Kennedy, in a portent of things to come, suggested that both options might simultaneously be pursued.[44] McCone on April 25 wrote that sabotage and attacks on Cuban shipping could help create the conditions for a military coup in Cuba, which he regarded as the United States' only hope.[45]

During the same weeks in April, the country faced another crisis half-way around the world. When Kennedy took office in 1961, Laos was threatened by Communist rule, but the President refused his advisers' suggestions to intervene militarily and opted for the formation of a neutral government in September 1962. That government was coming under renewed pressure from the Communist group Pathet Lao in April 1963, after two factions traded assassinations of important men and the Pathet Lao left the government coalition. As they had in both 1961 and 1962, McNamara and Rusk recommended putting American troops in Southeast Asia.

Kennedy refused these demands again, as he had done two years earlier. In his view, Southeast Asia was not a good place for U.S. forces. He still saw the Laotian crisis as part of a worldwide competition with the Soviets, but he wanted to retaliate in a region where the United States held more cards. The Soviets, he commented in an April 19 meeting, were "continuing the type of harassment effort in Laos" that the administration had put a stop to in Cuba. He suggested specifically that the United States should resume low-level reconnaissance flights over Cuba to put pressure on the Soviets, and the next day he questioned once again whether such a careful policy toward Cuba was necessary.[46]

The President's change of heart appears to have had an immediate effect. On April 19, CIA headquarters cabled the Hague in the Netherlands, announcing that a program for the sabotage of Cuban shipping had been approved. Such measures had been listed only as a contingency plan in the program the National Security Council approved in January, but the President apparently agreed to implement them without further ado. A second cable to various European ports on April 24 had broader implications: "US Govt. policy calls for all feasible forms pressure on Castro Regime to inhibit its success and culminate in disorder leading to its downfall. Realize motivation of assets will be major key to success ops, and that difficulties will be encountered due their interpretation USG policy. Burden of positive motivation thus rests on case officers involved who must decide each case on own merits and use considerable judgment to induce cooperation."[47] Case officers, in short, would have to persuade agents that the United States would intervene to overthrow Castro, provided Cubans themselves could create the necessary preconditions for action. By May the sabotage program was under way.

In a series of medium- and high-level meetings in late April and May, the administration addressed the same issues, with roughly the same results, as it had eighteen months earlier. On April 23 McNamara told the Standing Group of the NSC (which did not include the President) that Castro must be overthrown, preferably by provoking an internal revolt that would allow the United States to intervene. The attorney general, who once again seemed to have the electoral calendar on his mind, asked for studies of how Castro might be overthrown during the next eighteen months, or how the United States might give him the maximum difficulty during that period.

An agenda for an April 30 meeting of the same body listed various contingencies, including interference with overflights, Castro's death, a failed revolt like the one in Hungary, Communist intervention elsewhere, or reintroduction of offensive weapons that might be used to achieve "wider political objectives." In the wake of that meeting, Bundy ordered the preparation of yet another study of "the possible developments in Cuba if Castro were to disappear from the scene"—clear evidence that assassination was back on the table.[48] In a replay of November 1961, the CIA's Office of National Estimates drafted a pessimistic study of that contingency on May 7.[49] Higher authority seems to have intervened, however, and by the time the estimate was published on June 14, it called "dependence on the person of Castro . . . a major vulnerability of the regime . . . his death could result in one form of disorder or another ranging from power struggles within the regime's leadership to open civil war."[50]

Two other pieces of evidence indicate quite clearly that the administration, including the President, was still counting on the assassination of Castro to solve its problems. On March 15 the Wall Street Journal's newsbox included an item with the headline "Castro's Assassination becomes the major U.S. hope for de-communizing Cuba"—the only time, as far as has been discovered, that the strategy leaked into print. "Some officials maintain rising public discontent is bound to bring a successful assassination attempt sooner or later. They figure total chaos would follow, communism couldn't keep its grip without Fidel as front man. Reports suggest original revolutionaries still in key posts would make a strong bid for power against old-line Communists."[51]

Five days later, during the summit of Central American leaders in

Costa Rica, President Kennedy talked with Guatemalan President Ydigoras, who agreed to allow Cuban exiles to establish new bases in his country. Kennedy "reiterated the situation of Cuba within the framework of the world situation and said that perhaps the elimination of Castro himself might lead to an improvement of the Cuban situation since Castro individually was of such great psychological importance."[52]

On June 8 the CIA submitted a long program of action against Cuba. It called for covert activities to prevent Castro from pacifying the population and consolidating his rule, on the assumption that this would "encourage dissident elements in the military and other power centers of the regime to bring about the eventual liquidation of the Castro/Communist entourage" and eliminate the Soviet presence. The agency specifically recommended intelligence collection, propaganda to encourage sabotage, "exploitation and stimulation" of disaffection in the Cuban military and other power centers, more economic pressure, "general sabotage and harassment," and continued support of both CIA-controlled and "autonomous" anti-Castro Cuban groups based outside the United States that would undertake sabotage operations. "We are undertaking an intensive probing effort to identify, seek out and establish channels of communication with disaffected and potentially dissident non-Communist elements in the power centers of the regime, particularly in the armed forces hierarchy." Significant portions of this program, such as the support being provided to Manuel Artime's MRR and Manuel Ray's JURE to establish bases in Central America and the sabotage program against Cuban shipping, were already well under way. The Standing Group approved the program on June 28, and the President blessed it the next day.[53]

In one of the most extraordinary episodes of the entire anti-Castro initiative, the CIA meanwhile had orchestrated yet another assassination attempt on Castro, one that involved mobsters, extreme right-wing authors and publicists, American mercenaries, *Time* magazine, the Senate Internal Security Subcommittee, and anti-Castro activist William Pawley. This attempt to land about ten men with the mission of assassinating Fidel Castro—which was actually sold to the agency under false cover—has now become known to history as the Bayo-Pawley raid.

Pawley—founder of the Flying Tigers, international air and transportation magnate, and friend of Trujillo, Batista, Eisenhower, and Nixon—

may have been the man who first suggested to Ike that Castro should be assassinated. He had worked with former Batistianos as a "special contact" for the CIA in 1960–61, but after the Bay of Pigs Pawley's use as contact apparently lapsed, although he retained the cryptonym QDDALE as late as 1963. On May 5, 1961, Pawley secured an appointment with President Kennedy through the good offices of Eisenhower, and during the meeting he recommended that 10,000 Marines be "dropped" on a sugar plantation in the environs of Havana to seize the city, release political prisoners, and install a provisional government. Pawley was shocked to hear JFK blame Castro's revolution on the American economic exploitation of Cuba (where Pawley himself once owned investments), and after he told Kennedy that the Alliance for Progress would fail, the President ushered him out.

Sometime later, he wrote Kennedy urging him to start a new private American organization like the Flying Tigers, and promising the service of ready, willing, but unidentified Americans in such a cause. In mid-1962, Pawley claimed, he had orchestrated the ransom of three Cubans from Castro's prisons for $175,000. On November 2, after the climax of the missile crisis, Pawley released a telegram he had sent Kennedy calling the deal with Khrushchev "a devastating blow to the prestige of the U.S. and set us back in the cold war . . . The premature agreement with Khrushchev has cost the United States one of the best opportunities offered in many years . . . There is no substitute for the overthrow of Castro."[54]

By April 1963, the Miami industrialist became a pawn in an elaborate scheme hatched by John Martino, whose ghostwriter, Nathan Weyl, belonged to a network of ex-Communists, including former spy Hede Massing, who had become violent anti-Communists. They were friendly with Jay Sourwine of the staff of the Senate Internal Security Committee, headed by James Eastland. Sometime in the spring of 1963 Weyl approached Sourwine with the story that several Soviet technicians were prepared to defect from Cuba and provide pictures of underground missile sites. Smelling a coup, Sourwine offered to spring the defectors on the public in testimony before the committee if their escape could be arranged. Sourwine had Senator Eastland call Pawley, who immediately recognized that this information would utterly discredit the Kennedy administration and revive plans to invade Cuba. He eagerly agreed to help.

On April 18 he came to the office of JMWAVE's Shackley in Miami to ask for assistance.[55]

Shackley told Pawley that he should turn the defectors over to the CIA, and Pawley called Sourwine, who asked for a promise that the Senate committee could have them within thirty-six hours. Shackley refused, and Pawley said he would call General Marshall Carter, the deputy director of Central Intelligence, to get his permission. (In an interesting example of CIA compartmentalization, Shackley, who had known Pawley since August 1962 and had used him to help ransom an agent from Cuba, support an operation, and provide information on exiles, does not seem to have been aware of Pawley's prior relationship with CIA headquarters or his cryptonym QDDALE.)[56] Later that day Pawley called Shackley to say that Carter had given his permission and had also suggested that Shackley make no written record of the operation.

Meanwhile, Shackley agreed that Pawley should contact Martino, whom Pawley had identified as the middleman between Weyl and the "Cuban underground." Martino, Shackley said, could "best be described as an unsavory character." Pawley agreed but said that he had to continue to use him. He also explained that he now planned to rendezvous with the team of Cubans that was supposed to bring out the defectors in his own boat, the *Flying Tiger,* which would carry the arms for the operation, and that he would fly air cover with his own plane. Weyl, who apparently saw the CIA as a bastion of left wingers, was furious, but Pawley told him the agency must be involved.[57]

Martino, meanwhile, approached Richard Billings, a reporter and photographer for *Life* magazine stationed in Miami (who later became the public relations director of the House Select Committee on Assassinations). He invited *Life* to cover the operation, and the magazine promised each of the three Soviet defectors $2,500 in return for their stories. Now it was the CIA's turn to be outraged, but Shackley explained to General Carter and Fitzgerald that attempts to buy off Martino and Pawley and get them to ditch the *Life* connection had failed.[58]

Ample evidence, however, shows that the raid was actually just another mob plot against Castro's life, having nothing to do with Soviet technicians. In late 1962 Gerry Hemming was back in his home town of Los Angeles when he was contacted by Trafficante's former Cuban cellmate, Loran Hall. After meeting John Rousselot, a southern California congressman with ties to the John Birch society, Hall and Hemming decided to return to Florida via Dallas and New Orleans, where Hemming had met with Cuban leaders the previous year. To pay for the trip, Hall pawned a set of golf clubs and Hemming pawned a 30.06 rifle with another friend, a private investigator named Richard Hathcock.[59]

Dallas was already a center of the southern brand of Republicanism that was destined to take over the politics of the United States during the next forty years. It boasted the only Republican congressman in Texas, an arch conservative named Bruce Alger, and was the home of multimillionaire oil man H. L. Hunt, who sponsored the national "Life Line" radio program and made his anti-government views known frequently in letters to the editor.[60] Congressmen Rousselot gave Hall and Hemming the name of Robert Morris, a Dallas attorney, former president of the University of Dallas, former counsel to the Senate Internal Security Committee, and unsuccessful candidate for the Republican nomination to the Senate in New Jersey in 1960.[61]

When they reached Dallas, Morris put them in touch with Lester Logue, a petroleum geologist who was also interested in conservative causes and became something of a financial angel for Hall and Hemming during the rest of 1963. Behind Logue, apparently, was H. L. Hunt, whom Logue in 1977 acknowledged as his fellow worker in various conservative causes.[62] Logue arranged for Hall and Hemming to meet with General Edwin Walker, who had been making a name for himself as a conservative anti-Communist agitator ever since President Kennedy relieved him of his command in West Germany in 1961 for promoting the views of the John Birch Society. But Walker provided no direct support.[63] Logue gave Hemming and Hall hundreds of dollars on several occasions during 1963, and Hall estimated that he might have gotten $2,500 total from Logue. Either Logue or Morris also apparently knew *Dallas Morning News* columnist Larry Grove, who wrote a rather fawning feature about Hall and Hemming's efforts to train men for the struggle against Cuba on January 23, 1963. Grove described the 6'7" Hemming as a larger version of the actor Rock Hudson.

Hall and Hemming proceeded to New Orleans, where they met once again with Larry Laborde and Frank Bartes, and then continued on to Miami. Hall was now trying to get back in touch with his distinguished cellmate, Trafficante. Back in Miami, Hall later told HSCA investigators, he participated in several raids on shipping around Cuba in February and March 1963 and was wounded in the leg. One of his fellow raiders was Eduardo Perez, known as Captain Bayo. Hall returned to Dallas to recuperate and talked to Logue again. Logue wanted "to land a couple of thousand people in Cuba with a recognized president-in-exile, and then appeal to the U.N. and the O.A.S. for assistance and help and recognition. Logue had contacts in Guatemala or Nicaragua who would recognize them immediately." Logue gave Hall enough money to drive back to Florida.

When he got there, Hemming introduced him to Martino, who asked Hall if he might be interested in something bigger than a raid, backed by "people" from Chicago and Miami. Martino outlined a plan to place demolition charges that could be detonated from remote locations at sites frequented by Castro, and a few days later, in April, he invited Hall, without Hemming, to a meeting at a Miami Beach hotel. There, Hall found Trafficante, who vouched for Hall and left. Two other men then entered, whom Hall later identified as Giancana and Roselli. They promised Martino the $20,000–30,000 he said he would need, and according to Hall, Giancana gave Bayo $15,000 as a down payment for equipment. Martino told Hemming that the assassination of Castro was the real object of the raid.[64]

By early June 1963, when the raid was almost ready to depart, Hall had left the area to go to New York, New Jersey, and Washington to discuss another project—a plan to overthrow the government of Haiti. Hemming, who by this time had surmised that the putative Soviet defectors did not exist, declined to take part as well. On May 23 Pawley came to see Shackley again. Worried by the involvement of *Life,* he did not know whether to proceed. At Shackley's suggestion, he secured an agreement that only one *Life* representative—Dick Billings—would go on the raid. Shackley, who estimated the chances of success at one thousand to one and could easily have brought the whole project to a halt, told him to go ahead, and Fitzgerald at CIA headquarters endorsed that decision.[65]

In 1976, when the story finally broke, Pawley told the *Miami Herald* that Martino and Bayo claimed to have received $15,000 from *Life.* That was far more than the $2,500 per defector Pawley had mentioned to Shackley, but it exactly matches the figure that Hall said Bayo and Martino had received from Giancana—and Hall's story had not yet come to light. Pawley apparently knew how much money had been provided, but he was still concealing the actual source as late as 1976.[66]

Shortly before the raid took off, a CIA agent reported that the estimated payload for the trip was 1,730 pounds, including 432 pounds of weapons, ammunition, and demolition equipment—further confirmation for Hall's story. That was 230 pounds more than the authorized load of the small boat in which the team of Cubans planned to land.[67] On the evening of June 8, after a complicated rendezvous between Pawley's yacht, with Billings and two CIA men on board, and a flying boat carrying Martino and the Cubans, the small boat took off for Cuba. Billings recalls today that he thought to himself that the boat was riding quite low in the water. The men did not return for the scheduled rendezvous the next day.

Rip Robertson, the CIA man who briefed the team, concluded that the men never had any intention of returning. In two memos for Shackley, he explained that neither Martino nor Bayo showed any interest in the exfiltration and recovery plan, and that Bayo told them to go home and not to worry if he was not back by 1800 hours the next day. Martino and Bayo, Robertson thought, had not even told the Cubans what the CIA plan really was. Martino, he said, "never seemed to have a moment of concern after the launching was accomplished, and was felt by those aboard to be bored with the waiting period for rendezvous." He also thought that Pawley had known the men were not coming back. But if Pawley knew the real purpose of the operation, he took the secret to his grave.[68]

On June 28 the Cuban Revolutionary Council, now led once again by Tony Varona, announced that it had sent men to invade Cuba. Queried by JMWAVE, Artime's MRR gave the names of six of Bayo's team as some of the invaders. Shackley concluded that Pawley, Sourwine, and *Life* had all been conned, but he put an optimistic face on the fiasco in a cable for headquarters. "QDDALE," he said, referring to Pawley by his crypt, "has gained renewed confidence [in CIA's] ability [to] handle P[olitical]M[ilitary] infil ops." He also had learned not to involve the press; and *Life,* knowing the difficulties first hand, would be less likely to criticize CIA operations. And in any event, "Ten well armed men have been put into Cuba. They should be short term irritant to Castro even if they rolled up in short order."[69]

Even this, apparently, was overly optimistic. According to Fabian Escalante, the Cuban counterintelligence chief turned author, the team never landed. If Escalante is correct, then the boat must have sunk with the loss of all hands thanks to its excessive load, as Billings feared it might. This did not prevent Martino from reporting to JMWAVE in September that an informant in Cuba told him the team had killed several Russians and Cuban militiamen in a firefight in Oriente province and lost two men of their own.[70] Alternatively, Bayo might have been a Castro agent himself. His behavior in September 1962, when he tried to bring a high-level American to Guantanamo to discuss a supposed uprising for which there was no evidence, suggests a provocation, and this time, too, he might have been trying to embarrass the United States while returning to Cuba. In his 1976 interview, Pawley himself raised the possibility that the Cubans were actually Castroites. The question remains open.

Yet despite its anti-climactic conclusion, the Bayo-Pawley raid makes certain things clear. First, despite considerable message traffic between JMWAVE and the highest levels of the CIA, there is no evidence that the raid was ever briefed to anyone outside the agency or submitted for approval to the 5412 Committee or the new Cuban Coordinating Committee. Fitzgerald and General Carter evidently felt that the plan fell within the rubric of existing policy. Second, if Hall's story was true, as evidence suggests it was, this was another episode in the long-running mob plot, but with a new twist. In 1960 the CIA used Robert Maheu as a cut-out to enlist the help of the mob; now Roselli and Trafficante were using Martino and Pawley as cut-outs to enlist the help of the CIA. (Interestingly enough, Roselli met Harvey in Washington around June 20. Perhaps the fate of the raid figured in their discussions.)[71] And finally, in 1975, when Shackley testified before the Church Committee under the alias "Halley," he stuck to the original cover story and claimed that Martino (whose name he took days to remember) had been involved in an attempt to bring Soviet technicians out of Cuba.[72] The Kennedy administration by the middle of 1963 had revived its attempts to overthrow Castro, but without bringing the CIA and independent operators—including the mob—under control.

A year earlier, in June 1962, a young ex-Marine named Lee Harvey Oswald had returned to Dallas—where Hall and Hemming had found useful patrons—and in May 1963 he moved to New Orleans, another center of Cuban exile activity and the city where he had grown up among members of Carlos Marcello's mob. In June of 1963 he created a false chapter of a pro-Castro organization, and he was about to make contact with the New Orleans branch of the DRE. He had become friendly in Dallas with a mysterious White Russian, George de Mohrenschildt, who was now, like Loran Hall, involved in a plot to overthrow the government of Haiti. In September or October he appeared with Loran Hall at the home of Silvia Odio and had been pegged as a possible assassin of either Castro or President Kennedy, and in late September he tried and failed to enter Cuba legally through Mexico City, most probably in order to try to assassinate Fidel. In short, as we shall now see in detail, Lee Harvey Oswald by the middle of 1963 had become entangled in several different aspects of the events we have been following so closely, and on November 22, he stepped forward for all time as the key figure in the whole drama.

1 Robert Kennedy and James R. Hoffa. (Corbis–Bettman)

2 Vice President Richard Nixon and Prime Minister Fidel Castro leave Nixon's office April 19, 1959, after a two hour and twenty minute chat behind closed doors. (AP Photo)

3 Dwight D. Eisenhower with William Pawley. (Eisenhower Library)

4 A sketch made with the help of Antonio Veciana of Veciana's CIA case officer, "Maurice Bishop." (National Archives)

5 CIA agent David Atlee Phillips.

6 John Roselli, the mob's main contact with the CIA during the Castro assassination plots. (National Archives)

7 President Kennedy with outgoing CIA Director Allen Dulles (left) and his replacement, John McCone (right), September 27, 1961. (JFK Library; photo by Robert Knudsen)

8   Frank Sinatra, Peter Lawford, and Robert Kennedy, spring 1961. (Corbis–Bettman)

9   The McGuire sisters enjoy a night out in London in 1961. Phyllis McGuire and Sam Giancana are at right. (Corbis–Bettman)

10 Rolando Cubela, whom the CIA recruited to assassinate Fidel Castro under the code name AMLASH in 1962. (Corbis–Bettman)

11 Judith Campbell. (Corbis–Bettman)

12   FBI Director J. Edgar Hoover with President Kennedy and Attorney
General Robert Kennedy. (Corbis-Bettman)

13   From left to right: Attorney Jack Wasserman, his client Carlos Marcello,
Santo Trafficante, and Attorney Frank Ragano, Stella's Restaurant, Queens,
1966. In 1963, Ragano had carried Jimmy Hoffa's request that President
Kennedy be killed to Marcello and Trafficante. (New York Daily News)

14 Gerry Patrick Hemming and Loran Hall in Dallas, January 1963. (Dallas Morning News)

15 John Martino (2nd from left), shown with Eduardo Perez ("Captain Bayo," 3rd from left), during the preparation of the Bayo-Pawley raid, 1963. (National Archives)

16 Marina Oswald in Minsk.
(National Archives)

17 One of the famed "backyard photos" of Lee Harvey Oswald, March 1963.
(National Archives)

18 George de Mohrenschildt,
the mysterious acquaintance
of Jacqueline Kennedy, George
H.W. Bush, and Lee Harvey
Oswald. (Corbis–Bettman)

19 A meeting of a New Orleans area Civil Air Patrol unit, 1955. David
Ferrie is second from left; Lee Harvey Oswald, age 15, is at far right. (John B.
Ciravolo, Jr.)

20   Oswald handing out FPCC leaflets in downtown New Orleans, August 16, 1963. (National Archives)

21   Silvia Odio. (National Archives)

22 Jack Ruby with two of his employees at the Carousel Club. (National Archives)

23 The Kennedys arriving at Love Field in Dallas, November 22, 1963. (Corbis–Bettman)

24 The presidential limousine during the motorcade. (Corbis–Bettman)

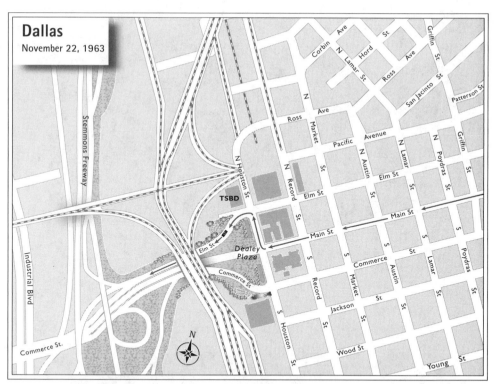

Dallas
November 22, 1963

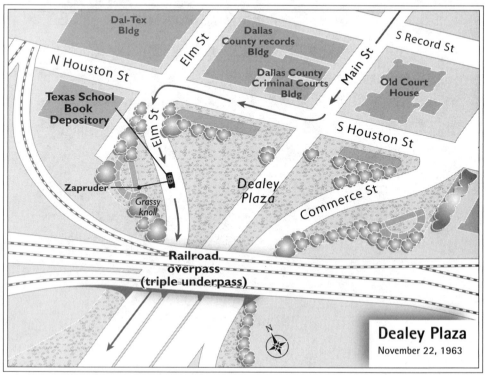

Dealey Plaza
November 22, 1963

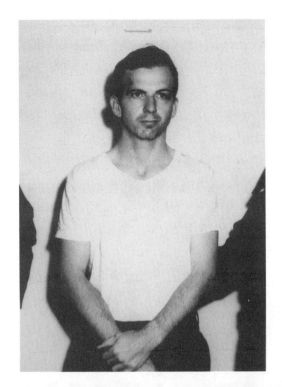

25 Lee Harvey Oswald
in custody after his arrest.
(National Archives)

26 Jack Ruby shoots Lee Harvey Oswald, November 24, 1963. (Bob Jackson)

27 Lyndon B. Johnson is sworn in as President on Air Force One, November 22, 1963. (JFK Library; photo by Cecil Stoughton)

28 Columnist Drew Pearson meets with President Johnson on January 16, 1967—the day he told the President about the CIA assassination plots against Castro. (LBJ Library; photo by Yoichi Okamoto)

PART II

Lee Harvey Oswald

8

A Defector Returns

On June 13, 1962, nearly three years after his defection to the Soviet Union in October 1959, Lee Harvey Oswald, aged twenty-two, returned to the United States with his young Russian wife, Marina Nikolayevna Prusakova, and their infant daughter, June Lee Oswald. Having first traveled from Minsk, where he was living, to Moscow in July 1961 to inform the American Embassy that he wished to return, Oswald spent the next ten months enduring bureaucratic delays, many of them related to a visa for his wife. At length, these problems were resolved, and on June 1, 1962, he borrowed $435.71 from the American Embassy (approximately $2,500 in today's dollars) to finance a train trip to Rotterdam and a boat to New York. While on the boat, he scribbled some extensive reflections on life in the Soviet Union, his purported disillusionment with it (which had struck the consular officer he saw in July 1961), and his reasons for leaving.[1]

No one, at this late date, will ever solve the Kennedy assassination by analyzing Oswald's character, and it will probably never be possible to know exactly why he went to Russia or why he returned. Despite numerous attempts by lone-assassin theorists to characterize him as a pathetic figure, he actually emerges from the FBI's lengthy investigation after November 22 as a most unusual and quite resourceful individual. His childhood was troubled: he never knew his father, his mother was an unstable personality, and—as Norman Mailer seems to have been the first to understand—he suffered a great deal in school, despite above-average intelligence, because of dyslexia, which was not properly understood during the 1940s and 1950s. Socially, he was withdrawn, and he had almost ascetic personal habits. Despite an occasional spree in the Marine

Corps, he never smoked and had apparently forsworn alcohol by the time he returned to the United States. He never showed any particular interest in food; only once did he show any desire for money; and he lived very cheaply throughout the last year and a half of his life.

Ultimately, his most important characteristics turned out to be secrecy, intrigue, and violence. From childhood onward, he was prone to sudden outbursts of aggression. In a 1952 interview with a New York City psychiatrist who saw him because of chronic truancy, thirteen-year-old Lee confessed to violent fantasies that he would not describe in detail. At about the same time, he pulled a knife on his sister-in-law, with whom he and his mother were staying in New York, causing Margaret and John Pic (Lee's half-brother) to ask them to leave. Mrs. Pic also said Lee struck his mother during an argument.[2] A schoolmate who knew him in junior high school later remembered that he was frequently involved in fights and was keenly interested in guns.[3]

During his Marine Corps service he was court-martialed twice, once for pouring a drink on a noncommissioned officer and once for possessing an unregistered revolver, with which he had inflicted a small wound on himself. When a fellow soldier was shot and killed by his own weapon while he and Oswald were on guard duty one night, some Marines evidently speculated that Oswald was responsible.[4] And in Dallas—although not, apparently, while in Russia—he beat his wife on several occasions, leading in one case to a brief separation.

Throughout his brief adult life, he showed a remarkable capability for hiding his thoughts, feelings, and plans. None of his family or acquaintances had the slightest idea that he was going to travel to Russia in 1958. He concealed a great deal from Marina during the last year of their life together, and he discouraged her from learning English in an evident attempt to remain her only contact with the outside world. His decision to leave Dallas for New Orleans in April 1963 was made suddenly, and no one in his intimate circle seems to have known that he was in Mexico during September of that year. Neither Marina nor any social acquaintance ever reported hearing Oswald express any hostility toward President Kennedy. After his arrest on November 22, he steadfastly denied having shot the President, or anyone else.

In 1967 Lee's older brother Robert Oswald published an interesting biography of Lee. While concluding that he had in fact killed President

Kennedy, he raised some important questions about his activities in the weeks before the assassination. He also provided an intriguing detail about his brother: that Lee's favorite television show, both in its original form and in daily syndication, was *I Led Three Lives,* the basically true story of Herbert Philbrick, a Boston advertising man who became a Communist and FBI informer during the 1940s.[5] The show ran weekly from 1953 until 1956 before going into syndication.

I Led Three Lives was inspired by the best-selling book of the same name that Philbrick published in 1952, several years after breaking cover to testify in the Smith Act trials of Communist leaders. Whether Lee Oswald ever read the book is not known, but since he was an enthusiastic reader and he loved the show, he may well have done so. The book tells how Philbrick unwittingly became involved in a Communist-front youth group in Cambridge, Massachusetts, in 1940–41. Philbrick contacted the Boston FBI office when he became aware of the Communists' role, and after he was asked to join the party, the FBI recruited him as a highly valued informant.

While the book (like the TV series) was undoubtedly screened by the FBI, Philbrick emerges as an intelligent and rather moderate man, who protests the bureau's persecution of well-meaning citizens innocently drawn into one front group or another.[6] More interesting, however, are certain aspects of his life as a spy that Oswald mimicked during the last seventeen months of his life. Like Philbrick, he tried to infiltrate several Communist organizations, including the Communist Party of the United States, the Trotskyite Socialist Workers Party, and, of course, the pro-Castro Fair Play for Cuba Committee. Like Philbrick, he evidently kept most of what he was doing entirely secret, even from his wife. (Philbrick's FBI handlers forbade him to tell his wife that he was working for them—that is, until they decided that she should join the party as well. They also told him repeatedly that the FBI would never acknowledge its relationship with either of them if they got into trouble.) And like Philbrick, Oswald found it convenient, at one point in his career as an infiltrator, to have the FBI call upon him and to tell them a largely fictitious story about his activities.

The critical question is whether Oswald undertook all these activities solely on his own initiative, or whether he was in fact guided by a governmental or nongovernmental sponsor. He did have contacts with both

the FBI and CIA in the months after his return from the Soviet Union—
directly with the FBI, and indirectly with the CIA through the enigmatic
George de Mohrenschildt, a White Russian petroleum geologist who
befriended Oswald not long after his return to the United States in the
summer of 1962. But it is far more likely that he embarked upon his career as a provocateur under unofficial supervision.

The truth about de Mohrenschildt's intelligence connections has
dribbled out over the last four decades, though some things may never be
known. What seems clear is that he contacted Oswald at the behest of
the Dallas Domestic Contacts Office of the CIA—with whom he had
had previous dealings—and that at the same time he was befriending
Oswald, he became involved in a CIA-sponsored attempt to topple the
Haitian government of François "Papa Doc" Duvalier in an effort to prevent Haiti from falling to Communism. Born to a White Russian family
of northern European descent in 1911, de Mohrenschildt lived in Belgium during parts of the 1930s before coming to the States in the early
stages of the Second World War. He already had some family connections there: his uncle, Ferdinand de Mohrenschildt, a tsarist diplomat, had
served in the legation in Washington during World War I and had married the daughter of Treasury Secretary William Gibbs McAdoo (who
was himself married to President Wilson's daughter) before dying of in-
fluenza during the great epidemic in early 1919.

Circumstantial evidence suggests that George de Mohrenschildt had
worked for Polish intelligence in Europe during the 1930s, and he apparently told his fourth wife that he had worked for French intelligence in
New York during the war.[7] When he attempted to join the OSS in 1942,
investigations turned up a number of serious allegations against him,
some relating to time he had already spent in Mexico.[8] After the war he
began a career as a "petroleum geologist" in Texas, Colorado, the Caribbean, and Yugoslavia.

De Mohrenschildt's personal life was stormy and exotic. His first two
marriages, in the 1940s and 1950s, each lasted less than a year. The third
one, in 1952, to Philadelphia socialite Winifred Sharples, an oil millionaire's daughter, ended in bitter divorce four years later. In 1964 Sharples
told the FBI that de Mohrenschildt had admitted to being a bisexual and
had complained that Americans were far too puritanical about that sort
of thing.[9] He also developed a reputation as a womanizer. His fourth

marriage in 1959 to a woman of White Russian descent—a dress designer named Jeanne LeGon—seems to have had a stronger foundation and lasted the remaining eighteen years of his life.

Wherever he went, de Mohrenschildt established himself as an extraordinarily sociable individual who could insinuate himself into almost any situation. While living in the New York area, he became well acquainted with Igor Cassini, brother of the dress designer Oleg Cassini, with William Randolph Hearst, Jr., with Mr. and Mrs. Hugh Auchincloss, the stepfather and mother of Jacqueline Bouvier Kennedy, and with Jackie herself.[10] His address book, now in the files of the House Select Committee on Assassinations, includes William Paley, the head of CBS; oilman and ambassador Ed Pauley; other leading Texas oil men such as Clint and Sid Murchison, who owned the Dallas Cowboys; civil engineer Ole Singstad, who built the Golden Gate Bridge; State Department official Angier Biddle Duke; and future president George H. W. "Poppy" Bush (the nickname appears in the book), whom the baron, as he liked to call himself, met through a nephew who had gone to preparatory school with Bush at Phillips Andover Academy in Massachusetts. In the spring of 1963 de Mohrenschildt claimed to know his fellow Texan, Vice President Lyndon Johnson, and he most certainly corresponded with Colonel Howard Burris, the vice president's military aide. Tall, handsome, and elegant, he spoke several languages fluently (including Spanish), and rarely failed to make a good impression. In 1976, when he contacted the CIA to complain that he was being followed, then-director Bush confirmed their long acquaintance and described him as a man who at one time had made and spent a very great deal of money.[11]

Despite many rumors of Communist, Nazi, and other sympathies, by 1957 de Mohrenschildt had established an intermittent relationship with the agency. The CIA may have helped him get a contract through the International Cooperation Administration—the forerunner of USAID—to do a petroleum survey of Yugoslavia, and J. Walton Moore, head of the Dallas Domestic Contacts Office, asked for a trace on him in late 1957. The reply forwarded certain derogatory information "which your Division will wish to consider in determining the extent and level of your use of Subject." Moore nonetheless commissioned de Mohrenschildt to write a series of reports on his trip to Yugoslavia and Poland, which reached CIA files. Moore also got to know him quite well socially.[12] By 1963 de Mohrenschildt had also come to the attention of Dallas FBI agent James Hosty, whose principal job was monitoring right-wing extremists but who knew the man as a relatively liberal member of the White Russian community.[13]

In 1960 one of de Mohrenschildt's children by Win Sharples died of cystic fibrosis. Late in that year, with his new wife, Jeanne, he embarked on a "walking tour" of Latin America that began in Central Mexico, took them to Guatemala in the weeks before the Bay of Pigs invasion, and ended in Haiti before their return to the United States in early 1962. De Mohrenschildt's son-in-law, Gary Taylor, later claimed they had spent much of the time at a friend's house in Guatemala, rather than walking.[14]

Yet a recently discovered document, combined with a revelation from Cuba, raises an astounding possibility about the trip through Mexico. The document involves Rolando Cubela, the anti-Batista revolutionary and Castro government official recruited into a conspiracy to poison Castro in December 1960. During that month Cubela traveled as Cas-tro's personal representative to international student meetings in Brazil and then Mexico.[15] On December 30 the FBI circulated a letterhead memorandum citing a Mexico City police source that Cubela had ar-rived in Mexico City from Brazil. For some unexplained reason, a copy of this memorandum was placed in de Mohrenschildt's CIA 201 file.[16] Cubela remained in Mexico City for about three months, and on March 9 he met a CIA contact who used the name Andrew Merton; they had a general discussion about the Castro regime.

Here the plot thickens. Andrew Merton's report referred to an earlier meeting with Cubela that had been aborted in Havana, though there is no specific evidence of de Mohrenschildt's having recently been in that city. Was Andrew Merton in fact de Mohrenschildt, or someone else? Cubela, years later, described his Mexico City interlocutor to Cuban au-thorities as "tall, an Anglo-Saxon type, more than 40, slim, [esbelto] large teeth, bags under his eyes, slightly receding hairline, well dressed, very so-ciable, good manners, and spoke perfect Spanish"—a description that matches de Mohrenschildt.[17] But it also matches David Atlee Phillips, who *was* in Havana in 1959–60 and was in touch with the DRE, of which Cubela had been a leader.[18]

In any case, exactly how de Mohrenschildt, who had been steadily employed for some time, and his wife, who had left her job, supported themselves during this long vacation is not clear. And during the period from 1960 through 1962 he was involved in an expensive lawsuit with Win Sharples over a trust fund her parents had established for their dead child, which eventually netted him about $10,000. Apparently, he was living on some combination of his wife's earnings and loans taken out from various Dallas financial institutions and regularly repaid with funds from unknown sources. After a business trip to Haiti, they returned to Dallas in late 1961 or early 1962. By that time, he had begun negotiations with the Haitian government on a substantial contract for geological exploration.[19]

The de Mohrenschildts became the Oswalds' best friends in Dallas, although at the time of the President's assassination they were in Haiti, where they had been since April. The baron gave some brief and somewhat misleading interviews to federal authorities right after the shooting, but it was not until March 1964, under pressure from the Warren Commission, that the FBI began thoroughly investigating his connection to Oswald. The bureau was not able to establish exactly how these two most unlikely friends met. The Oswalds had settled in Fort Worth in June 1962, living initially with Oswald's brother Robert, then moving in July into an apartment with Oswald's mother, and then in mid-August into an apartment of their own. While the Oswalds immediately made contacts among the Russian community in the Dallas–Fort Worth area, many of whom tried to help Marina in various ways, the baron himself claimed that he first met Oswald through a friend of his, retired Colonel Lawrence Orlov. Orlov apparently denied this in an interview with Edward Jay Epstein in the 1970s.[20]

De Mohrenschildt gave a very different version of the story to Epstein on March 29, 1977, which turned out to be the last day of his life. Epstein, a journalist writing his third book about the assassination, had agreed to pay $4,000 for a series of interviews. Now living in Florida, de Mohrenschildt was broke, and he believed that unidentified people were following him. He told Epstein that he had given the CIA assistance on certain matters for years in exchange for help in making contacts overseas for his oil business—for instance, in Yugoslavia in 1957. He had dealt, he said, with Moore of the CIA's Dallas office.

And Moore, he claimed, had begun telling him in late 1961 about a young ex-Marine, Lee Harvey Oswald, who had defected to the Soviet

Union, lived in Minsk, and would soon be returning to live in the Dallas area. De Mohrenschildt told Epstein that in the summer of 1962 an un-named associate of Moore's had given him the Oswalds' address and sug-gested that he meet them. The baron thereupon called Moore to ask for help in getting the lucrative oil exploration contract he was seeking in Haiti. He told Epstein that he would never have contacted Oswald with-out Moore's approval.[21]

Although the Warren Commission, the CIA, and the FBI became quite suspicious of de Mohrenschildt after the assassination, they cooper-ated to conceal Moore's identity. On March 13, 1964, the FBI asked de Mohrenschildt about a letter to a Dallas acquaintance in which he claimed that "an FBI man" had told him that Oswald was "harmless." De Mohrenschildt explained that he had met Moore in the late 1950s and thought he was in the FBI. He added, carefully, "I do not know anyone personally now with the FBI, the U.S. Immigration and Naturalization Service, or the Department of Justice," leaving out one critical three-let-ter agency.[22] De Mohrenschildt told the Warren Commission that he re-called talking about Oswald with Mr. "Walter Moore" [sic], whom he described in his April 23, 1964, testimony.

> Walter Moore is the man who interviewed me on behalf of the Govern-ment after I came back from Yugoslavia—G. Walter Moore. He is a Gov-ernment man—either FBI or Central Intelligence. A very nice fellow, ex-ceedingly intelligent who is, as far as I know—was—some sort of an FBI man in Dallas. Many people consider him head of FBI in Dallas. Now, I don't know. Who does, you see. But he is a Government man in some ca-pacity. He interviewed me and took my deposition on my stay in Yugo-slavia, what I thought about the political situation there.[23]

This forced Moore, on May 5, to write a long memorandum explain-ing that he had been put in touch with de Mohrenschildt in late 1957 by CIA headquarters to debrief him on his trip to Yugoslavia, and that he got to know him quite well. He stated, however, that he had not seen de Mohrenschildt since the fall of 1961, although he admitted having re-ceived a Christmas card from him in December 1963. The commission accepted that explanation, and no CIA evidence showing any other 1962–63 contact between de Mohrenschildt and Moore has ever come to light.[24] Moore was apparently using standard CIA practice: anything not actually documented in the files could safely be denied.

As Epstein argued in *Legend: The Secret World of Lee Harvey Oswald,* the story de Mohrenschildt told him in 1977 suggests that Moore used the baron to debrief Oswald. Circumstantial evidence further supports this argument. The FBI, apparently, had initial responsibility for debriefing Americans who returned to the United States after defecting to unfriendly countries. Thus, in 1959, the bureau had initially debriefed ex-Army soldier Loran Hall when he returned from Cuba and then informed the CIA that they could talk to him as well. Oswald's case was most similar to that of two other Americans, Robert Webster and Libero Ricciardelli, both of whom had also defected in 1959 and returned, respectively, in 1962 and 1963. The similarity in the three cases was sufficiently striking for a Defense Department official, Adam Yarmolinsky, to point it out in a call to the FBI on the evening of President Kennedy's assassination, without speculating about exactly what it might have meant.

Oswald was interviewed twice by FBI agent John Fain and two different companions, first on June 26, 1962, and then on August 16. On both occasions he was arrogant and largely unresponsive, denying making anti-American statements in Moscow or having any contacts with Soviet authorities. He promised to let the FBI know if any Soviet representatives approached him. During these interviews he denied, falsely, that he had either declared his intention to renounce his U.S. citizenship while in Moscow in 1959 or told U.S. authorities that he was going to give the Russians secrets he had learned during his Marine Corps service. Nonetheless, agent Fain eventually decided to close his case.[25] The CIA—specifically the SR/6, or "Soviet Realities" branch of the Soviet Russia division—had planned to contact Oswald if he returned, but according to his CIA file the agency made no attempt to debrief him directly, as they had both Webster and Ricciardelli.[26] Three days after Kennedy's assassination, a former SR/6 chief recalled that the agency had been thinking about approaching Oswald "through KUJUMP or other suitable channels . . . We were particularly interested in the OI [operational intelligence] Oswald might provide on the Minsk factory in which he had been employed." KUJUMP was the cryptonym for the agency's Domestic Contacts office.

On his boat trip home, Oswald had written what purported to be a diary of his experiences in Russia, and immediately upon his return he hired a typist to type up some of his recollections of working in Minsk. She produced about twenty pages. De Mohrenschildt told Epstein in 1977 that he personally encouraged Oswald to complete it, supplied photographs for it, received the final draft, and told Moore about it by October 1962.[27] And although de Mohrenschildt evidently did not say that he had given it to Moore, a CIA employee who has not been identified told the HSCA that in the summer of 1962 he had seen a contact report from a CIA field office describing the experiences of a former Marine who had worked in a radio factory in Minsk. But when the HSCA examined agency files on the factory, they did not find such a report.[28]

During the fall of 1962 Oswald moved from job to job and from place to place, but suddenly he came up with a large sum of money. Almost immediately after arriving, he had gone to the Texas State Employment Commission. Semi-skilled minimum wage jobs ($1.25 an hour) were plentiful in 1962, and Oswald's first employer was Leslie Welding Company in Fort Worth. From his earnings he began paying back the money he owed the State Department and his brother Robert, who had paid for his travel from New York to Fort Worth. But on October 7 de Mohrenschildt suddenly dropped Marina and their tiny daughter, June, at the home of his own daughter, Alexandra Taylor, and Oswald moved to Dallas. Mrs. Taylor had the distinct impression that her father was behind Oswald's move. Marina and Lee had been experiencing severe discord, and Lee had already beaten her at least once. Rather than tell Leslie Welding that he was leaving, Oswald simply failed to show up for work on October 8 and wrote a letter asking for his wages to be forwarded to Dallas. Marina later moved to another household where Russian was spoken.

Two days later, on Tuesday, October 10, Oswald went to the Texas Employment Commission office in Fort Worth and—skipping over his stay in the Soviet Union and claiming an honorable discharge from the Marines, which he did not have—immediately secured a new job at a typesetting firm, Jaggers-Stiles-Stovall. At $1.35 an hour, he worked with equipment that reduced photographs, arranged advertising displays, and photoset type. The company, curiously enough, also did a good deal of work for the Army Map Service, though its security was quite lax. Oswald used the equipment to fabricate several pieces of false identification for himself, including a draft card under the name A. J. Hidell and a driver's license for an O. H. Lee. His career as a secret operative had begun.

For the next two weeks, Oswald worked in Dallas and visited his family on weekends at the Taylors' in Fort Worth. On Sunday, October 28—the day the Cuban missile crisis was resolved—Oswald visited Marina again and told her that he wanted her to come to Dallas to live with him. No one knows where Oswald lived during much of October. He was registered at the YMCA from October 15 to October 19 but then effectively vanished, except on weekends. On November 4 the Oswalds moved into an apartment on Elsbeth Street in Dallas. But they separated again just a few days later after repeated arguments, and Marina moved in with yet another family, telling de Mohrenschildt, apparently, that she did not plan to return to her husband. Nonetheless, Oswald persuaded her to come back after another week or so. Young, very pretty, with an infant in hand and an obviously difficult husband, Marina showed a knack for attracting sympathy and gifts in her new home country—a talent that Oswald clearly resented.[29]

Meanwhile, his courtship of American Communist and Trotskyite organizations got under way. Oswald consistently complained to the de Mohrenschildts and others about his life in Russia, and he certainly could have been under no illusions as to the stature of the Communist Party of the United States of America in 1962. But in August of that year he began subscribing to the bi-weekly *Worker,* receiving it at a rented Dallas post office box. Several months later, in November or December, he sent the Hall-Davis Defense Committee—a Communist organization defending Gus Hall and Benjamin Davis, two Communist leaders—an offer to provide reproductions of any materials they might desire, and enclosed two prints of their leaflets. He apparently sent a similar offer to *The Worker,* and both the committee and the paper replied warmly but noncommittally on December 13 and December 19, respectively.[30] Here Oswald was following in the footsteps of Herbert Philbrick, who had produced materials for Communist organizations in his advertising office. The U.S. Communist Party, already shot through with informers and struggling with the FBI's COINTELPRO disruption campaign, was not about to trust an unknown volunteer from one of the most conservative parts of the country.

Simultaneous with his decision to subscribe to *The Worker,* on August 12 Oswald wrote the headquarters of an even weaker organization, the Trotskyite Socialist Workers Party in New York, using his home address. "Please send me some information as to the nature of your party, its policies etc.," he wrote, "as I am very interested in finding out all about your program." The embattled Trotskyites, also targets of a sustained FBI campaign, replied with a pamphlet on August 23, and Lee promptly ordered a copy of *The Teachings of Leon Trotsky,* which the SWP informed him on September 29 was unfortunately out of print. Upping the ante after his move to Dallas and his temporary disappearance, Oswald in late October sent an application to join the SWP, giving his Dallas post office box as his address.

National Secretary Farrell Dobbs replied on November 6, regretfully informing him that at least five members were required to form a branch, that individual memberships were not accepted (very possibly to screen out informers), and that no branches existed in the whole Lone Star State. They suggested, however, that he begin selling subscriptions to the SWP's weekly *Militant* and securing orders for other publications as a means of recruiting membership, and invited him to subscribe to two party publications. Oswald does not seem to have taken up this suggestion, and indeed there is no evidence of his proselytizing Marxism during this period at all. Not until December did he spend $1.00 on a four-month introductory subscription to *The Militant.* Early in the same month he apparently wrote a letter to the Socialist Workers Party headquarters offering to help with reproductions and enlargements, and he received a lengthier and friendlier but still noncommittal reply on December 9. In January he asked for, and received, an English translation of the *Internationale.*

He wrote the SWP in New York again on March 24, enclosing a clipping and apparently making a plea for affiliation, and they informed him in return that his name had been given to their youth branch, the Young Socialist Alliance, whose address they provided. Unfortunately, these last two letters and the accompanying clipping were apparently thrown out.[31] Oswald seems to have been trying to create a paper trail tying himself to

both the Communist Party USA and the SWP. His simultaneous courtship of both organizations—whom he must have known were bitter enemies—is rather suspicious. Nor did he ever apparently contact a single
member of either one. As it turned out, Dallas had a Communist Party
chapter of about seven members, but when the FBI used its "excellent
coverage" of the cell to ask early in 1964 if Oswald had ever contacted
them, the reply was negative.[32]

Oswald's move to Dallas brought a financial windfall—apparently
connected to de Mohrenschildt. In December 1962 and January 1963 he
suddenly paid off the remaining $396 of the $435 he had borrowed from
the State Department in Russia, making two payments of $190 and $206.
Epstein's analysis of his first six months back home suggests that, based
on what we know of his sources of support, Oswald could have paid this
debt off from his own resources only if he limited his expenses for his
family (excluding known rent but not accounting for his unknown accommodations in October) to just $53.32 a month. The Warren Re-
port's analysis basically reached the same conclusion, estimating that, as a
result of these payments, Oswald at the end of January 1963 had a total of
just $8.59 to his name. Even if Oswald and his family could have lived so
frugally, we have no explanation for the decision to pay $190 in Decem-
ber and another $206 in January, a month in which his known receipts
exceeded his known expenses by only $140.[33]

Another possible explanation came from Jeanne de Mohrenschildt,
George's wife, on November 22, 1963, when the two of them first heard
Oswald identified as the assassin at a cocktail party in Haiti. "Don't we
know someone by that name?" an airline stewardess heard her say to her
husband. "Yes, now I remember. He used to come to our house regularly
and you gave him money."[34] Shortly after the assassination, Gary Taylor
told the FBI that his father-in-law might have given Oswald money and
that he had an enormous influence over the much younger man.[35] In
2005 an old friend of de Mohrenschildt's, Nicholas Anikeefe—a former
CIA and State Department official—reported that de Mohrenschildt acknowledged giving the Oswalds financial help.[36]

Oswald's career as an assassin began between January and April 1963.
On March 3 the Oswalds moved yet again, to an apartment on Neely
Street in the same Oak Cliff section of Dallas. Sometime in mid-March
Oswald ordered a Smith & Wesson revolver from Los Angeles and a

Mannlicher-Carcano carbine from a mail-order house in Chicago, using the alias A. J. Hidell. Both items were shipped on March 20. On the last weekend in March, Oswald posed as Marina took the notorious photographs of him holding the pistol, the rifle, and copies of *The Worker* and *The Militant*. A day or two later, Oswald was given a week's notice at Jaggers-Stiles-Stovall, partly for poor performance and partly, it seems, because a Russian magazine he brought to work set off security concerns.[37] According to Marina, Oswald also persuaded her to write to the Soviet authorities requesting permission to return to the Soviet Union.[38]

By that time, Oswald had already been taking pictures of the home of retired General Edwin Walker, a right-wing activist now living in Dallas. General Walker had suddenly become a national figure in the spring of 1961 when a weekly in Germany, where he was commanding the 24th Division of the U.S. Army, reported that he was indoctrinating his troops in the ideology of the John Birch Society. That small organization, led by Robert Welch, a candy manufacturer from Belmont, Massachusetts, was warning the United States about the worldwide Communist conspiracy, whose ranks, according to Welch, included no less a figure than Dwight D. Eisenhower. After a brief investigation disclosed that the charge against Walker was true, President Kennedy relieved him of his command and had him transferred to Hawaii. The general immediately retired, went on the offensive, and was adopted by then-Democratic Senator Strom Thurmond of South Carolina as exhibit A in a campaign to prove that civilians were exercising too much control over the military and failing to take the Communist threat (which Thurmond identified with racial integration) seriously enough.

By December, the general was making speeches claiming that he had left the Army so as not to collaborate in the surrender of American sovereignty to the United Nations and suggesting that the United States had Communists in government.[39] Meanwhile, Drew Pearson reported having obtained a copy of a Defense Department legal opinion that the general's indoctrination of his troops during the 1960 election campaign clearly violated federal law, but the administration had declined to prosecute.[40]

Walker's statements became more and more shrill during 1962. Early in that year he went on a twenty-nine-city speaking tour with Billy James Hargis, a right-wing minister and founder of the Christian Crusade. In late September he showed up at Oxford, Mississippi, to encourage an insurrection against the Kennedy administration's ultimately successful attempt to get a black student, James Meredith, admitted to the University of Mississippi. Arrested and charged, Walker was freed on bond and returned to speak to the Mississippi legislature two months later. The government ultimately dropped the charges.[41]

Why Oswald decided to go after Walker is not entirely clear. The general had established a significant local reputation since settling in Dallas and had been mentioned more than fifty times in the *Dallas Morning News* between July 1962 and April 1963. His exploits had also received some coverage in *The Worker*, to which Oswald now subscribed, most recently in the April 2 edition in a story reporting Walker's call for an invasion of Cuba.[42] For whatever reason, Oswald appears to have visited Walker's neighborhood repeatedly during the first week in April. He returned on the night of April 10, and, it would seem, fired one shot at Walker while the general was sitting at his desk. Although this must have been a much easier shot than the ones Oswald fired on November 22 of that year, he missed, possibly because the bullet deflected, and he did not fire again. The FBI was unable to match the bullet to Oswald's rifle because of its deformity, but confirmed that it was fired by a Mannlicher-Carcano rifle and reportedly found a number of specific similarities with test bullets, though not enough for a definite match. Still, overwhelming evidence indicates that Oswald fired the shot.[43]

Earlier, Oswald had left Marina a long note in Russian giving her instructions on what to do if he did not return. When he did return very late that night—hours after the shot was fired around 9:00 p.m.—he evidently told her what he had done, saying that he was not sure whether he had hit the general or not. Oswald's role came to light because Marina hid the note in a Russian book, which the Secret Service discovered among her belongings shortly after the assassination. She told the whole story to Secret Service agents on December 3, 1963, describing Walker as "the head of the Fascist Organization in the United States." She also claimed to have told Oswald's mother, Marguerite, about the assassination attempt, but Marguerite denied that to the Warren Commission.[44]

Although neither the Warren Commission, the HSCA, nor any known secondary source has mentioned it, the FBI in the weeks after the assassination turned up evidence of an indirect connection between Oswald

and Walker. In the second week of December 1963, a Dallas lunch counter operator named Joe Loria told the FBI that he thought he saw
Oswald with an acquaintance of his named "Scottie" in March or April
of 1963. Bureau agents established that Scottie was actually an immigrant from Scotland named William Duff. Duff—sometimes known as
McDuff—was the leading suspect in the Walker shooting.[45] The Dallas
police got his name from an associate of Walker's, Robert Surrey, who
claimed he had seen at least two men with a 1963 Ford "lurking" around
the back of Walker's house on the Saturday evening before the shots were
fired. He said the car had no license plate.

If Surrey's story was true, Oswald evidently had an accomplice; if it
was false, Surrey was apparently trying to turn the attack on Walker into
some kind of conspiracy. He also explained that Duff had gone to work
in Walker's home office in December 1962 but had been discharged for
laziness on March 10. A certain Mrs. Whitley, who was briefly engaged
to Duff, reported having seen him driving four different cars, including a
1963 Ford. Walker himself reported that Duff visited him on April 13
and said he was in Phoenix at the time of the shooting.[46] Walker evidently did not believe him. He claimed to have received a phone call
from someone who said Duff confessed to taking the shot at him.

On June 6, 1963, Dallas police spoke to two private investigators hired
by an Oklahoma City law firm, evidently at Walker's request, to investigate Duff. They had made contact with him in late May and tried to entrap him by offering him money to kill Walker. Duff agreed to do so on
the night of June 10. Instead, however, Duff called James Hosty of the
FBI and told him about the arrangement. A few days later, Duff took a
polygraph examination at Dallas police headquarters and denied (1) having a grudge against Walker; (2) talking a shot at Walker; (3) remember-
ing who he was with on the night someone took a shot at Walker; (4)
providing information about the layout of Walker's house; (5) owning a
high-powered rifle; or (6) knowing who took the shot at Walker. The
examiner said he had answered all questions truthfully—with the exception of no. 3.[47]

The Dallas police dropped the case against him. When the FBI investigated him in January 1964 after the Kennedy assassination, several acquaintances described him as a hopeless liar. By the time bureau agents
found Duff himself on January 24, he was serving in the American Army
at Fort Sill, Oklahoma. He denied ever knowing or seeing Oswald—but

the coincidence that the lunch counter owner, who had no ax to grind, placed them together within a month of the shooting is striking.[48]

Another long-standing mystery relates to one of the pictures Oswald took at the back of Walker's house, which clearly shows the rear end of a 1957 Chevrolet sedan. The license plate has been cut out. While there is some controversy about whether it was cut out before the picture was discovered in the aftermath of November 22, 1963, or later, in either case one would like to know what Oswald or Dallas law enforcement wanted to hide.[49]

Remarkably, just a couple of weeks before he took his potshot at Walker, Oswald asked Marina to take the photos of himself with his rifle, his pistol, and copies of *The Worker* and *The Militant*. Had he been apprehended, the nation's newspapers would have featured those photographs as proof that a Marxist-Leninist and former defector had tried to kill one of the country's most notorious anti-Communists. Walker undoubtedly would have enjoyed the publicity, and many Dallas citizens voiced the opinion that the general had staged the whole thing. Six days after the assassination, on November 28, Marina Oswald actually told Secret Service agents that Lee had planned to send the pictures to *The Militant*. They might have proved extremely embarrassing to the paper, had he ever gotten around to it.[50]

The de Mohrenschildts, meanwhile, were planning a move to Haiti, and George's new contacts with the CIA were intensifying. His theoretically lucrative contract was printed in the Haitian paper *Le Moniteur* on March 13 as a governmental decree authorizing him to make a thorough geological survey of the island, for which he would receive $270,000 out of the profits of a sisal plant that he would operate. The American Embassy immediately expressed some skepticism that the plant could yield that kind of profit. When the de Mohrenschildts returned to Dallas to prepare for their move, they apparently found an envelope from the Oswalds that contained one of the pictures Marina had taken of the heavily armed Lee. Oswald had inscribed it to "George," and someone had written on the back, in Russian, "Hunter of Fascists, Ha-ha-ha." Handwriting experts later failed to definitively identify the writing as Marina's. The photograph was dated April 5, just five days before Oswald fired at Walker.

On the following weekend, the de Mohrenschildts stopped by to see the Oswalds yet again. "Lee," George said, according to Marina, "how did you miss General Walker?" Oswald flashed his wife a very disturbed look.[51] In March 1977 de Mohrenschildt told Edward J. Epstein that he had confided his suspicions about Walker's shooter to Moore at the CIA. After the assassination of the President, George obviously realized that he could be accused of withholding critical knowledge of Oswald's character. Not only did he conceal his inscribed copy of the Oswald photograph (which Epstein secured only after de Mohrenschildt's death), but he even told the first U.S. officials who interviewed him in Haiti after the assassination that his last meeting with the Oswalds had been in January 1963, when in fact he had seen them in April. Confronted with Marina's account a few weeks later, he said that he had been joking and that everyone assumed Walker had staged the shooting himself to get favorable publicity.[52]

De Mohrenschildt left for Haiti shortly after his conversation with Oswald—to help, apparently, in CIA efforts to overthrow the Haitian government. Considerable documentation on de Mohrenschildt's Haitian adventures is now available from two sources: CIA files and military Counterintelligence Source Files, or IRR files on both him and his Haitian associate, the banker Clemard Joseph Charles. Some of the most interesting documents survived only in Charles's files. Thus, for example, the CIA's file on Charles contains an August 2, 1962, memorandum by de Mohrenschildt on their projected joint enterprises. Their new Haitian Holding Company, he explained, "will bring native and American capital together, working thus along the lines of the Alliance for Progress." Each member would have the opportunity to participate in a large number of projects planned by the Charles Banque Commerciale, including tobacco, cheap housing, a wharf, a hydroelectric plant, lobster tail canning, coconut candy, a cotton wool plant, a local insurance company, a sisal plant, other factories already in existence, the telephone system, vegetable oil refining, oil container manufacturing, margarine manufacturing, sugar plants, and the "building of a casino." It also foresaw a dam and hydroelectric plant to be constructed by Brown & Root, the Texas contractors and long-time contributors to the campaigns of Lyndon Johnson. "This is the first attempt of bringing together the local Bank, capital, American financing and US Government help together. One should not forget the highly important geographical position of Haiti," he concluded.[53] The Holding Company does not seem to have gone very far.

On April 26, 1963, Gale Allen, a case officer from the CIA's Domestic Operations division, requested an "expedite check" on de Mohrenschildt from the CIA's Office of Security. The request itself is not contained in any of the CIA files on him released by the agency, but it is referred to in a December 1974 memorandum by Jerry Brown of the Office of Security Analysis. (Why that memorandum was written is a mystery, since no assassination-related investigations were in progress at that time.) On April 29, 1963, Allen received a summary of the 1958 trace reply, stating that certain derogatory information might be used to determine the appropriate level of contact with de Mohrenschildt.[54] In June 2004 Allen confirmed that he had been working in Domestic Operations, whose tasks included the establishment of U.S. companies abroad that could serve as fronts. He claimed to have no recollection of de Mohrenschildt and was quite sure that he was not involved in anything having to do with Haiti at that time. Allen therefore speculated that he made the request for the expedite check (which he did not recall) on behalf of someone else who had plans for de Mohrenschildt.[55]

Who that may have been we will probably never know, but the nature of de Mohrenschildt's mission emerged at once. The baron had managed to insert himself into another dramatic episode in the U.S. government's Caribbean policy: an attempt to overthrow Duvalier, the dictator who had terrorized Haitians for many years. Obsessed with the possible spread of Communism, the Kennedy administration by late 1962 had definitely established the objective of removing Duvalier before a Communist revolution could do so when his term of office expired on May 15, 1963. Having cut off most aid and encouraged contacts between the military attaché and dissident officers, the administration since October 1962 had hoped to provoke (although not run) a coup, and the CIA was thinking about sponsoring various exile groups.[56]

De Mohrenschildt had apparently become a player in this process. On April 26—the same day that Allen requested the "expedite check" on the baron—he returned from Haiti to Florida with Clemard Joseph Charles and immediately contacted Joseph Dreyer of West Palm Beach, Florida, who had met Charles in the late 1950s while Dreyer was helping Cubans grow jute in Cuba. Dreyer contacted an Army Intelligence operative named Dorothe Matlack in Washington, and she alerted Colonel Sam Kail, an Army Intelligence officer now living and working in Florida.

Kail spoke to Dreyer and found that Charles was traveling with George de Mohrenschildt, who "was arranging [an] appointment with VP Johnson who Morinshield [sic] knew from Texas and also from some business in which they are associated." Dreyer called Matlack to set up a debrief of Charles in New York City, his next stop. He also gave Charles a letter of introduction for Senator Ken Keating of New York, and another one for a Florida congressman.[57] Charles was in Washington on April 30 and visited the Executive Office Building but failed to get past one of the vice president's appointments secretaries.[58] Not wishing to stay in Washington because of segregation, Charles went on to New York.

The debrief was handled by a CIA operative from the New York Domestic Contacts office named Balog on May 3. Charles quickly got down to business. President Duvalier's lawful term would expire on May 15, and Charles hoped "that President Kennedy and other high U.S. government officials will give him an opportunity to present his plan to save Haiti from Duvalier and Communism." He asked for the utmost discretion, however, fearing that his family might be killed if anything leaked out. After some discussion he insisted on bringing de Mohrenschildt into the meeting, and the baron expressed complete confidence in Charles as "a potential leader in a democratic Haiti."[59] On May 6 Charles saw Balog again and requested that future conferences with U.S. officials take place without de Mohrenschildt present. He also claimed to have secured a $2 million, USAID-guaranteed loan from the Chase Manhattan Bank, subject only to a return to stability in Haiti. On May 7 he flew to Washington to meet with CIA personnel.[60]

On May 7 in Washington, Charles, de Mohrenschildt, Matlack, and Tony Czaikowski of the CIA met for lunch. The conversation, according to Matlack's record, dealt mainly with de Mohrenschildt's 1958 visits to Yugoslavia and Poland, but Czaikowski promised Charles another meeting with a "Mr. Green" later in the day. Shortly thereafter, however, Matlack heard by telephone that the State Department viewed Charles as shady and pro-Duvalier and that the CIA's Western Hemisphere branch had no further interest in him.[61] Army intelligence, however, cabled their representative in Haiti urging him to listen sympathetically to Charles, should he ever want to chat.

While in Washington, de Mohrenschildt also took Charles to meet an old friend of his, Nicholas Anikeefe, who now worked for the State Department, and Anikeefe took them to meet with Senator Claiborne Pell of Rhode Island, who spoke French.[62] Two weeks later, on May 21, de Mohrenschildt was back in New York speaking to a CIA contact code-named WUBRINY/1—apparently a cryptonym for a business, possibly the Chase Manhattan Bank. De Mohrenschildt said that Charles was back in Haiti and could be a great president "as soon as Duvalier can be gotten out . . . de Mohrenschildt said that he has obtained some Texas financial backing and that he has visited interested people in Washington regarding M. Charles candidacy."[63]

Whether de Mohrenschildt really knew Vice President Johnson is not entirely clear, although he easily could have. During 1964, while the CIA was covering (but not opening) his mail, he received one or two letters from a retired Colonel Howard Burris, who had been Johnson's military aide during his vice presidency. In any case, he had clearly involved himself in an attempt to overthrow the Duvalier government—a step the Kennedy administration considered a necessary prophylactic against the spread of Communism. We have no archival data on de Mohrenschildt's Haitian activities between June 1963 and early December, when he became of interest to the U.S. government because of his friendship with Lee Harvey Oswald.

Within days of de Mohrenschildt's departure from Dallas, the Oswalds set off for New Orleans. The FBI had recently become interested in him and Marina again. Agent Fain, who had been on the verge of retirement when he interviewed Oswald twice back in the summer of 1962, closed the Oswald case in August of that year—a decision that puzzled both Church Committee members and agent Hosty, who, in testimony before the committee in 1975, claimed that he inherited the case from Fain. But that was not the whole story. As early as July 19, 1962, Hosty had become interested in Marina, whom he suspected of being an intelligence agent, and suggested that a case be opened on her.[64] Hosty had placed both cases in "pending inactive" status, indicating that they would be taken up after six months. In March 1963, when he began searching for the Oswalds again, he discovered they had moved to Neely Street, but by the time he got there in May, they had left.[65]

The Oswalds moved to Louisiana, a center of anti–Castro activity, where Lee went to work for a leading anti-Communist activist, established and helped discredit a phony chapter of the Fair Play for Cuba Committee, and then in September left for Mexico, on a mysterious mission to reach Cuba that has never been satisfactorily explained.

9

The Big Easy

In late April 1963, Oswald suddenly left Dallas for New Orleans. In February the Oswalds had met a young woman named Ruth Paine, a Quaker pacifist who wanted to learn Russian. Arriving at the Oswalds' Neely Street apartment on April 24, Ruth discovered the Oswalds packed and ready to take a bus to New Orleans, where, Lee claimed, he would have a better chance of finding work. When Ruth offered to take in Marina (now pregnant again) and baby June at her house in Irving, Oswald cashed in Marina's bus ticket, shipped some belongings ahead, and left. After arriving in the city, he stayed for a few days with his Uncle Dutz and Aunt Lillian Murret, found work and an apartment, and asked Ruth Paine to drive his family to New Orleans, which she did. They remained there until September 23, when Ruth drove Marina and the baby back to Irving, Texas, and Oswald vanished for about sixty hours before reappearing on a bus between Houston and Laredo on his way to Mexico City.

During his five months in New Orleans—the city where he had lived until age four, and then on and off from junior high school until he joined the Marines—Oswald found work at the Reily Coffee Company and held that job until late July. Not long after arriving he began writing letters to V. T. Lee, the national director of the pro-Castro Fair Play for Cuba Committee (FPCC), about forming a chapter in New Orleans. He printed large numbers of handbills announcing his new chapter and began distributing them in at least three locations around New Orleans—Tulane University, the port of New Orleans area, and Canal Street—in May and June of 1963.[1] In July he secured a new passport.

In early August Oswald appeared at the store of Carlos Bringuier,

head of the New Orleans branch of the militant anti–Castro student organization DRE, and a day or two later he became involved in a street altercation with Bringuier and two other Cuban exiles over the FPCC
handbills, which outraged them. Arrested for disturbing the peace, he
spent one night and part of a day in jail. While there, he asked to see an
FBI agent and gave him a fanciful account of the extent of his FPCC activities. Later that month, he participated in a broadcast debate over Castro, Cuba, and the FPCC organized by New Orleans journalist William
Stuckey. On September 17 he obtained a tourist visa for Mexico, and a
week later he departed, apparently without telling anyone, including
Marina, where he was going. While in Mexico City, he tried and failed
to get a visa for immediate travel to Cuba.

New Orleans at this time was a major center of organized crime. Its
local boss, Carlos Marcello, was desperately fighting Robert Kennedy
and the federal government for the right to remain in the United States
and at liberty. He had been indicted on fraud charges in connection with
his forged birth certificate, and the trial was scheduled for the fall. But
New Orleans was also a center of Cuban exile activity, and Louisiana in
the summer of 1963 was the scene of two new operations mounted
against Castro by the DRE, organized crime elements, and a coalition of
other Cuban organizations. Just as these operations fell into a broader
pattern of anti–Castro activity headquartered in Miami, Oswald's key
moves that summer, including his altercation with the DRE, his radio
appearance in support of Castro, and his attempt to enter Cuba via Mexico, also fall squarely into a larger pattern of FBI and private right–wing
attempts to discredit Communist fronts and of continuing plots to assassinate Fidel Castro.

In May 1962, Stuckey had written in the *States-Item* that local Cubans
were raising money and sending arms to Florida for anti–Castro activities, working through unidentified soldiers of fortune and ex–Marines.
Those evidently included Gerry Patrick Hemming and his friend, former CIA asset Lawrence Laborde, who was trying to acquire a boat in
the area. Hemming wanted to build a training camp in Louisiana, and the
Cubans behind this operation were trying to affiliate with the DRE.[2] In
addition to offices in Miami and various Latin American capitals, that organization had branches in several American cities, including New Orleans, where a steady flow of Cuban refugees had settled since 1959. In

late 1962 the Kennedy administration began cracking down on the independent military activities of exile groups, insisting that any anti-Castro training bases be located outside the United States.

Early in 1963, as various sponsored and unsponsored exile groups started scrambling to find new homes in friendly Caribbean countries, the lower Mississippi Delta emerged as an alternative staging area for certain kinds of proscribed activities. The New Orleans FBI and Customs offices were far less vigilant than their Miami counterparts, and the two operations in Louisiana that were detected did not suffer any severe adverse consequences. But New Orleans was attractive to dissidents for another reason: as in Miami, Cuban exile activity in the city had been linked at least since 1960 to the deep pockets and underground connections of organized crime.

Leaders of the Miami headquarters of the DRE wanted to strike directly against Castro. But the CIA—its covert financial sponsor—insisted that it confine its activities to propaganda. Having scored a public relations and financial coup with its shelling of Havana on August 25, 1962, the Cuban student organization was determined to preserve a military role, and was using Miami Mafia contacts to procure arms. The DRE's New Orleans delegate, Bringuier, was a young, very anti-American Cuban who had settled in New Orleans in 1961, joined the Cuban Revolutionary Council in early 1962, and become head of the DRE's New Orleans branch in July of that year. Twelve months later, during the third week of July 1963, the FBI discovered a plan to bomb Cuba from a staging area near New Orleans. The operation involved both DRE members and organized crime elements with connections to Havana and the New Orleans area.[3]

In late July 1963 the FBI received a tip from a Miami Cuban named Orlando Pedroso Armores. Pedroso claimed to have inspected some practice bombs filled with sand at a house in Louisiana. The Cubans who took Pedroso there were expecting to find two B-26 aircraft, along with dynamite and fuses to make real bombs. Pedroso said the DRE was behind a plan to attack Cuba from an airstrip located some miles from the house. The CIA immediately denied any connection to the operation, and the Justice Department ordered the FBI to investigate it.[4] Pedroso further described three Cubans who had driven him to the site, two from Miami and one from New Orleans, and the FBI discovered that the station wagon he had traveled in had been rented in Miami by a DRE member named John Koch Gene. Koch, as he preferred to be called, appeared on a CIA list of DRE infiltrators for a November 1961 operation and had attended the World Youth Festival in Helsinki with other DRE members in July 1962.[5]

The case broke wide open on July 23, when U.S. Customs agent Wallace Shanley informed the FBI that the rented Chevrolet had been sighted with three prominent DRE members—Victor Espinosa Hernandez, Carlos Hernandez Sanchez, and Jose Basulto Leon—inside. The last two had taken part in the notorious DRE raid on Havana in August 1962, and in early June 1963 Espinosa and Hernandez had been arrested in Florida as they were about to launch a bombing raid on a Havana oil refinery. This new operation was clearly an independent raid of the sort the CIA had ordered the DRE not to conduct.[6]

Nevertheless, the New Orleans FBI office showed a notable lack of interest in the case. Even after Pedroso described the location in sufficient detail for agents to find it, the bureau did not bother initially to determine who owned the property. In the meantime, Pedroso had become frightened and now refused to sign an affidavit that could be the basis for a search warrant, though he agreed to accompany agents to the site. There, they discovered a padlocked trailer which had been rented in Chicago. On July 31, agents searched the property and discovered twenty practice bombs, twenty-five homemade fuses, twenty-six striker assemblies, twenty-five pieces of primer cord, twenty-four blasting caps, and a fifty-pound bag of nudoex, a chemical used to turn gasoline into napalm. The trailer contained forty-eight cases of dynamite, each including twenty-five sticks and weighing fifty pounds.[7]

By late July the FBI had discovered that the property was co-owned by William Julius McLaney of New Orleans, who had worked at the casino of the Hotel Nacional in Havana before Castro came to power. His brother Mike McLaney was part owner of the casino. But the key man in this latest plot to bomb Cuba turned out to be Victor Espinosa Hernandez, who had a long history as a revolutionary. He had worked with Rolando Cubela and Jose Luis Echeverria of the original DRE in 1957–58, acquiring arms for assassination attempts on Batista officials. By the time he left Cuba in 1960, he had come to know the McLaney brothers at the Hotel Nacional, and he listed McLaney as a reference when he arrived in the United States. He had also met Carlos Tepedino, who owned a jewelry store at the Nacional and whom he correctly identified as a CIA contact. He had trained in Guatemala in 1960–61 and infiltrated in and out of Cuba several times during 1961. He did not ac-knowledge belonging to the DRE, but in April 1961 the CIA assigned him the cryptonym AMHINT-25, using the standard designation for DRE members. His CIA operational approval had lapsed in May 1963, just two months before the plot was discovered.[8]

In 1963 Espinosa denied that Mike McLaney had financed the opera-tion or that he himself had driven the trailer to New Orleans. His con-federates Koch and Hernandez denied that the DRE had anything to do with the discoveries on the property, and the FBI, accepting this, dropped the DRE from the caption of the case.[9] No one was arrested. The bu-reau's conclusion, however, was mistaken. Backed by the McLaneys and assisted by other right-wing elements, the DRE was continuing its war against Castro. In 1978, testifying before the HSCA, Espinosa finally ad-mitted that Mike McLaney had put up the money for the operation and that Espinosa had purchased the weapons in the trailer from Richard Lauchli, an arms dealer in Collinsville, Illinois, who, he claimed, had come to his attention through the John Birch Society and their allies, the Minutemen. Lauchli had apparently sold weapons to several Cuban groups in Miami, sometimes working through Hemming.[10] Espinosa also eventually acknowledged driving the trailer to Louisiana.[11] But the DRE member from New Orleans whom Pedroso had met was not identified, and Bringuier was never even questioned.

The McLaney brothers had a variety of interesting connections. In addition to the Louisiana property where Espinosa stored his dynamite, William McLaney owned Gibbons Race Track Feed, which presumably serviced race tracks in the vicinity.[12] Mike McLaney claimed numerous famous acquaintances in the world of sports, including Baltimore Colts owner Carroll Rosenbloom, who in 1958 put up more than a quarter of McLaney's $800,000 interest in the Hotel Nacional and apparently took a financial bath himself when Castro shut the casinos down.

In later years Mike McLaney vehemently denied any mob connec-tions and even claimed never to have paid off Batista to keep his casino in operation.[13] Rosenbloom knew the Kennedys well, and McLaney told HSCA investigators in 1979 that he had played golf with both Joseph P.

Kennedy, Sr., and John F. Kennedy in Palm Springs. McLaney also engaged in a series of high-stakes golf games with New York Yankees co-owner Dan Topping.[14] Regarding Castro, McLaney told the HSCA investigators in 1979, "I believed in fighting Communism and thought the SOB should be killed." He acknowledged helping the exiles, including Tony Varona—the principal in the Roselli plot. Another player in the Louisiana plot was Sam Benton, a private investigator who was born in Poland and had lived in Cuba. When questioned by the FBI in August 1963, Benton admitted helping Espinosa look for a bomber and acknowledged an acquaintance with Juan Orta—the associate of former Cuban president Carlos Prio who was recruited to poison Castro in late 1960—but Benton lied about the source of Espinosa's funds.[15]

The DRE-backed bombing plot was only one of two elaborate exile operations in Louisiana during the summer before President Kennedy's assassination. The second was a training camp in Lacombe, Louisiana, led by Victor Paneque Batista. Known as Commandante Diego, Paneque had been a Castro revolutionary and high police official in Cuba before defecting in November 1959. Like Eloy Gutierrez Menoyo, he had drawn some suspicion as a possible undercover agent for Castro, but the CIA registered him as a source in August 1962. Paneque worked with Frank Sturgis and Orlando Bosch of the MIRR, and journalist Jack Anderson described him in his 1961 *Parade* article about Sturgis.[16] He was now working with the Christian Democratic Movement (MDC) and its leader, Laureano Batista Falla.

The MDC in early July had made a unity pact with Commandos L, led by Tony Cuesta, to make naval and air strikes against Cuba. They were also seeking $50,000 from Prio for military aid, and they were talking to the DRE about joining the unity pact as well.[17] These independent exile groups had evidently gotten the message that their bases now must be moved outside the United States, and (like Manuel Artime's MRR and Manuel Ray's JURE) were seeking locations in other Caribbean countries. In early July several MDC leaders met with Luis Somoza, the Nicaraguan dictator, who offered them a base. From there, they planned raids that would provoke Castro to retaliate and provide a pretext for military intervention by Caribbean countries.[18]

The MDC and Commandante Diego evidently decided to get things going in the lower Mississippi Delta before negotiations with Somoza were complete. On July 18 an MDC member told the CIA in Miami that thirteen men were training at an MDC camp on a ranch in Mississippi, pending their transfer to the projected new base in Nicaragua. A few days later the CIA learned that another nine men had left for New Orleans, bound for a training camp nearby, and that Commandante Diego was looking for more recruits in Chicago.[19] Apparently all these men were headed to the same facility. In 1967, when the camp came to light in the course of District Attorney Jim Garrison's investigation into the Kennedy assassination, an internal CIA memorandum quoted a June 25, 1963, report of a camp about fifteen miles from New Orleans, "after crossing a very long bridge right at entrance of state of Louisiana." The site was on a ranch "which belonged to some American millionaires who were defraying expenses for maintenance of men in training and providing equipment." The millionaires were not identified.[20]

On September 1, JMWAVE in Miami got a call from a Cuban close to the MDC. He reported that one of the organization's members at the Louisiana camp, Fernando Jose Barcena, had been caught writing a letter to Carlos Lechuga, a Cuban Communist diplomat who was once ambassador to Mexico and was now ambassador to the United Nations. Barcena had been brought to Miami immediately, where a group led by Laureano Batista Falla was beating a confession out of him. JMWAVE promptly informed the FBI, which sent agents to the site to free Barcena. He repudiated much of what he had just confessed to the MDC.[21] This incident evidently came to the attention of Bringuier, indicating that the New Orleans branch of DRE was in contact with the training camp as well.

Warren DeBrueys of the New Orleans FBI office heard about the camp through informants in late July but was repeatedly assured by them that the men had been recruited to work in the lumber business in Guatemala by one Rudolf Richard Davis. Although DeBrueys never bothered to visit the camp and apparently put the case aside in early August, he interviewed Davis on October 2 and submitted a full report. Davis explained that he had been born in New York in 1934 but lived in Cuba from 1936 to 1961. He moved to New Orleans and become involved in lumber and insurance late that year. He assured DeBrueys that the men should have understood they were going to a lumber camp, and that they had been persuaded to return to Miami after the well-publicized seizure of dynamite on Bill McLaney's property. DeBrueys was satisfied.[22]

Four years later, when Davis was interviewed in Houston as a result of the Garrison investigation, he finally told the truth. The camp, he said, had been established on the "DeLaBarre estate" with help from the John Birch Society, partly to give prominent members a chance to see training taking place. He also said that he had met Lee Harvey Oswald twice during 1963 in New Orleans, once while passing out leaflets and once at Oswald's apartment, where Davis claimed he was trying to get information about Oswald's pro-Castro activities.[23] No one ever pursued this important connection between Davis and Oswald.

Anti-Castro organizations, then, were operating in Louisiana with assistance both from gambling figures like Mike McLaney and from wealthy arch-conservatives who have never been identified. The same network included Carlos Marcello, one of the richest mob bosses in the country; David Ferrie, his personal pilot, who had known Lee Harvey Oswald in the 1950s and had worked with anti-Castro Cubans; and Guy Banister, a retired FBI agent who was assisting Marcello and who also had patronized Cuban causes. Marcello had been involved in the CIA-Mafia plots against Castro from the very beginning and thus would have been quite likely to encourage these and other new efforts being launched from his territory.[24]

In 1976, a key witness gave the Church Committee explicit information about Marcello's connection with the anti-Castro murder plot. Edward P. Morgan was a Washington criminal attorney of the stature of Edward Bennett Williams, the attorney for Hoffa, John Connally, and many others. He never became quite as famous because he preferred to avoid having his cases come to court, but his credentials were in some ways more impressive. A former FBI agent, he was counsel in two of the most famous congressional investigations of the mid-twentieth century, the Pearl Harbor investigation of 1946 and the Tydings Committee investigation of 1950, which examined Senator Joseph McCarthy's charges that the State Department was infested with Communists. Morgan represented his fellow former FBI agent Robert Maheu and Johnny Roselli in the 1960s and 1970s. In early 1967 he leaked a version of the story of their assassination plot against Castro to Drew Pearson and gave the story to the FBI.

The Church Committee called Morgan in March 1976, months after it had issued its assassinations report, because committee members had found his 1967 FBI interview and wanted to analyze the bureau's response to the Kennedy assassination. He repeated that Roselli had heard, sometime after the capture of his assassination squad in Havana in March 1963, that Castro had expressed a desire to retaliate against Kennedy. Then he said, suddenly, that just in the last forty-eight hours he had heard some "startling" information from a client that bore upon this matter, and offered to discuss it on or off the record. Unfortunately, he provided the name off the record but promised to contact his client as soon as the hearing was over to see if he would testify.

Later in the session, Morgan became somewhat worried about his client's reaction to this request and asked if the committee might go to him, rather than have him come to Washington. Counsel Paul Wallach said that they might. Later, asked again for specific knowledge about a retaliatory team, Morgan slipped up and revealed an important piece of information. "Certainly what I told you today about this New Orleans man may provide some information on it," he said, "but not I."[25]

Three attorneys for the committee—Wallach, Michael Epstein, and James Johnson—took part in this questioning. Wallach and Epstein have since died, and Johnson does not recall the exchange. Yet it seems significant that when John Roselli was called back for his fourth and last interview just one month later, Wallach (who knew the name of Morgan's source off the record) suddenly raised the name of Carlos Marcello and asked if he had been involved in any assassination conspiracies. After spontaneously denying that he had ever met Marcello, Roselli said he had no knowledge that Marcello had been involved in any assassination plots against Castro, the President, or Robert Kennedy.[26]

It would have made perfect sense for Marcello to have consulted Edward P. Morgan in 1976 about his long-running deportation case, all the more so since Marcello had been close to Jimmy Hoffa, whom Morgan had represented while Hoffa and Marcello were desperately trying to get Louisiana Teamster Ed Partin to recant his testimony against Hoffa. In short, there is every reason to believe that Marcello was the "New Orleans man" to whom Morgan referred, and that he, along with Roselli, Giancana, Trafficante, and Russell Bufalino of Buffalo, was involved in Mafia plots against Castro as late as the summer of 1963.

Around that time, Marcello was also involved with two other New Orleans men who worked with anti-Castro Cubans: his pilot David Ferrie, and private investigator Guy Banister, formerly of the FBI. Both men had been employed since 1961 by Marcello's New Orleans attorney, G. Wray Gill, to help prepare Marcello's defense in his forthcoming trial on fraud charges. These men had a variety of underworld connections, and Ferrie certainly—Banister, quite probably—knew Lee Harvey Oswald.

Despite being a rather bizarre individual, in both appearance and behavior, Ferrie had nonetheless become a pilot for a major airline and won the confidence of one of the leading mob bosses in America. Born in Cleveland in 1922, he graduated from college, tried several times to join the Catholic priesthood, and studied medicine. Because he suffered from a rare disease that caused all his body hair to fall out, he wore a striking red wig and false eyelashes. Eastern Airlines hired him as a pilot in 1951 and transferred him from Miami to New Orleans. His file at Eastern included a 1953 letter from airline president Eddie Rickenbacker thanking him for his effective work promoting air travel in the Southwest.[27] He was active in the Civil Air Patrol there in the early through the mid-1950s, where he worked with young boys and frequently socialized with them in his home. He was forced to give up his CAP affiliation after numerous complaints from parents about his homosexual advances toward cadets, but he continued to attend meetings for some time. Meanwhile, he became a rabid right-winger who frequently criticized presidents Roosevelt, Truman, Eisenhower, and Kennedy for being too soft on Communism.

Ferrie owned a plane of his own, in which he traveled around the South. Between 1959 and 1961 he struck up an alliance with Sergio Arcacha Smith, head of the New Orleans branch of the Cuban Revolutionary Council. According to another local Cuban exile, Carlos Quiroga, Ferrie was supplying Arcacha Smith with funds in denominations of $100. Ferrie took a vacation at the time of the Bay of Pigs invasion, but nothing is really known about what he was doing. On July 18, 1961, Arcacha Smith wrote Rickenbacker a remarkable letter, claiming that Ferrie's unspecified efforts had "revitalized" the CRC in the wake of the Bay of Pigs and that as a result "the re-harassment of Castro has begun . . . At this time our efforts are reaching a climax." Time, however, was growing short. He continued:

> The reinvigorating of our program was the result of the prodding of Captain Ferrie, and his associates, here in New Orleans. Through him we

have been able to get the best advice in affairs political, economic and military. Further, he has helped us straighten other affairs. As a result our organization is running smoother every day and our operations have begun. In addition Captain Ferrie has been assisting in obtaining needed equipment. Likewise, he has been assisting in the handling of the refugees.

Since events are approaching a climax we sorely need his advice on a day to day basis. Knowing your own often demonstrated patriotism, we are requesting that Captain Ferrie be given either a 60 or 90 day leave with pay so that the work at hand can be completed. At this time he holds in his hands so many threads which pertain to the security of the Caribbean area that no reasonable substitution could be made.[28]

Rickenbacker denied the request. About a month later, Ferrie's troubles began when he was arrested for homosexual activities with three teenage boys, leading to an FAA investigation that drew in the FBI. When the bureau interviewed him on August 22, Ferrie said he had been spending about three days a week helping the CRC obtain food and medicine but denied trying to procure arms. In October, after an Eastern Airlines superior questioned him about his arrest, he wrote a long letter detailing his anti-Castro activities and implying that he was the victim of a Communist conspiracy. Some Civil Air Patrol personnel acknowledged that while Ferrie at times seemed crazy, he had done excellent work building up the local organization. In late October the bureau heard from a Border Patrol official that Ferrie was trying to purchase a C-47 to help dispose of an arms cache he was holding.[29]

In 1967 an informant confirmed that Ferrie had been holding weapons, and a young Marine who had known Ferrie reported that in late summer 1961 Ferrie had offered to send him and a companion to an undisclosed location in Latin America to prepare to invade Cuba.[30] Carlos Bringuier told the New Orleans *Times-Picayune* that Ferrie had also worked with the New Orleans DRE, but the organization dropped him because of his homosexuality.[31]

In early 1961 Ferrie was hired by Marcello or his lawyer to shadow John Duiguid, a Justice Department attorney assigned to the Marcello case, on a trip to Guatemala where Duiguid was investigating Marcello's famous fake birth certificate.[32] In early 1962 the Border Patrol heard rumors that Ferrie had flown Marcello back into the United States in June 1961.[33] The sex charges against him were dropped in the fall of 1962 when the young witnesses suddenly recanted their statements, but Eastern Airlines began proceedings to terminate his employment.[34] Gill agreed to represent Ferrie in a grievance hearing in exchange for any additional help Ferrie might provide in preparing Marcello's defense, and Ferrie made more trips to Guatemala during 1963. Gill eventually made a similar arrangement with private eye Guy Banister, who was also assisting in Marcello's defense. Meanwhile, lengthy hearings at Eastern in the summer of 1963, in which Banister appeared as a character witness for Ferrie, failed to reverse the suspension, and Ferrie was terminated for making false statements on his original employment application and for moral turpitude.[35]

Banister had served in the FBI for twenty years, until 1955, when he retired as special agent in charge of the Chicago office. Afterward, he worked for two years for the New Orleans police as a deputy chief. In 1956 Banister helped coordinate New Orleans hearings by a subcommittee of the Senate Internal Security Committee designed to expose Communists in the New Orleans area. In a typical performance, the subcommittee, led by Senator James Eastland and accompanied by committee counsel Robert Morris, called about half a dozen suspected Communists who refused to answer questions based on their First and Fifth Amendment rights.[36]

After leaving the police department because of erratic public behavior, Banister opened his own detective agency. His clients included the Louisiana Sovereignty Commission, which was designed to neutralize civil rights activists, and the New Orleans Cuban Revolutionary Council. In 1967 a former FBI agent and firearms expert named I. A. Nitschke told the New Orleans District Attorney's Office that he had met two Cubans in Banister's office in late 1961 who were looking for arms to buy, and four different witnesses, including Nitschke, mentioned meeting David Ferrie there. One, a typist named Mary Helen Brengel, who did some work for Banister relating to Marcello's trial, expressed her surprise that her employer was helping the local mob boss. He replied that they were defending Marcello because his rights were being violated.[37]

That Oswald might have been connected to Ferrie was suggested to the New Orleans police and the FBI on November 24 and 25, 1963, by an unreliable New Orleans private investigator named Jack Martin, who had worked with Banister. (Banister, in fact, had pistol-whipped Martin on the evening of the Kennedy assassination.) On Sunday, November 24, Martin told the police that Ferrie had known Oswald and given him firearms instruction at the Civil Air Patrol. When confronted the next day by FBI agents, he said this was all speculation.

Ferrie, who had left town on November 22 for a visit to the Houston, Texas, area with two friends, finally came back to New Orleans to face the district attorney, the Secret Service, and the FBI on Monday, November 25, when Oswald was safely dead. To the best of his knowledge, he said, he had never met Oswald in the CAP or elsewhere. Ferrie on November 25 emphatically denied to Secret Service agents that he had been in Dallas for the last eight or ten years.[38] In a second interview on November 27, Ferrie discussed his work for Arcacha Smith and the CRC. He also acknowledged that he might have said publicly that Kennedy should be shot for failing to provide air cover at the Bay of Pigs, but he once again denied any connection with Oswald.[39]

Although the FBI essentially accepted Ferrie's denial, he was not telling the truth, and the bureau immediately found a witness who contradicted him. On November 23 a childhood friend of Oswald's named Edward Voebel appeared on television to say that he and Oswald had been in CAP, and Ferrie had been their commander.[40] Voebel, who turned out to be probably Oswald's best friend in that period, repeated his story to FBI agents two days later.[41] Two years earlier, the FAA had found that Ferrie had successfully encouraged at least two other cadets to join the Marine Corps, as Oswald did.[42]

Still, on November 28, the New Orleans FBI office dismissed Martin's allegations entirely.[43] Fifteen years later, however, the impressive HSCA investigation found no less than five people who confirmed that Oswald and Ferrie were active in the CAP squadron at Moisant Airport in the second half of 1955, even though Ferrie, by that time, had officially been dropped from CAP.[44] And the question was apparently resolved beyond any doubt in the 1990s, when a photo surfaced clearly showing both Ferrie and Oswald at a picnic for CAP cadets and instructors.[45]

During the FBI's brief investigation of Ferrie, attorney Gill confirmed that he had hired him at $300 a month, but precisely what Ferrie did for Gill remains somewhat mysterious. The telephone records of Gill's office, originally obtained by the Garrison investigation and later analyzed by a researcher named Peter Whitney, showed that Ferrie called Gill's office from the Dallas–Fort Worth area at least twelve times in 1962–63, half of them in 1963. He also made several calls from the Houston area. Meanwhile, he called a great many numbers in Dallas–Fort Worth and Houston, as well as numbers in Miami and in Opa-Locka, Florida, whose owners were never identified. Most of the month of November 1963 was missing from the records.[46] Nevertheless, from all the available evidence it is clear that Oswald knew Ferrie, and Ferrie in turn was closely linked to both Marcello and the New Orleans anti-Castro Cuban community.

More specific but controversial data are available relating to Oswald's possible links to Banister. Some of his FPCC leaflets—apparently from June 1963 onward—bore the address "FPCC 544 Camp St." This was one of two addresses used by a corner building, the other being 531 Lafayette Street, where Guy Banister Associates had offices. The New Orleans Cuban Revolutionary Council also used that address, though the CRC had vacated its office space by the summer of 1963. The New Orleans FBI office must have had one of Oswald's leaflets on hand at the time of the assassination, because by November 25 they had already interviewed the building's owner, Sam Newman, who had no memory whatever of Oswald but who had received a mysterious call from an unidentified man claiming he wanted a room in which to hold meetings. The Secret Service discovered those leaflets in the days after the investigation and also spoke to Newman and others in the building but could not get any information on the man who had supposedly tried to rent an office. On November 25 the FBI interviewed Banister for the first and last time, but only to confirm that he had helped the CRC rent space in the building.[47]

Banister died of a heart attack only six months after the assassination, and fifteen years later four witnesses told the HSCA that Oswald had varying degrees of connection to him. The first two witnesses—Banister's brother Ross, also a law enforcement officer, and Banister's friend and former FBI man Ivan Nitschke—said Banister was aware of Oswald's leafleting during the summer of 1963, although they had no information that he knew him.[48] The third witness, Banister's secretary and long-time friend Delphine Roberts, gave two interviews, on July 6 and August 27,

1978. In the first she claimed that Banister had been angry at the owners of their building for allowing Oswald to use the 544 Camp Street address but denied ever seeing Oswald. In the second interview she claimed to have held back critical information because she thought both Banister and the now-dead Ferrie, once a frequent visitor to the office, had been murdered shortly after the assassination. Now she claimed that Oswald visited the office twice, once with Marina, and asked for employment.[49]

The HSCA report stated discreetly that Roberts's reliability could not be determined. But her actual interviews leave little doubt that she was an extreme right-wing nutcase, a paranoid anti-Communist and segrega-tionist whose testimony cannot be taken seriously. A political activist and sometime candidate for local office in her own right, she explained to in-vestigators in her first interview that she "became concerned about our country when President Roosevelt and his Negro wife Eleanor got the U.S. into the United Nations which has its charter based on the Com-munist Manifesto." She had eventually worked with Leander Perez, the arch-segregationist boss of Plaquemines Parish, who was excommuni-cated from the Catholic Church because of his violent opposition to in-tegration. In the second interview she corroborated some of Jim Garri-son's fantastic accusations against businessman Clay Shaw as well.[50]

Another more intriguing witness, however, confirmed to the HSCA that Banister knew Oswald. He was William Gaudet, a New Orleans journalist with long experience in Latin American affairs and an on-going relationship with the CIA. As Gaudet explained in 1978, he had worked on South America for Nelson Rockefeller when he was assistant secretary of state during the Second World War, and he had written for David Lawrence, the conservative Republican editor of *U.S. News & World Report*. In 1948 Gaudet began writing a newsletter on Latin American affairs that was purchased in bulk by the CIA and, he added (perhaps facetiously), the KGB.

The FBI interviewed Gaudet after the assassination because he and Oswald had received Mexican tourist cards on the same day in Septem-ber 1963, but they did not ask him anything else about Oswald. Now Gaudet said that he had seen Oswald handing out leaflets around the New Orleans Trade Mart on several occasions that summer. He added, "I saw [Banister] in deep conversation with Lee Harvey Oswald on Camp

Street right by the post office box. They were leaning over and talking and it was an earnest conversation . . . It seemed to me that Guy Banister wanted Oswald to do something. This is the way it seemed to me."[51]

When Oswald first arrived in New Orleans, he immediately went to see his most direct contact with Marcello's organization—his Uncle Dutz Murret. Although the Warren Commission was content with vague and inaccurate characterizations of Murret's occupation in his and his wife's testimony, the HSCA established clearly that Murret was a bookie working with Sam Saia, one of Marcello's closest associates.[52] Certainly it would have been easy enough for Murret to have passed it through the grapevine that his somewhat notorious nephew, the ex-Marine who had defected to Russia and returned with a Russian wife, was back in town.

The job that Oswald found within two weeks of arriving in New Orleans connected him to yet another anti-Castro movement. Cleaning coffee machines at the Reily Coffee Company was certainly a step down from the commercial photography positions he had held in Dallas, but the company's president, William Reily, was deeply involved in a private propaganda organization attempting to combat Communist influence in Latin America and the United States, the Information Council of the Americas. INCA was the brainchild of Edward Butler, a young drop-out from Loyola University in New Orleans who had become interested in psychological warfare while serving in the Army from 1957 to 1959. A member of a distinguished New Orleans family, Butler had become devoted to the cause of the late Senator Joseph McCarthy, and after discharge from the Army he wrote an article suggesting (as William Pawley did some years later) that Communism was winning the global propaganda battle by default.

The Cuban revolution of 1959 hit the New Orleans business community and shipping industry hard, and Butler took advantage of their frustration to form two successive anti-Communist organizations. The first was Free Voice of Latin America, founded in 1960, which was intended to function like Radio Free Europe and broadcast anti-Communist material southward; it collapsed in early 1961. In May, about a month after the Bay of Pigs, he started INCA. Although personally Butler belonged to the extreme right, he made sure that his new organization took relatively moderate positions and stayed away from hot-button right-wing issues such as segregation—rather like a Communist front in reverse.

Butler's leading financial angel was Dr. Alton Ochsner, founder and head of the Ochsner Clinic, whose many Latin American patients included members of several ruling families. In 1964 Ochsner—an extreme right-wing segregationist—wrote a Mississippi acquaintance, agreeing that the real extremists in America were men like Nelson Rockefeller and Senators Jacob Javits and Ken Keating, not the John Birch Society or the Ku Klux Klan. He also endorsed an anti-Semitic white supremacist tract by Wilmot Robertson, *The Dispossessed Majority.* Ochsner apparently helped recruit a number of prominent businessmen as supporters, including William B. and H. Eustis Reily of the Reily Coffee Company.[53] During the summer of 1963 Butler also made contact with Gene Methvin, editor of *Reader's Digest,* and, through him, with General Edward Lansdale, former head of Operation Mongoose, and perhaps with Frank Hand of the CIA, who had been detailed to Lansdale.[54]

Butler planned to fight Communism by creating a "conflict corporation" that would train "conflict managers" who could master the arts of propaganda and subversion. Some years later, after securing the patronage of Schick Razor millionaire Patrick Frawley (the founder of Moral Re-Armament) and moving to Los Angeles, Butler explained his concept to a young journalist named Garry Wills. "The conflict manager," he said, "will infiltrate troublemaking groups, try to divert them from their goals, break up their structure, create internal dissension . . . All the years I practiced in New Orleans, we never had any trouble."[55]

Butler's proudest moment in New Orleans turned out to be a successful campaign to "expose" and discredit Lee Harvey Oswald's chapter of the Fair Play for Cuba Committee. Butler's behavior fell squarely into a pattern of FBI activities against that organization from 1961 to 1963, and it raises a number of questions about Oswald's own motives. In 1963 the FPCC was the target of a full-scale FBI counterintelligence operation, aided by the anti-Communist committees of the House and Senate. W. R. Wannall of the FBI summarized the bureau's relationship to the FPCC in a hastily produced memorandum for his boss, William C.

Sullivan of the Domestic Intelligence division, on November 23, 1963, the day after Kennedy's assassination and Oswald's arrest.

The bureau had learned about the new organization in 1960, when The *New York Times* carried a seven-column advertisement for it on April 6. By October the bureau had established that $3,500 of the money that paid for the ad (about 80 percent of the total) had been given to one Charles Santos Buch by Raul Roa of the Cuban mission to the United Nations. "On a confidential basis," the memo continued, "we arranged to have Buch appear before the Senate Internal Security Subcommittee (SISS) in January, 1961." The bureau also induced Buch to register as an agent of the Cuban government in January 1961, but the FPCC refused to register in the following month, opening up the possibility of legal prosecution.[56]

Sullivan also directed the COINTELPRO program which the FBI started in the late 1950s to disrupt and embarrass organizations deemed to be subversive. The program was essentially an attempt to adapt counter-intelligence techniques to domestic subversive groups, and it began by targeting the Communist Party USA in 1956. Senior bureau officials explained to the Church Committee that restrictive Supreme Court interpretations of the Smith Act and the failure of Congress to pass new anti-subversive legislation had made the prosecution of subversive organizations difficult, and COINTELPRO was designed to deal with them in another way. The FBI expanded its target list in 1960 to include supposedly Communist-influenced groups such as the anti-nuclear organization SANE and the NAACP, and added the Socialist Workers Party in 1961. The attorney general was not informed of these new targets.[57] What the FBI evidently did *not* tell the Church Committee was that COINTELPRO targeted the Fair Play for Cuba Committee as well. The FBI's newly released file on that organization leaves absolutely no doubt that it did.

COINTELPRO techniques included sowing suspicion among members of the targeted organization, leaking unfavorable publicity about the group, and identifying its members to friendly journalists in the press. To achieve these and other ends, bureau agents cooperated with federal and state legislative investigating committees. Crucially, they also used private anti-Communist organizations such as the American Legion, and the program even set up fictional organizations or chapters of targeted organizations, such as a fraudulent W. E. B. Du Bois Club (a leftist civil rights organization) in an unidentified southern city. The Church Committee found that supervision was very lax, and that field offices often failed to report what they were doing to headquarters.[58]

And indeed, while FBI files meticulously documented all purely *investigative* activities, the FPCC file that has been released to the National Archives, while including the Wannall memo describing the COINTELPRO operation against the FPCC, does not include any documents reporting in real time about any of its details. Using cut-outs like the American Legion and leaks to friendly newsmen, the FBI was behaving more like the CIA in its COINTELPRO operations, rather than following its own standard operating procedures.

As Wannall explained to Sullivan on November 23, 1963, the bureau in 1961 had discovered considerable friction between the Communist and Socialist factions of the Fair Play for Cuba Committee. "We were able to take advantage of such friction in December, 1961," he wrote, "when we prepared an anonymous pamphlet and mailed it to selected FPCC members throughout the country. The pamphlet was aimed at discrediting FPCC leadership and was written in a manner to create the impression it had been prepared by dissident Socialist Workers Party members of the FPCC." Wannall continued:

> As of February, 1962, membership in and activities of the then existing branches of the organization had been greatly curtailed . . . To a large measure, the decline in the FPCC was brought about by the aggressive FBI investigation of the organization coupled with an effective campaign of exposure of subversive influences in the group by the public press. In May, 1961, we had made effective use of our news media program to alert reliable news sources to the Communist Party and Socialist Workers Party influences in the FPCC. Thereafter, the press both on a nationwide and local basis carried out a vigorous barrage of exposure aimed at discrediting this group and revealing it for what it was; namely, a puppet of subversive elements.[59]

During 1961 and 1962 the FBI prepared extensively for a possible prosecution of the committee for failing to register as a foreign agent, but by the time of JFK's assassination the Justice Department had not approved the case. The issue became moot after November 23, when Oswald's association with the FPCC effectively discredited it all over the United States. Three days after Wannall's memorandum, J. Edgar Hoover forwarded an edited version to Robert Kennedy. That version omitted Wannall's account of the COINTELPRO actions against the FPCC.[60]

Since the second half of 1962, Lee Harvey Oswald had been trying to establish relationships with the Communist Party USA, the Socialist Workers Party, and now, in the spring of 1963, the Fair Play for Cuba Committee—all three targets of the FBI's COINTELPRO program. Yet during all that time, not one shred of evidence indicates that he had a single personal contact with any member of any of those organizations, or, indeed, with any leftist activists at all. The question arises, then, whether he made all these contacts while actually working in the COINTELPRO program himself, or in an allied effort run by private right-wing groups in Dallas and New Orleans. And in particular, we must ask whether Oswald's formation of a fake chapter of the Fair Play for Cuba Committee was from the beginning an attempt to both publicize and embarrass that organization, similar to the formation of a phony chapter of the Du Bois Club. Such an initiative might have been mounted by the FBI (although the evidence suggests it was not) or by INCA, whose leader, Butler, also endorsed exactly this kind of deception. The mystery deepened as Oswald's FPCC activities came to a climax in the summer of 1963.

10

Oswald Exposed

Oswald's association with the Fair Play for Cuba Committee began in early April 1963, when—still in Dallas—he wrote a letter to its New York City headquarters.

> L. H. Oswald
> P.O. Box 2915
> Dallas, Tex.
>
> Dear Sirs,
>
> I do not like to ask for something for nothing but I am unemployed.
>
> Since I am unemployed, I stood yesterday for the first time in my life, with a placard around my neck passing out fair play for Cuba pamphlets, ect. [sic] I only had 15 or so. In 40 minutes they were all gone. I was cursed as well as praised by some, my home-made placard read:
>
> HANDS OFF CUBA!
> VIVA FIDEL!
>
> I now ask for 40 or 60 more of the five basic pamphlets.
>
> Sincerely,
> L. H. Oswald[1]

No evidence confirms that Oswald actually handed out literature in Dallas. And we do not know exactly how he obtained the address of the FPCC offices. Although stories about Cuba (and occasionally about pro-Castro activists) appeared in both *The Worker* and *The Militant* from time to time, the FPCC itself did not advertise in those publications. A note on this letter indicates that the New York office sent literature to Oswald on April 17, shortly before he left for New Orleans. Once there, it took him two weeks to find a job at the Reily Coffee Company, whose owners were involved with the right-wing Information

Council of the Americas.[2] Oswald took the job on May 10, even though on May 8—after appealing his case—he began receiving $33 per week in·unemployment compensation following the loss of his Dallas job. Oswald rented an apartment at 4905 Magazine Street on May 9. Marina, now in her fourth month of pregnancy, and little June arrived on May 11.[3]

On May 26 Oswald wrote the FPCC in New York again, asking to join the organization. "Now that I live in New Orleans," he wrote, "I have been thinking about renting a small office at my own expense for the purpose of forming a FPCC branch here in New Orleans. Could you give me a charter?" He also asked for information on bulk purchases of literature and blank membership applications and requested a picture of Fidel, "a welcome touch." Offices, he said, rented for about $30 a month—the amount of one unemployment check—and he hoped to hear from the FPCC soon.

The national director, V. T. Lee, wrote a long, cordial, but cautious reply on May 29, enclosing the FPCC's constitution and by-laws and offering to certify Oswald's chapter if a certain number of members—approximately twice the number required for an executive board—could be found. He offered Oswald literature on credit, but warned him that the Southeast was hostile territory—the only FPCC branch in the region was in Tampa—and that an office would probably arouse a great deal of hostility. A post office box, the director said, was essential for the chapter to function, and he advised against using anyone's name in the return address on envelopes used for committee business. Oswald immediately replied:

Dear Mr. Lee,

I was glad to receive your advice concerning my try at starting a New Orleans F.P.C.C. chapter. I hope you won't be too disapproving at my innovations but I do think they are necessary for this area.

As per your advice, I have taken P.O. Box. (*NO* 30061)

Against your advice, I have decided to take an office from the very beginning.

As you see from the circular I had jumped the gun on the charter business but I don't think its [sic] too important, you may think the circular is too provocative, but I want it too [sic] attract attention, even if it's the attention of the lunatic fringe. I had 2000 of them run off.

Then followed a lengthy discussion of Oswald's intention to collect just $1.00 a month from his members and to forward $5.00 a year per member to the New York office from these funds.

> In any event I will keep you posted, and even if the office stays open for only 1 month more people will find out about the F.P.C.C. than if there had never been any office at all, don't you agree?
>   Please feel free to give advice and any other help.
>
>   Yours truly,
>   Lee H. Oswald.

The enclosed leaflet read "HANDS OFF CUBA! Join the Fair Play for Cuba Committee NEW ORLEANS CHARTER MEMBER BRANCH. Free Literature, Lectures. Location: _____ EVERYONE WELCOME!" A short membership application followed. The FPCC's national director must have concluded that Oswald was probably a *provocateur,* because he sent no reply to this letter or to several more that followed a couple of months later. In his brief Warren Commission testimony, V. T. Lee claimed not to have any specific memory of this correspondence.[4]

Oswald had not actually rented an office, but he had obtained a thousand handbills from a local company, Jones Printing. When the FBI interviewed two of its employees on December 3, 1963, they discovered that the man who ordered the leaflets had used the name "Osborne" and that neither employee thought Osborne looked like the FBI's photograph of Oswald—a detail the Warren Report omitted. An employee at a different company that had printed the blank membership cards and applications did identify Oswald from a photo and said he had used the name "Lee Osborne."[5]

While working at Reily Coffee, Oswald made frequent lunchtime visits to the Crescent City garage next door. He had been reading gun magazines, and he talked obsessively about firearms with the proprietor, Adrian Alba. Oswald promised Alba a generous price for a 30-caliber carbine that Alba might purchase for him through the National Rifle Association.[6] He also began to contemplate more foreign travel, and he and Marina apparently discussed having her and their child return to the Soviet Union. On June 24 he applied for a new passport, which he received within two days. About a week after that, both Oswalds sent letters to the Soviet Embassy asking for immediate Soviet visas for Marina and their child.[7] In late July he made a trip to Mobile, Alabama, with the Murrets to talk about his Russian experiences at a Jesuit college where a cousin was studying.[8]

Meanwhile, Oswald distributed some of his leaflets in at least three locations. On Sunday, July 16, he stationed himself at a New Orleans dock where the U.S.S. *Wasp* was berthed. He visited the Tulane University campus, where at least one student remembered seeing the leaflets lying about.[9] That, however, was not all. A newly discovered document reveals that Oswald was handing out leaflets in the middle of New Orleans more than a month earlier, and that his activities (although not his name) were brought to the attention of J. Edgar Hoover himself. On about July 8, 1963, the following letter addressed to Hoover—dated June 29, 1963— arrived at FBI headquarters.

> Dear Mr. Hoover:
>
> The writer, Rafael Aznarez Costea, Cuban refugee former chief Accountant of Lykes Bros. S. S. Co. at Havana until the office was closed in Dec. 1960. Actually working for the same company in New Orleans.
>
> Attached hereto please find a panflet [sic] given to me by a young American that was at Canal Street with a big advise [sic] 'HAND OFF CUBA" you know that is a Communist slogan agains [sic] the United States. I argued with him and called him communist, but you know they denie [sic] belong to the party.
>
> The American communists want to go to Cuba with the only purpose to make something like of the Abraham Lincoln brigade, similar to the one was in Spain, on account to confuse the American people again.
>
> When Fidel Castro disembarked in Cuba, he did so by the zone where the communist party was strong, *"MANZANILLO"*, in the province of Oriente. He went to Cuba not to fight Batista. He went to fight the U.S.A. He was unknown by that time, but he was *made* or built by Herbert Matthews and The New York Time. I just remember the letter sent to Mr. Matthew by the Cuban Ambassador at that time—"Mr. Matthew, what do you want in Cuba? *Another Argelia?*" [sic—Algeria.]
>
> How much cost a small advertise in that News paper? Who paid for those big articles in favor of Castro at that time?

The author continued with complaints about Communist tactics in general and described how he and his two sons had come to the United States with the help of Lykes Bros. He had arrived in January 1963. Insisting that the Cuban people opposed Castro, he concluded with a plea for the invasion of Cuba. The enclosed FPCC flyer (entitled "The Truth about Cuba Is in Cuba!") protested State Department restrictions upon travel to Cuba and encouraged the public to ask for permission to go (something that Oswald had not done when he applied for his passport) and to protest the ban.[10]

The young American who gave Aznarez the pamphlet must surely have been Lee Harvey Oswald (whose next sighting was also on Canal Street). Aznarez himself was apparently politically active and knowledgeable, and Lykes Bros.—a steamship company with Latin American interests that Castro had hurt—was the kind of business that supported INCA. The letter seemed designed to interest Hoover in the Communist menace posed by the New Orleans FPCC. It raises at least two difficult questions. First, despite the FBI's great interest in the FPCC, the file in which it was placed shows no evidence of any follow-up. Second, since Aznarez had seen Oswald on Canal Street and taken the trouble to write to Hoover about his leafleting, one might expect that other anti-Castro activists in New Orleans would have heard about him or seen him as well. But Carlos Bringuier of the DRE, whose store was not far away, claimed later that he had not heard of Oswald before late July—even though several years later he mentioned having discussed Oswald with Aznarez in a letter to Hoover of his own.[11]

In late July and early August Oswald began making contacts with local anti-Castro Cubans. His new activity began after he was discharged from the Reily Company on July 17, reportedly for poor performance. He visited a Spanish language teacher named Arnesto Rodriguez, head of a language school. Oswald, Rodriguez remembered after the assassination, came to see him around this time to inquire about Spanish lessons and asked a great many questions about Cubans in New Orleans.[12]

Somehow, Oswald secured the addresses of three "Cuban stores" which he wrote in his address book. One address, 107 Decatur Street, belonged to Bringuier and the DRE. The second store, at 117 Camp Street, was owned by Orlando Piedra, a leading Cuban security official under Batista whom a CIA report had once described as being in charge of all matters relating to "gambling, rackets, and contraband." Piedra explained to Miami FBI agents in December 1963 that he had sold the store to someone else at an undisclosed point in time, and managed to give the

impression that he had long since left New Orleans.[13] That was false—
Piedra had still been in New Orleans as recently as September 9, when
he spoke to the FBI.[14] The FBI found nothing of interest at the third address after the assassination, and never found out where Oswald got these
addresses.

On August 1 Oswald resumed his now one-sided correspondence
with V. T. Lee in New York.

> Dear Mr. Lee,
>
> In regards to my efforts to start a branch F.P.C.C. in New Orleans.
>
> I rented an office as I planned and was promptly closed three days later
> for some obscure reasons by the renters. They said something about re-
> modeling ect., [sic]. I'm sure you understand. After that I worked out of a
> post office box and by using street demonstrations and some circular
> work have substained [sic] a great deal of interest but no new members.
>
> Through the efforts of some Cuban-exil [sic] "gusanos" a street dem-
> onstration was attacked and we were officially cautioned by police. This
> incident robbed me of what support I had leaving me alone.
>
> Nevertheless thousands of circulars were disturbed [sic] and many,
> many pamphlets which your office supplied.
>
> We also managed to picket the fleet when it came in and I was sur-
> prised by the number of officers who were interested in our literature.
>
> I continue to receive through my post office box inquiries and ques-
> tions which I shall endeavor to keep answering to the best of my ability.
>
> > Thank you.
> > Lee H. Oswald.[15]

This letter included one at least partially true fact—that Oswald had
distributed leaflets to sailors from a Navy ship. Aznarez's letter suggests
that he had a confrontation with Oswald in late June, but no anti-Castro
Cubans supported this account after the assassination. Yet such a confrontation was *about* to occur just a few days later, with the help, whether
witting or unwitting, of Bringuier and the DRE, and Oswald personally
made sure that this one came to the attention not only of the FPCC but
of the Federal Bureau of Investigation. And Bringuier, with the help of
New Orleans journalist Bill Stuckey and Ed Butler of INCA, made sure
that it came to the attention of the general public.

On August 5 Oswald presented himself at a clothing store run by

Bringuier.[16] The head of the DRE was talking to a young American named Philip Geraci and his friend, Vance Blaylock, both fifteen years old. Geraci had raised $10 for the organization, and Blaylock came with him to turn it in. According to Bringuier's well-prepared testimony before the Warren Commission in April 1964, he was explaining to Geraci that he was too young to do anything but hand out literature when Oswald came into the store and introduced himself. Oswald, Bringuier said, then expressed support for the Cuban cause and offered either to help train men to oppose Castro or to go to Cuba himself to fight. He launched into a long and apparently not very sophisticated discussion of demolition and sabotage techniques and the manufacture of home-made guns and explosives, perhaps for the benefit of the two young Americans.

Bringuier explained to the Warren Commission that he was immediately suspicious of Oswald for two reasons. First, he said, nearly a year earlier, after the DRE's notorious attack on a Havana hotel, FBI agent Warren DeBrueys had sought information from him about his chapter and threatened to infiltrate it after Bringuier insisted that he was its only member.[17] (Curiously enough, when Bringuier was first interviewed by the FBI on November 27, 1963, he attributed that threat to Oswald.) Second, he claimed to have heard from two trainees at the MDC's Lake Pontchartrain camp about the informer who had been discovered there not long before. For both reasons, he said, he suspected that Oswald might be an informer/infiltrator himself and did not take him up on his offer. Oswald promised to give him a Marine Corps training manual, and apparently stopped by to leave it the next day. Bringuier claimed that Oswald continued the conversation with his brother-in-law, Rolando Pelaez, who was impressed by Oswald's commitment to the anti-Castro cause. For some reason Pelaez was neither interviewed by the FBI nor called by the Warren Commission. When Oswald left, the two young Americans decided to follow him briefly to see where he lived.

The Warren Report accepted Bringuier's account at face value, even though the young men who happened to be present did not, in one key respect, back it up. Both Geraci and Blaylock stated definitely, in response to specific questions, that Oswald said nothing about either training Cubans or going to Cuba himself. They also did not mention any other participant in the conversation, such as Bringuier's brother-in-law.[18]

More remarkably, Geraci recalled Oswald asking Bringuier if his organization were connected to the "Cosa Nostra," and Blaylock confirmed this. Warren Commission counsel Wesley Liebeler created some confusion by suggesting that Oswald was referring to a Cuban organization called the "Casa Nostra," though nothing suggests that such an organization exists. The phrase "Cosa Nostra" as a synonym for the Mafia had broken into public awareness on that day and the two days before as newspapers around the country reported that the Justice Department was hiding informant Joe Valachi, who was about to become the first Mafia member to confirm the existence of a national crime syndicate. Stories about Valachi that included the phrase "Cosa Nostra" had appeared in the *Washington Star* on August 3, the *Los Angeles Times* on August 4, and the *Chicago Tribune,* the *New York Times,* and the *Washington Post* on August 5. Evidently, Oswald asked Bringuier if he was connected to the mob, but Geraci and Blaylock denied that he offered to help train Cubans, as Bringuier has claimed ever since. By the time Bringuier testified before the Warren Commission in April 1964, he was arguing that Oswald was a Castro agent—an idea that became the basis for a book he published in 1967 as a counterpoint to the Garrison investigation, entitled *Red Friday.*[19]

Just three days later, on August 8, according to Bringuier's account, a Cuban friend of his, Celso Hernandez, came into his store during the afternoon to report that a young American was standing on Canal Street handing out leaflets (which Hernandez could not read) and wearing a large placard that read, "Viva Fidel." Bringuier grabbed another friend, Miguel Cruz, and a sign of his own showing a dagger in the back of the Statue of Liberty and ran out to find him. On their second attempt, they discovered that the leafleteer was Oswald.

Bringuier—in a fury, he said—began haranguing Oswald, accusing him of treachery, and inciting passersby, who joined in cursing Oswald. Staying cool and initially offering a hand in friendship, Oswald then folded his arms in front of him and finally said, "OK, Carlos, if you're going to hit me, hit me." Bringuier thought better of it and did not hit him, and the New Orleans police eventually arrived and arrested all four of the men.[20] A lieutenant who did not witness the incident but interviewed Oswald shortly thereafter concluded that his calm behavior suggested he purposely set up the incident.[21] Bringuier later ran into journalist Bill Stuckey and told him that he had discovered a pro-Castro activist. He gave Stuckey Oswald's address.[22]

The four men were charged with disturbing the peace, and the three Cubans immediately posted bond. Oswald did not. After spending the night in jail, he was interviewed the next morning (Saturday, August 10) by Lieutenant Francis Martello, formerly of the Intelligence Division of the New Orleans Police Department, who, as he explained to the Warren Commission, wanted to learn about the scope of Oswald's activities and organization and what might be expected from it in the future. Oswald's moment had come: like Herbert Philbrick, he had won the attention of the authorities, and he had a story to tell.

As Martello explained to New Orleans Secret Service agents in the very early morning hours of November 23, 1963, Oswald began by providing a great deal of personal information, and eventually admitted that his wife was an "alien M-1." He claimed to have become interested in the FPCC while in the Marine Corps in 1958—a lie, since the committee was not founded until 1960. Oswald claimed about thirty-five members of this chapter, when in fact he was the only one. Martello, whose Intelligence Squad work had introduced him to local Communist fronts, told the Secret Service that he had identified a Dr. Reissman, who lived on Pine Street, a Dr. Dombroski, and another unidentified man as leftists because they were "active in the integration movement" in New Orleans. Dombroski, Martello said, had been identified as a Communist in the 1956 Eastland Committee hearings. When he asked Oswald whether he knew Dr. Reissman and whether the FPCC met on Pine Street, Martello claimed on November 23 that Oswald had answered yes.

Oswald had apparently at least heard of Reissman. Lillian Murret, Oswald's aunt, spontaneously told the Secret Service just days after the assassination that when Ruth Paine arrived at her house with Marina, June, and the Paines' own children in tow, she mentioned her acquaintance with Dr. Reissman, and Oswald added that he knew him too.[23] The FBI located Dr. Reissman in Palo Alto, California, in early December 1963, and he denied any recollection of Oswald or any knowledge of a New Orleans FPCC chapter—especially in his own neighborhood.[24]

In his interview with Lieutenant Martello, Oswald omitted any mention of his travels to Russia and said he had gone to Fort Worth after discharge from the Marines. Later, when Oswald's aunt came to the jail house to pick him up, Martello learned the truth from her about his years in Russia, and Oswald then confirmed it.

And now, Oswald—going yet another step down the path his hero Philbrick had walked—asked to see an FBI agent. Police officials contacted the local bureau, which sent agent James Quigley, who prepared a full report. Oswald told Quigley that after writing the FPCC in New York he received a membership card—which was true. He added that he was subsequently contacted by one A. J. Hidell, whom he never met and who alerted him to a series of small meetings of the local FPCC chapter, which he attended. Hidell did not exist. This was Oswald's favorite alias, which he had used in forging a draft card and ordering a rifle from Klein's Sporting Goods in Chicago. Oswald also said that Hidell's phone was now disconnected and that he did not know the names of any of the other members he had met.

Hidell, he said, asked him on August 7 by mail to distribute FPCC literature, and he accepted. It is interesting that Oswald chose to make the August 7 incident the centerpiece of his activity, given that he had been handing out leaflets since June. Coincidentally, back in April 1961 Quigley had reviewed Oswald's Naval Intelligence File at the Algiers Naval Station near New Orleans after Oswald expressed his desire to return to the United States, but Quigley's August 1963 report gives no sign that he had made the connection, and he did not challenge Oswald's lie that he married Marina in Fort Worth.[25]

When Oswald called the Murrets' home from jail, he spoke with their daughter, Joyce O'Brien, whom he asked for the $25 bond. She went to the jail but declined to post it when she saw that he had been demonstrating in support of Castro. Informed by the police that he could be released at the request of a politician or elected official, she called a friend of her father's named Emile Bruneaux, who owned a liquor store and apparently had the necessary connections.[26]

By the time Oswald and his Cuban pursuers appeared in court on August 12, their confrontation had attracted some notoriety. Continuing to wring the maximum publicity from these events, he pled guilty to disturbing the peace and paid a $10 fine. The Cubans pled innocent, and the charges against them were dismissed. On that very day, Oswald once again wrote V. T. Lee in New York, enclosing a copy of his summons and a press clipping.

Dear Mr. Lee,

Continuing my efforts on behalf of the F.P.C.C. in New Orleans, I find that I have incurred the displeasure of the Cuban exile "worms" here. I was attacked by three of them as the copy of the enclosed summons indicates I was fined ten dollars and the three Cubans were not fined because of "lack of evidence" the judge said.

I am very glad I am stirring things up and shall continue to do so. The incident was given considerable coverage in the press and local R.B. news broadcast.

I'm sure it will all be to the good of the Fair Play for Cuba Committee.

Sincerely yours,

Lee H. Oswald[27]

Curiously, Oswald in this true account substituted the English "worms" for the Spanish word "gusanos" that had appeared in his August 1 letter, which seemed to describe events that had not yet happened. Once again, V. T. Lee, who now had proof that Oswald was bringing discredit upon his organization, did not reply.

Oswald and Bringuier were now working toward the same goal—giving Oswald's pro-Castro activities maximum publicity. On August 16, still out of work, Oswald went to the Louisiana State Employment Service and hired two other men to help him distribute leaflets in front of the New Orleans Trade Mart.[28] A television crew covered him. On that day, another Cuban exile and sometime informant, Carlos Quiroga, called the police again, but they did not arrive to arrest Oswald. That night, at the suggestion of Bringuier, Quiroga went to Oswald's home on Magazine Street to offer to join the FPCC. He claimed that Oswald invited him to do so, but that he did not join because he got no encouragement from Lieutenant Martello to infiltrate the organization. Oswald told Marina that Quiroga was probably a federal informant, as indeed he was.[29]

During the next week Bringuier, with a little help from Bill Stuckey and Ed Butler, managed to use Oswald to pursue the mission the DRE had been given by their sponsor organization, the CIA: to propagandize against Castro all over the Americas. Stuckey, a journalist, had graduated from Southern Methodist University in the early 1950s, served a hitch in the Marines, spent the better part of a year tramping around Latin America, and then had gone into journalism. His stories on Latin America for the New Orleans *Times-Picayune* included an admiring column about "Jerry Patrick" (actually Gerry Patrick Hemming) and a purported Louisiana training camp a year earlier, and he now hosted a weekly radio program on Latin America. As Stuckey explained to the Warren Commission in June 1964, he had a continuing relationship with the FBI, and he had used Bringuier as a source for some time.[30] Butler's Information Council of the Americas, which claimed to broadcast anti-Castro material to over one hundred radio stations in sixteen Latin countries, focused on disrupting subversive organizations.

On Saturday morning, August 17—the day after the Trade Mart leafleting—Stuckey went to see Oswald at his address on Magazine Street. Oswald, wearing Marine fatigue trousers, immediately agreed to talk with him on the porch. He explained to Stuckey that he was secretary of the New Orleans chapter of the FPCC, and that Hidell was president. Stuckey described his first impression to the Warren Commission.

> He appeared to be a very logical, intelligent fellow, and the only strange thing about him was his organization. This was, seemed, incongruous to me that a group of this type—or he should associate with a group of this type, because he did not seem the type at all, or at least what I have in my mind as the type. I would like to mention this. I was arrested by his cleancutness. I didn't expect this at all. I expected a folk-singer type, something of that kind, somebody with a beard and sandals, and he said— I found this fellow, instead I found this fellow who was neat and clean, watched himself pretty well.
>
> Mr. JENNER. You mean he watched his—
>
> Mr. STUCKEY. He seemed to be very conscious about all of his words, all of his movements, sort of very deliberate. He was very deliberate with his words, and struck me as being rather articulate. He was the type of person you would say would inspire confidence. This was the incongruity that struck me, the fact that this type of person should be with this organization. That is the gist of the first meeting.[31]

Stuckey arranged for Oswald to come to his NBC radio station that very evening for an interview. Oswald immediately wrote yet another letter to national director V. T. Lee announcing this new step forward. Dated August 17, it seems to have been finished the next day.

Dear Mr. Lee,

Since I last wrote you (Aug 13) about my arrest and fine in New Orleans for distributing literature for F.P.C.C., things have been moving
pretty fast.

On August 16th I organized an F.P.C.C. demonstration of three people. This demonstration was given considerable coverage by WDSU-TV
channel 6, and also by our channel 4 T.V. station.

Due to that I was invited by Bill Stucke [sic] to appear on his T.V. show
called "Latin American Focus" at 7:30 P.M. Saturday's [sic] on WDSU-
channel 6.

After this 15 minute interview which was filmed on magnetic [sic]
type [sic] at 4:00 P.M. for rebroadcast at 7:30 I was flooded with callers
and invitations to debates ect. As well as people interested in joining the
F.P.C.C. New Orleans branch.

That than [sic] is what has happened up to this day and hour.

You can I think be happy with the developing situation here in New
Orleans.

I would however, like to ask you to rush some more literature particularly the white sheet "Truth about Cuba" regarding government restrictions on travel, as I am quickly running out.

Yours truly,

Lee H. Oswald[32]

"The Truth about Cuba" was the leaflet that Rafael Aznarez had forwarded to Hoover.

Stuckey's show customarily ran for only five minutes, but when
Oswald arrived that evening Stuckey decided, as he told the Warren
Commission, to let him talk for as long as he wanted. His introduction
indicates that he planned to make this the first of a number of shows featuring various Cuban factions, in order to educate the local citizenry.

This is the first of a series of Latin Listening Post of persons more or less
directly concerned with the conflict between the United States and
Cuba. In subsequent programs, we will present talks with people who are
connected with the Cuban refugee organizations, people who are connected with President Batista, and United States citizens with direct
stakes in the outcome of the Cuban situation. Tonight we have with us a
representative of probably the most controversial organization connected

with Cuba in this country. The organization is the Fair Play for Cuba Committee. The person, Lee Oswald, secretary of the New Orleans chapter for the Fair Play for Cuba Committee. This organization has long been on the Justice Department's black list and is a group generally considered to be the leading pro-Castro body in the nation. As a reporter of Latin American affairs in this city for several years now, your columnist has kept a lookout for local representatives of this pro-Castro group. None appeared in public view until this week when young Lee Oswald was arrested and convicted for disturbing the peace. He was arrested passing out pro-Castro literature to a crowd which included several violently anti-Castro Cuban refugees. When we finally tracked Mr. Oswald down today and asked him to participate in Latin Listening Post, he told us frankly that he would because it may help his organization to attract more members in this area.[33]

Although Oswald certainly rambled and was often evasive during the thirty-minute discussion that followed, he gave a reasonably good account of himself. He insisted that the FPCC had only one interest, the fair treatment of Cuba and the right of Cubans to develop as they saw fit, without interference from the United States. He disclaimed any Communist associations or support for the Soviet Union and criticized Soviet imperialism and Soviet intervention in Hungary. He also cleverly noted that Castro had shown that he was no Russian puppet "during the October [missile] crisis" by refusing to allow UN weapons inspectors to enter Cuba. "We do not support the man," Oswald said, referring to Castro. "We do not support the individual. We support the idea of an independent revolution in the Western Hemisphere, free from American intervention."

Oswald asserted, incorrectly, that Castro was not yet a Communist, claimed that he had tried and failed to get information on the FPCC into the two local papers, the *Times-Picayune* and the *States-Item,* and admitted that he had never been in Latin America, except in Mexico.[34] When Stuckey challenged him to explain the tens of thousands of Cuban refugees who had come to the United States, Oswald replied that some of them were "people who are wanted in Cuba for crimes against humanity and most of those people are the same people who are in New Orleans and have set themselves up in stores with blood money and who engage in day to day trade with New Orleanians." That sounds suspiciously like a reference to Orlando Piedra, the Batista security policeman who owned one of the other stores in Oswald's address book. Asked about his own background, he omitted any mention of his stay in Russia and claimed to have been a buck sergeant in the Marine Corps.

Stuckey ran five minutes of the interview on the show that evening. On Monday, his news director, who had not yet heard the interview, suggested that he arrange a debate between Oswald and anti-Castro Cubans on a daily program called *Conversation Carte Blanche,* which ran for thirty minutes. When Oswald called him at a pre-arranged time (for what purpose Stuckey did not explain to the Warren Commission), Stuckey suggested this debate, and Oswald accepted. For the other panelists, Stuckey selected Bringuier and Butler, and scheduled the debate for Wednesday afternoon.[35]

Whether or not Stuckey's anonymous "news director" did in fact suggest this radio debate, it was not an original idea. Radio debates were a preferred tactic of the DRE, which had staged one between a pro- and anti-Castro student in Guatemala in December 1961, and apparently had planned another one in New York in April 1962. Just two weeks after Oswald's appearance in New Orleans, the Miami DRE headquarters was busily arranging a radio and television debate with some American students who had just made a visit to Cuba.[36]

On the morning of the debate, August 21, Stuckey called the New Orleans FBI office. He began by mentioning that he was no longer in the newspaper business—clearly indicating that he already had some relationship with the bureau—and told them about his contacts with Oswald. He asked whether the FPCC was listed as a subversive organization—something he had asserted in his interview with Oswald a few days before. He told the agent about the forthcoming debate that evening and suggested that he might want to listen. According to the agent's record of the call (initials HRH), he declined to answer the question about the FPCC but telephoned another agent, Milton Kaack, to let him know about the debate.[37]

Stuckey did not tell the Warren Commission about this call, but he did testify that during the same day "one of my news sources called me up and said, 'I hear you are going to have Oswald on Carte Blanche.' I said, 'Yes, that is right.' He said, 'We have some information about Mr.

Oswald, the fact that he lived in Russia for 3 years' . . . this individual who called me and gave me this information gave me dates of Washington newspaper clippings that I could check, which were stories about his leaving for Russia, or rather his appearance in Moscow in 1959." By the time Butler arrived at the station, Stuckey continued, he too had been given this information about Oswald. "His source," Stuckey said, "apparently was the House Un-American Activities Committee or something like that."[38]

In 1976 Stuckey told a completely different story about how he learned of Oswald's Russian past. In a letter to journalist Priscilla Johnson McMillan, he claimed that he phoned the FBI on the day of the debate—as indeed he did—and was read portions of Oswald's file. He was then invited to the office to examine it and to drop off a copy of his taped interview with Oswald. He claimed that Butler heard about Oswald's Russian past from Quiroga, who had heard Oswald's daughter, June, speak to him in Russia during a brief visit to Oswald's apartment.

This version of Stuckey's story does not seem to be true. Contemporary FBI documents show that the agent to whom Stuckey talked gave him no information, and although Special Agent Kaack might have called him back, the information that Butler read on the radio program was not in the FBI's files in New Orleans. Oswald did not tell Quiroga about his trip to Russia, claiming instead that he had studied Russian at Tulane, and files also show that the FBI got its copy of Stuckey's thirty-minute interview of Oswald from Butler, not from Stuckey, on August 26.[39]

Warren Commission staffer Albert Jenner was not curious enough to ask Stuckey to identify his "news source," and Butler, amazingly, was not called by the commission or, apparently, even interviewed by the FBI—although he did appear before the Senate Internal Security Subcommittee just a few days after the assassination to suggest that Oswald's deed was Communist-inspired. Stuckey's "news source" was either Butler, who had called the House Un-American Activities Committee, or an American intelligence agency, or possibly the Senate Internal Security Subcommittee, which had held hearings on Communism in New Orleans in 1956 and had more recently held hearings on the FPCC. The subcommittee was by now deeply involved with Cuba policy, including the Bayo-Pawley raid.

The so-called debate actually turned out to be more of an ambush. Stuckey told the Warren Commission that when Oswald and Bringuier arrived at the studio, Bringuier played the role of jilted lover.

> Bringuier, as well as I recall, started out with a remark like this, saying, "You know, I thought you were a very nice boy. You really made a good impression on me when I first met you." Referring to Oswald's visit to Bringuier in the store when Oswald was posing as an anti-Castro enthusiast, and Bringuier said, "I cannot understand how you have let yourself become entangled with this group." He said, "I don't think you know what you are doing." Oswald said something to the effect that, "I don't think you know what you are doing," and back and forth such as this. Bringuier said, "Anytime you want to get out of your organization and join mine there is a place for you," and he says, "I hope one day you will see the light." And again Oswald says, "I hope you see the light," and that was about all there was to that.[40]

Given that Bringuier later claimed in his book and in his Warren Commission testimony that he had sized up Oswald as an informant and infiltrator from the start, it is hard to avoid the conclusion that both he and Oswald were now exaggerating their roles in this drama for greater effect. When the show began, Stuckey's co-host, Bill Slatter, began by introducing the four participants: Stuckey, Oswald (described as head of the local FPCC, "generally recognized as the principal voice of the Castro government in this country"), Butler (distributor of "anti-Communist educational materials throughout Latin America"), and Bringuier (head of the local DRE chapter). He passed the mike to Stuckey, who summarized his previous contact with Oswald and then let fly.

> Following another line I asked Mr. Oswald if he had ever, or was a member of the American Communist Party and he said that the only organization to which he belonged was the Fair Play for Cuba Committee. Mr. Oswald also gave me this run down on his personal background. He said that he was a native of New Orleans, had attended Beauregard Junior High School and Warren Eastern High School. Had entered the U.S. Marine Corps, in 1956 and was honorably discharged in 1959. He said during our previous interview that he had lived in Ft. Worth, Texas before coming here to establish a Fair Play for Cuba chapter several weeks

ago. However, there were a few items apparently that I suspect that Mr. Oswald left out in his original interview which was principally where he lived after, between 1959 and 1962. We, er, Mr. Butler brought some newspaper clippings to my attention and I also found some too through an independent source, Washington Newspaper clippings to the effect that Mr. Oswald had attempted to renounce his American citizenship in 1959 and become a Soviet citizen. There was another clipping dated 1962 saying that Mr. Oswald had returned from the Soviet Union with his wife and child after having lived there three years. Mr. Oswald are these correct?

OSWALD. That is correct. Correct, yes.[41]

Recovering quickly, Oswald commented that "the fact that I did live for a time in the Soviet Union gives me excellent qualifications to repudiate the charges that Cuba and the Fair Play for Cuba Committee is Communist controlled." Slatter turned to Bringuier, who began with an abusive question that Oswald declined to answer, and then launched into a lengthy statistical diatribe on the economic decline of Cuba under Castro. Oswald replied that "the facts and figures from, oh a country like Pakistan or Burma would even reflect more light upon Cuba in relation to how many TV sets and how many radio and all that." Slatter and Butler pressed Oswald to identify the other members of his chapter, which he refused to do.

Butler then asked whether the FPCC "is not a Communist front organization," and Oswald replied that the "Senate Subcommittee," which had investigated the matter, found no connection. "Well, I have the Senate Hearings before me," Butler replied, "and I think what I have in front of me refutes precisely every statement that you have just made." After Butler and Oswald sparred over that point for a moment, Slatter interjected to ask whether Oswald had once asked to renounce his U.S. citizenship and become a Soviet citizen, and Oswald refused to answer. Asked whether he was a Communist, he affirmed, in response to Stuckey's question, that he was a Marxist, leading to another exchange in which Oswald rather elliptically tried to convey that Marxism was not necessarily Soviet-style Communism.

After a break, Stuckey returned to the charge, suggesting that other local members of the FPCC would like to know more about Oswald's stay in the Soviet Union and how he supported himself. Oswald replied that he had worked, and that he had never lost his American citizenship. When Slatter (who had obviously been briefed as well) asked if he had tried to lose it, Oswald become evasive, and Butler quoted from the *Washington Evening Star* of October 31, 1959, p. 1, to the effect that he had. He also quoted from a November 16, 1959, *Washington Post* story that the Soviets had refused him citizenship and asked for an explanation, which Oswald did not provide. Butler, who actually had the clippings, was never questioned by the Warren Commission about where he got them—or about anything else.

The discussion then returned to Cuba and Cuban-American relations, and Oswald did much better, claiming that the ideas of the FPCC were "very clear and in the best keeping with American traditions of democracy," disagreeing specifically with Castro's characterization of President Kennedy as "a ruffian and a thief," arguing that the United States in 1958 should have given arms to Castro rather than simply withhold them from Batista, and stating that Cuba was suffering from the cutoff of the vast majority of its exports to the United States. Slatter then wrapped up.[42]

What followed was even more interesting. Having just destroyed any credibility that Oswald might have had—certainly in 1963 New Orleans—and having concluded, as he told the Warren Commission, that Oswald had no more chance of attracting any members to the FPCC, Stuckey invited him out for a beer.

> The others left, and Oswald looked a little dejected, and I said, "Well, let's go out and have a beer," and he says, "All right." So we left the studio and went to a bar called Comeaux's Bar. It is about a half-block from the studio and this was the first time that his manner kind of changed from the quasi-legal position, and he relaxed a little bit. This was the first time I ever saw him relaxed and off of his guard. We had about an hour's conversation, 45 minutes to an hour, maybe a little more, maybe a little less, and, by the way, I mentioned his suit being rather gawky cut, and he told me afterward the suit was purchased in Russia, and they didn't know much about making clothes over there . . .
>
> We covered a number of points because I was relaxed, as far as I was concerned professionally I had no other occasion to contact Oswald. He

was off the spot. So we just had a little conversation. During that conversation he told me that he was reading at that time about Indonesian Communism, and that he was reading everything he could get his hands on. He offered an opinion about Sukarno, that he was not really a Communist, that he was merely an opportunist who was using the Communists.[43] We had a discussion about alcohol. I noticed he wasn't doing very good with his beer, and it was a hot night, and he made a reference to that. He said, "Well, you see, I am not used to drinking beer. I am a vodka drinker." And he said, "My father-in-law taught me how to drink vodka," and then he proceeded to tell me that his father-in-law, who was the father of his wife Marina, was a Russian Army colonel, and mentioned that as an army colonel he earned quite a bit more money than Oswald was earning in Russia. Oswald told me at that time he was making about 80 rubles a month as a factory worker, whereas his father-in-law, the Colonel, was making something like 300 rubles a month, so he could afford all the vodka he wanted, and he says—that is who taught him to drink vodka . . .

I asked him at that time how he became interested in Marxism and he said that there are many books on the subject in any public library. I asked him if he, if his family was an influence on him in any way. He says, "No," and he kind of looked a little amused. He said, "So," he says, "They are pretty much typical New Orleans types," and that was about all he said.

Mr. JENNER. Did you question or discuss with him whether he found that the system in Russia was a Marxist society or whether it was—

Mr. STUCKEY. Yes; he wasn't very pleased apparently with some of the aspects of Russian political life. Particularly in the factories he said that a lot of the attitudes and this sort of thing was the same sort of attitude that you would find in an American factory. There was a lot of deadheading, as we say in Louisiana. I don't know what your expression is.

Mr. JENNER. Goldbricking.

Mr. STUCKEY. Goldbricking. The boss' relatives on the payrolls at nice salaries.

Mr. JENNER. Nepotism.

Mr. STUCKEY. Nepotism, this sort of thing. Anybody with any authority at all would just use it to death to get everybody extra privileges that they could, and a lot of dishonesty, padding of production figures and this sort of thing. He said he wasn't very impressed . . .

He said that nobody—everybody seems to be almost alike in Russia because, after all, they had eliminated a lot of the dissenting elements in Russian society and had achieved fairly homogenous blend of population as a result.

Mr. JENNER. That was an observation on his part, was it, of an aspect of Russian society that disappointed him?

Mr. STUCKEY. I don't know. I don't recall him expressing an opinion as to whether he was disappointed by that. It was a comment. His tone was slightly acid as if he did not like it, but again this is my impression. He did say this which was interesting, he said that they wouldn't allow any Fair Play for Cuba Committees in Russia.

Mr. JENNER. He did?

Mr. STUCKEY. Yes: he said they just would not because it is the type of organization that Russian society would just suppress.

Mr. JENNER. Russian society?

Mr. STUCKEY. The Russian authorities would suppress . . .

He was relaxed, he was friendly. He seemed to be relieved it was all over. My impression was he was relieved that he did not have to hide the bit about the Russian residence any more, and that it had been a strain doing so, because his manner was completely different. There wasn't the stiffness or the guarded words and guarded replies. He seemed fairly open, and I have no reason to believe that everything he told me that night was not true. I think it was true.[44]

This conversation is notable for several reasons. Oswald emerges, as he does from de Mohrenschildt's reminiscences, as a disillusioned ex-Communist who has become cynical about virtually all institutions. Meanwhile, the Marine within him was still alive, and he preferred to claim that he customarily drank vodka than to admit that he did not drink at all. But most remarkably, Oswald, having apparently suffered a devastating defeat in the debate, suddenly seemed relieved and relaxed—an attitude that would make perfect sense if his whole escapade, from the first letters to V. T. Lee through the radio debate, had been a deception, designed to discredit the FPCC rather than to recruit for it. If that was his true job, it was now finished and he could relax.

The episode of Oswald's FPCC "chapter" bears all the marks of a COINTELPRO operation carried out by or with the witting or unwitting help of two private organizations, INCA and the DRE—from Oswald's founding of the chapter, through his distribution of leaflets over a period of at least six weeks (as proven by Aznarez's letter to Hoover), leading eventually to his confrontation with Bringuier (which Bringuier over-dramatized afterward by claiming—falsely, it seems—that Oswald had actually offered to join the DRE), and climaxing in the radio debate during which the purported leader of the New Orleans FPCC was exposed as a former defector to the Soviet Union. Arrested and questioned by local and federal authorities, Oswald stayed totally in character, just as Herbert Philbrick had done in so many spine-tingling episodes of *I Led Three Lives.* And then, over the New Orleans airways, Stuckey and Butler, with the help of some government entity that supplied clippings from Washington newspapers that it had kept in its files, revealed the clean-cut and articulate chairman of the FPCC to have been a defector—something which, as Stuckey said over the air, was bound to alienate any unwitting members or prospective acolytes of the FPCC. Butler and Bringuier had every reason to feel proud of themselves for destroying the chapter, even if its membership had in fact never exceeded the grand total of one, and Oswald had every reason to feel relief that he had played his own part successfully.

The behavior of the New Orleans police and the FBI certainly suggests that they knew Oswald's chapter was bogus. Lieutenant Martello was not sufficiently curious after Oswald's arrest to have Quiroga join his chapter as an infiltrator. The bureau did nothing, apparently, to follow up on Aznarez's letter to Hoover about FPCC leaflets on June 29. Nothing has ever been released showing that the New Orleans office was even informed of it. On July 29 the Dallas FBI office once again queried New Orleans about the Oswalds' whereabouts, and on August 13 New Orleans replied that they were living on Magazine Street.[45] Quigley on August 15 submitted his report on his August 10 jail house interview with Oswald—five days was the standard deadline for reports—but made no recommendation for any further investigation.[46]

On August 21 FBI headquarters in Washington, which somehow learned about Oswald's arrest, directed New Orleans to undertake further investigation "including nature of pamphlet following which contact should be made with established sources familiar with Cuban activities in the New Orleans area to determine whether subject involved in

activities inimical to the internal security of the U.S.," with results prepared for dissemination to other agencies.[47] New Orleans replied in two
stages. On August 23 they reported Oswald's August 9 arrest, the text of
his handbills, and his distribution of leaflets at the Trade Mart on August
16, complete with descriptions of his two helpers but without discussing
the purported FPCC branch. Meanwhile, on September 10 Dallas officially transferred the open case on the two Oswalds back to New Orleans.[48] Then, on September 24, more than a month after Washington's
query (and a day after the Oswalds left New Orleans), an additional report stated that neither Frank Bartes of the New Orleans CRC or another unnamed informant had any knowledge of Oswald. The report
said nothing about the existence or nonexistence of a New Orleans
FPCC chapter (although it had an appendix describing the FPCC), did
not mention the radio debate, and did not reflect any interviews with
Butler, Stuckey, or Bringuier. The New Orleans branch seems to have
done the minimum necessary to satisfy FBI headquarters without raising
any broader issues.[49]

Oswald's subsequent behavior was also suspicious. He did not write
yet another letter to V. T. Lee to tell him about the radio debate. But he
did write to the headquarters of the Communist Party of the United
States on August 28. This letter actually continued, in a way, an existing
correspondence. In June he had written *The Worker* about his FPCC
chapter and requested literature, and he received a brief reply in July
from Arnold Johnson, director of the party's Information and Lecture
Bureau. He wrote Johnson directly on August 13, enclosing a clipping
about his arrest.[50] Now, having been discredited for visiting the Soviet
Union and having vehemently denied being a Communist himself, he
wrote the party an incriminating letter, confirming, in effect, that he was
working on its behalf.

Comrades;
    Please advise me upon a problem of personal tactics.
    I have lived in the Soviet Union from October 1956 (?) to July 1962.
    I had, in 1959, in Moscow, tried to legally dissolve my United States
citizenship, however, I did not complete the legal formalities for this.
    Having come back to the U.S. in 1962 and thrown myself into the
struggle for progress and freedom in the United States, I would like to

know whether, in your opinion, I can continue to fight, handicapped as it were, by my past record, can I still, under these circumstances, compete with anti-progressive forces above ground or weather [sic] in your opinion I should always remain in the background, i.e. underground.

Our opponents could use my background of residence in the U.S.S.R. against any cause which I join, by association, they could say the organization of which I am a member, is Russian controlled, ect. I am sure you see my point.

I could of course openly proclaim, (if pressed on the subject) that I wanted to dissolve my American citizenship as a personal protest against the policy of the U.S. Government in supporting dictatorships, ect.

But what do you think I should do? Which is the best tactic in general? Should I dissociate myself from all progressive activities?

Here in New Orleans, I am secretary of the "Fair Play For Cuba Committee," a position which, frankly, I have used to foster Communist ideals. On a local radio show, I was attacked by Cuban exile organization representatives for my residence ect. in the Soviet Union.

I feel I may have compromised the F.P.C.C., so you see that I need the advice of trusted, long time fighters for progress. Please advise.

With Fraternal Greeting
Lee H. Oswald[51]

Just four days later, on September 1, Oswald wrote the CPUSA again, referring to plans for a move that have never been explained.

Dear Sirs,

Please advise me as to how I can contact the party in the Baltimore-Washington area, to which I shall relocate in October

Sincerely,
Lee Oswald[52]

The idea of relocating to the Baltimore-Washington area inevitably raises the question of whether a confrontation with President Kennedy was already on Oswald's agenda.

Oswald's caricature of a loyal Communist soldier in his August 18 letter stands in stark contrast with his lone wolf letters to V. T. Lee and with his anarchistic remarks to Stuckey at the bar. Only one of them, at most, could have been sincere. Three days after the assassination, an FBI informant at CPUSA headquarters in New York reported a discussion of Oswald's two letters among the party leaders. They concluded "that Oswald was a 'nut' used by the FBI to send letters to the CPUSA office in order to get answers."[53] While we have no evidence that the FBI itself was behind Oswald's letter-writing, the party's conclusion that it was seems understandable, especially given that Oswald had made no attempt to contact local Communist Party branches in either Dallas or New Orleans. As the Communists at party headquarters surely understood, a reply that encouraged him to join other leftist causes would have effectively discredited them once again, and when Arnold Johnson got around to sending a note on September 15, he was noncommittal.

Dear Mr. Oswald:

Your letter of August 28th to Elizabeth G. Flynn was turned over to me for reply.

Since I received your letter of September 1st indicating that you are moving to Baltimore, I suggest that when you do move that you get in touch with us here and we will find some way of getting in touch with you in that city. While the point you make about your residence in the Soviet Union may be utilized by some people, I think you have to recognize that as an American citizen who is now in this country, you have a right to participate in such organizations as you want, but at the same time there are a number of organizations, including possibly Fair Play, which are of a very broad character, and often it is advisable for some people to remain in the background, not underground, I assume this is pretty much of an academic question now and we can discuss it later.

Sincerely yours,

Arnold Johnson

By September 15, however, Oswald had interrupted his career as a political activist. What he did during the month between August 21, the day of the radio debate, and September 23, when Marina left New Orleans with Ruth Paine, is an almost complete blank in the official record. In 1967, however, in the course of New Orleans District Attorney Jim Garrison's investigation of the Kennedy assassination, about half a dozen residents of Clinton, Louisiana, a small town a hundred miles from New Orleans, reported having seen Oswald at four different but related locations. The Garrison investigation destroyed its own credibility on many points, and Clay Shaw, whom Garrison charged with murder, was acquitted in 1969. Yet, another decade later, in 1978, these same witnesses once again convinced the House Select Committee on Assassinations that they saw Oswald in Clinton during August 1963, and it is not difficult to understand why the committee decided to believe them.

The story began, apparently, when a young man stopped at Edwin Lee McGehee's barbershop in neighboring Jackson, Louisiana, one afternoon in August 1963 and asked for a haircut. While sitting in the barber chair, he mentioned that he came from New Orleans and was looking for a job. McGehee mentioned that East Feliciana State Hospital, a mental institution, was nearby, and specifically mentioned a possible opening in the electrical department. McGehee also referred him to the local state representative, Reeves Morgan, and told him how to find Morgan's house. Immediately after the assassination, McGehee said, he recognized Oswald as that man in the barber chair. He did not see the car he was riding in or anyone he was with.[54]

Reeves Morgan remembered Oswald coming to see him to ask about a job as an electrician at the hospital sometime in late August 1963. He suggested to Oswald that he might improve his chances by registering to vote. And Morgan, too, said he recognized Oswald after the Kennedy assassination, and he confirmed that McGehee had acknowledged at the time having sent Oswald to him. He alone of the Clinton witnesses claimed to have called the FBI after the assassination, and he stated that they told him they already knew Oswald had been in the area. Reeves had not seen anyone with Oswald either.[55]

The next four witnesses claimed to have seen Lee Harvey Oswald trying to register to vote in Clinton—an event they remembered easily because during most of that August Clinton was the target of a voter registration drive by the Congress of Racial Equality (CORE), a civil rights organization. The drive came to the attention of the FBI in early August, after the arrest of a white CORE leader, Michael Lesser.[56] The four witnesses, curiously enough, came from opposite sides of what was apparently a rather large political divide that received extensive coverage in the local press.

Henry Earl Palmer, the registrar of voters, remembered seeing a strange black Cadillac one day during the registration drive when he went out for coffee, and he noticed Corrie Collins, a black CORE leader, standing near it. Thinking that its occupants might be federal agents, he asked John Manchester, a deputy sheriff, to check its license plate. Manchester reported that it belonged to a representative of the International Trade Mart in New Orleans. Shortly thereafter, Palmer recalled, Lee Harvey Oswald came into his office, claimed to be working at East Feliciana State Hospital, and asked to register to vote. He showed his Marine discharge papers and stated, Palmer thought, that he was living on Camp Street in New Orleans. Palmer refused to register him.[57]

Palmer could not identify either of two men he saw inside the black Cadillac, but Manchester, who approached the car, did. He said the driver identified himself as Clay Shaw of the International Trade Mart, and later Manchester identified the other passenger from a photograph as David Ferrie. He then said, more vaguely, that he thought he saw Oswald getting into the car subsequently. He added that he had discussed the incident with Palmer immediately after the assassination.[58] William Dunn, a local CORE member, also remembered the black Cadillac, recognized Shaw and Ferrie from news photos, and saw Oswald standing in the voter registration line.[59]

The HSCA found Corrie Collins, the local leader of CORE who was standing near the black Cadillac, living in Dearborn, Michigan, in October 1978. An Army veteran, he explained that he had become involved in the registration drive after being turned away by the registrar upon his return from service in Vietnam. He easily remembered Oswald in the registration line because so few white people were standing there, and he remembered Deputy John Manchester talking to the two men in the black Cadillac. Several witnesses made clear that any strange car inevitably attracted attention. Collins remembered that he and Manchester used to tail one another around town, and he thought that Palmer respected what he was doing even though Palmer refused to register him. Collins could not really explain, however, why he did not talk to the FBI at the time. Relations between local FBI agents and southern civil rights workers were generally bad in 1963, and that might explain the lack of ready communication.[60] Another Clinton witness who identified Oswald was a nurse named Bobbie Dedon. She claimed to have remembered Oswald coming to East Feliciana State Hospital to ask about a job in August 1963, but her testimony was the least compelling.[61]

One of Jim Garrison's investigators, a state policeman from the Clinton area named Francis "Jack" Fruge, originally located all these witnesses, although he did not make clear exactly how Garrison learned about their stories in the first place. It also developed that Clay Shaw had a niece living in the Clinton area. The Shaw prosecution was one of the most disgraceful episodes in the history of American justice.[62] As a reporter present at the trial pointed out, Garrison gave the Clinton witnesses who identified Shaw an opportunity to see him in the courtroom.[63] The two identifications of Ferrie—by Deputy Manchester and CORE worker Dunn—were inevitably suspect after so many years, despite Ferrie's distinctive appearance. But all of these witnesses, including both civil rights demonstrators and law enforcement officials, were quite certain they saw Oswald in Clinton during August or possibly early September 1963, a period when he was not known to be working elsewhere. Their identification of Oswald leaves behind a real mystery about exactly what Oswald was doing in Clinton, Louisiana, three months before he killed the President, and who was with him.

The Clinton sightings are virtually the only evidence we have of what Oswald was up to between his radio appearance in mid-August and his departure from New Orleans in the last week of September. At that point he embarked on an even more secretive mission—an attempt to enter Cuba via Mexico City, for reasons no one has yet understood.

11

The Odio Incident

The event that definitely ties Oswald to anti–Castro Cubans and indicates that he had been recruited to travel to Cuba and assassinate
Fidel Castro occurred either on September 24 or 25 or on October 3,
1963, in Dallas. On one of those evenings, Oswald, in the company of
two Spanish-speaking men who called themselves Leopoldo and Angelo,
arrived at the home of a Cuban refugee, a beautiful young mother
named Silvia Odio, who lived in an apartment on Magellan Circle in
Dallas. This event—quickly discovered but initially neglected by the
Dallas FBI—became the focus of intense investigation designed to discredit Silvia Odio's story during the late summer of 1964, on the eve
of the release of the long-awaited Warren Report. It remains the single most important piece of evidence in the case, and the one that
definitively links Oswald to the broader story of anti-Castro intrigue that
we have explored at such length in earlier chapters of this book.

Unlike other events associated with that intrigue, the story of this
critical episode must be told from a post-assassination perspective, both
to understand the incident itself and to see why the one opportunity
to crack the case was completely missed by the Warren Commission.
Examining the investigators' behavior in the days and weeks following
November 22, 1963, also helps us understand why the three men who
visited Silvia Odio in late September or early October can now be identified with confidence. They were Loran Hall, the mob-connected mercenary who had shared Santo Trafficante's Trescornia cell in 1959; his
friend Lawrence Howard; and Lee Harvey Oswald.

Exactly one week after the assassination of President Kennedy, the
Dallas FBI was contacted by Mrs. C. L. Connell (Lucille), who was active

in the Dallas Catholic Cuban Relief Committee. She described a conversation she had with a friend, Silvia Odio, a divorced Cuban refugee of twenty-six with four children. According to Connell, Odio said that she had seen Lee Harvey Oswald speaking to Cuban refugees in Dallas, and that Oswald was "brilliant and clever." Odio added that she had heard indirectly from a Cuban source in New Orleans that Oswald was suspected of being a double agent.

Connell added that according to Cubans she knew, General Walker and a certain Colonel Castor, whom she later identified as Robert I. Castorr, had been speaking to Cuban refugees in Dallas and inciting them against President Kennedy in recent months. Connell also told the agents that Silvia Odio had been receiving psychiatric care from Dr. Burton Einspruch. She did not add that Silvia and another friend of hers named Marianne Sullivan were romantic rivals for the affections of Walter Michael Machann, a Catholic priest with a relaxed attitude toward his vows who was active in the Cuban refugee community. Ms. Sullivan revisited that situation at great length thirty years later in a memoir, *Kennedy Ripples*.[1]

Another three weeks passed before agents James P. Hosty and Bardwell Odum, neither of whom had interviewed Connell, located Silvia Odio. She turned out to be from a wealthy Cuban exile family. Her father, Amador Odio, had been a member of Manuel Ray's MRP in Cuba and had participated in Antonio Veciana's assassination plot against Castro in early fall 1961. He and his wife had been arrested after the discovery of the plot and were now serving long prison terms on the Isle of Pines.

Silvia had attended high school in the United States in the 1950s. She and her husband, a doctor, had initially left Cuba for Puerto Rico after the revolution but separated after he went for a time to Germany. She was now working in a Dallas office and living with the couple's four children in very modest circumstances. She had been a founding member of Manuel Ray's new group, JURE, which established a base in Venezuela with the covert help of the CIA and was preparing some sort of invasion of Cuba as well as attempting to arrange the assassination of Castro. Her sisters Sarita (Sara) and Annie had preceded her to Dallas and also lived there in the early fall of 1963. A page 1 story on Sarita, Annie, and their imprisoned parents, complete with photographs of all four, had run in the *Dallas Morning News* on May 5, 1962, undoubtedly making them well known within the Dallas refugee community.[2]

On December 18, Silvia told FBI agents her own story:

> Miss Silvia Odio, 1816 W. Davis Street, Dallas, Texas, advised she is a Cuban refugee and a member of the organization known as Junta Revolucionaria or JURE.
>
> Miss ODIO stated that in late September or early October, 1963, two Cuban men came to her house and stated they were from JURE. They were accompanied by an individual whom they introduced as LEON OSWALD. Miss ODIO stated that based upon photographs she has seen of LEE HARVEY OSWALD she is certain that LEON OSWALD is identical with LEE HARVEY OSWALD. Miss ODIO stated she is not certain if she misunderstood the first name of LEON or if the two Cuban men who introduced OSWALD as LEON misunderstood him. Miss ODIO stated the purpose of their visit was to ask her to write some letters to various businesses in Dallas and request funds for JURE.
>
> Miss ODIO stated that both of her parents are presently in prison in Cuba and for this reason she declined for fear her parents would be possibly harmed. These two individuals together with OSWALD then left. A few days later one of the two Cuban individuals contacted her by telephone and stated they were leaving town presumably to return to either Miami, Florida or Puerto Rico, the headquarters for JURE. The individual who called Miss ODIO who only gave his name as LEOPOLDO stated he was not going to have anything further to do with LEON OSWALD since he considered him to be "loco." This individual known only as LEOPOLDO stated that OSWALD did not appear sincere. He told them he was an ex-marine and could help them in the underground however he appeared to be very cynical and seemed to think that all Cubans hated all Americans. According to LEOPOLDO, OSWALD stated "I'll bet you Cubans could kill KENNEDY for what he did to you at the Bay of Pigs." According to Miss ODIO, LEOPOLDO told him that the Cuban people bore no malice toward President KENNEDY because of the Bay of Pigs episode.

Hosty said later that Silvia Odio did not seem inclined to talk to the FBI, and he got the erroneous impression that her English was poor.[3] His report told quite an abbreviated version of the story, omitting, for example, that Silvia's sister Annie had also been in the apartment on the day when the three men appeared and would vouch for Oswald's presence. Hosty contacted Dr. Burton Einspruch, Odio's psychiatrist, the next day. He confirmed that he was treating her for "certain psychiatric problems" but "advised she does not have any problems concerning hallucinations and that if she related information concerning the association of LEE HARVEY OSWALD with certain Cuban individuals he believes based upon his knowledge of Miss ODIO that she is telling the truth and is not exaggerating."[4] Despite this, the FBI, which had already submitted what it had intended to be its final report on the assassination, essentially dropped its inquiry into the Odio incident.

On April 6, 1964, Warren Commission staffer David Slawson raised the issue of Odio's testimony in a memorandum to Leon Hubert and Burt Griffin, two other staffers who were apparently on their way to Dallas to question witnesses. He obviously took it seriously and suggested that Mrs. Odio might easily be frightened into changing her story (which, as it turned out, she was not). Eight days later in Dallas, Griffin, accompanied by a Secret Service agent (the Secret Service, rather than the FBI, was apparently lending investigative resources to the Warren Commission at this stage), interviewed Mrs. Connell, who provided more detail about Silvia Odio. She described her as somewhat hysterical, partly as a consequence of her numerous romantic involvements, including her affair with Father Machann, who, she said, had left the priesthood.

On April 16 Griffin also saw Dr. Einspruch, who repeated that he believed Silvia's story, and added that she said she had seen Oswald more than once. On the same day, Griffin and Hubert met an Alcohol, Tobacco and Firearms agent named Frank Ellsworth, who discussed an attempt by a Cuban, Manuel Rodriguez, to purchase arms through a network of John Birchers and Minutemen. Rodriguez was connected to both Alpha-66 and to the DRE. Ellsworth also speculated that the Minutemen were most likely to have been involved in the assassination.[5]

The Secret Service decided to find the mysterious priest, Father Machann. An inquiry in Miami went nowhere, and a Miami monsignor could not find Machann in a directory of all Catholic priests in America.[6] On April 30, however, they located him in New Orleans, where he had begun studying at Loyola University, having left Dallas not

long before the Kennedy assassination. He acknowledged three years'
worth of work among Cuban refugees in Dallas and identified the principal Cuban groups there, but insisted that he had been careful not to
join any of them or take sides among them.

After a long discussion of Silvia Odio, Machann offered to phone her
to ask for the names of the men she claimed had visited her with Oswald.
But he insisted on making the call in private. Afterward, he returned to
tell the agent that while she did not know the real name of Leopoldo, she
had identified the other one as Rogelio Cisneros, one of the leaders of
JURE. That turned out to be untrue—Cisneros promptly explained to
the Secret Service in Miami that his one trip to Dallas, during which
Silvia Odio introduced him to a Uruguayan arms dealer named Juan
Martin, had taken place in June 1963.[7] Given Machann's insistence on
making the call alone, and given that Odio never identified Cisneros as
one of the three men to anyone else, it is quite likely that Machann, who
had left Dallas after becoming Odio's lover, might have known more
than he was letting on and was trying to divert suspicion from where it
belonged. Machann has subsequently disappeared.

These interviews led the Secret Service, the Warren Commission,
and, at the commission's request, the FBI to look into the presence of
Cuban refugees in Dallas, which numbered in the hundreds.[8] Exile organizations included the offices of Manuel Ray's JURE, to which Odio
belonged; a small chapter of the DRE, led by Sara Castillo and the Second National Front of the Escambray, or SNFE, closely affiliated with
Alpha-66 and headed by Manuel Rodriguez Orcaberro. The FBI interviewed Rodriguez, who denied any anti-Kennedy feelings, and submitted a report on Dallas Cuban activity in late June. They still had not followed up Silvia Odio's story.[9]

Not until July 22, 1964, two months before the Warren Report was
due, did Wesley Liebeler of the commission finally take Odio's testimony
in Dallas. She explained that she now believed the three men had come
to her home in late September—either Thursday the 26th or Friday the
27th. Two were Cubans and rather seedy, she said. One called himself
Leopoldo, and the other, she thought, might have called himself Angelo.
Leopoldo had done most of the talking. They had introduced the third
man, an American with a considerable growth of beard, as Leon Oswald.
Later she identified him as Lee Harvey Oswald. Her sister Annie had an-

swered the door and spoken briefly to Leopoldo and Angelo. They first asked for Sarita Odio, who was a student at the University of Dallas, but when Silvia came to the door and identified herself as the oldest sister, they said she was the person they wanted to talk with.

The two men tried to establish their bona fides with Silvia by referring to her father, Amador Odio.

One of them said, "We are very good friends of your father." This struck me, because I didn't think my father could have such kind of friends, unless he knew them from anti-Castro activities. He gave me so many details about where they saw my father and what activities he was in. I mean, they gave me almost incredible details about things that somebody who knows him really would or that somebody informed well knows. And after a little while, after they mentioned my father, they started talking about the American. He said, "You are working in the underground." And I said, "No, I am sorry to say I am not working in the underground." And he said, "We wanted you to meet this American. His name is Leon Oswald." He repeated it twice. Then my sister Annie by that time was standing near the door. She had come to see what was going on. And they introduced him as an American who was very much interested in the Cuban cause.

The two men asked Silvia to translate a fundraising letter they wanted to submit to various Dallas businesses. She declined, and asked them if they had been sent by local or national JURE leaders. When they said no, she began to become suspicious.

And I said, "Well, is this on your own?"

And he said, "We have just come from New Orleans and we have been trying to get this organized, this movement organized down there, and this is on our own, but we think we could do some kind of work." This was all talked very fast, not as slow as I am saying it now. You know how fast Cubans talk. And he put the letter back in his pocket when I said no. And then I think I asked something to the American, trying to be nice, "Have you ever been to Cuba?"

And he said, "No, I have never been to Cuba."

And I said, "Are you interested in our movement?" And he said, "Yes."

This I had not remembered until lately. I had not spoken much to him and I said, "If you will excuse me, I have to leave," and I repeated, "I am going to write to my father and tell him you have come to visit me."

And he said, "Is he still in the Isle of Pines?"

Silvia Odio did, in fact, write her father about the incident, and received a reply which she brought to her Warren Commission deposition. Written from prison on Christmas day, it confirmed that he had received a letter from her in early November. "Tell me who this is who says he is my friend—be careful, I do not have any friend who might have been here in Dallas, so reject his friendship until you give me his name."[10]

The men mentioned that they were leaving to go on a trip, although they might stay one more day. The next evening, Leopoldo telephoned her.

> The next day Leopoldo called me. I had gotten home from work, so I imagine it must have been Friday. And they had come on Thursday. I have been trying to establish that. He was trying to get fresh with me that night. He was trying to be too nice, telling me that I was pretty, and he started like that. That is the way he started the conversation. Then he said, "What do you think of the American?" And I said, "I didn't think anything." And he said, "You know our idea is to introduce him to the underground in Cuba, because he is great, he is kind of nuts." This was more or less—I can't repeat the exact words, because he was kind of nuts. He told us we don't have any guts, you Cubans, because President Kennedy should have been assassinated after the Bay of Pigs, and some Cubans should have done that, because he was the one that was holding the freedom of Cuba actually. And I started getting a little upset with the conversation.
>
> And he said, "It is so easy to do it." He has told us. And he [Leopoldo] used two or three bad words, and I wouldn't repeat it in Spanish. And he repeated again they were leaving for a trip and they would like very much to see me on their return to Dallas. Then he mentioned something more about Oswald. They called him Leon. He never mentioned the name Oswald.
>
> Mr. LIEBELER. He never mentioned the name of Oswald on the telephone?
>
> Mrs. ODIO. He never mentioned his last name. He always referred to the American or Leon.

Mr. LIEBELER. Did he mention his last name the night before?

Mrs. ODIO. Before they left I asked their names again, and he mentioned their names again.

Mr. LIEBELER. But he did not mention Oswald's name except as Leon?

Mrs. ODIO. On the telephone conversation he referred to him as Leon or an American. He said he had been a Marine and he was so interested in helping the Cubans, and he was terrific. That is the words he more or less used, in Spanish, that he was terrific.

The references to the possible assassination of Kennedy, of course, got the most attention after this testimony was released, but an equally critical passage occurred later, when Liebeler mentioned Hosty's December 1963 report that Leopoldo had said he wasn't going to have anything further to do with Leon.

> You told Agent Hosty that Leopoldo told you he was not going to have anything more to do with Leon Oswald since Leon was considered to be loco?
>
> Mrs. ODIO. That's right. He used two tactics with me, and this I have analyzed. He wanted me to introduce this man. He thought that I had something to do with the underground, with the big operation, and I could get men into Cuba. That is what he thought, which is not true.
>
> When I had no reaction to the American, he thought that he would mention that the man was loco and out of his mind and would be the kind of man that could do anything like getting underground in Cuba, like killing Castro. He repeated several times he was an expert shotman. And he said, "We probably won't have anything to do with him. He is kind of loco."
>
> When he mentioned the fact that we should have killed President Kennedy and this I recall in my conversation—he was trying to play it safe. If I liked him, then he would go along with me, but if I didn't like him, he was kind of retreating to see what my reaction was. It was cleverly done.[11]

We must keep in mind that while Liebeler, Odio, and everyone else understood that they were meeting because of the assassination of President Kennedy, the other matters to which she alluded were closely guarded CIA secrets about which Liebeler did not have a clue. "The big operation" referred, presumably, to Manuel Ray's CIA-sponsored JURE plans for another landing in Cuba. And the idea of getting Oswald into Cuba to shoot Castro was just one among dozens of assassination plots, some CIA-sponsored, some not, that had been mounted by Americans and Cuban exiles since 1959. Later in her testimony Odio volunteered that the three men had come from New Orleans, where Oswald had just left his lodgings. And as a matter of fact, while she and Leopoldo were speaking by phone, Oswald may have been on his way to Mexico to try to secure legal entry into Cuba. On the other hand, it is also possible, as we shall see, that her meeting with Oswald took place not in late September but on the evening of October 3, immediately after Oswald's return from his Mexican adventure.

A few days after Silvia gave her testimony, in late July 1964, her sister Annie, now living in Miami, told FBI agents that when Oswald first appeared on television after the assassination she felt sure she had seen him before. When Silvia reminded her of the incident in her apartment, Annie "realized that this was in fact the same person of whom she had been thinking when she saw Oswald on television" and that she was still "almost certain" that it had been Oswald.[12]

Another month passed and the September deadline for the submission of the Warren Report was closing in. Finally, on August 28, J. Lee Rankin of the commission pointedly asked J. Edgar Hoover to investigate Odio's story more thoroughly. Five days later, on September 2, Hoover wrote the Dallas office stating that it was "highly improbable, if not impossible" for Oswald to have been in Dallas on September 24–26, and ordered further investigation to disprove her statements by developing more information on her "mental status" and establishing her "reputation for veracity."[13] Agents in Dallas, Miami, and Puerto Rico worked hard on this task for the next few weeks with decidedly mixed results.

Three anti-Castro activists in Dallas belittled her story, but Ray and Cisneros, the leaders of JURE, reported her to be intelligent, dedicated, of good character, and unlikely to fabricate the episode of her meeting with Oswald.[14] A Dallas doctor confirmed that he treated her at a hospital on November 22 after she fainted upon hearing the news of the assassination, and her employer, James Dyer, confirmed that she had told the story of Oswald and the two men to him. When she had made clear that she thought the men might have been involved in the Kennedy assassination, he had become so angry that he suggested she find another job, which she did. He had never found her to be untruthful or suffering from delusions.[15]

Several acquaintances described how Silvia Odio had left Cuba with her husband and four children after her parents' arrest and had separated from and divorced her husband in Puerto Rico in 1962 before coming, penniless, to the United States, a situation that inevitably caused enormous strain. She had also, apparently, undergone a pregnancy, a miscarriage, and a hysterectomy early in 1964. Lucille Connell, the friend who brought Silvia to the FBI's attention in the first place, quoted Silvia's psychiatrist to the effect that she suffered from "grand hysteria" and a tendency to make things up.[16] But Dr. Einspruch himself said that despite her chronic and understandable nervous disorders, "There has never been any evidence of psychosis, inasmuch as she exhibited a 'good grasp of reality,' understands her responsibilities, and has attempted to be an 'adequate citizen and provider' for her family." If she gave any incorrect testimony, "it probably was the result of her misunderstanding the inquiries posed to her rather than a deliberate attempt to prevaricate."[17]

Silvia's uncle by marriage, Dr. Augustin Guitart, a professor who lived in New Orleans and had actually been present at Oswald's appearance in a New Orleans court, had looked after her children for a while in New Orleans and had heard her story about Oswald's visit, apparently even before the assassination took place. He believed her and found her generally truthful.[18] And even her ex-husband, Guillermo Herrera, while describing her as an excellent actress, said "that he is of the opinion that she would not be able to fabricate a story regarding any connection with Oswald and be able to stick to it through all the various inquiries to which she must have been subjected."[19] Taken together, the twenty-five interviews leave no reasonable option but to believe that she told the truth as she knew it. This, clearly, was not what Hoover had hoped to find.

In the midst of these last-minute interviews, on September 16, 1964—just eight days before the release of the Warren Report—the FBI discovered evidence in its files that Silvia Odio had apparently been visited by two American mercenaries, Loran Eugene Hall and Larry Howard, around the time in question. They had stopped in Dallas in late

September and early October 1963, on their way from California to Florida, transporting a trailer full of arms. Hall was an Army veteran and gambler living in Wichita, Kansas, when Castro came to power in 1959. Leaving behind a troubled personal life, he suddenly went to Cuba to join Castro's army—an odd decision, since by 1963 he was an extreme right-winger. While in Cuba, he was arrested and spent several months in the Trescornia detention center, sharing a cell with Santo Trafficante.

When he was released in 1960, Hall was interviewed by the FBI, but the CIA never took up the bureau's invitation to debrief him. Then Hall essentially dropped out of sight for more than two years, until he made contact with Gerry Hemming in Los Angeles in late 1962. He drove with Hemming to Florida in early 1963, stopping over in Dallas, where they had met the oil geologist Lester Logue, Robert Morris, and General Walker and received some funds from Logue, a political associate of H. L. Hunt. They also saw anti-Castro figures when they stopped in New Orleans. According to Hall, he was wounded during a raid on Cuba in March 1963 (presumably an Alpha-66 raid) and went to Dallas again to recuperate. While there, he and Logue apparently discussed a plan to stage a big raid on Cuba and seize enough territory to form a government in exile. Logue gave similar encouragement to Hemming in July 1963, promising eventual help in mounting one major raid, which, Logue believed, would bring forth a flood of donations.[20]

By spring 1963, the idea of some kind of pre-emptive military strike against Castro was becoming popular among right-wing exile groups and their American supporters. The Free Cuba Committee announced its foundation on April 10 in Washington, and its members included re-tired chief of naval operations Arleigh Burke, along with John Fisher, president of the conservative American Security Council, and William Pawley's friend the former congresswoman Clare Boothe Luce. In its in-augural press conference, the committee talked about cooperating with the administration to work out a program to eliminate Castro. In July a State Department official heard from a Cuban reporter that the commit-tee was planning to seize an island off Cuba and appeal for help. They expected Castro to crush the invasion, at considerable political cost to President Kennedy.[21]

Hall later said that after his recuperation in Dallas in March, he met with John Martino, Santo Trafficante, and Sam Giancana in Miami to discuss the Bayo-Pawley raid, but he left the Miami area in spring 1963 before the raid took off.[22] Hall had been involved in a planned invasion of Haiti. Federal agents were apparently watching the telephone line of a Haitian exile named Leon Cantave in New York City, and when Hall telephoned Cantave collect on April 6, they began looking for him. Hall telephoned the FBI office in Miami a few days later to give his address.

The planned invasion of Haiti involved Irving Davidson, the Washington lobbyist and friend of Jimmy Hoffa and Carlos Marcello, and Rolando Masferrer, the Batistiano exile. John Martino recruited two hundred Cubans for the venture. The involvement of both Martino and Davidson suggests that while Masferrer reportedly hoped to establish an anti-Castro base in Haiti after overthrowing Duvalier, mob interests were looking forward to building some new casinos there.[23] The plan reportedly secured the support of Dominican President Juan Bosch during the summer, but the attempt to land in Haiti in early September proved abortive.[24] Hall traveled to New York in connection with it, stopped in Washington, and saw Senator Kenneth Keating, an important critic of Kennedy's Cuba policy who was in contact with the DRE via Clare Boothe Luce and Pawley.[25]

Hall drove to Dallas for the third time in June 1963 on his way out to California. He stayed briefly with a certain Wally Yeats, who had learned about him and Hemming from a January story in the *Dallas Morning News*. Yeats, Hall told the HSCA in 1977, was trying to form a racist, anti-Semitic group in Dallas, where the Minutemen were already active. Mrs. Yeats made it clear that Hall was not welcome, and he moved to the Salvation Army. This was the point, he claimed, when Lester Logue invited Hall to a meeting in his office with some well-heeled Texans.

The meeting included three other well-dressed wealthy men, one a trucker named "Jack," another with Texas Instruments or Texas Optical, and another an associate of H. L. Hunt. Hall said he needed $50,000 for four boats to make the Cuba landing. Jack the trucker rose and said, "Here's $50,000 and if the rest of you will match it we'll give it to this man to blow Kennedy's ass off. With Kennedy dead, we'll have a Texan in office, and Texans take care of Texans." Hall jumped up and said he might blow someone's head off outside the country, but "I don't pull that shit here." Logue angrily told Jack that he never wanted to hear talk like that in his office again.[26] In early 1978 Logue "absolutely and categorically denied" to HSCA investigators ever hearing such an offer, although he acknowledged meeting and paying Hall several times during 1963.[27]

Hall then moved on to southern California, where he spent the next several months. As he told the HSCA, he became involved with a very right-wing anti-Castro organization, the American Committee to Free Cuba, headed by a Cuban refugee physician, Dr. Tirso Del Junco. Its members included Jose Norman and Congressman John Rousselot of the John Birch Society and Lee Harvey Oswald's hero, former Communist and FBI informer Herbert Philbrick.[28] Hall began speaking at various John Birch Society fundraisers. He was apparently in close touch with conservative exile groups, and he began trumpeting a rumor about the Kennedy administration, based on its support for Manuel Ray and Manuel Artime.

On September 18, he claimed, the administration was planning to back an invasion by Communists who would overthrow Castro and set up a new Communist regime. This scheme would allow Kennedy to claim, during the following year's campaign, that he had dealt with the Castro problem. Hall wanted money for his own invasion, to forestall the Kennedy-backed coup. One of his John Bircher associates, a certain Bill Tennyson, was sufficiently exercised by these rumors to ask Hall to take a lie detector test. The administrator of the polygraph examination, which Hall passed, gave the story to a U.S. Treasury investigator, who in turn gave it to the local CIA Domestic Contacts office. It is not clear whether any follow-up occurred.[29]

By early September, Hall had managed to raise enough money to buy a trailer full of arms and medical supplies for his proposed Cuba operation. Showing an unfortunate lack of curiosity, the HSCA in 1977 did not question him closely about where the arms, money, or medicine had come from, or even exactly what they were for. Hall left for Florida again, planning to stop in Dallas to raise more money and speak to someone about a boat. With him were two other men, Larry Howard, a Mexican-American, and a Cuban named Celio Castro Alba, who had driven out from Miami earlier in the month. When these three men were interviewed a year later, Hall said they left California in "late September," Castro Alba implied the same, and Howard gave the most specific testimony, stating that they headed out "on or about" September 17, 1963. Castro Alba told the FBI that the men had enjoyed themselves on the way, and that Hall and Howard had spent a day in Juarez, Mexico, while he remained quietly in El Paso. Alba also said they had checked into a motel in Dallas, where they remained about a week—a lead that the FBI apparently never followed up.

When the three men left Dallas for Miami, Hall parked his trailer full of arms and medicines at Lester Logue's house. He returned in mid-October with another man, William Seymour, to pick it up.[30] Anti-Castro activities in Dallas were proceeding on a number of fronts during these weeks. On October 1, Martino, whom Hall had met during the planning of the Bayo-Pawley raid, spoke in Dallas to promote his new book, *I Was Castro's Prisoner*. Father Walter Machann helped arrange the meeting.[31] Martino had flown from Miami to New Orleans on September 27. He spoke in various Texas cities from October 1 to October 3 and was in New Orleans on October 4 before returning to Miami.[32] He could have provided information about Odio's father to the men who visited her in late September or early October. Martino had done most of his prison time in La Cabana prison, and Amador Odio had spent some time there before being transferred to the Isle of Pines.[33] Amador Odio's December 1963 letter to Silvia suggests that "Leopoldo" had claimed to be in prison with him, and such a claim could have been based on a story told originally by Martino.

Meanwhile, the DRE, through its Dallas chapter, was attempting to acquire some weapons through a gun dealer named John Thomas Masen, who belonged to the Minutemen. Masen had apparently developed a source of stolen arms at a nearby Army base with the help of a Colonel George Nonte. The potential availability of more arms could easily have led Hall to leave his trailer with Logue in early October, travel to Miami, and return a couple of weeks later with Seymour to pick it up. (Leopoldo told Silvia Odio in his phone call that he would be returning to Dallas.)

Hall and Seymour evidently arrived in Dallas again in mid-October. On October 17—one day, Hall estimated, after their arrival—a Dallas police officer pulled them over and discovered a large cache of amphetamines in their car. After his arrest, Hall used his one phone call to reach college president Robert Morris, formerly of the Senate Internal Security Subcommittee and former counsel to General Walker. Morris in turn called Logue, who secured the services of a young attorney named Michael Rohde. Then Hall asked to see an FBI agent, and J. Harlan Brown of the Dallas office interviewed him on October 18.

Hall told Brown that he was a "group captain" in the Cuban Revolutionary Council in Miami and gave Tony Varona, now its head, as a reference. He said he had raided Cuba several times, both to attack targets and to exfiltrate resisters. With him was also a movie camera that he claimed had been donated by the John Birch Society in Dallas and film given by a local television station. He mentioned the story about him and Hemming that had run the previous January in the *Dallas Morning News* identifying him as "Lorenzo Hall." (As Hall explained, he often called himself "Lorenzo Pascillo" while dealing with Cubans.) Hall's attorney, Rohde, meanwhile got him released on a $200 bond, and Seymour was not charged. When the HSCA interviewed Rohde in 1977, he remembered the episode vividly and claimed, as did Hall in the same year, that officials of the CIA and military intelligence also visited Hall after his arrest. No record of those interviews has emerged.

Hall and Seymour impressed Rohde as "two extremely dangerous, committed individuals." While he could not exclude the possibility that they were "nuts," at a minimum they were tough, mean, and vicious. When Rohde checked out Hall's trailer at Logue's and found that it was full of weaponry, he had his father, a mover, take it to a warehouse. After Hall was released, Rohde told him to get it out of town, and Hall did. A few days later, Rohde learned that the charges would be dropped and Hall's bond would be returned. He became suspicious during the investigation that Hall had gotten a prescription from a Los Angeles physician, Stanley L. Drennan, airmailed to him from Las Vegas on the day after his arrest. In 1968 Hall told New Orleans District Attorney Jim Garrison that Dr. Drennan had been present at Birch Society meetings in Los Angeles where the assassination of Kennedy was discussed.[34]

When the Warren Commission demanded a more thorough investigation of the Odio incident on August 28, 1964, Dallas FBI agents apparently searched their files and discovered the record of Hall and Seymour's October 17, 1963, arrest, which they confirmed with Dallas police. The bureau had renewed its interest in Hall's anti-Castro activities the previous June and knew that he was now living in Kernville, California. During the spring of 1964 he had reportedly worked for the congressional campaign of an extreme anti-Communist Republican, Guy Gabaldon, who was defeated in the Nineteenth District. In September 1964, when the record of Hall's arrest the previous October came to light, the Dallas office of the FBI realized that he might possibly have been the "Leopoldo" or "Angelo" who had visited Silvia Odio with Oswald in late September 1963.[35]

Agent Leon Brown of the Los Angeles office interviewed Hall on September 16, 1964. Hall reported that he was now working as a truck driver and running the Rainbow Motel in Kernville. (Thirteen years later he told the HSCA that he had borrowed most of the money to buy the motel from a Pasadena bank.)

> HALL stated that during the latter part of September, 1963, he was in Dallas, Texas in company with LAWRENCE HOWARD and WILLIAM SEYMOUR. HALL had gone to Dallas to solicit aid in the anti-CASTRO movement. HALL said they contacted three professors at the university of Dallas who are Cuban refugees. One of these professor's name HALL recalled, was ODIO. These professors furnished HALL with a list of Cubans living in the Dallas area who could be contacted to solicit assistance in this movement.

This was not quite correct. No such professor existed, though Silvia Odio's younger sister Sara (or Sarita) was a student at a Dallas university, and Silvia testified that the three men who visited her had originally asked for Sarita. Hall said that he, Howard, and Seymour had contacted forty or fifty people, whereupon he and Seymour were arrested, held for a day, and interviewed by several federal intelligence agencies. He went on:

> HALL said that he recalled that while in Dallas on this particular occasion, the three of them, HALL, HOWARD, and SEYMOUR, had gone to the apartment of a Cuban woman who lived in a garden style apartment located on Magellan Circle in Dallas. HALL said that he could not picture this woman in his mind now. He said that her name was possibly ODIO. He said that he seemed to recognize this woman's name as ODIO because of the association with the name of the Cuban professor who had the same name, ODIO.

HALL stated that this Cuban woman lived in Apartment A of the same apartments located on Magellan Circle where a Cuban friend of his by the name of KIKI FERROR was living with two or three other Cuban men. He visited KIKI FERROR and on one occasion was introduced to this woman in passing, outside of the apartments. Later, HALL, in company with WILLIAM SEYMOUR and LARY HOWARD, went to her apartment to ask her assistance in the movement. HALL did not recall whether she was on the list given by the professors or if their previous introduction to her had prompted them to contact her. He said this contact was very brief and he did not believe that they even went into her apartment . . .

HALL said that the above described incident would undoubtedly be the same incident which has been referred to by SILVIA ODIO, but that he certainly would not have been the person whom SILVIA ODIO could have mistaken as LEE HARVEY OSWALD. HALL explained that it now occurs to him that WILLIAM SEYMOUR is a person who might be said to generally resemble OSWALD. HALL described SEYMOUR as being white, male, American, age about 25 or 26, five nine to five ten in height, 155 to 160 pounds, slender build, light hair and blue eyes. HALL said that he does not know where SEYMOUR is at the present time. He said that SEYMOUR is from Phoenix and is probably living some where at Phoenix, Arizona.

Hall then mentioned that he used the name Lorenzo Pascillo in the anti-Castro movement, and that he had a full beard at the time he was in Dallas. He said that both he and Howard spoke fluent Spanish and that he had been taken to be a Cuban by various Cubans. Howard had a Mexican mother and could easily be taken for a Mexican.[36]

Working frantically against a deadline of September 21 to hand in the final Warren Report to President Johnson, the FBI set about confirming Hall's story, which, it seemed, might relieve them of the possibility that Mrs. Odio was telling the truth. The investigation did not go well, however. On September 20 (four days after Hall's interview), Howard told a Los Angeles agent a different story about his trip to Dallas with Hall and Celio Castro Alba, and added what he knew about Hall and Seymour's return trip and arrest in October. He emphatically denied that he had visited any Cuban woman in Magellan Circle named Odio. He estimated that they had remained in Dallas from approximately September 20 to September 30.[37]

Seymour was able to prove that he had not been there at all. In an interview on September 18, he declared that he had been employed by a Miami welding company all through September and early October 1963. On September 22, the day after the Warren Report was handed to President Johnson, the manager of Beach Welding and Supplies showed the FBI pay records that confirmed this, eliminating any possibility that Silvia Odio had mistaken William Seymour for Lee Harvey Oswald.[38]

Someone, meanwhile, had spoken to Loran Hall. When agent Brown reinterviewed him on September 20 at his home, Hall "said he had been in error in previously stating that the incident referred by SILVIA ODIO had probably involved a contact by himself, WILLIAM SEYMOUR AND LAWRENCE HOWARD." He now remembered that those two men had been with him on separate trips, but he affirmed that he had visited Kiki Ferrer, whom he believed lived in Magellan Circle. This time he told the story of his October arrest much more fully, mentioning that an unnamed Dallas citizen had provided $5,000 bond. He acknowledged five different visits to Dallas in 1963, and admitted that "the name ODIO and information concerning a father being a prisoner on the Isle of Pines is familiar to him, but that he is now unable to relate this to any experience which he had in Dallas." He added that he now thought Celio Castro Alba was a Castro agent.[39]

The Warren Report was released to the public on September 27, 1964. Its attempt to discredit Odio's story relied mainly on an analysis of Oswald's movements, but it also discussed Hall's testimony.

On September 16, 1964, the FBI located Loran Eugene Hall in Johnsondale, Calif. Hall has been identified as a participant in numerous anti-Castro activities. He told the FBI that in September of 1963 he was in Dallas, soliciting aid in connection with anti-Castro activities. He said he had visited Mrs. Odio. He was accompanied by Lawrence Howard, a Mexican-American from East Los Angeles and one William Seymour from Arizona. He stated that Seymour is similar in appearance to Lee Harvey Oswald; he speaks only a few words of Spanish, as Mrs. Odio had testified one of the men who visited her did. While the FBI had not yet completed its investigation into this matter at the time the report went to press, the Commission has concluded that Lee Harvey Oswald was not at Mrs. Odio's apartment in September of 1963.[40]

The commission's failure to indicate that interviews with Seymour, Howard, and Castro Alba had now completely discredited this version of the story was a disgrace.[41] On October 1, 1964—four days after the Warren Report was released proclaiming that Oswald had acted alone and that he had not been to Mrs. Odio's apartment—FBI agents showed photos of Hall, Howard, Castro Alba, and Seymour to Silvia and Annie Odio in Miami. Silvia, who surely knew how hard the bureau had been working to try to establish that she was mentally unsound, said now that she could not identify any of them as the men she had seen, although Castro Alba resembled Leopoldo. She added that because of the passage of time and the difficulty of recognizing photographs, she was not certain that she could still identify the two men who had accompanied Oswald. Annie Odio, who had confirmed her sister's recollection of the meeting and the identification of Oswald back in December, did not identify any of them either.[42]

Yet Silvia Odio provided a detail which proved that the key part of Hall's original story—that he had visited her—was true. In his first interview, Hall had stated that his friend Kiki Ferrer lived in the same apartment complex at Magellan Circle. In his second interview, he acknowledged some confusion between Kiki Ferrer and a more prominent exile, Kiki Masferrer, the brother of Rolando Masferrer, who did not live in Dallas. On October 1, 1964, Silvia Odio said that although she did not know the name Kiki Ferrer, "there was a Cuban family of a man, wife and two children with the surname Masferrer who also lived in the Crestwood Apartments on Magellan Circle." Unfortunately, with the Warren Report put to bed, the bureau apparently did not follow up this lead to establish the relationship between this gentleman and Loran Hall.

Based on what we can reconstruct of his movements, could Oswald have been in Dallas in late September as Odio described? Despite some obfuscation by the Warren Commission, the answer is yes—indeed, there is no proof of where he was from September 23, the day that Marina left New Orleans with Ruth Paine, until very early in the morning of September 26, when an English couple saw him board a bus in Houston on the way to Mexico City. Paine told the FBI that she arrived in New Orleans after visiting Birmingham on September 20 and left with Marina on the morning of September 23.[43] A motel registration card confirmed that Ruth and Marina spent the night of September 23 in Waskom, Texas, 357 miles away from New Orleans.[44] A neighbor named Eric Rogers said that he saw Oswald running with two suitcases to catch a city bus the day after Marina left—that is, September 24.[45]

Oswald's last unemployment check was forwarded from his post office box in Austin, Texas, to New Orleans on September 23 and, according to the FBI, arrived in New Orleans around 6:00 p.m. on the 24th.[46] Someone cashed it at a Winn-Dixie supermarket in New Orleans, but no one could tell exactly when.[47] Exhaustive searches by the FBI found no evidence of Oswald's having stayed in any New Orleans hotel on the night of the 24th or of his taking any bus out of New Orleans on the 24th and 25th.[48] Some evidence suggested that the check might have been cashed several days after Oswald left town, that is, by someone else. It seemed to have reached the National Bank of Commerce on September 29, a Saturday (the date was not fully legible, according to the FBI).[49] But the manager of the Winn-Dixie where Oswald cashed the check said checks usually went to the bank in an armored car the next day.[50] Other evidence suggests that Oswald usually received his unemployment checks on Tuesday, and the Tuesday of that week was September 24.[51]

New Orleans is 528 miles from Dallas, but if Oswald left on September 23, the day Marina left, he could have been at Silvia Odio's house one or two days before the evening of Wednesday the 25th. Leopoldo told Silvia that the three men had just come from New Orleans and that they were about to leave on a trip. Even if Oswald had been at her apartment on the 25th, he could have reached Houston by 2:00 a.m. to board the bus to Laredo—a distance of 240 miles. But there is another possibility altogether, one that official investigations and other researchers have ignored, but which seems just as likely.

As we shall see, Oswald returned from his trip to Mexico City by bus, arriving in Dallas on the afternoon of Thursday, October 3. He did not appear at Ruth Paine's house in Irving until the next day. Silvia Odio's lease on her Magellan Circle apartment was up on September 30, but what everyone has missed is the evidence that she might not yet have moved out on that day. When Hosty interviewed Odio in December 1963, she told him that the three men had visited her in late September or early October. Seven months later, she and her sister settled on the last week of September, in part because of the move, but they could have been mistaken. The manager of the Crestwood Apartments, where Silvia lived, said that she assumed she had left either on September 30 (a Monday) or "a few days following" September 30, allowing her to leave on the weekend.[52]

The possibility that the meeting with Hall, Howard, and Oswald actually took place on October 3 takes on enormous significance because it was on September 26, while Oswald was on the bus to Mexico City, that the *Dallas Morning News* first reported the President's plans to visit Texas on November 21–22 and the possibility that Dallas might be on his itinerary.[53]

Hall and Howard probably had three reasons for their visit to Odio's house, whenever it occurred. They wanted her help in soliciting money from wealthy Cubans. They wanted information about JURE, an organization they regarded as Communist. (Hall had already warned John Birchers in southern California about a possible invasion of Cuba by Kennedy-backed Communists.) And finally, when Hall called Silvia the next day after their meeting, he wanted her help in getting Oswald into Cuba so that he might take a shot at Castro, just as Hall had briefly helped Martino (who was visiting Dallas at about the same time) try to set up the Bayo-Pawley assassination raid the previous spring. Since he knew Odio's father was in prison for participating in another assassination attempt on Fidel, he might easily have expected her to be sympathetic. And Leopoldo dropped a tantalizing hint to the effect that Oswald might be willing to take a shot at President Kennedy as well. Had Silvia Odio been able to tell Hall how he could get Oswald into Cuba, history might have taken an entirely different turn. But she did not, and as we shall see, Oswald's attempts to travel to Cuba legally via Mexico City failed as well.

In 1970 an Army intelligence officer interviewed Roy Hargraves, another one of Hemming and Hall's fellow mercenaries.

According to Jerry [sic] Hemming, both Howard and Hall met with Lee Harvey Oswald in Texas while en route to Florida prior to the John Kennedy assassination. After President Kennedy was killed, Hemming related to Source that he felt that the assassination was a Central Intelligence

Agency (CIA) plot to do away with Kennedy since Howard and Hall were believed to have been connected with the CIA. Source, at a later date, confronted Howard with the question concerning his part in the alleged connection with the Kennedy assassination. Howard "clammed up" and became nervous concerning the matter and avoided the subject completely.[54]

Hemming was apparently wrong about Hall's CIA connection, but the evidence suggests that his story of the meeting of Hall, Howard, and Oswald was true.

John Martino's role in this incident will never be exactly known, although he eventually admitted to having helped arrange the assassination of President Kennedy.[55] But in the midst of her Warren Commission testimony, Silvia Odio dropped a tantalizing hint that Martino was a man in whom the commission should take some interest. It came when Wesley Liebeler asked her about what Lucille Connell had told the FBI in late November 1963—that Silvia Odio said she saw Oswald in several meetings of anti-Castro Cubans and that he was "brilliant and clever." She replied:

> This is something when you talk to somebody, she probably was referring—we did have some meetings, yes. John Martino spoke, who was an American, who was very clever and brilliant. I am not saying that she is lying at all. When you are excited, you might get all your facts mixed up, and Martino was one of the men who was in Isle of Pines for 3 years. And he mentioned the fact that he knew Mr. Odio, that Mr. Odio's daughters were in Dallas, and she went to that meeting. I did not go, because they kept it quiet from me so I would not get upset about it. I don't know if you know who John Martino is.[56]

This testimony raises a great many questions. Since Martino, by his own account, was never at the Isle of Pines, it tends to confirm that Silvia did not, in fact, hear his speech on October 1. But he easily could have met her father at La Cabana fortress, and he might actually have been the "friend" about whom she wrote her father. By the time she testified, she may have learned more about Martino and exactly who he was and may have hesitated to be specific about his role in bringing Leopoldo to her house. Unfortunately, Liebeler did not take the hint, and her testimony remained the only reference to Martino in the entire Warren Report and evidence.

Oswald's contact with Loran Hall links him at one remove to both Martino and Santo Trafficante. Leopoldo's references to possible assassination attempts against both Castro and Kennedy, moreover, echo both Hall's and Hemming's testimony to the HSCA. Hall said that a Dallas discussion about assassinating Castro had led to an offer of $100,000 to assassinate Kennedy, and Hemming claimed that he had been in a number of discussions of plots against Fidel in which someone had suggested that the same goal might more easily be accomplished by killing Kennedy.[57] Such talk was cheap, of course, by 1978, but an extraordinary piece of contemporary evidence indicates that Hall and Hemming had talked freely about assassinating the President in 1963.

On Saturday, November 23, 1963, Richard Hathcock—the Los Angeles private investigator and owner of a pawn shop where Hemming and Hall had hocked a camera and Hemming's 30.06 rifle—contacted the FBI. He told them about his contacts with Hemming and Hall and reported that Hall had redeemed the rifle on September 18, just before he left for Dallas. Both Hemming and Hall, he told the agent twice, were "violently anti-Communist and anti-Castro." The text of the report said nothing about the President, but it was captioned "Assassination of President Kennedy." Unfortunately, the FBI failed to pursue the lead that Hathcock had been so eager to give them.[58]

Nor is this all. On September 12, 1963, the CIA Station in Miami reported that the November issue of a magazine called *See,* already on newsstands, featured a wanted poster for Fidel Castro on the cover. "The CIA needs men, can you qualify?" a headline inside asked, and the DRE offered a $10 million reward "to person or persons who with the help of the DRE will assassinate Fidel Castro." It was signed by DRE leader Luis Fernandez Rocha.[59] As we shall see, a disinterested witness placed Oswald at a DRE meeting in Dallas in October. And in early November Oswald claimed that he expected shortly to come into a considerable sum of money.

By late September, Lee Harvey Oswald was evidently involved in a plot to kill either Fidel Castro or John F. Kennedy. Which one it would turn out to be would depend on what happened in Mexico.

12

Journey to Mexico

Sometime in August of 1963, Lee Harvey Oswald decided to travel to Cuba via Mexico City. Having received a new passport back in July, he went to the Mexican consulate in New Orleans for a tourist visa on September 17. He specifically requested a transit visa, indicating an interest in travel to an unidentified third country, and declared his intention to take $300 with him. The visa was valid for fifteen days, that is, until October 2.[1] He received it on the same day that William Gaudet—the author of a newsletter on Latin American affairs whose main customer was the CIA—received his visa. But when the FBI found Gaudet at his Mississippi home on November 27, 1963, he denied having seen Oswald.[2]

Traveling to Cuba was illegal and dangerous, and Oswald knew it. The House Un-American Activities Committee had held a series of hearings on travel to Cuba during the last few years, focusing on trips sponsored by the leftist Fair Play for Cuba Committee. In Washington on May 6, 7, 23, August 5, and September 12 and 13, 1963, and in Los Angeles on July 1 and 2, HUAC interrogated various travelers, most of whom had failed to validate their passports and many of whom had traveled to Cuba via Mexico City. The May 23 hearings featured Oswald's FPCC correspondent V. T. Lee, who had received permission to go as a journalist in late 1962 and early 1963. The September hearings involved a large group of American students who had reached Cuba by way of Europe in summer 1963.[3] Several of them, upon their return, had debated the situation in Cuba on the radio with representatives of the DRE—a debate encouraged by the CIA.[4] *The Militant,* to which Oswald subscribed, had covered these hearings.

Much of the propaganda Oswald handed out in New Orleans during the summer before JFK's assassination, including the leaflet that Rafael Aznarez Garcia sent to J. Edgar Hoover in June, called specifically for lifting the travel ban in order that Americans might find out the truth about Cuba. Yet in his numerous letters to V. T. Lee, Oswald never asked him how to be included in the next FPCC-sponsored trip. Instead, he struck out on his own. And leading up to his departure, Oswald observed strict operational security. Ruth Paine believed he was going to Houston or Philadelphia to look for work, and a great deal of evidence suggests that his wife had no idea where he was actually headed, either.

From 1964 until the present, lone-assassin theorists have relied a great deal on the testimony of Marina Oswald to explain her husband's behavior in 1963. But the release of the original FBI investigative reports has cast considerable doubt on the story she told the Warren Commission in February 1964, and even more on the detailed account of her life with Oswald that she gave to Priscilla Johnson McMillan during the next fourteen years.[5] As it turns out, the story that Marina told the commission on February 3, 1964 (and which she then expanded considerably on June 11 and again on September 6) simply cannot be trusted because it differs so fundamentally from what she told the Secret Service and FBI in twenty-one different interviews during the previous two months (on November 22, 24, 27, 28, 30, December 1, 2, 3, 4, 6, 9, 11, 16, 17, 19, 20, and January 15, 16, 21, 22, 31). The files also suggest why her story might have changed so dramatically by the time of the Warren Commission investigation.

Beginning on November 28, when she spontaneously brought up the subject herself after seeing something about it on television, she repeatedly and emphatically denied knowing that her husband had traveled to Mexico in September. She generally pleaded ignorance of his activities and denied any knowledge of his owning ammunition for his rifle or practicing with it, and she said she had no idea why he would have fired at Kennedy or Connally. (She did, on the other hand, readily reveal all her knowledge about the Walker shooting as soon as the FBI confronted her with the note Oswald had written for her in Russian on the day of the incident.) The FBI repeatedly pressed her regarding the Mexico visit in late January as she prepared to testify before the Warren Commission, but she stuck firmly to her story that she knew nothing.[6]

Meanwhile, Marina was experiencing great changes in her financial status and her personal life. Within two days of JFK's assassination, she suddenly became a widow. The American people were evidently as moved by the image of a lonely foreign widow with two tiny children as they were traumatized by the death of a popular president, and by mid-January Marina had received $54,000 in donations from strangers—the equivalent of several hundred thousand dollars today.

At the local Six Flags Motel, where she, daughter June, and her new baby had been put immediately after the assassination, she met the motel manager, James Herbert Martin, who, as it happened, had known her husband's murderer, Jack Ruby, for many years. Martin promptly invited her and her children to Thanksgiving dinner and then persuaded them to take up residence in his home.[7] On New Year's Eve, Martin kissed Marina and told her he loved her. He also gave her a few gifts. But Marina said she would not have sex with him until she was living in her own house.

Martin engaged a lawyer for Marina, John M. Thorne, and persuaded her to sign an agreement making Martin and Thorne her agents for book and magazine deals. The two men must have realized, however, that her story would not be worth much if she continued to insist that she had known nothing about what her husband was doing. In the first week of February, when Martin and Thorne accompanied her to Washington for her first appearance before the Warren Commission, she suddenly reversed herself, claiming to have known all about the trip to Mexico. She even stated that Oswald had tried to recruit her to help hijack an aircraft to get there. On February 6, after testifying, she asked the Secret Service to stop its surveillance of her, after which she and Martin took a walk, returned to their hotel, and slept together for the first time.[8]

Marina apparently had second thoughts when she returned to Texas, and Robert Oswald, her brother-in-law, persuaded her to move in with him. On February 14 by registered letter she officially fired Martin and Thorne. Meanwhile, she further embellished her story, telling Robert that in spring 1963 Lee had tried to leave their apartment wearing a suit and carrying his pistol because he wanted to see Richard Nixon, who was coming to town. That part of her story, which she eventually repeated to the Warren Commission, collapsed when it turned out that

Nixon had never contemplated making any such visit during the first half of 1963.[9]

Marina told the Warren Commission that she had withheld all this information from the FBI because she disliked them. J. Edgar Hoover normally pursued with a vengeance anyone who lied to his agents, but in this case he decided that discretion was the better part of valor. The evolution of Marina's story after the assassination suggests that her Warren Commission testimony, and also the far more extensive interviews she later gave to McMillan, should be viewed with considerable skepticism. The bulk of all the other evidence available suggests that neither Marina nor anyone else knew that her husband was leaving for Mexico right after she and Ruth Paine left the city on September 23.

Oswald essentially disappeared that day or the next. It is not yet clear whether he appeared at Silvia Odio's apartment in Dallas on the night of September 24 or 25 or on the day he returned, October 3. Despite an exhaustive search, the FBI was never able to establish how Oswald got from New Orleans to Houston, where he turned up at 2:00 a.m. on the morning of September 26. There, he boarded a Flecha Roja bus and made the acquaintance of a young British couple named McFarland. The travelers entered Mexico in the morning and, apparently after a layover of several hours in Nuevo Laredo, boarded a second bus for Mexico City in the afternoon. They arrived in Mexico City on the morning of September 27.[10]

Two young Australian women, Patricia Winston and Pamela Mumford, boarded the second bus in Monterrey—several hours after it left Laredo—and met Oswald, the McFarlands, and an elderly British man who was sitting next to Oswald. Evidently feeling relaxed, Oswald identified himself to his fellow travelers as the chairman of the New Orleans Fair Play for Cuba Committee and said he intended to travel to Cuba via Mexico City. He recommended the Hotel Cuba in Mexico City and showed them what must have been his old passport, since it indicated his previous travel to Russia. "I gather the young man sitting next to me has been to Mexico City before," said the elderly gentleman—which, of course, Oswald had not. A Flecha Roja manifest identified the Englishman as John Howard Bowen.[11]

The search for Bowen made fools of several FBI agents and ultimately left behind a minor mystery. A few weeks after identifying him as a passenger, they discovered an address for him in Texmelucan, Mexico. An agent from the Mexico City legal attaché's office went there on January 7, 1964, and discovered an elderly gentleman named Albert Osborne. Osborne politely explained that Bowen was traveling in the United States.[12] By early February, the bureau had learned that Osborne was some sort of Protestant missionary and that he and Bowen were in fact the same person.[13]

By that time, Osborne/Bowen had really left Mexico for the United States and was traveling around the middle South.[14] When the FBI finally caught up with John Howard Bowen in Florence, Alabama, on February 11, he said that he had been born in Chester, Pennsylvania, in 1885 and was now a Baptist missionary, an "itinerant gardener and preacher." He had never, he said, been to Canada or England. He explained that he had met Albert Osborne around 1958 and borrowed his identity card because a Mexican census was in progress. He had not seen Osborne for several years. He confirmed boarding the bus at Laredo and remembered a traveler of Oswald's description and a British couple but denied having any conversation with Oswald. He said he had remained in Mexico preaching and distributing Bibles until sometime in November 1963. The agent believed him.[15]

Meanwhile, an agent in New Orleans found that the Reverend Albert Alexander Osborne had applied for a Canadian passport in New Orleans on October 10, giving a birth date of November 12, 1888, in Grimsley, England.[16] When attempts to locate Osborne failed, another agent reinterviewed Bowen on February 17 in Laredo, and this time he denied that there had been any other Americans or English speakers on his bus to Mexico City on September 26, and he refused to identify pictures of Oswald. He once again denied being Osborne and described a complicated itinerary around the southern states during the last few months.[17]

One mystery was solved and another one opened up on February 17, when Osborne's brother Walter identified pictures of Bowen as Albert Osborne, and then added that his brother had visited England during November and December. On the same day, the agent who interviewed Bowen identified photos of Osborne as the man he had questioned. Osborne, it turned out, had developed a network of American women who provided regular donations to his mission. On March 3 another FBI agent finally got him to admit, in Memphis, that he had been using the

Bowen alias for years. He had served in the British army from 1908 to 1914 and in the Canadian army from 1916 to 1918. He had indeed flown to England and Spain on a twenty-one-day excursion from mid-November through December 5, 1963.[18]

On March 5 Hoover asked the Dallas office to prepare a full report on Osborne and said he planned to suggest that the Warren Commission subpoena him. A week later, however, Hoover informed the Mexico City office that headquarters had concluded there was no connection between Oswald and Osborne, and that Osborne's "hesitancy and vagueness during interview is attributable to the fact that he is a con man."[19] So he apparently was, but the lack of follow-up left three questions unanswered.

First, in his final interview, Osborne continued to deny having met or spoken to Oswald, though he obviously had. Second, an alert Dallas agent remembered that some of Oswald's FPCC handbills had been ordered by a man who used the name Osborn, and that two of the New Orleans printers had said that Oswald was not the man with whom they had dealt. The agent sent photos of Albert Osborne to the FBI's New Orleans office, asking that they be shown to the printers for a possible identification. There is no evidence that this was ever done, or any indication of why it was not done.[20] And finally, no one has yet explained how an itinerant preacher who lived on $20 monthly donations from lonely widows could have afforded a three-week trip to Europe, which cost at least five times more in constant dollars in 1963 than it does today.

In any event, Oswald arrived in Mexico City on Friday, September 27, around 10:00 a.m. and went directly to the Cuban consulate to attempt to get a visa to enter Cuba. In crossing that threshold, he entered an arena of intense scrutiny by American intelligence agencies. Their photographic and telephone surveillance brought him to the attention of the CIA in Mexico City by October 1 at the latest. Exactly what they learned and how they learned it during his stay in Mexico City became the subject of a long, separate investigation by staffers of the House Select Committee on Assassinations in 1977–78. The final document became known as the Lopez Report after its principal author, Edwin Lopez.[21] Oswald's Cuban and Soviet contacts in Mexico City also became the basis for accusations that the intelligence services of those countries were behind the assassination of President Kennedy—accusations revived in a German television documentary in 2006.

Available sources on what actually happened inside those embassies include four transcripts of intercepted phone calls; testimony by a CIA transcriber about a fifth transcript that has never been found; the testimony of two officials each in the Cuban consulate and the Soviet Embassy about their conversations with Oswald; and an entirely different story that an American Communist and FBI informer claimed to have heard from Fidel Castro himself in spring 1964.

The first person Oswald saw in the Cuban consulate was Silvia Duran, a young Mexican woman of leftist sympathies who handled visa applications there. As the CIA immediately acknowledged in the days after the assassination, she was already of considerable interest to the agency because she had been the mistress of Cuba's ambassador to the United Nations, Carlos Lechuga, when he was stationed in Mexico City during 1962.[22] Duran was interrogated twice by Mexican authorities in the days after the assassination but was never interviewed by representatives of the Warren Commission. When the HSCA interviewed her in June 1978, they put in front of her Oswald's application for a Cuban visa, confirming that he had come in on September 27. She explained that he had stopped by three times that day. She was not certain whether he immediately announced that he wanted a transit visa that would enable him to go to the Soviet Union via Cuba or whether that emerged as a possible alternative during their conversation. She customarily told applicants that a visa to Cuba required only a reference from a Cuban who would take responsibility for the visitor while there.[23] She explained to Oswald that he would need four photographs in any case, told him where he might get them, and bid him good day.

When Oswald returned shortly thereafter with the pictures, she filled out his application. Then, apparently in an attempt to win political favor, he presented a dossier designed to prove his support for Communism in general and the Cuban Revolution in particular. It included his Russian labor card, his Russian marriage license, correspondence with the Communist Party USA, his Fair Play for Cuba Committee card, and a clipping from a New Orleans newspaper describing his arrest for disturbing the peace. When he claimed, falsely, to be a member of the CPUSA, Duran pointed out that American Communists usually arranged to travel to Cuba with the party's help, and she explained to HSCA investigators that the CPUSA could have arranged to have his visa waiting. Duran was obviously beginning to smell a rat, and Oswald did not help by protesting that he had not had time to make these arrangements. As she explained later, the Mexican government was so anti-Communist that American Communists usually arrived without *anything* that suggested their affiliation. Oswald had done just the opposite.[24] She repeated that he would need a Soviet visa in order to get a transit visa for Cuba, and he left to get one.

Neither the Warren Commission in 1964 nor the HSCA in 1977–78 managed to get any authoritative information from the Soviet Union about these transactions. But thanks to the collapse of Communism, we may now pick up the story with the help of a KGB officer who was serving in the Soviet consulate at the time, Oleg M. Nechiporenko, whose memoir, *Passport to Assassination,* appeared in 1993.[25] As Nechiporenko explained, Oswald arrived at the Soviet consulate at about 12:30 p.m. and initially saw another consular officer-cum-KGB agent, Valery V. Kostikov. Oswald said nothing about Cuba but described his previous life in the Soviet Union and his marriage, complained that he was under surveillance by the FBI, added that they were persecuting his wife, and asked to return to Russia.

Since Nechiporenko was a counterintelligence specialist, Kostikov handed Oswald off to him. Oswald seemed very tired—not surprisingly, since he must have been traveling more or less continuously for at least three days and had spent the last two nights on a bus. He repeated the same story to Nechiporenko, adding that he had asked the Soviet Embassy in Washington to be allowed to return but had been refused. This was at best a half-truth. In February, Marina had written the Soviet Embassy asking to return to her homeland and had submitted extensive documentation. Sometime around July 1 she had written a long and anguished plea asking that it be approved, and adding that her husband now wanted to return to the Soviet Union as well. "I enclose with this letter an application of my husband for permission to enter into the USSR," she concluded. But the enclosure was evidently a note from Oswald asking the embassy to "rush the entrance visa for the return of Soviet citizen Marina N. Oswald . . . As for my return entrance visa please consider it separately." No evidence that he had formally applied has ever been found.[26] He also said, according to Nechiporenko, that he had come to Mexico City because the FBI might arrest him if he wrote the Soviet Embassy in Washington. And he mentioned that he wanted to go to Cuba first, in case the Soviet Union refused to admit him.

Nechiporenko, like his FBI counterpart John Fain fourteen months earlier, asked Oswald why he left the Soviet Union in the first place, but Oswald refused to answer. Becoming suspicious, the officer eventually decided that he had no reason to help Oswald. He simply explained that normally any visa would have to be granted by the Soviet Embassy in the United States, where Oswald lived, and that it would take at least four months. He was willing to give Oswald the necessary paperwork and send it to Moscow, but the reply must come through Washington. "That won't do for me!" replied an agitated Oswald. "This is not my case! For me, it's all going to end in tragedy!" Nechiporenko then escorted him out.[27]

Oswald—upset by the difficulties he was encountering and undoubtedly exhausted—decided to try a bluff. Late that afternoon, possibly after checking into the Hotel Comercio and taking a nap, he returned to the Cuban Embassy, which was now closed, and demanded to see Silvia Duran again. A doorman brought him to her, and he announced that he had secured his Soviet visa and wanted his Cuban one. She replied that Havana would have to approve it in any case, and asked to see the Soviet one, which he, of course, could not produce. Once again Oswald became angry, declaring that since he had already been to jail for the Cuban Revolution, he deserved to enter the country.

At that point Duran decided to call the Soviet consul. The conversation, in Spanish, was recorded through a CIA phone tap and transcribed. "There is an American here," the English transcript reads, "who has requested an in-transit visa because he is going to Russia. I sent him to you thinking if he got a Russian visa that I could then issue him a Cuban visa without any more processing. Who did he speak to? He claims he was told there were no more problems." The Soviet on the other end took her name and number and said someone would call back.

Another Soviet called back twenty minutes later. According to Nechiporenko, it was Kostikov. Once again, the conversation was in Spanish.

SOVIET. Has the American been there?
DURAN. Yes, he is here now.
SOVIET. According to the letter he showed from the consulate in Washington, he wants to go to Russia to stay for a long time with his wife who is Russian. But we have received no answer from Washington,

and it will probably take four to five months. We cannot give a visa here without asking Washington. He says he belongs to a pro-Cuban organization and the Cubans cannot give him a visa without his first getting a Russian visa. I do not know what to do with him. I have to wait for an answer from Washington.

DURAN. We have to wait too, because he knows no one in Cuba and therefore it's difficult to give him a visa. He says he knew it would take a long time to process the Soviet visa but hoped to await that in Cuba.

SOVIET. The thing is that if his wife is now in Washington [sic] she will receive the visa for return to Russia. She will receive it and then can send it any place but right now she does not have it.

DURAN. Naturally, and we can't give him a visa here because we do not know if his Russian visa will be approved.

SOVIET. We can issue a visa only according to instructions.

DURAN. That is what I will put in my plans.

SOVIET. We can't give him a letter of recommendation either, because we do not know him. Please pardon the bother.

DURAN. No bother. Thank you very much.[28]

After November 22, as soon as Oswald's trip to Mexico City and his Soviet and Cuban contacts there became known, many conservative Americans and intelligence professionals concluded that the Soviets, the Cubans, or both had been behind the assassination. Within a week, on November 29, Lyndon Johnson was asking J. Edgar Hoover about possible Cuban involvement, and on the same day, while demanding that his friend Senator Richard Russell join the Warren Commission, he spoke specifically about the need to quash such suspicions. "We've got to take this out of the arena where they're testifying that Khrushchev and Castro did this and did that and kicking us into a war that can kill forty million Americans in half an hour," he said.[29] According to agent James Hosty, Dallas FBI agents heard from their boss on November 23 that higher authority was insisting that the foreign element of the investigation be downplayed. Yet several years later Hosty heard that an FBI assistant director told a class of new recruits that Kostikov, who had since been identified as a member of KGB Department 13, which handled assassinations, was probably responsible for Kennedy's death.[30]

As we shall see momentarily, Oswald may have said something at the Cuban consulate about possibly trying to assassinate Kennedy. But the Warren Commission, which was privy to the telephone conversation between Kostikov and Duran and to Oswald's possible remark as well, understandably concluded that the Cubans and Soviets had nothing to do with the assassination. And based on the transcript of that September 27 phone conversation, it is difficult to conclude that Oswald undertook the trip to Mexico for any reason other than to secure entry into Cuba. Duran's comment that "He says he knew it would take a long time to process the Soviet visa but hoped to await that in Cuba" explains how Oswald intended to parlay a transit visa into a stay in Cuba of several months.[31] The Soviets and Cubans must have assumed their embassies were watched and their telephones were tapped, and it does not seem possible that, if they had already recruited Oswald for some kind of plot against the President, they would have concocted such an elaborate deception, rather than simply meeting him in a secure location. Nor was he making a very good impression on anyone as a candidate for recruitment. All the evidence, in short, suggests that the Cubans and Soviets viewed him as unstable at best and a provocateur at worst.

Oswald refused to take no for an answer. Increasingly frustrated, Duran got the Cuban consul, Eusebio Azcue, to speak to him. As Azcue told the HSCA in 1978, once again he explained the requirements to Oswald and, when the disagreement devolved into a shouting match, showed him the door.[32]

Another highly controversial account of Oswald's visit has been attributed to Fidel Castro. The story first surfaced in print in a 1967 article in the *National Enquirer*. Its author, Comer Clarke, claimed to have traveled to Cuba and to have fortuitously encountered Castro on a Havana street on July 15 of that year. He claimed that Castro struck up a conversation with him after hearing him speak English and spontaneously agreed to an interview. Clarke, by his account, asked Fidel about possible Cuban involvement in Kennedy's assassination and got this reply.

Yes, I heard of Lee Harvey Oswald's plan to kill President Kennedy. It's possible that I could have saved him. I might have been able to—but I didn't. I never believed the plan would be put into effect.

Lee Oswald came to the Cuban Embassy in Mexico City twice. The first time, I was told, he wanted to work for us. He was asked to explain but he wouldn't, he wouldn't go into details. The second time he said he wanted to free Cuba from American imperialism. Then he said something like "Someone ought to shoot that President Kennedy." Then Oswald said, and this is exactly how it was reported to me, "Maybe I'll try to do it."[33]

According to Clarke, after this spontaneous revelation, Cuban authorities refused to allow him to interview Castro formally. Not surprisingly in light of where it appeared, the story does not seem to have received any attention until 1975, when Daniel Schorr referred to it in his book *Clearing the Air.*[34] By that time Clarke had been dead for three years, and his widow reportedly admitted that Clarke had not written the story himself and had never even met Castro.[35] As it turns out, however, an account of a similar conversation with Castro had been in the files of the FBI and the Warren Commission for some time. It was given to the bureau in 1964 by a long-time American Communist and FBI informant named Jack Childs, who claimed that Castro discussed the assassination with him in Havana in spring of 1964. Castro said that when the Cubans denied Oswald his visa, Oswald stormed out, exclaiming, "I'm going to kill Kennedy for this."[36] Citing a "confidential source," Hoover forwarded this story to the Warren Commission on June 17, 1964, but the commission did nothing with it.[37]

The year 1967 was full of intense controversy regarding the Kennedy assassination, and Jim Garrison's investigation was front page news. American intelligence might well have decided that it was time to get Childs's story into print, and that might have been the impetus for Clarke's article in the *National Enquirer.* Schorr no longer remembers exactly how he became aware of Clarke's article in the mid-1970s. But nonetheless, both Duran and Azcue, testifying before the HSCA in 1978, denied hearing anything like this from Oswald, and when HSCA members visited Havana to interview Castro, he denied ever saying it.[38] He also denied giving Clarke an interview at all. Only the Cuban government can release any cable traffic between Mexico City and Havana about Oswald's visit, and it has never done so.

Oswald certainly seemed capable of making such a statement. "Leopoldo," Silvia Odio's visitor, claimed that Oswald made a similar remark in his presence as well. The comment could also have been, as many have suggested, an implied reference to something Castro told an Associated Press reporter on September 7, 1963, in Havana—that "United States leaders should know that if they are aiding plans to eliminate Cuban leaders, they themselves will not be safe." This story appeared in the New Orleans *Times-Picayune* on September 9, and Oswald could easily have seen it.[39] But if Oswald did make a statement about killing Kennedy, it simply would have tended to confirm Azcue's and Duran's belief that he was some kind of provocateur. Only the original Cuban documentation will reveal what he did or did not say.

Other evidence confirming that Oswald was *not* working for Cuban intelligence came in the spring of 1964 from a defector from the Cuban General Intelligence Directorate (DGI). Code-named AMMUG-1, the defector remembered a conversation about Oswald with a number of officers in the DGI, including two who had actually represented the directorate in the consulate in Mexico City. According to AMMUG-1, agents always interviewed visa applicants because the applicant could identify himself as an agent by using a prearranged phrase. If he used the proper phrase, he received his visa immediately, but if he did not, he was asked to return in a few days while Havana was asked for authorization. It seems that the latter procedure was followed in Oswald's case, and he certainly did not receive a visa. AMMUG-1 did not hear anything about Oswald threatening to shoot President Kennedy.[40]

Perhaps because the Duran-Kostikov conversation involved an American, it was immediately transcribed. To understand what happened next, we must look, with the help of the Lopez Report, at CIA procedures in Mexico City. The agency combined phone taps on the Cuban and Soviet embassies with photographic surveillance. The Cuban Embassy had two entrances, a main entrance and a consular entrance. A live agent watched the main entrance from a secure location during business hours and was supposed to photograph everyone going in and out. The consular entrance had recently been closed and then reopened. According to CIA documentation shown to the HSCA, new equipment designed to cover the consular entrance had been installed on September 27, 1963, the exact day that Oswald visited Silvia Duran three times, presumably through that very entrance.

The equipment included a pulse camera that would automatically take a photograph whenever anyone went up to the door. Documents read by the committee seemed to show that the pulse camera was already operating on September 27. The CIA, however, insisted they were not yet working and denied having any photographs from that day. If indeed the camera was working, as the documents seemed to suggest, it should have photographed Oswald at least three times.[41] The Soviet Embassy's entrance received similar photographic coverage. Moreover, the HSCA found that CIA personnel listening in on telephones routinely contacted photographers to alert them to any visitors of particular interest who needed to be photographed.

Silvia Duran's conversation with Kostikov on the afternoon of September 27 about an American who had lived in Russia, married a Soviet woman, and intended to travel to Cuba and back to the Soviet Union immediately triggered intense interest among American authorities. The CIA station carefully monitored Americans traveling to and from Cuba to Mexico City and kept an active list of them. Between five and ten Americans made the trip in each direction each month.[42] The conversation between Duran and Kostikov certainly should have been part of the summary that agents compiled at the end of every work day for submission to the station chief, Winston Scott, the next morning. It might also presumably have triggered a consultation with at least one of the penetration agents the CIA had inside the Cuban Embassy or consulate.[43] One such agent routinely reviewed the photographs the CIA took to help identify the individuals in question.

Duran, known to be of operational interest to the CIA because of her affair with Carlos Lechuga, may well have been one of those penetration agents. After the assassination, the CIA's attempts to prevent her arrest and interrogation by Cuban authorities led U.S. Ambassador Thomas Mann to conclude that she was probably one of its agents.[44] Cuban intelligence chief Fabian Escalante claims that the Cuban Embassy had poor counterintelligence in 1963 and had been thoroughly bugged.[45] And as a matter of fact, when station chief Scott read the transcript of the September 27 conversation within a few days, he wrote in the margin, "Is it possible to identify?"[46] Given the CIA's resources, it seems that the answer was probably yes, especially since the Cubans were in no mood to protect Oswald's identity. But it seems to have taken several days for CIA officers to figure out who the mysterious American was.

The next morning, Oswald made another try at the Soviet Embassy. Late on the previous day, Kostikov had told Nechiporenko about Duran's phone call, and they had agreed to send a cable to the KGB's main office the next day informing Moscow Center of Oswald's visit. The two men arrived at the embassy in the morning for their weekly volleyball match against the team from the Military Attaché's office—essentially a KGB-GRU contest. But before the game could begin, Oswald showed up wearing a gray suit and began to tell his story, in English, to another embassy officer, Pavel Yatskov. Yatskov handed him off to Kostikov as soon as he could. Oswald once again began his story in English, although he eventually switched to "broken Russian," Kostikov said, at Yatskov's suggestion.

This time, describing his life in the Soviet Union and his return to the United States, he "even dropped some hints that he had supposedly carried out a secret mission"—an exaggeration characteristic of Oswald. Once again he claimed that the FBI was persecuting him, that he had lost his job, and that he feared for his life. In the midst of this desperate presentation, he pulled out his pistol, laid it on the desk in front of him, and began to cry. Yatskov, rather taken aback, picked up the revolver, unloaded it, and gave Oswald a glass of water. However, he could do no more than offer to give him visa application forms.

Oswald repeated his request for a letter recommending him for a Cuban visa, but Yatskov explained that the Cuban government must decide for itself. Oswald declined to take the forms, and Yatskov returned his revolver and his bullets and escorted him out. After some discussion, the three KGB men agreed that Oswald was obviously mentally unstable and decided to inform Moscow Center of his visit at once, even though it meant missing their volleyball game. Two months later they were very glad they had done so.[47] The Soviet and Russian governments have never released the contents of that cable.

Nechiporenko's book quotes some Soviet documents that amplify his own recollections and others that cast doubt on them. In early 1963, after Marina Oswald had requested permission to return to the Soviet Union with her child, the first chief directorate of the KGB asked the Minsk KGB office about the request on April 9. The Minsk office responded on April 16 with information about the Oswalds' stormy married life in Minsk (which had been recorded by KGB bugs) and excerpts from

letters that Marina and Lee wrote from the United States. The Minsk office saw "no reason to impede" Marina's return, but no action seems to
have been taken.

On October 8, a letter from the Registry and Archives Department of
the KGB to the Ministry of Foreign Affairs referred to "Special Communication No. 550 from Mexico," dated October 3, and asked that Lee
Harvey Oswald's "petition requesting immigration" be checked over.
That certainly seems to contradict the recollection of Pavel Yatskov, reported by Nechiporenko, that Oswald refused to fill out any forms. But
Nechiporenko also claims to have seen a report from the Ministry of
Foreign Affairs dated November 16, 1963, stating that the ministry had
not yet received a copy of Oswald's petition. Perhaps Oswald's repeated
references to a nonexistent application had managed to convince a Soviet bureaucrat that he had actually made a formal request. The same report stated that Marina's separate request had been refused on October 7,
1963, as it had previously been refused by the Leningrad KGB, because
Marina's stepfather in Leningrad had declined to take responsibility for
her and her child.

On October 25, a deputy chairman of the KGB wrote the Ministry of
Foreign Affairs that Oswald had come "to the Embassy in Mexico to request permanent immigration to the Soviet Union," and declared it "in-
advisable" to grant the request. On November 22 the same message to
the KGB in Minsk that denied Marina's request stated that Lee Oswald
"did not declare his intention to immigrate to the USSR." (This must
have been written and dispatched before any news of the assassination
reached Moscow early in the evening.)[48] The Warren Report did not
specifically state whether Oswald had actually applied to return to the
Soviet Union or not.[49] Nechiporenko's book sometimes seems to indicate that he did, but an actual application has not been found. In the
tense political atmosphere of 1963–64, it is quite possible that both the
Soviet and American authorities wanted to downplay any attempt by
Oswald to secure permission to return to the Soviet Union just two
months before he assassinated the U.S. President. In any case, the bulk of
the evidence we have available suggests that his real goal in late September was to get into Cuba, not to return to Russia.

One or two hours after Oswald visited the Soviets on September 28,
the CIA picked up another call from the Cuban consulate to the Soviet

Embassy. The transcriber, Boris Tarasoff, eventually, although not initially, identified the caller as Duran. The transcript reads as follows:

> SILVIA DURAN. There is an American here who says he has been to
>   the Russian consulate.
> RUSSIAN CONSULATE. Wait a minute.
> [Silvia Duran is then heard to speak in English to someone apparently
>   sitting at her side. This conversation goes as follows:]
> DURAN. He said wait. Do you speak Russian?
> [MAN]. Yes
> DURAN. Why don't you speak with him then?
> [MAN]. I don't know . . . [The person who was at the side of Silvia
>   Duran and who claimed to speak some Russian then got on the line
>   and spoke in what the transcriber described as "terrible, hardly recog-
>   nizable Russian."]
> [MAN]. I was in your Embassy and spoke to your Consul.
> RUSSIAN EMBASSY. What else do you want?
> [MAN]. I was just now at your Embassy and they took my address.
> RUSSIAN EMBASSY. I know that.
> [MAN]. I did not know it then. I went to the Cuban Embassy to ask
>   them for my address, because they have it.
> RUSSIAN EMBASSY. Why don't you come by and leave it then, we're
>   not far.
> [MAN]. Well, I'll be there right away.[50]

This September 28 call presents several mysteries. First, the text does not make much sense, although that might have to do with the man's broken Russian. Probably he meant to say "they asked for my address," not "they took my address." Second, Oswald, who had spent more than two years in the Soviet Union and had been married for more than two years to a Russian woman who spoke no English, did not speak "terrible, hardly recognizable Russian." And third, Duran, who was interrogated twice by Mexican police in the week after the assassination and interviewed by the HSCA at some length, always insisted that Oswald visited her three times on Friday, September 27, but never again. Although she acknowledged working on Saturdays, she insisted that the consulate was closed to the public on September 28 and that Oswald had not come back. She had no obvious reason to lie about this, certainly not during her initial interrogations by Mexican authorities. And finally, while the clandestine transcriber immediately and correctly identified Duran in the call she made to the Soviets on Friday afternoon, it took several days to identify her in this Saturday call.[51]

How can the phone call on September 28 be explained? The Soviet Embassy was one of two major centers of Soviet espionage in North America (Ottawa was the other) and had therefore become a critical target of U.S. counterintelligence. As the historian John Newman first pointed out, the CIA was using its real-time coverage of the Cuban and Soviet telephone lines in Mexico City to identify and contact Americans who phoned them. One was Eldon Hensen, a Texan who on July 19, 1963, called the Cubans. He declined to discuss his business over the telephone or go to the Cuban Embassy, but he mentioned where he was staying. As a released CIA cable explains, the CIA station immediately had a contact pose as a Cuban official, get in touch with Hensen at his hotel that very afternoon, and check him out. When Hensen offered to provide Castro unspecified help in the United States in exchange for money, the CIA immediately turned the matter over to the local FBI.[52] The CIA explained its intense interest in Americans in contact with the Soviet and Cuban embassies in an internal memorandum on December 13, 1963: "Our Mexico City Station very often produces information like this on US citizens contacting Soviet bloc embassies in Mexico City. Frequently the information we get is extremely incriminating, and on one or two occasions we have even been able to apprehend and return to the USA American military personnel who are attempting to defect."[53]

It certainly seems possible that, having learned by Saturday morning about the mysterious American with a Soviet past who had just been to the Soviet and Cuban embassies the previous afternoon, CIA officials were trying to identify him. Quite probably they had also alerted their real-time photographer at the Soviet Embassy to watch for him. The photographer would have seen Oswald leaving the embassy on Saturday morning. Following up on that information, an agency officer might have recruited a Spanish-speaking woman and man who spoke a little Russian to pose as Duran and the mystery man and make another call to the Soviet Embassy, just to confirm that the man photographed on Saturday morning at the Soviet Embassy was really the American they were interested in. That was about all that the Saturday call could have accomplished, but it was a start in obtaining some kind of identification of Oswald. Had the caller managed to elicit from the Soviets the address Oswald had left with them, the agency would probably have sent someone to find him.

The last two transcripts we have involving Oswald date from three days later, on Tuesday, October 1, at 10:31 a.m. and 10:45 a.m. The first caller reached the Soviet military attaché in the embassy and said that he had been at the consulate on Saturday. He asked if the Soviets had gotten an answer from Washington. He was referred to the consulate. At 10:45 another call come in from a man who identified himself as "Lee Oswald." He told an official named Obyedkov that he had been at the consulate on Saturday and that the consul had said he was sending a telegram to Washington. Obyedkov asked if the man he had talked to was Kostikov, and the caller said he was "dark." Obyedkov put him on hold, returned, said no answer had been received, and hung up on him.[54] At 1 p.m. the next day, October 2, Lee Harvey Oswald boarded a bus for Nuevo Laredo en route to Dallas.

The weight of the evidence suggests that these two calls, like the one on September 28 that supposedly came from the Cuban consulate, were also made by a CIA-sponsored impostor in an attempt to learn more about Oswald's Soviet contacts. To begin with, the CIA's transcriber, Boris Tarasoff, in a note on the 10:45 transcript, specifically identified this "Lee Oswald" as the same man whom he had heard on September 28 speaking "terrible, hardly recognizable Russian." And yet as we have seen, Duran's testimony, along with other evidence, leads to the reasonable conclusion that the September 28 caller was not Oswald at all. Second, it seems surprising that Oswald, who had presented himself at the door of the Cuban and Soviet embassies five times in two days, would now telephone and immediately identify himself instead. Third, the idea behind the call—that Oswald was waiting for a reply from Washington—receives no support from Nechiporenko's recollections. He said nothing about either sending a telegram to Washington or waiting for a possible reply. But the CIA's transcript of the September 27 conversation between Kostikov and Duran does have Kostikov saying, "We have no answer from Washington," and this could have led the CIA to believe that the Soviets were still waiting for one.

A further mystery arises from a story in the *Washington Post* on November 26, 1976, describing what seems to be a completely separate *fifth* conversation with Oswald. The story quoted an unnamed interpreter and stenographer—obviously Boris Tarasoff and his wife, Anna—concerning a conversation in which Oswald offered the Soviets unspecified information in return for money to travel to the Soviet Union. David Atlee Phillips, who had been the Special Affairs Section officer in the Mexico City station and was now the head of a new Association of Retired Intelligence Officers, confirmed on the record that this conversation took place. But the CIA, the *Post* said, had never given a full transcript to the Warren Commission. "When asked to explain the Agency's actions," the story read, "some CIA officials stationed at the time in Mexico City said the CIA may have had a relationship with Oswald that it sought to conceal. The CIA has denied this."[55]

The work of the HSCA was just getting under way when this story appeared, and the committee counsel, Richard Sprague, a well-known criminal prosecutor from Philadelphia, sent two staffers to investigate. They interviewed the Tarasoffs, now retired, at Guadalajara on November 26, 1976. Both of them, in contrast with so many intelligence officers involved in the case, seemed to remember events with the clarity befitting what was by far the most important episode in which they had ever been involved.

At that time, the Tarasoffs testified to having transcribed two conversations involving Oswald. The last conversation, in English, they said, had been given to them for immediate transcription, along with a request to do whatever they could to identify the caller. Its transcript was about two pages long, and the caller had requested financial assistance to help him get back to the Soviet Union. Anna, the Tarasoffs agreed, had transcribed the conversation because it was in English, and they both categorically denied writing any editorial comments on it like the note Boris had written on the transcript of the 10:45 conversation with Obyedkov, in which he had identified the caller as the same man who had phoned on Saturday, September 28.[56] Anna also said she did not remember the English-speaking caller offering any information about his identity.

During the next few months Sprague incurred the wrath of his elected congressional bosses and was forced to resign. Another year and a half passed before the Tarasoffs came to Washington to testify in closed session on April 12, 1978. By that time Boris had been shown the transcript of the October 1 call at 10:45, on which he had said the caller, "Lee Oswald," was the same man who had called on September 28. But in his testimony, Boris reversed himself about any long conversation in English, saying that he must have been mistaken about the existence of this transcript.

Anna Tarasoff, however, stuck to her story about the English transcript. David Atlee Phillips, testifying the day after the *Washington Post* story appeared, confirmed his quote but claimed that he had heard about the conversation from another source.[57] Both the CIA and FBI were rife with rumors exaggerating Oswald's connection to foreign intelligence agencies in the decades after the assassination, and it would be easy to dismiss the story of the missing English transcript as another one of those legends—except for Anna Tarasoff's highly specific memory of exactly what she had seen and done.

In my opinion, by October 1 the CIA, with the help of human sources in either the Cuban or Soviet embassy, had identified Oswald as the mysterious American.[58] An agency-sponsored impostor made the October 1 calls and in the 10:45 conversation identified himself as Oswald for two reasons: to find out whether the Soviets had gotten Oswald a visa, and to put Oswald's name on record in a form in which it could safely be reported to Washington and to the FBI without compromising a sensitive human source.

The CIA now tried to match Oswald with one of the photographs it had taken of persons entering and leaving the Soviet Embassy, and here the plot thickened yet again. Such photographs should have been available from Friday and Saturday, September 27 and September 28, but agency operatives either did not find any promising ones from those days or did not use them.[59] The photograph they eventually found of a tall, heavy-set Caucasian with a receding hairline was not taken until October 2 (the day Oswald left Mexico City), and it was not a photograph of Oswald.[60]

On October 8 the Mexico City station sent the following cable to headquarters at Langley, drafted by a member of the Soviet section.

1. Acc [source], 1 Oct 63, American Male who spoke broken Russian said his name Lee Oswald (phonetic), stated he at Sovemb on 28 Sept when spoke with Consul whom he believed be Valeriy Vladimirovich

Kostikov. Subj asked Sov guard Ivan Obyedkov who answered, if there anything new re telegram to Washington. Obyedkov upon checking said nothing received yet, but request had been sent.

2. Have photos male appears be American entering Sovemb 1216 hours, leaving 1222 on 1 Oct. Apparent age 35, athletic build, circa 6 feet, receding hairline balding top. Wore khakis and sport shirt. Source: [blanked out.]

3. No local dissem.[61]

This cable is extraordinary for both what it says and what it does not say. First, it actually overstates what the caller said, since it was Obyedkov, not the caller, who asked whether he had spoken to Kostikov, and the caller failed to confirm that. Its description is based on the photograph taken October 2, even though it places the timing on October 1, the day of the reported conversation. But most important, it tells only a fraction of what the CIA almost surely knew about Oswald's stay in Mexico at that time, since it omits the evidence that he had been at the Cuban consulate and that he was trying to travel to Cuba and the Soviet Union. Fortunately, some testimony explains exactly what was said and why the cable was so discreet. Other testimony raises even more sinister possibilities about CIA involvement with Oswald.

Based on the testimony of the Tarasoffs and Win Scott's scribbled request to identify the "American" whom Duran discussed with Kostikov on September 27, it seems clear that the Mexico City station had wanted an identification as soon as possible. If it was truly Oswald's voice in the phone call of September 28 and if he really did telephone the Soviets and identify himself on October 1, then a comparison of the transcripts would have told the CIA that Oswald had been physically present in the Soviet and Cuban embassies on September 28, since Boris Tarasoff specifically identified the two voices as coming from the same man on his October 1 transcript. The CIA officer who drafted the cable about the October call claimed to HSCA investigators that he did not check the earlier transcript, but that simply does not seem credible.[62]

Alternatively, if the calls on September 28 and October 1 were made by an impostor trying to figure out what was going on, even the first one had to be based on the knowledge that Oswald had been in the Cuban

Embassy on September 27 as well as the Soviet one. In addition, it is very hard to believe that agency analysts in Mexico City, having matched the two calls, did not realized that Duran had been talking to Kostikov about Oswald on September 27. Yet the cable not only failed to mention any contacts between the Cuban and Soviet embassies but also failed to mention Oswald's intention to travel to Cuba or the Soviet Union.

The best clue as to why the cable was sent in this truncated form comes from John Whiten, a CIA officer who testified to the HSCA under the pseudonym John Scelso. Whiten, whose testimony reveals a man of intelligence, integrity, and strong opinions, was the chief of the Western Hemisphere branch in 1963 and therefore, as he explained, one of Scott's superiors. Testifying in May 1978, Whiten explained that the CIA had detected a number of American servicemen trying to contact the Soviets through their embassy in Mexico City, and that J. Edgar Hoover had enormously appreciated the information the station had managed to provide. Contacts with Americans, he testified, "were detected enough so that J. Edgar Hoover used to glow every time that he thought of the Mexico station. This was one of our outstanding areas of cooperation with the FBI."[63]

The cable was sent by an officer with Soviet rather than Cuban responsibilities within the station because headquarters, and through headquarters the FBI, would want to know about such a Soviet contact. (The cable was marked "No local dissem," indicating that the information was withheld from the legal attaché, or local FBI agent.) Information relating to Oswald's Cuban plans, apparently, fell into a different category, partly because CIA coverage of the Cuban Embassy was undoubtedly more sensitive than its coverage of the Soviets. The cable tends to confirm, however, that the story of Oswald asking the Soviets for financial assistance or offering information was false, since this would have been exactly the kind of information, one should think, that J. Edgar Hoover would have most liked to have received.

As the Lopez Report and John Newman described in detail, the October 8 cable got Washington's attention. Elsie Scaleti of the Mexican desk received it, searched for Oswald's name, and retrieved his file from Ann Egerter of the Counter-Intelligence/Special Investigations group, James Angleton's mole-hunting unit. The draft of the Lopez Report anticipated that the final report of the HSCA would try to explain why the file was there, but it did not.[64] After reading the file, Egerter prepared the following cable, which went to Mexico City on October 10.

> 1. Lee Harvey Oswald who called Sovemb 1 Oct probably identical Lee Henry Oswald (201–289248) born 18 October 1939 New Orleans, Louisiana, former radar operator in United States Marines who defected to USSR in Oct. 1959. Oswald is five feet ten inches, one hundred sixty-five pounds, light brown wavy hair, blue eyes.

Two paragraphs followed detailing Oswald's defection, his statements in the Soviet Union, his return, and his current status. The cable concluded:

> 4. Station should pass info ref and par; one to (U.S. Embassy, Navy, Federal Bureau of Investigation and Immigration and Naturalization) locally. Info paras two and three originates with (State).
> 5. Ref and possible identification being disseminated to HDQS of (FBI, State, Navy and I&NS). Pls keep HDQS advised on any further contacts or positive identification of Oswald.[65]

The Lee "Henry" Oswald in paragraph one was a slip that probably reflected the fatigue of the typist and has generated more heat than it deserves. Oddly, however, in 1988 I watched a tape of the original NBC news broadcast of November 22, and I distinctly remember that the very first report of the arrest of the President's assassin referred to him as Lee *Henry* Oswald.

At the same time Scaleti sent the following teletype to the Department of State, the FBI, and the Department of the Navy:

> 1. On 1 October 1963 a reliable and sensitive source in Mexico reported that an American male, who identified himself as Lee Oswald, contacted the Soviet Embassy in Mexico City inquiring whether the Embassy had received any news concerning a telegram which had been sent to Washington. The American was described as approximately 35 years old, with an athletic build, about six feet tall, with a receding hairline.
> 2. It is believed that Oswald may be identical to Lee Henry Oswald, born on 18 October 1939 in New Orleans, Louisiana, a former U.S. Ma-

rine who defected to the Soviet Union in October 1959 and later made arrangements through the United States Embassy in Moscow to return to the United States with his Russian wife, Marina Nikolaevna Prusakova, and their child . . .

3. The information in Paragraph One is being disseminated to your representative in Mexico City. Any further information received is being made available to the Immigration and Naturalization Service.[66]

Although much has been made of the teletype's use of the incorrect description of Oswald in the Mexico City cable of October 8 rather than the correct one that Scaleti had sent to Mexico City on the very same day, this has an odd bureaucratic logic, since the intent of the teletype was simply to pass the original Mexico City report on to other interested agencies. The cable, however, omitted the detail of Oswald's having spoken to Kostikov. It took about three weeks for the teletype to lead to a renewed investigation of Oswald—who was back in Dallas—by FBI agent Hosty.

In response to its own cable from headquarters, the Mexico City station opened a "P" file on Oswald. As agents explained to HSCA investigators in 1977–78, they normally assisted the FBI in investigating suspicious Americans in Mexico City. The Lopez Report tentatively concluded that between October 11 and October 15 CIA personnel went back and compared the transcripts, and very likely the tapes, of all the calls that might have involved Oswald. In any event, the report categorically states, based on the testimony and depositions of various officers, that by October 15 at the latest "the 10/1 10:45 call, the 9/28 11:51 call, the 9/27 4:05 call, and the 9/27 4:26 call had been linked to Oswald." In my opinion, they had probably been linked to him during the first week of October. In any case, another memorandum circulated to other agencies in Mexico City on October 16 continued to say nothing about any visits to the Cuban Embassy or about Oswald's travel plans.[67]

After the assassination, the CIA based its official position on the paper record, as it customarily did in response to any outside inquiries about its activities, and insisted that it had not realized that Oswald was in the Cuban Embassy until reviewing transcripts after November 22. It stuck to the same story during the HSCA investigations, although various CIA

personnel told the committee that they remembered seeing actual photographs of Oswald, or that they remembered a cable reporting that he
had been in the Cuban Embassy before the assassination. In an unpublished manuscript now on file at NARA, Scott said that the station had
known all about Oswald's visits to the Cuban consulate, and Richard
Helms told John Newman roughly the same thing in the early 1990s. It
is the contemporary evidence, however, that clearly indicates what the
agency must have known.

Two hypotheses might explain the Mexico City station's discretion.
The first would suggest simply that since the Cuban Embassy was the responsibility of the CIA rather than the FBI, and specifically the responsibility of David Phillips, that it was not necessary to risk exposing the
sources and methods of Phillips's men regarding the Cuban Embassy
simply for the purpose of informing other agencies about what they
had learned there. Any revelation of CIA surveillance of the Cuban Embassy would probably have been more sensitive diplomatically in Mexico,
which was making a point of keeping relations with Cuba open, than
CIA surveillance of the Soviet Embassy would have been. The second is
more sinister: someone in the station, probably David Phillips, knew exactly what Oswald was trying to do, namely, get a visa to travel to Cuba,
where he would be provided a weapon with which to assassinate Fidel
Castro. That hypothesis has been supported, in very different ways, by
two sources: Antonio Veciana, the Cuban exile head of Alpha-66, who
in 1976 testified that he had seen "Maurice Bishop" (later identified
as Phillips) meeting with Oswald in Dallas, and, tantalizingly, Phillips
himself.

Veciana, as he explained to Church Committee investigators in March
1976, was recruited in Havana in 1960 by an American who called himself Maurice Bishop. He organized an unsuccessful assassination plot in
the summer and fall of 1961 that resulted in the arrest and imprisonment
of Silvia Odio's father and mother. After escaping to the United States,
Veciana was officially recruited by the CIA and became the leader of Al-
pha-66, the sabotage organization that began staging raids on Russian
and Cuban shipping in 1962 and continued into 1963. According to
Veciana's testimony, he continued working with Bishop until 1971.

In 1973 Veciana was convicted of a drug smuggling charge—which
he always denied—and spent two or three years in federal prison. A

sketch of Bishop made according to Veciana's instructions bore a striking resemblance to David Phillips, and the former CIA contract agent Ross Crozier, who was the DRE case officer in Miami in 1962, told the HSCA that Phillips used the name Maurice Bishop. Gaeton Fonzi, the investigator for the Church Committee and the HSCA who dealt with Veciana, said in a 2003 interview that Veciana identified Phillips as Bishop off the record, although he always refused to do so on the record. In March 1976 Veciana spontaneously volunteered that he met with Bishop in the lobby of an office building or bank in Dallas, where they had several rendezvous, sometime in August, he thought, of 1963—and that Bishop was simultaneously meeting with a young American whom Veciana later recognized as Lee Harvey Oswald.[68] When Sprague questioned Phillips in November 1976, he did not ask about Veciana, but Phillips later denied any connection with him, and even filed a libel suit against a media outlet that identified him as Bishop. Phillips denied the allegation that he was Bishop in his second HSCA appearance in 1978.

Phillips gave careful but often informative testimony during that appearance, though he also had to acknowledge an extraordinary fabrication in his November 1976 testimony. On that occasion Sprague questioned him at length about Oswald's visit to Mexico City and the preparation of the October 8 cable in which the CIA station had informed Washington of Oswald's contact with the Soviets. Although Phillips did not sign the cable, he claimed to have remembered preparing it and speaking to the officer responsible for reporting on the Soviet Embassy to make sure it went out. Like so many other CIA officers, he assured the committee that the written record reflected everything there was to know. But during his second appearance, when a committee counsel presented him with another cable proving that Phillips was in Washington, D.C., from at least September 30 until October 7, 1963, and spent the next two days in Miami, he had to admit that his earlier testimony must have been incorrect.[69] If Veciana told the truth and Phillips was indeed connected to Oswald, his absence from Mexico City during much or all of Oswald's visit would have left his colleagues in the dark as they tried to identify Oswald and determine what he was doing there.

Phillips was one of the most successful and mysterious of the CIA's Cold War agents. He began his career as an actor and a playwright, and at least one Church Committee counsel thought his acting skills were still very much in evidence during his testimony. He rose eventually to be head of the Western Hemisphere branch of the CIA, and when he appeared before the Church Committee in 1975 he denied, falsely, that the CIA had anything to do with the overthrow of Salvador Allende in Chile two years earlier.[70] In retirement, with several children to send through college, he launched a career as an author. His autobiography, *The Night Watch* (1977), was followed by a novel about intelligence, *The Carlos Contract* (1978), and *The Great Texas Murder Trials* (1979), a work of nonfiction. At some point before his death from cancer in 1988, he wrote an outline for another novel, entitled *The AMLASH Legacy,* dealing specifically with the Kennedy assassination.[71]

The outline carefully identified the characters with the real figures on which they were based: Mexico City station chief Winston Scott, HSCA investigator Gaeton Fonzi, Antonio Veciana, long-time assassination conspiracists Mark Lane and Bernard Fensterwald, and Phillips himself, who went by the name of Harold Harrison. The novel focused on Harrison's son Don, who begins looking for his father's journal after his father's death. A Mexican woman who attended his father's funeral gives Don a letter written by his father. The letter explains that Harrison had been one of two case officers who recruited Lee Harvey Oswald, helped establish his credentials as a Marxist, and then attempted to send him to Cuba through Mexico City in order to assassinate Fidel Castro, using a sniper rifle from an upper floor of a high-rise to shoot Castro in his jeep. Harrison does not know whether Oswald was a double agent, the letter continues, but this was the same plan Oswald used to kill Kennedy. Allen Dulles, the letter stated, provided Harrison and the other unidentified agent with $400,000 to set up Oswald after he succeeded in assassinating Fidel.

In the novel, Harrison has the last laugh when his son discovers that his father's posthumous letter is a forgery concocted by the Fensterwald character and a KGB agent whom Harrison had repeatedly outwitted during their spying careers. The real David Phillips might simply have concluded that since so many others had irresponsibly cashed in on the Kennedy assassination, he might as well do the same. Yet his outline of this novel was the only document I know in existence before 1998 to suggest that Oswald might have been trying to go to Cuba to assassinate Castro. In that year, I wrote a short article to introduce the idea that—as

"Leopoldo" suggested to Silvia Odio a few days before or a few days after Oswald's visit to Mexico City—Oswald's first assassination target may well have been the Cuban premier. We will probably never know whether Phillips was drawing on anything more than his imagination, but the plot of his novel, until the spectacular revelation at the end, tracks key events leading up to the Kennedy assassination almost perfectly.

I am certainly not thoroughly convinced that Phillips or any other CIA operative had anything to do with an assassination plot against Castro that involved Oswald. The plot might just as easily have been mounted by mob and right-wing elements such as John Martino, Loran Hall ("Leopoldo"), Guy Banister, David Ferrie, and Carlos Marcello in New Orleans—as well as, perhaps, the DRE, which had infiltrated at least one member, Isidro Borja, into Cuba through Mexico City as well and placed its ad for a Castro assassin in *See* magazine. Yet we cannot be sure that the CIA was not involved, especially since Martino had agency contacts of his own. Some evidence, including testimony from John Whiten and the recollections of British counterintelligence officer Peter Wright, suggests that James Angleton, the legendary chief of counterintelligence, was actually behind the Mafia plots against Castro, and Oswald's CIA 201 file was sitting in Angleton's shop when the report of his contacts with the Soviet Embassy reached headquarters.[72]

In another suspicious coincidence, in July 1963 the agency infiltrated an informer from the New York chapter of the Fair Play for Cuba Committee, a Puerto Rican named Victor Thomas Vicente, into Cuba, probably through Mexico City. Vicente declined to settle there, as the CIA hoped he might, but he met both Castro and Che Guevara and was debriefed after he returned.[73] Ironically, because Oswald's FPCC chapter was bogus from the beginning—and probably designed to discredit the organization in the New Orleans area—it could not successfully be used to get him into Cuba.

In 1988 the journalist Richard Billings—who covered JFK's assassination and the Garrison investigation for *Life* magazine, participated in the Bayo-Pawley raid on Cuba, served as public relations director for the HSCA, and co-authored *The Plot to Kill the President* with committee counsel G. Robert Blakey—received a luncheon invitation from David Phillips in Washington. The conversation turned out to be somewhat rambling, and Billings could not quite figure out why Phillips wanted to see him. A few weeks later, he read Phillips's obituary in the *Washington Post*. Many secrets undoubtedly died with him.

Oswald took a bus out of Mexico City on October 2 and reached Dallas on the afternoon of October 3. His discussions with "Leopoldo" had already touched on the possible assassination of both Castro and Kennedy. His almost hysterical behavior in the Soviet and Cuban consulates—behavior not typical of him in public settings—might have had something to do with what awaited him if he returned to the United States without getting into Cuba. The last, most secretive, and most critical phase of his short life was about to begin.

PART III

Converging Paths

13

Making Everyone Unhappy

about Cuba

Three related stories—American policy toward Castro's Cuba and the role of Cuban exiles, the Justice Department's attack on organized crime, and the activities of Lee Harvey Oswald—all reached a climax during the second half of 1963, culminating in the assassination of President Kennedy in Dallas on November 22. The Kennedy administration continued to pursue the overthrow of Fidel Castro, while managing to enrage various exile organizations, who either feared its plans or believed the government was not doing enough. Independent exiles' activity also surged in the Dallas area during the second half of 1963, and both Lee Oswald and his murderer, Jack Ruby, may have been involved with them.

The Kennedy administration's deliberations during the first half of 1963 led to a four-pronged policy toward Cuba in the second half of that year. The National Security Council bureaucracy for Cuban affairs included the Interdepartmental Committee on Cuba, headed by Gordon Chase, coordinator of Cuban Affairs, which handled propaganda and relations with allies and refugees; the Standing Group, responsible for contingency plans; and the Special Group responsible for covert activities.

The first prong of the United States' Cuba policy covertly established two leftist exile groups, Manuel Artime's MRR and Manuel Ray's JURE, in Nicaragua and Venezuela, respectively, to plan sabotage, raids, and possible military intervention in Cuba. In late May, Artime traveled through Central America and, without acknowledging his American sponsorship, received pledges of support from the Costa Rican and Nicaraguan governments.[1] On June 28, CIA headquarters decreed that Artime would now receive support directly from Washington within a new program called AMWORLD. Although Artime's CIA contact would remain in Miami, the rest of the station would have nothing to do with him in order to preserve deniability of U.S. government support. "[The U.S. government], it should be emphasized, is willing to accept the risks involved in utilizing autonomous [Cuban] exile groups and individuals who are not necessarily responsive to [CIA] guidance and to face up to the consequences which an unavoidable lowering in professional standards adhered to by autonomous groups (as compared with fully controlled and disciplined agent assets) is bound to entail," headquarters explained.[2]

As Desmond Fitzgerald, chief of the agency's Special Affairs Staff, explained to Dean Rusk, Robert McNamara, McGeorge Bundy, and John McCone in meetings in late June, the agency wanted to continue sabotage actions both by sponsored groups based outside the United States and by directly controlled assets operating from within the United States. They hoped to delegitimize Castro's rule by striking at economic targets and bring about a military coup. The administration was now somewhat divided over such measures, with Rusk in particular skeptical about their value and Bundy willing to abandon any hope of getting rid of Castro. But McCone was determined that more had to be done, and Robert Kennedy was still disinclined to let Castro alone.[3] The President approved sabotage measures on June 19.[4]

Artime and Ray were soon actively recruiting men for the job. In addition, Nicaraguan dictator Luis Somoza, who was hosting Artime, came to the United States in July, met with Florida exiles, and claimed that the Kennedys had authorized him to try to provoke a conflict with Castro. On July 14 Hal Hendrix of the *Miami News,* who had CIA connections, suggested that Robert Kennedy and Somoza were sponsoring Artime and three other veterans of the Bay of Pigs. He also reported Somoza's claim that he could provoke Castro into retaliating against Nicaragua, after which the United States would come to his aid and invade Cuba.[5] In an effort to damp down these rumors, Artime met with the Miami press in July and announced that he was leaving the United States because it was providing nothing but "beautiful words," and that he would henceforth seek support from wealthy Americans and certain Latin American governments and political parties.[6]

So tight was security regarding support for exiles that neither the ambassador to Nicaragua, where Artime was training, nor the State Department representative in Miami who was dealing with exiles seemed to know that Artime was actually receiving U.S. funds.[7] When Artime inadvertently let the cat out of the bag in Costa Rica in late September, his CIA case officer concocted an elaborate scheme to reassure Costa Rican President Ohrlich that Artime had been misinformed about U.S. government support.[8] By August, Fitzgerald was clearly concerned about Somoza's aggressive plans, and he suggested that Artime be encouraged to relocate his bases to Costa Rica and focus on building up internal Cuban resistance.[9]

The second prong of administration policy involved new strikes by exiles against Cuba itself. The CIA staged several air raids on Cuban economic targets during August and September, and on August 30 a State Department spokesman told the press that the U.S. government would not stand in the way of raids by exiles, provided they were not aimed at third-country shipping or insignificant seashore targets and did not originate within the United States.[10] These air raids provoked a military alert in Cuba and a strong protest from the Soviet Union, but President Kennedy told State Department Counselor Llewellyn Thompson to assure Soviet Ambassador Dobrynin that the United States had nothing to do with them.[11] In an effort to show more balance, U.S. Customs in Miami on September 15 publicly warned six Americans, including Frank Sturgis, sometime journalist Alex Rorke, and pilot Bill Johnson, against further raids.[12]

The militant Cuban exile Orlando Bosch claimed that one bombing raid on a refinery was launched by his organization from Central America—quite possibly at the CIA's behest. Several CIA reports from Miami mercenary informants (including Sturgis) confirmed that Bosch and Johnson carried out the raid, and suggested that JMWAVE was using the radically anti-American Bosch.[13] The situation was so potentially explosive that Bundy asked Chase to list all the American officials who knew that the United States was behind the raids. There turned out to be at least thirty, Chase replied, including Thomas Hughes of the State Department's Bureau of Intelligence and Research, Assistant Secretary of Defense Cyrus Vance, and Vance's two deputies for Cuban matters, future Secretary of Health, Education and Welfare Joe Califano and future Secretary of State (then Lieutenant Colonel) Al Haig.[14]

A few weeks later, on September 29, Chase asked subordinates to consider the possibility that Castro might somehow retaliate, as he had publicly threatened to do early in the month.[15] And on October 21 he suggested that the government might do well to lift some of its restrictions on autonomous raids, so that the CIA would not be held solely responsible for every action that took place.[16] On October 31 Castro himself identified the 174-foot boat *Rex,* moored in Palm Beach, as the mother ship for a recent attack that resulted in the capture of several raiders in small boats. Reporters discovered that the *Rex*'s berthing fees were paid by the Sea Key Shipping Company, a mysterious entity with a post office box address. The owner of the *Rex,* J. A. Belcher, was an oil company executive who bought the ship from a Nicaraguan company owned by the Somoza government. He denied any involvement in raids.[17]

On November 8, 1963, the Venezuelan government indicated that it had discovered a cache of about three tons of arms, with serial numbers removed, on a beach. They accused Castro of having sent the weapons into the country, and an OAS delegation later claimed to have seen Cuban insignia on them.[18] Evidence from American archives, however, suggests that the cache may have been a plant, the execution of a long-discussed plan dating back to August 31, 1962. The first hint comes in a memorandum written by General Edward Lansdale, head of Operation Mongoose, listing possible psychological actions against Cuba.

Psychological Activity: 24. Make available to the International Narcotics Commission documented evidence of Cuban exportation/importation of narcotics. (State)

Purpose: To create increased awareness in Latin America of Cuban subversive activities.

Considerations: Documented evidence available or obtainable should be fully exploited for impact upon hemisphere and world opinion.

Psychological Activity: 25. [4 lines of source text not declassified]

Purpose: To sow and increase distrust in Latin America of the Castro/Communist regime.

Considerations: This activity will be undertaken only on a spot basis, co-ordinated with U.S. objectives in the specific country.[19]

The September 6 comments of Thomas Parrott, General Maxwell Taylor's assistant at the White House, on this point are somewhat more enlightening despite deletions in the released version.

I would suggest a couple of additional activities: (a) under number 25, calling for the [less than 1 line of source text not declassified] Bloc arms in Latin American countries, this could be extended to include [less than 1 line of source text not declassified] propaganda materials and perhaps sabotage materials; (b) the possibility of [less than 1 line of source text not declassified] incidents which could lead to the breaking of diplomatic re-lations by selected countries. (This, of course, would have to be carefully considered in the sense of weighing the intelligence advantages of con-tinued diplomatic representation against the political/psychological gain from severance.)[20]

Paragraph 25 was deleted in its entirety from a revised September 12 version that Lansdale submitted for Bundy's approval. In a September 14 meeting of the Mongoose task force, "the 12 September addendum to the Phase Two Mongoose Operation was discussed and the entire Phase Two was approved in principle as a platform from which to proceed. Ac-tivities which may be especially sensitive are to be brought before the Group, and this body wishes to be kept generally advised on progress."[21] The minutes continue:

[1 paragraph (3 lines of source text) not declassified]
    CIA Headquarters and all WH stations are to be especially alert for any shipments of arms or other subversive material from Cuba to other Latin American countries. (Chief, Task Force W says this alert has been laid on and is in force.)

In May 1963, an undated list of "Additional Actions Against Cuba" included the following (the second paragraph apparently consists of CIA comments):

    7. Deception operation involving the laying down of arms caches con-taining Soviet, Czech and Chicom arms in selected areas of Latin Amer-ica, ostensibly proving the arms were smuggled from Cuba.

7. [comments] The key consideration in such an operation is the possibility that the 'discovery' of such arms caches might lead to embarrassment for the Administration since arms smuggling is one of the points most often stated for the U.S. possibly taking a more aggressive action against Castro. This type of operation, while feasible, is an extremely difficult and dangerous one to undertake in terms of making the operation completely plausible and foolproof.[22]

Then, six months later, three tons of arms turned up on a northwestern Venezuelan beach. The story broke in the newspapers on November 12, and on November 27—five days after JFK's assassination—Rusk informed the new President, Lyndon Johnson, that Venezuela planned to make a public announcement that the arms were of Cuban origin.[23]

In Richard Helms's fifth appearance before the Church Committee, on September 11, 1975, the former director described the incident this way:

> Mr. KELLEY. Mr. Ambassador, was it your perception that the Kennedy Administration's program against Cuba and the pressure to implement that program vigorously was any different in 1963 than it was in 1962?
>
> Mr. HELMS. Well, I find this a difficult question to answer for the simple reason that I don't have any recollection in 1963 once the operations—put it this way—cranked up again, that there were any particular limitations placed on what we were attempting to do. I realize that the character of some of them were changed. I think they must have been changed because conditions in Cuba had changed, the Cuban Missile Crisis had changed relations. We learned a great deal about Cuba because of the Cuban Missile Crisis itself.
>
> So I would imagine that the plans of 1963 were devised to try to treat the existing situation in Cuba, so they were in some respects different than those under Mongoose. But I do not recall having been told by anyone in authority that there is any less interest or intention on the part of the Kennedy Administration to unseat the Castro government. And I do recall that sometime, I guess it was in the summer or fall of 1963, talking to Mr. Robert Kennedy about the problem of Castro's efforts to send arms and trained guerrillas and so forth into other Latin American and Central American countries. And it just seemed to me that this was dangerous indeed, particularly after the

difficulties we'd had with Castro and the Cuban Missile Crisis, and my general recollection is that Mr. Kennedy said, yes, but what can the President do? If you can bring him evidence that Castro is sending arms and trained guerrillas and so forth to Latin American countries, then you give him something to work with. But under the circumstances, what can he do, what can any of us do?

Well, by chance, sometime after that, and I don't recall how long but it wasn't a terribly long time. The Venezuelan authorities, as I recall it, or maybe it was one of the Agency operations in Venezuela in conjunction with the Venezuelan security people or police, found a large arms cache on, I think way out in the country in Venezuela, and they also found through some penetration or agent, rather, a plan of some guerrillas, Venezuelan guerrillas, in touch with the Cubans to tie off certain sections of Caracas with armed men and so forth, and bring the city to a halt. There were some tunnels, or as I recall, this was also vague in my mind, now, I have not been in Caracas, but there are some vehicular tunnels where large numbers of automobiles go through during rush hour from one part of town to another. And they were going to tie this off.

Parenthetically, please don't hold me to the details because it was so long ago, I just don't remember. But that was the general thrust of it. But out of this cache were found some weapons and among those weapons I actually was given a submachine gun, which I believe was manufactured in Belgium, and on that submachine gun there was a place where there had been an insignia and the insignia had been brazed off, so that to the naked eye you could see nothing. But when the technicians in the Agency actually [began] to work with the chemicals and so forth, they were able to bring up for very short periods what was underneath. In other words, what the insignia had been long enough to photograph it.

And so we had photographs of what was on that thing, and it was the insignia of Castro's Cuba. So that these had obviously been sent from Belgium manufacture for the Cuban account. In other words, they had manufactured for them and sent to Cuba.[24]

Given the sensitivity of planting an arms cache, we do not know whether any documents showing that the CIA was actually behind the Venezuelan operation ever existed, much less if they will ever be released.

But when the arms cache was discovered, it did not, for reasons we shall examine, lead to any major new action against Castro.

Helms, who had undoubtedly supervised more than a few disinformation operations during his career, may have been trying in 1975 to rehabilitate his agency's reputation by once again making use of a deception. He would not have been the only CIA man to have done so. Just two months earlier, David Phillips, testifying about his role in American attempts to unseat Salvador Allende, had told the committee in reference to the September 1973 coup, "When Allende died it was because there was a coup against him by Chileans, and not because they were supported or abetted or encouraged or even winked at by the CIA."[25] That statement, as a recent book based on declassified documents has shown, was entirely untrue. The CIA station worked for years to create a political crisis conducive to a coup, closely monitored the development of the coup all through 1973, and had exact information about when and how it would take place. Phillips himself had expressed some doubts about the project early on, but only because he feared it would not succeed.[26] When a nation creates an agency whose task is to manipulate foreign perceptions and realities while hiding the role of the United States government, it should not be surprised to learn that high officials of that agency employ the same techniques to fend off domestic inquiries, even by other branches of the government.

President Kennedy attended his last high-level meeting about Cuba on November 12. McCone and Fitzgerald vigorously defended the sabotage program against the reservations of Rusk, who argued that "hit and run" operations were complicating relations with the Soviets and causing too much trouble internationally. Fitzgerald had to admit that it had become almost impossible to infiltrate agents into Cuba, and noted that about twenty-five of them had been apprehended during the last year. He claimed to have about 150 agents and subagents in Cuba and talked hopefully of drawing as many as a third of Cuba's top 150 military leaders into a coup. In his vague allusions to indirect contacts, Fitzgerald was referring to an agency operation called AMTRUNK aimed specifically at inducing military leaders to defect, and to Rolando Cubela (codenamed AMLASH).[27] Rusk was much more interested in catching Cubans exporting arms elsewhere in Latin America, possibly as a pretext for intervention.[28]

The administration counted on the raids merely to arouse hopes of liberation within Cuba and to force Castro to respond. It had other plans for his actual removal. An extensive paper trail shows that Fitzgerald, McCone, and the President himself were still counting on the sudden disappearance of Castro to provoke an internal coup or provide a pretext for American intervention—the third prong of its Cuban policy. In the late spring, pressure from the White House secured a National Intelligence Estimate from the CIA arguing that Castro's death might in fact doom the regime.[29] On August 1 Fitzgerald briefed the Joint Chiefs and stressed the need to prepare plans for a quick invasion in the event of an uprising in Cuba.[30] On October 31 someone in the agency wrote an unsigned memo suggesting that a faction within the Cuban army or militia might "neutralize the top leadership" and call for American help.[31] This was not merely idle speculation. A plot involving Castro's close associate, Rolando Cubela, had swung back into high gear during the second half of 1963 under Fitzgerald's direct control.

The CIA had recruited Cubela in Helsinki in July 1962 and met with him extensively in Paris the following month but lost contact in late 1962 and early 1963.[32] In September 1963, however, they managed to arrange another meeting with "AMLASH" at Porto Alegre, Brazil, through Cubela's friend Carlos Tepedino. "AMLASH cocky totally spoiled brat who will always be control problem but feel his feelings against regime sincere and he basically honest," his CIA interviewer reported. Washington replied that while Cubela was undisciplined and hopeless as an intelligence collector, he might still be able to recruit a network of friends who could progress "to sabotage and more serious matters on orderly basis."[33]

In mid-September the agency got another report on Cubela from a new potential recruit, Herminio Diaz Garcia, who had recently reached the United States. According to headquarters, Diaz was a former member of the Union of Revolutionary Insurrection, "an alleged gangster organization," during the 1950s and was involved in plots to assassinate Batista and to kidnap liberal Costa Rican President Jose Figueres. He was in and out of Castro's prisons in the early 1960s, including a stint in La Cabana, where he may have met John Martino, and he was reportedly close to Efigenio Amejeiras Delgado, the vice minister of Cuba's armed forces. According to Diaz, Amejeiras and Cubela belonged to the same group of dissident officers. Diaz reportedly arrived in the United States with a message for former President Carlos Prio Socarras, who was stepping up his own anti-Castro activities in the last half of 1963.[34]

During the second week in October Cubela met more than once with his case officer, a CIA man using the alias Ontrich. On October 13 Cubela demanded a meeting with none other than Robert Kennedy as a token of the U.S. government's genuine support. Because Cubela had "excellent entrée to highest target level which believe we cannot overlook," Ontrich recommended either flying him to Washington and granting his request or breaking off all contact with him.[35] Five days later a Paris CIA officer relayed Cubela's request again and recommended that Fitzgerald, who apparently was already scheduled to visit Paris, might be of sufficient stature to satisfy him. "Great minds think alike," Washington replied, and scheduled Fitzgerald's meeting with Cubela for the late afternoon of October 29.

A subsequent memo declared that Fitzgerald, code-named Dainold, "will represent self as personal representative of GPFOCUS [Robert Kennedy] who traveled Paris for specific purpose meeting AMLASH [Cubela] and giving him assurances of full United States support if there is a change of the present government in Cuba." If that meeting did not do the trick, the agency might make arrangements to bring Cubela to Washington to meet "with another high government official."[36] At their meeting, Fitzgerald said that the United States "is prepared to give full support to [Cubela] and his group if they are successful in real coup against the [Castro] regime." Fitzgerald now instructed the case officer to offer a cache of sabotage material, C-4 equipment, rifles with scopes, hand grenades, and pistols at his next meeting with AMLASH.[37] Paris arranged the meeting for the late afternoon of November 22.

No record indicates whether Fitzgerald briefed the attorney general on these contacts, but his intense personal interest in Cubela reflected the Kennedy administration's policy. The Kennedy administration had most certainly not given up on eliminating the Castro regime and had repeatedly concluded that the sudden death of Castro, followed by a period of chaos, would provide the best opportunity for American intervention to rid the island of Communism. During October the Pentagon was also consulted about a plan to insert an intelligence team immediately upon hearing of a coup, in order to assess the prospects for its success and contribute to a decision about introducing American forces.[38]

According to his deputy Sam Halpern, Fitzgerald was desperate to arrange Fidel's death. But his plan was not the only Castro assassination plot in the works during 1963—not by a long shot. Fabian Escalante, the former Cuban G-2 chief turned historian, identified many more, including the one carried out by John Roselli's team (which was captured in March) and the bombing raid planned in Louisiana (which, Mike McLaney confirmed to the HSCA, was aimed at Fidel).[39] In late July the CIA was also monitoring an assassination plot involving car bombs by a network code-named AMFAUNA. A "key figure" in AMFAUNA was CIA agent David Cabeza, who was subsequently linked to John Martino, whom Loran Hall had also reported to be interested in car bombs.[40] But Cubela was by far the highest-ranking Cuban official with whom the CIA had made contact. Given the number of agency personnel he contacted in different Latin American and European capitals and the number of Cubans (at least half a dozen) who knew about his plans, it seems incredible that he was not apprehended by Castro until 1966, when the CIA, of course, denied having had anything to do with him. Even after Cubela's imprisonment, the Cubans claimed not to have learned the full story of his CIA contacts until the release of the Church Committee Report in the fall of 1975.

The fourth prong hinted at a completely different policy. A lone American diplomat, William Attwood, was exploring the possibility of normalizing relations with Castro. In 1959, during his previous career as the foreign editor of *Look* magazine, Attwood had visited Cuba, interviewed Castro, and heard about Mafia assassination plots against him at a party in the home of Cuban sugar magnate Julio Lobo. From 1961 through 1963 he had served as ambassador to Guinea, where he had built a good relationship with leftist President Sekou Touré. After returning, he had been assigned to the American mission at the United Nations in late August. He immediately heard from the Guinean representative there and from Lisa Howard, an ABC reporter, that Castro might be interested in normalizing relations with the United States.

On September 18 Attwood wrote a memorandum for the White House suggesting that Castro might be willing to expel all Soviet military personnel, end subversive activity in Latin America, and pursue a nonaligned foreign policy in exchange for normalization of relations. Attwood advocated the deal on grounds that the United States did not intend to invade Cuba anyway and that its present policy was ineffective and unpopular around the world. He suggested that he return to Havana to discuss it with Castro.

Attwood had stumbled on a Castro initiative that was already about five months old. James Donovan, who ransomed the Bay of Pigs prisoners, had brought a similar if vaguer message back from Castro in early April, and McCone had told the President about it.[41] When the CIA debriefed Howard in late April or early May, she evidently told them that Castro wanted a rapprochement with the United States, accompanied by the expulsion of all Soviet personnel, but that the U.S. government would have to make the first move. Castro offered to meet with any "progressive" American emissary and told Howard she could arrange this through his associate, Rene Vallejo. Helms's May 1 memorandum of her report, which went to Bundy and RFK, also explained that while Raoul Castro and Che Guevara opposed a rapprochement, two other Castro intimates favored it. He also relayed Howard's opinion that "neither Guevara nor Raul Castro would be able to rule Cuba if Fidel were assassinated." On June 5 Helms reported that two more sources had confirmed Castro's interest in a rapprochement, as had diplomatic rumors from six other sources. Nothing was done in response, however, until Attwood started his discussions in New York.[42]

In September Attwood consulted with his boss, Adlai Stevenson, Undersecretary of State Averell Harriman, and Robert Kennedy and arranged through Lisa Howard to meet socially with Cuban delegate Carlos Lechuga in New York. Lechuga indicated that Castro would be quite happy to resume his conversations with Attwood in Havana. In late October Attwood managed to contact Castro himself through Howard and Major Vallejo, the top-level aide Howard had met in Havana. Vallejo relayed a message that while Castro could not leave Cuba at this time, even to go to the United Nations, he would welcome Attwood's visit. Five weeks later, two other sources confirmed Castro's interest.[43] Meanwhile, the CIA heard from another person who had met with Castro sometime in late September or early October 1963 that if the United States would lift the economic blockade against Castro, he would evict the Soviets from Cuba. The CIA informed Deputy Defense Secretary Vance, but neither the State Department, Attwood, nor Bundy seems to have gotten this news.[44]

Although in retrospect much has been made of Attwood's initiative, contemporary documentation shows that it was going nowhere. The possibility of normalizing relations with Castro came up several times in high-level meetings during 1963. McCone put the alternatives of normalization or invasion in front of President Kennedy back in April, and Kennedy suggested, prophetically, that both courses of action might simultaneously be pursued.[45] No high-level official, however, showed any interest in a deal with Castro in subsequent discussions, and in June a State Department paper flatly rejected it as too encouraging to Communist regimes.[46]

When McGeorge Bundy brought Attwood's initiative before the Special Group on November 5, those present, including McCone, U. Alexis Johnson from State, Vance from Defense, and the attorney general, agreed that it would be better for Attwood to return to private life before meeting again with Castro, and they suggested that Vallejo fly to Mexico City, perhaps to meet with U.S. Ambassador Thomas Mann. RFK also argued that Castro would have to end subversive activities and arrange the evacuation of all Soviet troops before the United States could discuss a détente. On November 12 Bundy telephoned Attwood in New York after speaking with the President.

> I talked this afternoon with William Attwood and told him that at the President's instruction I was conveying this message orally and not by cable. I told him that the President hoped he would get in touch with Vallejo to report that it did not seem practicable to us at this stage to send an American official to Cuba and that we would prefer to begin with a visit by Vallejo to the U.S. where Attwood would be glad to see him and to listen to any messages he might bring from Castro. In particular, we would be interested in knowing whether there was any prospect of important modification in those parts of Castro's policy which are flatly unacceptable to us: namely, the three points in Ambassador Stevenson's recent speech of which the central elements are (1) submission to external Communist influence, and (2) a determined campaign of subversion directed at the rest of the Hemisphere. Reversals of these policies may or may not be sufficient to produce a change in the policy of the United States, but they are certainly necessary, and without an indication of readiness to move in these directions, it is hard for us to see what could be accomplished by a visit to Cuba.[47]

During his presidency, John F. Kennedy was far more interested in moderating the Cold War than in intensifying it. By the second half of 1963 he was actively pursuing détente with Khrushchev, and on numerous occasions he disagreed with all his advisers on the wisdom of putting American combat troops into Laos or South Vietnam.[48] He brilliantly managed the missile crisis of October 1962 to avoid escalation into nuclear war. Yet the records show that he never accepted the continued existence of the Castro regime in Cuba, that he regarded Cuba as falling within America's sphere of influence, and that he hoped, through a mixture of economic pressure, covert action (very possibly including the assassination of Castro), and sudden American intervention, to remove it. Kennedy was not a leader who foreclosed his options, and had he lived he might possibly have decided on normalization of relations with Castro. In November 1963, however, the evidence proves that this was not yet his preference.

Still, by the second half of that year, the administration's policy toward Communist Cuba was not satisfying most Cuban exiles. Working covertly rather than openly toward Castro's overthrow made sense politically, but it inevitably heightened the dilemma that the administration had faced since the Bay of Pigs. With the exception of Artime and Ray, Cuban exile leaders and their American patrons assumed either that the administration was doing nothing about Castro or that it was trying to replace him with some form of leftist "Fidelismo sin Fidel" under either Artime or Ray. To many exiles, John Kennedy was a traitor to their cause. At least four distinguishable elements from the exile community were now acting on their own, both politically and in some cases militarily, to bring about the overthrow of Castro. They were former President Carlos Prio, who was trying to put together some kind of center-right coalition; Paulino Sierra Martinez, a lawyer now living in Chicago; the action groups Commandos L, SNFE, and Alpha-66; and, most interesting of all, the DRE.

After being overthrown by Batista in 1952 and escaping to the United States, reportedly with millions of dollars, Prio spent the 1950s trying to return to power. In 1956 he made a critical alliance with Fidel Castro, and several years later he was indicted for sending arms to Cuba. He returned there at the time of the revolution in 1959 but came back to the United States in early 1961, having fallen out with Castro. Between 1961 and 1963 Prio emerged as a significant player in Cuban exile politics.

Unfortunately, the U.S. government seems not to have released most of its documentation about this key figure in events leading up to JFK's assassination.[49] We know that Prio was closely connected to Antonio Varona, John Roselli's contact in the assassination plots, and he had evidently enjoyed a cordial relationship with Mafia elements during his time in power. John Martino knew him but did not trust him because he thought Prio was addicted to cocaine.[50] As Cuba's former president, he could, and did, arrange meetings with other Central and South American leaders, and he made a number of trips around the region from 1961 to 1963 asking for their support. In August 1961 Prio reportedly tried unsuccessfully to interest General Maxwell Taylor, Kennedy's special military representative, in a plan to train a new Cuban force in Florida that would invade Cuba with American help after a suitable provocation was arranged.[51]

In March 1962 Teamster leader Frank Chavez told the FBI that Prio had approached him to get Jimmy Hoffa's help to land a couple of hundred men on an island off the Cuban coast and shell the mainland. Chavez refused to make the introduction, he said. Prio himself told a Miami group that he had put together a band of 250 men, and Sturgis claimed that he was going to lead it.[52] A year later, a confidential source told the FBI that Hoffa had offered Prio fifty men to infiltrate Cuba as guerrillas, but Prio denied it.[53] According to an FBI informant, Prio also gave Gerry Hemming some money in mid-1963 and discussed forming a new training camp with him.[54]

In fact, during that summer Prio kept in touch with a variety of exiles, including Paulino Sierra Martinez, Luis Fernandez Rocha of DRE, and Eloy Gutierrez Menoyo of SNFE. Prio also visited the Dominican Republic's leftist president, Juan Bosch. He gave Army intelligence an alarming report about Bosch's plans to confiscate estates, nationalize industries, and leave the OAS. The Dominican military actually did overthrow Bosch in late September. He also reportedly was accompanied by Jose Aleman, a Florida businessman who told the FBI about a housing project in the Dominican Republic he was involved in with Santo Trafficante.

In September 1963 Prio and Varona visited Luis Somoza in Nicaragua, apparently in an attempt to become the leaders of Somoza's plan to topple Castro with American backing. Prio also met with Artime, but they did not manage to reach any accommodation, according to Artime.[55]

Another report claimed that Prio gave Artime some money in the spring. Artime denied it.[56] Somoza was spreading the story that President Kennedy had authorized him to establish anti-Castro bases in Nicaragua. In early September, Prio told a group of Cuban exiles that he had assembled a broad center-right coalition of exiles, including Sierra, and that he had Somoza's support. In an effort to get wealthy Cuban exiles to contribute to him, he was evidently threatening that an American-sponsored assault on Castro would fail to restore their property.[57]

The CIA and other American authorities consistently argued that Prio's own corrupt record made him an unsuitable symbol of the Cuban resistance, and in late September the Special Affairs Staff asked David Phillips, their man in Mexico, to put an unfavorable story about him in the press. In early October the Mexico City office planted an item suggesting that Prio could best help the Cuban people by returning his stolen millions.[58] Prio, meanwhile, got the drift of Washington's policy and was meeting with a mixture of activists like Laureano Batista Falla of the MDC and former members of Batista's government such as Carlos Marquez Sterling and Emilio Nunez Portuondo, two old friends of William Pawley.[59]

By the first of October, Prio was pushing the same line that Loran Hall had trumpeted in Los Angeles: that Kennedy was determined to replace Castro with a new left-wing government, presumably under Artime or Ray. Prio told wealthy exiles that he already had $10 million to establish bases around the Caribbean and overthrow Castro before Kennedy could carry out his plans.[60] By mid-October Prio claimed to have the support of a number of leading activists, including Nino Diaz and Eloy Gutierrez Menoyo, and on November 6 he stated that Kennedy and Khrushchev had agreed to replace Castro with a Tito-style leader after the 1964 U.S. elections.[61] A later report said that he was indirectly in touch with Richard Nixon, who hoped to make Cuba a big issue in the campaign.[62] Prio, in short, was competing with the Kennedy administration for Somoza's cooperation in Nicaragua and hoping to outflank the government's plans to overthrow Castro with the help of Artime and Ray. On December 15 Prio eulogized Kennedy in Los Angeles but criticized his policy of "international coexistence" with Russia.[63] Two months after JFK's assassination Prio informed the CIA that he was sending a team into Cuba to try to assassinate Castro during a duck hunt.

The agency made no comment, but his team was apprehended on the high seas.[64]

Rolando Masferrer, a leading Batistiano activist in the United States, was having thoughts similar to Prio's. In mid-August he told a Cuban that he hoped his planned invasion of Haiti would lead to the overthrow of Juan Bosch in the Dominican Republic with the help of Trujillo's surviving sons, enabling him to establish an anti-Castro base there. Without such a scheme, he explained, he "would be lost because the Batistianos have not been included in any plan directed by the United States regarding Cuba."[65]

Prio may have been working through a far more mysterious figure, a fifty-three-year-old Cuban lawyer named Paulino Sierra Martinez who now worked for the Union Tank Car Company in Chicago. Sierra initially came to the attention of the Chicago CIA Domestic Contacts office in March and April of 1963, and he told them that he had $10 million worth of backing to create a unified Cuban government in exile. Sources reported that Sierra was dealing with Americans for Cuban Freedom, based in Los Angeles, and that he might also be in contact with gambling interests. That committee seems to have been the same group that Loran Hall was working with during the very same summer.[66]

On May 9 Sierra met with forty representatives of various exile groups at the Royal Palms Hotel in Miami. He claimed that he wanted to unify all military action against Castro and said he had the "indirect" backing of the U.S. government. He then gave the floor to an American, William Trull, who claimed that he had $30 million available from an unidentified Chicago group of investors.[67] Shortly thereafter, the *Miami News* identified Trull as a gambler, and the FBI opened a file on Sierra. That in turn got the attention of the attorney general.[68]

Things became even stranger when FBI agents actually interviewed Sierra and Trull. Sierra claimed that Trull approached him after reading a story in a Chicago paper and offered $30 million from unidentified sources. Trull, on the other hand, identified himself as an entertainer and said that Sierra contacted *him* after seeing his performance before Cuban audiences, and asked him to pose as a wealthy American banker in Miami. According to Trull, Sierra claimed $14 million in backing from Cleveland gangsters in return for 50 percent of the casino profits after

Castro was overthrown. Trull actually spoke to Prio on Sierra's behalf to plead for unity. The FBI found Trull more convincing than Sierra.[69]

Sierra successfully established the Cuban Governing Junta in Exile (JGCE), a coalition of various center and right-wing Cuban groups, and continued to travel around the country making various pitches. Neither the FBI nor the CIA, who clearly were not behind him, could figure out who, if anyone, was actually backing him, and by September the State Department's Miami Coordinator of Cuban Affairs had concluded that he was nothing but a con man.[70] Meanwhile, in July and August Sierra had traveled to Nicaragua to promise mob money to one of Artime's associates in exchange for gambling concessions, and he told another Cuban that Chicago gambling interests had $30 million ready.[71] In October, CIA reported that Sierra had a boat stored at the home of Manuel Aguilar, and that Loran Hall, Aguilar's close associate, was planning a raid on Cuba.[72]

On November 20, JMWAVE gave CIA headquarters a long report on recent developments, prepared at the request of the Cuban coordinator in Miami. Sierra, it said, had been ubiquitous since May, filling a vacuum left by the dissolution of the Cuban Revolutionary Council. He apparently had received $650,000 from various American businesses, and in recent months, with the help of Alpha-66, SNFE, and Commandos L, he had been trying to arrange a major raid, which was the best way (as the DRE had discovered a year earlier) to attract publicity and funds. Sierra claimed support from Standard Oil, Sears and Roebuck, Union Carbide, United Fruit, Dupont, ATT, and U.S. Steel, and had gone on his own odyssey around the Caribbean planning bases in various countries.[73]

Six days later a memorandum on FBI letterhead reported that many Cuban exiles were losing faith in Sierra but confirmed that he had spent thousands of dollars on arms for some of the action groups, purchased from the right-wing Illinois arms dealer Rich Lauchli.[74] Sierra continued traveling and talking big for another six months or so, but no one ever discovered who, if anyone, was backing his operation.

The report of the boat at Aguilar's house becomes more interesting in light of an incident in the Florida Keys on October 30. The Customs Office, whose agent Wallace Shanley was the point man in federal attempts to stop unauthorized raids, had apparently been keeping track of Aguilar's boat, the *Pitusa II*. At 6:00 p.m. on October 29 it was loaded onto a trailer that headed for the Keys, "accompanied by another auto-mobile and a station wagon." The trailer turned off about a mile north of Jewfish Creek on Key Largo and went to a launching area. The two cars initially continued south but turned around and rendezvoused with the boat after midnight. At that point Customs officers approached the cars and boat. In a 1954 Mercury they found two Cubans, arms, munitions, explosives, and supplies. The other car, an Oldsmobile, was driven by its owner, Loran Hall. The weapons and supplies, presumably, were those he had initially obtained in California and brought from Dallas a week or two earlier. What kind of mission he was on has never been discovered, and the Customs men simply confiscated the trailer and weapons and let him go.[75]

In 1978 Hall told the HSCA that he traded a cannon to Aguilar for the boat, and that he got some dynamite from Artime. He said he was in-tercepted on No Name Key, not Key Largo, and he suspected that Gerry Hemming might have tipped the government off. After trying for more than a week to borrow another boat, he sold a rifle, flew back to Califor-nia around November 10, and gave up anti-Castro activity.[76]

Still other independent action groups among the exiles were busily scrambling for money, weapons, boats, and bases to continue their attacks on Fidel. Antonio Veciana, who kept a much lower profile in 1963 than in 1962, was reported in July to be planning to infiltrate a team into Cuba.[77] On June 8 Veciana, Tony Cuesta, and Luis Fernandez Rocha of the DRE were all featured in a long *Saturday Evening Post* article on ex-iles, and all of them spoke very frankly about the connection between spectacular, well-publicized attacks and fundraising.

A July report said that Evelio Duque of the Ejercito Cubano Anti-communista, or Cuban Anti-Communist Army, who had fallen out with the CIA in spring 1962, planned to land a force on keys north of Cuba to provoke a conflict with Castro. According to earlier reports, he had purchased one hundred semi-automatic rifles on the black market in Miami. The CIA's informant thought he was being supported by Fulgencio Batista, who was now living in Spain. Duque was violently anti-American.[78]

Enrique Molina and Victor Paneque of the MDC (Christian Demo-cratic Movement), who had established a Louisiana training camp in July, traveled to Nicaragua to see Somoza and were offered a base. The CIA heard that the Louisiana trainees were in fact projected to relocate to Nicaragua.[79] The agency dropped its connection with Laureano Batista Falla of the MDC in August, but reports in the fall suggested that he was well-financed, busily acquiring arms, and in touch with Prio.[80]

Santo Trafficante was also quite deeply involved with the independent exiles. On June 24, according to an FBI report in late August, a Cuban exile told an agent that Trafficante "wants to have Eloy Gutierrez Menoyo, leader of the Second National Front of the Excambray, killed . . . Some time in April, 1963, a representative of Trafficante approached Enrique Molina and another person, who were seeking arms and equipment for anti-Castro purposes. They did not have sufficient money to pay," and Trafficante's representative suggested they could get what they needed if they killed Gutierrez Menoyo outside the United States. Trafficante claimed that Gutierrez Menoyo failed to pay for $250,000 worth of arms and equipment that he received in April. The same report quoted Molina to the effect that if he had known how things would go in the United States, he would have remained in Cuba.[81]

The ubiquitous Frank Sturgis continued to report on plans by Pedro and Mario Diaz Lanz to bomb Cuba. In October Artime claimed that the Diaz brothers had the support of the "Goldwater movement."[82] But the most noteworthy independent exile was Orlando Bosch of the MIRR, who claimed responsibility for several bombing raids against Cuba during September 1963. Despite publishing violent attacks on the American government in general and the CIA in particular during 1961, Bosch worked with JMWAVE during 1962, but his clearance expired near the end of that year.[83] The agency eventually told the FBI that Bosch's raids were "not a CIA operation," but they originated in Fort Lauderdale—landing in Bimini before bombing Cuba—and no one was doing anything to stop him.[84] In another incident, on October 20, federal authorities seized a ship carrying twenty members of Commandos L on a raid in Cuba. "I don't understand it," said Santiago Alvarez, the boat's captain. "The U.S. government couldn't contribute more to Castro's cause if it tried."[85]

Alvarez would have been even more puzzled had he known of a recent proposal from within the CIA to support and direct Commandos L covertly. Apparently dating from June 1963, it proposed making the wherewithal available for two raids on Cuban ships per month. "A wealthy

American who has been deeply involved in Cuba and Latin America for many years and who has cooperated closely with CIA in the past," it read, "would be asked by CIA to present the program to an eminent and respected Cuban exile who in turn would be asked to act as a funding and cover front for the support to be furnished Commandos L." Commandos L would never learn where the money actually came from.[86]

The American certainly sounded like William Pawley, who had just run his own abortive raid on Cuba and was supporting the DRE. As active as ever, Pawley told the CIA in August that Somoza wanted an American to coordinate exile activities in Nicaragua, and generously volunteered himself for the job.[87] Although Tony Cuesta, the leader of Commandos L, expressed great distrust of the Kennedy administration in a *Saturday Evening Post* article of June, the proposal to support him apparently went before the Special Group in August. It was finally disapproved in October because raids were already becoming too controversial.[88] The whole episode suggests that Pawley was still dealing directly with headquarters and acting as a cut-out.

The DRE remained the most troublesome anti-Castro organization in the United States. It had concluded 1962 by publishing verbal attacks on President Kennedy and securing the replacement of its case officer, Ross Crozier, with George Joannides, who went by the name of Walter Newby. The change did not improve the DRE's relationship with the U.S. government, however. Its February Cuban report assailed Secretary McNamara and claimed that Soviet missiles remained in Cuba.[89] In the same month the group's leader, Luis Fernandez, told the CIA he intended to resume armed raids. His contact replied that the United States could not allow this.[90] On April 1 and 2 Fernandez announced both publicly and privately that the CIA was responsible for the arrest in Cuba of the DRE's leader, Alberto Muller, and for the failure of the Bay of Pigs, and that the DRE would regretfully carry on the struggle alone. But agency headquarters, still patient, ordered JMWAVE not to terminate its relationship simply based on a statement of intent, but only in response to an overt act.[91]

In late August the CIA received a tip from its Chicago informant, sheriff's office investigator and Mafia man Richard Cain, that a local Cuban had been approached by the DRE and asked to join a guerrilla force that would operate somewhere in Latin America. When the Cuban replied that he would do nothing not authorized by the U.S. government, the DRE man telephoned Miami, where Manuel Salvat Roque, the organization's military chief, claimed that they were backed not by the CIA but by the Pentagon.[92] In early September the DRE, which was still receiving CIA funds for propaganda activities in the United States and Latin America, arranged a radio debate with some American students who had just returned from a trip to Cuba under the auspices of the Fair Play for Cuba Committee. That debate had clear parallels with the one a few weeks earlier in New Orleans involving Carlos Bringuier and Lee Harvey Oswald.[93]

In another even more striking incident, on September 12 JMWAVE reported the appearance in newsstands of the November issue of the men's magazine *See,* which featured a cover photo of Fidel Castro captioned "Wanted, Dead or Alive, Fidel Castro for Crimes against Humanity, $10 Million Reward." The story inside was headlined, "The CIA needs men—can you qualify?" and included a statement by Fernandez that the DRE had deposited the reward in the Banco Santo Domingo. Queried, the DRE leadership denied they had authorized the ad. On October 23 the *Miami Herald* reported new DRE complaints about the CIA's failure to support its raids—complaints that DRE officials promptly told Joannides they had not made.[94]

The climax of the long and difficult relationship between the DRE and the CIA began on October 22, when the DRE gave Joannides its plan for a military base on a Caribbean island. (The island name is redacted in the released document.) In a long cable on November 8, Joannides reviewed the history of the last year. Although the agency had cut out its support for DRE military operations in March and threatened that any new raids would cost the group all its support, the organization's leaders remained restive and now, with the emergence of Ray's bases in Central America, wanted to make sure they did not lose their role "in what appeared to be the new ODYOKE [US government] putsch to oust AMTHUG-1 [Castro]." Now they asked to set up a substantial force at a base, "Martha," near Trinidad, to operate autonomously and infiltrate small numbers of men into Cuba.

JMWAVE, Joannides explained, opposed this plan. The DRE lacked the skill or personnel for unconventional war along these lines, the base was too far from the target, the American involvement would surely surface, and the monthly budget would increase from $20,000 to hundreds of thousands. "A freewheeling AMSPELL [DRE] with a chameleon sense of loyalty and an arrogant contempt for OKYOKE [U.S. government] is an unsuitable basket for the eggs of the autonomous group concept," Joannides wrote. The DRE was viewed by the exile community as the "enfant gaté and the enfant terrible." The cable recommended against support for the plan and asked permission to convey the negative message.[95]

Permission was granted, and Joannides met Fernandez on November 19. He informed him that the CIA was not inclined to support any part of the DRE's military plan, and that he was instructed to suggest that the group ally with Artime, whose organization was ideologically and militarily compatible with the DRE, was based outside the United States, and had the means and facilities for operations against Cuba. When Joannides was about half way through this delivery, Fernandez smiled and then burst out laughing. When he finished chuckling, he declared, "I just knew you were going to say something like that." "Meaningful glances were exchanged," Joannides wrote, "and the subject was dropped. The parting was most amicable."[96]

What JMWAVE did not know was that the DRE was not putting all its eggs in one basket either. Denied support from CIA, it had obviously found some patrons elsewhere, including Pawley and Clare Boothe Luce. And as a matter of fact, at the same time that Fernandez was getting nowhere with Joannides, the DRE was trying to swing a major arms deal in Dallas, Texas.

On Sunday evening, October 13, 1963, the DRE held a fundraising meeting in a bank at a North Dallas shopping center. The featured speakers were Manuel Salvat, the DRE's military chief, known to the CIA for his violent temper, and Anna Silveira, another DRE representative from Miami. They were accompanied by a third leading DRE figure, Joaquin Martinez de Pinillo, publisher of the DRE's bi-weekly *Cuban Report*.[97] The *Dallas Morning News* gave the meeting a warm preview on the morning of October 13, and General Edwin Walker also attended.[98]

During his stay in Dallas, which lasted several days, Salvat introduced Martinez to a local exile and Bay of Pigs veteran named Fermin de Goicochea Sanchez. He told Goicochea that he wanted him to buy enough arms to outfit several PT boats, and introduced him to a young

Dallas gun dealer, John Thomas Masen, who was also affiliated with the
John Birch Society. Martinez, who already knew Masen, told him that
Goicochea would be his contact from then on. Goicochea specifically
asked Masen for .50-caliber machine guns, 20-mm anti-aircraft guns, ba-
zookas, recoilless rifles, and C-3 or C-4 explosives. Masen said he could
get everything but the explosives. During their discussions Goicochea
also met a man whom he believed to be a retired army officer who was
offering to help—a man about 5'7", with reddish hair and a handlebar
mustache.[99]

The man was Colonel George Nonte of the U.S. Army, who ran
an armory in Fort Hood, Texas, near his home in Killeen. He might
have been involved in previous arms thefts, of which there had been
many from the armory recently, but when Masen approached him he
apparently decided to buy some insurance with the authorities. On
October 23, he told an Army intelligence representative that Masen
wanted to meet him about a forthcoming "large exercise in the Caribbean." The officer promptly informed the San Antonio FBI.[100] Nonte
met Masen that night with two other men. Masen said he heard about
the Caribbean operation from a certain Martinez—obviously Martinez
de Pinillo—who had recently come through Dallas looking for weapons.
Masen hoped to learn the exact time of the forthcoming attack on Cuba,
he told Nonte, and to sell the date, because one could make a lot of
money in the stock market with it. Masen, Nonte informed the FBI the
next day, was always looking for a score, was completely unscrupulous,
and would do anything for money except white slavery or drugs.[101] A
week later, Nonte got a call from a self-identified friend of Martinez
who called himself George Perrel and said he would be his contact from
now on. Masen confirmed that Perrel, who was actually Fermin de
Goicochea, was a Bay of Pigs veteran who was living in New York and
working with Martinez.[102]

The San Antonio FBI did not know that Masen had also come to the
attention of Frank Ellsworth, a Dallas agent in the Bureau of Alcohol,
Tobacco and Firearms, who often worked with FBI agent James Hosty
because they both kept track of right-wing subversives. On November
14 Ellsworth, along with another agent named William Fuller and an
Irving policeman known to Masen, went to Masen's gun shop to sound
him out on a weapon's purchase and entrap him. Ellsworth claimed to be

a crooked cop, and the policeman helped them satisfy Masen as to their bona fides by fabricating a teletype about Fuller. Masen called Nonte and claimed Nonte would take $30,000 for a large stock of weapons cached in Mexico. Fuller later claimed that he had also seen a list of the weapons the DRE wanted in Masen's shop.[103] In an effort to verify Masen's story, Ellsworth, who knew nothing about Nonte's conversations with the FBI, went to Fort Hood and found that someone had been robbing the armory blind lately.[104]

On the evening of November 18, two Dallas men, Lawrence Miller and Donnell Whittier, became the targets of a high-speed chase through city streets before crashing their Thunderbird into a telephone pole. The men in the car survived, and inside the vehicle the police found a load of weapons stolen from a National Guard Armory in Terrell, Texas.[105] On the next morning, when Ellsworth and Fuller arrived at the gun shop to close their deal, Masen, shaken, reported that Miller and Whittier had been working for him and that he had planned to offer the guns in their car to Fuller. Masen called Nonte again, and they worked out the price for the Mexico arms cache in a three-way conversation. Nonte said that Masen badgered him about where he could find a load of various weapons and claimed recently to have sold a load of M-1s with bayonets and scabbards.[106]

On Thursday, November 21, Ellsworth and Fuller arrested Masen for selling parts to convert semi-automatic M-1s into automatic rifles—a popular item in the illicit arms market in those days. Masen immediately identified George Perrel as the DRE's arms buyer.[107] Ellsworth concluded by early December that Nonte and a friend of Nonte's at an arsenal in Texarkana, Texas, had indeed furnished Masen with weapons, but Nonte was never charged.[108] It took until February 1964 for Ellsworth to discover that Fermin de Goicochea lived at the address Masen gave for Perrel, and Goicochea himself was not interviewed until October 1964, when he told the whole story.[109] Masen eventually pled guilty to one count of illegal arms sales.

What gives this story more than passing interest are two possible links to the leading figures in the Kennedy assassination, Lee Harvey Oswald and Jack Ruby. The first is one of the most extraordinary of all omissions from both the Warren Report and the HSCA Report. On December 19, 1963, FBI agent Hosty interviewed a civil engineer named Edward Stieg,

who must have contacted the FBI. Stieg told Hosty that he had attended
the public DRE meeting at the North Lake Shopping Center in October at which Salvat had spoken. He sat at the back, and he thought that
he saw Lee Harvey Oswald sitting there quietly as well. Hosty, following
up, met with Sara Castillo, the Dallas DRE leader, who acknowledged
the meeting and gave the date of October 13. She said she did not
remember Oswald but that most of the guests had signed a register that
Anna Silveira and Manuel Salvat had taken back to Miami. The Miami
office interviewed Silveira and located the register, but found neither
Oswald's nor Stieg's name on it.[110] Dallas apparently made no attempt to
contact everyone on the list.

In 2004—after some effort, because agent Hosty had misspelled his
name—I located Edward Stieg living elsewhere in Texas. He confirmed
that he had lived at the Garland, Texas, address noted by Hosty and that
in 1963 he had recently returned from several years in Venezuela, where
he had worked for an American oil company as a civil engineer. This fact
suggested why he might have attended a meeting on Latin American affairs. Stieg was friendly and gave every evidence of having a sound mind
despite having passed his eightieth birthday. But in several conversations
he insisted that he had absolutely no memory either of the meeting or
any conversation with the FBI. There can be no doubt, however, that his
conversation with Hosty took place, and the file suggests that Stieg must
have initiated it.

Stieg may have been mistaken in his identification, however. Frank
Ellsworth, the ATF agent who arrested Masen on November 19, saw
Oswald at the Dallas police station and was immediately struck by the remarkable resemblance between Masen and Oswald. Masen himself told
the HSCA in 1978 that he attended a DRE fundraiser, although he was
not asked to identify it.[111] But the meeting was publicized in the *Dallas
Morning News* and it would hardly have been out of character for Oswald
to show up. Oswald's appearance at the meeting would explain the contention of Lucille Connell, Silvia Odio's friend who had first called Odio
to the attention of the FBI, that Oswald had attended Cuban meetings in
Dallas. If indeed he managed to do so, that would call into question the
idea that his contacts with the DRE in New Orleans were genuinely
hostile.

Jack Ruby's possible connection emerges from two pieces of evidence, one somewhat speculative and the second from a question-able witness who nonetheless came up with a critical detail. In April 1964 the Dallas police discovered that Whittier, the weapons thief, had serviced Ruby's car at the Texaco service station where he worked.[112] Four months later, in August, a man named John Elrod contacted the FBI in Memphis to tell the story of his arrest in Dallas on November 22. Elrod, who was one of four tramps picked up by the Dallas police in the rail yard behind Dealey Plaza, told how Whittier's partner, Miller, had been brought down the jail corridor where he and a cellmate could see him. The cellmate told Elrod that he had been present at a meeting of five men in a motel in which Miller had received some money, and that Ruby had been present as well.[113]

The second story is even more tantalizing. On November 27, 1963, just two days after Ruby's name became a household word, a woman named Nancy Elaine Perrin contacted the FBI in San Francisco, where she lived. Admitting to prostitution, she said she worked briefly for Jack Ruby at the Carousel Club in 1961. She tended bar, and he threw her against the bar one evening because the glasses were not clean enough. As Perrin explained to the Warren Commission, she went to the police station and attempted to swear out a complaint against him but they re-fused to listen to her.[114]

Some months later, she and her husband, Dick Perrin, attended a number of meetings with Ruby involving running guns to Cuba and picking up refugees. In several interviews, she told the FBI to talk to Eddie Mark, a hoodlum from St. Louis, and Buddy King, a comic. She said a man named Dick Cherry, a bartender in another Dallas club who had been her pimp, was probably the man behind the meetings that dis-cussed gun-running. Most interesting, she said that the meetings were at-tended by an army colonel who claimed he could get the guns for Cuba in Mexico. Nothing came of the deal. Her husband, who she said was also present, had died in 1962.[115]

Perrin was obviously mentally unstable and had been hospitalized for mental illness more than once. A polygraph taken at the request of the FBI in San Francisco gave inconclusive results. She claimed to know both Teddy and Jackie Kennedy (she was, in fact, from New England and had lived in Boston before coming to Dallas).[116] The bureau eventually located a Dave Cherry in Dallas, who admitted being her pimp but denied her entire story about guns.[117] Yet the FBI identified a St. Louis hoodlum named Vito Cusamanno who, an informant said, went to Dallas in the summer of 1961 under the name of Eddie Marks, hoping to make a big score.[118] And her story remains troubling both because we know that Ruby had already tried to get involved in gun-running in 1959, and because the Army colonel sounds suspiciously like George Nonte.

The extent of Ruby's gun-running activities will almost certainly never be known. After his conviction for murdering Oswald, Ruby reportedly told Wally Weston, a comedian who had worked for him, "Wally, they're going to find out about Cuba. They're going to find out about the guns, find out about New Orleans, find out about everything."[119] And within a week of Ruby's murder of Oswald, two unrelated witnesses linked Ruby to arms deals involving Cuba. One, a convict named Blaney Mack Johnson, specifically tied him to Edward Browder, one of the era's leading illegal arms traders. In April 1964 the Warren Commission asked the FBI to pursue this lead, but the bureau apparently failed to do so.[120]

A Detroit woman remembered visiting her brother and sister-in-law, James and Mary Lou Woodard, in Florida in March 1958 and finding them in the company of a man named Jack. He was from Chicago, ran "a drinking place in Dallas," and had a trunk full of guns he planned to supply to Cubans. The Woodards' daughter, who was also there, said Ruby's pictures looked like Jack. James Woodard turned out to be a former U.S. Customs informant who indeed trafficked in arms and explosives but had a reputation for unreliability. The FBI never actually located him.[121] Ruby apparently acknowledged some acquaintance with another arms dealer, Thomas Eli Davis of Beaumont, Texas, who in the spring of 1963 was caught in Los Angeles trying to recruit mercenaries to take part in the overthrow of the Haitian government.[122] While each of these stories, like Perrin's, has problems of its own, the combination suggests that Jack Ruby had more to do with arms deals for Cuba than has ever come to light.

The DRE's arms purchase in Dallas never came off, but the organization was once again proving itself a highly motivated and uncontrollable organization, determined to eliminate Fidel Castro with or without the cooperation of the U.S. government, and utterly enraged by President

Kennedy's failure to do more to help. CIA reporting was relatively discreet regarding the statements of exiles about the personnel and institutions of the U.S. government, but at least one officer, Calvin Thomas, who had worked with the DRE in Miami for more than two years, from the spring of 1961 to the late summer of 1963, heard enough to write an extraordinary memo for the record on March 8, 1967, when Jim Garrison's New Orleans investigation was making the news. Noting that Garrison had already touched on the "Cuban Student Directorate" and Carlos Bringuier's contacts with Oswald, Thomas continued:

> I have assumed that, since the time I was transferred from Miami and scheduled for my next assignment as [redacted], officers better and more recently informed than myself have probably examined in detail all aspects of the DRE involvement with OSWALD, in order to rule out any slight possibility that compromise of the CIA sponsorship of this organization might in any way embarrass the Agency. Recent news reports of investigations centering in New Orleans on the assassination have once again brought to mind the concern I felt in November 1963, by which time, however, I was far removed from current knowledge of the operation.
>
> I do retain a distinct recollection that the DRE leadership, specifically Luis FERNANDEZ Rocha, whom I met several times, did hold sentiments of chagrin and embitterment that President Kennedy had not more forcefully pursued a "liberation" of Cuba. Whether or not this animus, which could be discerned as occasional signs of anger or of contempt or of discouragement, might have been translated into a wish for revenge, may be better known to other officers, who dealt with this group after the summer of 1963.[123]

By November 1963, the DRE's principal case officer, Joannides, shared the low opinion of the organization's reliability that had cost his predecessor his job a year earlier. Certainly the record gives no indication that Joannides was cooperating with the DRE in any nefarious scheme, as *Washington Post* reporter Jefferson Morley has speculated. Yet it is quite extraordinary, as Morley discovered, that the CIA in 1977–78 chose Joannides as its liaison with the HSCA, and that Joannides was commended by his superiors for resisting the importunate demands for documentation of the committee staff. Years later, committee counsel G. Robert

Blakey was incensed to discover that the CIA never revealed the critical vantage point that Joannides occupied in 1963.

From a broader perspective, the DRE's stance reflected the mess that the Kennedy administration had maneuvered itself into with respect to Cuba by the fall of 1963. While determined to overthrow Castro, it decided to support only relatively liberal exile groups and to keep its ultimate goal a secret from the world. This behavior deeply antagonized nearly all the exiles except Ray's JURE and Artime's MRR, which were now out of favor with more conservative elements in the exile community. Nor had the administration made a determined effort to eliminate the zone of illegality within which so many different exile groups were operating.

One other extraordinary story links Cuban exiles around Miami to the Kennedy assassination. On December 17, 1963, a Miami area doctor told the FBI to contact a woman named Lillian Spingler, who had information about the assassination. When reached, Spingler said that her husband and employers did not want her involved in the investigation, but she agreed to meet agents on December 19, her day off. She explained that she was a clerk in the gift shop of a Miami tourist attraction, the Parrot Jungle. Some time in early November, she said—most likely Friday, November 1—a man, apparently Cuban, came into the shop and engaged her in conversation. He wrote a note with his left hand, then said he could write with either hand. He also wrote her name, Lillian, with both hands, but spelled it Lilian, as in Spanish.

The man began complaining about the U.S. government and President Kennedy and referred to "shooting between the eyes." According to the FBI report of the interview, the man said he "had a friend who was smarter than himself who could speak more languages than himself, including Russian. He said this friend was a Marxist and an American citizen, who had served in the armed forces. At this point, he mentioned that Lee [only mention of name] is a sharpshooter, and that he has a very good eye. He further remarked that his friend was brilliant, but that he did not know where his friend was at that time, although he believed he was either in Texas or Mexico."

Spingler definitely remembered the name Lee, she said, because it reminded her of Robert E. Lee. She mentioned the incident to her boss, who "later stated that the Cuban probably had too much to drink." She saw the man again outside the shop on Tuesday, December 10, when one of the other clerks said, "There's your man." She spoke about it to the boss, who was coming out to take down the American flag. The man was in his twenties or thirties, about 5'8", medium build, dark hair, lighter eyes, rather wild, and spoke good English with an accent. She thought he was Cuban but had no proof.

Two other clerks in the gift shop also remembered the incident, including the man's ability to write ambidextrously and his references to a good shot, although they had not heard the name Lee or the remarks about President Kennedy. The FBI took Spingler's story sufficiently seriously to show her several thousand photos of Cuban refugees, but she could not identify any of them.[124] The FBI did not report that the Parrot Jungle was very close to another tourist attraction, the Monkey Jungle. Nor did they know that a year earlier, in November 1962, Cuban papers reported the confession of a refugee anti-Castro raider, Miguel Angel Orozco Crespo, who had been captured by Cuban security forces and had confessed to operating out of a base "south of Miami on Highway 4, in a building near the tourist attraction called 'The Monkey Jungle.'"[125]

In 1967 this incident was investigated by Alfonso Sepe, then an assistant state's attorney and later a circuit court judge. He took sworn testimony from Spingler and her fellow employees, all of whom seem to have told the exact same stories they had told the FBI four years earlier. As magazine writer Dan Christensen reported: "Sepe said the incident was relayed to the FBI in late December 1963 when Mrs. Spingler called them. After a quick investigation, FBI agent in charge, James O'Connor told her to 'just drop it and not mention it.' Mrs. Spingler is still taking O'Connor's advice and has refused to comment, saying only, 'They told me not to talk about it. Goodby.' The FBI would say nothing."

But Sepe also found that the investigation had not stopped there. A few weeks after interviewing Spingler, Special Agent O'Connor called her to say that he had identified the man as Jorge Soto Martinez, who was a bellhop at the mob-controlled Fontainebleau Hotel in early November. He admitted his conversation with her but denied threatening the President or saying he knew Oswald. "Agent O'Connor asked Mrs. Spingler if she wanted to come to the FBI office and identify the man. Agent O'Connor and Mrs. Spingler both state that Mrs. Spingler refused to go to the FBI office to identify Martinez because she was afraid of personal harm." O'Connor, Christensen wrote, closed the investigation because he did not think Soto Martinez was involved. Certainly he never filed a report on this second phase of his inquiry. No further information is available about Soto Martinez.[126]

We shall return later to the possibility that exiles played a key role in the President's assassination. The role of organized crime is much clearer, and it is to the motives of this mobster underworld that we now turn.

14

Turning Up the Heat

The Kennedy administration's offensive against organized crime was getting into high gear in 1963. Its biggest targets included Sam Giancana in Chicago (despite the continuing inhibitions against actually prosecuting him), various New York mobsters, and Carlos Marcello, whose indictment for submitting a false Guatemalan birth certificate came to trial in the second half of the year. Preparations were also continuing for new trials of Jimmy Hoffa on two different charges, and Johnny Roselli remained under intense federal surveillance as well. In August and September the Justice Department sprang another surprise on the public and the mob: the Senate testimony of Joseph Valachi, the first mobster to confirm in public the existence of a nationwide criminal organization. Meanwhile, the Senate Rackets Committee held revealing hearings about the American Guild of Variety Artists, a strippers' union whose unlucky membership included the dancers at Jack Ruby's Carousel Club in Dallas. All of these initiatives contributed to, or later shed light on, the assassination of President Kennedy in Dallas on November 22, 1963.

During the summer, the FBI's intense surveillance of Giancana, including a phone tap on one of his closest political associates and bugs in his favorite hangout, the Armory Lounge, focused on his relationships with Phyllis McGuire and Frank Sinatra. In June a new informant close to the McGuires told the bureau that Giancana had arranged for McGuire to get a part in Sinatra's new movie, *Come Blow Your Horn*. Using informants and surveillance, the bureau found that Giancana had taken a golfing holiday with Sinatra in Honolulu in June. Sam was keeping on the move both to explore casino opportunities outside the States and to avoid surveillance. On June 25 Hoover informed Attorney General Kennedy that Giancana had recently visited Hawaii, the Dominican Republic, western Canada, California, Florida, Pennsylvania, and New York.[1] He had stopped in Miami on the way back from the Dominican Republic in May, where he reportedly attended the meeting that launched the Bayo-Pawley raid. In August, reporter Sandy Smith of the *Chicago Sun-Times* described Giancana's attempts to set up a casino in the Dominican Republic with the help of the playboy Porfirio Rubirosa—a report confirmed by the FBI.[2]

The FBI's battle with Giancana escalated in late June. On the 23rd, Chicago agents began obvious and intrusive twenty-four-hour surveillance, parking their cars just outside his home and following him around the golf course. This initially caused him to behave erratically—once, getting out of his car without putting the brake on, and, on another occasion, losing the police in a high-speed nighttime chase. On June 26 two of Giancana's attorneys approached the agents and demanded that they end their excessive surveillance. They filed a petition in federal court asking for an injunction against the FBI the next day, and Hoover, who hated bad publicity, immediately told the Chicago agents to reduce their coverage.[3] On June 29 Sam's associate Chuckie English struck up a conversation with FBI agent Buddy Roemer outside the Armory Lounge. English denied that organized crime existed and returned to the building, but as the agents were leaving, he ran back out with a message from Giancana: "If Bobby Kennedy wants to talk to me I'll be glad to talk to him and he knows who to go through." They inferred that he meant Sinatra, whose name had come up earlier.[4]

The attorney general was in no mood for a sit-down. Convinced as always of its own righteousness, the Criminal Division of the Justice Department went into the court hearing confidently, and its chief, William Hundley, ordered FBI agents not to testify or even to acknowledge their presence in photos taken by Giancana and his lawyers. Giancana, however, had somehow managed to get the case heard by a friendly judge, Richard B. Austin, who on July 16 criticized the special agent in charge for ordering agents not to answer questions and made it clear that he was going to limit FBI surveillance severely. Kennedy declared himself "incensed" by the judge's decision and immediately called the special agent to thank him, but Hoover complained privately that the FBI, rather than the Justice Department, was taking the heat.[5]

The bureau promptly turned the Giancana watch over to the Chicago sheriff's office, and on July 22 Judge Austin fined special agent Johnson $500 for contempt. Two days later, the FBI director passed along evidence that the judge himself was under the influence of organized crime, but meanwhile Hoover had issued orders against "rough shadowing" or "mass saturation" of any top hoodlums and had commented on a memo that the coverage of Giancana had been "excessive" and "I don't want a repetition of it."[6] The Justice Department won the next round on July 26, when a panel of circuit court judges stayed Austin's order, allowing surveillance to resume.[7]

Giancana suffered an indirect setback after the FBI received evidence of his visit with Frank Sinatra at the Cal-Neva Lodge in Lake Tahoe, of which Sinatra was officially part owner, late that same July. Smith published the story on August 1 as part of a series in the *Chicago Sun-Times* on the national crime syndicate. The Nevada State Gaming Control Board also heard about the visit—which included a fist-fight between Sam and Phyllis McGuire's business manager that Sinatra and his valet had to break up—and scheduled a hearing because Giancana was on the list of hoodlums banned from casinos.[8] Sinatra's mob connections were disturbing some of his own associates, such as Charles Moses, a Hollywood press agent, who complained in July that all the singer's enterprises were gradually coming under the control of the mob.[9]

When Sinatra met the Control Board during the first week of August, he admitted meeting Giancana several years previously in Miami and seeing him a number of times every year since. He also acknowledged that they were together at the Cal-Neva on July 26 and that Sam and Phyllis McGuire had stayed with him in Palm Springs on different occasions. He promised never to associate with Giancana again within the state of Nevada, and he tried to brazen things out when the *Los Angeles Times* asked him about the incident on August 31, denying that he was under investigation.[10] Unfortunately for him, the FBI agreed to furnish information to the Nevada Control Board.[11]

On September 22 the well-connected gossip columnist Dorothy Kilgallen mentioned the appearance of Sinatra and the Rat Pack at Sam's Villa Venice in Chicago, Phyllis McGuire's role in *Come Blow Your Horn* ("a favor to Sam"), and Sam's earlier hopes to move into "rarefied political circles when the Democrats won last time around and Frank became big with the White House set."[12]

On October 22 the Nevada Gaming Control Board ordered Sinatra to sell all his Nevada gambling properties, valued at $3.5 million. An official of the board also accused him of using vile and abusive language during the investigation, and Sinatra declined to mount a defense against the charges.[13] If Sinatra were actually fronting for Giancana at the Cal-Neva Lodge, as many suspected, this sell-off would leave him with a debt to Giancana.

Meanwhile, on August 16, 1963, Smith published a story claiming that in 1959–60 Giancana had been recruited by the CIA to get intelligence out of Cuba. Although Smith garbled various dates and never mentioned assassination, he discussed the mob's gambling interests and its links to Batista and claimed Giancana bragged about his connections to anti-Castro Cubans. He also told the story of the Las Vegas bugging designed to uncover the relationship between Phyllis McGuire and an unnamed male entertainer, and mentioned that the FBI's new Mafia informant, Joseph Valachi, had named Giancana as the mob boss of Chicago and a member of the "national commission," or crime syndicate. Smith got his story from Ed Guthman and other officials of the Justice Department, who became very communicative after Smith arranged a private meeting with Robert Kennedy at his home.[14] When Smith called the CIA for comment on these leaks—having been referred to them, he said, by the Justice Department—Assistant Director Stanley Grogan "told him that we would neither confirm nor deny nor discuss this because we never would comment on any operation or an alleged operation, even though his information was completely erroneous."[15] Nevertheless, Smith's story led the former deputy director for plans, Richard Helms, to inform the current director, John McCone, for the first time about Giancana's role in the 1960–62 plot to assassinate Castro, which he falsely claimed was terminated during 1962.[16]

The Valachi hearings before the Senate Rackets Committee kicked off on September 25 with testimony from the committee's former counsel, now the attorney general. RFK summarized the state of organized crime and asked for new wiretap legislation to turn the FBI's current bugging operations into useful sources of evidence. Valachi himself testified for well over a week, riveting the public with details of his own career as a murderer, the organization of New York's five families, and what he knew about other cities. The hearings, like the Kefauver hearings a decade earlier, ran on national television and attracted enormous attention, with the press's leading columnists critiquing Valachi's performance as though he were an Oscar nominee. The hearings represented yet a further step in Kennedy's strategy of giving maximum publicity to allegations against mobsters that could not be proven in a court of law.

On October 11, after Valachi had finished testifying, the committee called two Chicago police officials, Orlando Wilson and William J. Duffy, who presented a lengthy history and analysis of the Chicago mob. "Sam [Mooney] Giancana led the list of mobsters named responsible for organized crime in Chicago when the top officials of the Chicago police department testified today," the *Chicago Tribune* story began the next day.[17] Although wiretaps were picking Giancana up somewhat less frequently than formerly, several intercepted conversations showed that he was definitely feeling the pressure from this unwanted attention.

On September 19, a week before Valachi testified, Sam was already claiming bitterly that Jimmy Hoffa had refused to provide a $3 million loan for a Nevada casino (possibly to buy out Sinatra at the Cal-Neva). Giancana said that at one time he got $1.75 million from Hoffa in two days, but "now all this heat comes on and I can't even get a favor out of him now. I can't do nothing for myself. Ten years ago I can get all the [obscene] money I want from the guy and now they won't settle for anything."[18] An informant close to the McGuire sisters told the FBI that Sam had talked about leaving the country for six to twelve months to get away from "the heat." After Valachi testified, a bug caught Giancana and English remarking that Valachi would do a lot of harm because he might encourage other informants to come forward as well.[19]

On October 17 a bug heard Giancana lose his temper when another associate, Butch Biasi, declined his offer of a loan for a land deal because federal authorities would immediately be all over him. "Giancana became extremely agitated at this and began to curse the government saying that he can't do a thing any more. He continued 'I'm just gonna hit and run, hit and run . . . take care of them . . . sneak here, sneak there . . . get nothing violent, (phonetic).'"[20]

But in fact Giancana still had resources of his own to tap. A *Chicago Tribune* story of November 3 described a long new report on organized crime that was given to the State Crime Commission, and named as one of its authors Richard Cain, the chief investigator in the sheriff's office who is now known to have been an undercover mobster himself.[21] And on November 7, a source close to the McGuires quoted Giancana to the effect that the Dominican playboy Rubirosa had a photograph of himself in a compromising position with Peter Lawford's wife, Pat, the President's and attorney general's sister. Sam speculated that it would "solve all of my problems" with the government if he could obtain it.

Phyllis meanwhile yielded to her sisters' repeated threats to close down the act if she did not break up with Sam. Taps during November revealed that he was spending time with another well-known singer, Keely Smith, and that the bartender at the Armory Lounge had given orders not to play the McGuire sisters' records on the juke box when Sam was around. Phyllis's resolve faded quickly, however, and she was back in Chicago by mid-December.[22]

Johnny Roselli, Giancana's man in Las Vegas, was among the large group of people that Frank Sinatra met at the Cal-Neva Lodge during the last week of July.[23] The FBI was following Roselli closely and reported numerous sightings in his two home bases, Los Angeles and Las Vegas, during late summer and early fall. By this time Roselli was having his own affair with Judith Campbell, the former lover of President Kennedy and Sam Giancana. According to Bradley Ayers—a young Army officer who was training anti-Castro Cubans that summer—Roselli was running a paramilitary camp for assassins in Florida at the time, but no documentary evidence has emerged to confirm it.[24]

The Tampa and Miami FBI offices were having less luck than Chicago in keeping track of Florida's mob boss Santo Trafficante, but he, too, was coming under pressure from federal law enforcement in the second half of 1963. An extortion case had developed out of a scheme that Florida financier Sam Kay and Denver banker James Egan put together to unload some of Trafficante's Batista-era Cuban pesos in Brazil. Felix Anthony "Milwaukee Phil" Alderisio had tried to muscle in on the operation by threatening Egan's daughter, and Trafficante interceded once or twice on his behalf. Alderisio was arrested for extortion in early November, but the government concluded it had too little evidence against Trafficante to proceed.[25] Alderisio went to trial a year later, together with Allen Dorfman and Chicago bail bondsman Irwin S. Weiner, a close associate of Jimmy Hoffa, but a Miami jury acquitted them.[26]

Despite the heat, Trafficante, working with Dominick Bartone, re-

mained active in arms-dealing with Cuban exiles.[27] And in early November an informant told the FBI that Trafficante and several partners
were negotiating with the new government in the Dominican Republic
for the construction of a casino, after a proposed housing project fell
through when the Juan Bosch government was overthrown in early September.[28] Trafficante was also reported to be the real owner, together
with Jimmy Hoffa, of the new Hotel Ponce de Leon in Puerto Rico.[29] In
November Trafficante's (and Hoffa's) attorney, Frank Ragano, taking a
leaf from Sam Giancana's book, threatened the FBI with a lawsuit if it did
not relax its surveillance of his client.[30] Meanwhile, Trafficante's old Havana associate, John Martino, was making a tour to promote his book *I
Was Castro's Prisoner*—a tour that took him to Dallas in early October.

On October 15 two Tampa police officers, Chief Neil G. Brown and
homicide sergeant Jack de la Llana, testifying before the Senate Rackets
Committee, identified Santo Trafficante (a.k.a. Louis Santos) as head of
the Tampa Mafia and discussed his numerous associations with Mafia
leaders around the country. They admitted that Trafficante's only conviction—for bribing local authorities—had been reversed, but they explained that witnesses would rarely if ever testify against mob figures because of very legitimate fears of reprisal. The testimony received ample
coverage in Tampa and other Florida papers, and was undoubtedly unwelcome to the mob chief.[31]

The FBI's intensified surveillance of mobsters in many cities around
the country and the numerous prosecutions brought by the Justice Department on any conceivable charge were having an effect. Earlier in the
year, on April 3, when the FBI monitored the funeral of the father of
Carmine Lombardozzi of the Gambino family in New York, mobsters
had beaten an agent, John P. Foley, and stolen his gun. Courtney Evans of
the FBI wrote Alan Belmont that Sam Giancana would be watching the
bureau's reaction to the incident carefully. The New York office apparently declined to make a paper record of what they decided to do, but at
least two bugs in different parts of the country captured the story for
posterity. New York FBI agents picked up another Lombardozzi associate in New York and beat him to within an inch of his life. On May 20
Angelo Bruno, the Philadelphia boss who was involved in deals with
Trafficante, quoted agents who had gone to see Carlo Gambino for a private talk.

Did you change the laws that now youse could hit FBI men; youse could
punch them and kick them and all that stuff. He said, I don't know what
you are talking about. Well, this is the test, that if you change the laws that
from now on you are going to hit the FBI everytime we pick one of your
people up, we are going to break their heads for them. And really, they
picked one guy up, they almost killed him, the FBI. They don't do that,
you know. But they picked one of the fellows up and they crippled him.
They said, that is an example. Now, next time anybody lays a hand on an
FBI man, that's just a warning. There is nothing else we got to tell you.
And they went away.[32]

Stefano Magaddino of Buffalo discussed the same incident with associates a month later. "We got from the President on down—against us
. . . but we got to resist . . . you have to do something material . . . They
beat up Carmine plenty. When his father died . . . When they beat up
that FBI . . . So after the beating . . . they said to him, 'We are even now. If
you others continue to do the same thing again, we will change our
methods with you people!' Four months later, in October, Magaddino's
son told him the President 'should drop dead . . . They should kill the
whole family, the mother and father too!'"[33] While the FBI was settling
its scores with the mob, the Kennedy Justice Department was pushing
for a new law to legalize wiretapping and thinking about a new immunity statute that could force mobsters to testify rather than take the Fifth
Amendment.

No Mafia figure, of course, received more concentrated attention
from the Kennedy administration than Carlos Marcello of New Orleans.
After a year of legal proceedings, Justice Department attorneys in the
summer of 1963 were preparing for his trial on charges of having pro-
cured a false Guatemalan birth certificate to prevent his deportation to
Italy. Marcello's empire extended to Dallas, where Jack Ruby—the operator of a mob-related strip club—was apparently experiencing some sort
of professional crisis.

Although Jack Ruby certainly was no full-fledged member of the
Mafia, he spent most of his adult life in enterprises closely associated
with it. For several years during the late 1940s he worked for a Chicago
local of the Scrap Iron and Junk Handlers Union, leaving after its head,
Leon Cook, was shot and killed.[34] Ruby's sister, Eva Grant, who seems to

have had at least as many mob connections as he did, invited him to Dallas to help her manage a club, the Silver Spur.[35] He came to Dallas in 1947, along with a number of Chicago mobsters who tried to muscle their way into local enterprises, including Paul Roland Jones, who did time for smuggling narcotics into Texas from Mexico and attempting to bribe the Chicago sheriff. Jack ran several different kinds of clubs during the 1950s, all of which failed. The Sovereign Club, which he operated in 1959–60 at the time of his visits to Cuba, became the Carousel in 1960, and Paul Roland Jones was listed as one of its owners.[36]

The Carousel—Ruby's last and most famous business—was a relatively up-scale strip club offering a variety of live acts, including comedians and magicians. But of course its most important employees were its frequently rotating dancing girls, whom Ruby recruited locally and from clubs all over the country. They belonged to the American Guild of Variety Artists, or AGVA—a mob-controlled union which the Senate Rackets Committee had investigated in the summer of 1962. While the hearings included only one indirect reference to Ruby—a statement by a witness who had seen two Dallas clubs with exotic dancers—they told an extraordinary story that provides essential background to understanding who Ruby was, what he was doing in Dallas, and, crucially, why he was busily complaining about AGVA to various leading mobsters around the country in the summer of 1963.[37]

AGVA, as various witnesses (including several former club employees) explained, was in theory a strong union that collected dues, membership fees, and contributions to a welfare fund from its members. It also required club owners to post substantial "salary bonds" to make sure the payroll could be met. Although the union collected approximately $1 million in dues and fees around the country every year, it did nothing for its members, failed to collect income tax deductions for the IRS, and allowed club owners to force their employees to work as B-girls or prostitutes. (B-girls mixed with the customers to entice them into buying them overpriced drinks—which, for the girls, contained no alcohol at all.) The welfare fund money seemed simply to disappear at the national office. Critical witnesses claimed that all the union's funds were going to managers' salaries, but mobsters, who owned many of the clubs, were surely siphoning off money directly from the union as well.

Jackie Bright, the national administrative secretary whom several witnesses identified as the real power in the union, let the cat out of the bag in an interview with a *Saturday Evening Post* reporter. Bright told the reporter there were times when he went to certain cities to ask a club owner for a bond, and the club owner said, "Come over and get it and you'll go out in a box." "What did you do?" asked the reporter. "I get on the phone and I call a few people who are friendly disposed to AGVA. In this particular instance, the next morning when I went downstairs to my desk to see if there was any mail, there was a note in my box, 'See the manager.' And the manager reported that the money had been delivered." Queried directly by the Senate Rackets Committee, Bright denied that this ever happened, but he also made the following comments: "While I say that AGVA has—is not dominated by any mobs, has no underworld connection, we have people who are friendly disposed, and I think that that's the proper way of stating it—toward AGVA, because they employ our members and they like our people and they can't see other people imposing their will upon us unjustifiably."[38]

The committee took extensive testimony about a network of strip clubs in Calumet City, Indiana, just across the Illinois border from Chicago, which the Chicago mob apparently controlled. An Illinois investigator confided his suspicions that organized crime was running a nationwide white slavery ring, shifting girls all over the country as needed.[39] A Chicago IRS agent who had tried to get withholding from the clubs reported that they always operated on a purely cash basis, and that the operator or manager "is never the true owner."[40] A witness from the Miami crime commission identified racketeers from Cleveland, Buffalo, and New York City as owners of Miami strip clubs (Miami, like Las Vegas, was notoriously an "open city") and said that strip clubs had replaced more traditional houses of prostitution since the Second World War.[41] And another witness told how in the summer of 1961, the New Orleans branch of AGVA had hired some pickets from the Teamsters Union, of all places, to force independent clubs to sign AGVA contracts, whose provisions with respect to members were then, of course, ignored.[42]

Those union officials called to testify did not take the Fifth Amendment, but either denied the various allegations or claimed that they had tried to do something about them, with no success. The hearings focused on AGVA's failure to do anything useful for its members, but enough information emerged to show that it fit the classic profile of a mob-dominated union such as the Teamsters. On the one hand, it was pocketing its members' dues without giving them anything in return, and on the other hand, it was using its control over its members to force club owners to cooperate, and, probably, to kick back as well. The Teamsters and other mob-dominated unions frequently used their power not only to fleece their membership, but to extort money from management in exchange for labor peace. That seems to be what AGVA was doing, and club operators like Jack Ruby were caught in the middle—as Jack's own problems during 1963 seem to confirm.

The FBI's post-assassination investigation of Ruby illustrated the strengths and weaknesses of the organization in the early 1960s. Helped by Ruby's own gregarious habits (he never missed an opportunity to promote himself) and the public's response to the assassination, the bureau found dozens of people all over the country who had known him at one time or another, as well as many of his associates and former employees in Dallas. But the agents seemed to have very little understanding of the milieu in which Ruby worked, and they showed an appalling lack of curiosity about the finances of the Carousel Club. Thus, although the FBI's reports quote many statements to the effect that Ruby was an anti-Communist and a loyal American (questions the bureau was wont to ask about almost anyone), Dallas agents made literally no attempt to figure out what happened to the thousands of dollars that the Carousel Club generated every month.

For example, they refused to follow a promising lead offered by Ruby's purported business partner Paul Roland Jones. Formerly of Dallas and now facing a perjury indictment in New York state, Jones told the Birmingham FBI in December that he was quite sure he could discover Ruby's true motives for shooting Oswald if they would take him back to Dallas for a few weeks. Jones said that in order to operate in the city, Ruby must have been paying off the police department, just as he himself had done years earlier. The Dallas FBI office declined Jones's offer.[43] Still, they uncovered enough information to show that, in all the major particulars, the Carousel resembled the other strip clubs that the Rackets Committee had described.

Ruby was undoubtedly part of a national network of operators. He secured strippers from St. Louis, San Francisco, New Orleans, and even Honolulu. Ruby's girls at the Carousel belonged to AGVA, but it treated them no better than it treated other members. Several witnesses confirmed that the girls who worked at the Carousel as dancers and strippers mixed with the clientele, encouraged them to order drinks, and worked as prostitutes after hours. Many years later, one former employee told Texas journalist Gary Cartwright that Ruby "would tell us to come on to the customers, promise them anything—of course he didn't mean for us to deliver, but sometimes we did on our own time . . . The price for a bottle of cheap champagne (the label covered with a bar towel) was anywhere from fifty to seventy-five dollars. We'd sit with the customer as long as the bottle lasted, drinking out of what we called spit glasses—frosted glasses of ice water. We worked for tips or whatever we could steal."[44]

To avoid other kinds of problems, Ruby relied on his connections with the police, whom he encouraged to patronize his club and treated generously. Meyer Panitz, a friend of Ruby's old associate Lewis McWillie, told the FBI that Ruby customarily asked a Dallas policeman to send off-duty officers to act as bouncers.[45] A boxer who had worked as a bouncer at his club said Ruby knew well over half of the DPD and frequently remarked that keeping the police happy was the way to run a club.[46]

But, apparently, Ruby could also count on the cooperation of the local AGVA representatives, James Henry Dolan (who held the job from 1958 through 1961) and Thomas Palmer (1961 through 1963). The FBI knew Dolan as a racketeer who had worked in Denver, beaten up *bolita* operators for Trafficante in Florida, and reportedly been associated with Marcello's associate Nofio Pecora in New Orleans.[47] Two different witnesses, one a stripper, told the FBI that they complained to AGVA after Jack hit them during arguments, only to be told to forget the whole thing, since Jack's standing with the police was much too high to get any satisfaction from them.[48] From 1949 through 1963, Jack himself was arrested once for disturbing the peace, twice for carrying a concealed weapon, twice for liquor violations, and once for civil assault. He paid a fine for his one conviction.[49]

It might be significant that Ruby opened the Carousel in 1960, less than a year after he met Trafficante in the Trescornia prison camp in Havana. In any event, the true ownership of the club turned out to be cloudy. Besides Ruby, various documents listed a restaurateur named Ralph Paul, who seems to have been Jack's closest business friend, Jack's brothers Sam and Earl, and Paul Roland Jones. Ralph Paul told the FBI that he had advanced Jack about $5,000 for the Carousel and had never gotten anything back, but he refused to confirm that he was legally part owner. Sam and Earl Ruby denied any involvement, and Jones apparently was never asked, even though he acknowledged talking to Ruby about the state of his business affairs as recently as November 11.[50] But whoever the owner was, he was evidently doing fairly well out of the club.

Ruby, like most strip-club operators, kept no accounts and ran his entire business on a cash basis. But two solid indicators of how well the Carousel was doing came to light after the assassination. The police found a letter to a New York AGVA official in Ruby's car claiming that the club had cleared about $5,300 in August 1963, less rent, which he did not specify, and about the same amount in September, implying an annual income of $50,000–60,000.[51] He had $2,020 on him when he was arrested for killing Oswald, and another $837.50 in his car, even though the Carousel had been closed that weekend.[52] In 1963, $60,000 a year would have been a very impressive income, but Ruby, according to all available evidence, lived cheaply and had virtually no assets at all. In the late 1950s, according to his accountant, he made between $2,000 and $10,000 per year.[53] He lived in a simple apartment with another man, paid cash for his rent, and drove used Oldsmobiles. Between 1959 and 1963 he took out six loans between $410 and $3,360, putting up his cars as security, and repaid them all on time.[54] He was a notorious soft touch, frequently lending money to his employees, but such generosity hardly accounts for his lack of assets.

Although Ruby paid his debts on time, he was remarkably delinquent in paying his taxes. On December 9, 1963, he owed the IRS $44,413.86, including about $4,400 in income tax and $40,000 in a "cabaret excise tax," which Ruby had claimed for years he did not owe because he was running a "dance hall," not a cabaret. After another club owner lost a case in federal court using that same argument, Ruby offered to settle the entire debt with the IRS at less than ten cents on the dollar by borrowing $3,000 from an unidentified friend. He claimed about $1,000 net assets, $3,900 annual income from the Vegas Club (operated by his sister), and $2,600 from the Carousel. In June and August, two IRS men suggested accepting the offer, on the grounds that they would never get any more.[55]

Since 1961, Ruby had complained about his financial problems to nearly everyone he knew, putting the blame particularly on the local of-fice of AGVA. He specifically argued that the union allowed his compet-itors (especially Abe Weinstein, who ran the Colony Club) to stage ama-teur nights, at which girls worked for less than scale, giving those clubs an unfair advantage. AGVA had supposedly banned the practice early in 1963 but Ruby claimed it was continuing. He officially complained both to the Western Regional Office in Los Angeles and the National Office in New York, which he visited in August 1963.[56] Ruby's complaints have puzzled many researchers, since the issue of amateur nights could hardly have been as financially critical as he made out. But what his complaints almost certainly meant was that Jack felt he was being squeezed unfairly by AGVA, which was taking too much of his money in the form of dues, welfare payments, and, quite possibly, simple extortion.

The $30,000–60,000 that the Carousel was apparently generating ev-ery year was probably evaporating because of payoffs to various mob in-terests with the power to put him out of business. These could easily have included AGVA (whose backers the Rackets Committee had un-fortunately failed to identify), the local organized crime barons, Joseph Civello and the Campisi brothers, and, quite possibly, Chicago mob fig-ures whom Ruby had known since his youth and who may have been involved in his original move to Dallas. Civello (who had been arrested at Appalachin in 1957) and the Campisi brothers had been the subject of FBI investigations and, in Civello's case, surveillance, since 1960 or so, but the bureau did not turn up very much, beyond numerous reports of sports betting at the Campisis' restaurant, the Egyptian Lounge.

Civello and the Campisis were not having much trouble with local authorities. Lieutenant Jack Revill of the DPD intelligence division told the FBI in 1961 and in 1964 that all rumors of the Campisis' illegal activ-ities were false, and Sheriff Bill Decker in 1957 had said that Civello had been induced to abandon illegal activities by a crackdown by local au-thorities.[57] Civello, a Louisiana native, was thought to be an underling in Marcello's empire, and was possibly his designated representative at the famous Appalachin conclave. Both Civello and Joe Campisi admitted knowing Jack Ruby—Civello even acknowledged having visited his club—and Joe Campisi told the HSCA that he was well acquainted with Marcello, to whom he sent a load of sausages annually as a Christmas present. Phone records showed that Campisi called New Orleans many times a day, presumably about betting matters.[58]

What makes these questions more acute is the pattern of Ruby's long-distance telephone calls during 1963. Throughout that year, but especially in the last few months before the assassination, he had substantial conversations with at least half a dozen major mob figures, including two with close ties to Jimmy Hoffa and the Teamsters Union. Another was his old friend Lewis McWillie, who now worked in Las Vegas. The FBI already knew enough about this relationship to interview McWillie on the very next day after Ruby shot Oswald.

McWillie told them that he and Ruby had continued to correspond, and that in early 1963 McWillie had asked Ruby to provide him with a handgun, to give him "some protection around the house." Ruby purchased one and sent it, but McWillie never picked it up at the post office. The gun was eventually returned.[59] McWillie acknowledged talking to Ruby during the last couple of months before the assassination about his union problems.[60] But Ruby's telephone records showed that he called McWillie six times during September alone. In 1978, McWillie told the HSCA that Ruby had asked if he could put him in touch with the president of AGVA—a rare hint of how strong his AGVA obsession had become.[61] As J. Edgar Hoover pointed out to the Warren Commission on March 27, 1964, McWillie had been associated with Santo Trafficante and Dino Cellini in Havana.[62]

On October 26, Ruby called Irwin Weiner, a notorious mob- and Teamster-connected bail bondsman in Chicago and talked to him for eight minutes. While nearly all the questionable characters Ruby called during this period told the authorities that he had requested help with his AGVA problems, Weiner on November 28 refused to discuss Ruby with FBI agents at all.[63] He had evidently known Ruby's brother Earl for a long time, and in 1978 he told the HSCA that Ruby asked him to write a bond for AGVA.[64]

On November 7, Ruby had perhaps his most interesting conversation of all, a seventeen-minute chat with Robert "Barney" Baker, a Chicago criminal who served as an enforcer to Jimmy Hoffa. According to Baker's ex-wife, who had testified about him before the Rackets Committee during the 1950s, Baker had pocketed some of the ransom money from one of the most sensational crimes of the 1950s, the kidnap-murder of seven-year-old Bobby Greenlease in Kansas City, Missouri, in 1953.[65] When Ruby reached Baker, who had been a union strongarm man in New York, he had just finished a prison term for extorting money from a trucking owner in Pittsburgh in exchange for heading off a strike. Baker referred him to another Hoffa associate, Murray Miller, who was staying in a Miami hotel. Ruby spoke to Miller for just four minutes the next day, and then reached Baker once again for another fourteen minutes. Both Baker and Miller claimed the conversations had concerned AGVA.

Ruby also claimed to have telephoned a notorious Chicago hoodlum, his childhood acquaintance Lenny Patrick. Both Patrick and David Yaras, Patrick's associate in a famous Chicago gangland slaying, acknowledged knowing Ruby but denied to the FBI that he had any true underworld connections.[66] And during all this time, Ruby received a number of mysterious incoming calls. Larry Crafard, a drifter who worked at the Carousel Club for room and board in October and November, told the FBI that the same man frequently called the club three or four times a day during that period but refused to leave his name. Ruby apparently knew who he was, but never identified him.[67]

The calls to Baker and Weiner suggest some connection between Ruby and Jimmy Hoffa. In December 1963 and March 1964, two different witnesses told the FBI that a man named Roy Pike, a former bartender at the Carousel, had said that Ruby was connected to Hoffa and the mob and made payoffs to the Dallas police. But when the bureau found Pike, he mentioned rumors that Teamster money had built the Cabana Motel in Dallas but denied having made any statements about Ruby.[68] Another Teamster-connected man named Krause linked Ruby to Lenny Patrick and Dave Yaras, and years later, James Hoffa, Jr., told crime investigative journalist Dan Moldea that he thought his father had known Jack Ruby.[69]

In retrospect, Ruby's many telephone calls probably had a dual significance. On the one hand, he was probably trying to line up whatever big-time muscle he could to back him in his ongoing dispute with AGVA and the mobsters behind it. Since the Teamsters had already picketed a strip joint in New Orleans that was trying to throw AGVA out, it is possible that Ruby was trying to straighten out his problems with the union by enlisting the Teamsters' help. Whatever his motives, in the process of complaining about his AGVA troubles, Ruby made himself known, if he was not known already, to a number of prominent mobsters who might conceivably need him to do an important job in Dallas some day.

By fall 1963, the outlines of a conspiracy among members of organized crime to kill President Kennedy were becoming clear. It involved
three of Robert Kennedy's principal targets: Santo Trafficante, Carlos
Marcello, and Jimmy Hoffa. Each one of those men had discussed assassinating the President or his brother privately (with Jose Aleman, Edward
Becker, and Edward Grady Partin), and they had discussed the matter
collectively through their intermediary, Hoffa's and Trafficante's attorney Frank Ragano. Links from Marcello to Oswald ran through Oswald's
Uncle Dutz Murret, Guy Banister, and David Ferrie, and links from
Trafficante to Oswald ran through Loran Hall, who accompanied Oswald
to Silvia Odio's house in late September or early October 1963 and
might easily have delivered new instructions to Oswald when he returned to Dallas from Mexico in late October. John Martino also visited
Dallas twice during October, at the very beginning and near the end of
the month.

Oswald's own behavior in the seven weeks after his return from
Mexico altered radically, and his movements during that time include
some major anomalies that the Warren Commission never managed to
explain.

15

Countdown to Catastrophe

Almost from the moment of his arrival back in Dallas on October 3, Oswald's behavior indicates that he had entered a new and more secretive phase of his life. More importantly, a series of events during the first weekend in November suggests very clearly that he already knew he was going to make an attempt on President Kennedy's life, that he expected to receive a substantial sum of money, and that he was hoping against hope he might be able to get out of it by successfully reaching Cuba instead. Two weeks later, on the last weekend before the assassination, excellent evidence places him in a rifle range in the Dallas area honing his marksmanship skills in preparation for the attempt. And other evidence suggests how, when, and from whom Oswald might have received his instructions.

The bus that brought Oswald back from Mexico arrived in Dallas on Thursday, October 3, and he may have appeared at Silvia Odio's apartment with Loran Hall and Larry Howard on that very evening, rather than on September 23, 24, or 25. On September 26, while Oswald was on his way to Mexico, the *Dallas Morning News* first announced on its front page that Kennedy would definitely be visiting Texas on November 21 and 22 and that Dallas might well be on the itinerary.[1] On Friday, October 4, Oswald suddenly materialized at Ruth Paine's home in Irving, where Marina—now more than eight months pregnant—and June were living. According to Paine, he said he had been in Houston for two weeks, and Marina in her many FBI interviews right after the assassination said she knew nothing about any trip to Mexico. He also said he had spent the previous night at the Dallas YMCA.[2]

The relationships among Ruth (who was still separated from her husband, Michael), Marina, and Lee had evolved into a highly charged emotional triangle, because Ruth disapproved of Lee and had become devoted to Marina, writing to her in July, "I love you, Marina, and want to live with you."[3] On Monday, October 7, Oswald went to Dallas and rented a room from Mary Bledsoe at 621 North Marsalis Street.[4] He went out for several hours every day looking for work. He spent the nights of Saturday, October 12, and Sunday, October 13, back in Irving. October 13 was also the date of the DRE meeting at the north Dallas shopping center at which Edward Stieg thought that he had seen Oswald.

Oswald returned to Marsalis Street the next morning, but Mrs. Bledsoe told him to move out because she disliked his eating habits and was disturbed by a telephone conversation he had in a foreign language. He rented another room just a bit further south in the Oak Cliff neighborhood, at 1026 North Beckley Street, the home of Earlene Roberts, where he continued to live, except on weekends, until November 21. Two days later, on Wednesday, October 16, he went to work filling orders at the Texas School Book Depository. Ruth Paine, who had heard about openings at the TSBD from a neighbor, steered him to the job. No one has ever provided much information about where he was and what he was doing during the days of October 7–11 and October 14–15.[5]

Oswald used his own name with Mrs. Bledsoe, but he rented the room at North Beckley under an alias, O. H. Lee. For the first time since his return to the United States he was making a real effort to conceal where he was. He might well have received new instructions. On October 17, the day after he went to work at the TSBD, Loran Hall and a companion, Thomas Seymour, were arrested in Dallas and charged with possession of amphetamines. They had returned after Hall's previous visit in late September and early October to pick up their truck full of arms. Although Hall in his 1977 testimony estimated that they had been back only one day when they were arrested, there is no proof of this. Possibly Hall, who almost certainly accompanied Oswald to Silvia Odio's house in late September or early October, met with Oswald earlier in the week of October 14 and renewed their conversation (reported by "Leopoldo" to Odio) about the possible assassination of President Kennedy. The front page of the *Morning News* had discussed Kennedy's November 21–22 trip to Texas again on October 5.[6] Hall did not leave Dallas for Miami until charges against him were dropped on October 23. A week later he was stopped by Customs agents as he tried to launch a raid from the Florida Keys, and shortly thereafter, in the first half of November, he flew back to the Los Angeles area, where he decided to start a new life.

Meanwhile, Oswald apparently remained in touch with someone in another city. A gas station operator across from his new rooming house remembered that he asked for change to make long distance calls on at least two occasions.[7] He returned to Irving for the weekend of October 19–20, and on the evening of Sunday the 20th, Marina began having labor pains and Ruth took her to the hospital. A second daughter, Audrey, was born that night, and Oswald went to work at the TSBD the next day. He initially did not want to visit the hospital but changed his mind when Ruth assured him that hospital officials would not try to make him pay for the delivery.

While Oswald was settling down incognito in Dallas, the FBI was belatedly trying to catch up with him and get back on his case. Oswald's August 8 arrest in New Orleans had led FBI headquarters to take a renewed interest in his whereabouts and activities.[8] Not until September 10, however, did Dallas formally transfer responsibility for the case to New Orleans, and it took six more weeks for New Orleans agent Warren DeBrueys to submit his report on Oswald and the FPCC on October 25.[9]

The CIA's cable about Oswald's conversation with the Soviet Embassy in Mexico City had reached Washington on October 8, and ten days later the agency (without mentioning Kostikov's name) informed other interested entities, including the FBI, that Oswald made this contact and that he was "probably identical Lee Henry [sic] Oswald" who had defected to the Soviet Union in 1959, married a Russian national, and returned to the United States.[10] Mexico City was a major center of Soviet espionage, and a former Marine who had already defected once had now been overheard contacting a KGB man in the Soviet Embassy. Yet the Washington FBI supervisor in charge of such cases did not react at all. He never opened an espionage investigation against Oswald or tried to find out where he was and what information he might have.

On October 18 the Mexico City legal attaché (local FBI agent), who had just heard the story from the CIA station, cabled headquarters and was given all recent information about Oswald, including his beatings of Marina in Dallas and his FPCC activities in New Orleans.[11] The bureau's

New Orleans office (now in charge of Oswald's file) received copies of those cables, but Washington did not ask agents either there or in Dallas to try to find out where Oswald was now. We have no idea why not. Instead, James P. Hosty in the Dallas office accidentally heard about the CIA cable from an agent of the Immigration and Naturalization Service. On October 22 he informed the bureau, noting that he had obtained a new address for Oswald's brother Robert four days earlier and was attempting to locate the Oswalds.[12] In response, New Orleans agent Kaack sent him Ruth Paine's Irving address, which he apparently got either from Mrs. Garner, the Oswalds' landlady on Magazine Street, or from his aunt, Lillian Murret.[13]

From the time he first took over the Oswald case from agent John Fain, Hosty had consistently shown more concern about the possibility that Marina might be a Soviet intelligence plant than about Oswald's activities.[14] Pretending to be an insurance agent, he dropped by West Fifth Street in Irving on October 29 and verified through a neighbor that Ruth Paine was living with a Russian woman and her two very young daughters next door. He reported that finding to Washington.[15] After two days during which he confirmed the Paines' identity—including the information that Michael worked for Bell Helicopter and had a security clearance—he returned on November 1 and knocked on Ruth's door.

Ruth explained that Marina and the children were living with her and that Lee was living at a Dallas address she did not know. After some hesitation she said he was working at the Texas School Book Depository, and Hosty, according to his recollection, was relieved to learn that Oswald was not doing sensitive work. Marina came out of the bedroom while they were talking, and Hosty, with Ruth interpreting, tried to reassure her that the FBI was there to protect her and would not contact Lee at work or attempt to get him fired, as Ruth and Marina both thought (without any real evidence) they had done in the past. Hosty apparently left his office address and phone number with Ruth. He claims he had no intention of making this a formal interview, if for no other reason than that it would have required an additional agent, and he wrote up no report. He told Marina, he says, that he would be back shortly.[16] Oswald called Marina from his boarding house almost every evening, and he must have heard about this visit almost at once.

On Tuesday, November 5, Hosty returned with another agent, Gary Wilson, but had an even briefer conversation this time. Once again, Ruth

told him that she did not have Lee's address, and he did not speak to Marina at all. But Marina apparently took the opportunity to write down
the license plate number of Hosty's car, which he had parked in the
driveway, and gave it to Lee later on. After Lee's arrest, Hosty's name, address, license number (with one letter wrong, a V in place of U) and office phone number were found in his address book. Some months after
the assassination, Marina confirmed that she had taken the license number down during Hosty's second visit, because Lee had asked her to. Yet
oddly, although according to this evidence Oswald would have learned
Hosty's name, address, and telephone number from Ruth and Marina
over the weekend of November 2–3, and the license number sometime
after November 5, in Oswald's address book Hosty's name, address, license number, and office phone number appear in a single entry, listed in
that order.[17]

Hosty wrote no formal report of this meeting. His October 30 report of his pretext interview next door had concluded, "Dallas and all
other offices should continue efforts to locate subject LEE HARVEY
OSWALD," but he did nothing more than call the book depository to
verify that Oswald was working there. They gave him the Irving address,
where he knew Lee was not living, but he apparently undertook no further investigation. After the assassination, Hosty told his superiors that he
had not reported this information because he knew it was false.[18]

From the assassination onward, agent Hosty has steadfastly claimed
that he would not have been able to ask Oswald about his trip to Mexico
without permission from Washington because that would have compromised FBI sources and methods. But rather than request permission or
approach Oswald to ask him to account for his movements since leaving
New Orleans, Hosty dropped the matter—probably because all along he
was more concerned about Marina than about Lee, and a single brief
contact with her was enough to suggest that she was not a dangerous
KGB plant. He had also determined that Oswald was not working with
classified information and thus appeared to pose no immediate threat to
national security.[19]

The FBI's failure to pursue Oswald more aggressively contrasts strik-
ingly with another pending criminal case. In 1960, an enlisted man in the
American Army named John George Gessner deserted his post at Fort
Bliss, where he worked with the Army's atomic cannon, and went to
Mexico City, where he made contact with Soviet intelligence. He later

told an undercover American agent (who must have discovered his contacts through American surveillance of the Soviet Embassy) that he had given the Soviets data on American nuclear weapons. The Soviets refused to let him defect to the Soviet Union, however, and his visits to the Czech, Polish, and Cuban embassies in Mexico City were also unsuccessful. He then traveled to Panama, where the United States arrested him, brought him back to the States, and imprisoned him for desertion. In early 1962 he was indicted for espionage, a charge that carried the death penalty. Gessner did not come up for trial until 1964, but responsible FBI authorities in Mexico City and Washington should surely have noticed the similarity in the two cases, since Oswald was also an ex-serviceman who had already defected and renounced his citizenship once and now had reopened contact with the Soviets at one of the two centers of their espionage effort in the western hemisphere.[20] But neither headquarters nor Dallas showed much sense of urgency in finding out what he was up to.

During the week before Hosty first met Ruth and Marina, Oswald had resumed his political intelligence work. On Wednesday evening, October 23, General Edwin Walker spoke to one thousand people at the Dallas Memorial Auditorium. Adlai Stevenson was scheduled to appear at the same venue to speak on United Nations Day, the 24th, and Walker took the opportunity to deliver a violent attack on the UN, on Stevenson, on Governor Connally (who had proclaimed United Nations Day in Texas), and on various American presidents. Oswald was in the audience.[21] The next day, Stevenson was picketed, taunted, spat upon, and hit with a sign when he appeared for his speech. The demonstrators outside the building included members of the local chapter of Alpha-66.[22] The story made national news, and when White House aide Arthur Schlesinger, Jr., called Stevenson to commiserate at President Kennedy's request, Stevenson talked about the hateful atmosphere in Dallas and suggested that the President should cancel his own trip.[23]

On Friday night Lee and Michael Paine had dinner at Ruth's house in Irving, and Lee talked about attending the Walker meeting. Michael spontaneously invited him to attend a meeting that evening of his local chapter of the American Civil Liberties Union at Southern Methodist University.[24] Then as now, the ACLU was the kind of liberal organization that made conservative Texans see red. Not surprisingly, the meeting discussed Stevenson's reception a few days previously, and an acquaintance of Michael's, Raymond Krystinik, later told the FBI that during the question period Oswald jumped to his feet and said "that General Edwin Walker was responsible for the trouble at the Stevenson meeting and stated emphatically that General Walker was both anti-Semitic and anti-Catholic." When Krystinik disputed that, Oswald called him a "petty capitalist," avowed Marxism, and accepted the epithet of Communist. Krystinik then asked what Oswald thought of the Kennedy administration, and Oswald stated, "They are doing a pretty good job as far as civil rights are concerned."[25] After the meeting, Oswald filled out an ACLU membership application and mailed it in. Driving home with Michael Paine, he speculated that one man they talked to might be a Communist and gave Paine the impression that he hoped to meet local Communists.

On Sunday, October 27, John Martino flew from Miami to Dallas for the second time that month. We have no information regarding why he went, where he stayed, or whom he saw.[26] Five days later, on November 1, Lee Harvey Oswald resumed his career as a left-wing provocateur, mailing yet another letter to Arnold Johnson of the Communist Party USA. It read:

Dear Mr. Johnson,

In September I had written you saying I expected to move from New Orleans, La., to the Philadelphia-Baltimore area. You advised me that I could contact you when I had gotten settled there and the party would contact me in that area.

Since then my personal plans have changed and I have settled in Dallas, Texas for the time.

Through a friend, I have been introduced into the American Civil Liberties Union local chapter, which holds monthly meeting on the campus of Southern Methodist University.

At the first meeting I attended on October 25, a film was shown and afterwards a very critical discussion of the ultra-right in Dallas.

On October 23rd, I had attended an ultra-right meeting led by General Edwin A. Walker, who lives in Dallas.

This meeting preceded by one day the attack on A. E. Stevenson at the United Nations Day meeting at which he spoke.

As you can see, political friction between "left" and "right" is very great here.

Could you advise me as to the general view we have on the American Civil Liberties Union?

And to what degree, if any, I should attempt to heighten its progressive tendencies?

This Dallas branch of the A.C.L.U. is firmly in the hands of "liberal" professional people, (a minister and two Law professors conducted the October 25th meeting.) However, some of those present showed marked class-awareness and insight.

Respectfully yours,
Lee H. Oswald[27]

Johnson did not reply. Having discredited his mythical FPCC chapter in New Orleans, Oswald apparently hoped to do the same to the Dallas ACLU by establishing some connection between it and the Communist Party USA—why, and on whose behalf, we do not know.

The first of several highly controversial incidents purportedly involving Oswald took place in early November. On December 16, Edith Whitworth, who worked at an Irving furniture store, told the FBI that the entire Oswald family came into her shop sometime late in the week of November 4–8. Oswald, she said, asked about gun repair because a sign outside the shop listed "furniture and guns," but she referred him to the Irving Sports Store, just a few blocks away. His foreign wife followed him inside with a toddler and a newborn baby, and Oswald mentioned that the baby had been born on October 20, which she remembered because her new grandchild had been born on that date. A friend of hers, Gertrude Hunter, who was visiting her in the shop at the time, confirmed the entire story and was sure the man was Oswald. They both remembered him driving the family away in a 1957 or 1958 Ford or Plymouth.[28]

Ruth Paine vehemently denied that this could have happened, as did Marina, and that the car was certainly not hers. At the nearby Irving Sport Shop, however, a repairman named Dial Ryder actually found a tag marked with the name "Oswald" that had been written sometime during the first half of November. His boss vouched for him, but he had no memory of the man or the job.[29] Oswald was not a licensed driver, although Marina had written Ruth from New Orleans that his uncle, Dutz Murret, or his cousin had taken him out in his car for a few lessons, and Paine also apparently admitted at one point that she had given him some lessons herself.[30] In the latter stages of the Warren Commission investigation, the FBI contacted every other Oswald in the area to try to link the repair tag to someone else, and agents even canvassed hospital records to identify other baby girls born on October 20, but to no avail.[31]

On Thursday and Friday, November 7–8, front-page stories in the *Dallas Morning News* announced, first tentatively and then definitely, that President Kennedy would come to Dallas during his November 21–22 visit to Texas. During the following weekend (November 8–10), a series of striking incidents occurred in Oswald's life, one of which the FBI spent weeks fruitlessly trying to refute. Both Marina and the Paines confirmed that Oswald did not come home on Friday the 8th as usual but showed up in Irving sometime Saturday morning and explained that he had been checking out another job. And as a matter of fact, according to the manager of a parking garage who contacted the FBI in early February 1964, Oswald came into the garage about two weeks before the assassination—that is, on about November 8—looking for work in response to a *Dallas Morning News* advertisement. The manager, Hubert Morrow, remembered that Oswald had asked how tall the building was and whether it had a good view of the city. The building—the Southland Hotel Garage—was at 1208 Commerce Street, just a few blocks from the Texas School Book Depository and one block over from Main Street, the normal parade route in Dallas and, as it turned out, part of the presidential motorcade route on November 22 (although that was only announced on November 15).[32]

On the day after the assassination the FBI heard a far more troubling story from Albert K. Bogard, a used car salesman at the Downtown Lincoln Mercury Dealership, a straight mile and a half southwest of the TSBD and directly on one of the two obvious routes between the TSBD and Oswald's boarding house. Bogard said that Oswald had come into the dealership on the afternoon of Saturday, November 9. Showing him every car on the lot, Bogard had to ask him twice to get his name—Oswald—and then brought him back inside to try to get him to put a deposit on a car. At that point Oswald announced that he had no money but expected to be receiving some soon. When Bogard asked him where he would get it, he said, "I've got it coming." They then went back out onto the lot and Oswald requested to test drive a $3,000 Mercury hardtop—a car worth about $18,000 in 2007 dollars. Bogard remembered that he was wearing a sweatshirt and "did not look like a $3,000 car man."

The eager salesman apparently did not bother to ask to see his driver's license (a point that never came up in his numerous FBI interviews), and Oswald immediately took the car onto Stemmons Freeway and began driving at high speed. Bogard had to call a halt to the escapade because the car was low on gas. He wrote Oswald's name on the back of one of his business cards. On the afternoon of November 22, when Oswald's name became known, Bogard's boss asked him if he didn't have a prospect by that name. Bogard took the card out of his pocket, confirmed that he did, exclaimed, "I guess he isn't a prospect any more!" and threw the card into the wastebasket, which must have been emptied that very night.[33]

That Oswald was expecting to receive a large sum of money was devastating evidence of a conspiracy, and the FBI and Warren Commission put a high priority on discrediting Bogard's story. Bogard insisted that the incident must have taken place on Saturday afternoon, November 9, but Ruth Paine swore convincingly that Oswald was in Irving at that time. She said she drove him to a Texas state office to take an examination for a learner's permit on that Saturday, but the office was closed.[34] Yet Oswald's visit to the dealership could easily have happened on Friday afternoon, since Oswald spent that Friday night at his boarding house and could have stopped by on his way home from work. (Regular work hours at the TSBD were not strictly enforced.) The testimony of Bogard's co-workers, moreover, seems to prove that the incident was not a fabrication. Another salesman, Oran Brown, said he also wrote down Oswald's name, and Brown's wife remembered seeing the paper with his name on it. The assistant sales manager, Frank Pizzo, confirmed having asked Brown on the 22nd if he didn't have a prospect named Oswald.[35] Bogard eventually took a polygraph and passed with flying colors.[36]

Another tantalizing piece of information came from an insurance agent whose office was right across the street from Oswald's boarding house. He remembered that Oswald came in about two weeks before the assassination and asked about auto insurance for a car he planned to buy. Oswald gave the name O. H. Lee (which he was using at the boarding house). The agent thought that Lee produced a Texas driver's license with that name, which has never been found.[37]

On the same day that he tried to take his driver's examination (November 9), Oswald typed a letter to the Soviet consulate in Washington,

D.C., that suggested he still hoped to go to Cuba. The letter, which he mailed several days later, read:

FROM: LEE H. OSWALD, P.O. BOX 6225, DALLAS, TEXAS
MARINA NICILAYEVA OSWALD, SOVIET CITIZEN
Dear sirs;

   This is to inform you of recent events since my meetings with comrade Kostin in the Embassy of the Soviet Union, Mexico City, Mexico.

   I was unable to remain in Mexico indefinily [sic] because of my Mexican visa restrictions which was for 15 days only. I could not take a chance on requesting a new visa unless I used my real name, so I returned to the United States.

   I had not planned to contact the Soviet embassy in Mexico so they were unprepared, had I been able to reach the Soviet Embassy in Havana as planned, the embassy there would have had time to complete our business.

   Of corse [sic] the Soviet embassy was not at fault, they were, as I say unprepared, the Cuban consulate was guilty of a gross breach of regulations, I am glad he has since been replaed. [sic]

   The Federal Bureu [sic] of Investigation is not now interested in my activities in the progressive organization "Fair Play For Cuba Committee", of which I was secretary in New Orleans (state Louisiana) since I no longer reside in that state. However, the F. B. I. has visited us here in Dallas, Texas, on November 1st. Agent James P. Hasty [sic] warned me that if I engaged in F. P. C. C. activities in Texas the F. B. I. will again take an "interest" in me.

   This agent also "suggested" to Marina Nicholayevna that she could remain in the United States under F. B. I. "protection", that is, she could defect from the Soviet Union, of course, I and my wife strongly protested these tactics by the notorious F. B. I.

   Please inform us of the arrival of our Soviet entrance visa's as soon as they come.

   Also, this is to inform you of the birth, on October 20, 1963 of a DAUGHTER, AUDREY MARINA OSWALD in DALLAS, TEXAS, to my wife.

Respectfully,
Lee H. Oswald.[38]

The Warren Commission concluded that this was merely a clumsy attempt to impress the Soviets. On the contrary, the text seems to suggest that Oswald had in fact submitted an application for a visa to the Soviet Union in Mexico City, as Nechiporenko's research indicated, and that he was hoping that he could go back to Mexico and travel to Cuba when his Soviet visa came through. And if the visa had come through—which it never did—that would have enabled him to go to Cuba rather than carry out an attempt on President Kennedy's life.

In fact, something else had happened during October that revived the issue of a Soviet visa. On October 15 the Cuban Ministry of Foreign Affairs had informed the Cuban consulate in Mexico City that Oswald's visa application had been denied because he did not have a visa for the Soviet Union.[39] We have no evidence that Oswald had learned about this, but something else in Oswald's letter suggests he might have: the reference to the replacement of the Cuban consul, Eusebio Azcue, with whom Oswald had a shouting match in Mexico City. It seems to imply that someone was keeping him informed of developments there. On the other hand, since Oswald had also been introduced to the man who became Azcue's replacement, Oswald may simply have been making a guess. The FBI intercepted the letter in Washington. On November 19 they forwarded the gist of it to Dallas, including the reference to "Comrade Kostin" but still without identifying him as Kostikov or asking for any specific action. "Information being furnished Dallas for whatever action deemed necessary," the bureau letter read. It apparently arrived on the morning of November 22.[40]

In another twist, Oswald left a longhand draft of his letter out in the open where Ruth Paine found it on Sunday, November 2. She later testified that this was how she learned, for the first time, that Oswald had been in Mexico, but she insisted that she said nothing about the trip to him or Marina.[41] Ruth and Oswald were wary of each other, and perhaps she was hoping that he would indeed take the opportunity to go to Cuba or return to the Soviet Union, leaving Marina and her children with her in Irving. But given how secretive Oswald usually was, it seems impossible that he could have simply left the draft out by mistake. Perhaps he wanted to find out whether Ruth would pass the information on to agent Hosty. For some reason, never explained, she made a copy in her own handwriting and kept it. She later claimed that she showed it to Michael but that he did not take it seriously.[42]

Hosty was very much on Oswald's mind. Sometime during the first half of November, Lee went to FBI headquarters (which, like everything else in downtown Dallas, was not far from the Book Depository) to confront him. Since Hosty was out, he left a note for him. When Hosty first testified about this incident before the Church Committee in 1975, he placed it between November 4 and November 8—that is, immediately after Hosty's visits to the Paine house and before Oswald wrote to the Soviets.[43] But in his 1996 book Hosty moved the incident a week forward, to approximately November 12—the following Tuesday, and the same day that Oswald mailed his letter mentioning "Hasty" to the Soviets. "In effect," Hosty wrote many years later, the note read: "If you want to talk to me, you should talk to me to my face. Stop harassing my wife, and stop trying to ask her about me. You have no right to harass her." Hosty claimed that the note was unsigned, and only when Oswald made a similar statement to his face at Dallas police headquarters on the afternoon of November 22 did he realize that the note had come from him.[44]

Because Hosty's boss, Gordon Shanklin, ordered him to destroy the note on November 25 to avoid embarrassing the FBI, we cannot be certain that it contained no signature. Not for the first time, Oswald's behavior here is open to contradictory interpretations. He might have been trying to get himself into trouble, perhaps to stop him from committing a terrible act; he might have been trying once again to make FBI files show him as a hostile leftist activist; or he might simply have been cracking under the strain of what he was about to do.

Oswald spent a routine week at work and in his room on North Beckley Street from November 11 through November 15. A *Dallas Morning News* story on Friday, November 15, stated that a presidential motorcade through Dallas was unlikely, but the next morning a page 1 story confirmed that there would be a motorcade after all, and predicted that it would travel down Main Street and *through* the triple underpass at Stemmons Freeway—a route visible from the Texas School Book Depository, although not nearly as convenient as the route the motorcade eventually took (see maps).

For the first time since early October, Oswald did not return to Ruth Paine's at all on the weekend of November 16–17. According to Marina, he explained that he did not want to encounter Michael, who would be there celebrating his daughter's birthday.[45] But in fact, he was evidently preparing to assassinate the President, with help from persons unknown.

Since Marina's return from New Orleans with Ruth, Oswald's rifle had been sitting wrapped in a blanket in the Paines' garage, known to Marina but not to Ruth. But that very Saturday afternoon, November 16—the same day that the *Dallas Morning News* previewed the motorcade route—a Dallas physician, Dr. Homer Wood, and his thirteen-year-old son, Sterling, visited the Sportsdome Rifle Range in the 8000 block of West Davis Street in Dallas—about two and a half miles from Oswald's boarding house in Oak Cliff. From approximately 3:00 to 4:30 p.m. they practiced target shooting. In the adjacent booth they could see the head and shoulders of a man whom both Dr. Wood and his son later claimed was Oswald. Sterling asked the man about his rifle and confirmed that it was a bolt-action 6.5-millimeter Italian carbine (like Oswald's Mannlicher-Carcano), with a sling and a scope. The boy could see Oswald's target from his booth, and he testified that Oswald scored several bull's-eyes at a distance of 100 yards. He thought he saw Oswald leave in a car parked nearby. Shown a photograph of Oswald's rifle, he said that the sling and the scope were not quite the same as the ones he had seen. The FBI recovered four Mannlicher-Carcano shells from the range, but they did not match Oswald's rifle.[46]

The Woods were highly credible witnesses, and the range was a short drive from Oswald's boarding house, where he was spending the weekend. If the Woods actually did see Oswald at target practice on that day, the episode helps answer the critical question of how Oswald could have performed an extraordinary feat of marksmanship six days later—a question raised by his brother Robert. Both Lee and Robert had learned to shoot in the military, firing semi-automatic weapons (the M-1). With a loaded clip in such a weapon, the shooter can simply squeeze off a number of consecutive rounds from a stationary position. The Mannlicher-Carcano, however, was a bolt-action rifle, requiring the shooter to use his right hand to work the bolt after every round before re-sighting. That made Oswald's feat on November 22—scoring two hits on Kennedy in three shots within a very few seconds—much harder. No one could have done that who had not had substantial practice with just this kind of weapon—and there is no other record of Oswald practicing with, or even firing, his own rifle.[47]

We have every reason to believe the Woods' story, and it confirms that

Oswald was involved in a conspiracy. Sterling Wood's testimony that the rifle he saw was not identical to the one used in the assassination is consistent with that interpretation, since everything we know indicates that Oswald's rifle was sitting in the Paines' garage on that Saturday. Someone else apparently provided him with a similar weapon to use for practice. It also helps explain why, after the assassination, the FBI never found any Mannlicher-Carcano ammunition at the Beckley Street address or at the Paines' house. The rifle had been shipped without ammunition, and the bureau searched far and wide to find where Oswald might have bought some, without result. Only two gun shops in the Dallas area sold it, and one of them belonged to John Thomas Masen, the Minuteman and would-be arms dealer who resembled Oswald and was arrested just a few days before the assassination. Someone, apparently, had lent Oswald a rifle for target practice and had given him just a few rounds of ammunition with which to make the attempt on the life of the President on November 22.

One more critical lead about Oswald's activities in the weeks before the assassination was never seriously pursued. On November 23 a Dallas Sheriff's Office investigator told the Secret Service about some Cubans who had been living at 3128 Harlendale Street in Dallas. He said they had been holding weekend meetings and were possibly affiliated with the "Freedom for Cuba Committee [sic] of which Oswald was a member." Three days later, the same man reported that the Cubans had vacated the house sometime between November 15 and November 23 and that Oswald had attended their meetings.[48] The FBI did not receive this report.

Not until May 1964, at the request of the Warren Commission, did the FBI report on Dallas anti-Castro Cubans, identifying branches of JURE, the 30th of November group, the DRE, and the SNFE. Manuel Rodriguez Orcaberro, the local SNFE head, had been reported by the CIA to be "violently anti-President Kennedy" immediately after the assassination, but when interviewed months later he denied this. The same CIA cable also quoted Eloy Gutierrez Menoyo, the SNFE leader, as having remarked on November 21, "Something very big would happen soon that would advance the Cuban cause."[49] But unknown to the Warren Commission, an unnamed Dallas informant told the FBI during 1964 that 3126 Harlendale had been the headquarters of the local Alpha-66 chapter, headed by Manuel Rodriguez, and the residence of one Jorge Salazar. But the Dallas office's sources claimed that Oswald was not known to any members of Alpha-66 and was not known to have visited 3126 Harlendale.[50] Neither that information nor any information on a Dallas Alpha-66 chapter, however, found its way into the bureau's report for the Warren Commission on Cuban exile activities in the Dallas area. Alpha-66 had picketed Stevenson's visit to Dallas, and its national head, Antonio Veciana, later claimed to have seen Oswald with "Maurice Bishop" in Dallas in August 1963.

The President's visit was by far the biggest story in Dallas for the entire week of November 18–22. The *Morning News* had eight different stories about it on Sunday, November 17, seven more on Tuesday the 19th, three on the 20th, and eight on the 21st. Several of them referred to the mobilization of extra police to handle the visit, the city's intense desire to avoid any replay of the Stevenson incident a month earlier, and, increasingly, the split in the Texas Democratic Party between Governor John Connally, a conservative (with whom Oswald had corresponded unsuccessfully to try to upgrade his Marine discharge while Connally was secretary of the Navy), and Senator Ralph Yarborough, a liberal. On Friday morning, the day of the event, eleven more stories dealt with the trip, including one that showed the motorcade route, without illustrating the turns from Main Street onto Houston and Houston onto Elm that took the presidential party right by the Texas School Book Depository.

On Monday evening, November 18, Ruth Paine telephoned the Beckley Street boarding house at Marina's request and asked for Lee, who apparently had failed to make his usual daily phone call. The landlady replied that no Lee Oswald lived there (she knew her boarder as O. H. Lee). On Thursday evening Oswald showed up suddenly at the Paines' house for the last time. That night he apparently spent some time in the garage. Before he left the next morning, he put his wedding ring and more than $100 on the dresser for Marina, who was still asleep. His neighbor and co-worker at the TSBD, Buell Frazier, noticed when he picked him up that he was carrying a package wrapped in brown paper. Oswald told him it contained curtain rods for his room.

Meanwhile, hundreds of miles away in New Orleans, another drama was playing itself out. After more than two years of legal wrangling,

Carlos Marcello finally came to trial during the first week of November for conspiracy to defraud the government by presenting a false Guatemalan birth certificate. Attorneys from the Justice Department itself handled the prosecution. A jury of seven men and five women was selected on November 5, and the New Orleans *Times-Picayune* printed the names of all the jurors on the next day. On Friday, November 8, the paper led with the sensational testimony of Carl Irving Noll, the ex-convict and cog in the Marcello machine who had first given the government the story of the forged certificate in a Pennsylvania prison more than three years earlier. Noll described the defendant's attempts to secure Guatemalan citizenship, culminating in his own trip to Guatemala in 1956 with $2,500 in Carlos Marcello's money for payoffs and his journey through the countryside until he found a town, San Jose Pinula, where a false entry of Marcello's birth could be put into the town ledger and a birth certificate filled out.

He had then returned to New Orleans with a Guatemalan lawyer, the law partner of the then-prime minister Eduardo Rodriguez-Genis, who gave the document to Marcello after it had been signed by the prime minister himself. On cross-examination, Marcello's lawyer, Washington attorney Jack Wasserman, implied that the birth certificate was not designed to defraud the government or prevent Marcello's deportation to Italy but merely to allow him to move immediately from Italy to Guatemala after a possible deportation. In a telling point, Wasserman also brought out that in April 1961 the government had already heard Noll's story that the birth certificate was false but nevertheless used it to deport Marcello to Guatemala.[51] Marcello was also represented by local council G. Wray Gill, whom both David Ferrie and Guy Banister had assisted in preparing his defense.

During the second week of the trial the government introduced a 1956 travel document that the Italian consulate in New Orleans had issued Marcello pending his deportation but that the Italian Embassy in Washington had suspended after he had shown them his new Guatemalan birth certificate. An Italian official also seemed to indicate that had Marcello been ordered deported, as he apparently feared he would be in 1956, the presentation of proof that he had been born in Guatemala, of Italian parents, might have led the Italian government to refuse him. Defense attorneys continued to argue that the birth certificate had never ac-

tually been used to defraud the U.S. government, as alleged in the indictment.[52]

When the defense began presenting its case on Monday, November
18, it argued that Marcello had successfully secured a stay of his deportation on October 30, 1956, before the Italian Embassy had refused to
revalidate his travel document, and this was the reason the Italian government had suspended it. On Thursday, November 21, the defense presented its last witness, Yvonne Klein of Wilmette, Illinois, a Chicago
suburb, who testified that Noll had traveled to Guatemala in 1956 on
business for her and had absconded with company funds. The judge sent
the case to the jury on the morning of Friday, November 22. At around
noon that day the jury returned a verdict of not guilty. After hearing the
news of the President's assassination in Dallas, David Ferrie and two
young male companions left New Orleans to spend the weekend in the
Houston area.[53]

A thousand miles or more away in Miami, John Martino and his family took advantage of local television schedules to watch both Walter
Cronkite on CBS and Huntley-Brinkley on NBC every evening. (Both
had been extended to a full half an hour the previous September.) Sometime during November 1963—perhaps during President Kennedy's visit
to Miami on November 18—the broadcast mentioned Kennedy's forthcoming trip to Dallas. "If he goes to Dallas," John Martino remarked,
"they are going to kill him."[54]

Back in Louisiana, in the town of Eunice, on US 195, a major east-
west artery in the south central part of the state, a prostitute and heroin
addict named Rose Cheramie was hit by a truck outside a bar and
house of prostitution called the Silver Slipper and taken to a hospital on
Wednesday, November 20. Since she had no money and was not seriously injured, the hospital called a State Police officer named Francis
Fruge, who had been on the force since 1948, and he put her in jail. That
night, however, he received a call that she was suffering from severe heroin withdrawal. After calling a doctor to sedate her, Fruge drove her to
the State Hospital in Jackson, more than two hours away, where records
later showed she was registered at about 6:00 a.m. on November 21.

The sedative calmed her, and during the drive, according to Fruge,
Cheramie told him she had been on her way to Texas with two Italians
or men who looked like Italians, who had thrown her out of the Silver

Slipper after a fight. She and the men had been on their way to Dallas, where they were going to get hold of some money, pick up her baby from a man who was looking after him, and kill President Kennedy. Years later, a resident at the hospital named Weiss said that a Dr. Bowers had heard the same story from Cheramie—once again, before the assassination actually took place.

Around November 25, 1963—about five days after hearing her story for the first time—Fruge went back to interview Cheramie, who had completed her withdrawal. At that point she diminished her credibility considerably by claiming to have worked for Jack Ruby and to have known both him and Lee Harvey Oswald. But with the help of other law enforcement agents, Fruge managed to confirm other parts of her story involving a big pending heroin deal in Houston, and even took her to Houston to try to break up the deal. The seaman who was supposed to be bringing in the heroin, however, failed to show. The town of Eunice, where she had her accident, was on the way to Houston, not Dallas, but Fruge claimed in 1978 to the HSCA investigators that he had confirmed that an underworld figure was watching Cheramie's baby in Dallas. Rose Cheramie died in another traffic accident in September 1965. When Fruge reinvestigated her story for District Attorney Jim Garrison in 1967, the manager of the Silver Slipper, Mack Manuel, told him that he remembered the incident of November 20, 1963, and that Cheramie's companions were pimps who frequently drove prostitutes across the South.[55]

During the late afternoon of Thursday, November 21, Lee Harvey Oswald made a surprise appearance at Ruth Paine's house in Irving, where he customarily visited only on weekends. On the same evening, Jack Ruby had dinner at the Egyptian Lounge, the steak house run by the Campisi brothers. The next morning, November 22, at about 10:45, Janet Conforto, also known as Jada, who had been the star attraction at the Carousel Club for several months, was driving east out of town in a 1963 Cadillac convertible when she accidentally hit a male pedestrian. The man's boss called the police, and she became impatient. "Let's hurry up and get this over with," she said, "I have to get to New Orleans."[56] By the time the police let her go, the President was landing at Love Field. When the FBI tracked her down in New York on December 4 to question her, she claimed Ruby had fired her during the last week of

October—but that appears to be questionable, since Ruby was still handing out advertisements for her act the day before the assassination.[57]

Meanwhile, in Miami, John Martino suggested to his son Ed that he take the day off from school. "I don't think you are feeling well today, Edward," he said, "I think you should stay home and rest." He told him to turn on the TV and let him know if there was any news. By 1:45 p.m. EST, there was.[58]

16

Three Days in November

Almost half a century later, no one can add very much about what happened on November 22, 1963. Although the Warren Commission's 1964 analysis of the shooting in Dallas's Dealey Plaza was not highly persuasive, much more detailed investigations by the House Select Committee on Assassinations in 1977–78 confirmed the commission's finding that Lee Harvey Oswald fired the shots that hit President Kennedy and Governor Connally. Its one critical new conclusion was that acoustic evidence seemed to prove a conspiracy, but that evidence has now become stuck in contradictions.

On the morning of November 22, Lee Harvey Oswald once again rode to the Texas School Book Depository with his co-worker and Ruth Paine's neighbor, Buell Wesley Frazier. Oswald carried a two-foot-long package wrapped in brown paper that he described as "curtain rods."[1] It evidently contained his rifle, which he took to the sixth floor of the building. One or two witnesses waiting for the President observed him standing near the window before the presidential motorcade came down Houston Street and turned on to Elm. For whatever reason, Oswald did not attempt a head-on shot as the motorcade came down Houston but waited until it had passed by him. Then he fired three times.

No aspect of the assassination has provoked more controversy than the sequence of gunshots that struck President Kennedy twice and Governor Connally once at approximately 12:30 p.m. Central Standard Time on November 22, 1963. The conflicts among three pieces of evidence—the Zapruder film, Governor Connally's own testimony, and Oswald's rifle—became perhaps the single most fertile ground for conspiracy theories during the 1960s and 1970s, and the controversy has never died out. The Zapruder film, taken by Abraham Zapruder, a well-placed spectator with an 8-mm camera, seemed to show President Kennedy responding to the first bullet that struck him in the back less than two seconds before Governor Connally obviously reacted to having a bullet pass through his body. This sequence suggested that two different shots were fired within about 1.33 seconds—less time than Oswald could have fired them with his bolt-action Mannlicher-Carcano rifle. Connally further complicated the issue by testifying until the end of his life that he realized the President had been hit before he felt the impact himself.

The Warren Commission created much of the confusion by deciding that Oswald had fired the first of three shots somewhere between Zapruder frames 210 and 225, that is, less than six seconds before the final, fatal head shot. They concluded tentatively that Oswald might have fired three shots within that period, but they also had to conclude that the first shot had also hit Governor Connally. The film seemed to show that Connally had been hit around frame 234, and it most certainly did not seem possible for Oswald to have fired twice in a maximum of twenty-four frames, that is, about 1.33 seconds, much less hit his target both times. They concluded that a single bullet had hit the President in the back, passed through his neck, hit Connally in the back, and come to rest in Connally's thigh after passing through his body and hitting his wrist. This so-called single-bullet theory was the only way to preserve the lone-assassin theory, to which the Warren Commission was strongly committed. Commission members adopted the single-bullet theory even though several of them made clear that they did not believe it.

Because a casual viewing of the Zapruder film shows that Kennedy had been hit by the time the limousine emerged from behind the Stemmons Freeway sign and that Connally reacted dramatically slightly thereafter, the film has been accepted by many Warren Commission critics and hundreds of thousands or millions of Americans as proof that Oswald could not have been the only shooter.[2] Very few of these critics have highlighted the implication of their argument: that two men would have had to fire at the limousine *from behind*.

The HSCA used far more technical resources to reach very different conclusions while still confirming the single-bullet theory. To begin

with, it appointed a panel of independent experts to use all available photographic evidence to find out if the back and neck wounds in President
Kennedy and the back, wrist, and thigh wounds in Governor Connally
were in fact lined up at a critical moment and thus could indeed have
been caused by one bullet. At frame 190 of the Zapruder film—about
1–2 seconds earlier than anyone had surmised—they did indeed discover
a straight bullet path whose trajectory led back to the corner sixth-floor
window of the TSBD, the floor on which Oswald's rifle was found. It
had therefore taken Connally about 44 frames, that is, about 2.5 seconds,
to react to being struck by a bullet that traversed his torso and punctured
his lung. Without inflicting similar wounds on a considerable sample of
individuals having no expectation of being shot, we really have no idea
how unusual such a delayed reaction might be. In any case, the panel
concluded that the two men's wounds had been aligned at that moment
along a trajectory leading to the TSBD window.

The panel reached the same conclusion about the entrance and exit
wounds in President Kennedy's head created by the last and fatal bullet
at frame 312, that is, 122 frames, or between 6 and 7 seconds, later.[3]
Somewhat more tentatively, the panel and the committee suggested that
Oswald had fired his first shot earlier still, between frames 162 and 167,
when they saw both Governor Connally and a small child running on
the grass react to what appeared to be a sudden sound.[4] That shot apparently missed, and Oswald had less than two seconds to fire the next shot,
which struck Kennedy in the back and then hit Connally. The committee concluded that Oswald might easily have done this if he had decided
not to use his telescopic sight at all and had used the rifle's open sights.
This would not have been surprising, since he would have used similar
open sights in the Marine Corps, where he had acquired nearly all of his
shooting experience.[5]

Other evidence is more definite. In 1977 Dr. Vincent Guinn, a chem-
ist, reviewed an enhanced neutron activation analysis of the bullets and
fragments recovered from the bodies of the two victims and from the
presidential limousine to determine how many actual bullets, and what
kind of bullets, they represented. His findings, presented to the HSCA,
have been recently re-analyzed by Drs. L. M. Sturdivan and Kenneth
Rahn.[6] They compared five pieces of evidence: the nearly whole bullet
found on Governor Connally's stretcher; a fragment taken from his wrist;
a fragment from President Kennedy's brain; two fragments from the

front seat of the limousine; and three smaller fragments from the rear seat floor. Traditional firearms tests and comparisons had already matched the nearly pristine bullet and the larger of the two fragments from the limousine to test bullets fired from Oswald's rifle. The neutron activation analysis analyzed in particular the concentrations of antimony in the five specimens—a metal added during manufacture to harden lead.

Dr. Guinn concluded, first, that the concentrations of antimony indicated that all the fragments were from Mannlicher-Carcano ammunition as opposed to other ammunition of the same 6.5 caliber. But he also found that the concentrations fell into two groups. They were sufficiently similar in the nearly pristine bullet found on Governor Connally's stretcher and the fragment from his wrist to confirm that the fragment came from the bullet. The other three fragments—one from Kennedy's brain and two from the car—differed from the first two but were sufficiently similar among themselves to confirm that they came from the same second bullet. These results seemed to prove that only two bullets struck the two men, both fired by Lee Harvey Oswald's rifle. And although no fragments of the bullet that struck Connally can be matched to Kennedy's back and neck wound, they further support the single-bullet theory since they indicate that only two bullets caused all the wounds.[7]

The autopsy of the President and its results have been the subject of even more controversy, partly because the Secret Service, in defiance of Texas law, insisted on taking President Kennedy's body back to Washington for autopsy rather than allowing the Dallas medical examiner to perform it. Yet there is still no documented or photographic evidence suggesting anything fundamentally wrong with the results reported by the original team of autopsy surgeons at Bethesda Naval Hospital and confirmed by a panel commissioned by the HSCA that looked at the original autopsy photos. The autopsy found two entry wounds in Kennedy's body, one in his back and one in the back of his head. The back wound exited through Kennedy's neck, and the massive wound in the right front of his skull, which is clearly visible in the Zapruder film, is characteristic of an exit wound, not an entrance wound. Using photographs and x-rays, the HSCA's very experienced panel agreed on the location of the President's two entrance and exit wounds, as well as those of Connally's wounds.[8]

The panel also concluded that the original autopsy surgeons had placed the entrance wound in Kennedy's head about four inches too low. They came to this conclusion partly because careful examination of the brain x-rays showed no evidence of a wound in the lower area. Dr. Humes, one of the original autopsy surgeons, appeared before the HSCA and agreed that his team had misidentified the location of that wound in the original report.[9] The panel of experts included one dissenter, Dr. Cyril Wecht of Pittsburgh, who had been critical of the Warren Commission's findings for many years. When he testified, Dr. Wecht argued that CE 399, the bullet found on Governor Connally's stretcher and identified as the famous single bullet, could not possibly have emerged in its nearly pristine condition after causing all the wounds that the other doctors believed it caused, and he vehemently disputed the trajectory analysis the panel used to conclude that one bullet could have taken such a path. But he agreed with all the rest of the panel's conclusions about the paths of the two bullets through President Kennedy, arguing only that it was *possible* (although he admitted there was no evidence to show it) that a second bullet might have struck President Kennedy's head from the front at the same time that another bullet struck the back of his head.[10]

As the motorcade sped off for Parkland Hospital, where the President was pronounced dead thirty minutes later, Oswald calmly and quickly walked downstairs to the second-floor lunchroom, where he bought a Coke. As policemen rushed into the building, supervisor Roy Truly identified Oswald as an employee.[11] He reached the front door of the building just as newsman Robin McNeil (later of the McNeil-Lehrer report) was coming into the building in a frantic search for a telephone. He directed McNeil to the nearest pay phone and then, apparently, left. His initial movements thereafter seem to show some confusion, but he evidently decided that he had to go back to his room on North Beckley Street to pick up his pistol. He had either not thought to bring it with him on the morning of the previous day, Thursday, or the problem of concealing it might have seemed too risky.

Oswald apparently began by walking about eight blocks *east* (that is, directly away from his rooming house) on Elm Street, proceeding further into downtown Dallas—a course that avoided the swarming crime scene in Dealey Plaza itself but apparently did not reflect his final plans at all. Then, at approximately Elm and Field Streets, he boarded a Lakewood-Marsalis bus, whose route normally went within seven blocks of his house in his Oak Cliff neighborhood. As Oswald must have known, another bus, the Beckley bus, also ran west along Elm Street and would have taken him directly to his rooming house. But after just a few blocks, the Lakewood-Marsalis bus got stuck in traffic owing to the jam-up in Dealey Plaza just ahead, and Oswald, taking his cue from a woman who was in a hurry, asked for a transfer (which was found on him when he was later arrested) and left the bus in the vicinity of Elm and Lamar streets.[12]

But instead of waiting for the Beckley bus, he began walking south on South Lamar Street, toward the Greyhound Bus Station—conceivably thinking about getting the first bus out of town. If that was his intention, however, he quickly changed his mind, hailed a cab that had just dropped a passenger at the Greyhound station, and asked him to take him to 500 North Beckley, about five blocks from his room. While the driver gave two different versions of where he left Oswald off, it seems to have been several blocks from the rooming house.[13] Oswald apparently walked the rest of the way to 1020 North Beckley.

In a coincidence that has never been explained, his landlady, Earlene Roberts, claimed she saw a police car stop in front of the house around 1:00 p.m. and then drive on. She identified it as car no. 207, but the Dallas Police Department established that no. 207 had been at City Hall or Dealey Plaza at that point, and the DPD could not place any other cars in the vicinity of Beckley Street.[14] Roberts said that Oswald stayed at the house for only a few minutes and left. She last saw him standing by the curb on the east side of the street, that is, by the northbound late of traffic, but he evidently began walking south and then east.[15]

Between ten and fifteen minutes later, Oswald encountered and killed Patrolman J. D. Tippit on Tenth Street just east of Patton, a little less than a mile from his boarding house. In 1998 the Tippit shooting became the subject of an exhaustive and careful study.[16] Its author, Dale K. Myers, successfully demolished most of the controversy surrounding the Tippit shooting and showed that Oswald without doubt was the killer. Yet Myers's account also leaves one important question that apparently will never be answered. Tippit had last touched base with headquarters via police radio at 12:55 p.m., twenty-five minutes after Kennedy was shot, when the dispatcher verified that he was still in the Oak Cliff area. By that time virtually every other available officer had gone to Dealey Plaza.

Tippit stopped at a gas station near the Houston Street viaduct over the Trinity River, south of downtown, where he remained for about ten minutes. During that period he failed to respond to a dispatcher's call, and a few minutes later he left, going south on Lancaster at high speed.[17] At about 1:14 p.m. Tippit was driving east on Tenth Street when he stopped to talk to Lee Harvey Oswald, who was walking on the sidewalk on the same south side of the street.

The Dallas police had not yet broadcast any description of a suspect in the President's assassination about forty-five minutes earlier. Why Tippit chose to speak to Oswald has long remained a mystery. Myers provides a good answer, citing eyewitnesses who had just seen Oswald walking *west* along Tenth Street, and others who saw that he was walking *east* when Tippit actually pulled up alongside him and began speaking to him through the passenger-side window. He hypothesizes that Oswald panicked when he saw a police car coming toward him and turned around, arousing Tippit's suspicion. His evidence is good, and this explanation makes sense, but it turns the question of Oswald's movements—already a puzzle—into a much bigger one.

The mystery of where Oswald was heading after leaving his rooming house has never been solved. Had he remained on Beckley Street, he might have taken a southbound bus that could have given him a connection to a bus south to Laredo, and even into Mexico (although he had not prepared for such a trip, as he had several months earlier, by obtaining an entrance visa). He was heading in the direction of Jack Ruby's apartment, but nothing suggests that the two men knew each other. He might have been heading for the Texas Theatre, where he actually wound up. We can only say that he seemed to be heading south, and that he had apparently decided to get off of any main road—even a two-lane through-street like Beckley. The distance from the rooming house to the place where he shot Tippit could have been reached easily in ten or fifteen minutes.[18] But if Oswald was actually walking *west* when Tippit first saw him—and two well-placed witnesses, including a cab driver behind Tippit's car, said he was—that complicates the picture considerably. To have reached that point from that direction he would have had to have walked three or four blocks east, an even longer distance south, and then doubled back. Still, that is apparently what he did.

Several witnesses watched Tippit roll down the passenger window,

speak to Oswald, and then step out of his car on the driver's side and begin to walk around the front. As he did so, Oswald suddenly drew his revolver and shot him three times in the chest. Then Oswald began to walk
away, stopped, went back to where Tippit was now lying on the ground,
leaned down, and shot him execution-style in the head. As he began
running west, witnesses saw him emptying and reloading his gun. Meanwhile, a witness used the police radio in Tippit's car to report the shooting, and within minutes police cars with sirens blaring were converging
on the scene.[19]

About twenty minutes later on Jefferson Boulevard, a main Oak Cliff
street six blocks away from the shooting site, a shoe salesman heard a police siren approaching and saw a somewhat disheveled young man who
appeared to have been running step into the well of the doorway of his
store and turn his back to the street. Curious, he stepped out behind the
man and watched him walk toward the Texas Theatre a few yards away,
where the ticket taker had emerged from her booth to see what was going on. The man ducked in behind her without buying a ticket. At 1:47
p.m. the theater operator called the police, who began to converge on
the theater. The shoe salesman, who had just found Oswald himself,
pointed him out in the second row. After initially appearing to surrender,
Oswald struck the first policeman who approached him, attempted to
draw his gun again, and apparently managed to pull the trigger as several
officers were taking it away. The gun misfired.[20]

Firearms evidence could not match the actual bullets that struck
Tippit to Oswald's revolver because Oswald had used ammunition that
did not fit his barrel properly. But the tests found the gun to be consistent
with the markings on the bullets. And tests did match four shells found in
the vicinity of the crime (where Oswald had dropped them as he fled) to
Oswald's revolver, which was still on him at the time of his arrest. Although only three of the bullets and three of the shells can be matched to
the same manufacturers, Myers pointed out that there are clear explana-
tions for this. In short, the evidence leaves no doubt that Lee Harvey
Oswald killed Officer Tippit as well as President Kennedy.[21]

Led by Captain Will Fritz of homicide, the Dallas police, Secret Service personnel, and, initially, FBI agent Hosty immediately began questioning Oswald at police headquarters. He admitted working at the
Texas School Book Depository, leaving the building after the assassina-

tion, going to his rooming house, getting his pistol, and going to the movies, but he denied shooting Kennedy or Tippit. He also denied owning a rifle, or that he carried a package with him that morning when he rode to work with Buell Frazier. When Hosty entered the room and was identified by name, Oswald yelled at him for "accosting my wife" and denied, in response to Hosty's question, that he had ever been to Mexico City. He also said that he was registered at North Beckley Street as O. H. Lee simply because the landlady made a mistake.

Staying in character as a left-wing activist, he reaffirmed his role as secretary to the New Orleans chapter of the Fair Play for Cuba Committee, expressed support for Fidel Castro's revolution, and indicated that he wanted to retain John Abt as his lawyer—a New York attorney well known for defending Communists. He never reached Abt. When Fritz noted that he answered questions quickly and asked if he had been interrogated before, he said that he had, by the FBI. He was paraded before the press several times and even answered a few questions, denying that he had shot anyone.

Oswald was interrogated on Friday afternoon and three times on Saturday. On late Saturday afternoon he was shown an enlargement of one of the photos Marina had taken of him with his rifle and pistol, and he insisted that it was a fake. Then he refused to answer any more questions. Interviews resumed at 9:30 on Sunday morning, and Oswald was shown a map of the city that the police found at North Beckley, including marks which, they claimed, showed where the President was shot. Oswald said he had used the map to mark the locations of jobs for which he had applied. He affirmed his Marxist, but not Leninist, beliefs, and denied that he had ever lived on Neely Street. Shortly after 10:00 a.m. on Sunday, Chief Curry came in to ask if they were ready to allow Oswald to go downstairs to be transferred to the county jail. Fritz said that he was.[22] By the time police detectives escorted Oswald into the basement, Jack Ruby was waiting there.

After his arrest for murdering Oswald, Ruby insisted that he had killed him on his own, simply to spare Jackie Kennedy the pain of having to return to Dallas for a trial. Because of money Ruby wired to one of his stripper employees only moments before he entered the police station, lone-assassin theorists have long maintained that he decided to kill Oswald on the spur of the moment. As the HSCA concluded, however, this theory cannot be reconciled with Ruby's behavior during the assassination weekend, much of which he spent fairly close to Oswald, even, at one point, trying to enter the room at police headquarters where the assassin was being interrogated. In fact, Ruby's behavior from November 21 through November 24 marks him as someone who had been given a key role in the great historical drama that was playing itself out in Dallas that weekend.

Ruby shared an apartment with another man, George Senator, but actually seemed to make his home at the Carousel Club, where he kept all but one of his beloved dogs, and in his car. He had evidently taken a considerable interest in the President's trip, since his car contained the front pages of both Dallas and Fort Worth newspapers laying out Kennedy's itinerary on November 20.[23] After eating dinner on Friday evening at the Egyptian Lounge with his close friend Ralph Paul, he had gone to the Cabana Motel to meet with a Chicago businessman named Lawrence Meyers, whom he had seen earlier at the Carousel Club.[24]

Another enigmatic figure was also staying at the Cabana Motel that night, a paroled convict named Eugene Hale Brading, who had recently changed his name to Jim Braden. Together with a certain Victor Emmanuel Perreira, Brading had worked a number of con jobs on wealthy widows, one of which had landed him in jail in the late 1950s. (He had previously been run out of Dallas by the sheriff.) He was now living in Los Angeles, where he had become a charter member of the Teamster-financed La Costa Racket Club, and was still working with Perreira and Earl Scheib, the owner of a nationwide chain of automobile body shops. He had married the widow of a Teamster official who had been accused of racketeering. He was also working in the oil business and had made several trips to New Orleans, listing his address as 1701 in the Pere Marquette building during the fall of 1963. Room 1707 of that same building was occupied by Attorney G. Wray Gill, who was representing Carlos Marcello in his deportation trial, with the assistance of David Ferrie.[25]

Brading, now Braden, got permission from his parole officer to travel to Dallas on November 17, promising to return on November 21—which he did not. The next day, the Dallas police picked Braden up in Dealey Plaza immediately after the assassination as he was coming out of the Dal-Tex building on Houston Street near the corner of Elm. Braden told both the DPD and the FBI that he had been looking for a pay phone, and neither organization ever realized that he was actually Eugene Hale Brading.[26]

Despite Ruby's interest in the presidential motorcade, which passed down Main Street just a few blocks from the Carousel Club, he did not attempt to view it. Between 12:00 and 12:30 p.m. on November 22 he was observed at the *Dallas Morning News,* where he often went to place ads for his club. He disappeared briefly during the assassination itself but reappeared immediately afterward and seemed quite affected by the news.[27] Then, apparently, he jumped into his car and drove to Parkland Hospital, where the motorcade had taken the wounded president and governor.

Seth Kantor was a former Dallas area newspaperman who was now the Washington correspondent of the *Fort Worth Star-Tribune.* Ruby, ever the publicity hound, had given Kantor several stories before he left Dallas in 1961. Kantor had accompanied President Kennedy to Dallas and ridden in the motorcade, and he was in Parkland just before 1:30 p.m., on his way to hear Assistant Press Secretary Matthew Kilduff announce the President's death, when Ruby suddenly tugged him on the shoulder. Ruby commented that the event was terrible and indicated that he planned to close his clubs for the weekend—as he, alone among downtown Dallas club operators, decided to do. Kantor told the FBI about this encounter on December 5, but Ruby denied that he had been at Parkland.[28] He could not have spent much time there, since he was back at the Carousel making phone calls before 2:00 p.m., but Kantor, an experienced and respected journalist who was in the middle of the biggest story of his life, could hardly have made a mistake. Yet the FBI and the Warren Commission apparently regarded the evidence that Ruby dashed to Parkland before the President was declared dead as too threatening to acknowledge, and arbitrarily decided that his encounter with Kantor could not have taken place. Fifteen years later, the HSCA corrected this mistake.[29]

Ruby called a number of close friends and family from the Carousel and dropped in on his closest relative, Eva Grant.[30] By the late afternoon or early evening he had worked his way into police headquarters, partly by exploiting his wide acquaintanceship with the police and the press and partly by claiming to represent a Yiddish newspaper. He was also, apparently, already attempting to kill Lee Harvey Oswald.

Victor Robertson was a radio and television reporter who had been to the Carousel Club quite a few times. On the afternoon of November 22 he had dashed to the scene of the Tippit murder, witnessed Oswald's arrest, and followed him to police headquarters. Sometime between 5:00 and 7:00 p.m. he saw Ruby try to enter the office in which Oswald was being interrogated. Two policeman stopped him, and one said, "You can't go in there, Jack."[31] Another reporter and a Vice Squad detective also saw Ruby in police headquarters around that time.[32] At some point in the evening Ruby returned to his own apartment and dropped into an evening service at his synagogue. Then, sometime before 11:00 p.m. he stopped at a delicatessen to buy sandwiches for policemen and reporters. He returned to headquarters by about 11:00.

Then occurred one of the more bizarre episodes of the weekend. Sometime after midnight, District Attorney Henry Wade and Police Chief Jesse Curry held a news conference and then presented Oswald to the press in the basement. Ruby was present at both events. At the news conference, Wade was asked whether Oswald belonged to any Communist Front organizations, and he said he did not know. When another reporter restated the question, Wade said the only organization he knew of was the "Free Cuba movement"—which was actually the name of a militant anti-Castro organization of right-wing Americans. "That's the Fair Play for Cuba Committee," Ruby corrected him simultaneously with one or two others. A newsreel camera swung around to catch Ruby making the correction.[33] Jack's awareness of the fine points of pro- and anti-Castro organizations—and which side Oswald was on—seems striking.

Seth Kantor, who was also present, wrote years later that Ruby was too far away, and Oswald was too surrounded by reporters, for him to have gotten off a clean shot when Oswald was brought forth in the basement. Ruby admitted to the FBI that he had his pistol with him that night, but later denied it to the Warren Commission. He continued driving around Dallas until very early in the morning.

On Saturday Ruby went again to his synagogue. Some people described him as upset and distraught over the assassination during the weekend, but others did not. Ruby visited the crime scene in Dealey Plaza on Saturday. He also spent some time looking at an "Impeach Earl Warren" sign—a popular item around the South ever since the chief justice penned the *Brown v. Board of Education* decision in 1954 that desegregated public schools. Ruby also complained about the hostile "Welcome, Mr. Kennedy" ad that had appeared in Dallas newspapers on November 22, paid for by a group of right-wingers including Nelson Bunker Hunt and Bernard Weissman, an associate of General Walker.[34]

Others of Ruby's movements were more suspicious, however. An NBC producer, Fred Rheinstein, encountered Ruby while parked in his remote television truck on Saturday morning, and then saw him walking the corridors of the Municipal Building, where Oswald was still held, on the truck's monitors as the day wore on.[35] Several other experienced reporters saw Ruby inside the building that day, bringing sandwiches to the police, as he often did.[36] Sometime between 2:00 and 3:00 p.m. Ruby went to his parking garage near the Carousel, and two men who knew him well overheard him discussing the transfer of Oswald to the county jail in a phone call to a local radio station. "You know I'll be there," Ruby said at one point.[37] And on the same afternoon, a Dallas policeman named Thomas Harkness saw Ruby in a crowd in front of Oswald's eventual destination.[38] Ruby's movements over the weekend are well documented because he was seen by so many newsmen with trained memories and by so many police officers who had known him for years. Through his many law enforcement connections he must eventually have learned that Oswald's transfer was postponed until sometime after 10:00 a.m. the next morning, as Chief Curry announced at 8:15 that evening.[39] All his attempts to get close to Oswald on Friday and Saturday failed, but the third day proved the charm.

Ruby spent the night at his apartment with his roommate, George Senator, who was in and out of the apartment Sunday morning doing laundry.[40] At 9:00 a.m. Ruby took a call from his cleaning lady, who wanted to schedule a visit. He seemed agitated to hear from her and insisted that she call again to confirm his presence before coming over. Kantor, who researched these issues more thoroughly than anyone else, concluded that Ruby was awaiting another call from a police contact regarding Oswald's transfer. It came, he concluded, from one of two detectives, L. D. Miller or W. J. Harrison, who were themselves summoned from the Delux Diner on Commerce Street (the home of the Carousel Club) at 9:00 to assist in the transfer. Both men were recalcitrant and evasive when called before Warren Commission investigators, and Harrison apparently failed a polygraph test.[41] The transfer was delayed while the local armored car company got its largest van in working order. It did not arrive at the Municipal Building until about 11:00.

At 10:20 Ruby got another call he had been expecting, from one of his strippers, Little Lynn, in Fort Worth. She had warned him that she would need an advance on her salary, and Ruby, always an easy mark for such requests, promised to wire her $25. He was abrupt but told her he was on his way downtown anyway to leave his favorite dog at the Carousel. The Western Union office was on the same block as the police station from which Oswald would depart. Senator had to leave the apartment about this time to continue doing his laundry, and Kantor hypothesizes that Ruby received another call getting the details of Oswald's departure. He stuffed his pockets full of money, put his pistol in his pants pocket, and set off for the city jail. Although Ruby and Senator both said he did not leave his apartment until 11:00 a.m., three television technicians thought they spoke to Ruby outside the Police and Courts building around 10:30. Back at the jail, Detective Harrison disappeared from his bureau's third floor office for at least fifteen minutes.

It is possible that Ruby parked across the street and spoke to one or more officers. When he learned that he had a few extra minutes, he went next door to the Western Union office to wire the money to Little Lynn.[42] From that location, he could see the armored van sticking out of the basement ramp. He completed his transaction at 11:17 and shot Oswald just four minutes later. The Warren Commission concluded that Ruby simply walked down the Main Street ramp and into the basement, fortuitously arriving just as Oswald did—but the two police officers watching the ramp swore that did not happen. Kantor established beyond any doubt that Ruby could have entered the Municipal Building on the first floor and reached the basement through a stairway that was not being watched, as several newsmen discovered on their own.

More ominously, as Kantor suggests, a police confederate might have waited for him to enter the building and then asked for Oswald to be brought down.[43] In the basement, Ruby stood directly behind his old friend, Detective Harrison. On December 1, 1963, Lieutenant Jack

Revill of the Dallas police, who was asked to investigate how Ruby got into the basement, interviewed him. Ruby refused to say how he got into the basement and became very angry when Revill asked him about Harrison, cursing Revill and accusing him of wanting to take away Harrison's job. Harrison denied knowing Ruby was behind him, but when asked by the Warren Commission for his opinion of the detective's reliability, Revill replied, "If this is being recorded, then I'd rather not state an opinion as to his truth and veracity." Revill also told the commission about a Dallas preacher named Ray Rushing, a man well known to him, who told him that he came to the jail on the morning of November 24 to offer Oswald spiritual guidance and rode in an elevator with Ruby. He refused to speak officially because he was afraid of the publicity.[44]

Ruby's later claim that he shot Oswald to spare Jacqueline Kennedy the pain of returning to Dallas for his trial was an oddly sentimental and considerate explanation for a man who lived off the exploitation of women. In any event, he admitted that his first attorney, Thomas Howard, had suggested the Jackie Kennedy explanation on the afternoon of his arrest.[45] Overwhelming evidence suggests that he accepted the assignment of eliminating Oswald (for which, apparently, he thought he would be acclaimed a hero) within hours of the President's death and that he spent most of the weekend trying to carry it out.

The Warren Report downplayed Ruby's organized crime associations, but we have seen that his business was surely mob-related and that he had been in frequent telephone conversations with leading mobsters all over the country for months before the assassination. Even J. Edgar Hoover sat up and took notice when Ruby almost immediately replaced his local counsel with Melvin Belli, a mob-connected San Francisco lawyer who had a long association with Mickey Cohen.[46] Ruby had attempted to become involved in Cuban arms deals, he had visited the island in 1959, and he had met Santo Trafficante at the Trescornia detention camp. Perhaps both of them remembered the meeting. Ruby's police contacts in Dallas made him an ideal choice to deal with Oswald. He subsequently denied that anyone asked him to carry out the crime, although in a well-publicized and rambling statement he also told Chief Justice Warren and other commissioners that he could tell them much more if they could bring him to Washington from Dallas.[47]

Ruby's role in eliminating Oswald, the Odio incident, and statements by John Martino and his son Edward, along with the testimony of Dr. Wood and his son Sterling and that of the car salesman Albert K. Bogard, are probably the most powerful direct pieces of evidence that the assassination of President Kennedy came about through a conspiracy. Some of them tie the assassination to the much broader web of circumstantial evidence involving organized crime, anti-Castro Cubans, and, more tangentially, extreme conservatives and right-wing organizations who were in close touch with Martino and Hall. And in 1978, as the HSCA was concluding its work, it seemed to come upon conclusive scientific evidence that more than one gunman had fired in Dealey Plaza. In subsequent years that evidence has been complicated by claims and counter-claims of sufficient weight to make it much less than conclusive, yet the questions it raises and attempts to answer are crucial and have never been resolved satisfactorily.

The possibility that a shot was fired at President Kennedy from the grassy knoll ahead of and to the right of the motorcade has been hotly debated since the Warren Report appeared. Initially, two kinds of evidence set off the controversy. To begin with, about one third of all eyewitnesses thought that some or all of the shots came from that area, and photos taken seconds after the shooting show a number of people, including at least one policeman, running up the hill in that direction.[48] One well-placed eyewitness who was watching the motorcade from the top of a building on Houston Street actually saw a man running into the rail yard from that area immediately afterward.[49] Second, the backward movement of President Kennedy's head after being struck by the fatal shot, clearly visible on the Zapruder film, seemed to indicate to many that the bullet came from the front. That belief was mistaken, but the possibility of a second gunman on the knoll persisted.

During the second half of 1978, as it wound up its work, the HSCA enlisted the help of experts in evaluating tape recordings made at Dallas police headquarters on November 22, 1963. After analyzing the original recordings and then re-recording shots from two locations in Dallas, three experts—James Barger, Mark Weiss, and Ernest Aschkenasy—concluded that the open microphone of a motorcycle policeman had recorded at least four shots during the assassination itself, and that there was a 95% probability that one of the shots had been fired from the grassy knoll to the right front of the motorcade. This led the committee to conclude that President Kennedy was probably assassinated by a conspiracy.[50]

Then several years later, a panel of the National Research Council (NRC), assisted by a tip from an independent researcher, concluded that words heard on the tape, which came from a separate recording channel, proved that the sounds Barger, Weiss, and Ashkenazy thought were shots must have occurred more than one minute *after* the assassination of President Kennedy.[51] In 2001 another independent researcher, Donald Thomas, published a paper in a British journal *Science and Justice* that attempted to explain this anomaly and once again establish that the original recording proved that someone had shot at the President from the grassy knoll.[52] Several years later some members of the original NRC panel wrote another as yet unpublished paper arguing that some of Thomas's data, and therefore, his conclusions, were invalid, and claiming once again that the sounds on the tape could not have been the shots in Dealey Plaza.

My argument—that Oswald shot and killed President Kennedy at the behest of organized crime, and specifically of Santo Trafficante, Carlos Marcello, John Martino, and possibly Sam Giancana—does not depend on proof of a second shooter on the grassy knoll, or anywhere else. But a review of the acoustic evidence, in my opinion, does show that the findings of the HSCA experts simply cannot be reconciled with the findings of the NRC panel, and that only some new insight or technical evidence can put the controversy to rest. Either Barger in particular made some fundamental scientific mistake from the beginning—which, given his qualifications, hardly seems likely—or there is some other explanation for the words on the tape. While this issue, like so many others in the case, has aroused strong emotions on both sides, no disinterested person, it seems to me, can regard the controversy about the acoustic evidence as settled yet.

To understand the disagreement, we must look first at who James Barger was and what he found. Barger worked for Bolt, Beranek, and Newman, perhaps the leading acoustics analysis firm in the United States at the time. BBN had done substantial work for the U.S. Navy, investigated the eighteen-minute gap for the Watergate special prosecutor, and analyzed a recording of the 1970 shootings at Kent State to determine how many shots were fired and where they came from. As Barger explained in his written report to the committee, the Dallas police had two different radio channels, 1 and 2, that allowed patrol cars and motorcycles to communicate with headquarters. During the presidential motorcade, officers were supposed to use channel 2, and Chief Curry did so from his car in the motorcade. But several officers may have mistakenly been using channel 1, and one of them, a motorcycle policeman, evidently had his microphone stuck in the "on" position for about five minutes around the time of the shooting. BBN filtered and analyzed his transmissions, recorded (as both channels were) on Dictabelts in police department headquarters, to search for any impulses that might have represented gunshots.[53]

Barger initially found four impulse patterns that looked like possible gunshots. After filtering out noise, a plot of remaining impulses showed "five impulse patterns introduced by a source other than the motorcycle. Upon closer examination, all but one of these patterns were sufficiently similar to have had the same source, and the impulses contained in these patterns appeared to have shapes similar to the expected characteristics of a shock wave and of a muzzle blast."[54] Using the dispatcher's periodic announcements of the time—which could have contained inaccuracies of as much as a minute—Barger determined that these events happened in the minute after 12:30 p.m., which Chief Curry's transmissions on channel 2 also confirmed as the minute of the assassination. He ascertained, critically, that the tape contained no other similar impulse patterns during the period of the recording. Using 0 seconds to represent the time of the first shot, the remaining three impulses occurred after a little less than 2 seconds, 8 seconds, and 8.5 seconds.

To find out whether the impulses actually represented gunfire, Barger led a team into Dealey Plaza in 1978 to run a new series of tests. They laid an array of 36 microphones along the motorcade route, and fired a series of shots at the positions of the limousine at the time of the actual shots from both the sixth floor of the TSBD and from the grassy knoll. They then digitized those results and compared them to the impulses on the tape. What they found was striking: the best matches between newly recorded impulses and the impulses on the tape occurred along the array of microphones moving in the direction of the motorcade and some distance behind the presidential limousine. In other words, the impulses on the tape did appear to be gunshots, recorded by a motorcycle in the motorcade as it moved through Dealey Plaza. The first two and the last impulses specifically matched shots fired from the TSBD. The third of the four, which came only half a second before the fourth shot and thus could not also have been fired by Oswald, matched a shot fired from the grassy knoll.

More specifically, a movie taken on Houston Street—the street the motorcade passed through before making a hairpin turn onto Elm, where the assassination occurred—showed a motorcycle policeman some distance behind the limousine. The committee identified the policeman on the motorcycle as Officer H. B. McLain, who testified on December 28, 1978, that his microphone could have been set to channel 1 and that the mike sometimes did become stuck in the open position.[55] Barger hypothesized that the motorcycle had sped up after the limousine made the turn, closing the gap. It had audibly slowed down shortly before the first shots were fired, indicating to him that it was about to make the hairpin turn, and had remained at the slower rate of speed during the time that the shots were fired. With the help of additional calculations, they concluded: "The complete motorcycle trajectory shows that the motorcycle traveled north on Houston St., at about 17 mph. It slowed to about 10 mph at a point about 40 ft south of the corner at Elm St., and then continued west on Elm St. at about 10 mph. This single diminution of speed is compatible with the single diminution of motorcycle noise about 3 sec before the first shot is heard."[56]

Barger had to allow for the possibility of random noise that might create false matches, and he employed statistical tests to try to calculate the probability that he had correctly identified impulses recorded through the microphone of a motorcycle traveling in the motorcade, and to estimate the probability that particular impulses actually represented gunshots. Based on a chi square test, he concluded that the probability of the best matches accidentally occurring along the array of microphones at a speed of 10 mph was only 1%. Based on further tests, he concluded that "the individual probabilities that shots occurred at each of the four times at which correlations exceeded threshold are 88%, 88%, 50%, and 75%, listed in order of increasing time." That meant two 88% probabilities of the first two shots from the TSBD at 0 and about 2 seconds (with 0 seconds indicating the first shot), a 50% probability of a shot from the grassy knoll (the source of the 1978 recording that matched) at 8 seconds, and a 75% probability of another shot from the TSBD at 8.5 seconds.[57] The matches for the first shot came from microphones placed on Houston Street shortly before the corner of Elm. Officer McLain told the HSCA that he remembered hearing only one shot, when he was about half way between Main and Elm on Houston. (He was facing the TSBD at that time.)[58]

Nor is this all. At the same time that Barger was conducting his investigation, an entirely independent team of experts was analyzing the Zapruder film in a separate attempt to time the shots. They used a combination of "panning error"—visual indications on the film that Zapruder had jiggled his camera in response to the sound of gunshots— and the reactions of Governor Connally and eyewitnesses. Using 0 seconds for the first panning error they found, they also found clear evidence of panning errors roughly 6.5 and 7.2 seconds later, and an additional, less strong indication of a second shot between 1.5 and 2 seconds after the first one. Their methods were inevitably less exact than a tape recording, but their independent results were very consistent with the sequence that Barger found on the tape.[59] The odds against such consistent results happening by chance are astronomically high.

As Barger explained, his computations were necessarily inexact because he had no way to know exactly where the motorcycle was at the time the various shots were fired. The test microphones were spaced 18 feet apart, and thus the motorcycle could have been as much as 9 feet or more from a microphone at the time a given shot was fired. That different distance from the source of the impulse would have changed the echo pattern that was part of the observed impulse, making a less than perfect match with the original transmission.

The committee was obviously most interested in the third impulse and its 50% probability of matching a shot fired from the grassy knoll. They enlisted two other scientists, Mark Weiss and Ernest Aschkenasy of Queens College, to see if they could devise a means of refining these results. Weiss and Aschkenasy did so by modeling how the echoes from shots would have bounced off the various structures in Dealey Plaza to produce the impulse patterns recorded from test shots. That allowed them to construct a model that could predict exactly what impulse patterns would be received at any point in Dealey Plaza, and not simply at the places where microphones had been placed. They found a location about 5 feet from the microphone that had generated the 50% probability of a match which, they believed, was the exact spot at which the motorcycle recorded the third shot. "The probability that they obtained their match because the two matched patterns were due to the same source (gunfire from the knoll) is about 95%," Barger said.[60] Unfortunately, by this point the HSCA had run out of time and money and could not ask Weiss and Aschkenasy to do the same kind of modeling for the three shots that they thought they had detected from the TSBD. The HSCA therefore announced a "high-probability" that President Kennedy was assassinated as a result of a conspiracy involving two gunmen, Oswald in the TSBD and an unidentified shooter on the knoll. That finding did not remain uncontested for very long.

The committee recommended further investigation by the FBI, but the bureau's Technical Services Division concluded in December 1980 that Barger, Weiss, and Aschkenasy had not proven that the Dictabelt recording contained any gunfire at all. The FBI then asked the National Research Council to convene a panel of experts to examine the evidence further, which it did. The panel, chaired by Professor Norman Ramsay of Harvard University, reported in 1982 that the recording was *not,* in fact, of gunfire. Not only did this panel question the methods and conclusions of Barger, Weiss, and Aschkenasy but it also presented new evidence that the impulses they had identified as gunfire had occurred one minute *after* the assassination of the President.[61]

The panel began by laying great stress on the sounds of approaching and retreating sirens that appeared on the channel 1 tape some time after the assassination, arguing that McLain's microphone should have picked up the sirens continuously from the time that they were turned on quite soon after the assassination when the motorcade set out at high speed for Parkland Hospital, and that the sirens on the tape seemed to have been recorded from a stationary microphone that the motorcade passed. Barger, however, had in fact already anticipated this argument, stating in his report that McLain's microphone would not have picked up the sirens over the noise generated by his engine, and also noting that more than one microphone tuned to channel 1 and stuck in the "on" position could have transmitted to police headquarters at the same time—a point that McLain had confirmed in his testimony.

Then the panel questioned the statistical reasoning that led Barger, Weiss, and Aschkenasy to conclude that the third impulse had a 95% probability of being a gunshot. Considering that shot totally in isolation, they argued that the HSCA experts had entertained only one alternative hypothesis, that the impulses might have been random (or "Poisson") noise, but that there were other possible sources for them, although they did not explain exactly what those might have been or why they might have mimicked shots in Dealey Plaza. This part of their analysis was seriously incomplete, because it did not ask how some other source might have produced not one but *four* impulses that not only matched those generated by shots fired from the TSBD and the grassy knoll but were spaced in the same time sequence as had been identified by the photographic expert analysis. (They might, of course, have argued that some other source generated the impulse matched with a shot from the knoll, even if the TSBD matches were genuine, but this was not specifically stated.)[62]

These arguments, however, faded into relative insignificance when the panel investigated another line of inquiry suggested by a private researcher who had copies of the channel 1 and 2 tapes. He pointed out, and the panel confirmed with the help of sophisticated spectrographic analysis (sometimes called "voiceprints"), that the channel 1 tape included cross talk from channel 2, which Chief Curry was using from the lead car in the motorcade. The cross talk had evidently been recorded through a channel 1 open mike—either McLain's or someone else's—from the speaker on a nearby motorcycle that was correctly set to channel 2. The first significant piece of cross talk on channel 1 is "Hold everything," which spectrographic analysis found to be identical with Sheriff Bill Decker's statement on channel 2, "Hold everything secure until the homicide and other investigators can get there." On channel 2, that statement occurred at least 50 seconds after Chief Curry, seeing that the President and Governor Connally had been hit, ordered the motorcade, "Go to the hospital"—in other words, at least a minute after the assassination. (The phrase "at least" applies to intervals between speech on channel 2, because the Dictabelt on channel 2 was voice-activated and would pause after 4 seconds of silence. Channel 1 was also being recorded by a voice-activated Dictabelt, but it was running continuously for five critical minutes because of the stuck-open mike.) But the "Hold everything" barely audible on channel 1 occurred almost exactly at the time of the last two impulses interpreted to be shots from the TSBD and from the grassy knoll. The cross talk evidence, therefore, seemed to indicate that those impulses, whatever they were, occurred about a minute after the President was assassinated.

A second, far more audible instance of cross talk occurred several minutes later and included the words "You want me . . . Stemmons." On channel 2 that statement came 189 seconds after the chief said "Go to the hospital," meaning that it was more than 189 seconds after the assassination, and on channel 1 it came 171 seconds after the last of the impulses interpreted to be shots, indicating once again that those impulses must have been generated after the assassination.[63] The panel then considered the possibility that the cross talk had accidentally been recorded on the channel 1 Dictabelt at a later date, but rejected this hypothesis on what certainly appear to be very sound scientific grounds.[64] For this reason the panel concluded unambiguously that the impulses on the tape could not have been gunshots and recommended against any further studies of the question.[65]

There the matter rested until 2001, when an independent researcher named D. B. Thomas, a scientist for the U.S. Department of Agriculture, published a new argument in the British forensic journal *Science and Justice*.[66] Thomas began by attacking some of the limitations of the NRC panel's approach, in particular their exclusive focus on the grassy knoll shot. He noted, for instance, that the best matches of test shots with the impulses on the channel 1 Dictabelt occurred along the array of microphones at an apparent speed of 18 mph—the speed of the motorcade. Thomas calculated the probability of finding the matches in a single topographic sequence accidentally at .008 or 125 to 1. That the spacing of the microphones matched a speed of 18 mph obviously made the probability of chance much lower, although he did not make an additional calculation.[67]

Thomas then took up the issue of cross talk, focusing on an important anomaly. Because "Hold everything" on channel 2 occurred one minute after Chief Curry ordered "Go to the hospital," the NRC panel had concluded that the sounds thought to be shots must have occurred after the assassination. Thomas, however, pointed out something else. The "You want me . . . Stemmons" broadcast on channel 2 occurred 180 seconds after Chief Curry said, "Go to the hospital"—words he must have spoken immediately after the assassination, and quite possibly even before the final fatal shot hit President Kennedy, since both Kennedy and Governor Connally were obviously wounded seconds before that. But on channel 1, "You want me . . . Stemmons" occurred only 171 seconds after the sounds the HSCA had found to be shots. Using evidence that the channel 1 recorder had been running about 5% too quickly—a point not disputed by the NRC panel—Thomas adjusted that figure to 179 seconds. That would have indicated that Chief Curry said "Go to the hospital" in the midst of the four impulses found to be shots.

Putting it another way, Thomas indeed identified a very important anomaly. On channel 1, an estimated 179 seconds of real time passed between the fragmentary "Hold everything" and "You want me . . . Stemmons," but on channel 2 only 120 seconds elapsed between the clear recordings of those two signals. Thomas therefore suggested that the "Hold everything" on channel 1 was a minute earlier than it should have been because the recording needle had skipped backward at that moment. Although he did not mention it, a book by a Dallas policeman confirms that both machines sometimes missed parts of transmissions, re-recorded the same transmission several times, or created "ghost signals."[68]

The NRC panel had acknowledged the 60-second difference in the spacing of the two events on the two channels but argued that the channel 2 recorder was operating on a voice-activated basis, and it could therefore have been stopped for a total of 60 seconds between those two events. While this was theoretically possible, Thomas cited findings from the original Barger report that seemed to rule it out. The dispatchers for both channels in Dallas police headquarters routinely attempted to announce the time every minute or two. Granted that they might be as much as 30 seconds off in any particular case, this had enabled Barger to check on the difference between recorded time and real time on channel 2, and the results were quite remarkable. A graph he produced showed that the tape was running for only about 2.5 minutes between the dispatcher's calls of 12:22 and 12:30 p.m., showing that it had indeed stopped for several minutes during that time. Yet the same graph shows almost exactly 6 minutes of recorded time between the dispatcher's calls of 12:30 and 12:36 p.m., indicating, as Thomas argued, that the tape did *not* stop recording during that time, certainly not for as much as a minute.[69] If that is true, then the critical "Hold everything" overdub on channel 1 must be chronologically in the wrong position.

For these reasons, Thomas concluded that the key impulses had in fact occurred at the time of the assassination and that they did represent three shots from the TSBD and one from the grassy knoll. He also hypothesized that the impulses showed a fifth shot or "rogue" shot of unknown origin, one that the original HSCA panel had dismissed. But neither Thomas nor the NRC addressed another problem. Barger placed the key sounds on the channel 1 tape at 12:30 p.m., the time of the assassination, based upon the dispatcher's previous announcements of the time on channel 1. The National Academy panel did not address the issue of how the dispatcher could have been off by a full minute in announcing the time, as their analysis implies.

Four members of the original National Academy panel and Richard Garwin of IBM published a rebuttal to Thomas in the same British journal in 2005.[70] Their analysis is by far the most complicated and intricate of the four that have been published, and it is impossible to summarize it fully here. But with respect to the critical issue raised by Thomas, they found a somewhat different time interval between the key recordings of "Hold everything" and "You want . . . Stemmons" than he and his predecessors had. They found an interval of approximately 144 seconds (plus or minus a few seconds) between those two events on channel 2, and an interval of about 35 seconds longer (correcting for the speed of the tape) between the two events on channel 1.

In other words, in contrast to the original NRC report (which four of them had helped to write), their new paper postulated only about 35 seconds of stopped recording on channel 2 instead of a full minute. The original panel, Lineker and his colleagues said, had miscalculated by making an improper adjustment for forward skips on channel 2 that were actually automatically corrected for. Such a gap of 35 seconds or so, they argued, was consistent with Barger's original graph. They also cited other sounds on the tapes and other technical evidence suggesting that the "Hold" on channel 1 did not result from a skip.[71]

Lineker and his colleagues made a strong argument that the impulses on channel 1 occurred a minute after the assassination and cannot therefore be shots, but they cannot prove that channel 2 was stopped for 35 seconds. And Thomas was right to raise another point. The odds against

Barger and his colleagues having identified a unique set of impulses on the channel 1 tape which just happened, by chance, to match the recordings of actual test shots in Dealey Plaza recorded along an array of microphones at a speed of 18 mph seem enormous. That probability in turn has to be multiplied against the chance that the time sequencing of the impulses would match quite closely with the timing of the three or four shots found by the separate panel that analyzed the panning error in the Zapruder film. Until someone can show that there was no basis for Barger's original conclusions, the issue of whether channel 1 actually recorded a shot from the grassy knoll will, in my opinion, remain open.

As Lineker and his colleagues note at the conclusion of their paper, the National Archives found in 2004 that the original recording of channel 1 could no longer be played, and the status of the original recording of channel 2 is not clear. All of their work was done from copies. NARA is now using a new "optical stylus" technology to produce a new and precise copy of at least channel 1, and eventually the issue may be resolved conclusively. Meanwhile, these investigators sensibly added that their findings in no way rule out a conspiracy to assassinate President Kennedy, even if Oswald, in the Texas School Book Depository window, fired the only shots.

17

Keeping Secrets

In 1975 John Martino told his business partner Fred Claassen that the original assassination plan called for Oswald to be met at the Texas Theatre, taken out of the country, and eliminated. Had he disappeared amid rumors of a mysterious plane flying into Mexico City late on the afternoon of November 22, with a passenger who then boarded a waiting plane for Havana, the pressure on the U.S. government to move against Castro would have been significant, especially after his contacts with Soviet and Cuban authorities in Mexico City had become known. Oswald's encounter with Tippit and his arrest at the Texas Theatre threw a monkey wrench into the works, but Martino, Frank Sturgis, the DRE, and Ed Butler of INCA all instantaneously launched an extensive disinformation campaign to place the assassination squarely on Castro's doorstep. Some intelligence personnel and high officials suspected foreign involvement, but these allegations were not seriously pursued.

Within hours of Oswald's arrest, the DRE in Miami was using Carlos Bringuier's confrontation with Oswald in New Orleans to suggest that Castro was behind the assassination. John Martino was making phone calls the same afternoon arguing that Oswald had to be tied to Castro. Jose Antonio Lanusa of the DRE immediately called his case officer, George Joannides, and passed on older reports from Bringuier about Oswald's Fair Play for Cuba Committee activities. Lanusa claimed that Joannides told him to sit on the information for at least an hour, but Lanusa did not wait and began calling the press. The next day, the DRE brought out a special edition of its newspaper, *Trinchera,* featuring paired photos of Oswald and Castro and clearly suggesting that Castro was behind the crime.[1]

Within two hours of Oswald's arrest, someone had briefed Hal

Hendrix, a Scripps-Howard newsman in Miami with extensive CIA connections. Hendrix had won a Pulitzer Prize for his reporting on the 1962 missile crisis for the *Miami News,* which included stories on the construction of Soviet missile bases weeks before President Kennedy confirmed them to the nation. The DRE was a critical intelligence source for those stories. In September 1963 Hendrix had written a story predicting the coup that overthrew leftist President Juan Bosch of the Dominican Republic—published the day before the overthrow took place. Earlier in the year he had written a series of articles suggesting that Bosch was too tolerant of Communists—articles which the American ambassador thought were designed to encourage Bosch's Dominican enemies. Evidence developed later suggested that Hendrix had a decades-long relationship with the CIA. His Scripps-Howard colleague, Seth Kantor, who was on the scene of the assassination, telephoned Hendrix in Miami at about 6:00 p.m. Dallas time—a little more than two hours after Oswald's arrest. Hendrix promptly gave Kantor the story of Oswald's radio debate with Bringuier and Stuckey in New Orleans and his FPCC activities.[2] That same night Lanusa called Daniel James, secretary of the Washington-based Citizens Committee for a Free Cuba, to give him the Oswald story, and James called the Washington field office of the FBI.[3]

On November 24, the day Ruby shot Oswald, the Senate Internal Security Subcommittee—which had been deeply involved in the Bayo-Pawley raid—began a brief investigation of its own designed to expose any links between Oswald and international Communism. Their first witness was Edward Butler of the Information Council of the Americas, one of the participants in the radio debate with Oswald back in August. Speaking authoritatively in a prepared statement, Butler said that Oswald showed no signs of insanity but had clearly been thoroughly indoctrinated in Communist propaganda. He argued that Oswald's "tremendous amount of Communist indoctrination" was his primary motivating factor, and asked the committee to consider "the responsibility here or the lack of responsibility for the assassination, they should consider the official responsibility of those who adhere to Communist doctrine," including "International Publishers, and all the other Soviet branches, and the news media, like radio Havana, who put this incendiary material on the airwaves, for people of this kind to hear."

Butler told the committee that he had decided Oswald was dangerous after hearing his interview with Bill Stuckey. But when asked whether hunting local Communists was part of his job, Butler denied it—a very different story from the one he told Garry Wills a few years later. When committee counsel Jay Sourwine asked him if Oswald might have been motivated by "directives he had been given," Butler declined to speculate. The SISS held no more hearings, but on December 5 one of its investigators had an interesting interview with Ruth Paine in Dallas. She repeated that Oswald had completely concealed his trip to Mexico from both her and Marina and added that she had never heard him discuss the FPCC. She also confirmed having taken him for two or three driving lessons in parking lots. She had never heard Oswald talk about President Kennedy at all, and she mentioned his fondness for football games and war movies on television.[4]

On Friday, November 29, Richard Cain—the Chicago mob's informant in the Sheriff's Office—dropped into the Chicago CIA Domestic Contacts Office, on a mission that put his mentor, Sam Giancana, squarely into the picture as part of the mob's disinformation campaign. Cain had been in touch with that office repeatedly over the years, most recently in September, when he passed on news of attempts by the DRE to make a major arms purchase—parallel to the similar effort they were making in Dallas.[5] Now Cain claimed that the Sheriff's Office had learned in February 1963 that the Chinese Communists had begun to control the Chicago Fair Play for Cuba Committee and that a February meeting of that committee had discussed the assassination of President Kennedy. He even claimed to have heard that Oswald had visited Chicago in April. Cain had already given this story to a local newspaper columnist, Margaret Daly, who published it.[6] When the CIA Domestic Contacts office suggested to Cain that he give his new information to the FBI, he indicated some reluctance to do so. A few days earlier, on November 27, FBI headquarters had received another rumor about the FPCC: that the head of the Chicago chapter, John Rossin, had known and subsidized Oswald.[7]

Other evidence suggests foreknowledge of the assassination in Chicago. On November 21, the day before Kennedy was shot, Chicago Secret Service agents heard a disturbing rumor about the DRE from one of their informants, Tom Mosely. He was planning the sale of arms to two Cubans: a local bus driver, Homero Echeverria, and a man from Miami whom the FBI later identified as Juan Francisco Blanco Fernandez, a member of the military section of the DRE. "We now have plenty of money," Echeverria told Mosely. "Our new backers are Jews. As soon as we (possibly they) take care of the Kennedys, we will be ready to move," which Mosely interpreted as referring to a return to Cuba. Echeverria identified his organization as the Student Federation of Revolutionaries, an obvious translation of the DRE.[8] The Secret Service wanted to pursue the case, but the FBI claimed jurisdiction over all assassination investigations and then dropped it.[9]

The Chicago mob was hopeful about the consequences of Kennedy's death. "I tell you in another two months the FBI will be like it was five years ago," remarked Giancana henchman Chuckie English in early December. "They won't be around no more. They're gonna investigate them Fair Play for Cuba's. They call that more detrimental than us guys. They'll say these local problems at home, let the local police handle it. The FBI won't be investigating competitive business. They won't be calling in businessmen and saying did they put the muscle on you and things like that. Are you scared? Did they use fear?" Giancana, meanwhile, seemed to be taking an intense interest in the Lake Tahoe kidnapping of Frank Sinatra, Jr., who was held from December 8 through December 10. Sam had reportedly visited Sinatra in November in Palm Springs, perhaps to secure payment for his interest in the Cal-Neva Lodge, which the singer's association with Giancana had forced him to sell.[10]

A sustained campaign involving some familiar names had begun in the Miami area as well. Within days of the assassination, Jerry Buchanan of the Pompano Beach *Sun-Sentinel* quoted Frank Sturgis to the effect that Oswald had been connected to Cuban G-2 agents in New Orleans and in Mexico City (the story of Oswald's September trip was broken by Mexican journalists over the weekend) and that he had tried to infiltrate anti-Castro organizations in Miami. When the FBI interviewed Sturgis on November 27, he said he had no proof.[11] Undeterred, Buchanan reprinted the same story on December 4.[12] Then radio personality Alan Courtney quoted John Martino, of all people, to the effect that Oswald had flown from Mexico City to Cuba in September or October of 1963 and repeated that Oswald had also visited Miami. Queried on November 29, Martino told the FBI that his information came from Cuban exiles whom he could not identify.[13]

Martino now had connections among the right-wing press thanks to his ghostwriter, Nathan Weyl, and in mid-December he published an extraordinary article on the assassination in the weekly *Human Events.* Drawing on rumors that had been circulating in right-wing circles for about six months, he argued that Castro had arranged the Kennedy assassination to forestall an invasion of Cuba that would coincide with a Titoist coup against Castro, led, he said, by former Castroite Huber Matos, now a prisoner on the Isle of Pines. He claimed that Kennedy had already cleared these plans with Khrushchev and that Soviet troops would have left Cuba after the coup so as to ensure Kennedy's re-election, which the Soviet leader avidly desired. He also elaborated on his claims about Oswald, stating that the assassin had offered his services to "Gerry Patrick," Hemming's usual alias, to the DRE, and also to JURE. The last suggestion sounds like a reference to the Odio incident, which had taken place in the same week that Martino himself had visited Dallas. Martino's comment appeared in print many months before the Odio incident became public knowledge, indicating that he had known about it.[14]

A disinformation bombshell dropped in Mexico City on November 26, when Gilberto Alvarado, a Nicaraguan intelligence operative and CIA source, told the agency that he had seen Oswald receive $6,500 in the Cuban Embassy in return for agreeing to kill Kennedy. Fortunately for the investigation, Alvarado had apparently been poorly briefed about Oswald's visit, and he dated the encounter on September 18, eight days before Oswald left the United States. He also claimed to have called the U.S. Embassy to warn them before the assassination, but no record of such a call was found. Although J. Edgar Hoover quickly concluded that the story was false, the U.S. ambassador to Mexico, Thomas Mann—a fellow Texan and friend of President Johnson—evidently believed it. On November 28 he cabled Washington that the assassination looked to him like the kind of thing the Cubans might do and urged a thorough investigation. The Alvarado report went right to the White House and may have helped convince President Johnson to appoint a commission to review the FBI report on the assassination. The allegation faded after Alvarado failed a polygraph administered by a CIA expert and recanted his story, although he revived it only days after the examination.[15]

On November 30, CIA headquarters received another alarming report. A foreign diplomat—probably an Italian—claimed that the Cubana

Airlines flight from Mexico City to Havana on November 22 had been delayed from 5 p.m. until 10 p.m., and that before departing it had taken on an extra passenger who arrived on a private plane from Mexico City at 9:30 p.m. This also turned out to be disinformation, when the CIA discovered with the help of its Mexico City phone taps that the flight had actually left at 8:35 p.m. after a normal four-hour layover at the airport.[16]

A number of people inside Cuba apparently decided to take advantage of the situation to spread a few rumors of their own. On November 28 an anonymous Cuban mailed a letter to Lee Harvey Oswald, General Delivery, Dallas, addressing him in Spanish as "friend Lee" and referring to plans to bring him to Havana to meet "the chief" after the "big job" was done. The letter, which bore the date November 10, was an obvious hoax, but Hoover referred to it as important evidence in a December 12 conversation with J. Lee Rankin, counsel to the newly appointed Warren Commission.[17] A similar letter from Cuba to Attorney General Robert Kennedy turned out to have been typed on the same machine.[18]

Another letter from a Cuban to a relative in Florida, passed to the FBI in the second week in December, developed longer legs. Dated November 27, it included the following passage: "On the other hand, you have the fact that our government agreed that Oswald had gone to the Cuban Embassy in Mexico to ask for a Cuban visa en route to Moscow. Could he have been trying to get a visa or money for services he was going to render? Besides, it is known here that Rubinstein was here a little less than a year ago visiting a Mr. Pranski, owner of a shop dealing in tourist articles, located on Prado Street between Animas and Trocadero, opposite the Sevilla Biltmore. In short, there is something rotten in Denmark." "Pranski" was reputed to be either a Czech or a Pole, and a friend of Fidel Castro.[19]

"Pranski," quickly renamed "Praskin," came to the attention of John Martino, who passed the story on to ghostwriter Weyl and his wife Sylvia. In January the story appeared in a New York anti-Communist sheet, *The Herald of Freedom,* and it was soon being circulated by another New York ex-Communist and ex-Soviet agent, Hede Massing. Although the FBI had already located the original source of the rumor, Weyl and Martino tried to inflate its significance by claiming that it had come from former Batista official Carlos Marques Sterling or from a contact of

Martino's in the Cuban underground.[20] Massing actually gave the FBI a garbled account of the Bayo-Pawley raid, and the New York office got a fuller report on it from the CIA, including Pawley's name. Unfortunately, no one in the bureau regarded the raid as having any broader significance.[21]

Carlos Marques Sterling did not back up Martino's story, and during April and May Martino stalled off the FBI (and brushed off a threat that the Warren Commission might subpoena him) on at least six different occasions, refusing to identify his source and telling various elaborate lies about him.[22] The bureau finally concluded that it could safely disregard the story, and the Warren Commission staff, which had considered calling Martino to testify, decided not to do so.[23] None of the FBI documents regarding this rumor ever referred to Martino's mob connections. Meanwhile, DRE leaders Manuel Salvat and Jose Lanusa also gave the story to an investigator of the Senate Internal Security Subcommittee. In 1978 the HSCA found Graziela Rubio Guerra, who had written the November 27 letter about Ruby, and she admitted that she had received the information from an unidentified Cuban underground organization.[24]

These disinformation campaigns launched by various mobsters and Cubans failed to goad the U.S. government into pursuing the Communist link, even though some of the nation's highest-level investigators and officials, including President Lyndon Johnson himself, had similar suspicions of their own. In setting up the Warren Commission during the week following the assassination, Johnson referred to the need to put an end to speculation that could plunge the United States into a world war, and in subsequent years he made many comments suggesting that Castro was responsible for the assassination—especially after 1967, when he received a fairly full account of the plots against Castro. In 1964 official Washington decided to let sleeping dogs lie.

In the eighteen months before the Kennedy assassination, Carlos Marcello, Santo Trafficante, and Jimmy Hoffa had all expressed the hope that such an event might relieve the government's pressure on organized crime. To a large extent, they got their wish. Robert Kennedy remained attorney general for only nine months after the assassination, resigning to run for the Senate from New York State, and the pace of the campaign against the mob fell off very quickly. In 1963, attorneys from the Justice

Department's Organized Crime section spent 1,081 days in court, 6,177 days in the field, and 1,353 days before grand juries, all roughly tenfold increases since 1960. But by 1966 the corresponding figures were 606, 3,480, and 373.[25] One high-profile case, however, still took its course. In his already-scheduled trial in Chattanooga, Jimmy Hoffa was convicted of jury tampering on March 4, 1964, and sentenced to eight years in prison. Three months later, on July 16, Hoffa was convicted in Chicago for misuse of union funds and given an additional five years.[26] And that conviction, ironically, led to the first leak of the CIA-mob plots against Castro.

Hoffa, Marcello, and Trafficante now launched a three-year campaign to keep the Teamster leader out of jail. Edward Grady Partin, the Louisiana ex-convict and Teamster who had initially approached the government in 1962 with his story of Hoffa's plans to kill Robert Kennedy, had provided the key evidence of jury tampering at the Chattanooga trial. Killing him would do no good. To save Hoffa, Partin must recant his testimony. Partin claimed that both a New Orleans municipal judge and Hoffa's "foster child" Charles O'Brien offered him six- or seven-figure sums to change his story, but he refused. On December 12, 1966, the Supreme Court denied Hoffa's appeal, although Earl Warren dissented on the grounds that Partin's background as a "jailbird" should have disqualified him as a credible witness.

Like Marcello, who was still successfully fighting his deportation, Hoffa knew how to drag out legal proceedings. His attorneys filed a new motion to reverse the conviction, based on the superficially credible but actually bogus accusation that the Justice Department had bugged the defense team and the jury room in the Nashville trial. And meanwhile, Hoffa started a fateful chain of events by hiring a new lawyer, Washington attorney Edward Morgan, to help with the appeal. Morgan (whose clients also included Johnny Roselli and Robert Maheu, the principals in the CIA-mob anti-Castro assassination plots in 1960–61) decided to use what he knew about CIA covert activities to put pressure on Robert Kennedy and the government to let Hoffa off.

Morgan had begun his career as an FBI agent but left the bureau in the early 1940s. He had served as counsel to two of the most famous congressional investigations of the postwar era, the Pearl Harbor investigation of 1945–46 and the Tydings Committee probe of 1950, which investigated Senator Joseph McCarthy's charges of Communists in the State Department. On January 13, 1967, Morgan came to see Washington columnist Drew Pearson, the only journalist of that era who would print anything that he believed to be true. Pearson, as Morgan well knew, was quite close to President Johnson, and his stepson Tyler Abell worked at the White House. After swearing Pearson to secrecy, Morgan told him that he was representing a man—obviously Robert Maheu—who was under pressure to testify before a congressional committee, the Long Committee of the Senate, about illegal wiretapping. As Morgan related the story,

> Around 1961 after the Bay of Pigs fiasco, Bobby Kennedy had concocted the idea of assassinating Fidel Castro. Bobby had approached Central Intelligency [sic], which in turn had approached this man. This man had hired two gunmen from the underworld, and they had spent about six months preparing to bump off Castro. They had made a very survey [sic] of the situation in Havana, working through members of the underworld who had run the gambling joints down there in the past. They had even gone to the point where the two gunmen were given pills to take in a hurry if they were captured.
>
> However, Castro's intelligence was smarter than theirs, and the two men were apprehended, tortured, and finally killed. Before they were killed, however, they confessed that they were put up to the job by Kennedy. At this point Castro decided that two could play this game, and he hired Lee Oswald to kill Kennedy.

We have no way of knowing whether it was Maheu or Morgan who made critical changes in the story: falsely dating it after the Bay of Pigs instead of before, and blaming Robert Kennedy rather than Allen Dulles and the Eisenhower administration for the plot. But Morgan's motive became clear as the conversation proceeded, when he began talking about his new client. "Ed [Morgan] has also collected some amazing facts, he says, regarding the bugging of Hoffa at the Chattanooga trial. It goes much further than the Justice Department has admitted. Apparently Ed got the information from his former FBI associates . . . Ed says that the FBI even tapped inside the jury at the Hoffa trial, clearly a criminal offense."

Morgan was a shrewd Washington insider who, according to his family, never made a move without a strategy. He followed up the next day, visiting Pearson at his farm in Potomac, Maryland, and announcing that he would like Pearson to give his story to both President Johnson and Chief Justice Warren. He then further sweetened the pot with this bit of news.

> Ed also said that when Jimmy Hoffa had come to see him to ask him to take his case, Ed had replied that he didn't like to be on the side of a loser and that the chance of getting a rehearing before the Supreme Court was about one out of five hundred. This was before he had learned that there had been bugs in the jury room.
>
> "However," said Ed, "you have a very big and efficient union. And I am a strong Lyndon Johnson man. I want your word that no matter what happens we can have your union support in 1968 if Lyndon Johnson runs."
>
> Ed said that Hoffa looked at him for about thirty seconds and didn't reply. Finally he said: "Okay, I'll put it in writing."
>
> "This is not something you put in writing," said Ed. "This is an agreement from man to man. I'll take your word."

Morgan was not only giving Johnson powerful ammunition against his bitter rival Robert Kennedy but also putting Johnson in his and Hoffa's debt. Pearson saw LBJ on Monday, January 16, and immediately "told the President about Ed Morgan's law client and also about the labor pledge for 1968. Lyndon listened carefully and made no comment. There wasn't much he could say."[27] When Pearson saw Earl Warren on January 19, the chief justice was appropriately skeptical but added that Morgan needed to give the information to the FBI. On the next day Hoffa himself came to see Pearson and played the role of the responsible labor leader.[28] Then Pearson lunched with Morgan again on January 23, and Morgan mentioned that one of the conspirators—presumably Johnny Roselli, although he did not say so—had recently been arrested in Las Vegas and had told part of the story to newspaper editor Hank Greenspun, who had arranged for his release. He again brought up the accusations of bugging in the Hoffa trial.[29]

During February Pearson wrote two columns about bugging by RFK's Justice Department.[30] Pearson shared an office building with Irving Davidson, the Washington lobbyist, arms dealer, and Caribbean intriguer who had long relationships with Marcello and Hoffa, and on February 15 Davidson dropped in to say that Teamster Ed Partin was ready to recant his evidence of Hoffa's jury tampering.[31] But on February 27 the Supreme Court denied Hoffa's motion for a stay of his sentence based on the wiretapping accusations, and after another last-minute appeal failed, he entered federal prison on March 7.

On March 3 Pearson and his collaborator, Jack Anderson, gave garbled, unattributed accounts of Morgan's story in columns published under Pearson's name in the *New Orleans States-Item* and under Anderson's name in the *Miami Herald,* and under both their names in the *Washington Post.* The CIA, they wrote, had concocted an anti-Castro assassination plot after the Bay of Pigs, and Robert Kennedy had approved it. He added the story of the three assassins who had been caught and tortured—although without giving a date—and the speculation that Castro had retaliated through Oswald. "Shortly after Kennedy was gunned down," they wrote, "the FBI handed President Johnson a memo reporting that Cuban leaders had hoped for Kennedy's death"—a detail that seems to be without foundation, unless it is a garbled reference to Jack Childs's intelligence about Castro's reaction. "One version" of the story, they wrote, said that underworld figures had been recruited to carry out the plot.[32] Pearson and Anderson were maverick journalists who now enjoyed the protection of the famous libel case, *New York Times v. Sullivan* (1964), and while many of their scoops were eventually vindicated, their more conventional colleagues often ignored them.

Morgan met with FBI agents on March 21, 1967, and gave them a somewhat fuller version of his story than he had given Pearson. He cited two unnamed clients as his sources—obviously Maheu and Roselli—and described the plot against Castro once again. He said Castro's reaction to the plot had come to his clients through sources close to Castro, some of which, he said, now lived in New Jersey. And he added that when one of his clients heard that Oswald was the sole assassin of President Kennedy, he "laughs with tears in his eyes and shakes his head in apparent disagreement." This could only have been Roselli. The FBI apparently informed President Johnson about this but made no move whatsoever to follow up the lead. The bureau also apparently told Johnson what it knew about the CIA plots against Castro. On March 23 Johnson saw Richard Helms on another matter and asked him for a full report. The inspector general went to work.[33] Pearson's column started the uncovering of the circumstances surrounding the assassination, one that has continued until this day.

Just two months earlier, on January 3, 1967, Jack Ruby, suffering from cancer, died of a blood clot in his lung at Parkland Hospital in Dallas. Convicted of Oswald's murder and sentenced to death in the spring of 1964, Ruby had appealed his conviction. His lawyers had mounted a defense based on a purported case of psychomotor epilepsy, and Ruby never implicated anyone else in his crime.

When Morgan's efforts to keep Hoffa out of prison failed, Marcello and Trafficante opened a new front in their campaign to free him. New Orleans District Attorney Jim Garrison had begun investigating the Kennedy assassination, making front-page headlines during the first half of 1967 with promises of sensational revelations. Newspapers around the country had reported the sudden death from a cerebral hemorrhage of David Ferrie, Garrison's prime suspect, on February 22. Although Garrison had linked Ferrie to anti-Castro Cubans and revived the story of the accusations against him in New Orleans immediately after the assassination, he had said nothing about Ferrie's much more extensive links to Marcello and the mob. Garrison's lack of interest in Marcello's organized crime empire had already disturbed independent investigator Aaron Kohn of the New Orleans Crime Commission, and some years later Garrison was tried for having collected payoffs from pinball operators. Despite overwhelming evidence presented during the trial, he was acquitted.[34]

Less than a month after Ferrie's death, Garrison began using his investigation of the Kennedy murder to help Jimmy Hoffa and Carlos Marcello solve their problem with Ed Partin. On March 13, Irving Davidson went to the Washington Field Office of the FBI to inform agents that Garrison was going to subpoena Partin to ask him about a photograph of him with Jack Ruby and about a trip he was supposed to have made to Cuba in 1960, after which he returned claiming to be a friend of Fidel Castro. Three months later, in June, Garrison told a Baton Rouge radio station that he was investigating reports that Oswald, Ruby, and Partin had driven around New Orleans together.[35]

Not long after that, Frank Ragano, who represented both Trafficante and Hoffa (and who had given Hoffa's message that John F. Kennedy had to be killed to Trafficante and Marcello in May 1963), went to see Partin and told him he could get Garrison off his back if Partin would sign an affidavit recanting his testimony against Hoffa. Partin refused.[36] In his own book, Ragano explained how Marcello had agreed to set up the meeting in exchange for Hoffa's long-delayed approval of a loan from Teamster funds. He also claimed that at the meeting, which Partin's lawyer attended, Partin offered to perjure himself—an offer Ragano rejected because he was sure Partin was wearing a wire and that the federal government was trying to entrap him, Ragano, into suborning perjury.[37] Partin, in any case, did not recant, and Hoffa remained in prison.

An independent researcher, Dan Moldea, author of *The Hoffa Wars* (1978), was the first to suggest that Marcello, Trafficante, and Hoffa had conspired in the assassination of President Kennedy. He did so without benefit of Ragano's statements to that effect, which did not appear for another sixteen years. Ragano made very clear that Marcello and Trafficante were depending on Hoffa for a steady flow of loans from the Central States Pension Fund, but it also seems that the secret they shared was another powerful incentive for them to continue their cooperation—and a potentially deadly threat to any one of them who ever thought about revealing it. They were determined to keep Hoffa out of jail, but this was one fight that Robert Kennedy won. Hoffa spent the next five years in Lewisburg Federal Prison in Pennsylvania.

The CIA inspector general submitted his report to Richard Helms on May 23, 1967. It provided a scrupulous but far from complete account of the Castro assassination plots during the Kennedy administration and of the AMLASH affair of 1963. The inspector general concluded that the plots had *not* been authorized by higher authority, and acknowledged that then-Attorney General Kennedy had been falsely informed in the spring of 1962 that they had been terminated. These details must have been unwelcome news to Lyndon Johnson when Helms briefed him on the report, since Pearson had led him to believe that RFK was behind the whole enterprise. Still, the AMLASH story confirmed that the Kennedy administration was trying to kill Castro, and Johnson remarked more than once that John Kennedy's death was the result of it. "I'll tell you something that will rock you," Johnson once told television correspondent Howard K. Smith during his presidency. "Kennedy was trying to get Castro, but Castro got to him first." After leaving office, Johnson in

1969 told Walter Cronkite during interviews for broadcast that he believed Oswald had been part of an international conspiracy, but then had second thoughts and had CBS delete the remark.[38]

Meanwhile, Johnny Roselli, who was being threatened with deportation, enlisted his old case officer William Harvey to try to get the government off his back. In December 1968 Roselli was convicted of running a fraudulent card game in Los Angeles and began threatening again to break open the Castro assassination story. He started serving a five-year sentence in 1969. In November 1970 Helms, still CIA director, declined to help secure his release, and on January 18, 1971, Roselli retaliated through Jack Anderson, who had become the sole author of *The Washington Merry-Go-Round* after Drew Pearson died suddenly in 1969. In a new column, Anderson named Roselli and Maheu, along with James O'Connell and William Harvey of the CIA—but not Sam Giancana or Santo Trafficante—as co-conspirators in the assassination plots against Castro before the Bay of Pigs. This was a much more accurate story than the one provided by Edward Morgan four years earlier.[39] Still, it went nowhere, even after Anderson named Giancana as well and got O'Connell and Harvey to admit their acquaintance with and admiration for Roselli in another column on February 23. (O'Connell and Harvey refused to discuss the plot.) The inspector general had concluded in May 1967 that too many people knew about the mob's anti-Castro plot for it to remain secret, but the agency successfully resisted Roselli's pressure and was still denying all press inquiries relating to the plot when he was released in October 1973.[40]

Assassination plots against Castro continued after Kennedy's death, and in 1967 a failed plot allowed Cuban intelligence to identify two new suspects in the Kennedy assassination. Rolando Cubela (AMLASH) received a cache of weapons from the CIA and in December 1964 met with Manuel Artime in Europe to coordinate their activities. But Cubela was finally arrested in Cuba in 1965 and jailed, even though Cuban authorities apparently had no idea of the extent of his CIA contacts until much later. In 1966 Tony Cuesta of Commandos L, Herminio Diaz, and two other men were intercepted trying to land a boat in Cuba to mount another assassination attempt on Castro. Diaz and another man were killed, and Cuesta was severely wounded and captured.[41] He lost limbs in the battle and remained imprisoned in Cuba for more than ten years before his eventual release and return to Florida. Fabian Escalante of Cuban G-2 (the author of three books on assassination plots) interrogated him at great length. In a conference in 1993 and in his 2004 book *El Complot,* Escalante reported that Cuesta eventually had identified two anti-Castro Cubans, Eladio del Valle and his dead fellow raider Herminio Diaz, as having been present in Dallas on November 22, 1963.

Eladio del Valle, a police official and legislator under Batista, has been linked to the assassination of President Kennedy since 1967. Del Valle was beaten and stabbed to death in Miami in February of that year, on the day before David Ferrie, then under investigation by Jim Garrison, died in New Orleans of a stroke. Del Valle had come to the United States in 1959, and in late 1960 William Pawley recommended him to the CIA, saying that del Valle was ready to lead one hundred men into Cuba.[42] Cuban intelligence and the FBI agreed that del Valle had long-time links to Trafficante and had smuggled drugs on his behalf. Cuban intelligence also claimed that he had been involved in anti-Castro assassination plots in 1962 and that he was working with the DRE.[43] In April of 1967, two months after del Valle's death, a Cuban-American journalist claimed that del Valle and David Ferrie had worked together running bombing raids against Cuba in the early 1960s in Miami, but this has never been confirmed.[44] Somehow, despite del Valle's notoriety, the Assassination Records Review Board neglected to request his 201 from the CIA along with those of many other Cuban exiles, and the agency now refuses to release it.[45]

Months before the Kennedy assassination, the CIA had identified Herminio Diaz as the former chief of security at the mob-controlled Havana Riviera Hotel from 1958 through 1960. Diaz had reputedly helped murder a Batistaite official in Mexico City years earlier and managed to escape from prison with the help of the muralist Diego Rivera. In the late 1950s he had been involved in a murder plot against Batista and another conspiracy to kidnap liberal Costa Rican President Jose Figueres. He had remained in Cuba after the revolution and was jailed twice by Castro, once at the time of the Bay of Pigs and once in 1962, before finally making his way to the United States. In April 1961 he had been held at the La Cabana fortress in Havana, where John Martino had also been incarcerated. He had reportedly arrived in the United States in 1963 with a message for Carlos Prio Socarras about an assassination plot against Fidel Castro, and JMWAVE in September 1963 was considering recruiting him as an agent because of his ties to Efigenio Amejeiras Delgado, Castro's vice-minister of the armed forces, who was reportedly conspiring with Rolando Cubela. It is not clear from available files whether he was in fact recruited.[46] Cuban intelligence reported more specifically that Diaz had been a gangster since the 1940s with long-standing links to Santo Trafficante, who owned the Havana Riviera, and that he received Richard Cain in Havana in 1960 when Cain visited as part of the Giancana–Trafficante assassination plot. Escalante quoted Tony Cuesta to the effect that Diaz and del Valle had arrived in Dallas on November 20 and returned after the assassination with a great deal of money, but Cuesta provided no further details before his death in Miami in the early 1990s.[47] Some day, perhaps, historians will be able to read the Cuban intelligence files upon which Escalante claimed to have based his book.

Despite his relatively high profile as an author and speaker, John Martino seems to have escaped the attention of Kennedy assassination researchers and also of the Garrison investigation during the remainder of the 1970s. Over the years he had become friendly with John Cummings, a reporter for the Long Island daily *Newsday,* to whom he had confided that he had been arrested in 1959 for trying to smuggle money out of Cuba. On one occasion Cummings encountered Trafficante in Martino's house. Martino laughingly told Cummings about the disinformation campaign he carried out after the assassination in an attempt to link Oswald to Castro.

Then, during the last year of his life, Martino turned to a more serious subject. Speaking cryptically, he told Cummings that he had helped organize the Kennedy assassination. Cummings got the impression that Martino transferred money to anti-Castro Cubans who were part of the plot. Martino also threw in what appears to be a red herring—that he had seen Lee Harvey Oswald meeting with FBI agent James O'Connor in Miami.[48] During that same year, in telephone conversations with the Fort Worth businessman Fred Claassen, Martino was more forthcoming.

As Claassen explained a few years later, he and Martino were involved in selling bulletproof vests to the Guatemalan government, and although they had never met face to face they had spoken on the telephone almost every day for about a year prior to Martino's death from a heart attack in

August 1975. Claassen claimed that Martino was still a "contract agent" with the CIA, and the bulletproof vests were manufactured by a Reston, Virginia, firm called Capps and Sons. The firm went bankrupt just a few months after Martino's death when a big deal with an unidentified foreign government fell through.[49] Claassen also reported that H. L. Hunt had paid for some of Martino's anti-Castro speaking engagements.

According to Claassen, after he and Martino began discussing the renewed interest in the Kennedy assassination, Martino acknowledged his involvement. He claimed that Oswald did not know who he was working for—that he thought he was working for pro- rather than anti-Castro Cubans. He also said that the conspirators had planned to get Oswald out of the country and eliminate him, but that everything went wrong after Oswald shot Tippit and was arrested. After that, "they had Ruby kill him." Claassen contacted the HSCA in 1977 and gave them the essentials of Martino's story but refused to give his own name out of fear. He also told his story to Earl Golz, a Dallas reporter, but apparently did not authorize its publication. Martino's wife eventually identified Claassen to HSCA investigators, but there is no record that they contacted him. He died in 2002.[50] Meanwhile, both Mrs. Martino and two long-time Martino associates from the casino business, Alan and Kenneth Roth, linked Martino to a CIA agent named David Cabeza.[51] The CIA has never released a 201 file on Martino.

In December 1974 Seymour Hersh of the *New York Times* published a sensational exposé of CIA domestic abuses. In the ensuing controversy, the gist of the 1967 CIA inspector general's report—that the agency had sponsored plots against Castro—came to light, partly through an indiscretion on the part of the new president, Gerald Ford. This sparked the formation of the Church Committee in 1975 and the House Select Committee on Assassinations in 1976. During the four years of their investigations and hearings, Santo Trafficante apparently managed to keep the complete story of the Kennedy assassination a secret through a mixture of intimidation and outright murder.

The events of 1975 were complicated by the re-emergence of two key figures, Hoffa and Giancana. Hoffa's attempts to win his freedom never stopped after his incarceration in 1967. Given his active support of Richard Nixon in 1960, many thought that Nixon's election in 1968 might lead to his release, but Attorney General John Mitchell apparently overruled long-time Nixon associate Murray Chotiner, a California attorney who pushed for Hoffa's release in 1969. During Hoffa's incarceration his replacement, acting Teamster president Frank Fitzsimmons, cemented relations with mob bosses in the Northeast, while Marcello and Trafficante remained loyal to Hoffa and continued to pressure Partin to recant his testimony. By late 1971 all the key mob bosses were apparently sharing in loans from the Central States Pension Fund, and Fitzsimmons had emerged as labor's strongest supporter of the Nixon administration.

On December 23, 1971, President Nixon paroled Hoffa on condition that he refrain from all union activity until 1980. Some of Nixon's White House aides, including Charles Colson and E. Howard Hunt—now the leader of the plumbers squad—apparently asked Fitzsimmons and the Teamsters for dirt about Edward Kennedy and other political opponents during 1972. Colson briefly served as Teamsters general counsel before his own legal problems became serious in 1973–74. Hoffa, meanwhile, began challenging the restrictions placed on him in court. That failed, but as 1975 dawned Hoffa, still only sixty-one years old, was plotting his return to power.[52]

Sam Giancana, meanwhile, had seen his own ups and downs. The Justice Department's vendetta against him continued into 1965, when the government used an immunity statute to try to force him to testify before a grand jury. When he refused, he spent a year in jail for contempt of court, and when he emerged in 1966 he left the country for Mexico, where Richard Cain had been preparing his new base of operations. During the next eight years Giancana evidently built something of a gambling empire in the Caribbean. Phyllis McGuire was frequently in his company. Cain was forced to return to Chicago to face trial on burglary charges in 1968, was convicted, and spent three years in jail.

When Cain was released, he approached Chicago FBI agent Buddy Roemer and began informing on Giancana's gambling activities. Cain was shot and killed in a Chicago restaurant on December 21, 1973.[53] Six months later, Mexican authorities suddenly arrested and deported Giancana. When he returned to Chicago, he told Roemer, who met him at the airport, that he had no intention of resuming local criminal activities. He lived quietly in Chicago for the next year, appearing several times before local grand juries. Government sources said he was uninformative.

As the story of the assassination plots against Castro finally leaked onto the front pages of major newspapers in the spring of 1975, several stories gave Giancana, along with Roselli, the leading role. None mentioned Trafficante, who prudently left the country for Costa Rica when the Church Committee hearings began in May.[54] William Colby, now director of the CIA, provided the committee with a copy of the IG report, and in short order it called James O'Connell, Sheffield Edwards, Robert Maheu (who successfully insisted on immunity), and various higher CIA officials. By mid-June committee staffers had contacted both Giancana and Roselli about testifying. On the night of June 20, 1975, Giancana was shot seven times in the face and head in the basement of his Chicago home. The crime was never solved.

Johnny Roselli appeared before the committee just four days later. He had now been living in South Florida for more than a year and had many contacts with Trafficante.[55] He had apparently been in touch with his CIA contacts, O'Connell and Harvey, and had a good idea of what the government knew and did not know. His testimony never went beyond what was already in the IG report and said nothing about the team he sent into Cuba in March 1963. He talked freely about the now-dead Giancana but, as his counsel explained, refused to refer to Trafficante by name. Roselli appeared again on September 22, going over much of the same ground but also discussing (with visible reluctance) the affair between Judith Campbell and John Kennedy. The committee issued its report on assassination plots on November 20, 1975.

Meanwhile, on the afternoon of July 30, 1975, Jimmy Hoffa, still trying to return to the presidency of the Teamsters, left his house to meet with two mob-connected Teamster officials, Anthony Provenzano of New Jersey and Anthony Giacalone of Detroit. The two men provided themselves with alibis for the afternoon, and Hoffa disappeared. His body has never been found, and in recent years forensic evidence has failed to confirm several sensational confessions regarding his murder. Both Giacalone and Provenzano were eventually convicted on other charges and served long terms. Provenzano died in prison.[56]

John Martino, coincidentally, died of a heart attack in the first few days of August 1975 without ever having come to the Church Committee's attention. Ted Shackley identified him before the committee just a few days later. During late 1975 and the first half of 1976 the committee undertook new phases of its investigation, including an enquiry into do-

mestic spying by intelligence agencies and a probe into the performance of the FBI and CIA during the investigation of President Kennedy's assassination. In March 1976 it heard from Edward Morgan, who
apparently linked Marcello to the mob plots against Castro and suggested a connection between those plots and the assassination of President Kennedy.

In April 1976 the committee called Roselli for yet another appearance to ask him about Morgan's "retaliation" theory of the Kennedy assassination. Over the years, Roselli had confided far more in journalist
Jack Anderson than he ever swore to under oath. He had been involved,
he said, in six different assassination plots against Castro from 1960
through 1963—two poisoning attempts and four shooting attempts, the
last one in March 1963. He also talked speculatively about how Kennedy
"might" have been killed—that it had something to do with the capture
and torture of Roselli's last assassination team, and that Oswald had to die
because he might have been linked to the Mafia. Ruby, he speculated,
was simply given an order he could not refuse.[57]

Sitting before the committee once more, a clearly nervous Roselli declined to give his Florida address for the record. Although he had told
the retaliation story to both Ed Morgan and Jack Anderson, he now denied knowing anything about it. His own attorney, Thomas Wadden, evidently worried that Roselli might be indicted for perjury and repeatedly
prompted him to admit that he had discussed Castro's possible involvement with various people, including Harvey and Maheu. The committee's questions were highly unspecific and never exactly asked Roselli
about the team of assassins he dispatched in March 1963, but he denied
having received any information from inside Cuba about Castro's plans
to retaliate, as Morgan had said. Roselli did refer to the Black Book Castro had given McGovern a year earlier that named the men Roselli sent
into Cuba in March 1963, but the committee investigators did not have
the report in front of them and did not ask him about the names.

Late in Roselli's testimony, committee counsel Paul Wallach, who had
elicited Morgan's story of a client from New Orleans who had information about anti-Castro plots, questioned Roselli about Marcello. The following exchange then took place:

> Mr. WALLACH. Did you ever hear that Carlos Marcello was involved in
> plots against either Robert or John Kennedy?

Mr. ROSELLI. No, sir.

Mr. WALLACH. The same question with respect to Santos Trafficante. Did you ever hear that he was involved in plots against Fidel Castro?

Mr. ROSELLI. No, sir. Against who?

Mr. WALLACH. Fidel Castro.

Mr. WADDEN (Roselli's attorney). Listen, if he's going to get knocked off, he would have gotten knocked off a long time ago, so you can answer that.

Mr. ROSELLI. I just used him for an—interpreting one or two times, that's all.[58]

For the first time in his testimony, Roselli had definitely linked Trafficante, in whose territory he now lived and with whom he was in frequent contact, to the assassination plots—though in a highly misleading fashion. When he returned to Florida after giving his testimony, Roselli was warned that a contract had been put out on his life. He disappeared on July 27. More than two weeks later his body was discovered floating in an oil drum near Miami. The killers, police stated, had made every effort to prevent the body from ever being discovered, but they had failed. Police immediately suspected Trafficante but never managed to make an arrest.[59]

Shaken by the death of their witness, the Church Committee called Trafficante himself on October 1, 1976. Incredibly, they agreed at the mobster's request not to make a transcript of the conversation. Trafficante essentially confirmed what was in the committee's already-released report—that he had put Roselli in touch with "Macho" Gener and with Juan Orta inside Cuba but that he had been phased out of the operation after that. He denied ever having met Jack Ruby, speculated that Castro had been behind the Kennedy assassination, and, according to the note-taker, showed an impressive knowledge of Lee Harvey Oswald. Trafficante confirmed having had dinner with Roselli a few days before his disappearance but denied that Roselli feared for his life. He claimed to be afraid for his own life, after the deaths of Giancana and Roselli.[60]

Roselli was the third (along with Giancana and Hoffa) of six key witnesses to die suddenly and violently in 1975–77. About two weeks after Trafficante's appearance before the Church Committee, the House of Representatives, after at least five months of wrangling, agreed to establish a committee to investigate the assassinations of John F. Kennedy and Martin Luther King, Jr. The House Select Committee on Assassinations hired a well-known Philadelphia prosecutor, Richard Sprague, as its counsel in the fall of 1976, and Sprague moved aggressively to hire staff and begin questioning witnesses. Sprague quickly alienated his elected bosses and had to resign in the spring of 1977, giving way to G. Robert Blakey. One of his investigators, a journalist named Gaeton Fonzi, had been working for the Church Committee and had been the first to hear the story of Antonio Veciana and Maurice Bishop.

In December 1976, Fonzi had taken charge of the Miami phase of the House Committee's investigations and put together a list of witnesses to interview. A garbled account of the Bayo-Pawley raid had now appeared in the press, and one of Fonzi's witnesses was Pawley. Now eighty, Pawley had been confined to bed with a nervous disorder for about a year, and on January 8, 1977, he shot and killed himself, leaving a note that he could no longer bear the pain.[61]

On March 29, 1977, Fonzi was looking for Oswald's old friend the White Russian George de Mohrenschildt, who was now living in Palm Beach, Florida. When Fonzi showed up at the home where de Mohrenschildt was staying, his daughter told him that he was out. Unbeknown to Fonzi, journalist Edward Jay Epstein had beaten him to the punch. At that very moment, de Mohrenschildt was giving a long interview to Epstein, telling him, among other things, that CIA Domestic Contacts Officer J. Walton Moore had asked him to become acquainted with Oswald in Dallas. Fonzi told de Mohrenschildt's daughter that he would return the next day. When her father got home and heard Fonzi's message, he sat down in front of his favorite television soap opera and killed himself with a shotgun.[62]

About a week later, on April 6, 1977, when Fonzi was preparing to interview former Cuban president and anti-Castro plotter Carlos Prio Socarras, Prio also shot himself to death. Family members said the seventy-three-year-old Prio had suffered recent financial reverses, but there was no suicide note.[63] He had been actively working among right-wing Cuban exiles all during 1963 and had ties to Trafficante through Tony Varona and Macho Gener, if not directly himself.

During the same month, a *National Enquirer* reporter named A. J. Weberman telephoned Loran Hall in California and recorded the conversation. Hall was hostile, profane, and apparently drunk, and his wife could be heard in the background urging him to terminate the conversation at once. "Hemming is a CIA punk, OK?" said Hall, when asked about his old companion. "I've known the SOB for fourteen years. He turned his own goddamn crews in so he wouldn't have to go to Cuba. He's fingered me on my own goddamn deals and caused me to get arrested." Then, however, Hall spontaneously dropped something more revealing. "Hey, man. Right as it stands right now, there's only two of us left alive. That's me and Santo Trafficante. And as far as I'm concerned, we're both going to stay alive, because I ain't going to say shit."[64]

When the HSCA asked Hall about this statement, he claimed he was referring to the Bayo-Pawley raid. But testifying in October 1977, he also acknowledged that in June, when he was still refusing to testify without a grant of immunity, he had received a mysterious anonymous call. "A friend of ours is taking a boat trip on the 6th," the caller said. "He hopes that he can come back on the 8th; and I said you can rest assured that he can." The friend, he confirmed, might have been Trafficante, although he quickly added that he did not know why he might have been concerned.[65]

Trafficante and Marcello survived the assassination investigations, but the 1970 Racketeer-Influenced and Corrupt Organizations Act (RICO), largely written by Blakey, made it easier to prosecute leading mobsters without tying them directly to illegal acts. From 1979 through 1981 the FBI mounted a complicated sting operation against Trafficante, using agents to open an illegal gambling establishment in Florida with the hope of making a deal. With the help of the sting, Trafficante was indicted in 1981 and again in 1983. After three years of delay, he finally came to trial in 1986 but beat the rap after the government was found to have concealed critical exculpatory evidence and two of the main witnesses against him were murdered.

In his 1994 book, attorney Frank Ragano—who had become estranged from Trafficante in the late 1970s but had returned to help get these new charges dismissed—described a last conversation with the mob boss. Trafficante reminisced about Cuba, Castro, and the trouble the Kennedys had brought him and his friends. Then suddenly he said in Italian, "Carlos fucked up. We should not have killed Giovanni [John]. We should have killed Bobby." He also explained that Hoffa had been killed because mob bosses had become more comfortable dealing with his successor, Fitzsimmons. Subsequent research, however, showed that this conversation could not have taken place when and where Ragano claimed it did.[66] Trafficante died in March 1987 without ever having been convicted on a federal charge.

Carlos Marcello continued to fight what became the longest and most expensive deportation case in the history of the United States. For thirty years, with his essentially unlimited resources, he managed again and again to exploit the loophole that allows candidates for deportation to file an unlimited number of motions in federal court. But beginning in 1979, the government made a bribery case against him thanks to the help of an informant who reached the mob boss through Irving Davidson. The government also began tapping Marcello's and Davidson's telephones as part of their sting operation (code-named BRILAB), and in 1980 it sprung the trap, indicting Marcello and Davidson and two others on various racketeering charges.

When the trial began, the government asked permission to introduce some of its surveillance tapes which, prosecutors claimed, touched on the JFK assassination. The judge refused to allow them. After a long trial, Marcello was found guilty in 1981 on one count of racketeering, although he was found innocent on all specific charges. Louisiana politician Charles Roemer was also convicted, but Davidson and the fourth defendant were acquitted on all charges. On the very next day, a Los Angeles grand jury indicted Marcello for trying to bribe a federal judge. In December 1981 he was convicted in that case as well and sentenced to a total of seventeen years in prison.

In 1989, an amazing incident in the Texarkana prison where Marcello was serving his sentence led the FBI to reopen the investigation of John Kennedy's assassination. On February 27 Marcello was admitted to the prison medical facility for dizziness, irregular heartbeat, and disorientation. During the next three days he suffered from the delusion that he was back home in New Orleans, and he began speaking to his attendants as though they were trusted associates. He discussed a meeting he had just held with "Provenzano" in New York, he suggested that his men visit a night club, and he spoke of an imminent celebration. And on three occasions during a two-day period Marcello remarked, "That Kennedy, that smiling motherfucker, we'll fix him in Dallas . . . we are going to get that Kennedy in Dallas."

On March 7 the FBI officially reopened the case and began monitor-

ing Marcello's mail and phone calls in the new facility to which he was
transferred in Minneapolis.[67] During the same month, the bureau got a
tip from Joseph Giarrusso, a former New Orleans police commissioner
who was now a city councilman. Giarrusso had received a call from an
unidentified Englishwoman who said that she had lived in New Orleans
from 1966 through 1968 and had worked briefly in the office of a lawyer
of Italian extraction. She had once typed a letter to Marguerite Oswald
(Lee's mother) that referred to the assassination and included a check.
The FBI eventually interviewed the woman in Britain, but the interview
remains classified.[68]

By the summer Marcello's mental state appeared to be alternating between lucidity and disorientation, although his roommate—another inmate—told the FBI that he understood far more of what was happening
around him than he let on. "Dallas, based on past statements made by
Marcello, feels that a failure to interview him in pursuit of his allegations
of personal culpability in the Kennedy Assassination could eventually
subject the bureau to criticism for failure to pursue every possible lead in
the investigation, even though the Bureau is on record as having officially
closed the investigation," an agent wrote on July 25.[69] To make the interview more interesting, the bureau dispatched agent Michael Wacks of
Los Angeles, who had gotten to know Marcello while working undercover in the BRILAB investigation, to help.

On October 13 Wacks met with Marcello in the Minneapolis prison
hospital library. The Mafia don recognized him at once and began talking both about his sentence and his new release date, which had been
moved up because of his health problems. The subject of his 1961 deportation also came up, and Wacks asked him if he still blamed Robert Kennedy. "Who else?" he replied. At that point Wacks, playing by the book,
informed Marcello that agents from Dallas had also arrived to interview
him about the assassination of President Kennedy. Marcello immediately
showed considerable concern, and when the formal interview began he
denied having any information that Robert Kennedy was responsible for
his deportation and claimed not to remember any of the men who had
known both himself and Lee Harvey Oswald.

Then an agent asked a most revealing question. "Marcello was advised
that in December, 1985, a conversation was overheard in which Marcello
stated that he (Marcello) had had John Kennedy killed, that he was not

sorry about it, and his only regret was that he (Marcello) did not kill Kennedy himself. Marcello stated that again, this was crazy talk and that he had never made any statement to that effect." No agent would ask such a specific question without documentation to back it up, and this exchange confirmed that someone had indeed heard Marcello claim responsibility for the assassination of John F. Kennedy.[70]

On February 6, 1990, the Dallas office reviewed these developments, including the as yet unreleased interview in Britain.

> It should be noted that [deleted—presumably the Britain interview] again place the Bureau in the dilemma of being presented facts 25 years after the event that can neither be confirmed nor discounted. Dallas is of the opinion that no additional investigation in this matter is warranted, in view of the fact that this subsequent investigation was initiated based on statements made by Marcello while in a semi-coherent state and that these statements were subsequently denied by Marcello when interviewed. In addition, volume upon volume of investigation has previously been conducted by the Bureau, as well as various Congressional subcommittees, and none of these investigations has ever established a positive connection between Marcello and the assassination. Any further pursuit of this investigation will merely give appearance of self-doubt regarding the original and subsequent investigations. Accordingly, UACB, Dallas, is closing DL 89-43 (the original KENNEDY assassination), as well as the current investigation (DL 175A-109) relating to captioned matter.[71]

Marcello died a free man in 1993. Law enforcement had run its course, and the assassination was now a matter for history.

Conclusion

The murder of John F. Kennedy emerged from two overlapping zones of illegality: American organized crime, which was defending itself against Robert Kennedy's relentless attack, and the U.S. government–sponsored or tolerated anti-Castro movement. Illegality and secrecy go together, but enough information emerged both before and after the assassination to trace the essence of the organized crime conspiracy. The most direct evidence points to Santo Trafficante, because of his connections to John Martino, who had advance knowledge of the plot, and to Loran Hall, who was evidently with Oswald at Silvia Odio's house and who spoke of protecting Trafficante in 1976–77. Trafficante's own lawyer, Frank Ragano, confirmed his boss's involvement and described giving encouragement from Jimmy Hoffa to both Trafficante and Carlos Marcello in the spring of 1963. Marcello bragged about his role at least twice. He was even more threatened by the government than Trafficante was, with deportation hanging over his head. Oswald and his family had lifelong connections with Marcello's mob, including David Ferrie, Oswald's Uncle Dutz Murret, and Guy Banister, who was working for Marcello by the summer of 1963.

Sam Giancana had also been fighting tremendous pressure from the government for three years and had spoken frequently about it. Jack Ruby's calls to Chicago mob figures such as Barney Baker and Irwin Weiner in the months before the assassination suggest that Giancana might have been involved in the conspiracy as well, as do the disinformation activities of his well-connected henchman, Richard Cain. Ruby had connections to all three of the most likely mob conspirators. He had visited Trafficante in jail in Cuba in 1959 and was still in touch with

Trafficante's old friend Lewis McWillie. He had grown up with Giancana's Chicago mob and still kept up with some of its members. And he now operated strip clubs in Dallas, which appears to have been a subsidiary branch of Marcello's New Orleans empire. All three of these hoodlums knew that Jimmy Hoffa's endorsement of their enterprise could prove useful. And John Roselli, although he cannot be linked directly to the assassination itself, worked closely with Giancana and Trafficante in the anti-Castro plots, and he indicated many times to Edward Morgan and Jack Anderson that there was more to the assassination of President Kennedy than Lee Harvey Oswald. He evidently was murdered in 1976 because he knew too much.

Where did these men find the audacity to kill a president of the United States? G. Robert Blakey and Richard Billings speculated convincingly in the 1970s that John Kennedy, because he accepted women as favors through Frank Sinatra (and perhaps in other contexts as well), had lost the immunity from retaliation that truly incorruptible public officials generally enjoyed.[1] By enlisting these very mob leaders to assassinate Fidel Castro in 1960, the CIA had inevitably weakened any inhibition about killing a head of government. In addition, Robert Kennedy's campaign against the mob—fought with every available weapon, and without many of the legal tools that later became available—fell outside traditional rules as well. The attorney general indicted suspected mobsters for any offense, no matter how trivial. When he discovered in 1962 that he could not indict Giancana because of his CIA connection, he pushed the FBI surveillance of him even harder. All these men knew that Hoffa's comment about the attorney general—that Robert Kennedy would not rest until Hoffa was behind bars—was true for them as well. These were desperate times that called for desperate measures.

That many anti-Castro Cubans, including one that had contact with Oswald, had very strong negative feelings about President Kennedy is also clear, but only a few pieces of evidence implicate any of them in the assassination itself. The first is the Rose Cheramie story of the two men who drove her from Miami to Louisiana on their way to Dallas to take part in the assassination, but there is no proof that they were Cuban. The second is Tony Cuesta's reported identification of Sandalio Herminio Diaz and Eladio del Valle as having been present in Dallas on November 22, but that cannot be confirmed. And the last is the tip the Dallas sheriff received after the assassination about meetings between Cubans and Oswald on Harlandale Avenue, a key lead that was never pursued.

Lee Harvey Oswald did kill President Kennedy all by himself. If someone fired a shot from the grassy knoll, he missed. The mob and the anti-Castro Cubans were part of a much broader nationwide network of right-wing activists, anti-Communists operating privately or within congressional committees, conservative businessmen like William Pawley and H. L. Hunt, and a few paramilitaries like the Minutemen. Many if not all of these men regarded the Kennedys as a mortal threat to America as they understood it. Pawley was close to John Martino, and Hunt reportedly subsidized Martino's book tour and was in touch with him through his security chief, former FBI agent Paul Rothermel.[2] But the only evidence that suggests such elements were directly involved in the assassination is Loran Hall's unconfirmed story of being offered $100,000 to kill Kennedy in Dallas in the summer of 1963.

Nothing suggests that the CIA was involved in the assassination. However, because of the nature of the CIA and its determination to conceal its connections to some of its operations, we cannot say anything with certainty about its possible connection with Lee Harvey Oswald. An agency officer, Scott Breckenridge, gave the following information to HSCA staffers in 1978.

> I said that [redacted] was another problem. The man had worked for us abroad under non-official cover. He had left the Agency and now works in a UN organization. He had run an agent into the USSR, that man having met a Russian girl and eventually marrying her. Our assumption is that the interest in the man is that the agent was successful in getting his Russian wife out of the country, as Oswald was in getting Marina out. We have no problem in arranging an interview with [redacted] but the name of the agent we do not wish to reveal, for reasons outlined at the meeting.[3]

Breckenridge acknowledged that the Soviet Russia division of CIA had indeed sent agents into Russia, perhaps in an effort to learn something about daily life there, to test Russian counterintelligence procedures, and perhaps to identify possible agents. Based on the way in which the agency resisted divulging numerous facts for as long as possible, we simply cannot rule out the possibility that Oswald was such an agent, all the less so since as we have seen the agency had plans to debrief him before he returned. That would explain the failure of any law enforcement or intelligence agency to challenge him regarding his public pledge to betray radar secrets in Moscow in 1959.

The CIA and its former agents cannot logically claim a presumption of innocence in matters like this. Many of them have proudly acknowledged the need to protect their agents from disclosure. Our inability to establish clearly whether the President's assassin had worked for the CIA—or whether the CIA had recruited him as part of a plot to assassinate Fidel Castro, as Antonio Veciana's story of seeing Oswald with David Phillips suggests—is simply part of the price we pay for maintaining a government agency that operates outside the law. Whether the price is worth the gain is a political question for all Americans to ponder.

The conspiracy did not go entirely according to plan. The conspirators were trying to provoke the invasion of Cuba, and in this they failed. Lyndon Johnson, who as vice president had opposed sabotage raids against Cuba, quickly cut them back when he assumed the presidency. Assassination plots against Castro continued, but the wide-ranging and coordinated campaign against him of 1960 to 1963 came to an end

Few events in American history have had more extraordinary short, medium, or long-term consequences than the assassination of John F. Kennedy. For the next eighteen months or so the assassination seemed to have cemented the liberal Democratic ascendancy in postwar America. President Johnson promptly seized the moment of national grief to break a legislative logjam, and by the middle of 1964 he had secured passage of the first major postwar tax cut, the omnibus Civil Rights Act, and his own proposals for a War on Poverty. And in November 1964 he defeated Barry Goldwater far more decisively than Kennedy probably would have, and substantially increased Democratic majorities in the House and Senate. That in turn enabled him to pass Medicare, a big education bill, the Voting Rights Act, and a great deal more during 1965. Not all this legislation would have passed under Kennedy. At the same time, since Kennedy had no intention of pushing for a "Great Society," he would not in all probability have provoked quite as much backlash as Johnson did.

In foreign affairs, the impact of Kennedy's death was even greater because of President Johnson's almost immediate decision to undertake the

Vietnam War, making it impossible to pursue the détente that Kennedy had just begun with the Soviets. JFK had repeatedly refused to fight a war in Southeast Asia.[4] In retrospect, however, the combination of a large draftee army, a never-ending series of Cold War trouble spots around the world, and the American political process would very likely have led to some similar war sooner or later. More important, with the coming of age of a new generation, the postwar consensus was doomed in any event. The Boom generation's rebellion was especially intense because of the Vietnam War, but it would have happened in any case because it reflected a deeper historical dynamic.

During the last forty years Boomers have undone their parents' work in one area of life after another, from the movies, television, and sports to academia, the corporate and financial world, and—beginning in the 1990s and continuing until today—politics, government, and foreign policy. The death of the most outstanding politician of the GI generation and the disastrous war that his successors waged accelerated this process, but they did not cause it. Perhaps because the established order was liberal and Democratic, the most powerful rebellion against it has been conservative and Republican, and this movement has destroyed much of the spirit and many of the institutions built up from the 1930s through the early 1960s. The assassination of a popular president with the help of a mail-order rifle started a gun control movement, but the backlash among gun owners has, ironically, been much more powerful. It played a significant role in the increasing Republican ascendancy from 1980 through 2004.

The Republican resurgence drew critical support from the Cuban-American community, much (though not all) of which has never forgiven the Democratic Party in general and John F. Kennedy in particular for failing to overthrow Fidel Castro. Indeed, in 1971 it was not difficult for E. Howard Hunt, by then retired from the CIA, to recruit several long-standing anti-Castro activists, including Bernard Barker, Frank Sturgis, and Eugenio Martinez, to work in the White House plumbers unit and to break into Democratic National Headquarters, partly, according to some of them, to investigate rumors that Castro was contributing to the Democratic Party.

Florida's population and electoral clout have grown dramatically in the last forty years, and Florida made the difference in the election and re-election of George W. Bush in 2000 and 2004. Certainly the Cuban-American community was decisive in at least the first of those momentous outcomes. The Bush family cemented its alliance with that community's conservative leadership in 1990 when President George H. W. Bush pardoned Orlando Bosch Avila, who had worked with the CIA in 1961–62 and continued his activities independently as head of the MIRR. Bosch had been convicted of a terrorist action against a Polish freighter in 1968. After his release he had planned a successful bombing of a Cuban Airlines plane in Venezuela in October 1976, which killed 73 people. After being held without trial in Venezuela for ten years, Bosch was released in 1988 with the help of Cuban-American ambassador to Venezuela Otto Reich, a power in the Republican Party. After Bosch came to the United States, Bush pardoned him of all American charges at the request of a Republican congressional candidate, Ileana Ros-Lehtinen, and her campaign manager, the President's own son and future Florida governor, Jeb Bush. In the long run, the Kennedy administration's attempt to promote liberal leadership among the exiles has been a failure.

Among the American left, especially within the younger generations, the Kennedy assassination gradually combined with Vietnam as evidence of vast, evil conspiracies within the government, or of immutable, corrupt tendencies in American society. Such beliefs peaked during the 1970s, partly with the help of the Church Committee investigation, which led to the creation of the House Select Committee on Assassinations in 1976. The executive branch of the federal government has refused to take conspiracy theories seriously since 1964, however, and when that committee concluded in 1979 that President Kennedy had probably been assassinated by a conspiracy involving organized crime figures, the FBI quickly found an excuse not to reopen the investigation. Conspiracy theories had a renaissance in the early 1990s after the release of Oliver Stone's film *JFK*. That film undoubtedly set back the public's understanding of the assassination for at least a decade, but it also led to the passage of the Kennedy Assassination Records Act and the vast releases of documentation that made *The Road to Dallas* possible. Too much time has now passed for any new legal proceedings.

Very few of the characters in this story remain alive today. Robert Kennedy was assassinated in 1968 by a Jordanian immigrant, Sirhan

Sirhan. Sam Giancana, Jimmy Hoffa, and Johnny Roselli were murdered in 1975–76. John Martino died in 1975 of natural causes, and Loran Hall died in California during the 1990s. Of the critical figures, the last to die were Santo Trafficante (in 1987) and Carlos Marcello (in 1993).

Fidel Castro Ruiz, whose 1959 revolution did so much to set these many events in motion, has now held power for forty-nine years, longer than any other political leader of the twentieth century. He has survived a strict U.S. economic embargo, hundreds of assassination plots, nine U.S. presidents, the fall of his Soviet Communist patrons, and, most recently, a serious intestinal ailment that required surgery in the summer of 2006 and forced him into at least temporary retirement. Largely because of American sanctions, Cuba remains a poor country, although its health care and educational achievements are much closer to first than to third world standards. The people enjoy relatively little freedom of expression and the Communist Party continues to rule, but Cuba's hemispheric isolation is easing. In recent years Latin American politics have swung to the left, and Venezuela has become a new and important Cuban ally.

During the twentieth century few countries had more closely intertwined destinies than Cuba and the United States. In 1898 the United States helped win Cuba's independence in a brief war with Spain, but promptly made that independence conditional. For sixty years no Cuban government was fully independent, and American business interests controlled much of the island's human and material resources. Castro's revolution reclaimed those assets and turned opposition to the influence of the United States into the organizing principle of Cuban political life. It is not only the fault of the United States that relations have never been re-established since 1960. On more than one occasion, Castro himself has spoiled a chance for improvement with some new initiative that was bound to anger his northern neighbor.

Like members of the same family, Cuba and the United States have left their imprint too deeply upon one another to ever live in complete isolation. To Americans, Cuba means not only the nineteenth-century war that made the United States a world power but also Hemingway's *Old Man and the Sea, Guys and Dolls,* Desi Arnaz, the Buena Vista Social Club, Minnie Minoso, Camilo Pascual, Tony Perez, Orlando Hernandez, and an ethnic minority that changed the face of the Southeast and wields considerable political clout. For Cubans, the United States means not only independence—first with North American help, and then in opposition to the region's strongest power—but also the source of Cuba's own national game, and the home of a huge expatriate community. Yet the chasm that has cost the two nations so dearly still divides them. I look forward to the day when Cubans and Americans will vacation freely in each other's land, when Cuban families are reunited, and when a major league baseball team makes Havana its home. But all this still seems far off as 2007 draws to a close, and unlikely to happen at once, even after Fidel Castro, too, has finally left the scene.

NOTE ON SOURCES

The basic published sources on the assassination are the reports, hearings, and selected exhibits of the Warren Commission and House Select Committee on Assassinations, all of which are now published online at http://www.history-matters.com.

The vast majority of unpublished sources used here come from the NARA JFK Assassination Records Collection in College Park, Maryland. That collection is abbreviated "JFK" the first time a certain document series is referred to. Within that collection, seven major sets of records were used.

FBI FILES

The NARA collection includes FBI files on numerous individuals and groups, including most of the major organized crime figures in the United States during the late 1950s and early 1960s. FBI files have a file number (such as FBI 92-2713) and an individual document number (FBI 92-2713-64). Occasionally, documents have been inserted into an existing file, and are labeled "1st NR," "2nd NR," and so on. All FBI files cited are FBI headquarters files unless otherwise indicated by a different prefix such as DL (Dallas) or NO (New Orleans). Some bug or wiretap evidence is in special files labeled "Elsur" (electronic surveillance) or "June mail." Most FBI documents are addressed officially from the special agent in charge (SAC) of the Field Office in question to the director, or vice versa.

When the FBI wants to communicate information to other agencies, it prepares something called a Letterhead Memorandum, abbreviated LHM in the notes.

CIA FILES

Four major collections of CIA files in the collection have been used.

CIA Segregated Collection

These documents—essentially those submitted by the CIA to the House Select Committee on Assassinations—are one of the two most important collections of CIA files. They are cited by box and folder. The collection suffers from an almost complete lack of organization.

CIA Printed Microfilm

This extremely important collection includes original CIA files on numerous individuals and groups, including leading Cuban exiles and exile organizations. It is much better organized (although the order of documents within files is rather random) and is also cited by box and folder.

CIA Miscellaneous Files

This is another separate collection of CIA files, cited by box and folder.

CIA Latin America Division Working Files

This extremely important collection was put together during the 1977 preparation of a task force report on possible Cuban connections to the assassination of President Kennedy. It is cited by box and folder.

HOUSE ASSASSINATIONS COMMITTEE NUMBERED FILES

Documents collected by the House Assassinations Committee are individually numbered and filed in over 200 boxes. They are cited by box and number.

SENATE SELECT COMMITTEE ON INTELLIGENCE ACTIVITIES

The Senate Select Committee on Intelligence Activities, or SSCIA, took testimony and collected documents in 1975–76. The testimony has been collected on a CD-Rom available from www.history-matters.com. These documents are cited by box and folder.

IRR (MILITARY INTELLIGENCE) FILES

These are also cited box and folder.

RIF NUMBERS

Every document in the JFK collection has an RIF (Record Identification Form) number, in three parts (separated by dashes), with about 12–15 digits total. Even though these numbers uniquely identify the document, they have not usually been used here, to save time and space. Very occasionally, however, I have included them because someone provided me the document online and I did not know what box and folder it was in. The NARA website includes a search engine for the entire collection which enables any researcher to locate a document by RIF number.

INTRODUCTION

1. See especially chapter 12, below.

2. Interview with Ed Martino, January 3, 2007. Martino's widow provided an airline ticket receipt for the October 27 Dallas trip to HSCA investigators in 1977; see memo to Cliff Fenton from Fonzi and Gonzales, October 7, 1977, JFK HSCA, numbered files (hereafter HSCA), Box 63/2572.

1. ORGANIZED CRIME IN THE 1950S

1. See Estes Kefauver, *Crime in America* (Garden City, NY, 1951), edited with an introduction by Sidney Shalett, for a summary of the hearings and findings.

2. *Ibid.*, pp. 10–34.

3. *Ibid.*, pp. 34–52, 76–8, 114–23, 141–59. Although Kefauver's book does not refer to Trafficante, Frank Ragano, and Selwyn Raab, *Mob Lawyer* (New York, 1994) indicates that the formal committee report did.

4. Dan Moldea, *Dark Victory: Ronald Reagan, MCA, and the Mob* (New York, 1986), pp. 87–92.

5. All three men acknowledged this within weeks of the murder of Oswald: see SAC New York, November 26, 1963; SAC Chicago, December 6; and SAC Chicago, December 18, JFK FBI 44-24016, nos. 201, 482, 787.

6. G. Robert Blakey and Richard N. Billings, *Fatal Hour: The Assassination of President Kennedy by Organized Crime* (New York, 1992), pp. 302–3.

7. *Ibid.*, pp. 303–4.

8. SAC Birmingham, December 14, 1963, FBI, 44-24016-724, and Blakey and Billings, *Fatal Hour*, p. 305.

9. SAC Birmingham, December 17, 1963, FBI 44-24016-778.

10. SAC Dallas, November 25, 1963, FBI 44-24016-634.

11. Interview of September 2, 1947, FBI 44-24016-1238.

12. SAC Dallas, December 5, 1953, FBI 62-97749-155.

13. McWillie deposition, April 4, 1978, HSCA numbered files, Box 203/11171.

14. *New York Times,* January 10, 1958.

15. SAC San Francisco, November 27, 1963, FBI 44-24016-658.

16. SAC Dallas, November 10, 1961, FBI 92-5704-1; SAC Dallas, September 26, 1960, FBI 92-2824-62, which reports Sheriff Decker's comments of November 1957, at the time of the Appalachin meeting; and SAC Dallas, FBI 92-5704-6, January 26, 1966, for Civello's comments on Decker.

17. On these associations see especially HSCA, Appendix to Hearings, vol. IX, pp. 93–117. A couple who reintroduced Mrs. Oswald to Termine in about 1970 reported that they spoke familiarly of a number of mob figures, and the New Orleans Crime Commission confirmed that Termine had been a significant Marcello associate.

18. Two excellent sources on basic Cuban history and the role of the mob are Thomas G. Paterson, *Contesting Castro: The United States and the Triumph of the Cuban Revolution* (New York, 1994), pp. 16–24, and Enrique Cirules, *El Imperio de Habana* (Havana, 1999), based partly on Cuban archives, pp. 3–62.

19. See the statement of Carl Noll, a long-time Marcello associate, SAC New Orleans, February 8, 1960, and Memorandum, Sam Papich, February 1, 1960, FBI 92-2713-64, 65.

20. Treasury Department memo, March 17, 1958, published at http://www.cuban-exile.com/doc_276-300/doc0288.html.

21. The monograph has been published by the FBI at http://foia.fbi.gov/mafiamon.htm.

22. See Arthur M. Schlesinger, Jr., *Robert F. Kennedy and His Times* (Boston, 1978), pp. 137–41.

23. On this point, and Robert Kennedy's "Silent Generation" in general, see William Strauss and Neil Howe, *Generations: The History of America's Future* (New York, 1991), pp. 279–94.

24. Robert F. Kennedy, *The Enemy Within* (New York, 1960), p. 33.

25. On Hoffa's early career see Dan E. Moldea, *The Hoffa Wars: Teamsters, Rebels, Politicians and the Mob* (New York, 1978), pp. 15–71.

26. Moldea, *Hoffa Wars*, pp. 72–6, 94–100.

27. *Hearings Before the Senate Select Committee on Improper Activities in the Labor or Management Field*, 86th Congress, First Session, Part 48, pp. 17215–19269.

28. *Ibid.*, part 53, pp. 18672–81.

29. *Robert Kennedy in His Own Words: The Unpublished Recollections of the Kennedy Years* (New York, 1989), p. 77; see also pp. 90–1.

30. *Chicago Tribune*, May 25, 1960, p. A2.

31. Frank Ragano and Selwyn Raab, *Mob Lawyer* (New York, 1994), pp. 140–52. Ragano represented Hoffa for many years. See also LBJ Library, Drew Pearson Diary, November 27 and December 10, 1963. Pearson describes working with Hoffa and John Connally at the 1960 convention to try to nomi-

nate Johnson and speculates that Hoffa contributed money to Johnson's campaign. Unfortunately Pearson's 1960 diaries have not yet been released.

32. Walter Sheridan, *The Fall and Rise of Jimmy Hoffa* (New York, 1972), pp. 139–42, 157–8, 166–7. According to Ed Partin, a Teamster official from Louisiana, convicted felon, and later a key government informant against Hoffa, Hoffa's support included a cash contribution of at least half a million dollars that originated with Carlos Marcello of New Orleans and went through Irving Davidson. Davidson denied it. See Moldea, *Hoffa Wars,* pp. 108, 260.

33. Kennedy, *Enemy Within,* pp. 74–5, 318–9.

2. CASTRO TAKES POWER

1. See Paterson, *Contesting Castro,* pp. 1–54, and SAC Miami to Director, April 6, 1961, FBI 109-430 NR.

2. Cirules, *Imperio de Habana,* pp. 261–9.

3. SAC New Orleans, February 8, 1960, FBI 92-2713-64.

4. FBI 97-4030-8, January 15, 1960, and 97-4030-12, March 21, 1960.

5. FBI reports of February 27, 1959, and August 11, 1960 (Norfolk office), JFK CIA Printed Microfilm, Box 117/14.

6. *Ibid.,* Miami reports of September 24 and November 7, 1958.

7. *Ibid.,* CIA Mexico City to Headquarters, November 24, 1958; CIA Santiago de Cuba to Headquarters, January 26, 1959; and SAC Miami to Director, April 6, 1959. See also New York *Daily News,* April 21, 1975, for a long interview with Sturgis.

8. JFK, IRR files, Boxes 5–8, contain numerous FBI reports on Prio from the early 1950s through the late 1960s.

9. Paterson, *Contesting Castro,* pp. 109–26.

10. FBI CR 109430-2011 (Houston, February 26, 1958); CR 109430-2075 (Miami, March 13); CR 109430-2086 (Houston, March 31, 1959).

11. On Davidson see FBI 2-1423-1, May 25, 1955; FBI 2-1423-53, May 21, 1961; and FBI 2-1453-54, May 28, 1961.

12. Legat Havana, November 11, 1958, FBI 2-1423 16th NR. (The abbreviation Legat, for Legal Attaché, stands for the FBI agent in an embassy abroad.)

13. SAC Detroit, August 23, 1962, FBI 29-31889-8.

14. Drew Pearson, *Diaries, 1949–59,* ed. Tyler Abell (New York, 1974), p. 449. Pearson continued his diaries—an extraordinary source about American political life—until his death in 1969, but his stepson and editor unfortunately halted their publication after the first volume appeared and gave most of the originals to the LBJ Library. There, with a few exceptions related to the JFK assassination, they languish, under privacy restrictions of which their author most certainly would never have approved.

15. Lyman B. Kirkpatrick, Jr., *The Real CIA* (New York, 1968), pp. 166–78.

16. Paterson, *Contesting Castro,* pp. 160–205.

17. On the Flying Tigers, see Duane Schultz, *The Maverick War* (New York, 1987), pp. 1–9, 124–5, and see also CIA Security Check on Pawley, July 24, 1952, NARA JFK, CIA Segregated Collection, Box 44, folder 39 (hereafter 44/39).

18. SAC Detroit, August 23, 1962, FBI 62-79985-9, Thomas Paterson papers, Thomas J. Dodd Center, University of Connecticut.

19. Memos of July 13 and August 8, 1954, CIA Segregated Collection, Box 2/1.

20. William Pawley oral history, Herbert Hoover Library.

21. Paterson, *Contesting Castro,* pp. 206–15; see also U.S. Department of State, *Foreign Relations of the United States* (hereafter *FRUS*), 1961–1963, vol. X, no. 169 (meeting of Taylor Board, April 22, 1961; hereafter *FRUS* are cited series, volume, number), for King's confirmation of this incident, and Mario Lazo, *Dagger in the Heart: American Policy Failures in Cuba* (New York, 1968), pp. 158–64.

22. Fabian Escalante, *The Secret War* (Australia, 1955), pp. 5–16.

23. CIA Santiago to HQ, January 5 and 6, CIA Printed Microfilm, Box 117/14.

24. M. A. Jones to Cartha DeLoach, April 1, 1959, at http://www.cuban-exile.com/doc_126-150/doc0147.htm.

25. See John Newman, *Oswald and the CIA* (New York, 1995), pp. 95–100.

26. Legat Havana, April 21, 1959; SAC Kansas City, April 30; Legat Havana, May 19; and J. Edgar Hoover to Allen Dulles, July 13, FBI 105-78016-1, 3, 6, 14.

27. *New York Times,* May 22, 1959, and December 10, 1959. The defendants, including Joseph Civello of Dallas, were convicted of obstructing justice by concocting false stories about the meeting. Civello received a five-year term. The conviction was overturned a year later.

28. Paterson, *Contesting Castro,* pp. 226–37.

29. Legat Havana, April 29, 1959, and June 10, FBI 92-2781-95, 102.

30. On Martino's background see Chief Inspector Atlantic City to SAC Newark, August 22, 1944, FBI 32-2980-744, and Miami Letterhead Memorandum (hereafter LHM), November 11, 1959, FBI 64-44828-4. Martino described his work on fraudulent gambling equipment to his son Edward; interview with Ed Martino, January 3, 2007.

31. Interview with John Cummings, August 23, 2003. Cummings, a reporter, had a long friendship with Martino.

32. Legat Havana, July 31, 1959, FBI 64-44828-1.

33. Interview with Loran Hall, August 20, 1977, HSCA, Box 1.

34. Dallas police arrest record, November 24, 1963, FBI 44-24016-634.

35. Three acquaintances of Ruby's now living in Las Vegas confirmed this after the assassination. The most definite was Meyer Panitz, whom Lewis McWillie later cited as an associate of Ruby's, who described how Ruby would call a police captain who would supply off-duty patrolmen. FBI 44-024016-775, interview of December 17, 1963. Dallas policemen also confirmed their acquaintance with him: SAC Dallas, December 4 and December 16, 1963, FBI 44-24016-461, 803.

36. FBI 44-24016-634, November 29, 1963.

37. SAC Dallas, December 31, 1963, FBI 44-24016-917, December 31, 1963; SAC Dallas, February 5, 1964, FBI 44-24016-1073, and Interview with Deputy Sheriff A. J. Ayo, and February 18, 1964, FBI 44-24016-1176.

38. McKeown's testimony of April 12, 1978, can be seen at http://jfkassassination.net/russ/m_j_russ/mckeown.htm.

39. Rosen to Belmont, February 27, 1964, FBI 44-24016-1155. The memo also says—apparently falsely—that the FBI, not Ruby, made the original approach.

40. As suggested by Blakey and Billings, *Fatal Hour*, p. 316.

41. The original records of Flynn's contacts with Ruby are in FBI DL 137-681.

42. On Martin Fox and the Tropicana, see Legat Havana to Director, FBI 62-9-210-1-15, December 29, 1958.

43. On the dinner see Ruby's testimony, Warren Commission, vol. V (hereafter WC, vol. no.), pp. 205–6. The commission failed to pursue this lead.

44. When McWillie was interviewed in Las Vegas the very next day—November 25—he remembered Ruby's and Mynier's visits but denied she had served as a courier. SAC Las Vegas, November 24 and 25, 1963, FBI 44-24016-26, 426.

45. SAC Dallas, December 3, 1963, FBI 44-24016-634, gives the July 1 date. Blakey and Billings, *Fatal Hour*, give a date of April 27.

46. London cables, November 26 and November 29, 1963, and Memorandum, DD/P to J. Edgar Hoover, December 12, 1963, CIA Segregated Collection, Box 2/10. Although a further cable a few days later reported that Wilson-Hudson in 1959 had struck Senator Eastland's Internal Security subcommittee as a psychopath, the CIA eventually reported that Wilson was very intelligent, although a heavy drinker, and confirmed the dates of his detention. In 1978, McWillie, whom Ruby was visiting, confirmed that he had made visits to Trescornia, although he denied that Ruby had come along. HSCA, *Final Assassinations Report*, pp. 186–7.

47. An Evanston, Illinois, attorney, John Marcus, brought this to the FBI's at-

tention on Sunday, November 24, FBI 44-24016-298. Ruby had identified himself as a Dallas club owner originally from Chicago.

48. HSCA, *Final Assassinations Report,* p. 183. Cuban tourist cards confirmed the last three trips.

49. On Martino's sentencing see the UPI ticker of December 18, 1959, FBI 64-44828.

50. Moldea, *Hoffa Wars,* p. 123.

51. SAC Miami, September 18, 1962, FBI 28-31889-20.

52. Attwood's July 10, 1975, SSCIA testimony is available online: the key passage is at http://www.gwu.edu/~nsarchiv/NSAEBB/NSAEBB18/08-11.htm. I knew Attwood for many years as a person of great intelligence, observation, and integrity.

53. SAC Miami, FBI 29-31889-20, September 18, 1963, and Legat Havana, August 3, 1959, FBI 105-80291-1.

54. Interview with Edward Browder, January 12, 1978, HSCA, Box 105/5081.

55. See Memoranda by Donahue, May 5, 1959, and Belmont, June 30, 1959, available at http://cuban-exile.com/doc_151-175/doc0155.htm and http://cuban-exile.com/doc_151-175/doc0153.htm.

56. *FRUS,* 1958–60, vol. VI, no. 348.

57. *Ibid.,* 250, 287, 300, 306, 322.

58. Barker's role is discussed in Fabian Escalante, *The Secret War* (Australia, 1995), pp. 30–40, and confirmed at great length in Barker's own CIA file, CIA Printed Microfilm, Box 100, folders 10–11. Barker was known as AMCLATTER-1.

59. CIA Printed Microfilm, Box 117/14.

60. New York *Daily News,* April 21, 1975, and interview with Frank Sturgis, April 3–4, 1974. Rockefeller Commission, JFK SSCIA, Box 36/7 and 41/4–5.

61. See the 201 file, CIA printed microfilm, 117/14. If documents dealing with Sturgis's involvement in assassination plots during 1959 ever existed, they never came to the attention of a team of CIA officials who wrote a long report on CIA involvement in Castro assassination plots in 1976, either. On February 9, 1973—at the height of Sturgis's Watergate notoriety—William Colby, then the CIA deputy director for plans, told another CIA official that Sturgis "has not been on the payroll for a number of years." Three years later, another official, Jerry Brown, noted that Colby's statement presented problems, since the agency had frequently denied any connection to Sturgis since the Watergate break-in. See memo for record by JRS and memo for record by Jerry Brown, February 2, 1973, and July 20, 1976, CIA Segregated Collection, Box 52/2.

62. *FRUS,* 1958–60, VI, 374, 376, 379, 387.

63. Stephen G. Rabe, *Eisenhower and Latin America: The Foreign Policy of Anti-Communism* (Chapel Hill, 1988), pp. 6–25.

64. The literature on these episodes has become enormous. See for example John Prados, *President's Secret Wars* (New York, 1986), pp. 91–170; Richard Immerman, *The CIA in Guatemala* (Austin, TX, 1982); Stephen Kinzer, *All the Shah's Men: An American Coup and the Roots of Middle East Terror* (New York, 2003); and on Cambodia and Laos, David Kaiser, *American Tragedy: Kennedy, Johnson, and the Origins of the Vietnam War* (Cambridge, MA, 2000), pp. 20–30.

65. JFK CIA Latin America Division Work Files (hereafter LA WF), Box 5/1. This critically important collection of files was apparently put together for a study of CIA assassination plots within the agency in 1975–76.

66. CIA LA WF, Box 5/1, cable of January 6, 1960.

67. "Request to install recording device in William Pawley's office," October 6, 1959, CIA Segregated Collection, Box 2/1.

68. Miami WH Rep to Chief WH, September 10, 1959; Memorandum for the Record, September 25; Report of Contact, January 23, 1960, CIA Segregated Collection, Box 2/4, and "Request to Install Recording Device," October 6, 1959, and Director of Security to DCI, December 29, 1959, *ibid.*, Box 2/1.

69. Nixon to Pawley, January 12, 1960; Pawley to Eisenhower, January 12; Pawley to Nixon, January 14; undated note, "Call Pauley [sic]," Nixon Vice Presidential Papers, NARA, Laguna Beach, CA, Box 582, William Pawley folder.

70. *FRUS*, 1958–60, VI, 423.

71. *Public Papers of the Presidents, 1960–1* (Washington, 1961), pp. 125, 134–6.

72. *Ibid.*, 453, 454.

73. CIA, LA WF, Box 5/3, memo by Rudolf Gomez.

74. *Public Papers of the President, 1960–1*, pp. 202–82.

75. Rabe, *Eisenhower and Latin America*, pp. 128–9, 136–7.

76. Rubottom Memorandum, March 9, *FRUS*, VI, 473.

77. *Ibid.*, 481, printed with deletions. The full text has been published at http://www.shafr.org/newsletter/2002/sep/covert.htm.

78. See Peter Kornbluh, ed., *Bay of Pigs Declassified: The Secret CIA Report on the Invasion of Cuba* (New York, 1998), pp. 70–1. The group was headed by a CIA agent working under the name Frank Bender, whose real name was Gerald Droller.

79. *FRUS*, VI, 486.

80. Tad Szulc, *Fidel: A Critical Portrait* (New York, 1986), pp. 514–5.

81. When the report was completed, Tracy Barnes and Richard Bissell wrote a lengthy and sometimes informative rejoinder to refute it. It too is published in Kornbluh, ed., *Bay of Pigs Declassified*.

82. *Bay of Pigs Declassified,* pp. 25–8.

83. *Ibid.,* pp. 42–44, 60–1.

84. *Ibid.,* pp. 33, 60–1, and Escalante, *Secret War,* pp. 74–5.

85. *FRUS,* VI, no. 529, June 10, 1960 (the full document has been released by the Eisenhower Library). Secretary of State Herter was delegated to tell Pawley to stop promoting former Batista officials, but Pawley continued to do so—see for example Memo for Record, August 3, 1960, CIA Segregated Collection, Box 4/2.

86. HSCA, *Hearings and Appendix volumes* (hereafter HSCA, vol. no), X, p. 57; *Bay of Pigs Declassified,* pp. 66–71.

87. Pawley to Thomas Mann, March 3, 1961, CIA Segregated Collection, Box 2/4.

88. *Bay of Pigs Declassified,* pp. 65–72.

89. *Ibid.,* pp. 58, 71–75. "The Agency," Kirkpatrick wrote, "and for that matter, the American nation is not likely to win many people away from Communism if the Americans treat other nationals with condescension or contempt, ignore the contributions and the knowledge which they can bring to bear, and generally treat them as incompetent children whom the Americans are going to rescue for reasons of their own." See also *FRUS,* 1961–63, X, 169.

90. The CIA's intense, complex dealings with the exiles during the year before the invasion can be followed in JFK, CIA Printed Microfilm, Boxes 71/9–10 and 121/12.

91. CIA Memo for record by Major Koch, September 15, 1960; CIA Printed Microfilm, Box 35/28.2; SAC Miami, November 2, 1960, FBI 97-4474-1; SAC Miami, November 11, FBI 97-4474-2.

92. Assistant AG to Hoover, January 24, 1961, FBI 97-4474-9; on Rorke's connections see Memorandum for the Record, June 30, 1960, CIA Printed Microfilm, Box 43/18.

93. SAC Miami, March 24, 1961, FBI 97-4474-14; WAVE to Director, March 26, CIA Printed Microfilm, Box 21/7.1; SAC Miami, March 27, FBI 97-4474-21.

94. CIA Information Report, November 18, 1959, and CIA Information Report, February 9, 1960, CIA Printed Microfilm, Box 101/22.2; Foreign Service Dispatch, March 31, CIA Printed Microfilm, Box 101/22.1.

95. Undated memorandum on the DRE, CIA Printed Microfilm, Box 45/5.2; JMASH to Director, September 3, 1960, *ibid.;* Memo for Record, June 2, 1961 (interview with Brian Crozier), LA WF, Box 5/2; JMASH to Director, November 18, 1960, CIA Printed Microfilm, Box 45/5.2; Rimm (?) to BELL, January 18, 1961, *ibid.;* WAVE to Bell, 610303, CIA Printed Microfilm, Box 45/

5.1; Chief, Washington office to Chief Contact Division, April 15, 1961, CIA Printed Microfilm, Box 70/4.2.

96. Szulc, *Fidel,* pp. 517–21.

97. *Public Papers of the President, 1960–1,* p. 655.

98. The issue did not die there, as Kennedy suggested a fifth debate and Nixon replied that it should be confined to Cuba alone. In an exchange of telegrams, each of the two men seemed to reverse their televised positions, with Nixon arguing that the United States should help exile forces—who, he falsely claimed, had until now received "virtually no support" from the government—while Kennedy denied that he advocated intervention in violation of American treaty obligations and refused to have a debate restricted to this issue. *Los Angeles Times,* October 24, 1960, p. 1.

99. *FRUS,* 1958–60, VI, 613; see also Memo to Richard Nixon by J. D. Hughes, May 11, 1960, Nixon Vice-Presidential Papers, Box 582, William Pawley folder. Pawley later claimed that Eisenhower had offered him a new position as undersecretary of state for hemispheric affairs, but had withdrawn the offer a few days later because of State Department opposition. See William Douglas Pawley oral history, Herbert Hoover Library.

100. *FRUS,* 1961–63, X, 19 (Staff Study, January 16); Rabe, *Eisenhower and Latin America,* pp. 170–1.

101. *FRUS,* 1957–60, VI, 616, 623, 627.

102. *FRUS,* 1961–63, X, 1, 2, 3, 7.

3. THE CIA ENLISTS THE MOB

1. *Public Papers of the President 1960–1,* pp. 403–4.

2. See 94th Congress, 1st Session, U.S. Senate, Senate Select Committee on Intelligence Activities (hereafter SSCIA), *Alleged Assassination Plots Involving Foreign Leaders* (Washington, 1975). The IG report is available in its original form at http://www.history-matters.com/archive/jfk/cia/80T01357A/pdf/104-10213-10101.pdf.

3. CIA, LA WF, Box 5/3, Memo for record by Rudolf Gomez, January 5, 1960.

4. *Alleged Assassination Plots,* pp. 114–6.

5. Memo for record, April 6, CIA, LA WF, Box 5/3. Another copy of the memo for record was prepared that omitted this exchange.

6. *FRUS,* 1957–60, VI, 453, 454.

7. Hunt Testimony, SSCIA, Box 25, folder 1, page 25; E. Howard Hunt, *Give Us This Day* (New Rochelle, NY, 1963), pp. 32–8. In his book, Hunt said the assassination conversations were with Bissell's deputy Tracy Barnes.

8. Interview with Edward Browder, January 8, 1978, HSCA, Box 105/5081, and Browder to John Hornbeck, February 21, 1978, Box 115/5726. Although the first scheme in particular seems rather fantastic, recently released documents confirm that the army had discussed developing a radiological assassination weapon as early as 1948. See the *Washington Post,* October 9, 2007, p. A8.

9. SSCIA, *Alleged Assassination Plots,* pp. 72–3. I have been unable to find these cables in CIA files.

10. See Richard D. Mahoney, *JFK: Ordeal in Africa* (New York, 1983), pp. 36–40.

11. The file ZRRIFLE/QJWIN is available in JFK, CIA Printed Microfilm, Box 54/10–11. QJWIN was apparently a European criminal named Jose Marie Andre Mankel. The files refer only to the "extreme sensitivity" of the objective for which he was recruited.

12. SSCIA, *Alleged Assassination Plots,* pp. 13–70.

13. Rabe, *Eisenhower and Latin America,* pp. 154–62; SSCIA, *Alleged Assassination Plots,* pp. 191–215.

14. Chicago office, Department of Justice, May 26, 1960, FBI 97-4030-12 2nd NR, and SAC Miami, June 17, 1961, FBI 97-4030-18. Drew Pearson had heard different versions of Rothmann's story about Nixon's gambling in 1952 and 1954: see Pearson, *Diaries,* pp. 227, 335.

15. SSCIA, *Alleged Assassination Plots,* p. 74 n.2.

16. See the testimony of John Whiten ("John Scelso"), May 16, 1978, at http://www.history-matters.com/archive/jfk/hsca/secclass/pdf/Scelso_5-16-78.pdf, and Peter Wright, *Spycatcher* (New York, 1987), pp. 159–60. Wright's conversation with Angleton also included William Harvey, who took over the position in 1962.

17. Eisenhower Library, White House Office, Office of the Special Assistant for National Security Affairs, Special Assistants series, Presidential subseries, Box 2, Presidential Papers 1955 (1), and Box 3, Pending Material (President) 1957 (4). The authors of the Church Committee report on assassinations do not seem to have been aware of this loophole. See *Alleged Assassination Plots,* pp. 10–1.

18. CIA 1967 IG Report, pp. 14–6 and see testimony of James O'Connell and Joseph Slimon, May 3 and September 12, 1975, Boxes 24/4 and 47.

19. See *Los Angeles Times,* July 24, 1948, p. 2; November 16, 1948, p. 1; April 22, 1950, p. 1; and October 8, 1950, p. 30; May 11, 1953, p. 1; August 19, 1954, p. 4; November 5, 1955, p. 10. Roselli was questioned in connection with Bioff's death by car-bombing. Some news accounts spelled his name Rosselli. The defendants secured their paroles with the help of a St. Louis mob lawyer, Paul Dillon, who had represented Kansas City boss Tom Pendergast and knew President Truman. Dillon became friendly with T. Webber Wilson, a Mississip-

pian and chairman of the Parole Board, and got more help from attorney Maury Hughes of Dallas, who knew Attorney General Tom Clark. See the well-researched biography by Charles Rapplye and Edward Becker, *All American Mafioso: The Johnny Rosselli Story* (New York, 1991), pp. 46–117.

20. FBI 92-3267-2 (LHM, January 16, 1958), 92-3267-4 (SAC Los Angeles, December 23, 1957), 92-3267-10 (SAC Los Angeles, March 28, 1958), 92-3267-18 (May 19, 1958), 92-3267-33 and 34 (September 10, 1958), 92-3267-42 (December 19, 1958), and 92-3267-52 (November 24, 1959).

21. Roselli testimony, June 24, 1975, SSCIA, Box 46; SSCIA, *Alleged Assassination Plots,* pp. 75–76; compare 1967 CIA IG Report, pp. 15–7.

22. Minutes, November 3, LA WF, Box 5/2.; SSCIA, *Alleged Assassination Plots,* p. 110.

23. See Maheu's testimony, SSCIA, Box 24/3; Harvey testimony, July 11, 1975, Box 35/5; Roselli testimony, September 22, 1975, Box 1/1; and Edward P. Morgan testimony, March 19, 1976, Box 26/5.

24. The best secondary source on Giancana is William F. Roemer, Jr., *Man Against the Mob* (New York, 1989). Roemer was another Chicago FBI agent working on organized crime cases.

25. See Giancana's FBI file, FBI 92-3171, especially nos. 1 (December 26, 1957), 33 (May 25, 1959), 36 (June 30, 1959), 41 (October 30, 1959), and 52 (September 12, 1960), all from SAC Chicago.

26. CIA IG report of 1967, pp. 24–5.

27. SAC Tampa, February 2, 1960, FBI 92-2781-120.

28. The summary of Trafficante's testimony, which at his request was not transcribed verbatim, is in SSCIA, Box 44. He testified on October 7, 1976.

29. O'Connell originally misdated the story, placing it in the 1960–61 period and claiming that it also identified Giancana. The Church Committee staff did not find it, but the HSCA staff did, in the issue of January 21, 1962. Its rogues' gallery included Trafficante but not Giancana or Roselli. See HSCA, Hearings and Appendix volumes, X, p. 166.

30. Trafficante's HSCA testimony is at http://mcadams.posc.mu.edu/russ/jfkinfo2/jfk5/traff.htm. On Orta's 1958 arrest see Paterson, *Contesting Castro,* pp. 83–5.

31. CIA IG Report of 1967, pp. 22–4.

32. Havana to Chief WH (J. C. King), September 21, 1959, and WAVE (Miami) to BELL, December 19, 1960. LA WF, Box 5/1.

33. Trafficante testimony, SSCIA, Box 44; his HSCA testimony is at http://mcadams.posc.mu.edu/russ/jfkinfo2/jfk5/traff.htm. Trafficante and Cubela may have met through a Havana jeweler, Carlos Tepedino, who had a store in the Havana Hilton, where Trafficante had an office. Tepedino, who had known

Cubela since 1953, later emigrated to New York and became an intermediary between Cubela and the CIA after Cubela had become known as AM/LASH. See also Fabian Escalante, *1963: El Complot* (Melbourne, Australia, 2004), pp. 55–60.

34. CIA IG Report, p. 80. Two original documents on this episode—BELL to WAVE, March 24, 1961, and JMRIM to Bell, March 30, will be found in JFK, CIA Printed Microfilm, Box 101, folders 23.1 and 23.2.

35. FBI 92-3171-89, p. 2V. In retrospect this story raises some rather fascinating questions. While it does not obviously track exactly with what we now know about the CIA conspiracy, it does tally quite well with stories told by Marita Lorenz, who had aborted a child fathered by Castro in 1959, and by Frank Sturgis to Gaeton Fonzi, a journalist and investigator for the Church Committee and the House Assassinations Committee, in 1977. Both Lorenz and Sturgis confirmed that Sturgis's friend Alex Rorke (of whom more later) had given her pills to poison Fidel, but she dated the incident in early 1960. Neither Lorenz nor Sturgis, moreover, has a very good reputation for credibility, and Sturgis had passed up a chance to give this story to the Rockefeller Commission a few months earlier. Gaeton Fonzi, *The Last Investigation* (New York, 1993), pp. 85–9. Sturgis—a notorious exaggerator himself—confirmed this story, but Lorenz subsequently discredited herself with fantastic stories about the assassination in Dallas. See Sturgis's Rockefeller Commission testimony, April 3–4, 1974, SSCIA, Box 36/7 and 41/4–5.

36. See SAC Chicago, February 28, 1962, FBI 105-93264-8, and CIA DDP to J. Edgar Hoover, July 10, 1962, FBI 105-93264-12.

37. CIA Printed Microfilm, Box 8/25, report of October 7, 1960; SAC Chicago report of November 1, FBI 105-93264-1; DDP (Richard Bissell) to Hoover, November 4, FBI 105-93264-2; CIA Printed Microfilm, 8/25, report of December 12. Cain's mob status is detailed by Roemer, *Man Against the Mob,* pp. 219–27.

38. Maheu testimony, July 29, 1975, SSCIA Box 24/3; O'Connell testimony, May 30, 1975, Box 24/4.

39. See Roselli's testimony, June 24, 1975, SSCIA, Box 46.

40. SAC Salt Lake to Director, November 11, 1960, FBI 139-1201-1, and November 4, FBI 139-1201-2.

41. *Ibid.,* SAC Miami to Director, December 23, 1960. FBI 139-1201-7.

42. Director to SACs, December 8, FBI 139-1201-3; SAC Miami, December 28, FBI 139-1201-15; SAC WFO, January 12, FBI 139-1201-11; SAC WFO, January 30, FBI 139-1201-19.

43. SAC Miami, January 28, 1961, FBI 139-1301-15; SAC Salt Lake, February 6, FBI 139-1201-17; SAC WFO, February 13, FBI 139-1201-19.

44. CIA IG Report of 1967, pp. 26–8. In April, on the eve of the Bay of Pigs operation, Orta sought asylum in the Venezuelan Embassy. When Venezuela broke off diplomatic relations with Cuba in November, Orta moved to the Mexican Embassy, where he remained for almost three more years before securing approval to leave for Mexico in October 1964. An undated CIA memorandum later confirmed that the CIA had used Orta "as a penetration of the top-level Castro Government circles for the purpose of collecting information on government policies and attitudes" and paid him $400 per month until the middle of 1966.

45. In December and January 1960–61, two FBI memoranda to the CIA reported that the Cellini brothers—former Havana casino owners—were working with Varona through Edward Moss, a Washington public relations consultant, to help overthrow Castro in exchange for the restoration of their gambling interests. CIA IG Report of 1967, pp. 29–31.

46. CIA Segregated Collection, Box 9/71, n.d., "Orlando Piedra," and CIA WH/4, "Anti-Castro Activities in the United States," January 15, 1960, CIA Segregated Collection, Box 44/6.

47. *FRUS*, 1957–60, VI, 614 (meeting of November 29, 1960), and *FRUS*, 1961–63, X, 37 (meeting of February 6, 1961). SAC Tampa, April 19, 1961, FBI 92-2781-177. CIA IG Report of 1967, pp. 31–2, and see also Roselli's testimony, SSCIA, June 24, 1975, Box 46, and O'Connell's testimony, May 30, Box 24/4. See also SAC Miami, October 3, 1961, FBI file 52-76826-29, in which Piedra guardedly vouched for Varona, denying that he had ever been a Communist.

48. Harrison might have been the alias of a CIA surveillance man whom O'Connell, presumably, had sent to help. He might also have been Joseph Shimon, a Washington policeman whose career had survived a wiretapping scandal in the late 1940s involving Howard Hughes, and whom Maheu, ironically, had brought into this plot. See the *Washington Post,* June 19, 1950, p. B1, for Shimon's wiretapping activities. See also SAC Los Angeles, March 13, FBI 138-1201-28; SAC Las Vegas, March 28, FBI 138-1201-32; SAC Miami, March 29, FBI 138-1201-33; Dodge to Director, April 12, FBI 138-1201-36.

49. FBI 131-2301-39 (LHM, April 20, 1961), and FBI 131-2301-40 (Rosen to Parsons, April 25).

50. Testimony of Lawrence Houston, SSCIA, June 2, 1975, Box 25/1.

51. *Bay of Pigs Declassified,* pp. 75–95.

52. The Black Book is not listed in the JFK on-line index or in the Church Committee records finding aid, but in 2004 I discovered a copy inserted as an appendix to the Church Committee testimony of Ted Shackley, the Miami Station Chief, who had testified under the name of Halley. See Halley testimony, SSCIA records, Box 46.

53. SSCIA records, Memo for the Committee, January 15, 1975, Box 28/2. See also Escalante, *The Secret War,* pp. 41–85, on infiltrations and plots during this period. Escalante apparently had access to Castro's Black Book or to the sources it was based on.

54. See the interview summaries of Veciana, March 22, 1976, SSCIA, Box 41, folder 06-M, and Box 43. See also Fonzi, *The Last Investigation,* pp. 117–71.

55. See the remarks of General Fabian Escalante during a conference in December 1995 in Nassau, published at http://cuban-exile.com/doc_026-050/doc0027-3.html. Gaeton Fonzi also confirmed the identification of Phillips as Bishop during this session of the conference. Crozier's identification is documented in Memorandum, February 4, 1978, Fonzi & Gonzales to G. Robert Blakey, JFK, HSCA numbered files, Box 105/5063.

56. Thus, when another case officer, Calvin Hicks, submitted Veciana's name for a security check in 1962, the security office found nothing about him in the files. Howard Gossage for CI/Operational Approval and Support Division, December 29, 1961, and Instruction Sheet, January 25, 1962, CIA Printed Microfilm, Box 46/16.

57. Richard Helms with William Hood, *A Look over My Shoulder* (New York, 2003), p. 177.

58. Sam Halpern testimony, April 22, 1976, SSCIA, Box 46.

59. Testimony of David Atlee Phillips, HSCA Security Classified testimony, April 28, 1978, at http://history-matters.com/archive/jfk/hsca/secclass/pdf/Phillips_4-25-78.pdf.

60. See below, chapter 11.

61. CIA LA Division WF, Box 5/4, December 9, 1960, and Box 5/5, December 13.

62. *Miami News,* January 23, 1961, clipping in CIA Printed Microfilm, Box 47/17.2.

63. *Time,* June 9, 1975 (originally quoted by Moldea, *The Hoffa Wars).*

64. Browder interview, January 12, 1978, HSCA numbered files, Box 105/5081.

65. FBI 92-2713-64, SAC New Orleans, February 8, 1960.

66. See SAC New Orleans, March 16, 1961, FBI 92-2713-125, and SAC New Orleans, April 13, 1961, FBI 92-2713-144. On Dalzell see SAC New Orleans, March 1, 1961, FBI 106-9670-4, and SAC New Orleans, June 6, 1961, FBI 106-9760-6. On Banister, see SAC Tampa, February 7, 1961, FBI 105-87912-182. As Frank Ragano, Trafficante's lawyer, discovered in 1963, Marcello and Trafficante were old friends. Both of them had also been involved in loans from Teamster pension funds, and both men had dealings with a Miami mortgage

broker named Sam Kay. See Ragano, *Mob Lawyer,* pp. 132–3, and SAC San Antonio, January 27, 1961, FBI 92-2713-78.

4. THE KENNEDYS TAKE OVER

1. Robert Dallek, *An Unfinished Life: John F. Kennedy, 1917–1963.*

2. On the latter point see Rabe, *Eisenhower and Latin America, passim.*

3. Dallek, *Unfinished Life,* p. 356. See also Richard Bissell's testimony about a briefing in late November 1960, cited in SSCIA, *Alleged Assassination Plots,* pp. 120–1. On JFK's briefing, see the memorandum by Allen Dulles, June 1, 1961, *FRUS,* 1961–63, Microfiche Supplement to volumes X–XII (hereafter "Supplement"), no. 265.

4. These developments can be followed in *FRUS,* 1961–63, X, 19, 20, 21, 24, 27, 28, 30, 31, 32, 35, 40, 45, 46, 48.

5. Bissell testimony, June 9, 1975, JFK, SSCIA, Box 41/4.

6. On Harvey see Powers, *The Man Who Kept the Secrets,* pp. 126–7. In 1978 a very forthright and impressive retired CIA official, John Whiten—who testified under the pseudonym John Scelso—told the HSCA that Harvey had been close to Guy Burgess, Donald McLean, and Kim Philby, the three British KGB agents who defected at various times during the 1950s and 1960s, and that he eventually had to be relieved from a job in Rome because of his alcoholism. Scelso/Whiten's testimony is available at http://www.history-matters.com/ archive/jfk/hsca/secclass/Scelso_5-16-78/html/Scelso_0001a.htm; see especially pp. 147–50. See Harvey testimony, June 25, 1975, SSCIA, Box 36/1. For some reason, no committee member or staffer raised the issue of the date of his note during Harvey's questioning. Harvey's notes have now been published: see Bayard Stockton, *Flawed Patriot: The Rise and Fall of CIA Legend Bill Harvey* (Dulles, VA, 2006), pp. 152–3. Unfortunately Stockton dated it incorrectly as 1962, not 1961.

7. SSCIA, *Alleged Assassination Plots,* pp. 181–4; CIA IG Report of 1967, pp. 37–8. The ZR/RIFLE-QJ/WINN file, now released in the CIA Printed Microfilm collection, begins with the recruitment of QJ/WINN in the fall of 1960.

8. SSCIA, *Alleged Assassination Plots,* p. 185.

9. *Ibid.,* pp. 123–4. The President's appointment log at the JFK Library confirms that Smathers met Kennedy privately twice during February 1961.

10. See Hunt, *Give Us This Day,* pp. 160–82.

11. *FRUS,* 1961–63, 61, 65, 66, 74, 114.

12. *Bay of Pigs Declassified,* pp. 71–5.

13. CIA, LA WF, Box 5/5, cables of March 29, April 4, April 5.

14. Aleksandr Fursenko and Timothy Naftali, *One Hell of a Gamble: Khrushchev, Castro and Kennedy, 1958–64* (New York, 1997), p. 91.

15. *FRUS,* 1961–63, X, 101.

16. *FRUS,* 1961–63, X, 84; on Masferrer's invasion attempt, see JFK, FBI file 2-1622. Masferrer was arrested in early April, but a sympathetic federal judge freed him pending a deportation hearing, claiming that justice was not served by arresting a man at the whim of the secretary of state (who had publicly attacked him) or the attorney general. SAC Miami, April 20, 1961, and April 27, FBI 2-1622-105 and 2-1622-108.

17. *FRUS,* 1961–63, X, 95.

18. Haynes Johnson with Manuel Artime, Jose Perez San Roman, Erneido Oliva, and Enrique Ruiz-Williams, *Bay of Pigs* (New York, 1964), pp. 75–6.

19. Hunt, *Give Us This Day,* p. 204.

20. *FRUS,* 1961–63, X, 102, 105, 108; see also *Bay of Pigs Declassified,* pp. 56–7. According to Hunt, *Give Us This Day,* Bissell returned from the White House and announced that Kennedy had overruled him regarding the air strike—a story other sources do not support.

21. *Bay of Pigs Declassified,* p. 73. Hunt, *Give Us This Day,* pp. 182–7, claims the sequestration was his idea, apparently because he did not trust Manuel Ray not to betray the plan to Castro.

22. *FRUS,* 1961–63, X, 157.

23. The battle can be followed in some detail in *FRUS,* 1961–63, X, nos. 118–55. For a summary see Fursenko and Naftali, *One Hell of a Gamble,* pp. 92–7, including details of Castro's reaction.

24. *Ibid.,* 158 (Chester Bowles memorandum, April 19), 159, 162, 178, 166, 167.

25. See *FRUS,* 1961–63, X, nos. 202 (Interagency Task Force Paper, May 5, 1961), 203 (Bundy to Kennedy, May 5), 204 (notes of meeting, May 5), 206 (Arleigh Burke memorandum, May 5), 213 (JCS to CINCLANT, May 9).

26. *Ibid.,* 234.

27. *Ibid.,* 259 (undated memo, August 1961), 260 (Memo for Record, September 9), 261 (Goodwin Memorandum, September 9), 262 (Kennedy letter, September 14), 263 (Kennedy-Kubitschek conversation, September 15).

28. *Parade,* May 15, 1961; a copy is in CIA Printed Microfilm, Box 8/15.2.

29. See WAVE dispatch (WAVE was now the CIA Miami station, also known as JM/WAVE), May 20, 1961; WAVE to Director, July 29; CIA Printed Microfilm, Box 8/15.2; Duque telegram to Maxwell Taylor, August 8, 1961, and Memo for Record, September 19, 1961, CIA Printed Microfilm, Box 20/6.1; and Memo to Chief, WH, January 29, 1962, CIA Printed Microfilm, Box 8/15.2.

30. FBI reports, July 31 and September 1, 1961, FBI 105-86406-4, 5. By the fall Hemming became involved with another controversial Cuban, Eloy Gutierrez Menoyo, who under Batista had been a leader of the Directorio Revolucionario and had founded the Second National Front of the Escambray. Working with Castro after the revolution, he had betrayed William Morgan's uprising to Castro in the fall of 1959. After Menoyo defected to the United States in early 1961, he was originally suspected of being a Castro agent and had to spend months in a Texas detention center before several leading exiles managed to secure his release. The CRC treated him coolly, but in October he was reported to be running some maritime operations with Hemming. By early 1962 the CIA concluded that he might be of use. CIA Office of Central Reference, undated (apparently January 1962), and CIA memorandum for record, October 25, 1960, CIA Microfilm, Box 109/15.

31. Hans Tanner, *Counter-Revolutionary Agent* (London, 1962), pp. 126–7.

32. INSCOM/CSF, January 23, 1961, Counterintelligence Source Files, Box 8/12.3; FBI LHMs, February 13 and February 23, *ibid.*, Box 7/9.3; Contact Report, April 2, *ibid.*

33. Tanner, *Counter-Revolutionary Agent,* pp. 115–7.

34. FBI Report, November 7, 1961, Counterintelligence Source Files, Box 7/9.3.

35. Dallek, *An Unfinished Life,* pp. 316–9. On the choice of Lyndon Johnson, see *ibid.,* pp. 267–74.

36. There are three basic sources on the Organized Crime program: Victor Navasky, *Kennedy Justice,* pp. 44–95, 357–440; Ronald Goldfarb, *Perfect Villains, Imperfect Heroes: Robert F. Kennedy's War against Organized Crime* (New York, 1995); and Sheridan, *Fall and Rise of Jimmy Hoffa,* pp. 165–304.

37. Hoover to all offices, May 22, 1961, FBI 92-2781-200 1st NR.

38. Schlesinger, *Robert F. Kennedy,* p. 263.

39. Sheridan, *Fall and Rise,* pp. 171–94.

40. Moldea, *Hoffa Wars,* pp. 123–4.

41. Ragano, *Mob Lawyer,* pp. 87–90, 132–9.

42. Blakey and Billings, *Fatal Hour,* p. 408, quotes a conversation suggesting this between Sam Giancana and Johnny Roselli. See below, chapter 6.

43. Edmund F. Kallina, Jr., *Court House over White House: Chicago and the Presidential Election of 1960* (Orlando, 1988).

44. *Ibid.,* pp. 29–38, 45–56, 69–79.

45. *Ibid.,* pp. 96–144. Although Vice President Nixon held himself aloof from the Republican challenge, other national party figures, including party chairman Thruston Morton, did not.

46. *Ibid.,* pp. 160–66. Kallina also points out that Nixon probably benefited

from some irregularities in other parts of Illinois and that the shift of Illinois alone would not have put Kennedy's election in jeopardy. Had Nixon taken Illinois, Kennedy would still have been elected, even if all eleven, instead of only six, of Alabama's unpledged Democratic electors had voted for Senator Harry Byrd instead of for JFK.

47. SAC Chicago Report of March 24, 1961, FBI 92-3171-167.

48. FBI LHM, September 20, 1960, in Otash file, posted by the FBI, http://foia.fbi.gov/otash_fred/otash_fred_part01.pdf.

49. Judith Exner, *My Story,* as told to Ovid Demaris (New York, 1977). Press accounts and FBI documents often confirm that Campbell's lovers—John Kennedy and Sam Giancana—were where she claimed they were on various dates.

50. *Ibid.* In one interesting slip, Exner (pp. 190–4) claims that FBI agents first came to see her about Giancana in Los Angeles in November 1960. According to Giancana's FBI file, that meeting occurred months later, on June 12, 1961, when she said, as she did in her book, that she had met him as "Sam Flood" in Miami Beach in March 1960.

51. Hoover memorandum, April 17, FBI 92-3171-192; Hoover memorandum, April 12, 92-3171-237 1st NR; SAC Chicago, May 5, 92-3171-225, Ralph Hill's huge 5/5/61; Hoover to Attorney General, May 18, 92-3171-224.

52. FBI LHM, April 20, 1961, FBI 139-1201-39, and A. Rosen to Mr. Parsons, April 25, FBI 139-1201-40.

53. Bissell's extensive remarks before the Taylor Board can be read in *FRUS,* X. For his testimony see SSCIA, *Alleged Assassination Plots,* pp. 122–3. Memo to the Attorney General, May 22, 1961, FBI 139-1201-53.

54. Attorney General's note, June 3, FBI 139-1201-54; Evans to Belmont, June 7, FBI 139-1201-54; and SAC Los Angeles, June 9, July 7, and July 14, FBI 139-1201-49, 67, 68–9.

55. FBI 139-1201-57.

56. Roemer, *Man Against the Mob,* pp. 145–61.

57. FBI 92-3171-314, July 13, 1961, and Memo to the Attorney General, July 14. The original FBI report reads "they can go [obscenity] themselves."

58. SAC LV to Director, September 7, FBI 139-1201-77.

59. SAC New Orleans, February 8, 1960, FBI 92-2713-64. France was Marcello's actual country of origin since he had been born in Tunis in 1910, but France had refused him also.

60. SAC New Orleans, January 3, 1961, FBI 92-2713-72; SAC Washington FO to Director, February 1, FBI 92-2713-83; SAC New Orleans, March 16, FBI 92-2713-125; Evans to Parsons, March 3, FBI 92-2713-109.

61. State Department, Deptel 2126 to Rome, January 31, 1961, and Asst Commissioner A. E. Loughran to Robert Wiley, April 21, INS File A-2 669-541.

62. *Washington Post,* April 7, 1961, p. A2; L'Allier to Belmont, April 7, FBI 92-2713-143.

63. *Washington Post,* April 10, 1961, p. B19.

64. Evans to Parsons, April 15, 1961, FBI 92-2713-151.

65. *New York Times,* May 5, 1961, p. 2.

66. Blakey and Billings, *Fatal Hour,* pp. 276-7.

67. *New York Times,* June 9, 1961, p. 67, and October 30, p. 6.

68. SAC Baltimore, September 2, 1961, FBI 92-2713-229.

5. OPERATION MONGOOSE

1. *FRUS,* 1961-63, X, 266 (memorandum for record, October 5).

2. Memorandum of October 6, 1961, *FRUS,* 1961-63, microfiche supplement to vols. X-XII, 275.

3. *FRUS,* 1961-63, X, 271.

4. *Ibid.,* no. 269. David Talbot, *Brothers: The Hidden History of the Kennedy Years* (New York, 2007), relies heavily on interviews with Goodwin to argue that JFK was not determined to overthrow or kill Castro. He ignores this published memo.

5. Editorial note, *ibid.,* 270. The participants at the White House meeting are listed in the Presidential Appointment Calendar, JFK Library. Halpern's testimony is in SSCIA, Box 25/2. Halpern remembered the meeting as taking place in October; he was only a few weeks off.

6. *Ibid.,* 272, and Sam Halpern testimony, SSCIA, Box 25/2.

7. *FRUS,* X, 275, 276.

8. See two articles by James G. Hershberg, "The United States, Brazil and the Cuban Missile Crisis (part I)," *Journal of Cold War Studies,* vol. 6, no. 3, p. 8, and "Before the Missiles of October: Did Kennedy Plan a Military Strike against Cuba?" *Diplomatic History,* vol. 14, no. 2 (spring 1990), pp. 163-99.

9. *FRUS,* X, 278, 292 [emphasis added].

10. *Ibid.,* 285, 287 (McCone memoranda of December 27 and January 12).

11. Harvey testimony, SSCIA, Box 36/1.

12. *FRUS,* X, 274.

13. Hershberg, "Before the Missiles of October," p. 173.

14. *FRUS,* IX-XI, microfiche supplement, no. 278. This is Szulc's original contemporary record.

15. Szulc testimony, SSCIA, Box 37/3.

16. *Public Papers of the President, 1961,* at http://www.presidency.ucsb.edu/ws/index.php?pid=8448&st=&st1=.

17. *FRUS,* IX–XI, supplement, no. 280; see also *FRUS,* X, 304, for Harvey's cover memo.

18. *FRUS,* X, 309, 310, 311, 314, 323. On the Joint Chiefs see Hershberg, "Before the Missiles of October," p. 174.

19. *FRUS,* X, 319.

20. CIA IG report, pp. 39–50; Harvey testimony, SSCIA, July 11, 1975, Box 35/5. FBI surveillance confirms Roselli's presence in Miami in April 1961: see SAC Los Angeles, April 17, 1962, FBI 92-3267-176.

21. Miller to Director FBI, January 31, 1962, FBI 139-1201-82; Rosen to Belmont, February 2, FBI 139-1201-83.

22. Sullivan to Brennan, April 5, 1962, FBI 139-1201-86.

23. Hoover memorandum, May 10, 1963, FBI 91-3171-735. Edwards memo is in *FRUS,* 1961–63, X, 337.

24. SSCIA, *Alleged Assassination Plots,* p. 134. The committee report falsely states that Edwards's memorandum mentioned Harvey's April 9 request to contact Roselli. This is not so; Harvey's name does not appear in it, nor does any indication that the operation was ongoing.

25. See Elder's testimony, SSCIA, Box 27/1, and McCone's testimony, Box 44. Harvey is quoted in SSCIA, *Alleged Assassination Plots,* p. 134.

26. IG Report, pp. 61, 63.

27. *Alleged Assassination Plots,* pp. 153–4. Harvey briefed the Special Group on May 3.

28. The first comment is from Harvey's second appearance before the SSCIA, July 11, 1975, Box 35/5; the second is from his first appearance, June 25, Box 36/1. Halpern's comment is from his interview of October 10, 1987, JFK, CIA Miscellaneous Files, Box 8. Harvey never claimed that he had received any additional authority from outside the agency to continue this project, but his deputy, Sam Halpern, told the Church Committee that Harvey felt he had a mandate from the attorney general to use the underworld in operations in Cuba. As he testified: "The underworld would be used in terms of the charge from the Attorney General to make use of any and all assets on the Island of Cuba. And the Attorney General made it clear that there obviously were existing assets left over from the days when the underworld was very strong in Cuba. And we were supposed to try to contact anybody in the underworld as well as anybody else who had any possibility of providing any kind of assets inside Cuba." Halpern testimony, June 18, 1975, p. 15, SSCIA, Box 25/2. Halpern admitted, however, that he had not *personally* heard this from the attorney general, and the committee unfortunately failed to ask Harvey to confirm or deny this statement when

he subsequently testified. As we shall see, however, it does not square with a subsequent statement by the attorney general to the general counsel of the CIA. What is more likely is that Harvey, like Helms, was interpreting a general injunction to use any available asset as he saw fit.

29. Lansdale to 5412 Committee, December 7, 1961, *FRUS*, X, 281.

30. Helms testimony, July 17, 1975, 25/3.

31. CIA IG Report, 1967, p. 48. Roselli's testimony referred only to Cubans nos. 1 (Varona), 2 (Rafael Gener), and 3 (the speedboat operator), and to my knowledge no. 3 has never been identified. No. 3 may have been a mysterious Cuban whom Harvey told the IG in 1967 used the name Maceo, a fairly prominent exile who spoke Italian.

32. JMWAVE to Director, July 18, 1962, CIA, LA WF, Box 5/2. A brief AP item describing the confession appeared in the *Chicago Tribune*, July 18, p. 8.

33. Escalante, *The Secret War*, pp. 125–6.

34. *FRUS*, X, 353.

35. DOD memo of July 23, 1962, and Harvey memo of July 24, *ibid.*, 358, 359.

36. *FRUS*, X, 360.

37. *Ibid.*, 360, 362, 364, 367. For RFK's note see Taylor testimony, SSCIA, Box 26/1, exhibit 6.

38. SSCIA, Box 244/13.

39. This whole paragraph is based on *Alleged Assassination Plots*, pp. 161–8. Of those present, Harvey, McCone, Goodwin, and Lansdale all remembered that assassination was discussed; and although only Harvey specifically remembered that McNamara had raised it, indirect evidence from McCone's deputy Walter Elder—who listened to McCone discuss the meeting with McNamara on the telephone shortly thereafter—confirmed this. (McNamara vehemently denied that he had raised it when the story broke in 1975 and has continued to do so, most recently in the documentary film *The Fog of War*.)

40. *FRUS*, 372, 374, 377, 380.

41. *Ibid.*, 431.

42. *Ibid.*, 385.

43. Escalante, *The Secret War*, pp. 115–27. CIA IG Report of 1967, pp. 51–2, and Harvey testimony, July 11, 1975, Box 35/5, pp. 32–4.

44. FBI LHM, April 21, 1962, CIA Printed Microfilm, Box 101/23.2. On Tepedino see Mexico City to Director, July 19, CIA Printed Microfilm, Box 101/23.1. For the code names see Director to WAVE, July 17, CIA Printed Microfilm, Box 101/23.1.

45. Memorandum by Richard Fallucci, Task Force W, September 1, 1962, CIA Printed Microfilm, Box 51/3.2.

46. Madrid to Director, October 11, 1962, CIA Printed Microfilm, Box 51/3.3.

47. Assistant Attorney General J. Walter Yeagley to John A. McCone, June 1962 (exact date illegible); WAVE to Director, June 10; and CIA Memo to Record, September 28, CIA Printed Microfilm, Box 71/8.1.

48. WAVE to Director, September 29, 1962; Director to WAVE, September 30; Harvey to AG, October 4, and Charles Ford memorandum, September 28, CIA Printed Microfilm, Box 71/8.1.

49. *Chicago Tribune,* September 5, 1962, p. 1. For some reason this statement has been omitted from *Public Papers of the President.*

50. *FRUS,* XI, 8, 9.

51. *FRUS,* X, 307.

52. June and August Progress Reports on the CRC, JMWAVE to Chief Task Force W (Harvey), September 1 and September 22, 1962, CIA Printed Microfilm, Box 121/11.

53. San Juan to Director, July 25, 1962; Information Report, August 8; CIA San Juan to Director, August 10; Director to San Juan, August (?) (illegible), *ibid.,* Box 72/19.1.

54. WAVE to Chief TF W, March 14, 1961, *ibid.,* Box 7/9.2.

55. WAVE to Chief, CI/OA, February 23, 1962, CIA Printed Microfilm, Box 8/21; WAVE to Director, April 30, *ibid.,* Box 20/5.2; WAVE to Chief Task Force W, September 18, *ibid.,* Box 8/15.2; Instruction Sheet, November 7, *ibid.,* Box 8/21.

56. CIA interoffice correspondence, June 1, 1962, CIA Segregated Collection, Box 1/4. Hemming's letter was dated March 25.

57. SAC Miami, April 25, 1962, FBI 105-110398-3.

58. CIA memorandum July 2, 1962, CIA Segregated Collection, Box 1/4; SAC Miami, July 26, 1962, FBI 105-110398-9.

59. *New Orleans States-Item,* July 21, 1962, *ibid.,* and *Miami Herald,* July 22, *ibid.,* Box 1/18.

60. Sixteen years later Hemming gave the House Select Committee on Assassinations some remarkable details regarding events in New Orleans. After the meeting with Bartes and Clarens, he said, they had been flown in a small Cessna to an Air National Guard base near Covington, on the north shore of Lake Pontchartrain, where the projected training camp would be. At the airport he claimed to have seen David Ferrie, an Eastern Airlines pilot and civil air patrol instructor who had known Lee Harvey Oswald as a cadet and who was now doing work for Carlos Marcello. The plane, Hemming testified, was owned by William Reily, a New Orleans coffee manufacturer who, he said, had a long-standing relationship with Frank Bartes. One year later,

Lee Harvey Oswald went to work at the Reily Coffee Company.

Hemming claimed that he met with Rabel, Bartes, an unidentified Cuban who was with Laborde, a European with an odd accent, and an American. He was not given the names of the last two men, but he claimed later to have identified them as George de Mohrenschildt, a Russian-born oil geologist from Dallas, and Guy Banister, an ex-FBI agent who did indeed have connections both to Cubans in New Orleans and to Marcello. And at that meeting, he said, someone—the committee counsel did not force him to say who—had offered him a large sum of cash in hundred-dollar bills to try to enter Cuba and arrange the simultaneous assassinations of Fidel, Raoul, and Che Guevara. Hemming explained that he declined on the grounds that such an operation was simply impossible. There was nothing inherently improbable about Hemming's having been offered a large sum of money in New Orleans to kill Castro, since Marcello was making similar offers a year earlier, but just how much of this story was true we can only guess. Hemming's testimony is at http://www.history-matters .com/archive/jfk/hsca/unpub_testimony/pdf/Hemming_3-21-78.pdf. See especially pp. 137–42.

61. SAC Miami, September 6, 1962, FBI 2-1693-62. See also Hemming's HSCA testimony, *ibid*.

62. FBI LHM, March 30, 1962, Counterintelligence Source Files, Box 7/9.2

63. See Ragano, *Mob Lawyer*, pp. 87–131.

64. HSCA Report, X, 51.

65. For CI/Operational Approval and Support, December 29, 1961, CIA Printed Microfilm, Box 46/16. See also WAVE to Director, December 29, *ibid.*, Box 47/17.2.

66. WAVE to Director, July 7, 1962, CIA Printed Microfilm, Box 47/17.2; Jay B. L. Reyes to Chief Contact Division, Support Branch, and Chief NYC, July 26, *ibid*.

67. *New York Times*, September 14, 1962, p. 13.

68. Fabian Escalante, *1963: El Complot* (Melbourne, Australia, 2004), pp. 28–30, and testimony of David Atlee Phillips, April 25, 1978, HSCA Security Classified Testimony, at http://history-matters.com/archive/jfk/hsca/secclass/pdf/Phillips_4-25-78.pdf, pp. 66, 77.

69. July 1962 DRE Progress Report, WAVE to Chief Task Force W, August 14, 1962, CIA Printed Microfilm, Box 70/6

70. CIA Memorandum, April 8, 1962, CIA Printed Microfilm, Box 45/5.1.

71. WAVE to Chief Task Force W, June 23, 1962; WAVE to Chief Task Force W, May 31; and April progress report, n.d., CIA Printed Microfilm, Box 70/5.

72. August progress report, WAVE to Chief Task Force W, September 19, 1962, CIA Printed Microfilm, Box 70/6.

73. WAVE to Chief Task Force W, September 14, 1962; Harvey to Helms, September 4; and *Meet the Press* transcript, September 2, CIA Printed Microfilm, Box 70/6; also JMWAVE to Director, September 26, CIA Segregated Collection, WF, Box 2/9.

74. WAVE to Chief Task Force W, August 30, 1962, CIA Printed Microfilm, Box 70/6.

75. HSCA, Hearings and Appendix Volumes, X, 81–88. Luce confirmed this story in a taped conversation with William Colby of the CIA: see the transcript, October 25, 1975, CIA Miscellaneous Files, Box 3/3.7. On Keating, who had been speaking forcefully about Cuba at least since early September but did not specifically argue that the Soviets were introducing missiles until October 11, see *Chicago Tribune,* October 11, 1962, p. 2.

6. CRUSADERS AND GANGSTERS

1. SAC Philadelphia to Director, August 29, 1961, FBI 92-3171-396.

2. SAC Chicago to Director: September 8, 1961, and Evans to Belmont, September 12, FBI 92-2993171-422 and 423.

3. SAC Chicago to Director: October 10, 1961, FBI 91-3171-440, and October 12, FBI 91-3171-441.

4. SAC Chicago to Director, January 11, 1962, FBI 91-3171-582, and January 16, FBI 91-3171-588.

5. See Director to Attorney General, December 11, 1961, and SAC Chicago to Director, December 9, FBI 92-3171-527; also Blakey and Billings, *Fatal Hour,* p. 414. The same report notes that Giancana was trying to get a new manager for heavyweight Sonny Liston, one who would not be seen as so close to Giancana that Liston would not be allowed to fight for the championship, as indeed he did, successfully, in the fall of 1962.

6. Quoted in Blakey and Billings, *Fatal Hour,* pp. 414–5.

7. SAC Chicago to Director, January 3, 1962, FBI 92-350-E-48.

8. SAC Chicago to Director, February 2, 1962, FBI 91-3171-620.

9. SAC Chicago to Director, February 10, 1962, FBI 91-3171-623.

10. Director to SAC Chicago, February 15, 1962, FBI 97-3171-626, and SAC Chicago to Director, February 28, 1962, FBI 91-3171-647.

11. See SAC Los Angeles to Director, February 22, 1962, and Hoover memorandum, February 27, FBI 92-3267-121, 122, 125. This memo went into the main FBI file on Roselli where many agents, presumably, could see it.

12. O'Donnell Testimony, SSCIA, Box 1/1.

13. Courtney Evans to A. Belmont, March 15, 1962, FBI 92-3267-158. The original report on Otash's conversation with Spindel has been posted online by the FBI: LHM on Fred Otash, September 2, 1961, http://foia.fbi.gov/otash_fred/otash_fred_part01.pdf.

14. Blakey and Billings, *Fatal Hour,* p. 414, and see also p. 406. The authors, who evidently found this transcript during the HSCA investigation, state that the bug involved an investigation of bookmaker Gil Beckley but do not say exactly when the conversation occurred.

15. SSCIA, *Alleged Assassination Plots,* p. 130.

16. Hoover to SAC Chicago, April 4, 1962, FBI 97-3171-678.

17. FBI 92-3171-735. The portion of the memo in this file—Giancana's— begins with this sentence. Apparently they had been discussing other organized crime cases as well, but I do not believe the full text is available.

18. Twelve years later a Church Committee witness, William Wilson, reported that he had heard most of this story from Hoover himself while working in the Justice Department early in the Nixon administration. According to Hoover, Wilson said, both Hoover and Robert Kennedy were furious that Giancana's CIA connection had made it impossible to proceed against him even at a later date. Wilson testimony, SSCIA, Box 40/5.

19. SAC New York to Director, November 9, 1962, FBI 97-3171-919, and SAC Chicago to Director, November 20, FBI 97-3171-931.

20. SAC Chicago to Director, December 1, 1962, FBI 97-3171-944, and December 5, FBI 97-3171-936.

21. SAC Chicago to Director, October 31, 1962, FBI 97-3171-917.

22. SAC Chicago to Director, January 16, 1963 FBI 97-3171-956.

23. SAC Chicago to Director, February 28, 1963, FBI, Criminal Intelligence Files, Elsur 92-350-E-147.

24. SAC Chicago to Director, April 2, 1963, FBI 97-3171-991.

25. This claim is from Roemer, *Man Against the Mob,* pp. 183–9.

26. On Sheridan and Hoover see Victor Navasky, *Kennedy Justice,* p. 412.

27. Moldea, *The Hoffa Wars,* p. 55.

28. Sheridan, *Fall and Rise,* pp. 205–6.

29. J. Edgar Hoover memorandum, August 13, 1962, FBI 92-3267-284, and SAC Los Angeles, August 17, FBI 92-3267-301.

30. Sheridan, *Fall and Rise,* pp. 198–216.

31. On Partin's previous legal problems see Navasky, *Kennedy Justice,* pp. 419– 20; Sheridan, *Fall and Rise,* pp. 195–6, 216; Chief Justice Warren's dissenting opinion, *Hoffa v. United States,* 385 U.S. 293 (1966); and *New York Times,* February 7, 1964, p. 61.

32. FBI LHM, October 4, 1962, and SAC New Orleans, October 10, FBI 63-9966-1 and 63-9966-6. Sheridan, *Fall and Rise,* p. 217, claims that Partin passed the polygraph first and was then released from jail. The opposite was true. On the FBI's skepticism, see Navasky, *Kennedy Justice,* p. 420.

33. Navasky, *Kennedy Justice,* p. 406 (based on Sheridan's own log).

34. Ben Bradlee, *Conversations with Kennedy* (New York, 1975), p. 126. Ken-

nedy told the story to Bradlee, then a *Newsweek* correspondent, in February 1963. The story emerged during Hoffa's jury tampering trial in the spring of 1964 but attracted remarkably little attention.

35. Interview with G. Robert Blakey, October 1983.

36. SAC Tampa, May 27, 1961, FBI 92-2781-218; McAndrews to Evans, September 20, FBI 92-2781-315; Labadie to Director, October 2, FBI 92-2781-323. The files do not make clear if bugs were actually implanted.

37. SAC Tampa, December 7, 1961, FBI 92-2781-390.

38. SAC Tampa, January 15, 1962, FBI 92-2781-425; SAC Tampa, February 2, FBI 92-2781-453.

39. SAC Miami, August 31, 1962, FBI 92-2781-600, and SAC Miami, September 11, FBI 92-2781-604.

40. John Martino and Nathan Weyl, *I Was Castro's Prisoner: An American Tells His Story* (New York, 1963), pp. 105–29.

41. SAC Miami to Hoover, November 2, 1962, FBI 64-44828-7; Acting Chief, Miami Field Office, October 23, 1962, CIA Segregated Collection, Box 15/11. The names of the Cubans are deleted from the latter document.

42. Hemming's HSCA testimony, March 21, 1978, p. 123, is at http://www.history-matters.com/archive/jfk/hsca/unpub_testimony/pdf/Hemming_3-21-78.pdf.

43. Martino and Weyl, *I Was Castro's Prisoner,* pp. 44–8. Although Pawley was quoted with regard to one suspected Communist, I am not aware that Pawley ever made accusations of homosexuality.

44. SAC Miami to Director, February 4, 1964, FBI 92-503-241.

45. E. A. Loughran to Robert Hale, February 21, 1962, INS file A2 669 541.

46. *New York Times,* June 9, 1961, p. 67; July 12, p. 20, and October 30, p. 6; SAC New Orleans, August 10, FBI 92-2713-215.

47. SAC New Orleans, December 14, 1961, FBI 92-2713-255.

48. SAC Baltimore, September 2, 1961, and March 14, 1962, FBI 92-2713-229, FBI 92-2713-294.

49. Irving Davidson interview, November 2, 1978, HSCA Box 232/13239.

50. John H. Davis, *Mafia Kingfish: Carlos Marcello and the Assassination of John F. Kennedy* (New York, 1989), pp. 111–2.

51. For the Milwaukee informant's report, see SAC Milwaukee, March 24, 1962, FBI 92-2713-299.

52. SAC New Orleans, February 7, 1962 FBI 92-2713-272, and January 10, 1963, FBI 92-2713-348.

53. SAC Los Angeles, May 11, 1967, FBI Los Angeles 137-2528-196; see also reports of May 16, FBI 137-2528-196, and June 5, FBI 92-2675-2, all in FBI files, Edward Becker. See also Ed Reid, *The Grim Reapers* (Chicago, 1966), pp. 157–9. Reid did not publish Becker's or Roppolo's names.

54. Ragano, *Mob Lawyer,* pp. 132–8.

55. *Ibid.,* pp. 140–5.

56. SAC Miami, September 25, 1963, FBI 92-2781-830, and SAC Miami, October 24, FBI 92-2781-871.

57. *Washington Post,* May 16, 1976, p. 29.

58. Aleman's testimony, September 27, 1978, at http://history-matters.com/archive/jfk/hsca/reportvols/vol5/html/HSCA_Vol5_0153a.htm.

7. THE MOB ENLISTS THE CIA

1. For full accounts of the crisis see Fursenko and Naftali, *One Hell of a Gamble,* pp. 198–290; Ernest R. May and Philip D. Zelikow, eds., *The Kennedy Tapes: Inside the White House during the Cuban Missile Crisis* (Cambridge, 1997); and McGeorge Bundy, *Danger and Survival* (New York, 1988), pp. 391–462.

2. See *FRUS,* 1961–63, X–XIII, supplement, and JFK Library, RFK Kennedy papers, Attorney General's papers, Box 1, Desk Diary, 1962.

3. Harvey Testimony, July 11, 1975, SSCIA, Box 35/5.

4. Fursenko and Naftali, *One Hell of a Gamble,* p. 284.

5. *Ibid.,* pp. 312–3.

6. Taylor Exhibit 11, SSCIA documents (copy in author's possession).

7. *FRUS,* XI, 197, 201.

8. CIA, LA WF, Box 1/1.

9. See Powers, *The Man Who Kept the Secrets,* pp. 88–91, 136.

10. *FRUS,* XI, 264.

11. *FRUS,* XI, 261, 262.

12. Memos by Cottrell, January 24, 1963, and Excom meeting, January 25, *ibid.,* 273, 274, 275.

13. *FRUS,* XI, 271.

14. *Ibid.,* 289.

15. *Chicago Tribune,* November 22, 1962, p. 24.

16. For the interview with Al Burt, see CIA Printed Microfilm, Box 69/27.2.

17. Dispatch, WAVE to Chief Task Force W (Harvey), November 13, 1962, CIA Printed Microfilm, Box 69/28.

18. Contact Report, November 16, 1962, LA WF, 2/9.

19. Memo for Record, November 15, 1962, CIA Printed Microfilm, Box 69/28.

20. See Jefferson Morley, "Celebrated Authors Demand that CIA Come Clean on JFK Assassination," *Salon,* December 17, 2003, http://www.salon.com/news/feature/2003/12/17/joannides/.

21. Luis Fernandez Rocha to John F. Kennedy, December 13, 1963, CIA Printed Microfilm, Box 69/27.2.

22. WAVE to Director, December 10, 1962, CIA Printed Microfilm, Box 69/27.2.

23. *Washington Post,* December 4, 1962; SAC Miami, December 6; Hoover to SAC Miami, December 13; and SAC Miami, February 19, FBI 2-1693-70, 75, 77.

24. Laurence Houston to J. Walter Yeagley, January 9, 1963, CIA Printed Microfilm, Box 72/20.1.

25. For two excellent accounts of the negotiations see Navasky, *Kennedy Justice,* pp. 327–39, and Johnson, *Bay of Pigs,* pp. 321–41.

26. *Public Papers of the President 1962,* no. 556, at http://www.presidency.ucsb.edu/ws/index.php?pid=9065&st=&st1=.

27. Terence S. Carabanc to chief SAS, January 31, 1963; Monroney, Robert F., Office of Security, January 23, and WAVE to Director, February 16, CIA Printed Microfilm, Box 3/16.2; WAVE to Chief SAS, March 13; WAVE to Director, March 14, and Managua to WAVE et al., March 25, CIA Printed Microfilm, Box 3/16.1.

28. On these meetings, which dealt mainly with the Alliance for Progress, see Martin, *Kennedy and Latin America,* pp. 104–14.

29. Laurence Houston to J. Walter Yeagley, January 9, 1963, CIA Printed Microfilm, Box 72/20.1, and Field Information Report, February 6, CIA Microfilm, Box 72/20.2.

30. San Juan to Director, January 4, 1963, CIA Printed Microfilm, Box 72/20.1.

31. CIA IG Report of 1967, pp. 52–3.

32. This information was provided indirectly to me in the fall of 2003 by General Fabian Escalante, the retired Cuban counterintelligence officer and author.

33. Pearson Diary, LBJ Library, January 13, 1967; Pearson and Anderson, "The Washington Merry-Go-Round," March 7, *Washington Post,* p. C13; Morgan interview, March 21, FBI 62-109060-4827. The Pearson/Anderson column referred to a 1963 plot, and Morgan indicated to the FBI that the assassins had been captured not too long before the assassination of the President.

34. *Washington Post,* January 18, 1971, p. B7; January 19, p. D15; March 10, 1975, p. D13.

35. SSCIA, *Alleged Assassination Plots,* pp. 84–5. Frederick A. O. Schwartz, the committee's chief counsel, explained in an interview with me on July 11, 2005, that the committee had decided to focus on the issue of authorization of the plots, rather than on their exact extent, and their report certainly reflected this approach.

36. HSCA, X, p. 177.

37. See Bradley Earl Ayers, *The War That Never Was* (New York, 1976), pp. 37–8, and Director CIA to Director FBI, June 25, 1963. FBI 92-3267-482.

38. Halpern Testimony, June 18, 1975, SSCIA, Box 25/2, pp. 22–8. See also CIA IG Report of 1967, pp. 75–7. A new book, Don Bohning, *The Castro Obsession* (New York, 2005), p. 183, edits an interview with Halpern to suggest that Halpern was claiming that Fitzgerald had gotten his orders from the Kennedys, but Halpern's own words, as reported by Bohning, do not say that.

39. Chief, CIA Operational Approval and Support, November 9, 1962, CIA Printed Microfilm, Box 47/17.2, and CIA Interagency memo, November 16, CIA Printed Microfilm, Box 46/17.1. See also Director to Withheld, April 8, 1972, CIA Printed Microfilm, Box 46/17.1, which states that Veciana's relationship with Army Intelligence lasted until 1966.

40. WAVE to Director, 630104, CIA Printed Microfilm, Box 72/20.2.

41. *Chicago Tribune*, March 19, 1963, p. 1, and *New York Times*, March 20, p. 2.

42. McCone memorandum, March 26, 1963, CIA Miscellaneous Files, Box 5/6.17, and *FRUS*, XI, 303, 304.

43. Memo by Joseph Califano, April 17, 1963, *FRUS*, X–XII microfiche supplement, no. 655.

44. *FRUS*, XI, 315.

45. *FRUS*, X–XII, microfiche supplement, no. 670.

46. See Kaiser, *American Tragedy*, especially pp. 198–200.

47. Quoted in CIA, Latin America Division/DDO, Memorandum to the Inspector General, "Latin America Division Task Force Report of Possible Cuban Complicity in the John F. Kennedy Assassination," June 29, 1977, LA WF, Box 3/1.

48. *FRUS*, XI, 322, 329, 330, 333.

49. CIA, LA WF, Box 1/9.

50. *FRUS*, XI, 347.

51. *Wall Street Journal*, March 15, 1963, p. 1.

52. Memcon, March 20, 1963, JFK Library, NSF, President's Trip to San Jose, 3/63, Memoranda of Conversations, Box 238A.

53. *FRUS*, XI, 346, and see Fitzgerald memo, June 19, 1963, CIA, LA WF, Box 1/1, for the President's approval.

54. See the chapter on Cuba from Pawley's unpublished autobiography, written in the early 1970s and unprophetically entitled "Russia Is Winning," in the Thomas Paterson papers, Thomas J. Dodd center, University of Connecticut. See also *Chicago Tribune*, November 10, 1962, p. N2, a UPI item of November 3 in Pawley's FBI file, FBI 62-79985, and the *Miami Herald*, November 4, 1962.

55. The unusually large and well-organized CIA file on this operation, with its pages numbered, will be found in JFK, CIA Segregated Collection, Box 51/

25. On the April 18 meeting see Shackley's May 23 memorandum, "Soviet Defectors," no. 18348.

56. See Chief, JMWAVE to Chief SAS, July 24, 1963, *ibid.*, no. 18460, and *Miami Herald,* January 8, 1976, p. 1, in which Pawley claimed to have been called by Eastland.

57. Shackley, "Soviet Defectors," CIA Segregated Collection, Box 51/25.

58. Interview with Richard Billings, July 11, 2005, and Shackley (COS JMWAVE) to Carter (DDCI) and Desmond Fitzgerald, June 5, 1963, CIA Segregated Collection, Box 51/25, no. 18355.

59. For Hall's account see the summary of his interview with HSCA Staff, HSCA, Transcripts and Steno Tapes of Immunized Executive Session, Box 1, August 20, 1977, and his testimony, October 5, 1977, *ibid.* Hemming's testimony of March 21, 1978, is at http://www.history-matters.com/archive/jfk/hsca/unpub_testimony/pdf/Hemming_3-21-78.pdf. The two men, who were no longer on speaking terms by the late 1970s, agreed on all these points.

60. For examples of Hunt's letters see the *Dallas Morning News,* October 2, 1962; June 29, 1963; and August 9, 1963. On Morris, *ibid.,* August 13, 1963, sec. 4, p. 1.

61. See *Washington Post,* November 21, 1962, p. A4.

62. Logue identified himself as a "professional associate" of Hunt, adding, "I regarded him as a great American. He worked in right-wing causes, some of which I admire very much." *Dallas Times Herald,* April 2, 1977, p. 4. Logue also acknowledged one meeting with George de Mohrenschildt, but it is doubtful that they knew each other well, since Logue does not appear in de Mohrenschildt's voluminous address book. On de Mohrenschildt, see Chapter 9.

63. On Walker see below, chapter 9.

64. See the staff summary of Hall's testimony, HSCA, Transcripts and Steno Tapes of Immunized Executive Session, Box 1, August 20, 1977, for the fullest account. By the time Hall gave this testimony in 1977, Giancana, Roselli, and Martino were dead, and no one could corroborate this part of the story. It certainly was possible, however—Giancana was detected flying to Caribbean destinations from Miami in this period—and there is no question, in any case, that Martino remained close to Trafficante and that Trafficante and Roselli had been involved in plots against Castro since 1960. According to Warren Hinckle and William Turner, "CIA sources" told them that Roselli and Martino were hanging out together that summer, but Turner does not now recall who the sources were, and I have discovered another case in which their source repudiated what they claimed he said. Warren Hinckle and William Turner, *Deadly Secrets: The CIA-MAFIA War against Castro and the Assassination of J.F.K.* (New York, 1992), p. 195.

65. Memo for record, June 4, 1963, CIA Segregated Collection, Box 51/25, no. 18354.

66. *Miami Herald,* January 8, 1976, p. 1.

67. Memo to DCOS, 6/6/63. Subject: "Load and Capacity of V-20 Intermediate Craft." CIA Segregated Collection, Box 51/25, no. 18362.

68. Robertson's memos are a memo to Shackley, June 15, 1963, CIA Segregated Collection, Box 51/25, no. 18451, and the more informal "Memo for Ted/Bob from Rip, June 15, 1963," CIA Miscellaneous Files, Box 8, JFK-M-08/2.

69. Chief of Station to Director, June 26, 1963, CIA Segregated Collection, Box 51/25/2, no. 18457, and WAVE to Director, June 26, CIA Miscellaneous Files, Box 8, JFK-M-08/2.

70. WAVE to Director, February 26, 1964, CIA Segregated Collection, Box 51/25/2.

71. SAC Richmond, June 21, 1963, FBI 92-3267-481.

72. Shackley Testimony, SSCIA, August 19 and 25, 1975, Box 46. Martino had died just two weeks earlier, on August 3. Shackley also denied knowledge of any assassination plots and said he was not surprised that Harvey, for whom he had also worked in Berlin, would have kept Harvey's contacts with Roselli from him.

8. A DEFECTOR RETURNS

1. Because Oswald's experiences in Russia have been frequently dealt with in considerable detail, this work will spend relatively little time on them. The most interesting accounts are Edward J. Epstein, *Legend,* as reprinted with a new afterword in *The Assassination Chronicles* (New York, 1992), especially pp. 378–437; Norman Mailer, *Oswald's Tale: An American Mystery* (New York, 1995); and Priscilla Johnson McMillan, *Marina and Lee* (New York, 1977), pp. 64–182. This last book, however, is based largely on interviews with Marina, whose memory had shown an astonishing improvement since the fall and winter of 1963–64.

2. SAC New York, November 27, 1962, FBI 105-82555-50 (p. 31); SAC San Antonio, December 12, FBI 105-82555-790.

3. SAC New Orleans, November 25, 1963, FBI 105-82555-454.

4. SAC St. Louis, November 29, 1963, FBI 105-82555-50 41st NR and SAC Milwaukee, November 30, FBI 105-82555-568.

5. Robert Oswald, with Myrick and Barbara Land, *Lee: A Portrait of Lee Harvey Oswald by His Brother Robert Oswald* (New York, 1967), p. 47.

6. Herbert Philbrick, *I Led Three Lives: Citizen, "Communist," Counterspy* (New York, 1952), especially pp. 20, 63–5.

7. Epstein, *Legend,* p. 460.

8. Ensign Horrigan to Commander Vanderbilt, CIA Printed Microfilm, Box 13/16B2 (undated).

9. Epstein, *Legend,* p. 463, and FBI report, March 3, 1964 (interview with Winifred Sharples), CIA Printed Microfilm, Box 13/16B1.

10. De Mohrenschildt has often been cited as the only man who knew both Oswald and Mrs. Kennedy. The journalist and author Priscilla Johnson McMillan is, I believe, the only person to have known both Oswald and President Kennedy.

11. The address book is in HSCA, Box 26/1193. For Bush's note see Russell Holmes's summary, April 4, 1977, CIA Segregated Collection, Box 34/20.

12. Moore's trace request is in CIA Printed Microfilm, Box 13/16B2. See two memos by Russell Holmes, April 4 and April 7, 1977, CIA Segregated Collection, Box 36/27 and Box 34/20.

13. Hosty mentioned this in Church Committee testimony, Box 42, December 7, 1975, p. 61.

14. Epstein, *Legend,* p. 471.

15. CIA, LA WF, Box 5/4, Director to Rio, December 16, 1960. Washington wanted to arrange a meeting between Cubela and representatives of the new DRE. It is not clear whether this happened.

16. For a clean copy of the FBI LHM, see CIA Printed Microfilm, Box 101/22.1. A largely illegible copy is in de Mohrenschildt's file from the same collection, Box 13/16B1. On his departure from Mexico see Epstein, *Legend,* p. 464. According to Epstein, de Mohrenschildt's tourist card showed that he had left Mexico in November, but it is not clear where he got this information.

17. Escalante, *1963: El Complot,* p. 58.

18. The plot is even thicker because Antonio Veciana, whom Phillips had recruited under the name Bishop, said that Bishop had referred him for training to a man named Melton, and Phillips more or less acknowledged knowing such a man in Havana without being able to identify him.

19. FBI Report, March 14, 1964, filed in CIA Printed Microfilm, Box 13/16A2.

20. On the Oswalds' movements, see *Report of the President's Commission on the Assassination of President John F. Kennedy* (Washington, DC, 1964) (hereafter *Warren Report*), pp. 714–8; on Orlov, see Epstein, *Legend,* pp. 457–8. Orlov recalled visiting the Oswalds with de Mohrenschildt but said that they were clearly acquainted with each other before that.

21. Epstein, *Legend,* pp. 558–9.

22. FBI Report, March 14, 1964, filed in CIA Printed Microfilm, Box 13/16A2.

23. Warren Commission, IX, p. 235.

24. Moore's memorandum may be found in CIA Printed Microfilm, Box 107/3.

25. The FBI reports of these debriefs were reprinted in WC, XVII, pp. 728–40. On Oswald's defection see Newman, *Oswald and the CIA,* pp. 15ff.

26. The HSCA summarized the experiences of various other defectors and their CIA contacts. The study is at http://jfkassassination.net/russ/jfkinfo4/jfk12/defector.htm.

27. Epstein, *Legend,* p. 559.

28. HSCA. *Final Assassinations Report,* p. 264.

29. On this period see Epstein, *Legend,* pp. 469–79, and *Warren Report,* pp. 714–22.

30. For the correspondence see WC, XXI, pp. 674–7.

31. This correspondence is in WC, XIX, pp. 573–80.

32. FBI Domestic Intel Division, February 14, 1964, FBI 105-82555-2143.

33. Epstein, *Legend,* p. 647; *Warren Report,* pp. 741–3. The commission analysis allows Oswald up to $100 a month in some fall months for food and miscellaneous expenses, but only by listing nothing in those categories for June and July.

34. CIA memorandum, June 23, 1964, CIA Printed Microfilm, Box 14/18.

35. SAC Dallas, December 3, 1963, FBI 105-82555-455.

36. Telephone interview with Nicholas Anikeefe, July 16, 2005.

37. *Warren Report,* pp. 184–5, 723–4.

38. *Warren Report,* p. 725.

39. *Chicago Tribune,* July 27, 1961, p. C6; *Los Angeles Times,* December 13, p. 2.

40. *Washington Post,* December 7, 1961, p. D23.

41. *Los Angeles Times,* December 7, 1962, p. 13; *Chicago Tribune,* January 22, 1963; *Washington Post,* May 3, 1963, p. A4.

42. *The Worker,* April 2, 1963, p. 2. In the late 1970s a German émigré named Volkmar Schmidt, who had met the Oswalds twice in February, claimed to Edward Jay Epstein that he had drawn Oswald out on the danger posed by men like Walker during that month. He also claimed that Oswald had bitterly attacked President Kennedy's policies toward Cuba. Epstein, *Legend,* pp. 483–5. Yet this story seems too good to be true, mainly because of Schmidt's failure to bring it to the attention of authorities in 1963–64, when it would have virtually clinched their case, even though Schmidt was interviewed by the FBI. In addition, Schmidt's story of how he met Oswald and where these conversations took place does not match that of de Mohrenschildt or of Everett Glover, his roommate, who was interviewed by the FBI and testified before the Warren Commission. See Warren Commission, IX, pp. 128–9, 256, 452 (testimony of George

and Jeanne de Mohrenschildt), and X, pp. 3, 20–30 (testimony of Everett Glover).

43. SAC Dallas, December 23, 1963, FBI 105-82555-1212.

44. The text of the note is in Mailer, *Oswald's Tale,* pp. 504–5. On Marina and the Secret Service see Forrest Sorrels to Jesse Curry, December 26, 1963, in the Dallas Police Department (hereafter DPD) files. Marguerite's denial is Warren Commission, I, pp. 243–4.

45. SAC Dallas, December 16, 1963, FBI 105-82555-1212.

46. Dallas Police Department (hereafter DPD), Supplementary Offense Reports, April 12 and April 16, 1963, Box 20, folder 9/2. This entire collection may be viewed (with an Opera browser) at http://jfk.ci.dallas.tx.us/.

47. *Ibid.*

48. SAC Los Angeles, January 23, 1964, FBI 105-82555-1492; SAC Oklahoma City, January 28, FBI 105-82555-1570.

49. See Gerald Posner, *Case Closed* (New York, 1993), pp. 116–7n. Posner claims the car was identified as belonging to one of Walker's associates but gives no source.

50. Secret Service Report, November 28, 1963, FBI 105-82555-929. It is possible, of course, that he did, and that the *Militant's* editors disposed of them.

51. See Epstein, *Legend,* pp. 491–2, 559–61.

52. State Airgram from Haiti, December 8, 1963, FBI 105-82555-342.

53. Memo by George de Mohrenschildt, August 1, 1962, CIA Printed Microfilm, Box 8/29.

54. Memorandum by Jerry Brown, Security Analysis group, December 30, 1974, CIA Segregated Collection, Box 41/15.

55. Interview with Gale Allen, June 19, 2004.

56. See A-135 Port-au-Prince, October 3, 1962; A-284 Port-au-Prince, January 20, 1963; State Memo, "Assessment of Haitian Opposition," JFK Library, NSF, Haiti, General, 9/62–2/63, Box 103.

57. Memorandum of Visit—Joseph W. Dryer [sic], Jr., May 1, 1963, Counterintelligence Source Files (IRR), Box 29/3. (The HSCA, which interviewed Dreyer in 1978, spelled his name with two Es.)

58. Subject: Charles, n.d., Counterintelligence Source Fills (IRR), Box 29/3.

59. Teletype, NY DCO Balog to Czaikowski, May 2, 1963, CIA Printed Microfilm, Box 8/29.

60. Balog to Czaikowski, May 7, 1963, CIA Printed Microfilm, Box 107/3.

61. CIA Memo to Record A. F. Czaikowski, May 10, 1963, CIA Printed Microfilm, Box 107/3.

62. Telephone interview with Nicholas Anikeefe, July 16, 2005. Mr.

Anikeefe said he met de Mohrenschildt in New York before the Second World War and remained friends with him until his death. He assured me, however, that their dealings did not involve CIA business.

63. Memo for Record, State, Office of Caribbean Affairs, May 23, 1963, Counterintelligence Source Fills (IRR), Box 29/2; Contact Report, May 21, 1963, CIA Printed Microfilm, Box 13/16A3.

64. Hosty to SAC Dallas, July 19, 1962, FBI 100-110461-29. Paul Hoch made this document available to me.

65. See SAC Dallas to Director, SAC Dallas, March 25, 1963, FBI 105-82555-31, and Hosty to SAC Dallas, May 23, 1963, DL 100-10461-35.

9. THE BIG EASY

1. This is well covered by John Newman, *Oswald and the CIA* (New York, 1995), pp. 310–3. See also Chapter 10, below.

2. See SAC New Orleans, May 23, 1962, FBI 105-110398-5, and SAC Miami, July 26, FBI 105-110398-9.

3. SSCIA, Testimony of Warren DeBrueys, January 8, 1975, Box 43. See Bringuier's testimony, WC, X, pp. 32ff.

4. SAC Miami, July 18, 1963, and Hoover to J. Walter Yeagley, July 24, FBI 2-1821-2.

5. Koch, as he preferred to be called, appeared on a CIA list of DRE infiltrators for a November 1961 operation and had attended the World Youth Festival in Helsinki with other DRE members in July 1962. See unattributed CIA memo, August 17, 1962, CIA Printed Microfilm, Box 110/9, and JMWAVE to Director, December 15, 1961, CIA Printed Microfilm, Box 45/5.1.

6. FBI LHM, SAC Miami, July 24, 1963, FBI 2-1821-10.

7. SAC New Orleans, July 26, 1963, FBI 2-1821-12; SAC New Orleans, July 26, FBI 2-1821-12; D. E. Moore to Sullivan, July 30, FBI 2-1821-17; Moore to Sullivan, July 31, FBI 2-1821-18; SAC Miami, July 29, FBI 2-1821-22; Moore to Sullivan, July 31, FBI 2-1821-19.

8. BELL to WAVE, April 1961, CIA Printed Microfilm, Box 22/12.1. Espinosa's HSCA testimony, June 7, 1978, is HSCA, Box 170/9265. On his clearance see Memorandum, February 19, 1968, CIA Segregated Collection, Box 41/53.

9. SAC Miami, July 31, FBI 2-1821-31.

10. Hoover to Customs Bureau, June 21, 1963, FBI 2-1693-90.

11. Espinosa HSCA testimony, Box 170/9265; SAC New Orleans, October 28, 1963, FBI 2-1821-51.

12. SAC New Orleans, 630814, FBI 2-1821-44.

13. See Dan Moldea, *Interference: How Organized Crime Influences Professional Football* (New York, 1989), pp. 94–5. For McLaney's claims see SAC Miami, September 20, 1973, FBI 92-14642-2.

14. SAC New York, October 16, 1967, FBI 162-1-202-167.

15. SAC Miami, August 8, 1963, FBI 2-1821-33. Curiously enough, Benton, who also did insurance investigations, and McLaney were now engaged in a lengthy attempt to blackmail or ruin Carroll Rosenbloom over charges that the Colts' owner had torched his own house in Margate, New Jersey, in 1950. In the course of the proceedings McLaney also accused Rosenbloom of betting against his own Baltimore Colts in 1953. Rosenbloom denied it. See Moldea, *Interference*, pp. 110–4.

16. See CIA Memo for record by Major Koch, September 15, 1961, CIA Printed Microfilm, Box 35/28.2, and Trace Request, November 18, 1963, CIA Printed Microfilm, Box 35/28.1.

17. WAVE Information Report, September 3, 1963, CIA Printed Microfilm, Box 12/6.

18. Information Report, CIA, 630726, CIA Printed Microfilm, Box 7/9.2.

19. Field Information Report, August 29, 1963, CIA Printed Microfilm, Box 73/7.

20. JMWAVE, December 30, 1967, CIA Segregated Collection, Box 1/2.

21. WAVE to Director, September 2, 1963, CIA Printed Microfilm, Box 73/7. Another copy is in CIA, LA WF, Box 1/4.

22. SAC New Orleans, October 3, 1963, FBI 109-584-3740.

23. J. Walter Yeagley, Assistant Attorney General for Internal Security, to Hoover, March 25, 1968, FBI 105-179794-1.

24. SAC New Orleans, April 13, 1961, FBI 92-2713-144.

25. Morgan testimony, SSCIA, March 19, 1976, Box 26/5, p. 62.

26. Roselli testimony, SSCIA, April 23, 1976, Box 46, pp. 49–50.

27. Rickenbacker to Ferrie, March 23, 1953, HSCA, Box 285/14904, FAA files, vol. III (folder C).

28. Sergio Arcacha Smith to Eddie Rickenbacker, July 18, 1961, HSCA, Box 285/14904 vol. IV.

29. FBI LHM, SAC New Orleans, September 21, 1961; Ferrie to Captain Greiner, October 30; and FBI LHM, New Orleans, October 30, HSCA, Box 285/14904, FAA file, vol. III.

30. See FBI interview with Gordon Novell, February 21, 1967, FBI 62-109060-4707, and INS to FBI, April 17, 1968, FBI CR 105-0-17960.

31. Memorandum of February 20, 1967, New Orleans Domestic Contacts, CIA, Office of Security Files, Box 1/2.2.

32. See Goldfarb, *Perfect Villains, Imperfect Heroes,* pp. 72–5.

33. Border Patrol, report of investigation, February 19, 1962, FBI 105-104340-4.

34. FAA Report, December 13, 1963, HSCA, Box 284/14904, Folder A.

35. See the House Committee report, "David Ferrie," HSCA, X, pp. 105–14, at http://www.history-matters.com/archive/jfk/hsca/reportvols/vol10/pdf/HSCA_Vol10_AC_12_Ferrie.pdf.

36. Hearings before the Subcommittee to Investigate the Administration of the Internal Security Act and Other Internal Security Laws of the Committee on the Judiciary, US Senate, parts 11–12, 84th Congress, 2nd Session, Washington, 1956. At the close of the hearing, Eastland expressed the subcommittee's thanks to "Mayor Morrison, the deputy police chief, W. Guy Banister, and his assistant, Sergeant Hubert Badeaux, Marshal Edward Petitbon and his assistants, in particularly Mr. Todd and Mr. Grace . . . The police department here, the major, Mr. Banister, have been very helpful in setting up the hearing and making preparations for this investigation."

37. See Newman, *Oswald and the CIA*, pp. 289–90, and HSCA, Box 236/13523 (Nitschke, Oster, Lewis, and Brengel interviews).

38. See James Kirkwood, *American Grotesque* (New York, 1970), pp. 125–8, for Ferrie's Secret Service interview. (Kirkwood's book is an acute, violent attack on the Garrison investigation and the trial of Clay Shaw.)

39. SAC New Orleans, November 27, 1963, FBI 105-82555-454.

40. Belmont to Rosen, November 29, 1963, FBI 105-82555-72.

41. SAC New Orleans, November 25, 1963, FBI 105-82555-454.

42. FAA Report, December 13, 1963, HSCA, Box 284/14904, Folder A.

43. HSCA Report, IX, p. 106, at http://www.history-matters.com/archive/jfk/hsca/reportvols/vol9/pdf/HSCA_Vol9_4_Oswald.pdf.

44. *Ibid.,* pp. 110–5.

45. The photo was first printed in Robert Grodin, *The Search for Lee Harvey Oswald: A Comprehensive Photographic Record* (New York, 1995), pp. 18–9.

46. See Peter Whitmey, "Did David Ferrie Lie to the Secret Service?" (*The Fourth Decade,* 1996), at http://mcadams.posc.mu.edu/whitmeyferrie.htm. This includes the full list of calls, although it is not completely clear how Whitmey determined which calls from the office (as opposed to collect calls placed from elsewhere) could be attributed to Ferrie.

47. SAC New Orleans, November 25, 1963, FBI 105-82555-454, pp. 680, 683. See also the Secret Service report of December 1, WC, XXVI, pp. 762–73.

48. HSCA, X, p. 128.

49. *Ibid.,* p. 129.

50. HSCA, Box 184/9979, and Box 204/11196.

51. HSCA, Box 190/10347 (deposition, June 15, 1978). A copy of Gaudet's 1963 FBI interview is *ibid.,* Box 236/13526.

52. HSCA Report, X, pp. 96–9.

53. See Arthur E. Carpenter, "Social Origins of Anticommunism: The Information Council of the Americas," *Louisiana History* no. 20 (1989), pp. 117–43, especially pp. 120–9.

54. See Newman, *Oswald and the CIA,* p. 342. Newman seems too definite, however, about a reference to Frank Hand and his relationship to Butler.

55. Garry Wills, *The Second Civil War: Arming for Armageddon* (New York, 1968), pp. 145–8.

56. Wannall to Sullivan, November 23, 1963, FBI 97-4196-876.

57. Final Report of the Select Committee to Study Governmental Operations with Respect to Intelligence Activities, United States Senate, Book III: Supplementary Detailed Staff Reports on Intelligence Activities and the Rights of Americans (Washington, DC, 1976; hereafter SSCIA, III), pp. 1–10.

58. *Ibid.,* pp. 35–6, 45, 49, 60–3.

59. Wannall to Sullivan, November 23, 1963, FBI 97-4196-876.

60. Hoover to the Attorney General, November 26, 1963, FBI 97-4196-877.

10. OSWALD EXPOSED

1. This and the following correspondence between Oswald and the FPCC are reproduced in WC, XX, pp. 511–33.

2. A CIA memorandum of January 1964 noted that the agency had a file on the company, which had been "of interest as of 1948," but no other information has ever been released. M. D. Stevens memorandum, January 31, 1964, NARA, JFK Collection, CIA, Office of Security files, Box 1/2.1. I am indebted to Malcolm Blunt for bringing this to my attention. Gerry Hemming also claimed to have met Reily on his 1962 trip to New Orleans to set up a training camp, but this is certainly unconfirmed.

3. *Warren Report,* pp. 725–6. It is not clear exactly when Oswald knew he had won his appeal, but he had written Marina and Ruth Paine on May 3 that he expected to receive his benefits.

4. Lee's testimony: WC, X, pp. 86–95.

5. SAC New Orleans, December 4, 1963, FBI 105-82555-455, p. 393, and see *Warren Report,* p. 728.

6. SAC New Orleans, November 23, 1963, FBI 105-82555-454, p. 264. The bureau subsequently found Oswald's fingerprint on one of the magazines and found that an ad for Klein's Sporting Goods, where Oswald bought his rifle, had been torn out of it: *Warren Report,* p. 455–6.

7. *Warren Report,* p. 727.

8. SAC Mobile, November 30, 1963, FBI 105-82555-383 1st NR.

9. On the *Wasp* see Newman, *Oswald and the CIA,* pp. 313–4. On the Tulane sighting, see interview with Hugh T. Murray, SAC New Orleans, November 26, 1963, FBI 105-82555-454.

10. Rafael Aznarez Costea to J. Edgar Hoover, June 29, 1963, FBI 97-4196-857.

11. Carlos Bringuier to J. Edgar Hoover, February 14, 1967, FBI 62-109060-4514.

12. SAC New Orleans, November 25, 1963, FBI 44-24016-634.

13. On Piedra see CIA Segregated Collection, Box 9/71, n.d., "Orlando Piedra," and CIA WH/4, "Anti-Castro Activities in the United States," January 15, 1960, CIA Seg 44/6. His FBI interview was SAC Miami, December 18, 1963, FBI 105-82555-813.

14. SAC New Orleans, October 25, 1963, FBI DL 105-1201-15. Thirty years later Piedra gave a series of interviews in which he recalled the FBI finding him in Miami, "on vacation." He said that Oswald's address book had included his name as well as his address—which was false—and that he had told the bureau about an unnamed friend of Oswald's whom he thought should be arrested. There is no such information in his interview. See Daniel Efrain Raimundo, *Habla El Coronel Orlando Piedra* (Miami, 1994), p. 191.

15. WC, XX, pp. 524–5, and see p. 533 for the envelope.

16. WC, X, pp. 32–50, for Bringuier's testimony, April 7, 1964, in New Orleans.

17. DeBrueys more or less confirmed this in his SSCIA testimony, Box 43.

18. See Geraci's testimony, WC, X, p. 78, and Blaylock's testimony, *ibid.,* p. 83. Their testimony tallies with what they told the FBI on November 29, 1963: see FBI 100-16601-98, pp. 532–5.

19. Carlos Bringuier, *Red Friday, November 22, 1963* (Chicago, 1969). According to one account, he had solicited money to finance the publication from Dallas oil billionaire H. L. Hunt: Dick Russell, *The Man Who Knew Too Much* (New York, 1992), p. 588.

20. Bringuier's testimony, WC, X, pp. 32–50. For his FBI interview see FBI NO 100-16601, pp. 696–7.

21. Francis Martello testimony, April 7–8, 1964, WC, X, p. 62.

22. See Stuckey's Warren Commission testimony, June 6, 1964, WC, XI, pp. 158–60. Based upon Stuckey's testimony, this encounter must have taken place on the day of the confrontation in the street.

23. For Martello's November 23 statements and Lillian Murret's statements see WC, XXVI, pp. 762–81 (CE 3119). This important document may have been neglected because it is almost illegible without computer magnification.

24. WC, XXVI, p. 791 (FBI report of December 4, 1964).

25. Newman, *Oswald and the CIA,* pp. 334–6.

26. SAC Houston, November 30, 1963, FBI 105-82555-50 46th NR, and SAC New Orleans, November 29, FBI 105-82555-454, p. 154.

27. WC, XX, p. 526.

28. Although only one of the other men, Charles Hall Steele, was ever identified, he told the FBI that the other helper had been hired at the same place. The two men bowed out when they realized what the leaflets were, and Oswald paid them each $2. SAC New Orleans, November 25, 1963, FBI 105-82555-454, p. 264.

29. SAC New Orleans, November 27, 1963, FBI 105-82555-454, p. 705, and SAC New Orleans, November 28, FBI 105-82555-50 39th NR. On December 5, Marina told the FBI that Oswald "thought the man was an FBI Agent or a man from some anti-Castro organization." Dallas, December 5, 1963, FBI 105-82555-455, p. 290. See also Secret Service report of December 1, WC, XXVI, pp. 762–73.

30. WC, XI, pp. 156–7.

31. WC, XI, p. 162.

32. WC, XX, pp. 529–30.

33. For the transcript see WC, XXI, pp. 621–32.

34. This referred apparently to a trip to Tijuana which he took during his Marine Corps service.

35. WC, XI, p. 166.

36. Chief Guatemala City for Chief Western Hemisphere, December 5, 1961, CIA Printed Microfilm, Box 70/4.1; WAVE to Chief Task Force W, April 4, 1962, CIA Microfilm, Box 70/5; and Chief JMWAVE to Chief SAS (DF), September 3, 1963, CIA Microfilm, Box 69/28.

37. Memo for file, August 21, 1963, FBI NO 100-16601-14.

38. WC, XI, pp. 166–7 [emphasis added].

39. McMillan, *Marina and Lee,* pp. 439–40; compare Newman, *Oswald and the CIA,* p. 343.

40. WC, XI, p. 169.

41. WC, XXI, p. 634.

42. *Ibid.,* pp. 633–41.

43. The U.S. State Department, as it happens, had reached the same conclusion at the time.

44. WC, XI, pp. 171–4.

45. SAC Dallas to SAC New Orleans, July 29, 1963, FBI NO 100-16601-9, and SAC New Orleans to SAC Dallas, August 13, FBI NO 100-16601-12.

46. SA John Lester Quigley, August 15, FBI NO 100-16601-13.

47. Director to SAC New Orleans (Bureau Letter), August 21, 1963, FBI NO 100-16601-15.

48. SAC New Orleans to Director, August 23, 1963, FBI NO 100-16601-17; SAC Dallas to Director, September 10, FBI NO 100-16601-24.

49. SAC New Orleans, September 24, 1963, FBI NO 100-16601-26. On September 9 an FBI agent had talked to Orlando Piedra: see SAC New Orleans, October 25, FBI DL 105-1201-15.

50. WC, XX, pp. 260–1.

51. *Ibid.,* pp. 262–4.

52. *Ibid.,* p. 270.

53. SAC New York, November 26, 1963, FBI 105-82555-50 17th NR. Peter Dale Scott, *Deep Politics and the Assassination of JFK* (Berkeley, 1993), pp. 77–90, raised some of the same questions about Oswald's activities in New Orleans.

54. See Megehee interview, January 19, 1978, HSCA Box 107/5121, and his testimony of April 19, 155/8500.

55. Interview with Reeves Morgan, January 19, 1978, HSCA, Box 107/5121, and testimony, April 19, 1978, HSCA Box 155/8501.

56. FBI report of August 9, HSCA, Box 171/9309.

57. Palmer testimony, April 19, 1978, HSCA, Box 155/8499.

58. Testimony of John Manchester, March 14, 1978, HSCA, Box 155/8503.

59. Testimony of William Dunn, April 18, 1978, HSCA Box 155/8497.

60. Interview with Corrie Collins, October 24, 1978, Box 230/013114.

61. Testimony of Bobbie Dedon, April 18, 1978, HSCA, Box 260/14568.

62. For a full account see James Kirkwood, *American Grotesque* (New York, 1970).

63. *Ibid.,* pp. 213–6.

11. THE ODIO INCIDENT

1. Marianne Sullivan, *Kennedy Ripples: A True Love Story* (Los Angeles, 1994). Although written to read like a romance novel, the book, as the title indicates, purports to be true. Machann is sometimes spelled McKann or MacChann.

2. *Dallas Morning News,* May 5, 1962, p. 1.

3. Interview with James P. Hosty, April 14, 2006.

4. For the interviews with Connell, Silvia Odio, and Dr. Einspruch, see SAC Dallas, December 23, 1963, FBI 105-82555-1212.

5. Slawson memorandum of April 6, 1964, and Griffin to Slawson, April 16 (three separate memos). These memoranda are four of a large number of documents generously provided by researcher Paul Hoch, hereafter cited as PHOF (Paul Hoch's Odio file), in cases where I did not read the original document in the archives myself.

6. Report of Ernest Aragon, Secret Service, May 5, 1964, WC, XXVI, p. 349.

7. *Ibid*. For Father Machann's interview see WC, XXVI, pp. 403–8.

8. SSCIA testimony, December 12, 1975, Box 42.

9. SAC Dallas, May 28, 1964, FBI 105-82555-4313.

10. WC, X, p. 373. I have corrected the translation that Silvia Odio provided the commission.

11. WC, XI, pp. 370–7.

12. FBI Miami LHM, July 30, 1964, WC, XXVI, pp. 362–3.

13. Hoover to SAC Dallas, September 2, 1964, FBI 105-82555-4743.

14. SAC Dallas to Hoover, September 5, 1964, FBI 105-82555-4793. SAC Miami, September 8, 1964, FBI 105-82555-4892.

15. SAC Dallas to Hoover, September 9, 1964, FBI 105-82555-4891, and interview with James Dyer, SAC Dallas to Hoover, September 15, FBI 105-82555-4855.

16. SAC Dallas to Hoover, September 15, 1964, FBI 105-82555-4855.

17. SAC Dallas, September 9, 1964, FBI 105-82555-4893.

18. SAC New Orleans, September 19, 1964, FBI 105-82555-4870.

19. SAC San Juan, September 11, 1964, FBI 105-82555-4927. Not surprisingly, perhaps, his mother disagreed: SAC Miami, September 12, 1964, FBI 105-82555-4868.

20. SAC Miami, September 30, 1963, FBI 2-1693-95. This is one of a series of informants' reports on Hemming's activities—so detailed that Hemming himself might have been the source.

21. State Memcon, July 19, 1963, JFK Library, NSF, Cuba, Subjects, Exiles, 7/63–9/63, Box 48. *Chicago Tribune,* April 11, 1963, p. 2.

22. On Logue's plans see Hall's HSCA testimony, October 15, 1977, HSCA, Box 269, and Jonathan Blackmer's notes of his interview with Hall, August 20, 1977, Box 1.

23. CIA Cable, August 13, 1963, in FBI 105-95677-337.

24. SAC Miami to Hoover, August 29, 1963, FBI 105-65100-9, and SAC New York to Hoover, October 17, FBI 105-65100-11. Hall also told the HSCA that he might have heard George de Mohrenschildt's name in connection with the Haitian operation.

25. Hall's HSCA testimony, October 15, 1977, HSCA, Box 269.

26. Jonathan Blackmer's notes of his interview with Hall, August 20, 1977, HSCA, Box 1.

27. This was a different organization from the Citizens Committee for a Free Cuba, which apparently involved Clare Boothe Luce, among others. Logue interview, February 18, 1978, HSCA, Box 118/5968. Hall himself said in 1977

that he assumed the offer had not been serious, because he did not believe he would still be alive if it had been real. Interview with Jonathan Blackmer, *ibid.* Hall had actually given the gist of this story to the *New Orleans States-Item* ten years earlier, on May 3, 1968.

28. A year later, Dr. Tirso Del Junco told the FBI that Hall had probably pocketed the money he had raised. SAC Los Angeles to Director, August 24, 1964, FBI 105-78016-23.

29. See Hall's testimony, October 15, 1977, HSCA, Box 269, and Memorandum by Michael Riley, investigator, U.S. Treasury, September 5, 1963, CIA Segregated Collection, Box 1/11.

30. See Hall's interview of September 16, SAC Los Angeles to Hoover, September 17, 1964, FBI 105-82555-4890; Howard interview, September 20, in Harry Whidbee to Hoover, September 25, 1964, FBI 105-82555-4993; and FBI Miami LHM, September 26, 1964, PLH Odio file.

31. Sullivan, *Kennedy Ripples,* p. 325. Ms. Sullivan dates the meeting on October 1. In June 1964, a Dallas anti-Castro Cuban, Raul Castro Baile, remembered Martino's visit as having taken place in September 1963. He confirmed Father McChann's involvement. The *Dallas Morning News,* which had given Martino's book a very favorable review a few months earlier, did not cover the meeting.

32. These dates came from records provided to HSCA investigators by Martino's widow. See Cliff Fenton memorandum, October 7, 1977, HSCA, Box 63/2572.

33. This information has been provided by Dr. Alberto Coll, a law professor at DePaul University, whose father, Silvio Alberto Coll, had been arrested in the same Castro assassination plot as Amador Odio in late 1961 and saw Odio in La Cabana prison.

34. On Hall's arrest see interview with Jonathan Blackmer, August 20, 1977, HSCA, Box 1; his FBI interview of October 18, 1963, SAC Dallas to Hoover, October 23, 1963, FBI 105-78016-17; and Michael Rohde's HSCA deposition, HSCA, Box 80/3499. See also *Los Angeles Times,* May 15, 1968, p. 3, on Dr. Drennan, and Hall's interview with Jim Garrison, May 6, 1968, HSCA Box 51/2171.

35. Undated memo, RJB, DL 100-10461, pp. 211–2, PLH Odio file. (Warren Commission Document 1546). Hoover to SAC Los Angeles, June 24, 1964, FBI 105-78016-20, and SAC Los Angeles to Hoover, August 4, 1964, FBI 105-78016-21. SAC Los Angeles to Director, August 24, 1964, FBI 105-78016-23. On Gabaldon see *Los Angeles Times,* May 3, 1964, p. V8.

36. SAC Los Angeles to Director, September 17, 1964, FBI 105-82555-4890.

37. Enclosure to Harry Whidbee to Hoover, September 25, 1964, FBI 105-82555-4993.

38. SAC Phoenix to Director, September 19, 1964, FBI 105-82555-4887; Miami LHM, September 26, 1964, PLH Odio file; see also Calvin Evans to Hoover, September 20, 1964, FBI 105-82555-4954.

39. Enclosure to Harry Whidbee to Hoover, September 25, 1964, FBI 105-82555-4993. The HSCA in 1978 interviewed agent Brown to ask him what he remembered about his two very different encounters with Hall, but he claimed that he had almost entirely forgotten them. Summary of testimony, May 15, 1978, HSCA, Box 1/8343.

40. *Warren Report,* p. 324.

41. Gerald Posner, *Case Closed,* pp. 177–8, nonetheless accepted this passage as correct almost thirty years later.

42. FBI Miami LHM, October 2, 1964, PLH Odio file (CD 1553D).

43. SAC Dallas, November 28, 1963, FBI 105-82555-505, p. 199.

44. J. Edgar Hoover to J. Lee Rankin, March 2, 1964, FBI 105-82555-2296.

45. SAC New Orleans, November 27, 1963, FBI 105-82555-454.

46. S. A. Dalrymple to Hoover, March 24, 1964, FBI 105-82555-2864.

47. SAC New Orleans, November 27, 1963, FBI 105-82555-454.

48. Stephen Callender to Hoover, September 23, 1964, FBI 105-82555-4981.

49. SAC New Orleans, November 28, 1963, FBI 105-82555-526.

50. SAC New Orleans, November 27,1963, FBI 105-82555-454.

51. This was pointed out by Vincent Bugliosi, *Reclaiming History: The Assassination of President John F. Kennedy* (New York, 2007), p. 1310. Bugliosi, remarkably, concludes that Oswald was at Odio's apartment, probably on September 24 or 25, but because he does not realize that Hall lied about Seymour's presence and because he knows very little about Hall's background and activities, he concludes that it does not prove a conspiracy.

52. SAC Dallas to Hoover, August 5, 1964, FBI 105-82555-4647.

53. *Dallas Morning News,* September 26, 1963, p. 1.

54. Hq Army Intelligence Ft Holabird FL, August 7, 1970, CIA Printed Microfilm, Box 109/17.

55. See below, chapter 17.

56. WC, XI, p. 380.

57. Hemming testimony, March 21, 1978, at http://www.history-matters .com/archive/jfk/hsca/unpub_testimony/pdf/Hemming_3-21-78.pdf.

58. SAC Los Angeles, November 23, 1963, FBI 105-78016 2nd NR.

59. WAVE to Director 4222, September 12, 1963, CIA, Latin America Division/DDO, Memorandum for the Inspector General, "Latin America Divi-

sion Task Force Report of Possible Cuban Complicity in the John F. Kennedy Assassination," June 29, 1977, p. 101. LA WF, Box 3/1.

12. JOURNEY TO MEXICO

1. SAC New Orleans, n.d., FBI 105-82555-454.

2. HSCA, Box 236/13526. Gaudet acknowledged his relationship to the CIA.

3. *Violations of State Department Regulations and Pro-Castro Propaganda Activities in the United States, Hearings before the Committee on Un-American Activities,* House of Representatives, 88th Congress, 1st Session, part 1, pp. 223–34; part 2, *passim,* and part 3, pp. 651–60.

4. Chief JMWAVE to Chief SAS (DF), September 3, 1963, CIA Printed Microfilm, Box 69/28.

5. The fruits of this long association were published in Priscilla Johnson McMillan, *Marina and Lee* (New York, 1977), which provides a day-by-day (and, at times, almost minute-by-minute) account of Lee's thoughts and feelings during 1963, including many details which Marina never shared with either the FBI or the Warren Commission.

6. All these interviews can be found in FBI 105-082555, serials 570 (November 22), 454 (November 24), 929 (November 28), 97 3rd NR (November 28), 668 (November 29), 454 (November 29, November 30, and December 1), 734 (November 30), 929 (December 1), 1053 (December 1), 249 (December 2), 702 (December 2), 455 (December 2, 3, and 4), 193 (December 2), 360 (December 6), 1212 4th NR (December 9, 16, and 17), 563 (December 9), 1172 (December 11), 713 (December 16), 861 (December 17), 868 (December 19), 1329 (December 20), 1144 (January 3), 1345 (January 3), 1567 (January 15 and 17), 1569 (January 18), 2027 (January 21), 1579 (January 22), and 1630 (January 31).

7. SAC Dallas, January 18, 1964, FBI 105-82555-1567 (interview with James Martin).

8. SAC Dallas, February 19, 1964, FBI 105-82555-2095 2nd NR.

9. Ibid., and see SAC Dallas, June 1, 1964, FBI 105-82555-3982.

10. Legat London to Director, December 13, 1963, FBI 105-82555-962.

11. SAC Los Angeles, December 17, 1963, FBI 105-82555-720.

12. Hoover to SAC Memphis, February 25, 1964, FBI 105-82555-2091.

13. SAC San Antonio, February 3, 1964, FBI 105-82555-2118.

14. Legat Mexico, February 10, 1964, FBI 105-82555-1833.

15. SAC Birmingham, February 11, 1964, FBI 105-82555-1983.

16. SAC New Orleans, February 13, 1964, FBI 105-82555-1953.

17. SAC San Antonio, February 17, 1964, FBI 105-82555-2075.

18. Legat London, February 17, 1964, FBI 105-82555-1995; SAC Birming-

ham, February 17, FBI 105-82555-1996; SAC Knoxville, February 16, 1964, FBI 105-82555-2176; SAC Portland, March 6, FBI 105-82555-2385; SAC Memphis, 640303, FBI 105-82555-2433.

19. Hoover to SAC Dallas, March 5, FBI 105-82555-2310, and Hoover, March 12, FBI 105-82555-2517.

20. SAC Dallas to New Orleans, 640229, FBI DL 100-10461-3823.

21. The Lopez Report is available at http://www.history-matters.com/archive/jfk/hsca/lopezrpt/contents.htm.

22. Legat Mexico City to Director, November 25, FBI 105-82555-967.

23. Duran's deposition is in HSCA, III, pp. 6–119.

24. Ibid., p. 35.

25. Oleg M. Nechiporenko, *Passport to Assassination: The Never-Before-Told Story of Lee Harvey Oswald by the KGB Colonel Who Knew Him* (New York, 1993).

26. This correspondence is in WC, XVI, pp. 10–32.

27. Ibid., pp. 66–71.

28. Newman, *Oswald and the CIA,* p. 358.

29. Michael R. Beschloss, ed., *Taking Charge: The Johnson White House Tapes, 1963–1964* (New York, 1997), p. 67.

30. Hosty testimony, December 12, 1975, Box 42, pp. 3–4, 43.

31. An account by Fabian Escalante, the former chief of Cuban G-2 who had access to Cuban sources, claims that Oswald hoped to remain in Cuba for several weeks. Fabian Escalante, *1963: El Complot* (Melbourne, Australia, 2004), p. 108.

32. Azcue testimony, HSCA, III, p. 133.

33. For the account of Morris Childs, known as "Solo" in the FBI—actually a fascinating and lengthy account of a long trip to both Moscow and Havana—see SAC New York to Director, June 11, 1964, FBI CR 100-428091-3930. See Newman, *Oswald and the CIA,* p. 526, for a letter passing the information along from J. Edgar Hoover to J. Lee Rankin of the Warren Commission, June 17, 1964. For Comer Clark's account see Daniel Schorr, *Clearing the Air* (New York, 1977), p. 177. For Castro's reaction see HSCA, Hearings, III, pp. 207–9.

34. Schorr, *Clearing the Air* (New York, 1977), p. 177.

35. See Peter Dale Scott, *Deep Politics II* (Grand Prairie, TX, 1996), p. 98, quoting Anthony Summers.

36. Ibid., pp. 93–4. Childs reported a very odd remark from Castro—that "nobody goes that way for a visa," that is, to Mexico City. The opposite was true—many Americans went there for visas.

37. Newman, *Oswald and the CIA,* p. 526.

38. Blakey and Billings, *The Plot to Kill the President,* pp. 164–6.

39. For the news item see the *Los Angeles Times,* September 9, 1963, p. 14.

40. Memo, Chief, Counterintelligence, SAS (name deleted), to Chief, counter Intelligence Staff, May 8, 1964, CIA Segregated Collection, Box 3/2 (RIF 104-10050-10091).

41. HSCA, Lopez Report, part 2, pp. 17–27.

42. CIA Mexico City, November 27, 1963, CIA, LA WF, Box 1/9.

43. David Atlee Phillips confirmed the presence (though not the identity) of at least two such agents to the HSCA in late 1976. See his testimony of November 27 at http://history-matters.com/archive/jfk/hsca/secclass/pdf/Phillips_11–27–76.pdf, pp. 125–6. The committee did not force him to identify them and because of redactions it is not clear how many there may have been.

44. Interview of Thomas C. Mann, November 29, 1977, HSCA Box 84/3966.

45. Escalante, *1963: El Complot,* p. 105.

46. HSCA, Lopez Report, part 2, p. 30, and part 3, p. 121. On the presence of two penetration agents see also *ibid.,* part 5, p. 188, citing a contemporary CIA cable.

47. Nechiporenko, *Passport to Assassination,* pp. 75–81.

48. *Ibid.,* pp. 92–9.

49. *Warren Report,* p. 301.

50. Newman, *Oswald and the CIA,* p. 364.

51. For Duran's two interrogations see Lopez report, pp. 186–7, and CIA cable, November 28, 1963, FBI 105-82555-1334; also HSCA, III, 49–51. See also her HSCA testimony, HSCA, III, pp. 49–51. Oddly, August Belmont of the FBI claimed in an internal memo on December 3, 1963, that Duran had said that Oswald had visited the Cuban consulate on the 28th as well as the 27th, but there is no evidence for this in any reports from Mexico City. See Belmont to Sullivan, December 3, 1963, FBI 105-82555-656. In 1978 the consul, Eusebio Azcue, told the HSCA that he thought Oswald might have come back on two successive days, but added, confusingly, that on Saturday the consulate would not have been open, and suggested that Oswald had come on Thursday (which was impossible) and on Friday. Duran was far more definite. See Azcue's testimony, September 18, 1978, at http://history-matters.com/archive/jfk/hsca/reportvols/vol3/pdf/HSCA_Vol3_0918_2_Azcue.pdf.

52. Newman, *Oswald and the CIA,* pp. 362–3.

53. CIA C/WH/3 to C/CI/SI, December 13, 1963, CIA file 201-289248, at http://history-matters.com/archive/jfk/cia/201/pdf/104-10004-10202.pdf.

54. Lopez Report, pp. 78–9.

55. *Washington Post,* November 26, 1976, p. 1.

56. HSCA, Interview with Boris and Anna Tarasoff, November 30, 1976, pp. 23–32.

57. The testimony of Boris and Anna Tarasoff and of David Phillips can all

be found at http://www.history-matters.com/archive/jfk/hsca/secclass/contents.htm.

58. FBI Director Clarence Kelley confirmed that the United States had human sources in the Soviet embassy. See Clarence M. Kelley and James Kirkpatrick Davis, *Kelley: The Story of an FBI Director* (Kansas City, MO, 1987), p. 268.

59. For a detailed discussion of the CIA's photographic coverage of these embassies and what it may have yielded, see HSCA, Lopez Report, pp. 72–115.

60. HSCA, Lopez Report, pp. 139–40.

61. Reprinted in Newman, *Oswald and the CIA,* p. 509.

62. Lopez Report, p. 136.

63. Testimony of "John Scelso," HSCA, May 16, 1978, p. 50; the Lopez Report quotes another CIA man, Allan White, to the same effect, p. 133.

64. HSCA, Lopez Report, p. 142.

65. HSCA, Lopez Report, pp. 144–5.

66. HSCA, Lopez Report, p. 146.

67. HSCA, Lopez Report, p. 170.

68. See Veciana's interview summary, March 22, 1976, SSCIA, Box 43.

69. Testimony of David Atlee Phillips, April 24, 1978, HSCA, Security Classified Testimony, at http://history-matters.com/archive/jfk/hsca/secclass/pdf/Phillips_4-25-78.pdf.

70. See below, chapter 13, text accompanying note 25.

71. *Washington Post* reporter Jefferson Morley provided me with a copy of the outline.

72. See p. 314.

73. See CIA, Memo for the record, Louis de Santi, SAS/CI/CP, July 10, 1963, LA WF, Box 2/9. See also "Task Force Report," June 29, 1977, LA WF, Box 3/1, p. 96. The city through which Vicente traveled to Cuba is blacked out, but it had Cuban diplomatic representation, making Mexico City a very likely candidate.

13. MAKING EVERYONE UNHAPPY ABOUT CUBA

1. Artime's own report, June 6, 1963, CIA Printed Microfilm, Box 4/17.2.

2. Chief, WH, to various stations, June 28, 1963, CIA, LA WF, Box 5/1. In *Ultimate Sacrifice* (New York, 2005, with Thom Hartmann), Lamar Waldron spins an elaborate fantasy based upon about a dozen documents selected from the tens of thousands now available in the archives. Ignoring this document, which clearly explains what AMWORLD was, he turns it into a plan for a coup led by Che Guevara, a contention for which there is no evidence whatever.

3. See Fitzgerald memorandum, June 22, 1963, *FRUS,* 1961–63, XI, 350, and Bundy to Standing Group, May 28, *ibid., 343.*

4. Memo for Record, June 19, 1963, *ibid., 348.* The minutes refer to the President as "higher authority."

5. This is explicitly reported in CIA Information Report, July 26, 1963, CIA Printed Microfilm, Box 7/9.2.

6. WAVE to Director, July 18, 1963, CIA Printed Microfilm, Box 4/17.1.

7. See Managua 59, August 8, 1963, JFK Library, NSF, Cuba, Subjects, Miscellaneous Cables, 4/63–11/63, Box 48A, and Coordinator Miami, August 9, *ibid.*

8. San Jose to Director, September 25, 1963, CIA Printed Microfilm, Box 4/19.2, and Heckscher memorandum, October 3, *ibid.,* Box 4/19.1.

9. *FRUS,* 1961–63, XI, no. 357, memo of August 9. Fitzgerald mentioned that Somoza was claiming pledges from support from both John and Robert Kennedy.

10. Washington *Post,* August 31, 1961, p. 1.

11. Llewellyn Thompson Memo, September 13, 1963, *FRUS,* 1961–63, XI, 366. The Kennedy conversation is *FRUS,* 1961–63, XI, 371.

12. *New York Times,* September 16, 1963, p. 39.

13. CIA Information Report, August 16, 1963, FBI 97-4474-33. For Bosch's claim of responsibility see the *New York Times,* September 9, 1963, p. 9.

14. Gordon Chase memo, September 6, 1963, SSCIA, Box 45/6.

15. Gordon Chase memo, September 29, 1963, SSCIA, Box 45/6.

16. *FRUS,* volumes X–XII, supplement, no. 713.

17. *New York Times,* November 1, 1963, p. 1.

18. *New York Times,* November 9, 1963, p. 5, and December 14, p. 10.

19. *FRUS,* X, no. 399.

20. *Ibid.,* 414.

21. *Ibid.,* 423, 431. Document 431, by Walter Elder, refers merely to a "Mongoose meeting." Robert Kennedy attended, but this does not seem to have been the same meeting as a Special Group meeting on the same day, reported in no. 430.

22. *FRUS,* X–XII, microfiche supplement, no. 675.

23. *FRUS,* XII, no. 169, and *New York Times,* November 8, 1963, p. 5. *New York Times,* December 14, 1963, p. 10.

24. Helms testimony, SSCIA, Box 247/4.

25. Phillips testimony, July 31, 1975, SSCIA, Box 27/2.

26. See Peter Kornbluh, *The Pinochet File* (New York, 2003), pp. 104–12.

27. On AMTRUNK see Memo, AMTRUNK operation, April 25, 1975, CIA, LA WF, Box 2/9. See also Fabian Escalante, *1963: El Complot* (Melbourne,

Australia, 2004), pp. 32–5. Escalante, a former chief of Cuban G-2, confirms the suspicion of the CIA memorandum that AMTRUNK was later betrayed by Jose Ricardo Rabel Nuñez, who returned to Cuba in 1965.

28. *FRUS,* 1961–63, XI, nos. 375, 376.

29. See above, chapter 7, text accompanying note 50.

30. Memo for Record, August 1, 1963, CIA, LA WF, Box 1/1.

31. Memo of October 31, CIA, LA WF, Box 1/1.

32. Information Report, undated, CIA Printed Microfilm, Box 101/24.1.

33. Porto Alegre to Director, September 9, 1963, and Director to Porto Alegre and JMWAVE, September 9, CIA Printed Microfilm, Box 101/24.1.

34. WAVE 4428 to Director, September 17, 1963, and see WAVE 4580 to Director, September 19, CIA Printed Microfilm, Box 101/24.2.

35. London to Director, October 15, 1963, CIA Printed Microfilm, Box 102/25.1.

36. Paris to Director, October 21, 1963; Director to Paris, October 21; and undated memo, "Contact Plan for Dainold Meeting with AMLASH-1," CIA Printed Microfilm, Box 102/25.2.

37. Memo for the Record, November 19, 1963, CIA Printed Microfilm, Box 102/25.2.

38. *FRUS,* 1961–63, X–XII, supplement, no. 714.

39. Escalante, *1963: El Complot,* pp. 33–4.

40. CIA memorandum, July 15, 1963, and Memo for Record 1977, quoting cable of July 24, CIA, LA WF, Box 2/6. Cabeza had been "employed by the agency in agent status" and was "a key figure in the AMFAUNA operation"; see Jacob D. Esterline to Deputy Director for Plans, February 4, 1967, CIA-DDP-Files, Box 7, folder 1. On Cabeza and Martino see HSCA memorandum, October 4, 1977, Box 63/2548.

41. *FRUS,* XI, 310.

42. *FRUS,* X–XII, supplement, no. 671.

43. *FRUS,* 1961–63, XI, 367, 373.

44. *FRUS,* X–XII, supplement, no. 717.

45. *FRUS,* XI, 315.

46. Memorandum, Bureau of Inter-American Affairs, June 20, 1963, *FRUS,* XI, 349.

47. *Ibid.,* nos. 368, 377. Talbot, *Brothers,* pp. 228–30, gives a misleading picture of JFK's attitude by ignoring these documents.

48. Kaiser, *American Tragedy, passim.*

49. The CIA 201 file released to NARA as part of the printed microfilm does not begin until mid-1963, even though Prio must have been of intense interest to the agency for decades. As for Prio's 12,000-page FBI file, it did not be-

come part of the JFK collection because of Prio's suicide on April 4, 1977, while an HSCA investigator was trying to find him for an interview. The committee lost interest in Prio after his death and never requested his FBI file, which was therefore left out of the FBI file release in response to the JFK Records Act. In 2005 I placed a FOIA request for the file, asking that it be designated a JFK record and therefore processed under the less restrictive rules used for such records, but the FBI Freedom of Information Office has so far released documents from the late 1950s that are too full of redactions to be of any use. Fortunately, the IRR (Military Counterintelligence) files in the JFK collection include a file on Prio, who became a source for army intelligence during this period, and that file includes a number of letterhead memoranda reporting the results of FBI investigations. I am much indebted to Malcolm Blunt for pointing me toward the IRR files. It is unfortunate that both the FBI and CIA have now stopped observing the JFK Assassination Records Act.

50. Interview with Ed Martino, January 3, 2007.

51. DA Intelligence Report, August 11, 1961, Counterintelligence Source Files, Box 7/9.1.

52. FBI LHM, March 30, 1962, Counterintelligence Source Files, Box 7/9.2.

53. FBI LHM, May 20 and June 6, 1963, Counterintelligence Source Files, Box 7/9.2.

54. SAC Miami, September 30, 1963, FBI, Box 2-1693-95.

55. FBI LHM, September 27, 1963, Counterintelligence Source Files, Box 7/9.2; see also Memo, David Stine III, August 20, 1963, Counterintelligence Source Files, Box 8/12.1.

56. WAVE to Director, August 8, 1963, Memo for Record, Henry Heckscher, August 30, CIA Printed Microfilm, Box 114/21.

57. CIA Information reports, September 27 and October 7, 1963, CIA Printed Microfilm, Box 114/21.

58. Director to Mexico City, September 24, and Mexico City reply, September 26, and October 7 CIA Printed Microfilm, Box 114/21.

59. WAVE to Director, September 26, 1963, CIA Printed Microfilm, Box 114/21.

60. CIA memorandum, date illegible but approximately October 1, 1963, CIA Printed Microfilm, Box 114/21.

61. WAVE to Chief SAS, October 19, 1963, and WAVE to Director, November 7, CIA Printed Microfilm, Box 114/21.

62. WAVE to Director Action C/SAS 3, December 5, 1963, CIA Printed Microfilm, Box 114/21. The contacts with Nixon reportedly were through two confederates, newspaper publisher Guillermo Marquez and Carlos Marquez Sterling. This report drew on a conversation of November 14. It also gave a

modified version of Prio's plan—that he would go back to Cuba and be re-elected president after Artime successfully invaded.

63. FBI LHM, December 24, 1963, and FBI LHM, March 31. Counterintelligence Source Files, Box 7/9.2.

64. WAVE to Director, January 28; Director to WAVE, February 5; and WAVE to Director, February 17, CIA Printed Microfilm, Box 68/18.

65. Information Report, August 16, 1963, CIA Printed Microfilm, Box 32/14.

66. Chicago Domestic Contacts report, n.d. (approximately April 14, 1963), CIA Printed Microfilm, Box 46/10. On the Christian Defense League and American Committee for Cuban Freedom see D. Boylan, "A League of Their Own: A Look inside the Christian Defense League," at http://cuban-exile.com/doc_026-050/doc0046.html.

67. CIA Information Report, May 7, 1963, JFK Library, NSF, Countries, Cuba, Subjects, Information Reports, 4/63–11/63, Box 48A.

68. SAC Miami, May 19, 1963, FBI 105-121010-1, and Director to Attorney General, May 28, FBI 105-121010 NR.

69. SAC Chicago to Director, June 4, 1963, FBI 105-121010-2.

70. Memorandum, September 17, 1963, FBI 105-121010 NR.

71. FBI LHM, September 23, 1963, FBI 105-121010-20.

72. CIA TDCS, October 15, 1963, FBI 105-121010-22.

73. JMWAVE to Director, November 20, 1963, CIA Printed Microfilm, Box 46/10.

74. FBI LHM, November 26, 1963, FBI 105-121010 NR.

75. SAC Miami, November 9, 1963, FBI 105-78016-18 1st NR.

76. Hall interview with Jonathan Blackmer, August 20, 1977, HSCA, Box 1.

77. Document Transfer and Cross Reference, June 27, 1963, CIA Printed Microfilm, Box 47/17.2.

78. See Document Transfer and Cross Reference, June 7, 1963, and Document Transfer and Cross Reference, July 12, CIA Printed Microfilm, Box 20/5.2.

79. Information Report, CIA, July 26, 1963, CIA Printed Microfilm, Box 7/9.2, and Field Information Report, August 29, CIA Printed Microfilm, Box 73/7.

80. Trace Request, August 22, 1963; Information Report, CIA, November 2, and Information Report, CIA, December 3, CIA Printed Microfilm, Box 7/9.2.

81. SAC Miami to Hoover, August 28, FBI 105-96551-20.

82. Daily summary, August 1, 1963, CIA Printed Microfilm, Box 117/16.1, and Memcon, October 8, 1963, Box 4/19.1.

83. See WAVE to Director, May 21, 1961, and January 16 and February 20, 1962, CIA Printed Microfilm, Box 8/15.2.

84. SAC Miami, December 13, 1963, FBI, Box 97-4474-55.

85. *Los Angeles Times,* October 22, 1963, p. 4.

86. *FRUS,* X–XII, supplement, no. 686.

87. WAVE to Director, August 6, 1963, CIA Printed Microfilm, Box 4/18.

88. *FRUS,* X–XII, supplement, no. 713.

89. DRE leadership, February 15, 1962, CIA Printed Microfilm, Box 70/2.

90. WAVE to Director, February 22, CIA Printed Microfilm, Box 70/2.

91. WAVE to Chief SAS, April 4, 1963, DRE press release of April 1, and Director to WAVE, April 4, CIA Printed Microfilm, Box 70/2.

92. "Information Concerning Directorio Estudiantil," August 26, 1963, CIA Printed Microfilm, Box 68/22.

93. Chief JMWAVE to Chief SAS (DF), September 3, 1963, CIA Printed Microfilm, Box 69/28.

94. CIA, LA WF, Box 2/9. JMWAVE to Director, September 12 and September 21, 1963, CIA Printed Microfilm, Box 69/28. My attempts to locate a copy of the November 1963 issue of *See* have been unsuccessful. See also WAVE to Director, October 23, 1963, CIA Printed Microfilm, Box 69/27.1.

95. JMWAVE to Chief SAS, 631108, CIA Printed Microfilm, Box 69/28.

96. JMWAVE to Director, November 19, 1963, *ibid.*

97. See SAC Miami, January 25, 1964, FBI 105-82555-1505.

98. *Dallas Morning News,* October 13, 1963, section 1, p. 7; SAC Miami, December 26, 1963, FBI 105-82555-1213.

99. SAC Dallas, September 18, 1964, FBI SA 105-2886-38.

100. 112th INTC Group, Dallas, October 24, 1963, FBI SA 105-2886-1.

101. SAC San Antonio, October 25, 1963, FBI SA 105-2886-6.

102. SAC San Antonio, November 1, 1963, FBI SA 105-2886-10. Goicochea confirmed all these details when the FBI interviewed him more than ten months later.

103. SAC San Antonio, March 17, 1964, FBI SA 105-2886-34.

104. Testimony of Frank Ellsworth, July 25, 1978, HSCA, Box 200/10903.

105. *Dallas Morning News,* November 19, 1963, and see Ray and Mary La Fontaine, *Oswald Talked: New Evidence in the JFK Assassination* (Gretna, LA, 1996), pp. 31–2.

106. See SAC Dallas, April 8, 1964, FBI DL 105-1686-47, and LHM, SAC San Antonio, November 26, 1963, FBI San Antonio 105-2886-17.

107. SAC Dallas, November 29, 1963, FBI San Antonio 105-2886-20.

108. SAC Dallas, December 12, 1963, FBI San Antonio 105-2886-21.

109. SAC Dallas, February 19, 1964, FBI San Antonio 105-2886-33, and SAC Dallas, September 18, FBI San Antonio 105-2886-38.

110. SAC Dallas, December 19, 1963, FBI 105-82555-1212.04, and SAC Miami, December 26, FBI 105-82555-1213.

111. Deposition of Frank Ellsworth, July 25, 1978, Box 200/10903, and deposition of John Thomas Masen, July 26, 1978, Box 200/10904.

112. A memo of April 17, 1964, to that effect is quoted in Ray and Mary La Fontaine, *Oswald Talked,* p. 34.

113. SAC Memphis, August 11, 1964, FBI DL 44-1639-1994.20.

114. WC, XIV, p. 343 (testimony of Nancy Perrin Rich).

115. See SAC San Francisco, November 27, 1963, FBI 44-24016-416; SAC San Francisco, December 5, FBI 44-24016-501, and SAC Dallas, December 18, FBI 44-24016-803.

116. SAC San Francisco, April 7, 1964, FBI 44-24016-1378.

117. SAC Dallas, December 16, 1963, FBI 44-24016-803.

118. SAC St. Louis, December 4, 1963, SAC Dallas, December 18, 1963, FBI 44-24016-803.

119. Quoted in Blakey and Billings, *Fatal Hour,* p. 323.

120. Rankin to Hoover, April 3, 1964, FBI 105-82555-3114. Browder claimed no memory of Ruby in an otherwise informative interview with HSCA investigators in 1978.

121. SAC Atlanta, November 30, 1963, FBI 44-24016-75; Browder HSCA testimony, January 12, 1978, HSCA, Box 105/5081; SAC Detroit, December 3, FBI 44-24016-308, and SAC Knoxville, December 4, FBI 44-24016-346.

122. On Davis and Ruby see Seth Kantor, *The Ruby Cover-Up* (New York, 1978), pp. 42–6. On Davis's Los Angeles activities see SAC Los Angeles, June 25, 1963, FBI 105-120907-9.

123. Memorandum for the record, Possible DRE Animus Towards President Kennedy, March 8, 1967, CIA Segregated Collection, Box 64-17/8. Another memo by Donovan Pratt, "Cubans and the Garrison Investigation," March 7, 1968 (copy in author's possession—released by CIA), identifies Thomas as the author of the memo.

124. SAC Miami, December 31, 1963, FBI 105-82555-1213.

125. Quoted in *The Worker,* November 18, 1962, p. 3.

126. See Dan Christensen, "JFK, King: The Dade County Links," *Miami Magazine,* vol. 27, no. 11, September 1976, at http://cuban-exile.com/doc_101-125/doc0122.html.

14. TURNING UP THE HEAT

1. SAC New York, June 6, 1963, FBI 92-3171-1015; SAC Honolulu, June 13, FBI 92-3171-1027; and Hoover to Attorney General, June 25, FBI 92-3171-1075.

2. *Chicago Sun-Times,* August 8, 1963, p. 35, FBI 92-3171-1192, and T. J. McAndrew to Courtney Evans, August 26, FBI 92-3171-1193.

3. SAC Chicago, June 27, 1963, FBI 92-3171-1059; SAC Chicago, June 26, FBI 92-3171-1053; Director to SAC Chicago, June 29, FBI 92-3171-1057.

4. SAC Chicago, July 1, 1963, FBI 92-3171-1096 ("Miscellaneous June references").

5. SAC Chicago, June 16, FBI 92-3171-1103 (including *Washington Star,* June 18); Courtney Evans to Belmont, July 16, FBI 92-3171-1114; SAC Chicago, July 17, FBI 92-3171-1117.

6. Courtney Evans to Belmont, July 22, FBI 92-3171-1122; Hoover to Attorney General, July 24, FBI 92-3171-1126 2nd NR; Director to all SACs, July 26, FBI 92-3171-1126.

7. SAC Chicago, October 16, 1963, FBI 92-3171-1231.

8. SAC New York, July 30, 1963, FBI 92-3171-1161; SAC Chicago, August 1, FBI 92-3171-1159; and SAC Chicago, August 2, FBI 92-3171-1154.

9. Moses declined to repeat these allegations when the FBI interviewed him, although he recalled meeting "Sam Mooney" on the set of *Come Blow Your Horn.* See SAC Chicago, September 10, 1963, FBI 92-3171-1202, and SAC Los Angeles, September 12, FBI 92-371-1203.

10. SAC Las Vegas, August 9, 1963, FBI 92-3171-1170 (the Gaming Control Board had leaked its hearing to the FBI), and *Los Angeles Times,* September 1, p. E1.

11. SAC Honolulu, October 4, 1963, FBI 92-3171-1228.

12. *Washington Post,* September 22, 1963, p. G3.

13. *Los Angeles Times,* October 23, 1963, p. 2.

14. See Courtney Evans to August Belmont, August 16, 1963, FBI 92-3171-1200.

15. Memo for Record, Stanley J. Grogan, August 16, 1963, SSCIA, Box 20/1.

16. See the *Chicago Sun-Times,* August 16, 1963, and SSCIA, *Alleged Assassination Plots,* pp. 107–8.

17. *Chicago Tribune,* October 12, 1963, p. 3.

18. SAC Chicago, December 6, 1963, FBI 92-3171-1270 (Miscellaneous June references).

19. SAC New York, September 27, 1963, FBI 92-9171-1224, and SAC Chicago, October 11, 1963, FBI 92-9171-1230.

20. SAC Chicago, October 17, 1963, FBI 92-3171-1234.

21. *Chicago Tribune,* November 3, 1963, p. 26.

22. SAC New York, November 6, 1963, FBI 92-3171-1248; SAC New York, November 7, FBI 92-3171-1249; SAC Chicago, November 16, FBI 92-3171-1252, and December 19, FBI 92-3171-1274.

23. SAC Los Angeles, November 9, 1963, FBI 92-3267-530.

24. Charles Rappleye and Ed Becker, *All American Mafioso: The Johnny*

Rosselli Story (New York, 1991), pp. 222–7, and Ayers, *The War That Never Was,* pp. 37–8.

25. See SAC Miami, September 5, 1962, FBI 87-66742-1; SAC Miami, August 2, FBI 87-66742-123; and Rosen to Belmont, October 8, 1963, FBI 87-67742-163.

26. *Chicago Tribune,* October 30, 1964, p. D7.

27. SAC Tampa, July 12, 1963, FBI 92-2781-740, and Wannall to William Sullivan, November 1, FBI 92-2781-922 1st NR.

28. SAC Miami, November 13, 1963, FBI 92-2781-905.

29. SAC San Juan, November 6, 1963, FBI 92-2781-901.

30. SAC Tampa, November 8, 1963, FBI 92-2781-911.

31. See 88th Congress, 2nd session, Senate Permanent Subcommittee on Investigations, *Organized Crime and Illicit Traffic in Narcotics,* part 3 (Washington, 1964), pp. 522–41.

32. SAC Philadelphia, May 20, 1963, FBI 92-1067-Sub A-8.

33. Quoted in Blakey and Billings, *Fatal Hour,* p. 273.

34. SAC Dallas, November 28, 1963, FBI 44-24016-542.

35. The best evidence of Eva Grant's connections is an interview with Paul Roland Jones, a thrice-convicted mobster, who told the FBI not long after the assassination that she had introduced him to her brother Jack in Chicago during 1946 while he was meeting with her and two now-dead men to discuss vending machines, a mob-dominated business. See SAC Birmingham, December 14, 1963, FBI 44-24016-724. Eva herself boasted to Dallas friends that she had been a member of the Capone mob in Chicago: see SAC Dallas, November 25, 1963, FBI 44-24016-634.

36. See SAC Dallas, November 29, 1963, FBI 44-24016-562.

37. See *American Guild of Variety Artists: Hearings before the Permanent Subcommittee on Investigations of the Committee on Government Operations, U.S. Senate, 87th Congress, 2nd session,* testimony of Clayton Hart, pp. 435–86.

38. *Ibid.,* pp. 612–20. The committee also elicited testimony that Bright had run up a large unpaid bill at the Concord Hotel in the Catskills, whose proprietor had apparently found it advisable to do the administrative secretary of AGVA a favor; *ibid.,* pp. 401–31.

39. *Ibid.,* pp. 133–42.

40. *Ibid.,* pp. 165–8.

41. *Ibid.,* pp. 375–400.

42. *Ibid.,* pp. 1–28.

43. SAC Birmingham, December 14, 1964, FBI 44-24016-724; SAC Birmingham, December 16, FBI 44-24016-741; and SAC Dallas, December 17, FBI 44-24016-766.

44. Quoted in Blakey and Billings, *Fatal Hour,* pp. 311–2. SAC St. Louis, November 29, 1963, FBI 44-24016-658; SAC San Francisco, December 2, FBI 44-24016-658; SAC New Orleans, December 30, FBI 44-24016-658; SAC Los Angeles, November 26, FBI 44-24016-16. SAC Dallas, November 26, 1963, FBI 44-24016-634 (interview with Robert Shorman, a musician); SAC Los Angeles, November 26, FBI 44-24016-634 (interview with Carl Maynard, another club owner).

45. SAC Las Vegas, December 17, 1963, FBI 44-24016-775.

46. SAC Los Angeles, December 26, 1963, FBI 44-24016-634.

47. Blakey and Billings, *Fatal Hour,* pp. 327–8.

48. SAC Dallas, November 25, 1963, FBI 44-24016-411, and SAC Dallas, November 25, FBI 44-24016-634.

49. SAC Dallas, November 24, 1963, FBI 44-24016-634.

50. SAC Dallas, November 25, 1963, FBI 44-24016-634, and SAC Dallas, November 29, FBI 44-24016-562.

51. SAC Dallas, November 25, 1963, FBI 44-24016-634.

52. SAC New York, December 11, 1963, FBI 44-24016-667, and SAC Dallas, November 25, FBI 44-24016-634.

53. FBI 44-24016-480, December 12, 1963.

54. SAC Dallas, November 29, 1963, FBI 44-24016-634.

55. See various tax documents, FBI 105-82555-1350.

56. SAC Los Angeles, November 29, 1963, FBI 44-24016-658, and SAC Dallas, November 25, FBI 44-24016-634.

57. SAC Dallas, November 10, 1961, FBI 92-5704-1; SAC Dallas, February 27, 1965, FBI 92-5704-4, and SAC Dallas, September 26, 1960, FBI 92-2824-62.

58. See Blakey and Billings, *Fatal Hour,* pp. 336–7.

59. SAC Las Vegas, November 25, 1963, FBI 44-24016-426, and SAC Dallas, November 24, FBI 44-24016-634.

60. Hoover to Rankin, March 10, 1964, FBI 44-24016-1183.

61. Quoted in Blakey and Billings, *Fatal Hour,* p. 325.

62. Hoover to Rankin, March 27, 1964, FBI 44-24016-1332.

63. SAC Chicago, November 28, 1963, FBI 44-24016-235.

64. Quoted in Blakey and Billings, *Fatal Hour,* p. 326.

65. Half the ransom money disappeared after the St. Louis police had initially recovered it. The actual kidnappers were executed.

66. Blakey and Billings, *Fatal Hour,* pp. 326–7, and see Kantor, *The Ruby Cover-Up,* pp. 72–4.

67. SAC Detroit, November 29, 1963, FBI 44-24016-658.

68. SAC Corpus Christi, December 27, 1963, FBI 44-24016-63 4; Dallas,

March 11, 1964, FBI 44-24016-1196; and SAC Los Angeles, March 10, 1964, FBI 44-24016-1216.

69. Petersen to Hundley, November 27, 1963, FBI 44-24016-490, and see Moldea, *Hoffa Wars,* pp. 427–8.

15. COUNTDOWN TO CATASTROPHE

1. *Dallas Morning News,* September 26, 1963, p. 1.

2. The YMCA confirmed this. See WC, X, pp. 281–3.

3. Thomas Mallon, *Mrs. Paine's Garage and the Murder of John F. Kennedy* (New York, 2002), pp. 34–40. Given the innocent atmosphere of 1963 and the subsequent history of the two women, there seems no reason to doubt Ruth's statements to her biographer that she was not suggesting a sexual relationship.

4. In an extraordinary coincidence, Mrs. Bledsoe recognized Oswald getting on and off a Dallas city bus on Elm Street on November 22, just minutes after he had assassinated the President. DPD files, 439-001, November 23, 1963, and Mary Bledsoe testimony, WC, VI, pp. 409–11.

5. The results of initial interviews are summarized in Moore to Sullivan, November 27, 1963, FBI 105-82555-381.

6. *Dallas Morning News,* October 5, 1963, sec. 1 p. 1.

7. SAC Dallas, November 24, 1963, FBI 44-24016-634.

8. Director to SAC New Orleans (Bureau Letter), August 21, 1963, FBI NO 100-16601-15.

9. SAC Dallas to Director, September 10, 1963, FBI NO 100-16601-24, and SAC New Orleans, October 25, FBI DL 105-1201-15.

10. Copies of these documents are in Newman, *Oswald and the CIA,* pp. 509, 512–3.

11. Legat Mexico to Director, October 18, 1963, and Director to Legat Mexico, October 22, FBI NO 100-16601-34.

12. SAC Dallas to Director, October 22, 1963, FBI NO 100-16601-35.

13. SAC New Orleans, October 31, 1963, FBI 105-82555-44, and SAC New Orleans to Director and SAC Dallas, October 25, FBI 105-82555-41.

14. James P. Hosty, Jr., *Assignment: Oswald* (New York, 1996), pp. 48–50. See also SAC Dallas to Hoover and New Orleans, November 3, 1963, FBI 105-82555-48.

15. SAC Dallas, October 30, 1963, FBI NO 100-16601-39.

16. *Ibid.,* p. 50. W. A. Branigan to Sullivan, February 3, 1964, FBI 105-82555-1652, definitely quotes Hosty that he had left his address and phone number on November 1, and this is confirmed by Ruth Paine, SAC Dallas, January 31, 1964, FBI 105-82555-2027.

17. SAC Dallas, February 18, 1964, FBI 105-82555-2287, and Hosty, *Assignment: Oswald,* p. 27.

18. Hosty to SAC Dallas, December 9, 1963, FBI 105-82555-671.

19. SAC Dallas, December 25, 1963, FBI DL 44-24016-634.

20. On Gessner see Hosty, *Assignment: Oswald,* pp. 214–5, and news stories from the *New York Times,* March 17, March 31, and June 6, 1962, and June 10, 1964, and the *Chicago Tribune* of May 30 and June 3, 1964. He was convicted and sentenced to life imprisonment, but the conviction was reversed on appeal: see the *New York Times,* March 9, 1966.

21. See the account of Walker's speech, *Dallas Morning News,* October 29, 1963, section 4, p. 1.

22. *Los Angeles Times,* October 25, 1963, p. 1.

23. See Kaiser, *American Tragedy,* p. 283.

24. SAC Dallas, November 22, 1963, FBI 105-82555-459.

25. SAC Dallas, December 3, 1963, FBI 105-82555-158. See also Michael Paine's Warren Commission testimony, WC, II, pp. 407–14.

26. Mrs. John Martino provided HSCA investigators with his airline ticket receipt in 1977. Cliff Fenton memorandum, October 7, 1977, HSCA Box 63/2572.

27. WC, XX, pp. 271–3.

28. Robert P. Gemberling to Hoover, May 28, FBI 105-82555-3899, and SAC Dallas, December 16, 1963, FBI 105-82555-1212.

29. SAC Dallas, December 16, 1963, FBI 105-82555-1212.

30. Mallon, *Mrs. Paine's Garage,* p. 44, and see SAC Dallas, February 3, 1964, FBI 105-82555-2027.

31. Robert P. Gemberling to Hoover, 640528, FBI 105-82555-3899; SAC Dallas, July 20, 1964, FBI 105-82555-4579.

32. SAC Dallas, February 1, 1964, FBI 105-82555-2027. Of two co-workers who were interviewed, one discounted the story but another had some recollection of it, although he could not identify the man as Oswald. All of them, coincidentally, knew Jack Ruby, whose club was nearby and who frequently parked his car there.

33. SAC Dallas, November 23, 1963, FBI 105-82555-505, p. 364. Embellishments of this incident to the effect that Oswald also praised Soviet Russia have no basis in the original investigative reports.

34. SAC Dallas, January 4, 1964, FBI 105-82555-1261.

35. SAC Dallas, December 23, 1963, FBI 105-82555-1212 (report of December 12); SAC Dallas, December 11, FBI 105-82555-572; SAC Dallas, November 23, FBI 105-82555-505, p. 362, and SAC Dallas, January 8, 1964, FBI 105-82555-1567.

36. SAC Dallas, February 25, 1964, FBI 105-82555-2250.

37. SAC Dallas, December 2, 1963, FBI 105-82555-455, p. 195.

38. WC, XVI, p. 33.

39. WC, XXV, pp. 586-7.

40. Washington Field Office to Director, New Orleans, and Dallas, November 19, 1963, FBI NO 100-16601-42. On the same day Dallas was finally designated the office of origin for the Oswald case once again.

41. W. A. Branigan to Sullivan, January 20, 1964, FBI 105-82555-1542.

42. Mallon, *Mrs. Paine's Garage,* pp. 45–9.

43. SSCIA testimony, December 13, 1975, pp. 84–91.

44. Hosty, *Assignment: Oswald,* pp. 21–3.

45. SAC Dallas, November 30, 1963, FBI 105-82555-454.

46. SAC Dallas, December 4, 1963, FBI 105-82555-456 (interviews with Dr. Homer and Sterling Wood); Dallas police report, L. C. Graves, December 2, DPD 5.5-1500; and FBI Lab to SAC Dallas, December 16, FBI 105-82555-766 2nd NR.

47. See Robert Oswald, *Lee,* pp. 205–10. I myself learned to shoot a semi-automatic M-16 rifle at Fort Leonard Wood, Missouri, in the spring of 1971 and achieved a higher proficiency than Oswald. I am quite certain, however, that I could not have done what he did with a bolt-action rifle (with which I have no experience) without extensive practice. Marina, after initially telling the FBI she knew nothing about her husband practicing with his rifle, later altered this aspect of her testimony, but the FBI was not able to confirm her vague accounts.

48. WC, XIX, p. 534.

49. WAVE to Director, November 24, 1963, CIA Office of Security, Box 1, folder 2/4.

50. SAC Dallas, May 28, 1964, FBI 105-82555-4313. SAC Dallas, May 28, 1964, FBI 105-82555-4313, and SAC Dallas, December 22, 1975, FBI 62-116395-1232, PLH Odio file.

51. New Orleans *Times-Picayune,* November 6, 1963, sec. 1, p. 11, November 8, sec. 1, p. 1, and November 9, sec. 1, p. 1.

52. New Orleans *Times-Picayune,* November 13, sec. 1, p. 10, November 14, sec. 1, p. 5, and November 15, sec. 3, p. 14.

53. *Ibid.,* November 19, sec. 1, p. 17, and November 22, sec. 1, p. 3.

54. Interview with Ed Martino (then seventeen years old), January 3, 2007. I have been unable to find any scripts or videos of NBC or CBS evening news broadcasts from this period.

55. See Staff Report, "Rose Cheramie," HSCA, X, pp. 198–205, and especially the testimony of Francis Fruge, April 18, 1978, Box 155/8502. Larry Hancock, *Somebody Would Have Talked* (JFK Lancer Productions and Publications,

2006), pp. 451–60, cites a Customs Department memo that confirms Fruge's account of the attempted drug sting in Houston.

56. DPD report, November 28, 1963, Box 1/8/36, and November 25, Box 7/8/7.

57. SAC New York, December 12, 1963, FBI 44-24016-463.

58. Interview with Ed Martino, January 3, 2007, and see Edward R. Martino, "Events I Witnessed July 1959 through November 1963," at http://www.larry-hancock.com/documents/chapter%2001/Events59-63.pdf. Ed Martino now speculates that his father kept him home for fear that he might blurt something out if he heard the news at school.

16. THREE DAYS IN NOVEMBER

1. Affidavit of Buell Wesley Frazier, DPD, Box 15/1.

2. The first and one of the most convincing treatments was by Josiah Thompson, *Six Seconds in Dallas* (New York, 1967), esp. pp. 59–81.

3. HSCA, VI, pp. 34–5.

4. *Ibid.*, p. 17.

5. See Blakey and Billings, *Fatal Hour*, p. 120, which states that two shots could be fired in as little as 1.2 seconds using the open sights.

6. See HSCA, I, pp. 491–567; K. A. Rahn and L. M. Sturdivan, "Neutron Activation and the JFK Assassination," *Journal of Radioanalytical and Nuclear Chemistry*, vol. 262, no. 1 (2004), pp. 205–22.

7. A recent article has questioned and disputed the conclusions of Guinn, Sturdivan, and Rahn, arguing that the fragments could have come from as many as five different Mannlicher-Carcano bullets. See Erik Randich and Patrick M. Grant, "Proper Assessment of the JFK Assassination Bullet Lead Evidence from Metallurgical and Statistical Perspectives," vol. 51, no. 4 (July 2006), pp. 717 ff. Kenneth Rahn has posted a rebuttal at http://www.Kenrahn.com/JFK/Scientific_topics/NAA/Review_of_RG/Review.html.

8. Their findings were summarized by Dr. Michael Baden, September 7, 1978, HSCA, I, pp. 180–322.

9. *Ibid.*, pp. 323–32.

10. *Ibid.*, pp. 332–73.

11. Roy Truly affidavit, November 22, 1963, DPD, Box 1/5.

12. Testimony of Cecil McWatters (bus driver), WC, II, pp. 262–74. Although it is not generally known, McWatters on the afternoon of November 22 told the Dallas police a completely different story—that he had picked up a man who he said resembled Oswald (whom he saw in a line-up) less than a block from the Depository and had let him off somewhere on Marsalis Street, much closer to his rooming house. Exactly how and why he changed his story is not

clear, but his second story makes more sense. See DPD, McWatters affidavit, Box 2/1. His second story was also confirmed by Oswald's one-time landlady, Mary Bledsoe: see her affidavit, November 23, DPD, Box 2/1.

13. Affidavit of William Wayne Whaley, November 23, 1963, DPD, Box 2/1.

14. SAC Dallas, June 12, 1964, FBI 105-82555-4003.

15. Earlene Roberts testimony, WC, VI, pp. 443A, and affidavit of Earlene Roberts, December 12, 1963, WC, VII, 439.

16. Dale K. Myers, *With Malice: Lee Harvey Oswald and the Murder of J. D. Tippit* (Milford, MI, 1998).

17. *Ibid.,* p. 45–6, 55.

18. I walked from the rooming house to the murder site in 1996 and had no trouble reaching it in the 10–15 minutes that Oswald had.

19. *Ibid.,* pp. 65–106.

20. *Ibid.,* pp. 141–76.

21. *Ibid.,* pp. 250–84.

22. Fritz's notes, made after Oswald's death, are in DPD, Box 5/3.

23. SAC Dallas, November 28, 1963, FBI 44-24016-634.

24. Blakey and Billings, *Fatal Hour,* pp. 355–6.

25. See Peter Noyes, *Legacy of Doubt* (New York, 1973), pp. 157–61, and Seth Kantor, *The Ruby Cover-Up* (New York, 1978), pp. 76–7.

26. See interviews with Braden, November 22, 1963, DPD, Box 5/2, and SAC Los Angeles, January 29, 1964, FBI 105-82555-1577. Braden was still using the name Eugene Brading in his dealings with the FBI.

27. Interview with reporter Hugh Ainsworth, SAC Dallas, November 25, 1963, FBI 44-24016-634.

28. Belmont to Rosen, December 5, 1963, FBI 44-24016-598.

29. The FBI made this decision early: see SAC Dallas to Hoover, February 4, 1964, FBI 44-24016-1090.

30. When interviewed by the FBI on November 25, the day Ruby shot Oswald, Eva Grant said merely that Jack had called her eight times on November 22 and dropped by three times. See SAC Dallas, November 25, 1963, FBI 44-24016-634. Later she told the Warren Commission that he had spent the whole late afternoon and early evening with her, but this, as we shall see, was not true.

31. When the Warren Commission investigated this incident, the Dallas police officers on duty claimed that the man in question was not Ruby, but Robertson stuck to his story. See Robertson's FBI interview, January 20, 1964, WC, XXI, pp. 309–10, and his Warren Commission testimony, July 24, WC, XV, pp. 347–54. Blakey and Billings, *Fatal Hour,* p. 340, misstate his name as Robinson.

32. Blakey and Billings, *Fatal Hour,* p. 340.

33. This can be heard, although not seen, at http://mcadams.posc.mu.edu/ ruby.htm. I have seen the clip of Ruby but have not been able to locate it.

34. SAC Dallas, November 28, 1963, FBI 44-24016-559.

35. Testimony of Fred Rheinstein, WC, XV, pp. 355–7.

36. Kantor, *The Ruby Cover-Up*, p. 116, identifies two reporters.

37. Testimony of Garnett Hallmark, WC, XV, pp. 488–92, and interview with Thomas Brown, November 29, 1963, WC, XXV, p. 680.

38. Testimony of Thomas Harkness, WC, VI, pp. 308–15. Harkness had already given this testimony at Ruby's murder trial.

39. Kantor, *The Ruby Cover-Up*, p. 120, quotes Curry as telling reporters (including Kantor himself), that they need only return by 10:00 a.m. the next morning to be sure of seeing the transfer.

40. Considerable evidence suggests that Senator was gay, but despite many rumors, Ruby seems to have been a heterosexual of somewhat unusual habits. He had had one long relationship in the late 1950s and often tried to date his girls, and he enjoyed phone sex with women. The most adored beings in his life were his dogs.

41. Kantor, *The Ruby Cover-Up*, pp. 125–31.

42. *Ibid.*, pp. 132–4, 138–9, and Blakey and Billings, *Fatal Hour*, pp. 343–4.

43. Kantor, *The Ruby Cover-Up*, pp. 138–43, 151–2.

44. WC, II, p. 82. Although Revill clearly remained skeptical, he indicated that Harrison had passed his polygraph. Seth Kantor refers to Warren Commission documents which I have not found indicating that he had *not* passed it.

45. Kantor, *The Ruby Cover-Up*, p. 425 16n.

46. See SAC Los Angeles, December 12, 1963, FBI 44-24016-727. The FBI later learned that a defense expert quit the case partly because he was suspicious about the source of the defense funds: SAC Washington Field Office, March 10, 1964, FBI 44-24016-1212.

47. Testimony of Jack Ruby, June 7, 1964, WC, VI, pp. 191–3.

48. The most thorough analysis of what witnesses heard is by John McAdams, available at http://mcadams.posc.mu.edu/shots.htm.

49. Statement of J. C. Price, November 22, 1963, DPD Box 5/2.

50. For a summary see the HSCA *Final Report,* pp. 63–82.

51. The NRC Panel's report, "Report of the Committee on Ballistics Acoustics," is at http://www.jfk-online.com/nas04.html#7.

52. D. B. Thomas, "Echo correlation analysis and the acoustic evidence in the Kennedy assassination revisited," *Science & Justice,* vol. 41 (2001), pp. 21–32.

53. Barger's report is in HSCA, VIII, pp. 33–127, and is available at http://www.history-matters.com/archive/jfk/hsca/reportvols/vol8/pdf/HSCA_Vol8_AS_2_BBN.pdf.

54. HSCA, VIII, p. 43.

55. McLain's testimony is HSCA, V, pp. 617–41, at http://www.history-matters.com/archive/jfk/hsca/reportvols/vol5/pdf/HSCA_Vol5_1229_3_McLain.pdf. On the stuck microphone see pp. 636–7. McLain subsequently changed his mind and argued that the tape was not from his motorcycle.

56. *Ibid.,* pp. 108–9.

57. *Ibid.,* p. 107.

58. McLain's testimony, HSCA, V, p. 629.

59. The photography analysis is in HSCA, VI, pp. 14–62, and at http://www.history-matters.com/archive/jfk/hsca/reportvols/vol6/pdf/HSCA_Vol6_2_Shots.pdf. See especially p. 26.

60. HSCA, V, p. 673–6.

61. NRC Panel report, "Report of the Committee on Ballistics Acoustics," at http://www.jfk-online.com/nas04.html#7.

62. "Report of the Committee on Ballistics Acoustics," sections II and III.

63. *Ibid.,* section IV-3.

64. *Ibid.,* Appendix D.

65. The NRC panel also laid great stress on sounds of a bell and of advancing and retreating sirens on the Channel 1 tape, arguing that Officer McLain was not in a position to pick up such sounds. This does not, however, prove anything, because it was very possible for the tape to have recorded through more than one open microphone at once, as Barger had pointed out. (I well remember this phenomenon from my own days as a radio-dispatched cab driver.)

66. D. B. Thomas, "Echo correlation analysis and the acoustic evidence in the Kennedy assassination revisited," *Science & Justice,* vol. 41 (2001), pp. 21–32.

67. *Ibid.,* pp. 28–9.

68. Gary Savage, *JFK First Day Evidence* (Monroe, LA, 1993), p. 321.

69. The graph itself, quite simple to read, is HSCA, VIII, p. 72 (p. 32 of the report). I have expressed this point in terms of actual time rather than in the different slopes of the regression lines before and after the assassination to which Thomas refers. The points on the graph appear to refer to the actual dispatcher time notations.

70. R. Lineker, R. L. Garwin, H. Chernoff, P. Horowitz, and N. F. Ramsay, "Synchronization of the acoustic evidence in the assassination of President Kennedy," *Science & Justice,* vol. 45, no. 4 (2005), pp. 207–26 (hereafter Lineker et al.).

71. *Ibid.,* pp. 224–5.

17. KEEPING SECRETS

1. See Jefferson Morley, "Revelation 19.63," *Miami Daily News,* April 12, 2001, and Martino, "Events I Witnessed," p.11.

2. Kantor, *The Ruby Cover-Up,* pp. 376–81. Hendrix's story of September 24, 1963, did not, as Seth Kantor wrote, actually describe the coup, but it both predicted and in effect endorsed it—something the American Embassy had *not* done. See also John Bartlow Martin, *Overtaken by Events* (New York, 1966), pp. 454–5. Hendrix left journalism to work for ITT in the early 1970s and was involved in CIA attempts to prevent Salvador Allende from taking power in Chile. He eventually had to plead guilty to giving false information to Congress in connection with those attempts.

3. Mohr to DeLoach, November 22, 1963, FBI 105-82555-405, and SAC Washington, November 23, FBI 105-82555-506.

4. Butler's November 24 testimony and Ruth Paine's December 5 statement are both in Record Group 46, Records of the US Senate, Senate Internal Security Subcommittee, 86th–88th Congresses, Kennedy Assassination Records Collection, Box 1.

5. Chief, Contact Support, September 4, 1963; Chicago Contact Division, September 9, and Chicago Contact Division, September 25, CIA Printed Microfilm, Box 8/24, and From Index (Thorne) to Lohmann, September 10, CIA Printed Microfilm, Box 8/25.

6. CIA Memo to Chief, LEOB/SRS, December 11, 1967, CIA Segregated Collection, Box 1/9; see also "Daly's Diary," n.d. but apparently November 26 or 27, 1963, CIA Printed Microfilm, Box 8/25.

7. Branigan to Sullivan, November 27, 1963, FBI 105-82555-244.

8. SAC Chicago, December 2, 1963, FBI 105-82555-761.

9. Blakey and Billings, *Fatal Hour,* pp. 194–5.

10. SAC Chicago, December 3, 1963, FBI 92-3171-1257. SAC Chicago, December 3, 1963, FBI 92-3171-1257. In the midst of the kidnapping, the Las Vegas FBI office heard a story that, if true, resolved a long-standing mystery. It came from an attorney, Harry Claiborne, who eventually became a judge but was convicted of tax evasion, and it was recorded in a high-level internal memo at FBI Headquarters in Washington: "The information which Claibourne [sic] furnished pertained to the primary which was held in West Virginia in which Kennedy was victorious prior to Kennedy's election to the presidency. Claibourne stated that a tremendous amount of money was spent in this primary. He said that Frank Sinatra, Sr., spent some time in Palm Springs with JFK. At the time Sinatra was with Kennedy in Palm Springs, Kennedy had lost his voice, as a result of which he had to write down every question . . . Kennedy allegedly told Frank Sinatra that he had spent a tremendous amount of money in West Virginia and that he was 'hurting' . . . Frank Sinatra in effect told him don't worry about it, that he would get ahold of some money . . . Sinatra, Sr., allegedly went to Sam Giancana in Chicago and 'got a bundle for JFK.' This money was

passed on from Giancana to Sinatra with the understanding that Sinatra would be able to keep the heat off of Sam Giancana. Frank Sinatra apparently was not able to deliver and the conjecture could be that this [the kidnapping] may be the way of getting back the money which Giancana had given to Sinatra. The above is all speculation and is merely furnished to the Bureau by [Las Vegas Special Agent in Charge] Elson as having been given to him by his source, Claibourne, and he wanted to be sure to label it speculative." A. Rosen to Mr. Belmont, December 10, 1963, FBI 192-3171 NR. The story, however, cannot be completely true, because Kennedy did not visit Palm Springs after the West Virginia primary on Tuesday, May 10, 1960. Kennedy campaigned in other states for much of the rest of the month. He spent Friday, May 27, through Monday, May 30, in California, appearing formally in Los Angeles on May 31, but he was apparently in the Pebble Beach–Monterey area, nowhere near Palm Springs.

11. SAC Miami, November 27, 1963, FBI 105-82555-510.

12. SAC Miami, January 25, 1964, FBI 105-82555-1505.

13. SAC Miami, December 10, 1963, FBI 64-44828-NR.

14. John Martino, "Cuba and the Kennedy Assassination," *Human Events,* December 21, 1963.

15. CIA Cable, November 26, 1963, FBI 105-82555-681; Branigan to Sullivan, November 29, FBI 105-82555-246; Hoover to Legat Mexico, November 27, FBI 105-82555-60; and Embassy Mexico, November 28, 1963, FBI 105-82555-2235. Johnson, who had opposed such a commission strongly in a conversation with J. Edgar Hoover on November 25, favored one while talking to James Eastland on November 28. Beschloss, *Taking Charge,* pp. 31–2, 46–7. The connection with Alvarado was suggested to me by Peter Dale Scott. See also Helms to Hoover, December 7, 1963, FBI 105-82555-347.

16. CIA Memorandum, "Flights from Mexico City to Havana on November 22, 1963," n.d., at http://www.maryferrell.org/mffweb/archive/viewer/showDoc.do?docId=32707&relPageId=2. A year later, in December 1964, the CIA received an even more bizarre story of a private plane carrying two "gangsters" that had supposedly landed late in the evening in Havana after flying from Dallas to Mexico City via Tijuana. The source, who claimed that the September *Warren Report* had jogged his memory, was now reported to be dead.

17. SAC Dallas to Hoover, December 5, 1963, FBI 105-82555-226.1, and Hoover memorandum, December 12, FBI 44-24016-667.

18. Wannall to Sullivan, December 11, 1963, FBI 105-82555-890.

19. The letter, dated November 22, 1963, is in FBI 44-24016-910.

20. See SAC New York, January 24, 1964, FBI 44-24016-1010; SAC New York, February 4, FBI 64-44828-NR; SAC Miami, April 4, FBI 105-82555-3103; SAC New York, February 26, FBI 44-24016-1135; and SAC New York, March 5, FBI 105-82555-2526.

21. SAC New York, March 17, 1964, FBI 64-44828 NR.

22. SAC New York, April 21, FBI 105-82555-3323.

23. SAC Miami, May 8, 1964, 64-44828 NR, and SAC Miami, June 1, 64-44828 NR. See also W. David Slawson to J. Lee Rankin, April 24, 1964, HSCA Box 65/2646.

24. See Gaeton Fonzi memorandum, August 11, 1978, HSCA, Box 196/10709.

25. Blakey and Billings, *Fatal Hour,* pp. 227–8.

26. Moldea, *The Hoffa Wars,* pp. 171–4.

27. Pearson Diary, January 13, 14, and 16, 1967, LBJ Library.

28. *Ibid.,* January 19 and 20.

29. *Ibid.,* January 23.

30. *Washington Post,* February 12 and 26, 1967, both p. E7.

31. Pearson diary, February 15, LBJ Library.

32. *Washington Post,* March 3, p. C13.

33. See FBI, WFO, Information Supplied by Attorney Edward P. Morgan, March 21, 1967, FBI 62-109060-4827. See also Powers, *The Man Who Kept the Secrets,* pp. 121–2.

34. See Blakey and Billings, *Fatal Hour,* p. 54.

35. WSAC WFO to Hoover, March 13, 1967, FBI 62-109060-4833; Moldea, *The Hoffa Wars,* p. 180.

36. Moldea, *The Hoffa Wars,* p. 180.

37. Ragano and Raab, *Mob Lawyer,* pp. 186–97.

38. *New York Times,* June 25, 1976, p. 12, and see Talbot, *Brothers,* p. 284.

39. See Rappeleye and Becker, *All-American Mafioso,* pp. 288–89, and *Washington Post,* January 18, 1971, p. B7.

40. On Roselli's indirect contacts with the agency see CIA Memo for Record, April 28, 1967, and Memorandum for the Record by Deputy Director of Security James P. O'Connell, June 29, 1971; O'Connell memorandum, July 7; and Memorandum to Executive Director, February 15, 1972, CIA Segregated Collection, Box 1/1.

41. See the "Black Book" given by Fidel Castro to George McGovern in 1975, SSCIA, Appendix to "Halley" testimony, Box 36/1.

42. See Jose Benitez to William Pawley, October 18, 1960, and Chief, Western Hemisphere Division, to Chief JMASH, November 4, JFK, CIA Segregated Collection, Box 2/4.

43. On del Valle's drug-smuggling see SAC Miami to Director, August 1, 1966, FBI 100-378541-27, and Escalante, 1963: *El Complot,* pp. 154–7.

44. "Miami Murder Linked to JFK Plot, Friend of Murdered Miami Man, Hiding in Fear of his Life, Tells His Story Exclusively for ENQUIRER Readers," by Diego Gonzales Tendera, *National Enquirer,* April 30, 1967. While

the source is obviously less than fully trustworthy, the author either had real knowledge or an extremely vivid imagination.

45. When I submitted a FOIA for it in 2003, he was able to provide the number of the file, but the agency, ignoring the JFK Records Act, now refuses to release any 201 files, and his request was denied. Files at NARA show that television journalist Dan Rather had requested files on del Valle as early as 1975.

46. WAVE to Director, September 17, 1963, CIA Printed Microfilm, Box 101/24.2. This document is from the AMLASH file; no file on Herminio Diaz has been released.

47. Escalante, *1963: El Complot,* p. 157.

48. Interview with John Cummings, August 23, 2003. Cummings had previously given the same story to British author Anthony Summers: see Anthony Summers and Robbyn Swan, "The Ghosts of November," *Vanity Fair,* December 1994, pp. 112, 117. Agent O'Connor denied ever having met Oswald in Miami.

49. *Washington Post,* November 22, 1975 [sic], p. A11.

50. See Belford Lawson memorandum, August 29, 1977, HSCA Box 61/02155, and notes by Earl Golz, late summer 1978, copy in author's possession (provided by Earl Golz to Anthony Summers, and thence to me). Cabeza had been "employed the agency in agent status" and was "a key figure in the AMFAUNA operation"; see Jacob D. Esterline to Deputy Director for Plans, February 4, 1967, CIA-DDP-Files, Box 7, folder 1.

51. Cliff Fenton memorandum, October 4, 1977, HSCA Box 63/2548.

52. Moldea, *The Hoffa Wars,* pp. 255–386.

53. Roemer, *Man Against the Mob,* pp. 230–48.

54. See for example *New York Times,* May 20, 1975, p. L1.

55. Rappleye and Becker, *All-American Mafioso,* pp. 304–5.

56. On the killing see Moldea, *The Hoffa Wars,* pp. 384–93.

57. Jack Anderson interview with Cliff Fenton and John Hornbeck. HSCA Box 84/3961 (Routing slip dated December 7, 1977).

58. Roselli testimony, April 23, 1976, Box 46.

59. See Rappleye and Becker, *All-American Mafioso,* pp. 2–5, 316–21.

60. Interview with Santos Trafficante, October 1, 1975, SSCIA, Box 44.

61. Fonzi, *The Last Investigation,* pp. 56–7.

62. *Ibid.,* pp. 188–93. For a detailed account of de Mohrenschildt's suicide—as it surely was—see Ray and Mary La Fontaine, *Oswald Talked: The New Evidence in the JFK Assassination* (Gretna, LA, 1996), pp. 118–37.

63. *Chicago Tribune,* April 6, 1977, p. B13.

64. The transcript is in HSCA, Box 28/1469.

65. Hall testimony, October 5 and 6, 1977, HSCA, Box 269.

66. Ragano and Raab, *Mob Lawyer*, pp. 328–49, dated this conversation just a few days before Trafficante's death. For the evidence against this, see Summers and Swan, "The Ghosts of November," p. 106.

67. SAC Dallas to Director, March 3, 1989, FBI DL 175A-DL-109-1, and SAC Minneapolis to Director, March 7, FBI DL 175A-DL-109-3. I thank Malcolm Blunt for calling this file to my attention.

68. SAC New Orleans to Director, March 15, 1989, FBI DL 175A-DL-109-11, and Legat London, September 20, FBI DL 175A-DL-109-36. The FBI's London office eventually found her and apparently interviewed her, but the entire account of the interview has been withheld by the bureau. My own mandatory review request is pending.

69. SAC Dallas to Director, July 25, 1989, FBI DL 175A-DL-109-26.

70. See Wacks's report, SAC Minneapolis, September 6, 1989, FBI DL 175A-DL-109-37, and the full report, SAC Minneapolis, September 6, FBI DL 175A-DL-109-30X2.

71. SAC Dallas, February 6, 1980, FBI DL 175A-DL-109-38.

CONCLUSION

1. See Blakey and Billings, *Fatal Hour*, pp. 402–15, for an excellent discussion on this point.

2. See Harry Hurt III, *Texas Rich: The Hunt Dynasty from the Early Oil Days through the Silver Crash* (New York, 1981), pp. 237–8, referring to a contact in March 1964.

3. Memorandum for the Record, "Meeting with HSCA Staffers," June 28, 1978, CIA Segregated Collection, Box 57/13.

4. As I have shown at length in *American Tragedy*.

ACKNOWLEDGMENTS

The assassination of John F. Kennedy has been a subject of enormous controversy for more than forty years, but this book would never have been written without the relatively recent release of enormous documentary archives. A good deal of the credit for that release must go to Oliver Stone. While I believe that his film *JFK* did more than anything else to promote the most irresponsible conspiracy theories about the case, it undoubtedly helped lead to the passage of the JFK Assassination Records Collection Act in 1992, one year after it appeared. That Act was very thoroughly administered by the Assassination Records Review Board, which worked for a very full release of the kind of background material that has allowed me to place the assassination in context. Professor Anna K. Nelson of American University, a board member, has also been an enthusiastic supporter of this project.

At the National Archives I have received enormous help from Matt Fulghum, Martha Murphy, James Mathis, and Marty McGann, who helped me navigate through their vast and complex waters and never failed to find what we were looking for. Special thanks must also go to Malcolm Blunt, a British amateur researcher (in every sense of the term!) who has no writing ambitions but who has tried to familiarize himself with every JFK document in the archives in College Park. I was fortunate to sit next to him during several of my trips there and found his tips to be invariably accurate and useful. Bill and Janie Strauss were wonderful hosts during numerous trips to the Washington area.

It was clear after my first trip to College Park that I would never be able to do the necessary research on my own, and with the help of Professor Arthur Epstein of the University of Maryland I managed to recruit a series of outstanding assistants, including Christian James, Pat Crawford, Nick Kimball, Meghan Lyon, Jennifer Stavish, and Abram Fox. Another Maryland student, Aidan Smith, wrote a computer program that enabled me to sort the results of the National Archives' own computer search engine into usable form. But my most tenacious researcher was my son, Tom Kaiser, then of George Washington University, who made his way through large portions of the Oswald and Ruby files. Tom, who also wrote a senior thesis on the subject, proved his credentials as a potential historian, but as he had already told me when he chose to major in history, "I'm not going to write it, I'm going to make it."

My brother Bob got me professionally involved in the Kennedy case for the first time in the fall of 1983, when he commissioned me to write a piece about the assassination for the twentieth anniversary edition of the *Washington Post's* "Outlook" section. While writing that piece, I had several very long conversations with G. Robert Blakey, who was an enormous help and who at the time encouraged me to go further into the case. In subsequent decades I have received enormous assistance from a number of other authors and independent researchers. Rex Bradford has performed an enormous service by putting tens of thousands of pages of basic documents on line at history-matters.com. Richard Billings, Bill Drenas, Mr. and Mrs. Earl Golz, Larry Haapanen, Larry Hancock, Paul Hoch, Jim Lesar, Gary Mack, John McAdams, Jefferson Morley, Ken Rahn, Peter Dale Scott, Anthony Summers, Josiah Thompson, and Gordon Winslow all provided invaluable help even though many of them differ with one another, and with me, about the case. I am sure they will have a lot to say about the finished product, and I am looking forward to hearing it. Dan Moldea was a continual source of important information about organized crime. I apologize to any of the many people who helped me whom I have unfortunately forgotten.

Several participants in the drama were also very helpful. James P. Hosty was unfailingly courteous and well-informed during three long telephone conversations. Frederick Schwartz and Jim Johnson shared interesting experiences from the Church Committee. Anne Sullivan, Linda Morgan, and above all Ed Martino generously provided information about deceased family members who had played various different roles in the drama. I believe there may be other members of younger generations like Ed Martino who may have important stories to tell, and I hope that eventually they will do so.

I owe a great debt to the Harvard University Press, not only because they have now published three of my books but because they have always allowed me to write them as I wished. In this case the credit goes to

Kathleen McDermott and Susan Wallace Boehmer, the two editors on the project, who both embraced the idea and did a great deal to make the final product read more clearly. While writing the book I received excellent editorial suggestions from my wife, Patti Cassidy, and from Don Lamm, John Schindler, and Alberto Coll. And last, I would like to acknowledge my debt to the late William Young, who in the 1970s got me interested in the case of Sacco and Vanzetti. After his death in 1980 I managed to complete his work on the case, and that experience convinced me that someday I should also tackle the greatest mystery of the twentieth century.